Stand!

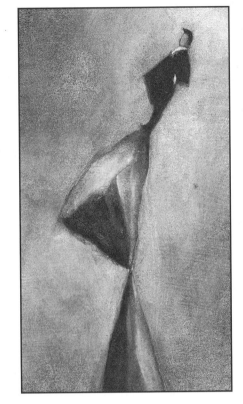

Educational Psychology

Contending Ideas and Opinions

Academic Editor

David M. Podell

College of Staten Island, City University of New York

coursewise
publishing
inc.

Bellevue • Boulder • Dubuque • Madison • St. Paul

Our mission at **Coursewise** is to help students make connections—linking theory to practice and the classroom to the outside world. Learners are motivated to synthesize ideas when course materials are placed in a context they recognize. By providing gateways to contemporary and enduring issues, **Coursewise** publications will expand students' awareness of and context for the course subject.

For more information on **Coursewise,** visit us at our web site: http://www.coursewise.com

To order an examination copy, contact Houghton Mifflin Sixth Floor Media: 800–565–6247 (voice); 800–565–6236 (fax).

Coursewise Publishing Editorial Staff

Thomas Doran, ceo/publisher: Environmental Science/Geography/Journalism/Marketing/Speech
Edgar Laube, publisher: Political Science/Psychology/Sociology
Linda Meehan Avenarius, publisher: **Courselinks**™
Sue Pulvermacher-Alt, publisher: Education/Health/Gender Studies
Victoria Putman, publisher: Anthropology/Philosophy/Religion
Tom Romaniak, publisher: Business/Criminal Justice/Economics
Kathleen Schmitt, publishing assistant
Gail Hodge, executive producer

Coursewise Production Staff

Lori A. Blosch, permissions coordinator
Mary Monner, production coordinator
Victoria Putman, production manager

Note: Readings in this book appear exactly as they were published. Thus, inconsistencies in style and usage among the different readings are likely.

Cover photo: Ian Lawrence/1998/nonstock

Interior design and cover design by Jeff Storm

Library of Congress Catalog Card Number: 99-64306

ISBN 0-395-97390-2

Printed in the United States of America by Coursewise Publishing, Inc.
7 North Pinckney Street, Suite 346, Madison, WI 53703

10 9 8 7 6 5 4 3 2 1

from the Publisher

Sue Pulvermacher-Alt
Coursewise Publishing

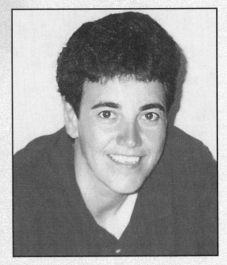

I grew up near a small town with one gas station. In this station was a small, refrigerated case with two tubs of ice cream—vanilla and chocolate. I'd go in the station with my dad and beg for an ice cream cone. Then I had to choose—chocolate or vanilla. I wanted both. Choosing only one was tough (and time consuming).

Eventually, the gas station got a soft-serve ice cream machine. Now my selection took only a second—the swirl, please. You know—the soft-serve ice cream flavor that is part chocolate and part vanilla woven together in one peaked spiral. I found nirvana. Unfortunately, my nirvana didn't last long. By the time I was six, the ice cream world got more complicated. Soft or hard? The 31 flavors of Baskin-Robbins. Waffle or regular cone? One, two, or three scoops? The swirl was still there, but now I had alternatives to carefully consider.

This *Stand! Educational Psychology* volume is a little like an ice cream shop. In your educational psychology course, you'll need to work your own way through many complicated and flavorful issues: Are American schools failing to educate young people? What's the best way to educate kids with special needs? Which approach—phonics or whole language—helps kids to be more effective readers? Why not group students by ability? Does television educate us?

For a few of the issues discussed in this volume, we've taken a chocolate or vanilla approach—you'll find two articles that explore opposing viewpoints. Other issues required more of a Baskin-Robbins approach—three to five articles that explore contending ideas.

I invite you to visit our ice cream shop like this: Taste each flavor. Ideally, taste each twice. Next go back and taste the flavor that *doesn't* appeal to you at first. Make sure you give that flavor extra careful consideration. From there, create your own cone. Or better yet, come up with your own flavor. This is your treat, and it's your responsibility to make sure it's right for you.

In addition to the readings in this volume, you'll find web sites (yup, more flavors) that we hope will expand your understanding of the issues. The R.E.A.L. sites you'll find throughout this *Stand! Educational Psychology* volume and at the **Courselinks**™ site for Educational Psychology are particularly useful sites. But it's your cone. Read our annotations and decide if the site is worth visiting. Do the activities so you can get to know the site better. Search our **Courselinks** site by key topic and find the information you need to be a more informed educator.

As publisher for this volume, I had the good fortune to work with David Podell as the Academic Editor. David had the final say on which 43 article flavors we included here. I've known David for several years, and we've worked together on other projects. He is a consummate professional—considerate, responsible, and knowledgeable. Members of the Editorial Board helped refine the ice cream selection by offering critical feedback and posing some interesting challenges. My thanks to David and the entire Editorial Board.

As you use our print and online resources and continue to build your understanding of educational psychology, I invite you to share your reactions to our materials. What worked and what didn't work in this *Stand! Educational Psychology* volume and the accompanying **Courselinks** site? What flavors should we add or take out next time? I'd really like to hear from you—as one ice cream lover to another.

Sue Pulvermacher-Alt, Publisher
suepa@coursewise.com

iii

from the Academic Editor

David M. Podell
College of Staten Island, City University of New York

Education is one of the most controversial topics in the United States today. Underlying the controversy is a sense of dissatisfaction in the education that we currently provide. People rightly ask, "Why can't we have a first-rate educational system that prepares students as citizens, gives them skills to join the world of work, fills them with knowledge, and stimulates their imagination?" Many look to the field of educational psychology, a field that bridges the disciplines of education and psychology, for some of the answers.

Finding the answers, however, is not so simple. As you might expect, different perspectives and beliefs lead people to different answers to the same question. If we ask, "What should we be teaching in school?" the answer will be radically different if you believe in multicultural education or if you believe that students should study the canon (that is, the "Great Books"). The answers to other important questions, such as "How should we teach children with disabilities?" and "How should we educate children who do not speak English?", are similarly influenced by personal beliefs.

As a college teacher, I used debates to help students better understand issues in educational psychology (for example, "Which method of teaching reading—phonics or whole language—is better?"). A colleague suggested that I initially ask students to state their position—and then assign them to the team advocating the opposite position! To succeed at the assignment, the students had to park their beliefs at the door and reason out the arguments supporting the position that they themselves opposed. That's when the debates really worked. I encouraged the students to anticipate the arguments of the opposing team and to find the flaws in those arguments. In preparing for this activity, the students did more reasoning, research, and teamwork than in any other assignment I gave. And in the end, they understood the issues better.

This book presents different sides of issues in educational psychology. I challenge you to put aside your personal beliefs and predispositions and then read and think about the articles critically to consider the merit of each position outlined by the authors. By truly understanding the arguments on both sides of an issue, you can analyze and evaluate and form your own position based on knowledge and reasoning.

As a professional educator, you should have positions on current educational issues. But your positions should be developed from knowledge and reasoning, rather than from information that others tell you. This book is designed specifically to create uncertainty. The authors of the articles present arguments to opposing positions. You, the reader, must examine the arguments and decide which ones are strongest. As you read, keep your mind open, think critically, and discuss the issues with your fellow students. Your understanding of the issues will deepen, and your beliefs about education will be more informed.

David M. Podell is Professor of Education and Dean of Humanities and Social Sciences at the College of Staten Island. He earned his master's degree from Harvard University and his Ph.D. from New York University. His research concerns factors influencing referrals and placement in special education. He is the co-author of Educational Psychology: Windows on Teaching and the academic editor of Perspectives: Educating Exceptional Learners.

Editorial Board

We wish to thank the following instructors for their assistance. Their many suggestions not only contributed to the construction of this volume, but also to the ongoing development of our Educational Psychology web site.

WiseGuide Introduction

Critical Thinking and Bumper Stickers

Question Authority

The bumper sticker said: Question Authority. This is a simple directive that goes straight to the heart of critical thinking. The issue is not whether the authority is right or wrong; it's the questioning process that's important. Questioning helps you develop awareness and a clearer sense of what you think. That's critical thinking.

Critical thinking is a new label for an old approach to learning—that of challenging all ideas, hypotheses, and assumptions. In the physical and life sciences, systematic questioning and testing methods (known as the scientific method) help verify information, and objectivity is the benchmark on which all knowledge is pursued. In the social sciences, however, where the goal is to study people and their behavior, things get fuzzy. It's one thing for the chemistry experiment to work out as predicted, or for the petri dish to yield a certain result. It's quite another matter, however, in the social sciences, where the subject is ourselves. Objectivity is harder to achieve.

Although you'll hear critical thinking defined in many different ways, it really boils down to analyzing the ideas and messages that you receive. What are you being asked to think or believe? Does it make sense, objectively? Using the same facts and considerations, could you reasonably come up with a different conclusion? And, why does this matter in the first place? As the bumper sticker urged, question authority. Authority can be a textbook, a politician, a boss, a big sister, or an ad on television. Whatever the message, learning to question it appropriately is a habit that will serve you well for a lifetime. And in the meantime, thinking critically will certainly help you be course wise.

Getting Connected

This reader is a tool for connected learning. This means that the readings and other learning aids explained here will help you to link classroom theory to real-world issues. They will help you to think critically and to make long-lasting learning connections. Feedback from both instructors and students has helped us to develop some suggestions on how you can wisely use this connected learning tool.

WiseGuide Pedagogy

A wise reader is better able to be a critical reader. Therefore, we want to help you get wise about the articles in this reader. Each section of a *Stand!* reader has three tools to help you: the WiseGuide Intro, the WiseGuide Wrap-Up, and the Frame the Debate review form.

WiseGuide Intro

In the WiseGuide Intro, the Academic Editor gives you an overview of the topics covered, and explains why particular articles were selected and what's important about them. In the "Introduction" to each issue, you'll also find questions designed to stimulate critical thinking. Wise students will keep these questions in mind as they read the articles for each issue. When you finish reading the articles for an issue, check your understanding. Can you answer the questions? If not, go back and reread the articles. The Academic Editor has written sample responses for many of the questions, and you'll find these online at the **Courselinks**™ site for this book. More about **Courselinks** in a minute. . . .

WiseGuide Wrap-Up

Be course wise and develop a thorough understanding of the topics covered in this course. The WiseGuide Wrap-Up at the end of each section will help you do just that with concluding comments or summary points that repeat what's most important to understand from the section you just read.

In addition, we try to get you wired up by providing a list of select Internet resources—what we call R.E.A.L. web sites because they're **R**elevant, **E**nhanced, **A**pproved, and **L**inked. The information at R.E.A.L. sites will enhance your understanding of a topic. (Remember to use your Passport and start at http://www.courselinks.com so that if any of these sites have changed, you'll have the latest link.)

Frame the Debate Review Form

At the end of the book is the Frame the Debate review form. Your instructor may ask you to complete this form as an assignment or for extra credit. If nothing else, consider doing it on your own to help you critically think about the readings for each issue.

Prompts at the end of each article encourage you to complete this review form. Feel free to copy the form and use it as needed.

The Courselinks™ Site

The **Courselinks** Passport is your ticket to a wonderful world of integrated web resources designed to help you with your course work. These resources are found at the **Courselinks** site for your course area. This is where the readings in this book and the key topics of your course are linked to an exciting array of online learning tools. Here you will find carefully selected readings, web links, quizzes, worksheets, and more, tailored to your course and approved as connected learning tools. The ever-changing, always interesting **Courselinks** site features a number of carefully integrated resources designed to help you be course wise. These include:

http://www.courselinks.com

- **R.E.A.L. Sites**   At the core of a **Courselinks** site is the list of R.E.A.L. sites. This is a select group of web sites for studying, not surfing. Like the readings in this book, these sites have been selected, reviewed, and approved by the Academic Editor and the Editorial Board. The R.E.A.L. sites are arranged by topic and are annotated with short descriptions and key words to make them easier for you to use for reference or research. With R.E.A.L. sites, you're studying approved resources within seconds—and not wasting precious time surfing unproven sites.

- **Editor's Choice**   Here you'll find updates on news related to your course, with links to the actual online sources. This is also where we'll tell you about changes to the site and about online events.

- **Course Overview**   This is a general description of the typical course in this area of study. While your instructor will provide specific course objectives, this overview helps you place the course in a generic context and offers you an additional reference point.

- **Take a Stand!**   Register your opinion about the issues presented in your *Stand!* reader online. You can see what students and faculty members across the country are thinking about the controversial issues presented in your text. Then add your own vote.

- **www.orksheet**   Focus your trip to a R.E.A.L. site with the www.orksheet. Each of the 10 to 15 questions will prompt you to take in the best that site has to offer. Use this tool for self-study, or if required, email it to your instructor.

- **Course Quiz**   The questions on this self-scoring quiz are related to articles in the reader, information at R.E.A.L. sites, and other course topics, and will help you pinpoint areas you need to study. Only you will know your score— it's an easy, risk-free way to keep pace!

- **Topic Key**   The online Topic Key is a listing of the main topics in your course, and it correlates with the Topic Key that appears in this reader. This handy reference tool also links directly to those R.E.A.L. sites that are especially appropriate to each topic, bringing you integrated online resources within seconds!

- **Web Savvy Student Site**   If you're new to the Internet or want to brush up, stop by the Web Savvy Student site. This unique supplement is a complete **Courselinks** site unto itself. Here, you'll find basic information on using the Internet, creating a web page, communicating on the web, and more. Quizzes and Web Savvy Worksheets test your web knowledge, and the R.E.A.L. sites listed here will further enhance your understanding of the web.

- **Student Lounge**   Drop by the Student Lounge to chat with other students taking the same course or to learn more about careers in your major. You'll find links to resources for scholarships, financial aid, internships, professional associations, and jobs. Take a look around the Student Lounge and give us your feedback. We're open to remodeling the Lounge per your suggestions.

Building Better Stand! Readers

Please tell us what you think of this *Stand!* volume so we can improve the next one. Here's how you can help:

1. Visit our **Coursewise** site at: http://www.coursewise.com
2. Click on *Stand!* Then select the Building Better *Stand!* Readers Form for your book.
3. Forms and instructions for submission are available online.

Tell us what you think—did the readings and online materials help you make some learning connections? Were some materials more helpful than others? Thanks in advance for helping us build better *Stand!* readers.

Student Internships

If you enjoy evaluating these articles or would like to help us evaluate the **Courselinks** site for this course, check out the **Coursewise** Student Internship Program. For more information, visit: http://www.coursewise.com/intern.html

Contents

section 1
Education and Learning in the New Millennium

WiseGuide Intro I

Issue 1 How Well Are Schools Doing the Job? 3

1 **In Defense of Schools,** David Berliner and Bruce Biddle. *Vocational Education Journal,* March 1996.
Berliner and Biddle take the position that, contrary to public opinion, schools are largely successful at educating young people. They contend that American education's biggest challenge is to succeed in spite of significant social problems, such as poverty and inequitable funding of schools. **4**

2 **A Nation Still at Risk: An Education Manifesto,** William Bennett and others. *Policy Review,* July/August 1998.
William Bennett and his colleagues take a look at American public education and find it woefully inadequate. They see the solution in accountability, school choice, charter schools, and merit pay. **7**

Issue 1 Summary **13**

Issue 2 Standards and Testing 14

3 **Standards Amidst Uncertainty and Inequality,** David C. Berliner and Bruce J. Biddle. *School Administrator,* May 1996.
Berliner and Bruce caution that American education is moving increasingly toward standards and accountability, focusing on how schools serve the job market. They note that schools have other functions, including fostering humanism in students and promoting students' understanding of social justice and citizenship. **15**

4 **Voluntary National Tests Would Improve Education,** Marshall S. Smith, David L. Stevenson, and Christine P. Li. *Educational Leadership,* March 1998.
Smith, Stevenson, and Li argue that voluntary national exams in key subjects such as reading and mathematics will motivate schools and students to achieve more. They believe that national testing would also promote better and more focused teaching. **19**

5 **National Tests Are Unnecessary and Harmful,** Monty Neill. *Educational Leadership,* March 1998.
Neill contents that further testing in schools wastes classroom time and taxpayers' money and provides redundant information. He sees the movement for greater testing as "an attempt to improve education on the cheap." **22**

6 **What's Wrong with Teaching for the Test?** Jack Kaufhold. *The School Administrator,* December 1998.
Kaufhold claims that "teaching to the test" may harm students, rather than help them. Teaching to the test promotes the learning of memorized information that may be obsolete, inhibits divergent and higher-order thinking, and excludes the affective domain and the arts. **24**

Issue 2 Summary **26**

At **Coursewise,** we're publishing connected learning tools. That means that the book you are holding is only a part of this publication. You'll also want to harness the integrated resources that **Coursewise** has developed at the fun and highly useful **Courselinks**™ web site for *Stand! Educational Psychology.* If you purchased this book new, use the Passport that was shrink-wrapped to this volume to obtain site access. If you purchased a used copy of this book, then you need to buy a stand-alone Passport. If your bookstore doesn't stock Passports to **Courselinks** sites, visit http://www.courselinks.com for ordering information.

Issue 3 Constructivist Approaches to Education   27

7 **From Behaviorist to Constructivist Teaching,** Geoffrey Scheurman. *Social Education,* January 1998.
Scheurman contrasts the role of teachers in a behavioral model, in which the teacher acts as a transmitter of knowledge, with their role in a constructivist model, in which the teacher acts as a facilitator or collaborator. He examines the nature of both teacher activity and student activity from the perspective of both models.   **28**

8 **Constructivist Cautions,** Peter W. Airasian and Mary E. Walsh. *Phi Delta Kappan,* February 1997.
Airasian and Walsh contend that constructivism, which continues to grow in popularity, is easier to deal with in theory than in practice. They warn that teaching from a constructivist perspective requires students to learn in an entirely new way and requires teachers to rethink every aspect of their instructional approach.   **33**

Issue 3 Summary   **39**

WiseGuide Wrap-Up   **40**

WiseGuide Intro   **41**

section 2
Controversies in Psychology

Issue 4 The Brain and Learning   43

9 **The Brain Revolution,** Robert Sylwester. *The School Administrator,* January 1998.
Sylwester claims that advances in our understanding of the brain and cognition make it necessary that educators explore new ways of teaching. While he acknowledges that brain research is in its infancy, he sees it as an opportunity to rethink our approach to promoting learning.   **44**

10 **The Sociology of the Gene: Genetics and Education in the Eve of the Biotech Century,** Jeremy Rifkin. Adapted from *The Biotech Century: Harnessing the Gene and Remaking the World* (Tarcher/Putnam, 1998).
Rifkin reflects on the social implications of our increased understanding of genetics. He notes that, because we increasingly find genetic causes for human characteristics, we risk promoting "genetic discrimination," segregation, and intolerance.   **48**

11 **Brain Science, Brain Fiction,** John T. Bruer. *Educational Leadership,* November 1998.
Bruer describes what we know about learning from brain science regarding the biological influences on learning and the interplay between the biological and environmental influences. He cautions that popular applications of brain research to education are not well grounded in science.   **56**

Issue 4 Summary   **60**

Issue 5 Nature and Nurture   61

12 **Do Parents Matter?** Sharon Begley. *Newsweek,* September 7, 1998.
Begley presents the arguments of Judith Rich Harris—that parental impact on children is less than we tend to believe. Begley also looks at the arguments of Harris's opponents, who question her methodology and her lack of scientific accuracy.   **62**

13 **Boys Will Be Boys,** Barbara Kantrowitz and Claudia Kalb. *Newsweek,* May 11, 1998.
Kantrowitz and Kalb examine the development and vulnerabilities of boys. They contend that, while girls have more choice in their behavior in today's society, boys' roles are becoming more narrowly defined.   **67**

14 **Why Smart People Believe That Schools Shortchange Girls: What You See When You Live in a Tail,** Judith Kleinfeld. *Gender Issues,* Winter/Spring 1998.
Kleinfeld challenges the widely held belief that schools shortchange girls and inhibit their academic achievement. She presents evidence that indicates that girls are not treated differently and, in fact, do well in school, and that gaps between males and females in higher levels of education are narrowing.   **72**

Issue 5 Summary   **80**

Issue 6 Being a Child in Today's Society   81

15 The Death of Child Nature: Education in the Postmodern World, David Elkind. *Phi Delta Kappan,* November 1997.
Elkind contrasts the views of childhood and education that emerge from modern and postmodern perspectives. He sees a consistency between the postmodern view and the ideas of such theorists as Dewey, Montessori, and Piaget.   **82**

16 Stop Blaming Kids and TV, Mike Males. *The Progressive,* October 1997.
Males argues that society is scapegoating children and teenagers for society's ills when, in fact, the evidence is to the contrary. He fears that, by focusing blame on children, we fail to address the problems of poverty, drug abuse, and violence that young people encounter.   **88**

Issue 6 Summary   90

Issue 7 Multiple Intelligences   91

17 How Teachers Interpret MI Theory, Linda Campbell. *Educational Leadership,* September 1997.
Campbell discusses how Howard Gardner's theory of multiple intelligences is being implemented in elementary and secondary classrooms. She describes the impact of the theory on curriculum, pedagogy, assessment, and apprenticeships.   **92**

18 Multiple Intelligence Disorder, James Traub. *The New Republic,* October 26, 1998.
Traub describes the instant popularity of Gardner's multiple intelligences theory and analyzes its appeal. He examines whether the theory contributes to improving education in schools that embrace it.   **97**

Issue 7 Summary   101

WiseGuide Wrap-Up   102

section 3
The Diversity of Society

WiseGuide Intro   103

Issue 8 Culture, Ethnicity, and Language   104

19 The Canary in the Mine: The Achievement Gap between Black and White Students, Mano Singham. *Phi Delta Kappan,* September 1998.
Singham examines the relationship between race and academic achievement, presenting socioeconomic, sociopathological, and genetic models to explain group differences. Singham notes that group work and discovery-based approaches to teaching and learning benefit all students.   **105**

20 Multiculturalism and Schools: The Struggle toward Open-Mindedness, Louis Denti. *Educational Horizons,* Spring 1998.
Denti grapples with the arguments for and against multicultural education. He concludes that multicultural education, while allowing for diversity, simultaneously promotes unity in shared beliefs in mutual respect, civility, and integrity.   **112**

21 Language Wars: Spanish Speakers Fight to Overturn Bilingual Education, Andrew Phillips. *Maclean's,* June 1, 1998.
Phillips reports on the controversy regarding bilingual education. Proponents of bilingual education contend that it provides students with an opportunity to learn in their native language while gradually learning English. Critics contend that bilingual education keeps non-English speakers segregated and unlikely to join English-speaking classes.   **118**

22 Bilingual Education: The Controversy, Richard Rothstein. *Phi Delta Kappan,* May 1998.
Many critics of bilingual education take the position that past generations of immigrants succeeded in an era when bilingual education did not exist. Rothstein argues that past generations were not as successful in school as we might think and that there were, in fact, forms of bilingual education in the past.   **121**

Issue 8 Summary   128

Issue 9 Inclusion of Students with Disabilities   129

23   **Inclusive Education: A Modern-Day Civil-Rights Struggle,** John A. Kovach and Don E. Gordon. *The Educational Forum,* Spring 1997.
Kovach and Gordon suggest that inclusive education is essentially a civil-rights issue. They contend that students with disabilities are marginalized and segregated and that only major structural change of schools will solve the problem.   **130**

24   **Inclusion: Time to Rethink,** David S. Martin. *The Educational Forum,* Spring 1997.
Martin supports inclusive education but advocates a continuum of placement options for students with disabilities. He argues that, for some children with hearing impairments, separate classes are the best choice.   **137**

25   **The Dismantling of the Great American Public School,** Karen Agne. *Educational Horizons,* Spring 1998.
Agne argues that the inclusion of students with disabilities in regular classes impedes the development of a truly excellent public school system. She contends that equality in education comes from helping students progress at their own rate.   **143**

Issue 9 Summary   **147**

WiseGuide Wrap-Up   148

section 4

Testing, Grouping, and Teaching

WiseGuide Intro   149

Issue 10   How We Test Children   151

26   **Continuing Tensions in Standardized Testing,** Thomas Haladyna, Nancy Haas, and Jeanette Allison. *Childhood Education,* Vol. 74, No. 5, 1998.
Haladyna, Haas, and Allison examine the history of standardized testing, the valid and invalid uses of test scores, and the effects of testing on students and teachers. They offer four propositions to ensure that standardized test scores are used responsibly.   **152**

27   **What Happens between Assessments?** Jay McTighe. *Educational Leadership,* December 1996/January 1997.
McTighe advocates the use of performance assessment, in which students apply what they have learned to solve meaningful, real-life problems. He further argues that instructional decision making should be based on assessment findings.   **163**

Issue 10 Summary   **168**

Issue 11   Ability Grouping   169

28   **Detracking for High Student Achievement,** Jeannie Oakes and Amy Stuart Wells. *Educational Leadership,* March 1998.
Oakes and Wells discuss ten high schools in which students were grouped heterogeneously as part of restructuring efforts. They describe the challenges that teachers encountered and the effects of detracking on the curriculum, the teachers, their pedagogy, and the students.   **170**

29   **A Response: Equal Does Not Mean Identical,** Sally M. Reis, Sandra N. Kaplan, Carol A. Tomlinson, Karen L. Westberg, Carolyn M. Callahan, and Carolyn R. Cooper. *Educational Leadership,* November 1998.
Reis and her colleagues take issue with the position of Oakes and Wells in Reading 28, arguing that detracking is an inadequate strategy for ensuring student success. They contend that teachers need to offer differentiated instruction that meets the individual needs of students.   **173**

Issue 11 Summary   **176**

Issue 12   The Reading Controversy   177

30   **Where's the Phonics? Making a Case for Its Direct and Systematic Instruction,** Patrick Groff. *The Reading Teacher,* October 1998.
Groff makes the case for phonics as the optimal way to teach children to read. He rejects the idea of an "integrated-balanced" approach to reading instruction that includes listening comprehension and making predictions about stories.   **178**

31   **Reading the Right Way,** Bill Honig. *The School Administrator,* September 1997.
Honig offers an approach to reading instruction that emphasizes basic phonemic awareness, decoding, and automatic recognition of words. He believes that effective instruction uses elements from both the phonics and whole-language traditions.   **182**

32   **What's Basic in Beginning Reading? Finding Common Ground,** Dorothy S. Strickland. *Educational Leadership,* March 1998.
Strickland presents a method of reading instruction that she calls "whole-part-whole" that attempts to balance the bottom-up and top-down approaches. Specifically, teachers should move from learning through whole written texts to learning about specific parts of the text and then applying what was learned from the text.   **188**

Issue 12 Summary   **191**

Issue 13   Learning Disabilities   192

33   **Why Kids Can't Read,** Robert Sheppard. *Maclean's,* September 7, 1998.
Sheppard examines the initial growth and more recent shrinkage of programs for students with learning disabilities. He also looks at the results of recent changes in educational services for this population, including increased litigation, greater use of technology, and increased need for advocacy.   **193**

34   **Curing Our "Epidemic" of Learning Disabilities,** Louise Spear-Swerling and Robert J. Sternberg. *Phi Delta Kappan,* January 1998.
Spear-Swerling and Sternberg contend that the category "learning disabled" is imprecise and misleading and should be dropped. They argue that all students who struggle with learning would be better served by learning specialists who address students' individual strengths and weaknesses.   **198**

Issue 13 Summary   **203**

WiseGuide Wrap-Up   **204**

section 5

The Impact of Technology

WiseGuide Intro   **205**

Issue 14   Television and Other Media   206

35   **The Politics of Teleliteracy and Adbusting in the Classroom,** Marnie W. Curry-Tash. *English Journal,* January 1998.
Curry-Tash takes the position that educators should promote students' ability to analyze and evaluate what they see on television. She encourages students to examine television advertisements to determine how advertisers seek to manipulate them and to consider how advertisements influence society.   **207**

36   **Teaching Television to Empower Students,** David B. Owen, Charles L. P. Silet, and Sarah E. Brown. *English Journal,* January 1998
Owen and colleagues advocate that teachers should help students to reflect on their television viewing habits and to recognize the profound effect that television has on viewers such as themselves. The authors conclude that students become empowered and less influenced by television when they become more critical viewers.   **213**

Issue 14 Summary   **218**

WiseGuide Wrap-Up   **219**

section 6

Growing Up Safe

WiseGuide Intro   220

Issue 15 Violence in Childhood   222

37 **The Kid No One Noticed,** Jonah Blank. *U.S. News and World Report,* October 12, 1998.
Blank reports the story of a fourteen-year-old boy who brought a gun to school and
killed three classmates. The boy, who seems to have never considered the
consequences of his actions, desperately wanted attention and respect.   **223**

38 **Facing Anger in Our Schools,** Dale Ann D. Roper. *The Educational Forum,* Summer 1998.
Roper highlights the pivotal role of anger in school violence and presents practical
strategies for dealing with anger and creating cooperative classrooms.   **226**

39 **Uneasy Days for Schools,** Timothy C. Brennan Jr. *Newsweek,* June 1998.
Brennan tells the story of a thirteen-year-old student who brought to school a list of
people he wanted to die, and the reaction of parents and educators. We need to
provide children, Brennan claims, with healthy role models to help them learn right
and wrong.   **231**

Issue 15 Summary   **232**

Issue 16 Character Education   233

40 **How Not to Teach Values: A Critical Look at Character Education,** Alfie Kohn.
Phi Delta Kappan, February 1997.
Kohn argues against the common practice of "telling" students what is right and
wrong. He proposes that teachers use literature and discussion to promote greater
understanding of values. He also notes the importance of changing the culture of
schools.   **234**

41 **The Character to Seek Justice: Showing Fairness to Diverse Visions of Character
Education,** Perry L. Glanzer. *Phi Delta Kappan,* February 1998.
Glanzer contents that Alfie Kohn, in Reading 40, has simplified a complicated issue.
Character education, Glanzer says, must recognize the diversity of families and try to
identify and promote shared values.   **247**

42 **Keeping in Character: A Time-Tested Solution,** Jacques S. Benninga and
Edward A. Wynne. *Phi Delta Kappan,* February 1998.
Benninga and Wynne disagree with Kohn (Reading 40), but for different reasons than
Glanzer (Reading 41). They contend that character education rests on promoting in
children a sense of belonging and responsibility for others.   **252**

43 **Ethics and Freedom,** Sanford N. McDonnell. *The School Administrator,* May 1998.
McDonnell argues that character must be built on knowledge and that we should
return to core values of American heritage. Among the methods he advocates are
use of moral dilemmas in literature, student decision making regarding classroom
rules, cooperative learning and team sports, and service-oriented projects in which
students meet the needs of others.   **261**

Issue 16 Summary   **264**

WiseGuide Wrap-Up   **265**

Index   **266**

Topic Key

This Topic Key is an important tool for learning. It will help you integrate this reader into your course studies. Listed below, in alphabetical order, are important topics covered in this volume. Below each topic you'll find the reading numbers and titles, and R.E.A.L. web site addresses, relating to that topic. Note that the Topic Key might not include every topic your instructor chooses to emphasize. If you don't find the topic you're looking for in the Topic Key, check the index or the online topic key at the **Courselinks**™ site.

Ability Grouping
29   A Response: Equal Does Not Mean Identical

How to Work Effectively with a Heterogeneous Classroom
http://www.maec.org/hetclass.html

American Education
1   In Defense of Schools
2   A Nation Still at Risk: An Education Manifesto

Are Public Schools in Decline?
http://homer.louiseville.edu/~tnpete01/church/vouch2b.htm

Empowering Our Schools
http://www.empower.org/html/campaigns/edreform/main.htm

National Testing
http://www.hslda.org/nationalcenter/alerts/nationaltesting/

Assessment
27   What Happens between Assessments?

Guidelines for the Development and Management of Performance Assessments
http://www.campus. cua.edu/www/ eric_ae/digests/tm9604.htm

Behaviorism
7   From Behaviorist to Constructivist Teaching

Bibliographies
Media Literacy Education Bibliography
http://www.indianapolis.in.us/maci/mlbib.html

Bilingual Education
21   Language Wars: Spanish Speakers Fight to Overturn Bilingual Education
22   Bilingual Education: The Controversy

Yahoo! Bilingual Education
http://dir.yahoo.com/Education/Bilingual/

Brain Research
9   The Brain Revolution
11   Brain Science, Brain Fiction

Brains.Org: Practical Classroom Applications for Current Brain Research
http://www.brains.org/

Character Education
40   How Not to Teach Values: A Critical Look at Character Education
41   The Character to Seek Justice: Showing Fairness to Diverse Visions of Character Education

42   Keeping in Character: A Time-Tested Solution
43   Ethics and Freedom

For-Character Education
http://www.uic.edu/~edaw/main.html

Childhood
15   The Death of Child Nature: Education in the Postmodern World

Hurry Up! It's Time to Go!
http://ericps.crc. uiuc.edu/npin/respar/texts/learning/n00038.html

Children
Children, Media and Violence
http://interact.uoregon.edu/MediaLit/FA/MLmediaviolence.html

Children and TV Violence
http://www.cmhc.com/factsfam/violence.htm

Classroom Environments
Brains.Org: Practical Classroom Applications for Current Brain Research
http://www.brains.org/

Constructivism
7   From Behaviorist to Constructivist Teaching
8   Constructivist Cautions

Cultural Diversity
Multicultural Education
http://www.ncrel.org/catalog/multicult.htm

Culture
Center for Educational Priorities
http://www.cep.org/

Desegregation
HORIZONS Newsletter
http://horizons.educ.ksu.edu/

Education
Center for Educational Priorities
http://www.cep.org/

Studies in Moral Development and Education
http://www.uic.edu/~lnucci/MoralEd/index.html

Educational Reform
Empowering Our Schools
http://www. empower.org/html/campaigns/edreform/main.htm

Effective Teaching
How to Work Effectively with a Heterogeneous Classroom
http://www.maec.org/hetclass.html

Elkind, David
Hurry Up! It's Time to Go!
http://ericps. crc.uiuc.edu/npin/ respar/texts/learning/n00038.html

Ethnicity
19   The Canary in the Mine: The Achievement Gap between Black and White Students

HORIZONS Newsletter
http://horizons.educ.ksu.edu/

Gender Equity
13   Boys Will Be Boys
14   Why Smart People Believe That Schools Shortchange Girls: What You See When You Live in a Tail

Initiative for Educational Equity Committee
http://www.mfrl.org/ compages/aauw/gequity.html

Genes
10   The Sociology of the Gene: Genetics and Education in the Eve of the Biotech Century
12   Do Parents Matter?

Government
Yahoo! Bilingual Education
http://dir.yahoo.com/Education/Bilingual/

Heterogeneous Grouping
28   Detracking for High Student Achievement

How to Work Effectively with a Heterogeneous Classroom
http://www.maec.org/hetclass.html

Inclusive Education
23   Inclusive Education: A Modern-Day Civil Rights Struggle
24   Inclusion: Time to Rethink
25   The Dismantling of the Great American Public School

Inclusive Education
http://www.uni.edu/coe/inclusion/index.html

Integration
HORIZONS Newsletter
http://horizons.educ.ksu.edu/

Internet Links

Yahoo! Bilingual Education
http://dir.yahoo.com/Education/Bilingual/

Inclusive Education
http://www.uni.edu/coe/inclusion/index.html

Phonics Research and Whole-Language
http://www.idsi.net/nyeducation/
phonicslinks.htm

For-Character Education
http://www.uic.edu/~edaw/main.html

Studies in Moral Development and Education
http://www.uic.edu/~Inucci/MoralEd/
Index.html

Law

Inclusive Education
http://www.uni.edu/coe/inclusion/index.html

Learning Disabilities

33 Why Kids Can't Read
34 Curing Our "Epidemic" of Learning
   Disabilities

Media

Center for Educational Priorities
http://www.cep.org/

Media Literacy

35 The Politics of Teleliteracy and Adbusting
   in the Classroom
36 Teaching Television to Empower Students

Media Literacy Education Bibliography
http://www.indianapolis.in.us/maci/mlbib.html

Postman Links
http://www.cs.umass.edu/~ehaugsja/z/tech/
postman/links.html

Children, Media and Violence
http://interact.uoregon.edu/MediaLit/FA/
MLmediaviolence.html

Center for Media Literacy
http://www.medialit.org/

Moral Development

For-Character Education
http://www.uic.edu/~edaw/main.html

Studies in Moral Development and Education
http://www.uic.edu/~Inucci/MoralEd/
index.html

Multicultural Education

20 Multiculturalism and Schools: The
   Struggle toward Open-Mindedness

HORIZONS Newsletter
http://horizons.educ.ksu.edu/

Multicultural Education
http://www.ncrel.org/catalog/multicult.htm

Multiple Intelligence Theory

17 How Teachers Interpret MI Theory
18 Multiple Intelligence Disorder

National Testing

4 Voluntary National Tests Would Improve
   Education
5 National Tests Are Unnecessary
   and Harmful

National Testing
http://www.hslda.org/nationalcenter/alerts/
nationaltesting/

Neuropsychology

Brains.Org: Practical Classroom Applications
   for Current Brain Research
http://www.brains.org/

Parenting

12 Do Parents Matter?

Hurry Up! It's Time to Go!
http://ericps.crc.uiuc.edu/npin/respar/
texts/learning/n00038.html

Children, Media and Violence
http://interact.uoregon.edu/MediaLit/FA/
MLmediaviolence.html

Performance-Based Assessment

Guidelines for the Development and
   Management of Performance Assessments
http://www.campus. cua.edu/www/ eric_ae/
digests/tm9604.htm

Phonics Approach

30 Where's the Phonics? Making a Case
   for Its Direct and Systematic Instruction

Phonics Research and Whole-Language
http://www.idsi.net/nyeducation/
phonicslinks.htm

Postman, Neil

Postman Links
http://www.cs.umass.edu/~ehaugsja/z/tech/
postman/links.html

Postmodernism

15 The Death of Child Nature: Education
   in the Postmodern World

Reading Instruction

30 Where's the Phonics? Making
   a Case for Its Direct and Systematic
   Instruction
31 Reading the Right Way
32 What's Basic in Beginning Reading?
   Finding Common Ground
33 Why Kids Can't Read

Phonics Research and Whole-Language
http://www.idsi.net/nyeducation/
phonicslinks.htm

Research

Multicultural Education
http://www.ncrel.org/catalog/multicult.htm

Yahoo! Bilingual Education
http://dir.yahoo.com/Education/Bilingual/

Guidelines for the Development and
   Management of Performance Assessments
http://www.campus.cua.edu/www/eric_ae/
digests/tm9604.htm

Phonics Research and Whole-Language
http://www.idsi.net/nyeducation/
phonicslinks.htm

Children, Media and Violence
http:// interact.uoregon.edu/MediaLit/FA/
MLmediaviolence.html

Resources

Inclusive Education
http://www.uni.edu/coe/inclusion/index.html

Separation of Church and State

Are Public Schools in Decline?
http://homer.louiseville.edu/~tnpete01/church/
vouch2b.htm

Sex Differences

13 Boys Will Be Boys
14 Why Smart People Believe That Schools
   Shortchange Girls: What You See When
   You Live in a Tail

Initiative for Educational Equity Committee
http://www.mfrl.org/compages/aauw/
gequity.html

Standards

3 Standards Amidst Uncertainty and
   Inequality

Television

35 The Politics of Teleliteracy and Adbusting
   in the Classroom
36 Teaching Television to Empower Students

Center for Educational Priorities
http://www.cep.org/

Media Literacy Education Bibliography
http://www.indianapolis.in.us/maci/mlbib.html

Postman Links
http://www.cs.umass.edu/~ehaugsja/z/tech/
postman/links.html

Children, Media and Violence
http:// interact.uoregon.edu/MediaLit/FA/
MLmediaviolence.html

Children and TV Violence
http://www.cmhc.com/factsfam/violence.htm

Testing

6 What's Wrong with Teaching
   for the Test?
26 Continuing Tensions in Standardized
   Testing

Violence

16 Stop Blaming Kids and TV
37 The Kid No One Noticed
38 Facing Anger in Our Schools
39 Uneasy Days for Schools

Center for Media Literacy
http://www.medialit.org/

Children, Media and Violence
http:// interact.uoregon.edu/MediaLit/FA/
MLmediaviolence.html

Children and TV Violence
http://www.cmhc.com/factsfam/violence.htm

Whole Language Approach

Phonics Research and Whole-Language
http://www.idsi.net/nyeducation/
phonicslinks.htm

section 1 | Education and Learning in the New Millennium

Learning Objectives

- Understand the political and philosophical arguments in the current debate on the effectiveness of American schools.

- Know the issues surrounding standardized testing as a strategy to improve education.

- Identify the advantages and disadvantages of behavioral and constructivist approaches to teaching and learning.

WiseGuide Intro

For a profession that has been around for rather a long time, you might think that education would have settled down to a quiet pace and predictable form. Instead, education is more controversial than ever. *How* do we teach? *What* do we teach? *How* do we know when teaching has been successful? *Who* should control education?

As we witness the turn of not only a century but a millennium, we are more than ever at odds about education. Many factors have promoted the debates in education; most prominently, people with differing points of view politically have focused their lens on education and have found themselves differing dramatically on the answers to the questions identified above. *Educational psychology,* the branch of psychology that seeks to examine questions related to school learning, has been brought into the fray by all sides in the debate, most of whom claim that research from educational psychology supports their argument.

In this section, we attempt to explore the major issues that are currently being debated in the fields of education and learning and to understand how educational psychology informs these debates. In the first issue, we enter into the debate regarding how well schools do their job. In Reading 1, David Berliner and Bruce Biddle defend American schools and try to dispel the myth that schools are failing to educate young people. The opposing position is argued in Reading 2 by William J. Bennett and others, who contend that American schools have been failing for years and need a major overhaul to be effective. If you read just slightly below the surface, you may detect the differing political values held by the authors of the two articles.

The section's second issue is standards and testing. When things go wrong in education (for example, when evidence indicates that American students score below their counterparts in other countries), many cry out for higher standards and more testing. In Reading 3, Berliner and Biddle (from Reading 1) warn that increased testing does not by itself solve the nation's educational problems or the social problems that underlie them. The opposing view is taken in Reading 4 by Marshall S. Smith, David L. Stevenson, and Christine P. Li, who argue that increased testing, albeit voluntary, would enhance academic achievement among American youth. Monty Neill, in Reading 5, counters that testing is, in fact, harmful to the very students it is designed to help. Finally, Jack Kaufhold, in Reading 6, tackles the concept of "teaching to the test" and highlights the important aspects of education that are lost when teachers opt to orient their teaching to improve student performance on standardized tests.

The third issue comes more directly from the field of educational psychology. For most of the twentieth century, psychologists argued whether learning could best be explained by *behaviorism,* an approach based on systematic rewards or punishments for demonstrating desired behaviors, or *constructivism,* an approach based on the notion that learners construct their own understanding of phenomena. These two schools of thought yield very different approaches to teaching and define the role of the teacher very differently. Increasingly, constructivist approaches are gaining in popularity, although they are, in fact, difficult to implement. In Reading 7, Geoffrey Scheurman examines the role of the social studies teacher in behaviorist and constructivist environments, favoring the constructivist model. Peter W. Airasian and Mary E. Walsh, in Reading 8, shine a critical light on constructivism and present teachers with a set of cautions regarding the use of constructivism in their teaching.

The purpose of presenting these three issues first in *Stand! Educational Psychology* is to bring the reader into the debates that are raging at this moment, debates which have enormous impact on how we educate youth in the new century and millennium.

How Well Are Schools Doing the Job?

Questions

1. Before you begin reading, write a single paragraph identifying your opinion, based on your experience, regarding whether or not American schools do what society asks them to do. After you have read the two articles, ask yourself again: do American schools do the job? Is your position the same or has it changed?

2. What appear to be the political positions of the authors of the two articles? How might the authors' arguments be used by those on the left and on the right?

3. Assume for a moment that you are suddenly appointed secretary of education in the president's Cabinet. Based on the positions presented in the two articles, what recommendations would you make to improve American public education in the twenty-first century?

Introduction

With the exception of the few children who are "home educated," all children in the United States are required to attend school. Schools eat up a significant part of state budgets and a healthy amount of the federal and local budgets. We look to schools to give children the skills they will need for jobs, to make them independent thinkers and learners, and to socialize them to enter society. While we expect schools to teach students to read, write, and do math, we also expect schools to teach children about the dangers of smoking, alcohol abuse, and drug use; to make them knowledgeable about AIDS and other sexually transmissible diseases; to make them computer literate; and to prepare them to live in a multicultural society. In other words, we ask quite a lot of schools.

Criticism of schools is always present, but one of the most influential critiques of American schooling of the recent past was *A Nation at Risk* (1983), which highlighted the failings of American public schools in preparing an educated citizenry who were ready for jobs. But is the crisis real? The two articles presented here take opposing views on this issue. At the turn of the new century, are American schools in a state of crisis or are they doing the job? You decide.

In Defense of Schools

Two professors take education critics to task in *A Manufactured Crisis.* Here they outline their reasons for celebrating the success of public schools.

David Berliner and Bruce Biddle

David Berliner is professor of curriculum and instruction and of psychology in education at Arizona State University. His research involves classroom teaching, teacher education and educational policy. Bruce Biddle is professor of social psychology and director of the Center for Research in Social Behavior at the University of Missouri.

In 1983, the United States government published *A Nation at Risk,* asserting that American industry and our leadership in the world were endangered because of our poor public school system and the ignorant students it was producing. Hundreds of similar reports followed, all used by politicians and business leaders to keep the putative crisis in American education before the American people. Some of these critiques were well-meaning and scholarly. But many were not, and in aggregate they succeeded in undermining faith in our nation's schools.

Evidence now suggests that the American public school system has actually performed remarkably well, and it has done so while it became harder to teach children than it was a generation ago. Today, many more families are faced with stressful situations. More neighborhoods cope with violence and drugs; many people are earning real wages that are lower than they were in 1970; and more children are raised in poverty. While some American schools are an embarrassment to a nation as rich in democratic traditions and fiscal resources as is the United States, the overall public system of schooling is much more worthy of praise than of blame.

Many myths about American education permeate discussions about schooling. In our new book, *The Manufactured Crisis* (Addison-Wesley), we seek to debunk attempts to undermine public education by forcing a distinction between reliable data and apocryphal myth.

Myth: Achievement and aptitude test scores are down: today's students are less able than ever before.

Scholastic Aptitude Test (SAT) scores, given to high school seniors who volunteer to take the test, did decline from the mid-1960s to the mid-1970s—and remained stable after that. But an aptitude test of about 140 multiple-choice verbal and mathematics items cannot assess 12 years of wide-ranging achievement. Moreover, since taking it is voluntary, the test cannot reflect national trends, and, according to studies done in the 1980s and 1990s by the College Board, the drop is almost all attributable to a change in the population that took the test. The 1941 norming group was 10,000 mostly white, mostly Northeastern, male students, almost half of whom had gone to private school; it is those elite students' scores that have been used to judge the performance of the 1.5 million remarkably heterogeneous test takers today. When you democratize access to higher education, as the United States has done, a drop in average performance is likely to ensue. The drop has amounted to only 5 percent of the raw score points over the course of about 30 years.

The federal government's own well-regarded longitudinal National Assessment of Educational Progress (NAEP), which tests 9-, 13- and 17-year-olds on a broad range of curricula, shows either stability or growth in average performance over the years from the 1970s to the 1990s—and rather large increases in scores for minority populations. Moreover, the commercially produced standardized tests are almost all at record highs in terms of average student score.

Longitudinal data analyses conducted by researchers at the University of Colorado of tests such as the Iowa Test of Basic Skills (ITBS), the Metropolitan Achievement Test (MAT) and the Comprehensive Test of Basic Skills (CTBS) suggest that the average student today is about 34 percentile ranks above where the average student scored 25 years ago. This is almost exactly the difference between the IQ scores of a representative sample of today's students and those of their grandparents—with the youth of today scoring about one standard deviation (34 percentile ranks) above their grandparents and about 20 percentile ranks above their parents. Every time the IQ test has been renormed, the average child has scored higher than the average child in the previous generation. Furthermore, the gains in IQ have been primarily in the sections of the tests assessing decontextualized, abstract thinking and problem solving. Finally, the four tests that measure aptitude for different graduate programs (GRE, LSAT, GMAT and MCAT) show stability or growth from the 1960s through the 1990s. Although it may be hard to believe, on average, kids today are a lot smarter than their parents. Even in international achievement comparisons, American schools look much better than portrayed by government, academic and media naysayers, according to the American Education Research Association in Washington, D.C.

Myth: America pays more for its schools than any other nation.

We are generally in the middle of the pack in comparisons of our K-12 expenditures with those of other industrialized nations. But those data do not tell the whole story. While average American spending on schools is moderate, half of our nation's school districts are below even that point because of the peculiarities of local school funding. We have districts that are not able to provide the texts, let alone the computers, their children need. Additionally, we have districts that pay their teachers abominably low salaries, as revealed in a report by the Economic Policy Institute, a liberal think tank based in Washington, D.C.

Myth: There is no relation between the amount of money spent by a school district and school achievement.

New research from the University of Chicago clearly shows that money and achievement are related. Estimates are that if the average district spent $500 more per child per year, and those funds were used on instruction, achievement test scores would rise over 20 percentile ranks, according to *Educational Researcher,* a journal published by the American Education Research Association. The increase in educational expenditures between 1967 and 1991, sometimes reported to be more than 100 percent, is actually more like 60 percent and three-quarters of that increase was for non-instructional or special educational programs, according to the Economic Policy Institute.

Teachers' salaries did go up from 1967–91 for people gaining seniority and advanced degrees. But the real salaries for teachers of equivalent experience and training showed no gains at all between the late sixties and the early nineties. Besides the increase in special education costs, one of the biggest reasons local taxpayers believed school expenditures were rising was the shrinkage in corporate property tax dollars that went into local school budgets, according to U.S. Labor Secretary Robert Reich. He says states like Louisiana provided tax breaks to corporations amounting to a loss of around one billion dollars for schools between 1980–1990.

Myth: Private schools are inherently better than public schools.

Private schools and public schools come in all varieties—some good, some bad. According to the National Center for Education Statistics, when students have the same rigorous coursework such as advanced algebra, calculus and physics, public school children have an edge of a few points in measured achievement over those in private schools.

Myth: American business spends a great amount of money on remedial education for students produced by public schools.

On the contrary, the Sandia National Laboratories, a federal government agency, found that of the roughly $40 billion spent on education in industry every year, about 97 percent of that money goes for non-remedial education. The money is spent primarily for the upgrading of skills for technical workers, the introduction of new technology to professionals and the education of sales people about new products.

Myth: The United States is not producing enough technically able workers for its economy.

In the mid-1980s, the National Science Foundation issued a report claiming future shortages of scientists, engineers and mathematicians would cripple the American industry. A congressional committee headed by Representative Howard Wolpe in 1992 declared the report a "fabrication" that resulted in the oversupply of these professionals, while demand for their services dropped.

The failure to understand the American economy has had schools madly pushing for higher levels of achievement for all of its students as the job market changes markedly. But at the start of this decade, the economy was creating nine new cashier jobs for every computer programming job, and the U.S. now has nine times as many janitors as it has lawyers, accountants, investment bankers, stockbrokers and computer programmers combined. The biggest sector of the job market is now service, not manufacturing.

What employers worry least about are the kinds of technical skills schools can provide students, according to a study conducted by the Sandia National Laboratories citing surveys done by the Rochester School District and the Michigan Department of Education in the late 1980s. What employers worry about most are the interpersonal skills of individuals, such as getting along with others, honesty, following directions, punctuality, dependability and sobriety. These personal characteristics are shaped at home and in neighborhoods more so than in schools. So if our nation is not producing the kind of workers desired by industry, then perhaps we need to look deeper at the kind of society we have become. Schools may sometimes be the scapegoat, not the source of these problems.

It seems to us that vocational education has recognized this double mission, though it has not always been articulated. Vocational educators must provide their students with the technical skills needed to do a job and they must provide them with the social skills that are needed to keep a job. Clearly the latter set of skills is related to success in the workplace. And just as clearly, if the former set of skills was deficient, then applicants would not be hired. Job seekers, however, are not always aware of the importance of the social and personal characteristics that lead to employment and personal success in life. Thus curriculum developers need to think about the school and extracurricular experiences that promote these skills.

On the other hand, it may sometimes be employers themselves who are responsible for encouraging the lack of responsibility and poor social skills that they say they require of workers. Increasingly, industry hires young people at low wages, part-time, with no benefits or opportunity to advance and treats them as disposables—like the dishware in fast-food restaurants. In settings such as this, a lack of commitment by young workers is to be expected. Blaming schools for such attitudes is disingenuous.

The overall problem with American education stems from social causes such as income gaps, deficiencies caused by local district funding and poverty.

Furthermore, while America was told that its workforce was not competitive, worker attitudes were poor and that its schools were at fault for all this, the productivity of the American worker hit all-time highs. According to the McKinsey Global Institute, an international management consulting firm, the American worker is the most productive in the world—leading our rivals Germany and Japan, each of which produce about 80 percent our capacity. The statistics were based on such criteria as GNP, the cost of producing one product unit and the percentage of product cost attributed to labor. Where are all those industrialists who bashed American schools in the eighties?

A Different Portrait

We have evidence that teachers are better qualified than the public believes; that school textbooks in use portray vividly mainstream moral values and even have the approval of some conservative religious organizations; that

after-school programs are an important part of development for many youngsters, providing an effective mechanism for building the character of inner city youth; and that American citizens with children in public schools have a very high regard for the schools that serve their children. It is Americans without children in school who are more inclined to have a low opinion of what is being accomplished. This becomes a big problem for an aging nation. According to a study from the Institute for Educational Leadership in Washington, D.C., in about half our states, more than 80 percent of family units are without children in school.

One reason for the negative opinions is the awful press that public schools have received in the U.S. If a child is shot, or drugs are found on a child at school, the papers have a field day. Yet the media seem never to report that children say schools are safer and more drug-free than their neighborhoods. Schools provide a safe haven for many children, a respite from the violence and despair that have settled in their neighborhoods. It is those neighborhoods—often poor and without much hope for improvement—that need help. America's public schools do not cause these problems, they reflect them. The media, however, seem to forget that. And the papers seldom report the miracles that occur daily in our schools, where caring teachers create safe environments in which children learn. That, of course, receives little public attention.

Some of the most vocal school critics are antidemocratic, working to undermine public schools. Many of the reforms they suggest, such as vouchers, privatization, greater accountability, intensification of teachers' and students' work, are not likely to succeed. The overall problem with American education stems from social causes such as income gaps, deficiencies caused by local district funding and poverty. Efforts toward reform could include better equalization of school funding, reduction in class size, increased use of performance evaluations, development of a more thinking-skill oriented curriculum and promotion of parent and community involvement.

We are not defending the status quo in education. There is a great deal of room for improvement. But America's public schools have not failed the American people, despite the misinformed campaigns waged by some business and government officials and the press. Given the circumstances in contemporary America, our public schools have done remarkably well, and our teachers have reason to be proud.

FRAME
the
DEBATE

Form at end of book

A Nation Still at Risk:
An Education Manifesto

On April 3, 1998—fifteen years after the release of the landmark education report, *A Nation at Risk*—a number of the nation's most prominent education reformers, business leaders and policymakers met at an event sponsored by The Center for Education Reform, Empower America, the Heritage Foundation and the Thomas B. Fordham Foundation. The purpose was to discuss the state of American education and recommend far-reaching reforms. The following manifesto results from that meeting.

William Bennett and others

Fifteen years ago this month, the National Commission on Excellence in Education declared the United States a nation at risk. That distinguished citizens' panel admonished the American people that "the educational foundations of our society are presently being eroded by a rising tide of mediocrity that threatens our very future as a Nation and a people." That stark warning was heard across the land.

A decade and a half later, the risk posed by inadequate education has changed. Our nation today does not face imminent danger of economic decline or technological inferiority. Much about America is flourishing, at least for now, at least for a lot of people. Yet the state of our children's education is still far, very far, from what it ought to be. Unfortunately, the economic boom times have made many Americans indifferent to poor educational achievement. Too many express indifference, apathy, a shrug of the shoulders. Despite continuing indicators of inadequacy, and the risk that this poses to our future well being, much of the public shrugs and says, "Whatever."

The data are compelling. We learned just last month that American 12th graders scored near the bottom on the recent Third International Math and Science Study (TIMSS): U.S. students placed 19th out of 21 nations in math and 16th out of 21 in science. Our advanced students did even worse, scoring dead last in physics. This evidence suggests that, compared to the rest of the industrialized world, our students lag seriously in critical subjects vital to our future. That's a national shame.

Today's high school seniors had not even started school when the Excellence Commission report was released. A whole generation of young Americans has passed through the education system in the years since. But many have passed through without learning what is needed. Since 1983, over 10 million Americans have reached the 12th grade not even having learned to read at a basic level. Over 20 million have reached their senior year unable to do basic math. Almost 25 million have reached 12th grade not knowing the essentials of U.S. history. And those are the young people who complete their senior year. In the same period, over 6 million Americans dropped out of high school altogether. The numbers are even bleaker in minority communities. In 1996, 13% of all blacks aged 16-to-24 were not in school and did not hold a diploma. Seventeen percent of first-generation Hispanics had dropped out of high school, including a tragic 44% of Hispanic immigrants in this age group. This is another lost generation. For them the risk is grave indeed.

To be sure, there have been gains during this past 15 years, many of them inspired by the Excellence Commission's clarion call. Dropout rates declined and college attendance rose. More high-school students are enrolling in more challenging academic courses. With more students taking more courses and staying in school longer, it is indeed puzzling that student achievement has remained largely flat and that college remediation rates have risen to unprecedented levels.

The Risk Today

Contrary to what so many seem to think, this is no time for complacency. The risk posed to tomorrow's well-being by the sea of educational mediocrity that still engulfs us is acute. Large numbers of students remain at risk. Intellectually and morally, America's educational system is failing far too many people.

Academically, we fall off a cliff somewhere in the middle and upper grades. Internationally, U.S. youngsters hold their own at the elementary level but falter in the

Reprinted with permission of *Policy Review*, a publication of the Heritage Foundation.

middle years and drop far behind in high school. We seem to be the only country in the world whose children fall farther behind the longer they stay in school. That is true of our advanced students and our so-called good schools, as well as those in the middle. Remediation is rampant in college, with some 30% of entering freshmen (including more than half at the sprawling California State University system) in need of remedial courses in reading, writing and mathematics after arriving on campus. Employers report difficulty finding people to hire who have the skills, knowledge, habits, and attitudes they require for technologically sophisticated positions. Silicon Valley entrepreneurs press for higher immigration levels so they can recruit the qualified personnel they need. Though the pay they offer is excellent, the supply of competent U.S.-educated workers is too meager to fill the available jobs.

In the midst of our flourishing economy, we are re-creating a dual school system, separate and unequal, almost half a century after it was declared unconstitutional. We face a widening and unacceptable chasm between good schools and bad, between those youngsters who get an adequate education and those who emerge from school barely able to read and write. Poor and minority children, by and large, go to worse schools, have less expected of them, are taught by less knowledgeable teachers, and have the least power to alter bad situations. Yet it's poor children who most need great schools.

If we continue to sustain this chasm between the educational haves and have-nots, our nation will face cultural, moral, and civic peril. During the past 30 years, we have witnessed a cheapening and coarsening of many facets of our lives. We see it, among other places, in the squalid fare on television and in the movies. Obviously the school is not primarily responsible for this degradation of culture. But we should be able to rely on our schools to counter the worst aspects of popular culture, to fortify students with standards, judgment and character. Trashy American culture has spread worldwide; educational mediocrity has not. Other nations seem better equipped to resist the Hollywood invasion than is the land where Hollywood is located.

Delusion and Indifference

Regrettably, some educators and commentators have responded to the persistence of mediocre performance by engaging in denial, self-delusion, and blame shifting. Instead of acknowledging that there are real and urgent problems, they deny that there are any problems at all. Some have urged complacency, assuring parents in leafy suburbs that their own children are doing fine and urging them to ignore the poor performance of our elite students on international tests. Broad hints are dropped that, if

there's a problem, it's confined to other people's children in other communities. Yet when attention is focused on the acute achievement problems of disadvantaged youngsters, many educators seem to think that some boys and girls—especially those from the "other side of the tracks"—just can't be expected to learn much.

Then, of course, there is the fantasy that America's education crisis is a fraud, something invented by enemies of public schools. And there is the worrisome conviction of millions of parents that, whatever may be ailing U.S. education in general, "my kid's school is OK."

Now is no time for complacency. Such illusions and denials endanger the nation's future and the future of today's children. Good education has become absolutely indispensable for economic success, both for individuals and for American society. More so today than in 1983, the young person without a solid education is doomed to a bleak future.

Good education is the great equalizer of American society. Horace Mann termed it the "balance wheel of the social machinery," and that is even more valid now. As we become more of a meritocracy the quality of one's education matters more. That creates both unprecedented opportunities for those who once would have found the door barred—and huge new hurdles for those burdened by inferior education.

America today faces a profound test of its commitment to equal educational opportunity. This is a test of whether we truly intend to educate all our children or merely keep everyone in school for a certain number of years; of whether we will settle for low levels of performance by most youngsters and excellence only from an elite few. Perhaps America can continue to prosper economically so long as only some of its citizens are well educated. But can we be sure of that? Should we settle for so little? What about the wasted human potential and blighted lives of those left behind?

Our nation's democratic institutions and founding principles assume that we would be a people capable of deliberating together. We must decide whether we really care about the debilitating effects of mediocre schooling on the quality of our politics, our popular culture, our economy and our communities, as dumbing-down infiltrates every aspect of society. Are we to be the land of Jefferson and Lincoln or the land of Beavis and Butthead?

The Real Issue Is Power

The Excellence Commission had the right diagnosis but was vague—and perhaps a bit naïve—as to the cure. The commissioners trusted that good advice would be followed, that the system would somehow fix itself, and that top-down reforms would suffice. They spoke of "reforming our educational system in fundamental ways." But they did not offer a political or structural-change strategy to turn these reforms into reality. They underestimated, too, the resilience of the status quo and the strength of the interests wedded to it. As former commissioner (and Minnesota governor) Albert Quie says, "At that time I had no idea that the system was so reluctant to change."

The problem was not that the Excellence Commission had to content itself with words. (Those are the only tools at our disposal, too.) In fact, its stirring prose performed an important service. No, the problem was that the Commission took the old ground rules for granted. In urging the education system to do more and better, it assumed that the system had the capacity and the will to change.

Alas, this was not true. Power over our education system has been increasingly concentrated in the hands of a few who don't really want things to change, not substantially, not in ways that would really matter. The education system's power brokers responded to the Commission, but only a little. The Commission asked for a yard, and the "stakeholders" gave an inch. Hence much of *A Nation at Risk*'s wise counsel went unheeded, and its sense of urgency has ebbed.

Today we understand that vast institutions don't change just because they should—especially when they enjoy monopolies. They change only when they must, only when their survival demands it. In other parts of American life, stodgy, self-interested monopolies are not tolerated. They have been busted up and alternatives created as we have realized that large bureaucratic structures are inherently inefficient and unproductive. The private sector figured this out decades ago. The countries of the former Soviet empire are grasping it. Even our federal government is trying to "reinvent" itself around principles of competition and choice. President Clinton has declared that "the era of big government is over." It should now be clear to all that the era of the big-government monopoly of public education needs to end as well.

The fortunate among us continue to thrive within and around the existing education system, having learned how to use it, to bend its rules and to sidestep its limitations. The well-to-do and powerful know how to coexist with the system, even to exploit it for the benefit of their children. They supplement it. They move in search of the best it has to offer. They pay for alternatives.

But millions of Americans—mainly the children of the poor and minorities—don't enjoy those options. They are stuck with what "the system" dishes out to them, and all too often they are stuck with the least qualified teachers, the most rigid bureaucratic structures, the fewest choices and the shoddiest quality. Those parents who yearn for something better for their children lack the power to make it happen. They lack the power to shape their own lives and those of their children.

Here is a question for our times: why aren't we as outraged about this denial of Americans' educational rights as we once were about outright racial segregation?

The Next Civil-Rights Frontier

Equal educational opportunity is the next great civil-rights issue. We refer to the true equality of opportunity that results from providing every child with a first-rate primary and secondary education, and to the development of human potential that comes from meeting intellectual, social and spiritual challenges. The educational gaps between advantaged and disadvantaged students are huge, handicapping poor children in their pursuit of higher education, good jobs and a better life.

In today's schools, far too many disadvantaged and minority students are not being challenged. Far too many are left to fend for themselves when they need instruction and direction from highly qualified teachers. Far too many are passed from grade to grade, left to sink or swim. Far too many are advanced without even learning to read, though proven methods of teaching reading are now well-known. They are given shoddy imitations of real academic content, today's equivalent of Jim Crow math and back-of-the-bus science. When so little is expected and so little is done, such children are victims of failed public policy.

John Gardner asked in 1967 whether Americans "can be equal and excellent, too?" Three decades later, we have failed to answer that question with a "yes." We have some excellent schools—we obviously know how to create them—and yet we offer an excellent education only to some children. And that bleak truth is joined to another: only some families have the power to shape their children's education.

This brings us to a fundamental if perhaps unpleasant reality: as a general rule, only those children whose parents have power end up with an excellent education.

The National Commission on Excellence in Education believed that this reality could be altered by asking the system to change. Today we know better. It can only be altered by shifting power away from the system.

That is why education has become a civil-rights issue. A "right," after all, is not something you beg the system for. If the system gets to decide whether you will receive it or not, it's not a right. It's only a right when it belongs to you and you have the power to exercise it as you see fit. When you are your own power broker.

Inside the Classroom

Fortunately, we know what works when it comes to good education. We know how to teach children to read. We know what a well-trained teacher does. We know how an outstanding principal leads. We know how to run outstanding schools. We have plenty of examples, including schools that succeed with extremely disadvantaged youngsters.

Immanuel Kant said, "the actual proves the possible." If it can happen in five schools, it can happen in five thousand. This truly is not rocket science. Nor is it a mystery. What is mysterious is why we continue to do what doesn't work. Why we continue to do palpable harm to our children.

Let us be clear: all schools should not be identical. There are healthy disagreements and legitimate differences on priorities. Some teachers like multi-age grouping. Others prefer traditional age-grades. Some parents want their children to sit quietly in rows while others want them to engage in hands-on "experiential learning." So be it. Ours is a big, diverse country. But with all its diversity, we should agree at least to do no harm, to recognize that some practices have been validated while others have not. People's taste in houses varies, too, yet all residences must comply with the fire code. And—while differing in design and size and amenities—all provide shelter, warmth, and protection. In other words: all provide the basics.

Guiding Principles

A. Public education—that is, the public's responsibility for the education of the rising generation—is one of the great strengths of American democracy. Note, however, that public education may be delivered and managed in a variety of ways. We do not equate public education with a standardized and hierarchical government bureaucracy, heavy on the regulation of inputs and processes and staffed exclusively by government employees. Today's public school, properly construed, is any school that is open to the public, paid for by the public, and accountable to public authorities for its results.

B. The central issues today have to do with excellence for all our children, with high standards for all teachers and schools, with options for all families and educators, and with the effectiveness of the system as a whole. What should disturb us most about the latest international results is not that other countries' best students outstrip our best; it is that other countries have done far better at producing both excellence and equity than has the United States.

C. A vast transfer of power is needed from producers to consumers. When it comes to education reform, the Port Huron Statement's formulation was apt: Power to

the people. There must be an end to paternalism; the one-size-fits-all structure; and the condescending, government-knows-best attitude. Every family must have the opportunity to choose where its children go to school.

D. To exercise their power wisely and make good decisions on behalf of their children, education's consumers must be well-informed about school quality, teacher qualifications, and much else, including, above all, the performance of their own children vis-a-vis high standards of academic achievement.

Strategies for Change

We urge two main renewal strategies, working in tandem:

I. *Standards, assessments and accountability.* Every student, school and district must be expected to meet high standards of learning. Parents must be fully informed about the progress of their child and their child's school. District and state officials must reward success and have the capacity—and the obligation—to intervene in cases of failure.

II. *Pluralism, competition and choice.* We must be as open to alternatives in the delivery of education as we are firm about the knowledge and skills being delivered. Families and communities have different tastes and priorities, and educators have different strengths and passions. It is madness to continue acting as if one school model fits every situation—and it is a sin to make a child attend a bad school if there's a better one across the street.

Ten Break-Through Changes for the 21st Century

1. America needs solid national academic standards and (voluntary) standards-based assessments, shielded from government control, and independent of partisan politics, interest groups, and fads. (A strengthened National Assessment Governing Board would be the best way to accomplish this.) These should accompany—and complement—states' own challenging standards and tough accountability systems.

2. In a free society, people must have the power to shape the decisions that affect their lives and the lives of their children. No decision is more important than where and how one is educated. At minimum, every American child must have the right to attend

Signatories of *A Nation Still at Risk*

Jeanne Allen
President
The Center for Education Reform

Leslye Arsht
Co-Founder
Standards Work

William J. Bennett
Co-Director
Empower America

Randy Bos
Superintendent
Waterloo Central School District

Stacey Boyd
Founding Director
Academy of the Pacific Rim Charter

Frank Brogan
Commissioner of Education
State of Florida

John Burkett
Former Statistical Analyst,
Office of Educational Research
and Improvement,
U.S. Department of Education

Murray Dickman
President
Pennsylvania Manufacturers'
Association

Denis Doyle
Senior Fellow
Hudson Institute

Dwight Evans
Pennsylvania House of Representatives

Willard Fair
The Urban League of Greater Miami

Chester E. Finn, Jr.
President
The Thomas B. Fordham Foundation

Rev. Floyd Flake
Pastor
Allen A.M.E. Cathedral and School

Howard Fuller
Director
Institute for the Transformation
of Learning,
Marquette University

Carol Gambill
Math Teacher

Mike Gambill
Business Leader

P.R. Gross
Biologist
Falmouth, Massachusetts

Scott Hamilton
Associate Commissioner of Education
Massachusetts Department
of Education

Roger Hertog
President
Sanford Bernstein & Co., Inc.

Eugene Hickok
Secretary of Education,
Commonwealth of Pennsylvania

E.D. Hirsch
Professor
University of Virginia

William J. Hume
Chairman
Center for Education Reform

Raymond Jackson
President
ATOP Academies
Phoenix, Arizona

Lisa Graham Keegan
State Superintendent of Schools
State of Arizona

Floyd Kvamme
Partner
Kleiner, Perkins, Caufield & Byers

Yvonne Larsen
Board President
California State Board of Education and
Vice-chairman, National Commission
on Excellence in Education

Thaddeus S. Lott, Sr.
Project Manager
Acres Homes Charter Schools
Houston Independent School District

Robert Luddy
CEO
Captive Aire Systems

Will Marshall*
President
Progressive Policy Institute

Deborah McGriff
Senior Vice President
The Edison Project

Michael Moe
Senior Managing Director,
Montgomery Securities

Paul Peterson
Professor of Government
Harvard University

Susan Pimentel
Co-Founder
Standards Work

Albert Quie
Former Governor
State of Minnesota and Member,
National Commission on Excellence
in Education

Diane Ravitch
Senior Fellow
Brookings Institution

Nina Shokraii
Education Policy Analyst
The Heritage Foundation

Jay Sommer
Former Teacher of the Year and
Member, National Commission
on Excellence in Education

Leah Vukmir
Director
Parents Raising Educational Standards
in Schools

Herbert J. Walberg
Research Professor of Education
University of Illinois at Chicago

* Mr. Marshall dissents from that portion of recommendation #2 that would have public dollars flow to private and parochial schools on the same basis.

the (redefined) public school of his choice. Abolish school assignments based on home addresses. And let public dollars to which they are entitled follow individual children to the schools they select. Most signers of this manifesto also believe strongly that

this range of choices—especially for poor families—should include private and parochial schools as well as public schools of every description. But even those not ready to take that step—or awaiting a clearer resolution of its constitutionality—are united in their conviction that the present authoritarian system—we choose our words carefully—must go.

3. Every state needs a strong-charter school law, the kind that confers true freedom and flexibility on individual schools, that provides every charter school with adequate resources, and that holds it strictly accountable for its results.

4. More school choice must be accompanied by more choices worth making. America needs to enlarge its supply of excellent schools. One way to do that is to welcome many more players into public education. Charter schools are not the whole story. We should also harness the ingenuity of private enterprise, of community organizations, of "private practice" teachers and other such education providers. Schools must be free to contract with such providers for services.

5. Schools must not harm their pupils. They must eschew classroom methods that have been proven not to work. They must not force children into programs that their parents do not want. (Many parents, for example, have serious misgivings about bilingual education as commonly practiced.)

6. Every child has the right to be taught by teachers who know their subjects well. It is educational malpractice that a third of high school math teachers and two-fifths of science teachers neither majored nor minored in these subjects while in college. Nobody should be employed anywhere as a teacher who does not first pass a rigorous test of subject-matter knowledge—and who cannot demonstrate their prowess in conveying what they know to children.

7. One good way to boost the number of knowledgeable teachers is to throw open the classroom door to men and women who are well-educated but have not gone through programs of "teacher education." A NASA scientist, IBM statistician or former state governor may not be traditionally "certified" to teach and yet may have a great deal to offer students. A retired military officer may make a gem of a middle-school principal. Today, Albert Einstein would not be able to teach physics in America's public school classrooms. That is ridiculous. Alternative certification in all its variety should be welcomed, and for schools that are truly held accountable for results, certification should be abolished altogether. Colleges of education must lose their monopoly and compete in the marketplace; if what they offer is valuable, they will thrive.

8. High pay for great educators—and no pay for incompetents. It is said that teaching in and leading schools doesn't pay enough to attract a sufficient number of well-educated, and enterprising people into these vital roles. We agree. But the solution isn't across-the-board raises. The solution is sharply higher salaries for great educators—and no jobs at all for those who cannot do the job well. Why should the principal of a failing school retain a paycheck? Why shouldn't the head of a great school be generously rewarded? Why should salaries be divorced from evidence of effectiveness (including evidence that one's students are actually learning what one is teaching them)? Why should anyone be guaranteed permanent employment without regard to his or her performance? How can we expect school principals to be held accountable for results if they cannot decide whom to employ in their schools or how much to pay them?

9. The classroom must be a sanctuary for serious teaching and learning of essential academic skills and knowledge. That means all available resources—time, people, money—must be focused on what happens in that classroom. More of the education dollar should find its way into the classroom. Distractions and diversions must cease. Desirable-but-secondary missions must be relegated to other times and places. Impediments to order and discipline must be erased. And the plagues and temptations of modern life must be kept far from the classroom door. Nothing must be allowed to interfere with the ability of a knowledgeable teacher to impart solid content to youngsters who are ready and willing to learn it.

10. Parents, parents, parents . . . and other caring adults. It is a fact that great schools can work miracles with children from miserable homes and awful neighborhoods. But it is also a fact that attentive parents (and extended families, friends, etc.) are an irreplaceable asset. If they read and talk to their children and help them with their homework, schools are far better able to do their part. If good character is taught at home (and in religious institutions), the schools can concentrate on what they do best: conveying academic knowledge and skills.

Hope for the Next American Century

Good things are already happening here and there. Most of the reforms on our list can be seen operating someplace in America today. Charter schools are proliferating. Privately managed public schools have long waiting lists. Choices are spreading. Standards are being written and rewritten. The changes we advocate are beginning, and we expect them to spread because they make sense and because they serve children well. But they are still exceptions, fleas on the elephant's back. The elephant still has most of the power. And that, above all, is what must change during the next fifteen years in ways that were unimaginable during the past fifteen. We must never again assume that the education system will respond to good advice. It will change only when power relationships change, particularly when all parents gain the power to decide where their children go to school.

Such changes are wrenching. No monopoly welcomes competition. No stodgy enterprise begs to be reformed. Resistance must be expected. Some pain must be tolerated. Consider the plight of Detroit's automakers in the 1980's. At about the same time the Excellence Commission was urging major changes on U.S. schools, the worldwide auto market was forcing them upon America's "big three" car manufacturers. Customers didn't want to buy expensive, gas-guzzling vehicles with doors that didn't fit. So they turned to reliable, inexpensive Asian and European imports. Detroit suffered mightily from the competition. Then it made the changes that it needed to make. Some of them were painful indeed. They entailed radical changes in job expectations, huge reductions in middle management and fundamental shifts in manufacturing processes and corporate cultures. The auto industry would not have chosen to take this path, but it was compelled to change or disappear.

Still, resistance to structural changes and power shifts in education must be expected. Every recommendation we have made will be fought by the current system, whose spokesmen will claim that every suggested reform constitutes an attack on public education. They will be wrong. What truly threatens public education is clinging to an ineffective status quo. What will save it are educators, parents and other citizens who insist on reinvigorating and reinventing it.

The stakes could not be higher. What is at stake—and what is at risk—is America's ability to provide all its daughters and sons with necessary skills and knowledge, with environments for learning that are safe for children and teachers, with schools in which every teacher is excellent and learning is central. What is at stake is parents' confidence that their children's future will be bright thanks to the excellent education that they are getting; taxpayers' confidence that the money they are spending on public education is well spent; employers' confidence that the typical graduate of the typical U.S. high school will be ready for the workplace; and our citizens' confidence that American education is among the best in the world.

But even more is at stake than our future prosperity. Despite this country's mostly admirable utilitarianism when it comes to education, good education is not just about readiness for the practical challenges of life. It is also about liberty and the pursuit of happiness. It is about preparation for moral, ethical and civic challenges, for participation in a vibrant culture, for informed engagement in one's community, and for a richer quality of life for oneself and one's family. Test scores are important. But so, too, are standards and excellence in our society. The decisions we make about education are really decisions about the kind of country we want to be; the sort of society in which we want to raise our children; the future we want them to have; and even—and perhaps especially—about the content of their character and the architecture of their souls. In the last decade of this American century, we must not be content with anything less than the best for all our children.

Form at end of book

Issue 1 Summary

Many are quick to blame the ills of American society on its schools. Berliner and Biddle reject these criticisms; American education, they say, is quite successful in preparing students. Bennett and his colleagues, on the other hand, see little to celebrate in American schools and much that needs changing. They view the educational system as a monopoly that is not amenable to change. These opposing positions frame many of the debates that are now raging in education—debates about charter schools, national testing, more stringent evaluation of teachers, and many other subjects.

Take a look at the educational issues that are being discussed in the courts, in the legislatures, and in professional organizations, as reported in newspapers and news magazines. Whether or not American education is in crisis, it certainly is in contention.

Standards and Testing

Questions

1. What are the primary arguments *for* national testing? What are the primary arguments *against* national testing?

2. What are the implications of the standards and national testing movement for teacher education? Put differently, if society were to demand higher standards and the introduction of national testing, how would the preparation of teachers need to be altered?

3. Congratulations—you are still the U.S. secretary of education. The president asks you to make a recommendation regarding the introduction of national testing. Write the president a memorandum responding to this request.

Introduction

When student performance declines, many call for increased standards and testing. The belief is that these actions will have a series of effects: states and school districts will focus their curricula more precisely on what is tested, teachers will take their responsibilities more seriously, and students will be more motivated because they fear failure. On the other hand, critics of this position argue that, when new tests are imposed, teachers necessarily teach to them and neglect other aspects of education; the author of the test consequently has an enormous influence on the content that students will be taught. Further, critics of large-scale testing argue that such tests typically emphasize memorized learning and fail to promote students' critical thinking and reasoning.

The authors of the four articles concerning standards and testing take differing views on the value of increased standards and testing as strategies for solving the problems of American education. Whether you agree or disagree, careful reading of the four articles will broaden your understanding of the standards and testing issue.

Standards Amidst Uncertainty and Inequality

David C. Berliner and Bruce J. Biddle

David Berliner is Regents professor of education at Arizona State University. Bruce Biddle is a professor of social psychology at University of Missouri-Columbia.

From *A Nation at Risk* in 1983 to now, many of those who criticize the public schools have made claims about evidence but often have not displayed that evidence or have bolstered their arguments with inappropriate, misleading, or simplistic analyses of data.

As demonstrated in our recent book, *The Manufactured Crisis,* and by other authors, those who argue that achievement test scores in America have declined or that the United States spends more on its schools than any other nation or that the country is not producing enough mathematicians and scientists for our economic needs are simply wrong.

Those who say that our international test scores show the weakness of our public schools or that our private schools have inherent advantages over public schools are misleading their listeners. Those who say money is unrelated to achievement or that spending on instruction in the schools is up dramatically are too simplistic in their analysis of the data.

Nobody says our public schools are all excellent, for they are not, and some are an embarrassment to a nation as rich as ours. And no thoughtful analyst wants the status quo, for our visions of teaching and learning have changed as has our economic system and thus our schools must change too. But school changes often recommended today to reflect the economic system seem to us to be misguided, and it is that issue to which we turn.

New Criticisms

Since the American public is just now beginning to learn how rarely the evidence supports some of the most damning recent criticisms of our schools, the critics have begun to argue that evidence is not the issue. Thus, the arguments of some school critics, such as Louis V. Gerstner Jr., chief executive officer of IBM, recently have shifted so that now the problem is that our children are not being prepared for the world of the next century.

This is an easier criticism to make, of course, since none of us knows what the world of the next century will bring. All the workforce analysts whom we know and believe claim that the vast majority of the jobs to be filled in the next century have not yet been created. So it is quite safe to say to parents that the schools are not preparing their children for the jobs of the next century. This keeps parents nervous and the schools on the defensive. What shall they do in the meantime?

"Perhaps it is time to rethink this pressure . . . to push higher standards for the sake of the economy . . ."

Some critics from industry and government claim to have the answer. They are saying that the way to improve the schools and prepare our students for the jobs of the next century is through better, clearer, tougher (but achievable) standards in the basic subjects. Somehow, this seems particularly reasonable to argue for when it comes to subjects Americans seem to worry about most, mathematics and science.

Promulgated along with tough content standards are demands for high performance standards. In this way American parents and educators will understand what standards their children should know and be able to do at different ages and at what level of skill they should be doing it. These high content and performance standards in mathematics, science, and other areas of the basic curriculum are intended to ensure our students are employable, that our industry will succeed.

This was the thesis of the March conference of governors and business leaders hosted by Gerstner. At least two things are left out of this analysis, however; the nature of the jobs of the future and making certain that students actually have opportunities to learn those standards. Unfortunately, these are truly crucial issues.

Preparing Students

Much of what we hear about the relationship of schooling to the jobs of the future today is, of course, hooey. What is ordinarily left out of the argument is that most jobs of the next century will not require many people with particularly high levels of mathematics or science. On that issue scholars have generated a reasonable concensus, something economists and labor-force analysts are not noted for achieving.

Present trends suggest that the jobs of the early part of the next century will be predominantly in the service area, with the hospitality sector of the economy employing more people than almost any other sector, and retail giants like Wal-Mart being among the largest non-governmental employers.

As America entered this decade, the economy was creating nine new cashier jobs for every computer programming job. While the Bureau of Labor Statistics recently predicted that paralegals were the fastest growing occupation with employment growth increasing from 1988 to 2000 by 75 percent, this growth turns into only 62,000 new jobs.

By way of contrast, the growth rate for jobs as custodians and housekeepers will only be 19 percent, but that will generate 556,000 jobs over that same period. In fact the United States now has 1.5 times as many janitors as it has lawyers, accountants, investment bankers, stockbrokers, and computer programmers combined! It is hard to look at these statistics and then follow the lead of President Clinton and writers like Ray Marshall and Marc Tucker who declare we should reform the schools to develop many more high-level "symbolic analysts"—to use Secretary of Labor Robert Reich's terms.

The symbolic analysts in our society use mathematical and scientific language in their jobs. These include architects, chemists, financial planners, marketing managers, and so forth. College degrees and advanced studies are needed by these individuals. School teachers and students are asked to work harder and longer to ensure they possess these technical skills.

According to this line of reasoning, the higher the average level of education in this country, the greater our economic might. But even Reich acknowledges that only 20 percent of the jobs of the future will require such high-level cognitive skills, while 80 percent of the jobs will be split among two other categories of workers: "routine production service" workers, such as data entry personnel—jobs

easily filled by those with basic literacy and numeracy—and "in-person service" workers, such as sales persons and tellers—jobs requiring a pleasing manner and on-the-job training.

Educational Laborers

Sometimes critics of public education argue that our society needs more highly educated workers to generate growth of our industries and the economy. Yet studies by McKinsey and Company, the prestigious management consulting firm, have shown no relationship between the level of education of the workforce and a nation's productivity.

What does matter is the education of the leaders of business and industry, not the education of the general population from which workers arise. If America turns out 20 percent of our youth to do symbolic analysis (and our rate of four-year college graduation is now about 30 percent of a cohort), that might be all that our nation needs for growth of its economic system.

Some figures compiled by Richard Rothstein, a research associate at the Washington-based Economic Policy Institute, make the national trends clearer. In 1968, 11 percent of those earning a college degree took work in jobs that did not require such a degree or found no work at all. In 1990, however, that rate had increased dramatically, with 20 percent of the college graduates not finding work in jobs that needed their degrees or finding no work at all. We now have 664,000 college graduates working as retail sales clerks, 83,000 laboring as housekeepers or custodians, and 166,000 driving trucks and buses. Blue-collar workers now number 1.3 million college graduates, double the rate of 15 years ago.

Why haven't all these talented people made the high-wage jobs grow? They cannot make the high-wage jobs grow because the economy is not in need of their talents. In fact, the oversupply of such talented workers has dropped real wages for the college educated just as dramatically as it has for those others the economy has declared unnecessary, those with only a high school education.

Let us be clear. We are not advocating any abandonment of the science and mathematics curriculum. We are not against working toward reasonable and rigorous content and performance standards. What we question, however, is whether it is honest for schools to be selling such courses to our students and their families as a way to guarantee high-paying work.

Perhaps it is time to rethink this pressure from some persons in industry and government to push higher standards for the sake of the economy and explore the many other reasons for wanting high levels of mathematics, science, history, geography, and many other subjects.

In *The Manufactured Crisis,* we defended English literature, music, and art not because they prepare us for work, but because they prepare us to be better human beings. Literature and the arts humanizine us and ennoble us, helping us to understand and feel a part of the great achievements of civilization.

Math and science do no less. In a complex world of environmental degradation, of financial complexity and computer wizardry, of chemical and biological wonders, of complex social forces and mass-media hype, we must have the literacy to understand and the emotional education to marvel at nature, detect fraud, practice good citizenship, and lead fulfilling lives.

But a high level of literacy for humanistic educational purposes is different than a push for higher levels of achievement to enhance employability or profitability. The proper role of educators is to articulate a vision of what the educated person should be like, but that process should not begin and end with a vision of what the employable person should know and be able to do.

In an age of overabundant information and too many low-wage jobs with little intellectual stimulation, the mission of the schools is to help students interpret their world and their obligations to it, to help students find joy in their outside-the-job pursuits, and perform well the role of citizen in a democracy. The push for ever higher content and performance standards in basic subjects seems remarkably free of such concerns, and that is wrong.

Equity Standards

What shall it take if students are to learn ever-higher levels of mathematics and science, history and language, geography, and social studies?

One must begin, of course, with teachers, curricula, and testing experts specifying the content to be learned and the performances that are acceptable. But content and performance standards for the nation do not mean a thing unless our country also achieves some kind of equity in opportunity to learn.

Standards in this area are of equal importance to standards in the other areas. Can we really improve American education as a whole when about 1 percent of the nation's population owns 40 percent of its wealth? Will the children in the schools serving impoverished sectors of society really have an equal chance to learn the content specified? Will they be able to reach the levels required for mastery? What might prevent them?

Children from disadvantaged backgrounds are more likely to have health problems than other children, with more rotting teeth and chronic diseases, because they cannot afford or rarely have access to medical or dental care. In addition, it is hard to come to school ready to learn algebra and the origins of the Civil War when your home is a rat-infested apartment in a rundown housing project, where drug sales and violent behavior are common.

How will content and performance standards raise the scores of these children when they know, in their hearts, they have been abandoned by society? How will the families of students in these communities help their children with the more rigorous academic demands that accompany the new standards? Many of these parents themselves are ill or working full-time at low-paying, physically exhausting jobs. Many are raising children alone. Others are immigrants without neighborhood schools to help them learn English, even when they want to.

America's system of unequal funding for public schools means our poorest students often receive the shoddiest education in the land. Many teachers in the urban and poor rural areas cannot help their students master the new standards because they lack qualifications, while the best-qualified teachers work mostly in advantaged metropolitan areas and wealthier suburbs. How will the development of new standards address this inequality?

And how will the standard setters compensate for the overcrowded classrooms and lack of textbooks, computers, and other teaching aids now characteristic of our poorer schools? In a rural school we know of in a poor district in Arizona—a state with surplus income and a large tax reduction program—the ceiling has fallen, and the rain drips in. Could this possibly interfere with learning?

The point is that merely to define content and performance standards nationwide, a goal that may be quite worthy, is not enough. While critics find it easier to deal with content and performance demands than with poverty, hopelessness, and inequities in school funding, school improvement cannot begin without opportunity-to-learn standards. In the end, it is impoverishment of the spirit of our young people that is our real challenge.

A Cautious View

Let us not get so caught up in the desire to serve the job market that we lose sight of the curriculum goals that are less specificable, those that foster humanistic ends, that catch our students up in the social, political, humanistic, and artistic issues of our times. Students who care more for their fellow citizens and their social and physical environment should ultimately produce a higher standard of living for us all than one obtained by educating only the advantaged members of society to score high on all the tests that accompany the new standards.

In fact, we think that without more concern for social justice, the standards so often touted today will be unobtainable by large segments of the population because of the circumstances of their lives. Despite their talent, these students will never have the opportunity to meet the standards so often promoted.

So let us be cautious of those who profess that they can both improve the schools and the economy through higher standards, for it may be that the economy cannot employ all of that talent at high wages, and it may be that the talent that is needed will only be cultivated among the advantaged families. In that direction lies oligarchy, not a continuation of our democracy.

Form at end of book

Voluntary National Tests Would Improve Education

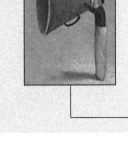

Voluntary national exams in reading and mathematics would mobilize Americans to increase student achievement.

Marshall S. Smith, David L. Stevenson, and Christine P. Li

Marshall S. Smith is Acting Deputy Secretary, David L. Stevenson is Senior Advisor, and Christine P. Li is Program Specialist for the United States Department of Education, 600 Independence Ave., S.W., Washington, DC 20202. For more information about this article, please contact Christine P. Li at christine_li@ed.gov. For more information on the voluntary national tests, please contact NAGB at http://www.nagb.org

At Crestview Elementary School, 4th grader Ashley reads voraciously and independently about fishing in the Yurok culture, while 8th grader Ricky devises and solves algebraic equations. At Del Mar Elementary School, Melanie struggles to make sense of her social studies textbook, while Scott multiples four-digit numbers in his 8th grade mathematics class. Why are Ashley and Ricky developing more advanced academic skills than Melanie and Scott? Why do schools hold such different expectations for what students can learn? To help ensure that *all* of America's children have the opportunity to achieve academic success in reading and mathematics, President Clinton has proposed the development of voluntary national tests in 4th grade reading and 8th grade mathematics.

Why 4th Grade Reading and 8th Grade Mathematics?

Reading independently by the 4th grade is the gateway to learning in all subjects. By 4th grade, teachers usually stop teaching reading and expect students to have made the transition from learning to read to reading to learn. As a poor reader, Melanie will likely experience school difficulties without intensive interventions. She may have diffi-

culty comprehending mathematics story problems, analyzing literature, and interpreting historical documents in the higher grades. She is more likely to be identified as learning disabled, receive lower grades, and not graduate from high school (Velluntino, Scanlon, and Spearing 1995; Natriello, McDill, and Pallas 1990; McMillan, Kaufmann, and Klein 1997). Melanie is not alone. Forty percent of 4th grade students read below the basic level on the National Assessment of Educational Progress (NAEP) and have trouble understanding the overall meaning of what they read (Campbell, Donahue, Reese, and Phillips 1994).

Learning some algebra and geometry by the end of 8th grade is the gateway to taking challenging mathematics courses in high school and college (Stevenson, Schiller, and Schneider 1994). Having learned some algebra and geometry by the end of the 8th grade, Ricky will enter high school prepared to study demanding mathematics. Upon entering college, he will be able to choose from a multitude of careers, particularly in rapidly growing industries such as information technology. Even if Ricky does not attend college, his higher math skills will yield benefits. Richard Murnane and Frank Levy have demonstrated that male high school graduates with higher math skills who do not go to college earn more than those with lower math skills (Murnane and Levy 1996).[1] However, many of our students do not have the same opportunities as Ricky. Only 25 percent of 8th grade students and fewer than 15 percent of low-income students take algebra by the end of 8th grade (National Center for Education Statistics 1996).

Voluntary National Tests Would Differ from Other Tests

The idea behind the proposed voluntary national tests is not simply to have another test, but to improve the chances that all children will receive high quality instruction in reading and mathematics. Unique features of the voluntary national tests would enable parents and teachers to use the tests as tools to improve education from the grassroots level.

Public and Independent

An independent, bipartisan board, the National Assessment Governing Board (NAGB), would develop the tests with extensive public involvement. The tests would be based on the highly respected NAEP frameworks, which NAGB also oversees, and which were developed through a broad-based consensus process. Under the guidance of NAGB, teachers, principals, business and community leaders, parents, and reading and math specialists would create the test items. Throughout this process, NAGB would hold public hearings. The tests would be free of racial, cultural, or gender bias and would make accommodations for disadvantaged, limited English proficient, and disabled students. In addition, the National Academy of Sciences would conduct three studies related to the tests. It would study the quality and fairness of the test results, and determine if an equivalency scale could be developed to link commercially available standardized tests and state assessments to NAEP.

Unlike NAEP, which is not an individual test and is given to a sample of students, the voluntary national tests would be given to individual students and yield individual student scores. The tests are strictly voluntary. The federal government would not withhold funding from a state or local education agency based on its participation, nor would the federal government receive individual test results. Under the current schedule, the pilot test would be conducted in March 1999, and the first test would follow in March 2000. The first voluntary national tests would be administered in March 2001, and the government would offer a new version of the tests on an annual basis.

Tied to Challenging External Standards

The voluntary national tests would measure student performance standards against challenging external standards of what students know and can do. The tests would be explicitly linked to NAEP performance levels and, in mathematics, also to the performance scale for the Third International Mathematics and Science Study (TIMSS).

The voluntary national tests would measure student performance against challenging external standards of what students know and can do.

The NAEP performance standards are challenging. In cases where states set performance standards, their standards are generally below the NAEP standards. A recent Southern Regional Education Board study revealed that in some states, more than 80 percent of the students are proficient on state assessments, but only 20 percent or fewer are proficient based on NAEP standards (Musick 1996).

The results of a standards assessment based on national and international benchmarks would be powerful tools for local change. With a clear picture of the performance of their children, communities could better invest their time, money, and energy in schools. Teachers could target students' needs and use test results for self-evaluations. Administrators could support the professional development their schools and teachers need. Parents could choose to become more involved in their children's education.

Public Release of the Tests

Within two weeks of the test administration in March, the test items, answers, and explanatory information would be widely distributed via the Internet and other avenues. In May, teachers would receive individual students' answers to every test item, along with explanatory information.

Before the end of the school year, teachers and parents would know how their students' performance measures against high academic standards, *and* they would have the tools to help improve their performance. Teachers and parents would have a clear explanation of what the NAEP standards are and detailed examples of proficient performance based on those standards. Teachers and parents could address individual student needs. Educators could evaluate their current teaching materials and instructional methods and make plans to help their students during the same school year. Principals and teachers could review the test results to evaluate the effectiveness of their instructional programs, to plan their summer professional development, and to mobilize school communities to improve performance.

Rich Supplemental Information

The annual public release of the tests would include rich supplemental information that clearly explains the performance standards and the content area of each item. For mathematics, the content areas include numbers and operations, geometry, and estimation. Parents and teachers would receive examples of student work for each item, as well as examples of the work needed to meet different levels of performance. Teachers would have access to instructional strategies, research-based curriculum materials, and a sample test a year before the first administration of the tests.

Through the Internet and other means, parents and teachers would have immediate access to test results and elaborative information. In fact, the power of technology would give parents and teachers innumerable opportunities to improve student performance in reading and mathematics. For example, through a Web site for the voluntary national tests, parents and teachers would be able to request technical assistance, join networks, access sample lesson plans, view reading lists recommended by the American Library Association and the International Reading Association, and learn about programs that provide assistance in improving students' reading and mathematics skills.

Helping Teachers Teach Challenging Content

The tests would provide educators with tools to teach challenging content. The rich supplemental information would give teachers a clear understanding of the content areas in reading and mathematics. Each year the tests are offered, the content areas would remain the same, but the items would be different. The tests would *not* be designed to encourage teachers to have students memorize items or master testing "tricks." With consistent content areas, but new test items each year, the tests would encourage teachers to teach students demanding content.

National Focus

The voluntary national tests would center the nation's attention on improving reading and mathematics education. The president and others would talk about the tests every week for the next two years. This national focus would help mobilize local communities to improve the quality of instruction in schools. Business and community organizations could form school partnerships, and community members could participate in campaigns to improve reading and mathematics. The Department of Education, with many partners, is already involved in such campaigns. The America Reads Challenge includes a corps of trained reading tutors, reading specialists, and tutor coordinators; parental support; and early intervention for our most disadvantaged children. The Department of Education and the National Science Foundation have developed an action plan to build public understanding of challenging mathematics, to help equip teachers with the skills and knowledge to teach challenging mathematics, and to assist communities in efforts to implement high-quality curriculums and instructional materials.

> **By ensuring that every 4th grader can read independently and every 8th grader can solve challenging mathematics problems, the tests would create a foundation for their school careers.**

The voluntary national tests would challenge students to achieve high academic standards at key points in their school careers. By ensuring that every 4th grader can read independently and every 8th grader can solve challenging mathematics problems, the test would create a foundation for their school careers. If we do not help them establish this foundation, students from schools like Crestview and Del Mar will be unequally prepared to enter the demanding workplace of the 21st century. Students like Melanie will continue to struggle to read, and those like Scott will continue to do rote computation. The voluntary national tests would give parents and teachers powerful tools to help *all* America's children excel academically, compete in a global economy, and become responsible citizens in our democratic society. The voluntary national tests alone would not change American education. But they could help mobilize local efforts or improvement in two of the most essential basics of American education: reading and mathematics.

Notes

1. For further discussion, see United States Department of Education Planning and Evaluation Service. (October 20, 1997). "Mathematics Equals Opportunity." White paper prepared for U.S. Secretary of Education Richard W. Riley.

References

Campbell, J. R., P.I. Donahue, C.M. Reese, and G.W. Phillips. (1994). *NAEP 1994 Reading Report Card for the Nation and the States.* Washington, D.C.: U.S. Government Printing Office.

McMillan, M., P. Kaufman, and S. Klein. (1997). *Dropout Rates in the United States 1995.* Washington, D.C.: U.S. Government Printing Office.

Murnane, R.J. and F. Levy. (1996). *Teaching the New Basic Skills.* New York: Free Press.

Musick, M.D. (1996). *Setting Education Standards High Enough.* Atlanta: Southern Regional Education Board.

National Center for Education Statistics. (1996) *NAEP Facts: Eighth-Grade Algebra Course-Taking and Mathematics Proficiency.* Washington, D.C.: U.S. Government Printing Office.

Natriello, G., E. L. McDill, and A. M. Pallas (1990) *Schooling Disadvantaged Children: Racing Against Catastrophe.* New York: Teachers College Press.

Stevenson, D.L., K. Schiller, and B. Schneider. (1994). "Sequences of Opportunities for Learning." *Sociology of Education* 67:187–198.

Velluntino, F. R., D.M. Scanlon, and D. Spearing. (1995). "Semantic and Phonological Coding in Poor and Normal Readers." *Journal of Experimental Child Psychology,* 59: 76–123.

Form at end of book

National Tests Are Unnecessary and Harmful

The proposed national exams in mathematics and reading are detrimental to student learning.

Monty Neill, Ed.D

Monty Neill is Executive Director of the National Center for Fair & Open Testing (FairTest), 342 Broadway, Cambridge, MA 02139 (e-mail to fairtest@aol.com;Web site: http://www. fairtest org).

Much of the debate over President Clinton's proposal for national exams has focused on issues of federalism and political control. Though Representative Bill Goodling (R-Pennsylvania) regularly reminded people that "you cannot fatten cattle by weighing them," too little discussion has center on the tests' likely educational consequences.

The administration and the U.S. Congress compromised on national testing in 1997 by agreeing to allow item development, but not field testing or other implementation, and by agreeing to conduct several studies. The issue will return to Congress this year, first with the reauthorization of the National Assessment of Educational Progress (NAEP), and then probably in the fall, when Congress will again debate funding for national tests. Given its weak rationale and the likely inequities and educational dangers associated with it, Congress should reject the national testing plan.

More Testing Is a Waste

Proponents of national tests claim they are needed to provide individual student test scores and to yield aggregate statewide and nationwide data. But we already have mountains of such information. U.S. schoolchildren are the most tested in the world, taking more than 100 million standardized tests each year.

These large-scale exams provide teachers or parents with little useful information about individual students. The more time teachers spend prepping for and giving standardized tests, the less time they have to spend on real teaching. The kind of assessment that can directly improve teaching and learning takes place in the classroom every day. Congress could usefully support ways to improve teachers' abilities to do strong classroom assessment.

As for comparing school districts to one another, that has long been the purview of state education departments. Most states now have or are implementing exams based on state standards. Clinton's proposed exam would not provide parents or educators with useful new information, which explains why only six states signed on to the plan.

Given its weak rationale and the likely inequities and educational dangers associated with it, Congress should reject the national testing plan.

But what of the claim that state standards vary considerably, and national tests are needed to make interstate comparisons? Wrong again. We already have such a national test. NAEP exams are given to a significant sample of students across the country, and the resulting data are used to make highly publicized interstate comparisons.

Finally, U.S. students also take exams that compare performance across countries. What we learn from these exams is that American children perform well above average in reading, but about average in math and science. Their greatest weakness is not in mastering the basics, but in understanding concepts and applying knowledge. Unfortunately, the proposed new national tests would primarily measure knowledge of the basics. They would not effectively measure—or encourage the teaching of—the kinds of higher-order thinking skills that U.S. students most lack.

The Tests Will Be Harmful

If the proposed tests were merely a waste of classroom time and taxpayer dollars, complaints about them might be muted. Unfortunately, they could well do more educational harm than good. Standardized tests have been used for decades as gatekeepers to deny low-scoring students access to high-quality programs and to track them into low-level classes. The administration refused to build safeguards into its testing and to prevent misuse, such as tracking or grade retention based on a single test score, though the congressional compromise calls for studying this issue. There were inadequate requirements to ensure that students with disabilities would be included fully and assessed fairly. Students with limited English proficiency either would not be assessed at all or would be assessed invalidly. There was also no requirement that schools provide all children with the opportunity to learn the material on which they would be tested.

The tests themselves were to be mostly multiple choice and short answer; a sort of "NAEP-lite" that would fail to assess whether students can actually think in a subject area. If Clinton's tests pass Congress and become important—as he clearly wants them to—they will perpetuate the tendency to reduce teaching to low-level drill-and-kill, particularly in schools serving poor kids. That will not only harm excellence, it will further undermine equity.

The unfortunate reality is that at the state and now the national level, testing is mostly an attempt to improve education on the cheap. Rather than measure student performance with basic skills tests once again, let's get down to the hard business of taking real action to improve teaching and learning in our public schools. A first step is to reject the false idea that we can test our way to better schools.

Form at end of book

What's Wrong with Teaching for the Test?

In a quest to show better performance, educators may be harming students in the long term.

Jack Kaufhold

Jack Kaufhold, a former superintendent, is a professor of educational psychology at Nova Southeastern University, 3301 College Ave., Fort Lauderdale, Fla. 33314. E-mail: kaufhold@fcae.acast.nova.edu

As the quest for high test scores goes on and the pressure mounts on educators to meet higher goals, many teachers have reconciled themselves to skipping traditional curriculum content and replacing it with only that material that is likely to appear on the next standardized test.

In some cases, this measure is one of self defense. Site administrators are told, "If your test scores don't go up, you may lose your job." Teachers also know that if their students' achievement test scores fluctuate too much from year to year, they too could be demoted or dismissed. Several school districts, including Broward County, Fla., have made test scores a part of teacher evaluation criteria.

Although teachers and administrators know they have no control over the academic preparedness of students when they begin their school careers, they realize they are expected to educate the students to an increasingly higher level of scoring. For many educators placed in this high-stakes position, the only recourse is to teach for the test. In other words, the only material taught is that which has appeared on similar tests in the past.

In fact, some people see nothing wrong with this practice. They offer a quick-fix type answer: "At least we can be sure that students have learned *something*." But have they really learned something? How much have they actually benefitted from digesting this required material? Those who would advocate teaching for the test need to examine first these deterrents.

Harmful Impact

The practice of teaching to the test has eight significant undesirable effects. That practice:

- *Invalidates the test.*

  Teaching for the test actually can invalidate test scores and defeat the purpose of the test. According to Robert L. Linn and Norman E. Gronlund, authors of *Measurement and Assessment in Teaching*, "This (teaching for the test) not only would be an undesirable narrowing of what is taught, but would be likely to inflate test scores and change the meaning of results, possibly changing the construct measured from problem solving to memorization ability."

  It is not inconceivable that an overly ambitious or competitive principal or teacher might drill students on test-term material in an effort to score higher than his or her colleagues' classes.

- *Promotes convergent thinking.*

  This practice also promotes convergent thinking while emphasizing that students need to search for the *one right answer*. Creative ideas or divergent thinking is discouraged as students narrow the scope of their thinking toward what will be on the test.

  How sad it is to think that many of our children with bright, creative minds have their divergent thought patterns curtailed in searching for a pre-established answer.

- *Promotes learning information that may be obsolete.*

  In 1970, Alvin Toffler, in his book *Future Shock,* made a point that is valid today as we approach the new millennium. He wrote, "For education the lesson is clear. Its prime objective must be to increase the individual's 'cope-ability'—the speed and economy with which he can adapt to continual change."

  Toffler claimed (even before the widespread use of powerful computers) that the "here and now environment" soon will vanish. "Johnny must learn to anticipate the directions and rate of change . . . and so must Johnny's teachers," he said.

  If Toffler is correct, there is little use in memorizing data in order to score high on a test.

- *Excludes the arts and extracurricular activities.*

An overzealous teacher might well ask, "Why take time to go on a field trip if it doesn't increase test scores?" In like manner, subjects such as art, music and physical education could be strongly de-emphasized in the competition for high marks.

One elementary school teacher in North Carolina reported that her request for a field trip was turned down because "the objectives of the trip did not coincide with the test material."

- *Excludes the affective domain.*

In 1973, psychologist Abraham Maslow wrote that there was another side to the student that was equally important as cognitive learning. This aspect was explained as the affective or personal side of education. It consisted of mentoring to a student's needs, feelings and interests in order to maximize learning and produce a mentally healthy student.

Since the standardized tests do not deal with affective material, this part of learning is omitted.

- *Overlooks discovery learning and promotes didactic instruction.*

Educators from John Dewey to Jean Piaget and Jerome Bruner have stressed the value of active learning. Numerous books by these individuals and others point to the fact students retain information longer if they actively participate in discovering knowledge. Dewey's famous quote, "What we have to learn, we learn by doing" would not be practical in teaching for the test.

". . . subjects such as art, music and physical education could be strongly de-emphasized . . ."

- *Involves only short-term memory.*

Author Jeanne Ormrod, who wrote *Educational Psychology—Developing Learners,* explained that each learner has to carefully "encode" or translate material that is taught in order to transfer that learning to the long-term memory where it becomes knowledge. Material that is taught for immediate use in a testing situation could likely wind up getting only as far as the short-term memory.

- *Excludes higher-order thinking skills.*

Psychologist David Elkind noted that the "aim of psychometric education, which is to produce children who do well on achievement tests, is in direct opposition to the aim of developmental education, which is to produce critical and creative thinkers." Elkind concluded that the "developmental approach seeks to create students who *want to know,* whereas the psychometric approach seeks to produce students who *know what we want.*"

Why Compare?

Faced with all these deterrents, a well-meaning school official could say, "Yes, but if we don't teach for the test, we will be low in comparison with other schools in other locations." A proper response to that might be "Why compare?" When demographics, student abilities, financial capability and community expectations differ from place to place, what valid reasons can there be for comparing schools, counties, states and even countries? What is gained by these comparisons and what do they prove? What is wrong with measuring each school, county or state against itself?

There is nothing wrong with establishing and maintaining proficiency standards for schools (provided that these standards can be achieved within the context of the school's funding and community support), but unilateral comparisons of these scores make no sense.

In our zeal to provide measures of accountability to the public it is well to remember that, unlike other professions, the product of teaching is not easy to quantify. While the best physician might be the one who performs the most successful operations and the best attorney might be the one who wins the most cases, this same yardstick cannot be applied to education. It is not necessarily true that the best educator is the one with the highest-achieving students.

In the case of the doctor or lawyer, each has clients who willingly place themselves in the hands of the professional and pay for his or her services. The educator, on the other hand, deals with students who may be unwilling to learn or whose parents or community do not provide proper support.

To return to the original question, "What's wrong with teaching for the test?" let me suggest a more apt query: "What's right about it?"

Form at end of book

Issue 2 Summary

The issue of raising standards and introducing national testing cuts to the heart of a critical problem in American education—the tension between excellence and access. On the one hand, we want an educational system that produces bright students who will help society move forward. On the other hand, we want to ensure that all students have access to education. By introducing higher standards and increased testing, we risk denying access to some students. However, if standards are kept low and failure is infrequent, the quality of education declines. Educators have been debating this issue for a long time; a solution has been elusive. To a great extent, one's political and social beliefs influence one's position on this difficult issue.

Constructivist Approaches to Education

Questions

1. How does the role of the teacher differ from the perspectives of the behavioral, information-processing, cognitive constructivist, and social constructivist approaches?

2. What problems can occur when teachers adopt a constructivist approach to teaching in their classrooms?

3. Which approach—behavioral, information-processing, cognitive constructivist, or social constructivist—or which combination of approaches is being used in this course? Which approach makes most sense to you in your future teaching, and why?

Introduction

This issue differs from the prior two in that it concerns more directly the applications of psychology to education. For the better part of the twentieth century, *behaviorism* was the school of thought in psychology that had the greatest impact on American education. Behaviorism is based on the idea that learning occurs as a function of external events, such as rewards and punishments. Much research was done with animals to demonstrate how external events control the learning of new behavior. The influence of *constructivism* emerged in the 1970s and grew in the 1980s and 1990s. Constructivism is based on the idea that learners create their own understanding of phenomena through experience, frequently guided by a more knowledgeable adult or peer. Underlying constructivism is the idea that human learners are rational and are active agents in their own learning.

The first of the two articles addresses how constructivism emerged in America and the impact of the two approaches—behaviorism and constructivism—on the role of teachers. The second article cautions readers about the constructivist approach, identifying potential problems that could prevent rather than promote learning.

From Behaviorist to Constructivist Teaching

Geoffrey Scheurman

Geoffrey Scheurman is associate professor in the Department of Teacher Education at the University of Wisconsin-River Falls, River Falls, Wisconsin. He taught high school social studies in Wyoming for 11 years before earning his Ph.D. in Educational Psychology from the University of Iowa. The author would like to thank Tom Russo, Mike Yell, several of his students, and especially Michael Simpson and Jennifer Rothwell for the constructive feedback and editorial assistance.

Constructivism refers to a set of related theories that deal with the nature of knowledge. The common denominator linking these theories is a belief that knowledge is created by people and influenced by their values and culture. In contrast to this view is the behaviorist belief that knowledge exists outside of people and independently of them, and that the major goal of a good education is to instill in students an accepted body of information and skills previously established by others.

When the constructivist view is applied to teaching and learning in the social studies, the goal of a good education includes the development of (1) deep understanding of social studies problems and procedures, and (2) rigorously defensible beliefs about important disciplinary issues. This developmental process is enhanced when students learn to view problems and issues from different angles and to identify multiple perspectives within and outside the field of study. Ultimately, knowledge is constructed when students form their own interpretations of evidence submitted to them for review.

The constructivist perspective has important implications for teaching and learning in the social studies. Much of social education has been directed toward the simple transmission of information and techniques for processing information. Constructivism has a natural affinity with approaches to teaching that are directed toward open-ended inquiry, and that encourage creative reflection on objects, events and cultural experience.

Constructivism, like other approaches, comes in varying shades. As one author stated, "the particular version of constructivism one adopts . . . has important implications for classroom practices, for the definition of knowledge, for the relative emphasis on individual versus social learning, for the role of the teacher, and for the definition of successful instruction."[1]

This introductory article provides a frame of reference for the special section on constructivism that follows, and for the debate about constructivism in social studies that appears imminent.

One way to examine constructivist approaches to social studies teaching is to contrast them to other world views on teaching and learning. I have designed a matrix around four hypothetical teacher roles (Table 1, row one), each derived from a philosophical view about the nature of knowledge (row two). These views reflect a theoretical background derived from psychological research (row three). They also imply a metaphorical view of learners (row four).

The categories in this matrix are neither exclusive (a teacher probably engages students in multiple ways within a lesson or unit), nor judgmental (different roles may facilitate important, albeit different, educational objectives). Nevertheless, it is possible to classify the nature of classroom activity when a teacher adopts a specific epistemology, or view of knowledge (rows five and six).

Teacher As Transmitter

According to the behaviorist view, reality exists independently of learners and knowledge is received exclusively through the senses. Learning functions like a switchboard, occurring when one person transmits the universal characteristics of reality to another. According to B. F. Skinner, knowledge is acquired when the bond between stimulus and response is strengthened by means of a reinforcer. The teacher's primary function is to break information and skills into small increments, present them part-to-whole in an organized fashion, and then reward student behaviors that mirror the reality presented by teachers and texts.

For the teacher as transmitter, classroom activity might include responding to questions in a chapter, taking notes from a lecture, or responding to cues provided by a computer. For example, students may use information

Table 1 Matrix of Teaching and Learning Approaches

Role of Teacher	Transmitter	Manager	Facilitator	Collaborator
Nature of Knowledge	Universal, objective, and fixed (independent of knower)	Universal and "objective" (influenced by knower's prior knowledge)	Individually constructed, "objective" (contingent on knower's intellectual development)	Socially constructed; "subjective" (distributed across knowers)
Grounding Theoretical Tradition	Behaviorism	Information processing	Cognitive constructivism	Social constructivism
Metaphorical View of Learner	Switchboard	Computer	Naive scientist	Apprentice
Nature of Teaching Activity	*Present* reality to students • disseminate information incrementally • demonstrate procedures • reinforce habits during independent practice	Help students *process* reality • assemble information-rich environments • model expert memory and thinking strategies • foster metacognition	*Challenge* students' conceptions of reality • promote disequilibrium with discrepant objects and events • guide students through problem solving activities • monitor reflective thinking *after* discoveries	Participate with students in *constructing* reality • elicit and adapt to student (mis) conceptions • engage in open-ended inquiries with students • guide self and students to authentic resources and procedures
Nature of Student Activity	*Replicate* reality transmitted by authorities • listen • rehearse • recite	*Manipulate* reality perceived through senses • practice thinking and memorizing activities • develop new schemes automatize skills • practice self-regulatory strategies	*Experience* reality during physical and social activity • assimilate information • develop new schemata and operations to deal with novel experiences • reflect on physical, social, and intellectual discoveries	*Create* reality during physical and social activity • manufacture "situated" (cultural) understandings • actively engage in open-ended inquiries with peers and teachers • reflect on co-constructed meanings

they receive during a lecture on events leading up to the American Revolution to place activities challenging British rule on a continuum called "Degrees of Disagreement," whose categories range from "dissent" and "civil disobedience" through "insurrection" and "rebellion." This and other class activities are described in more detail in the next article.* The skills of classification that students practice in such an activity are important, but the questions require responses that can be termed right or wrong rather than interpretations that are justified on the basis of critically-examined evidence

Teacher As Manager

The behaviorist paradigm has undergone a dramatic shift over the past several decades. A major challenge to behaviorism in the field of linguistics was launched by Noam Chomsky, who argued that children possess an innate capacity to acquire language, and that their minds should not be considered passive receptacles into which knowl-

*Does not appear in this publication.

edge about language is transmitted. With the help of computers, cognitive scientists have fueled a "revolution" in the psychology of learning by modeling how learners' prior knowledge (stored in clusters called *schemata*) not only filters, but actually modifies, sensory activity as it is experienced.[2]

Given that pre-existing memory structures influence the learner's interaction with stimuli, an important function of teaching, in this view, is to help students become aware of their prior knowledge and conceptions, and then to provide them with increasingly expert methods for dealing with an information-rich environment. The teacher as manager might model strategies for "chunking" information, encourage students to build connections using advance organizers and concept maps, and eventually help students acquire techniques for regulating their own thinking processes.

In a unit on the American Revolution, for example, the teacher could have students practice critical reading using a heuristic for engaging in the evaluation of historical accounts. This heuristic involves remembering what a historian actually says about events (the literal reading of the account), examining what a historian may have implied by his or her narrative (reading between the lines), and evaluating what biases or values may be reflected in a historian's record of events (generalizing beyond the lines). By managing an environment in which students gain experience at consuming information and asking questions about it, teachers help students develop their own independent abilities to review historical materials.

Teacher As Facilitator or Collaborator

While the teacher as manager may allow students a more active role than the teacher as transmitter, learning is still based on the twin premises that (1) knowledge is a possession of "truths" that reside outside the knower, and (2) learning is the process of acquiring those truths. There is a qualitative shift in epistemology, however, when one abandons the requirement that knowledge "represent an independent world" and accepts the constructivist premise that knowledge "represents . . . what we can *do* in our *experiential* world."[3]

Although constructivist theories are too numerous to delineate here, the field can be categorized into two basic views: *cognitive* and *social* (Table 1, columns three and four).[4] The most influential figure in cognitive constructivism is Jean Piaget, who believed that people develop universal forms or structures of knowledge (i.e., prelogical, concrete, or formal) that enable them to experience reality. This view holds that while an autonomous "real" world may exist outside the learner, he or she has limited access to it. The emphasis in learning is on how people assimilate new information into existing mental schemes, and how they restructure schemes entirely when information is too discrepant to be assimilated.

The most influential figure in the social constructivist camp is Lev Vygotsky. Accepting Piaget's view of how individuals build private understandings of reality through problem solving with others, Vygotsky further explained how social or cultural contexts contribute to a *public* understanding of objects and events. In this view, reality is no longer objective, while knowledge is literally co-constructed by, and distributed among, individuals as they "interact with one another and with cultural artifacts, such as pictures, texts, discourse, and gestures."[5]

The conceptual relationship between the two forms of constructivism is so close that I have chosen to discuss them together. If, as Piaget suggested, knowledge is acquired when cognitive stability is directly challenged, then the primary role of the teacher as facilitator is to pose problems that stretch learners to a point of intellectual disequilibrium (perturbation). Once this point is reached, the teacher provides students with opportunities to manipulate objects and work together on solving problems

(action), and to think about and discuss new-found properties of "reality" as they experience it (reflective abstraction).

If, as Vygotsky suggested, cognitive development is "the transformation of socially shared activities into internalized [thought] processes,"[6] then the primary role of the teacher as collaborator is to monitor classroom learning and participate actively with students in its evolution. Two further recommendations on the nature of teaching derive from social constructivism. First, what teachers have traditionally viewed as errors in student thinking should be understood as misconceptions that both indicate a student's readiness to learn and offer an entry point for teachers to provide scaffolding (expert support) for that learning. Second, students should have frequent opportunities to interact with peers and more experienced people, including the teacher, who becomes another collaborator in the creation of meaning.

One kind of activity that would enhance a constructivist classroom, with the teacher adopting the role of facilitator or collaborator, would be for students to collectively assemble a variety of historical documents about an event, review the evidence and perspectives that they offer, and construct their own description and interpretation of the event.

Connections and Concerns

In one sense, the teaching roles depicted in the Table 1 matrix are additive from left to right. For example, it is difficult to imagine any learning encounter without a certain amount of transmission on the part of the teacher. Even the most collaborative exercise requires instructions and prerequisite information to help students follow procedures and to reinforce thinking skills. Also, to suggest that a teacher challenge students' conceptions of reality with novel experiences (the role of facilitator) is not to assume that the teacher does not or should not have clear standards for judging better and worse versions of reality as well as what constitutes a good strategy for approaching the problem (role of manager).

There are many connections between constructivist models of teaching and other theoretical ideas. For example, a growing body of evidence suggests that people construct representations of the world using multiple intelligences—from musical and spatial to linguistic and logical.[7] In the constructivist lesson on Lexington Green that follows in the next article,* students make use of linguistic skills to interpret language usages in old documents, analytical skills to deduce the relative certainty of an author's claim, spatial skills to interpret maps, and interpersonal skills to act as lead historians or witnesses to the event.

*Does not appear in this publication.

Emotional intelligence is another construct gaining attention in educational circles.[8] Students with highly-tuned levels of emotional intelligence may readily empathize with the feelings expressed in a poignant song about a dying friend—even if the tragedy occurred in 1775. More importantly, the simple act of assuming a first person role in a conflict involving different versions of truth is sure to evoke an affective response from many teenagers. This creates an opportunity for teachers to *develop* emotional intelligence by exposing students to the ideas that (1) having a vested interest in a situation influences individual perceptions of reality, and (2) emotional responses may figure as largely as reason in interpreting historical evidence.

There are several concerns to consider in adopting constructivist reforms. Some research suggests that American college students are disposed to see problems in dualistic terms and to seek simple answers from authorities such as teachers and texts.[9] If, as Newmann suggests,[10] these dispositions are brought about by how students are and have been taught, a move toward constructivist teaching methods in the pre-college years may be essential. Some questions that arise are:

- What are the developmental limits of adolescents in constructing knowledge?

- How much time should be devoted to the process?

- To what extent should we trade breadth of knowledge for depth of understanding?

- On what basis will students justify "personal meanings"?

- How can teachers collaborate in the construction of meanings, and still serve as objective evaluators of their quality?

Perhaps the most critical concern in adopting constructivist reforms is the possibility of the wholesale abandonment of traditional instruction and assessment. In the zeal to eradicate the mindset of "one-right-answer reductionism," teachers may adopt an "anything-goes constructivism."[11] Bandwagon mentality has never served teachers or students well in the long run. As with any educational reform, there must be standards and criteria for what constitutes a reasonable student construction in order to avoid rampant relativism in what counts as acceptable.

Authoritative expertise exists in history and the social sciences, just as it does in math and science. It is important to realize that some constructions—call them realities, truths, arguments, representations, schemes, or simply elements of acquired knowledge—are better than others.[12] Richard Prawat refers to a "constructivist dilemma," which he defines as "striking the right balance between honoring the individual student's own effort after meaning while steering the group toward some 'intellectually honest' (i.e. disciplinarily correct) construction of meaning. . . ."[13]

In spite of my affinity for many of the claims in the constructivist camps, I am doubtful that a willy-nilly appeal to "personal meaning" will do anything to aid in the powerful learning of social studies. As teachers, our moral obligation to decide what children ought to know does not disappear when we discard one theoretical paradigm in favor of another, even if the new one invites students to participate actively in the construction of disciplinary knowledge.

Recognizing these concerns, there may be a greater danger if we *don't* make an effort to adopt constructivist reforms. To many students, the past is seen as a "dry compilation of 'facts' and 'data,' a closed catechism, or a set of questions already answered" when it really is an ongoing conversation and a "place to invent."[14] Woodrow Wilson once criticized examinations in history as a meaningless ritual of listing "one damn fact after another." In continuing to encourage this kind of activity, teachers may be contributing to many students' perception of social studies as the least interesting, most irrelevant subject in the school curriculum.[15] Worse, teachers may be losing the joy inherent in the exercise of their own chosen profession. In either case, the evidence is too strong, and the stakes are too high, not to consider constructivist approaches in social studies instruction.

Notes

1. P. W. Airasian and M. E. Walsh, "Constructivist Cautions," *Phi Delta Kappan* 78, 9 (1997), 445.
2. A review of schema and connectionist theories, among others, can be found in R. E. Reynolds, G. M. Sinatra, and T. J. Jetton, "Views of Knowledge Acquisition and Representation: A Continuum from Experience Centered to Mind Centered." *Educational Psychologist*, 31, 2 (1996).
3. E. von Glasersfeld, "A Constructivist Approach to Teaching" in L. P. Steffe and J. Gale, eds., *Constructivism in Education* (Hillsdale, NJ: Erlbaum, 1995), 6–7.
4. Although constructivism has been categorized in numerous ways (at least twelve by my count). I have chosen to ally myself with others who identify two main perspectives presented here (e.g., see Airasian and Walsh, 1997). The cognitive constructivist perspective is sometimes referred to as "radical constructivism," of which Jean Piaget and Ernst von Glasersfeld are primary champions, even though the next column in the matrix, "social constructivism," departs from traditional theories in ways that might be considered even more radical than Piaget or von Glasersfeld. For a valuable discussion on the roots of constructivist thinking and applications to classrooms, free of such fine grained distinctions, see J. G. Brooks and M. Brooks, *In Search of Understanding: The Case for Constructivist Classrooms* (Alexandria, VA: Association for Supervision and Curriculum Development, 1993).

5. L. S. Vygotsky, *Mind in Society: The Development of Higher Psychological Processes* (Translation edited by M. Cole, et al., Cambridge, MA: Harvard, 1978), 90. Some researchers make fine-grained distinctions between social constructivist theories that emphasize the general importance of cultural context and theories that specify the mental operations of learners as they interact with particular conditions in the environment. For a review of "situated cognition" (the latter variety), see the discussion by Reynolds et al. (footnote 2).

6. V. John-Steiner and H. Mahn, "Sociocultural Approaches to Learning and Development: A Vygotskian Framework," *Educational Psychologist* 31, 3/4 (1996), 192.

7. I speak of the varied works by Howard Gardner, including *Frames of Mind: The Theory of Multiple Intelligences* (New York: Basic, 1983) and *Multiple Intelligence: The Theory in Practice* (New York: Basic, 1993). During a recent conversation I had with Gardner, he referred to multiple intelligences as the "tools" a person has to represent and ultimately understand the world. He believes that understanding is in turn consistent with a constructivist view of knowledge.

8. Daniel Goldman, *Emotional Intelligence: Why It Can Matter More Than IQ,* (New York: Bantam, 1995).

9. Patricia M. King and Karen S. Kitchener review over two decades of research on adult intellectual development associated with the Reflective Judgment Model in *Developing Reflective Judgment,* (San Francisco: Jossey-Bass, 1994).

10. See Fred M. Newmann, "Higher Order Thinking in the Teaching of Social Studies: Connections between Theory and Practice" in J. F. Voss, D. N. Perkins and J. W. Segal (eds.), *Informal Reasoning and Education* (Hillsdale, NJ: Erlbaum, 1991).

11. For an excellent discussion of cautions in the constructivist movement, see Airasian and Walsh, *op cit.* (footnote 1). These descriptive terms can be found on pp. 448–49.

12. A similar concern is discussed by K. T. Spoehr and L. W. Spoehr, "Learning to Think Historically," in *Educational Psychologist,* 1994. For example, they state "not all facts—and not all opinions—are created equal."

13. R. S. Prawat and R. E. Floden, "Philosophical Perspectives on Constructivist Views of Learning." *Educational Psychologist,* 29, 1 (1994), 47.

14. Tom Holt, *Thinking Historically: Narrative, Imagination, and Understanding* (New York: The College Board, 1990), 13.

15. J. M. Shaughnessy and T. M. Haladyna, "Research on Student Attitudes Toward Social Studies," *Social Education* 49 (1985): 692–695.

Form at end of book

Constructivist Cautions

The authors point out the difference between the theory of constructivism and its practical application, and they argue that the consequences of implementing constructivism in the classroom will be considerably more challenging than might be anticipated from the simple slogans that advocates repeat.

Peter W. Airasian and Mary E. Walsh

Peter W. Airasian and Mary E. Walsh are professors in the School of Education, Boston College, Chestnut Hill, Mass.

Recently, the concept of "constructivism" has been receiving a great deal of attention. At the conceptual level, constructivists debate such questions as, What is knowledge? What is teaching? What is learning? And is objectivity possible?[1] At the practical level, these complex issues have, in many cases, been reduced to catch phrases such as "Students construct their own knowledge" or the slightly narrower "Students construct their own knowledge based on their existing schemata and beliefs." Many efforts are under way to translate constructivist epistemology into classroom practices that will enable students to become "constructors of their own knowledge." While readily acknowledging that constructivism has made and will continue to make a significant contribution to educational theory and practice, we wish to sound a cautionary note about the euphoria surrounding constructivism.

What Is Constructivism?

Constructivism is an epistemology, a philosophical explanation about the nature of knowledge. Although constructivism might provide a model of knowing and learning that could be useful for educational purposes, at present the constructivist model is descriptive, not prescriptive. It describes in the broadest of strokes the human activity of knowing and nowhere specifies the detailed craft of teaching. It is important to understand at the outset that constructivism is not an instructional approach; it is a theory about how learners come to know. Although instructional approaches are typically derived from such epistemologies, they are distinct from them. One of the concerns that prompted us to undertake this discussion is the rush to turn the constructivist epistemology into instructional practice with little concern for the pitfalls that are likely to ensue.

Constructivism describes how one attains, develops, and uses cognitive processes. Multiple theories, such as those of Piaget and Vygostky, have been proposed to explain the cognitive processes that are involved in constructing knowledge. While constructivism provides the epistemological framework for many of these theories, it is not itself an explanation for the psychological factors involved in knowing.

In general, constructivist compare an "old" view of knowledge to a "new," constructivist view. In the old view, knowledge is considered to be fixed and independent of the knower. There are "truths" that reside outside the knower. Knowledge is the accumulation of the "truths" in a subject area. The more "truths" one acquires, the more knowledge one possesses. In sharp contrast, the constructivist view rejects the notion that knowledge is independent of the knower and consists of accumulating "truths." Rather, knowledge is produced by the knower from existing beliefs and experiences. All knowledge is constructed and consists of what individuals create and express. Since individuals make their own meaning from their beliefs and experiences, all knowledge is tentative, subjective, and personal. Knowledge is viewed not as a set of universal "truths," but as a set of "working hypotheses." Thus constructivists believe that knowledge can never be justified as "true" in an absolute sense.

Constructivism is based on the fundamental assumption that people create knowledge from the interaction between their existing knowledge or beliefs and the new ideas or situations they encounter. In this sense, most constructivists support the need to foster interactions between students' existing knowledge and new experiences. This emphasis is perceived to be different from the more traditional "transmission" model, in which teachers try to convey knowledge to students directly.

These fundamental agreements among constructivists are tempered by some important areas of difference about the process of constructing knowledge. These differences are reflected in two versions of constructivist theories of cognition: developmental and sociocultural. Developmental theories, such as Piaget's, represent a more traditional constructivist framework. Their major emphasis is on describing the universal forms or structures of knowledge (e.g., prelogical, concrete, and abstract operations) that guide the making of meaning. These universal cognitive structures are assumed to be developmentally organized, so that prelogical thinking occurs prior to concrete logical thinking in a developmental sequence. Within this framework, the individual student is considered to be the meaning maker, with the development of the individual's personal knowledge being the main goal of learning.

Critics of developmental theories of cognition point out that this perspective does not take into account "how issues such as the cultural and political nature of schooling and the race, class, and gender backgrounds of teachers and students, as well as their prior learning histories, influence the kinds of meaning that are made in the classroom."[2] Cognitive-developmental theories, it is claimed, divorce meaning making from affect by focusing on isolating universal forms of knowledge and thus limiting consideration of the sociocultural and contextual influences on the construction of knowledge.[3]

A second version of constructivism is reflected in the social constructivist or situated social constructivist perspective. As its name suggests, this type of constructivism puts its major emphasis on the social construction of knowledge and rejects the individualistic orientation of Piagetian theory. Within the sociocultural perspective, knowledge is seen as constructed by an individual's interaction with a social milieu in which he or she is situated, resulting in a change in both the individual and the milieu. Of course, it is possible for an individual to "reside" in many milieus, from a classroom milieu through a much more general cultural milieu. The point, however, is that social constructivists believe that knowledge has a social component and cannot be considered to be generated by an individual acting independently of his or her social context.[4] Consequently, recognition of the social and cultural influences on constructed knowledge is a primary emphasis. Because individual social and cultural contexts differ, the meanings people make may be unique to themselves or their cultures, potentially resulting in as many meanings as there are meaning makers. Universal meanings across individuals are not emphasized.

Critics of this perspective have pointed to the chaos that might be inherent in a multiplicity of potential meanings. While the social constructivists' concern with particular contextual or cultural factors that shape meaning enhances their recognition of differences across meanings, it limits their recognition of the universal forms that bring order to an infinite variety of meanings. Arguably, the critics of each version of constructivism exaggerate the positions espoused by these theories; however, they do set into relief the relative emphasis of each theory on the individual or the context.

This brief overview of constructivism omits many of the nuances and issues that characterize the debate over constructivist theory. However, our purpose is not to provide an in-depth portrait of constructivism, but rather to identify fundamental tenets that most constructivists would endorse and to point out that constructivism is not a unitary viewpoint. This latter fact is often overlooked in practice-oriented activities that derive from the slogan "Students are constructors of their own knowledge." The conflicts between the two versions of constructivism is not merely "a matter of theoretical contemplation. Instead, it finds expression in tensions endemic to the act of teaching."[5] The particular version of constructivism one adopts—developmental or social constructivist—has important implications for classroom practices,[6] for the definition of knowledge,[7] for the relative emphasis on individual versus social learning,[8] for the role of the teacher,[9] and for the definition of successful instruction.[10]

Why Is Constructivism So Readily Accepted?

In the broad sense, constructivism represents a shift in the perspective of the social sciences and humanities from a view in which truth is a given to a view in which it is constructed by individuals and groups. There has been an inevitable spillover of this view from the social sciences and the humanities to education.

However, most educational theories and innovations are adopted with high levels of uncertainty. The wisdom of their adoption and the range of their impact are rarely known in advance of their implementation. Thus the justification for adopting a theory or innovation must come from outside the theory or innovation per se.[11] Typically, the justification is supplied by the existence of a pressing need or problem that requires quick amelioration or by the moral symbolism inherent in the theory or innovation. This is as true for constructivism as it has been for all educational theories and innovations that have sought to make their way into practice. However, it is very important to emphasize that there is a crucial difference between evidence that documents the need for change and evidence that documents the efficacy of a particular strategy of change. The specific strategy selected to produce change must seek its own validation, independent of the evidence of the need for change of some kind.

To understand its rapid acceptance, we must examine both present educational needs and the symbolic aspects of constructivism. The pressing educational need that fuels interest in constructivism is the perception that what we have been doing in schools has failed to meet the intellectual and occupational needs of the majority of our students; schools seem not to be promoting a sufficiently broad range of student outcomes. In particular, "thinking" or "higher-order" skills are not receiving sufficient instructional emphasis. A large part of the explanation for the perceived deficiency in pupil learning is thought to be an emphasis on "reductionist" or rote outcomes and forms of instruction. Reorienting instruction to nonrote outcomes makes such skills as generalizing, analyzing, synthesizing, and evaluating very important. From an instructional point of view, it puts much more of the onus on the student to construct personal meanings and interpretations. There is a link, then, between an epistemology that focuses on students' constructing their own knowledge and an education system that seeks to promote higher-level learning outcomes.

Also linking constructivism and educational need is the current emphasis on bottom-up as opposed to top-down approaches to reform. Thus recent reforms have increasingly allocated discretion for reforming the educational process to individual schools, teachers, students, and parents. In particular, teachers are given more discretion to construct their own meanings and interpretations of what will improve classroom teaching and learning. Moreover, because constructivism is an epistemology of how people learn, its focus is logically on classroom practice. The increased teacher discretion over teaching and learning, combined with the classroom orientation and higher-level focus of constructivism, has sparked teachers' interest in the potential of constructivism for classroom practice.

Constructivism seems to pass the onus of creating or acquiring knowledge to the student.

Of course, it is not just increased teacher discretion and the classroom focus of constructivism that prompt interest. Constructivism is also appealing for other, more symbolic reasons. First, the rhetoric that surrounds constructivism is seductive. It plays off the metaphor of "lighting the flame" of student motivation (constructivism) against that of "filling the bucket" of students' heads with facts (present methods).[12] Constructivists claim that they emphasize autonomy as opposed to obedience, construction as opposed to instruction, and interest as opposed to reinforcement.[13] The implication is that, if one is opposed to constructivism, one is opposed to student autonomy, construction of meaning, and interest. Thus opponents are viewed as being against lighting the flame of student motivation. Such rhetoric plays a potent role in the reception of all innovations, including constructivism.

Second, since knowledge consists of what is constructed by the learner and since attainment of absolute truth is viewed as impossible, constructivism makes the implicit assumption that all students can and will learn—that is, construct knowledge. The vision of the constructivist student is one of activity, involvement, creativity, and the building of personal knowledge and understanding. This is an appealing symbol in an education system that is perceived to be inadequate for meeting the learning needs of many students. However, our consideration of constructivism should extend beyond process to an examination of the nature of the knowledge actually constructed.

Third, in a variety of ways and with a variety of potential consequences, constructivism symbolizes emancipation. From one perspective, constructivism can be interpreted as a symbol of the emancipation of teachers from the primary responsibility for student learning, since constructivism passes the onus of creating or acquiring knowledge from the teacher to the student. This notion is mistaken. The teacher will no longer be a supplier of information, but he or she will remain very much involved in the learning process, coordinating and critiquing student constructions, building his or her own knowledge of constructivism in the classroom, and learning new methods of instruction. Constructivism can also be interpreted as a symbol of the emancipation of teachers from the burden of dealing with the difficult issue of motivation, since many constructivists view the student's sense of ownership of and empowerment over the learning process as providing its own intrinsic motivation.[14]

Constructivism certainly is emancipatory and dovetails well with the agendas of many interest groups through its social constructivist emphasis on context as a critical feature of knowledge construction. When context becomes an important aspect of knowledge construction, it is logical to conclude that involvement in different contexts will lead to the construction of different knowledge, even if the same set of "data" is presented in the different contexts. Given a problem or an issue, a context—which is often designated in social, economic, racial, and gender terms—will influence the interpretations, conclusions, motives, and attitudes of individuals in that context. When confronted with the same problem or issue, individuals in different milieus may construct different interpretations and conclusions. In this case, "truth" becomes what those in a given milieu construct. And since different milieus vary in their constructions and since there is no absolute truth to search for, knowledge becomes relative to the milieu one inhabits.

This view is certainly symbolically emancipatory for many disempowered groups, but with what effect on the classroom? It would be naive to ignore the sociopolitical agendas and potential consequences for education that constructivism can evoke, particularly those emanating from the social constructivist version of constructivism.

Thus there are strong forces that underlie the growing interest in and acceptance of the constructivist epistemology. These forces stem from the perceived need to alter educational practice from an associational approach to one that emphasizes the higher-level knowledge construction needed to cope with the rapid expansion of information. They also stem from symbolic features of constructivism, particularly the symbols associated with the rhetoric of constructivism.

Cautions

Despite the persuasiveness of the above forces, it is important to be aware that the application of constructivism in classrooms is neither widespread nor systemic. This is not to suggest that there are no successful applications of constructivism. In fact, a number of writers have described approaches to constructivist teaching in special education classrooms, in largely African American classrooms, and in after-school programs.[15] With the exception of Ann Brown's Community of Learning schools, however, most applications of constructivism have tended to be recent, narrowly focused pilot studies. In discussing her ongoing work, even Brown indicates that, "for the past 10 years or so, my colleagues and I have been gradually evolving learning environments [to foster grade school pupils' interpretive communities]."[16] Accentuating the need for gradual development is important, because in simultaneously mounting constructivist teaching and endeavoring to remain faithful to constructivist tenets, teachers and administrators will be confronted with a number of obstacles and issues.

We turn now to some cautions that need to be kept in mind as teachers attempt to implement constructivism in their classrooms. Some of these cautions are pertinent to any classroom innovation. Others are specific to constructivism.

Do not fail to recognize the difference between an epistemology of learning and a well-thought-out and manageable instructional approach for implementing it. We do not have an "instruction of constructivism" that can be readily applied in classrooms. There are suggestions for methods that are likely to foster student construction of knowledge, primarily those that emphasize nonrote tasks and active student participation in the learning process (e.g., cooperative

learning, performance assessments, product-oriented activities, and "hands-on" learning, as well as reciprocal teaching and initiation-reply-evaluation methods). However, it is not clear how such methods relate to learning in different content areas or whether these methods will be equally successful across all subject areas.[17]

It is even more important to recognize that the selection of a particular instructional strategy represents only part of what is necessary in the constructivist approach. Selection of a strategy does not necessarily lead to appropriate implementation or to the provision of individual feedback to students regarding their constructions. Implementing constructivism calls for a "learn as you go" approach for both students and teachers; it involves many decisions and much trial and error. Commenting on the relevance of this theory for contemporary practices and procedures in education, Kenneth Gergen writes:

There is no means by which practical derivatives can simply be squeezed from a theory of knowledge. As has been seen, theories can specify neither the particulars to which they must be applied nor the contexts in which they may be rendered intelligible. There are no actions that follow necessarily from a given theory. . . . Thus, rather than seeking clear and compelling derivatives of constructionist theory, we should explore the kinds of practices that would be favored by the perspective within current conventions of understanding.[18]

Do not fall into the trap of believing that constructivist instructional techniques provide the sole means by which students construct meanings. This is not the case. Students construct their own knowledge and interpretations no matter what instructional approach is implemented and no matter what name is given to it. What teacher has not taught a didactic, rote-oriented topic or concept only to find that the students constructed a variety of very different meanings from those anticipated by the teacher? Thus no single teaching method ought to be used exclusively. One of the leading advocates of constructivism in education has compellingly argued that, from a constructivist point of view, it is a misunderstanding to consider teaching methods such as memorization and rote learning useless. "There are, indeed, matters that can and perhaps must be learned in a purely mechanical way."[19] One's task is to find the right balance between the activities of constructing and receiving knowledge, given that not all aspects of a subject can or should be taught in the same way or be acquired solely through "hands-on" or student-centered means.

Because students always make their own meaning from instruction, the important curricular and instructional choice is not a choice between making and not making personal meaning from instructional activities, but a choice among the ideas, concepts, and issues that we want our students to construct meaning about. It is in this area that states such as Kentucky, California, and Vermont, among others, are redefining the expectations for student learning and reinforcing those expectations through statewide assessments. Similarly, it is in this area that such organizations as the National Council of Teachers of Mathematics are promulgating and advocating newer, more performance-oriented goals in their subject areas. The issues addressed by states and professional organizations are much more focused on the outcomes than on the means of instruction.

Do not assume that a constructivist orientation will make the same demands on teaching time as a nonconstructivist orientation. Time is an extremely important consideration in implementing constructivist education in two regards.

1. Time Is Needed for Teachers and Pupils to Learn and Practice How to Perform in a Constructivist Classroom

If criticisms of "reductionist" education are valid, then substituting another approach, whether in part or in toto, will call for a redefinition of both teachers' and students' roles. In a constructivist approach, teachers will have to learn to guide, not tell; to create environments in which students can make their own meanings, not be handed them by the teacher; to accept diversity in constructions, not search for the one "right" answer; to modify prior notions of "right" and "wrong," not stick to rigid standards and criteria; to create a safe, free, responsive environment that encourages disclosure of student constructions, not a closed, judgmental system.

Students will also have to learn new ways to perform. They will have to learn to think for themselves, not wait for the teacher to tell them what to think; to proceed with less focus and direction from the teacher, not to wait for explicit teacher directions; to express their own ideas clearly in their own words, not to answer restricted-response questions; to revisit and revise constructions, not to move immediately on to the next concept or idea.

It is easy to *say* that constructivist teachers must create an open, nonjudgmental environment that permits students to construct, disclose, and expose their constructions to scrutiny. But listening and responding to student constructions will be difficult and time-consuming.[20] Teachers will have to become accustomed to working with quite different and more general goals, since the instructional emphasis will be on the viability of varied, idiosyncratic student constructions. Teachers will need to serve as initiators of activities that will evoke students' interest and lead to new constructions and as critics of the constructions that students produce. In a sense, much of the responsibility for learning will be turned over to the students through "hands-on" experiences and activities designed to spur their constructions of meaning. The more teachers become engaged in this process, the more the resulting constructions will be theirs, not the students'.

Finding a balance between teacher involvement or noninvolvement in the process of learning will be a challenge. It is legitimate to ask how well—and how soon—teachers will be able to create such an environment and reorient their practice. In this regard it is noteworthy that, with few exceptions,[21] there is considerably less discussion about the role and activities of the *teacher* in constructivist education than there is about the role and activities of the *students*. But changes in orientation in both teacher and students will not occur immediately, especially for those who have had a long time to become accustomed to the current norms of classroom practice. New ways of thinking, acting, organizing, and judging will always take time to develop.

2. In the Shift to Constructivist Teaching, Considerable Time Will Be Required for Responding to the Individual Constructions of Students

Student constructions have two important properties: 1) they are complex in form, and 2) they differ from student to student. Because constructions represent understandings and connections between prior and new knowledge, they cannot be conveyed in a word or a phrase. To convey one's construction of meaning will require an in-depth presentation about one's knowledge and how one arrived at or justifies that knowledge. If constructions are reduced to multiple-choice items or to some other truncated representational form, the richness and meaning of constructivism will be lost. Hence, to review, understand, and respond to student constructions will require substantial teacher time and perhaps the involvement of parents and community members as well.

Moreover, different students are likely to produce quite different constructions, making it difficult to apply the same frame of reference to the review of their constructions. Each construction and its underlying logic will need to be examined, understood, and reviewed. Hence, the amount of time needed to respond to these constructions will be further increased. Responding to student constructions will be more like reading essays or viewing oral reports than like scoring multiple-choice or short-answer tests.

Implicit in the need for increased time are other important time-related issues, such as the tradeoff between coverage and depth. It is likely that the quality of students' knowledge constructions will depend in part on the time they are given to construct. More time will mean richer and deeper constructions. Teachers and schools will have to face the question of whether it is better to cover a large amount of content at a rather shallow level or to cover a smaller amount of content in great depth. The constructivist approach fits much better with the latter choice, since it aims for personal meaning and understanding, not rote associations.

Do not believe that the opposite of "one-right-answer" reductionism is "anything-goes" constructivism. Implicit in any form of classroom instruction guided by any theory of learning is the need for standards and criteria of judgment. This matter is both important and challenging in constructivist thought and application. Among the questions that constructivist teachers will have to confront regarding standards and criteria are: On what basis should students have to justify their constructions? Can the teacher who facilitates the constructions also be an objective evaluator of them? What constitutes a "reasonable" or "acceptable" student construction? Should the teacher try to avoid transmitting standards and criteria that end up influencing or controlling the nature of student constructions? If so, how? Are evaluation standards and criteria independent of context or are they contextually bound?

A teacher who accepts the constructivist tenet that knowledge is constructed by individuals and that knowledge and experience are subjective must inevitably face the relationship between truth and meaning. In practical terms, the teacher must decide how much emphasis will be placed on the relative "truthfulness" of students' constructions or on their "meaningfulness" to the student. Since there is no one best construction and since people must construct their own meanings from personal experiences and understandings, there are many viable constructions.[22] Further, if it is assumed that knowledge is ego- and context-specific, the likelihood of agreeing on common standards of evaluation is diminished greatly. This perspective could create many problems when applied in classrooms

A rejoinder to this view argues that the lack of one best construction does not mean that some constructions cannot be deemed better than others. Moreover, sole reliance on personal meaning to justify constructions leads to rampant relativism and potentially biased, self-serving, and dishonest constructions.[23] In this view, the role of the teacher is to challenge students to justify and refine their constructions in order to strengthen them.

At the opposite end of the spectrum from meaningfulness is truthfulness. Absolute certainty is alien to the tenets of constructivism. However, there can be intermediate positions between absolute and relative truthfulness. Thus it is possible to evaluate some constructions as being more truthful (i.e., reasonable) than others. If a position of modified or relative truthfulness is adopted, as it inevitably will be in real classrooms, the teacher is directly confronted by the need to establish standards and criteria for evaluating the merits of students' constructions.

However, in facing this need, the teacher also faces an issue that should be approached with awareness and caution. In evaluating some constructions as being better than others, the teacher will find that the more explicit the evaluation standards and criteria, the greater the likelihood that they will be transmitted to and adopted by the students. When standards and criteria are constructed jointly by teachers, students, and parents, transmission and adoption become desirable. However, if the teacher is the sole determiner of standards and criteria, he or she is likely to have the primary influence on the nature of classroom constructions. Students may not construct meaning on their own, for they know that high grades derive from meeting the teacher's standards and criteria. Constructivism is thus compromised. The problem of guiding and evaluating students without undermining their constructivist activities is a thorny one. The development of standards and criteria that are clear but that allow variance in evaluation is paramount, and each teacher will have to find his or her appropriate balance, given that few external guidelines for defining such standards and criteria exist.

In the preceding discussion we have pointed out the difference between the theory of constructivism and its practical application. In particular, we have argued that the consequences of implementing constructivism in the classroom will be considerably more challenging than might be anticipated from the simple slogans that advocates repeat. But our comments and cautions should not be taken as criticisms of the constructivist viewpoint. Indeed, we recognize and appreciate the positive role that this orientation can play in changing educational practice. Rather, our comments are meant to illuminate and anticipate important issues that will inevitably arise in attempts to implement constructivism in practical, classroom settings. These are not reasons to avoid trying to implement constructivism; they are efforts to help readers know something about what they are adopting at a more substantive level. Knowing some of the nuances and problems of a theory or innovation makes one better able to move beyond rhetoric to consider the implications for one's own practice.

Notes

1. Richard S. Prawat, "Teachers' Beliefs About Teaching and Learning: A Constructivist Perspective," *American Journal of Education,* vol. 100, 1992, pp. 354–95. Carl Bereiter, "Constructivism, Socioculturalism, and Popper's World 3," *Educational Researcher,* October 1994, pp. 21–23; Rosalind Driver et al., "Constructing Scientific Knowledge in the Classroom," *Educational Researcher,* October 1994, pp. 5–12; and Neil M. Agnew and John L. Brown, "Foundations for a Model of Knowing: II. Fallible but Functional Knowledge," *Canadian Psychology,* vol. 30, 1989, pp. 168–83.
2. Michael O'Loughlin, "Rethinking Science Education: Beyond Piagetian Constructivism Toward a Sociocultural Model of Teaching and Learning," *Journal of Research in Science Teaching,* vol. 29, 1992, p. 792.
3. Martin L. Hoffman, "Development of Moral Thought, Feeling, and Behavior," *American Psychologist,* vol. 34, 1979, pp. 958–66.
4. Kenneth J. Gergen, "Exploring the Postmodern: Perils or Potentials," *American Psychologist,* vol. 49, 1994, pp. 412–16; and James V. Wertsch and Chikako Toma, "Discourse and Learning in the Classroom: A Sociocultural Approach," in Leslie P. Steffe and Jerry Gale, eds., *Constructivism in Education* (Hillsdale, N.J.: Erlbaum, 1995), pp. 159–74.
5. Paul Cobb, "Where Is the Mind? Constructivist and Sociocultural Perspectives on Mathematical Development," *Educational Researcher,* October 1994, p. 13.
6. Deborah L. Ball, "With an Eye on the Mathematical Horizon: Dilemmas of Teaching Elementary School Mathematics," *Elementary School Journal,* vol. 93, 1993, pp. 373–97.
7. Virginia Richardson, "Constructivist Teaching: Theory and Practice," paper presented at the annual meeting of the American Educational Research Association, New Orleans, 1994; and Bereiter, op. cit.
8. Driver et al., op. cit.
9. Ibid.
10. Ginnette Delandshire and Anthony J. Petrosky, "Capturing Teachers' Knowledge: Performance Assessment," *Educational Researcher,* June/July 1994, pp. 11–18.
11. Peter W. Airasian, "Symbolic Validation: The Case of State-Mandated, High-Stakes Testing," *Educational Evaluation and Policy Analysis,* vol. 4, 1988, pp. 301–13.
12. David Elkind, "Spirituality in Education," *Holistic Education Review,* vol. 5, no. 1, 1992, pp. 12–16.
13. Rhete DeVries and Lawrence Kohlberg, *Constructivist Early Education* (Washington, D.C.: National Association for the Education of Young Children, 1987).
14. Aire W. Kruglanski, *Lay Epistemics and Human Knowledge* (New York: Plenum Press, 1989); Penny Oldfather, "Sharing the Ownership of Knowing: A Constructivist Concept of Motivation for Literacy Learning," paper presented at the annual meeting of the National Reading Conference, San Antonio, 1992; and O'Loughlin, op. cit.
15. Ann Brown, "The Advancement of Learning," *Educational Researcher,* November 1994, pp. 4–12; Richardson, op. cit.; Gloria Ladson-Billing, *The Dreamkeepers: Successful Teaching of African-American Children* (San Francisco: Jossey-Bass, 1994); and Wertsch and Toma, op. cit.
16. Brown, "Advancement of Learning," p. 7.
17. Susan S. Stodolsky, *The Subject Matters* (Chicago: University of Chicago Press, 1988); and Cobb, op. cit.
18. Kenneth Gergen, "Social Construction and the Educational Process," in Steffe and Gale, pp. 17–39.
19. Ernst von Glasersfeld, "A Constructivist Approach to Teaching," in Steffe and Gale, p. 5.
20. Peter W. Airasian, "Critical Pedagogy and the Realities of Teaching," in Henry Perkinson, *Teachers Without Goals, Students Without Purposes* (New York: McGraw-Hill, 1993), pp. 81–93.
21. See, for example, Brown, "The Advancement of Learning"; and Ladson-Billing, op. cit.
22. Geraldine Gilliss, "Schön's Reflective Practitioner: A Model for Teachers?," in Peter Grimmett and Gaalen Erickson, eds., *Reflection in Teacher Education* (New York: Teachers College Press, 1988), pp. 47–54.
23. Bereiter, op. cit.; and Karl Popper, *Objective Knowledge: An Evolutionary Approach* (Oxford: Clarendon, 1972).

Form at end of book

Issue 3 Summary

Constructivist theories grew in influence toward the end of the twentieth century. These theories highlight the value of teaching through guided experience, in which students are given opportunities to create their own understandings and test their own ideas. Despite the popularity of constructivism, many classrooms are still run on behavioral principles, with teachers acting as transmitters of knowledge. Constructivist teaching requires a complete redefinition of the teacher's role, and many teachers are uncomfortable with that type of change.

WiseGuide Wrap-Up

As we come to the end of the twentieth century, we are engaging in many important debates that will define our educational approach of the twenty-first century. Some of these debates, such as the debate about national testing, have significant political components. These debates touch on the central issue of *what* is the curriculum of schools—that is, what we should teach students. As one might expect, the political left and the political right differ dramatically on this question.

A perhaps less political debate centers on *how* we teach: do we follow a behaviorist model in which teachers act as transmitters of knowledge, or do we follow a constructivist model in which teachers are responsible for creating learning experiences in which students construct their own knowledge? Together, these two debates—*what* we teach and *how* we teach it—are at the heart of the debate in American *education* today. In the next section, we look at the central debates in American *psychology* today.

R.E.A.L. Sites

This list provides a print preview of typical **Coursewise** R.E.A.L. sites. (There are over 100 such sites at the **Courselinks™** site.) The danger in printing URLs is that web sites can change overnight. As we went to press, these sites were functional using the URLs provided. If you come across one that isn't, please let us know via email to: webmaster@coursewise.com. Use your Passport to access the most current list of R.E.A.L. sites at the **Courselinks** site.

Site name: Are Public Schools in Decline?

URL: http://homer.louiseville.edu/~tnpete01/church/vouch2b.htm

Why is it R.E.A.L.? This home page addresses the issue of the decline of American public schools. It is produced by an organization whose goal is to ensure that the church and state are separated, as guaranteed in the United States Constitution; the point of view expressed reflects that of the political left. According to the authors of this home page, the evidence does not support the claim that American schools have declined.

Key topics: American education, separation of church and state

Try this: Visit "The Case against School Vouchers," then click on "Are School Vouchers Needed?" Read the segment "Are Public Schools in Decline?" If aggregate SAT scores have been declining since the 1960s, how does this site argue that U.S. public schools are actually getting better?

Site name: Empowering Our Schools

URL: http://www.empower.org/html/campaigns/edreform/main.htm

Why is it R.E.A.L.? This home page focuses on educational reform, as well as cultural and economic change, from the perspective of the political right. William J. Bennett, a co-author of two of the articles in this section, is co-director of the "Empower America" organization. Bennett and his colleagues make specific recommendations regarding how American schools should be reformed, including the adoption of charter schools and voucher plans.

Key topics: American education, educational reform

Try this: This site offers many reasons why American elementary and secondary schools have fallen "from world superiority to the back of the class." Name two reasons that are given.

---

section 2 | Controversies in Psychology

Learning Objectives

- Know the major findings of brain research pertaining to teaching and learning, as well as the limits of these findings.

- Understand the impact of parents on children's development and how gender relates to learning and development in the home and in the school.

- Grasp the relationship between the needs and characteristics of children on the one hand and society's expectation and view of children on the other.

- Comprehend Gardner's theory of multiple intelligences and the issues surrounding its application in the classroom.

Just as educational psychology is a branch of education, it is also a branch of psychology. Not surprisingly, given its name, educational psychology is, in fact, where education and psychology overlap. In Section 1, we examined some of the most controversial topics in education today. In Section 2, we examine major issues in psychology that have a significant impact on education and teaching.

Our first issue is the question of how much we know about the brain and how our knowledge about the brain informs teaching, if at all. In the past few decades, psychologists' understanding of the brain has grown enormously, and the study of the brain has been one of the most exciting branches of research in psychology. Among the findings of researchers have been the identification of the different functions of the left and right parts of the brain, the localization of specific areas in the brain that control particular activities, and the isolation of chemicals that control brain functions. From these findings, some educators have gleaned lessons for education. Others argue that, despite the revolution in understanding of the brain, we are still far away from applying our knowledge of the brain to educational methods. In Reading 9, Robert Sylwester argues that brain research presents educators with opportunities to improve schooling. Jeremy Rifkin, in Reading 10, confronts the dilemmas presented to society by an increased understanding of genetics. Finally, in Reading 11, John T. Bruer critically analyzes some of the major claims emerging from research into the brain to determine whether such claims are valid. These three articles present both the excitement and the caution in educators' response to brain research.

What controls who we are—nature (our biological makeup) or nurture (how we are brought up)? This question has troubled educators, psychologists, and even philosophers long before we understood what genes and chromosomes were. The "nature/nurture" debate has been one of the most central debates in the field of educational psychology. Although practically everyone agrees that both nature and nurture contribute to our psychological makeup, psychologists still argue about *how* and *how much* each contributes. Sharon Begley, in Reading 12, tries to answer the question "Do parents matter?"—in part, in response to a recent book that argues that almost everything about us is determined by our DNA. The next two articles look specifically at the growth of boys and girls. In Reading 13, Barbara Kantrowitz and Claudia Kalb struggle with the question of how best to bring up boys, focusing on the vulnerabilities, such as reading disorders, successful suicide attempts, and aggression, that are more common among boys than among girls. Judith Kleinfeld, in Reading 14, questions the widely held belief that schools are shortchanging girls.

Next, we examine a dilemma facing all children, both boys and girls, in today's world: how to be a child in today's society. In Reading 15, David Elkind argues that society expects children to conform to a model of the "universal child" and allows little room for children's individuality. Mike Males, in Reading 16, contends that society should stop attributing society's ills to children and adolescents and the forces that are believed to influence them—namely, sex and violence on television and computer screens—and should look instead at the rate of adult violence.

The final issue in this section pertains to Howard Gardner's theory of multiple intelligences. This theory, which has garnered the support of many educators across the nation, is based on the notion that we have many types of intelligence, rather than a single intelligence that can be measured in an IQ test. The many types of intelligence can then be identified in children and nurtured by schools that are willing to value types of intelligence that differ from the traditional type. In Reading 17, Linda Campbell presents how Gardner's theory of multiple intelligences can be implemented by classroom teachers. However, James Traub in Reading 18 describes the controversy that surrounds both the theory itself and its application to the classroom.

The four issues presented in this section are some of the most contentious issues in psychology today, issues that have direct bearing on how we educate young people in our society. Although the issues surrounding brain research, the relative roles of nature and nurture, the differing needs of boys and girls, and new ideas such as multiple intelligence theory are unresolved, we must struggle to understand these issues better to move ahead in the improvement of teaching and learning.

The Brain and Learning

Questions

1. What issues do policymakers face when considering emerging brain research as it applies to education?

2. Why does the development of a better understanding of genes suggest to some a threat of discrimination and segregation?

3. In what ways has brain research been misapplied or applied too hastily to the improvement of education?

Introduction

For centuries, the brain has been a mystery. Only in the past century and, to a greater extent, in the last decades of the twentieth century have we developed an understanding of how the brain functions. We know that the brain is involved in learning, thinking, language development, and social-emotional development; we also know that the brain is involved with variations from the norms in each of these areas. Naturally, educators have looked to brain research to shed light on how we can promote learning, thinking, and development among typical and atypical learners.

Despite the pace at which brain research progresses, have we reached a point where brain research can intelligently inform our approaches to teaching and learning? And what is the social-political implication of brain research? These issues are at the heart of the articles you will now read.

The Brain Revolution

Spectacular developments in cognitive science, reminiscent of Dewey's progressive movement, open a world of new challenges for school leaders.

Robert Sylwester

Robert Sylwester, author of A Celebration of Neurons: An Educator's Guide to the Human Brain, *is a professor of education at University of Oregon, Eugene, Ore. 97403-5267. E-mail:bob_sylwester@ccmail.uoregon.edu*

An old adage suggests those who ignore history are doomed to repeat it. We're now confronting an explosion of new information about the workings of our brain that will profoundly affect educational policy and practice. Yet our profession, oriented as it is toward the social and behavioral sciences with only limited understanding of biology and cognitive science, stands unready at the moment to take advantage of this learning revolution.

Several key policy and administrative issues now are emerging from the cognitive science revolution. How might educational leaders begin to deal with these issues? Our search for direction can begin with an intriguing historical parallel.

Democracy and Education

In retrospect, it seems such an obvious idea. Why then did it take so long for someone to think of it, and so much longer for people to accept it and to incorporate it into our schools?

By the beginning of the 19th century, the U.S. Constitution had codified the basic principles that were to define and govern our representative democracy. But it took almost 100 years for a dominant voice to suggest that the schools demonstrate the emerging democratic principles that future voters must understand if they are to function as intelligent citizens in a democratic society. John Dewey's *School and Society,* published in 1899, and *Democracy and Education,* published in 1916, built on the previous work of others, such as the European educators Johann Pestalozzi and Frederich Froebel, but Dewey became this century's most powerful American voice in the educational revolution.

Rereading his books, it all seems logical. Why wouldn't a fledgling democratic society demand that its public schools be laboratories for democratic behavior—tuned to the needs and abilities of students? Why use the 12,000 hours that students spend in school from kindergarten to grade 12 to demonstrate the competing authoritarian societal perspective that our founders rejected in our war for independence? One would think that Dewey's ideas (or something similar to them) would have been enthusiastically embraced and instituted.

In one way they were. The Progressive Education Movement led to a wide range of enthusiastic implementation strategies (such as the Gary Plan, the Dalton Plan and the Winnetka Plan) that were widely hailed. I was born in 1927, and so I went to school during the period when these new approaches had an opportunity to become integral to the schools. Unfortunately, my schools, like most schools at the time, didn't function on democratic principles.

Far from it. We didn't even explore representative democratic values. These were not bad schools, but democracy was something we studied in civics class, where we learned to write down how our total government was organized. But we didn't learn how to democratically organize our small classroom community.

By mid-century, when I entered the education profession, progressive education was in serious decline, severely buffeted by its critics. In 1938, when he was 79, John Dewey published *Experience and Education,* a somewhat poignant title for a book in which he analyzed what went wrong with his dream to incorporate democracy into education.

The interesting thing is that now, at the end of the 20th century, many of Dewey's ideas quietly have been incorporated into American schools.

Reprinted with permission from the January 1998 issue of *The School Administrator* magazine.

Cognition and Education

Our profession is in a transformational state. A cognitive science revolution, which has been under way for some time (with a major escalation during this decade), threatens to shortly explode with a new perspective of what it means to be (and teach) a human brain.

Dramatic advances in brain imaging and other research technologies are moving scientists toward an unprecedented view of our brain at the cellular and systems levels. This has led to an immense interest in the development of a comprehensive brain theory that will be of the scientific magnitude of $E = MC^2$, in that it will spark a revolution in the brain sciences analogous to the revolution in the physical sciences sparked by Albert Einstein's relativity theories. It may profoundly alter our view of ourselves, as democracy altered our view of society.

"The comprehensive brain theory will emerge out of Charles Darwin's discoveries about natural selection . . ."

The comprehensive brain theory will emerge out of Charles Darwin's discoveries about natural selection as a scientific explanation for biological diversity (about 150 years ago), Einstein's theoretic reconceptualization of energy/time/space/matter (about 100 years ago) and James Watson and Francis Crick's discoveries about DNA as the cellular mechanism for Darwinian developmental principles (about 50 years ago).

Predicting when such a major theory actually might emerge is difficult, but it probably won't occur before the turn of the century and, when it does, it will contain elements that will be culturally and professionally controversial. The global brain theory inevitably will lead to the emergence of a new John Dewey, a new Jean Piaget, a new B. F. Skinner—someone who will translate the biological theory into an educational theory. This is the theory that will transform current educational thought and practice.

Our profession may thus have a few years of lead time. During this period educators should begin to do two things:

- shift from our current social and behavioral science orientation to one that includes the biological sciences that are now beginning to answer the teaching/learning questions that long have mystified us, and

- focus our energy on trying to understand the development before we seek and promote practical educational applications.

Educational leaders ought to read several fine nontechnical books to begin this study (see related story, page 16*). In doing so, realize that this is a rapidly developing field, so one's reading should focus on materials published within the past five years.

Our growing understanding of the theory and research into the workings of the human brain inevitably will lead us to imaginative and useful classroom explorations since knowing why generally leads to knowing how to. To bypass the knowing why component virtually guarantees the best we can hope for is to stumble blindly onto a good idea, but then not to know why it is cognitively sound.

Educators therefore must explore how best to respond to the cognitive science revolution. It won't go away if we just ignore it. This exploration should include the study of the errors of previous failed movements that sought to transform education and the identification of educationally significant cognitive science developments that will play important roles in the educational theory that will emerge.

The task of school leaders is to make a prospective exploration of the cognitive science revolution, which may well spark the dominant educational movement of the 21st century. These exciting discoveries are occurring on our watch, and so we get to participate in the beginnings of all of the revolutionary fervor, decision making, failures and successes.

One never knows how a revolution will develop. Could Einstein have predicted the mid-century dropping of atomic bombs and the end-of-the-century video games? Atomic energy and the electronic revolution both emerged out of his theories. The Chinese word for stress has two characters: One means danger; the other means opportunity. Expect both in this revolution.

Starting Points

Our profession tends to seek immediate practical applications of new theories and research findings, but useful applications generally don't emerge immediately from major scientific developments. The DNA code was discovered in 1953, yet most genetic engineering has occurred during this decade, and cloning did not emerge until mid-1997. Further, it's quite a leap from the tightly controlled variables of cognitive science laboratory research to messy classroom research, where the variables bounce off the walls.

What are the practical applications of an infant? It's a wet noisy pet, at least 20 years from a clear sense of how it will turn out. What we do with infants is observe them carefully and nurture them. We might try out things such as music lessons and ball hitting if we note interest and ability, but we don't make wild promises about

*Does not appear in this publication.

accomplishments (except perhaps in end-of-year, holiday letters). As childhood merges into adolescence, real interests and abilities become clearer, and we then invest more heavily and decisively in practical applications.

This is also true with the brain sciences, which really are still in their infancy but are growing rapidly. It's a time to put our energy into getting acquainted with this infant that will change our professional lives—to observe, explore and nurture. Our discoveries about children don't generally surprise us because we've provided them with their genes and their jeans.

Similarly, many discoveries from the brain sciences don't surprise us either because we've been working with a room full of brains for a long time, and although we may not understand neural networks and neurochemicals, we do know a lot about how minds function. Call it folklore knowledge if you wish, but our professional instincts generally have served us well.

The Search for Resources

However, we also must get beyond our folklore knowledge. Our profession is grounded in the social and behavioral sciences, and most educators fulfilled the minimum natural science requirements in their teacher-preparation programs. Since the cognitive sciences now provide some answers to many of our questions, we must elevate our professional understanding of brain biology.

" . . . we must elevate our professional understanding of brain biology."

Pushing for change in teacher education program requirements is an important long-range solution but, in the short term, we need to start tapping into our (typically unused) best local resource, the top secondary school biology, chemistry and psychology teachers and the few committed "brain junkies" that every school district seems to have. They understand cellular and systems biology better than anyone else, and they are usually effective teachers.

It's a lot cheaper and better to identify and convene this group, to discover how best to use them in a vigorous staff development program, than to depend entirely on outside consultants. Investing a little in improving their knowledge will pay big dividends because you then will have local staff members constantly available to (1) assist teachers who want to teach units on our brain, (2) critique proposed programs that purport to be based on brain research and (3) set up and run understandable workshops on how our brain works.

Staff development will be more complex and continuing than in some other areas because brain research (like computer technology) is so dynamic. What's true this year may not be true next year. To wait to get involved until we know everything for sure makes about as much sense as waiting until the ultimate computer is developed before purchasing one.

Some argue that we've successfully used our brain for eons without knowing how it works, and most of us use cars and computers without really understanding them, so it's not important that educators understand the human brain. I disagree. Understanding the workings of our brain is important because an uninformed profession will be vulnerable to pseudoscientific fads, inappropriate generalizations and dubious programs that certainly will emerge (if they're not already knocking on your door). It's also difficult to imagine why a person who educates brains would not want to understand them and to explore ways of enhancing their effectiveness, now that such information is available.

Emerging Policy Issues

We need to start thinking now about several thorny issues that will emerge. No simple answers exist for any of them at this point, but it's better to contemplate them now than to first confront them during an unexpected community uproar fueled by divergent religious, political or cultural beliefs. Two examples illustrate the importance of prior planning.

First, the dramatic advances in the brain sciences are all predicated on evolutionary theory, and this will be disquieting to those who are deeply committed to a design view of life that precludes Darwinian developmental principles. These patrons already are upset that evolution is included in science courses, and they will be more riled to learn that Darwinian principles underlie almost everything we're now discovering about our brain (even though they may be fascinated by the discoveries).

People have a right to their various religious, philosophical and scientific beliefs in a democratic society, and one would hope that the discussions and debates that are sure to occur will be civil and productive—that is, a search for the ground that connects rather than the construction of walls that separate. Let's take the lead in sensitivity and civility in this and other areas of potential controversy.

Second, while cognitive research probably will support many current policies and practices, we can expect it to question others. For example, the visual, aural and movement arts have taken a terrible beating in this cost-conscious era, and yet evidence is amassing that they play a central role in the development and maintenance of a brain. So how will we deal with this problem if cheaper-is-better continues to rule when it's much cheaper to fund a spelling program than an arts program?

I expect that we'll have similar problems with such other issues as emotion and evaluation, rigid standards and rigid curricular sequences and the role of computers in instruction and drugs in behavior management. Expect more challenges as the implications of the cognitive revolution become clear.

A Nurturing Process

It's a good time, not a bad time. We're in this for the long haul. We shouldn't rush to claims that brain research supports something if we can't cite the research that proves it.

It's not necessary to add the totem of brain research immediately to every successful educational practice.

If our evidence is shaky, it simply funnels criticism from our patrons. Let's rather take the time and expend the energy to do it right.

Observe. Imagine. Explore. Research. Implement. It's a good sequence for nurturing our biological infants—and also for nurturing our marvelously new professional infant.

Form at end of book

The Sociology of the Gene:
Genetics and Education in the Eve of the Biotech Century

Genetic engineering gives us unprecedented power over human life. But, Mr. Rifkin asks, to whom should such power be entrusted?

Jeremy Rifkin

Jeremy Rifkin is president of the Foundation on Economic Trends, Washington, D.C. This article has been adapted from his new book, The Biotech Century: Harnessing the Gene and Remaking the World *(Tarcher/Putnam, 1998). The book is available in bookstores or by phoning 800/788-6262. © 1998, Jeremy Rifkin.*

While the 20th century was shaped largely by spectacular breakthroughs in the fields of physics and chemistry, the 21st century will belong to the biological sciences. Scientists around the world are quickly deciphering the genetic code of life, unlocking the mystery of millions of years of biological evolution on Earth. As a result of the new breakthroughs in molecular biology and biotechnology, our way of life is likely to be more fundamentally transformed in the next several decades than in the previous thousand years. By the year 2025, we and our children may be living in a world utterly different from anything human beings have ever experienced in the past. Long-held assumptions about nature, including our own human nature, are likely to be rethought. Ideas about equality and democracy are also likely to be redefined, as well as our vision of what is meant by such terms as "free will" and "progress."

Already the shift from an industrial economy that is based on the exploitation of fossil fuels and metals to a biotechnical economy that is based on the exploitation of genes is radically changing our concept of social reality. Researchers in the field of molecular biology are beginning to discover an increasing genetic basis for a wide range of mental diseases, moods, behaviors, and personality traits. The new findings, in turn, are creating the context for a new sociobiology that favors a genetic interpretation of human motivations and drives. While genetic researchers are quick to add that environment plays at least a mitigating role in shaping mental outlook and emotional development, many biologists have come to believe that one's genes are a far more important factor in determining one's future. The new biological fundamentalists are convinced that personality is largely predetermined and written into one's genetic program—and only slightly modifiable by the environment in which one is raised.

It seems that every week or so a new study is published showing a likely connection between genotype and personality. In a study published in 1996, researchers report finding a genetic basis for "novelty seeking," "thrill seeking," and "excitability." Two separate research teams—one led by Richard Ebstein of the Herzog Memorial Hospital in Jerusalem and the other by Jonathan Benjamin of the National Institute of Mental Health's Laboratory of Clinical Science—associated differences in novelty seeking and thrill seeking with lower levels of dopaminergic activity. Dopamine plays a critical role in stimulating euphoria. Researchers found that high novelty seeking is "strongly associated with high plasma prolactin levels, which reflect low dopaminergic activity."[1]

Researchers at the National Institutes of Health in Bethesda, Maryland, say they have located genes that predispose people to "high anxiety." Individuals who inherit one form of a gene on chromosome 17, says Dennis Murphy of the NIH, are more likely to worry, according to a study reported in *New Scientist*. The gene linked to anxiety influences the production of a protein known as the serotonin transporter. This particular protein controls the brain's level of serotonin, a chemical that affects mood.[2]

In 1997, scientists at the Institute of Child Health in London reported that they had located what they believed to be a cluster of genes on the X-chromosome that predispose girls to better "social skills" than boys. The researchers found significant differences in social skills between two groups of girls who suffered from Turner's syndrome (a rare condition in which a copy of the X-chromosome is inherited from only one parent). The girls who inherited the paternal X-chromosome were far more socially expressive, had an easier time making friends, got along better with family and teachers, and were found to be generally

Adapted from *The Biotech Century: Harnessing the Gene and Remaking the World* (Tarcher/Putnam, 1998).

happier and better adjusted than those who inherited the X-chromosome from their mother. The scientists concluded that when the X-chromosome is inherited from the mother, it is apparently inactive, whereas when it is passed along from the father, it is active and fosters higher levels of social interaction.[3]

Genetically Correct Politics

The accumulating body of studies on the genetic links to personality and behavior is having an effect on public discourse. It is important to remember that, from the end of World War II through the 1980s, most social scientists argued that it is only by instituting changes in the environment that social evils can be addressed. The orthodox political wisdom favored nurture over nature. Now, plagued by deepening social crises, the industrial nations no longer seem able to make significant changes by the traditional path of institutional and environmental reform. The sociobiologists and others of their persuasion contend that attempting to overhaul the economic and social system is at best palliative and, at worst, an exercise in futility. The key to most social and economic behavior, they contend, is to be found at the genetic level. To change society, they claim, we must first be willing to change the genes, for, while the environment is a factor, the genes are ultimately the agents most responsible for individual and group behavior.

The radical shift from nurture to nature is attributable, in part, to the intense interest generated by the Human Genome Project and the steady barrage of hyperbolic statements in the media by its most prominent advocates. Dr. James Watson, who served as the first director of the government-funded effort to decipher the human genome, summed up the enthusiasm of many of his colleagues involved in the multibillion-dollar government program. In an interview with *Time* magazine, Watson boldly asserted that "we used to think our fate was in our stars. Now we know, in large measure, our fate is in our genes."

Others in the molecular biology community have been equally effusive. Biologist Walter Gilbert calls the Human Genome Project the "Holy Grail of Genetics," while biologist Norton Zinder refers to the human genome sequence as the "Rosetta Stone." Biologist Robert Sinsheimer goes even further, saying that the sequence "defines a human."[4]

Much of the rhetoric is no doubt politically motivated, designed to keep public attention focused on the great potential benefits that are likely to flow from the Human Genome Project. Ensuring continued congressional funding for the project is probably never far from the thoughts of its champions in the fields of molecular biology and business, who have much to gain financially from the genetic data being collected at the taxpayers' expense.

The very idea that the genes are "at the root of many current societal problems" would have been unthinkable and summarily dismissed by academicians and policy makers just a generation ago. When Arthur Jensen, a professor of education and psychology at the University of California, Berkeley, attempted to raise the genetic arguments in an article titled "How Much Can We Boost IQ and Scholastic Achievement?" which was published in the *Harvard Educational Review* in 1969, the American intellectual community responded with a vitriolic attack, warning that such thoughts were likely to bring us back to the eugenics dogma that spread throughout the country and around the world earlier in the century. Jensen responded to his critics by charging that reasonable debate was being "stifled [by the] *zeitgeist* of environmentalist egalitarianism."[5]

Today, what was until recently regarded as sheer heresy has gained increasing intellectual currency and is fast becoming orthodoxy, at least in the medical field. Writing in the journal *Science,* editor Daniel Koshland argued that a number of genetic diseases are "at the root of many social problems." Koshland points to the growing "ranks of the homeless," many of whom suffer from mental disease, as an example of the need to tackle social problems at their genetic roots, through preventive measures. Koshland's genetic argument for homelessness left liberal social reformers aghast but raised few eyebrows within the scientific community, where many had already been won over to the genetic-causation camp. The idea that homelessness might also have some relationship to the question of educational opportunity, income distribution policies of the marketplace, the marginalization of the work force resulting from corporate downsizing and the introduction of new labor-saving technologies, and the increasing disenfranchisement of the poor was curiously absent from Koshland's remarks, leaving the clear impression that our last best hope resides with the molecular biologists and their efforts to decipher the "Holy Grail" of biology—the human genome.

The troubling social and economic consequences of shifting to genetic causation as an all-encompassing explanatory model were dramatically illustrated several years ago in the firestorm of controversy that surrounded a federal government decision to co-sponsor a national forum on the genetic links to criminal behavior. The theme of the conference was "Genetic Factors in Crime," and it was funded by the NIH Human Genome Project. In a brochure prepared for the meeting, conference organizers said that "genetic research holds out the prospect of identifying individuals who may be predisposed to certain kinds of criminal conduct." When news of the planned meeting leaked out in the press, African American groups protested and called on the NIH to withdraw its funding for the gathering.

If the social reformers of the 1950s and 1960s gave short shrift to the genetic basis of human development in their zeal to right the wrongs of society, the new genetic reformers seem poised at the opposite extreme, attributing far too much of human and social behavior to the genes.

The growing nature/nurture debate has polarized much of the academic community in recent years. However, biologists working in the new field of developmental genetics may provide some much-needed middle ground for understanding the many subtle relationships that exist between genotype and phenotype and between genetic expression and environmental triggers. Developmental geneticists would disagree with the belief held widely among such molecular biologists as Dr. Alexander Rich and Dr. Sung Hou Kim, who claim that "the instructions for the assembly and organization of a living system are embodied in the DNA molecules contained within the living cell."[6]

Biologists in the new field acknowledge that genes encode important information for the development of an organism, but they argue that genes do not, in themselves, determine or control that development. Cell biologist Dr. Stuart Newman of the New York Medical College points out that living beings are "dynamical systems" and are "sensitive to inputs from their environments and, unlike machines, for example, can exhibit very different behavior and take on different forms under slightly different environmental conditions."[7] Newman says it's more appropriate to think of DNA as "a list of ingredients, not a recipe for their interactions."[8] He cites the example of a developing embryo in the womb.

Now, with the emergence of the genetic revolution, society entertains the prospect of a new and more serious form of segregation.

The "environment" of the genome includes not only externally controllable factors like temperature and nutrition, but also numerous maternally provided proteins present in the egg cell at the time of fertilization. These proteins influence gene activity, and by virtue of variations in their amounts and spatial distribution in the egg can cause embryos even of genetically identical twins to develop in uniquely different ways.[9]

Newman and others in the field of developmental genetics argue that genes don't generate organisms. Rather, the very existence of genes already presupposes the existence of the organism in which they're embedded, and it is the organism itself that interprets, translates, and makes use of the genes in the course of its development.

This is a far different approach to the working of genes from the reductionist argument of such biologists as Richard Dawkins who contend that an organism is little more than the orchestrated program created by the genes.

The idea of genes as "master molecules" or "causal agents" is giving way to a more sophisticated understanding of genes as integral components of more complex networks that make up both an organism and its external environment. An article in *Scientific American* sums up much of the current thinking of biologists on the cutting edge of developmental genetics research.

The mystery of how developing organisms choreograph the activity of their genes so that cells form and function at the right place and at the right time is now being solved. Hundreds of experiments have shown that organisms control much of their genes, most of the time, by regulating transcription.[10]

Despite the fact that new experimental research is undermining the arguments and assumptions based on simple genetic reductionism, the idea of the "master molecule" that controls our biological destiny has proved so useful in advancing the interests of the molecular biologists and the many commercial firms that make up the biotech industry that it continues to gather momentum, both in the media and in public discourse, as an explanatory tool for understanding adolescent behavior, personality development, ethnic and racial differences, collective psychology, and even the workings of culture, commerce, and politics.

Dr. Jonathan Beckwith, a professor of microbiology and genetics at Harvard University and one of the early pioneers in the field of molecular biology, argues that a more balanced presentation of the relationship between genetics and environment needs to be made in the public arena, or we run the risk that the new science will become the handmaiden for a eugenics-based politics. Beckwith points out that many diseases, such as cancer and depression, are the result of the subtle and not so subtle interactions of genetic predispositions and environmental triggers and to ignore the relationships and concentrate only on the gene is tantamount to abandoning any idea of moderating or reforming the environment as a remedial strategy.

Genetic Discrimination

Societies have always been divided between the haves and the have-nots, the powerful and the powerless, the elite and the masses. Throughout history, people have been segregated by caste and class, with myriad rationales used to justify the injustices imposed by the few on the many. Race, religion, language, and nationality are all well-worn methods of categorization and victimization. Now, with the emergence of the genetic revolution, society entertains the prospect of a new and more serious form of segregation. One based on genotype.

A 1996 survey of genetic discrimination in the U.S. conducted by Dr. Lisa Geller and her colleagues in the Department of Neurobiology and the Division of Medical Ethics of the Harvard University Medical School, suggests that the practice is already far more widespread than previously thought. Genetic discrimination is being practiced by a range of institutions, including insurance companies, health-care providers, government bodies, adoption agencies, and schools.

Employers are particularly interested in using genetic tests to screen prospective employees. Employers who invest heavily in long-term education and on-site training want to know if prospective employees—especially those destined for advancement on the executive track—will be free of potentially debilitating diseases over the lifetime of their work contracts. With education and retraining costs increasing, employers are understandably anxious to ensure that they are not wasting their time and resources on an employee who won't be able to continue working a few years down the line. An extensive survey of 400 employers, conducted by the Northwestern Life Insurance Company in 1989, reported that 15% of the companies planned to conduct routine genetic screening tests of their prospective employees and dependents before the year 2000.[11] With health and disability compensation costs mounting each year, employers are going to feel increasingly pressured by their own bottom lines to genotype workers in the hopes of cutting costs and increasing profit margins.

Genetic discrimination is also beginning to penetrate other institutions in society. Children, for example, are increasingly being classified, segregated, and treated in a discriminatory manner in the nation's schools, based on only vague understandings—and sometimes misunderstandings—of the role played by genetic inheritance in academic and classroom performance.[12]

In the 1950s and 1960s, academic success or failure was largely attributed to environmental factors, including parental nurturing, family dynamics, community support, and economic background. Breakthroughs in cognitive psychology and molecular biology in the 1970s and 1980s set in motion a series of profound changes in the American education system, with educators placing greater emphasis on biological, as opposed to environmental, causes of student performance. Writing in the *American Journal of Law and Medicine*, Dorothy Nelkin, a professor of sociology and law at New York University, and Laurence Tancredi, a New York psychiatrist and lawyer, noted: "Increasing research on human genetics has encouraged the assumption that learning and behavioral problems reflect biological deficits. Problems lie less in a student's environment and social situation than in the biological structure of his or her brain."[13]

Today, reading difficulties, short attention span, and behavioral problems are increasingly seen as biological deficits and classified as illnesses to be treated by pharmacological means and other forms of medical intervention. Nowhere is the shift in emphasis more apparent than in the reclassification of behavioral problems. In the 1960s and 1970s, "hyperactivity" was considered a psychological and social problem and was dealt with by attempting to understand the child and reform his or her environment. In 1980 the editors of the *Diagnostic and Statistical Manual of Mental Disorders* replaced the term "hyperactivity" with a new term, "attention deficit disorder," thereby signaling a new belief that the problem lies in the brain chemistry and genetic endowment of the child and, therefore, should be treated as an illness. Millions of children with short attention spans who exhibit hyperactive behavior have been classified as suffering from attention deficit disorder and are now being treated for their illness with Ritalin and other drugs.[14]

Other behaviors have also been redefined in the medical literature, reflecting the new bias toward biological deficits as an explanatory model for student performance. A number of new biologically based disabilities, including "expressive writing disorders" and "stereotype habit disorders," have found their way into the *Diagnostic and Statistical Manual of Mental Disorders*.[15] While it is only fair to acknowledge the genetic basis of many learning disabilities, education reformers are concerned that the shift in emphasis to "genetic causation" has left little or no room for the obvious role played by the environment in shaping a child's mental abilities and behavioral orientation.

I.Q. tests, which purport to measure inherited intelligence, have been used for much of the 20th century to classify, place, and track children, establishing a discriminatory scheme in the classroom. What's new is a generation of testing procedures designed to isolate and measure specific biological deficits in children for potential medical intervention. The "neural efficiency analyzer," for example, measures the speed with which the brain processes information. Brain electrical activity mapping (BEAM) is used by neurologists to diagnose students with learning disorders. With computer brain scans, neurologists can follow the flow of blood in the brain while a child is reading or thinking and detect differences in youngsters with dyslexia. Doctors using position emission tomography (PET) can visually track brain activity by tracing radioactive substances. Researchers are using the PET technology to monitor brain activity in the frontal region of the brain and to correlate it with children's behavior patterns in order to identify "at-risk" youngsters.[16]

The array of new neurotechnologies gives further impetus to efforts in the schools to classify youngsters on the basis of their genotype, often allowing educators to sidestep or ignore the role that environment plays in triggering or exacerbating genetic predispositions for learning and behavioral problems. The shift to genetic determinism is occurring despite years of scientific studies showing that such things as diet, lifestyle, family and class background, and socializing experiences also significantly affect learning skills, classroom performance, and personal behavior.

The increasing "genetization" of children has begun to undermine the traditional mentoring relationship in the classroom, substituting the practitioner/patient relationship for the teacher/student one. The evidence of this change is everywhere. Millions of children are currently being treated for learning disabilities and behavioral disorders with a range of pharmacological drugs, including Librium and Valium for anxiety, Prozac and Zoloft for depression, Dexedrine for behavioral disorders, and Phenobarbital and Benadryl for purposes of sedation.[17] Prescribed drugs have become major factors in the educational process and have been increasingly used to segregate and stigmatize children in the classroom.

Some teachers are less tolerant of children who have been diagnosed with a genetic disorder and more likely to give up on them, believing that their genetic "handicaps" make them less likely to keep up with "normal" children. Less attention, supervision, and support from teachers often translate into a downward learning spiral, diminution of personal confidence and self-esteem, and the further marginalization of genetically branded students. The discriminatory biases can follow children through school and into the workplace. Poorly educated and often improperly socialized, these youngsters are likely to be discriminated against a second time around by would-be employers for psychological and intellectual deficits created, in part, by the school systems that unfairly genotyped and stereotyped them in the first place.

Segregating individuals by their genetic make-up represents a fundamental shift in the exercise of power. In a society in which the individual can be stereotyped by genotype, institutional power of all kinds becomes more absolute. At the same time, the increasing polarization of society into genetically "superior" and "inferior" individuals and groups will create a new and powerful social dynamic. Families that can afford to program "superior" genetic traits into their fetuses at conception will ensure their offspring an even greater biological advantage—and

thus a social and economic advantage as well. For the emerging "genetic underclass," the issue of genetic stereotyping is likely to lead to growing protests and the birth of a worldwide "genetics rights" movement as an ever-growing number of victims of genetic discrimination organize collectively to demand their right to participate freely and fully in the coming biotech century.

Some genetic engineers envision a future with a small segment of the human population engineered to "perfection," while others remain as flawed reminders of an outmoded evolutionary design. Molecular biologist Lee Silver of Princeton University writes about a not too distant future made up of two distinct biological classes, which he refers to as the "Gen Rich" and the "Naturals." The Gen Rich, who account for 10% of the population, have been enhanced with synthetic genes and have become the rulers of society. They include Gen Rich businesspeople, musicians, artists, intellectuals, and athletes—each enhanced with specific synthetic genes to allow them to succeed in their respective fields in ways not even conceivable among those born of nature's lottery.

At the center of the new genetic aristocracy are the Gen Rich scientists, who are enhanced with special genetic traits that increase their mental abilities, giving them power to dictate the terms of future evolutionary advances on Earth. Silver writes:

With the passage of time, the genetic distance between Naturals and the Gen Rich has become greater and greater, and now there is little movement up from the Natural to the Gen Rich class. . . . All aspects of the economy, the media, the entertainment industry, and the knowledge industry are controlled by members of the Gen Rich class. . . . In contrast, Naturals work as low-paid service providers or as laborers. . . . Gen Rich and Natural children grow up and live in segregated social worlds where there is little chance for contact between them. . . . [Eventually,] the Gen Rich class and the Natural class will become the Gen Rich humans and the Natural humans—entirely separate species with no ability to crossbreed and with as much romantic interest in each other as a current human would have for a chimpanzee.[18]

Silver acknowledges that the increasing polarization of society into a Gen Rich class and a Natural class might be unfair, but he is quick to add that wealthy parents have always been able to provide all sorts of advantages for their children. "Anyone who accepts the right of affluent parents to provide their children with an expensive private school education cannot use unfairness as a reason for rejecting the use of reprogenetic technologies," Silver argues. Like many of his colleagues, Silver is a strong advocate of the new genetic technologies. "In a society that values human freedom above all else," he writes, "it is hard to find any legitimate basis for restricting the use of reprogenetics."[19]

Difficult Choices

Even with all the excitement being generated around the new genetic technologies, we sense, though dimly, the menacing outline of a eugenics shadow on the horizon. Still, we would find it exceedingly difficult to say no to a technological revolution that offers such an impressive array of benefits. Thus we find ourselves ensnared on the horns of a dilemma as we make the first tentative moves into the biotech century. One part of us, our more ancient side, reels at the prospect of the further desacralizing of life, of reducing ourselves and all other sentient creatures to chemical codes to be manipulated for purely instrumental and utilitarian ends. Our other side, the one firmly entrenched in modernity, is zealously committed to bringing the biology of the planet in line with engineering standards, market forces, and progressive values. Not to proceed with this revolution is unthinkable, as it would violate the very spirit of progress—a spirit that knows no bounds in its restless search to wrest power from the natural world.

The biotech revolution represents the culmination of the Enlightenment vision, a world view that has provided a philosophical and social road map for modern man and woman for more than 200 years. Finding new, more powerful technological ways of controlling and harnessing nature for utilitarian and commercial ends has been the ultimate dream and central motif of the modern age. It was Francis Bacon, the founder of modern science, who urged future generations to "squeeze," "mould," and "shape" nature in order to "enlarge the bounds of human empire to the effecting of all things possible." [20] Bacon laid the groundwork for the Enlightenment era that followed by providing a systematic vision for humanity's final triumph over nature. Isaac Newton, René Descartes, John Locke, and other Enlightenment philosophers constructed a world view that continues to inspire today's molecular biologists and corporate entrepreneurs in their quest to capture and colonize the last frontier of nature, the genetic commons that is the heart of the natural world.

The biotech century promises to complete the modernists' journey by "perfecting" both human nature and the rest of nature, all in the name of progress. The short-term benefits of the emerging Biotechnological Age appear so impressive that any talk of curtailing or preventing their widespread application is likely to be greeted with incredulity, if not outright hostility. Who could oppose the engineering of new plants and animals to feed a hungry world? Who could object to engineering new forms of biological energy to replace a dwindling reserve of fossil fuels? Who could protest the introduction of new microbes to eat up toxic wastes and other forms of chemical pollution? Who could refuse genetic surgery to eliminate crippling diseases? How could anyone in good conscience oppose a technology that offers such hope for bettering the lot of humanity?

In the years to come, a multitude of new genetic engineering techniques will be forthcoming. Every one of the breakthroughs in biotechnology will be of benefit to someone, under some circumstance, somewhere in society. Each will, in some way, appear to advance the future security of an individual, a group, or society as a whole. The point that needs to be emphasized is that bioengineering is coming to us not as a threat but as a promise, not as a punishment but as a gift. While the thought of engineering living organisms still conjures up sinister images in the movies, it no longer does so in the marketplace. Quite the contrary, what we see before our eyes are not monstrosities but useful products and hopeful futures. We no longer feel dread, but only elated expectation at the great possibilities that lie in store for each of us in the biotech century.

For its most ardent supporters, engineering life to improve humanity's own prospects is, no doubt, seen as the highest expression of ethical behavior. Any resistance to the new technology is likely to be castigated by the growing legion of true believers as inhuman, irresponsible, morally reprehensible, and perhaps even criminally culpable.

On the other hand, the new genetic engineering technologies raise one of the most troubling political questions in all of human history. To whom, in this new era, would we entrust the authority to decide what is a good gene that should be added to the gene pool and what is a bad gene that should be eliminated? Should we entrust the federal government with that authority? Corporations? The university scientists? From this perspective, few of us are able to point to any institution or group of individuals we would entrust with decisions of such import. If, however, we were asked whether we would sanction new biotech advances that could enhance the physical, emotional, and mental well-being of people, we would not hesitate for a moment to add our support.

We appear caught between our instinctual distrust of the institutional forces that are quickly consolidating their power over the new genetic technologies and our desire to increase our own personal choices and options in the biological marketplace. While control of the new genetic technologies is being concentrated in the hands of scientists, transnational companies, government agencies,and other institutions, the products and services are being marketed under the guise of expanding freedom of choice for millions of consumers.

In the early stages of this new technological and commercial revolution, the informal bargain being struck between the governing institutions of society and consumers appears to be a reasonable one. Biotechnology has much to offer. But, as with the introduction of other technological innovations throughout history, the final costs have yet to be calculated. Granting a specific institution or group of individuals the power to determine a better-engineered crop or animal or a new human hormone seems a trifle in comparison with the potential returns. It is only when one considers the lifetime of the agreement that the full import of the politics of the Biotechnological Age becomes apparent.

Throughout history, some people have always controlled the futures of other people. Today, the ultimate exercise of power is within our grasp: the ability to control, at the most fundamental level, the future lives of unborn generations by engineering their biology in advance, making them "partial" hostages of their own architecturally designed blueprints. I use the word "partial" because, like many others, I believe that environment is a major contributing factor in determining the course of one's life. It is also true, however, that one's genetic makeup plays a role in helping to shape one's destiny. Genetic engineering, then, represents the power of authorship, albeit "limited" authorship. Being able to engineer even minor changes in the physical and behavioral characteristics of future generations represents a new era in human history. Never before has such power over human life been even a possibility.

Should power of this sort be granted to any public or commercial institution or, for that matter, even to consumers? Whether institutionally motivated or consumer driven, the power to determine the genetic destiny of millions of human beings yet to come lessens the opportunities of every new arrival to shape his or her own personal life story.

Still, at the dawn of the biotech century, the authorial power, though formidable, appears so far removed from any potential threat to individual human will as to be of little concern. Many of us will be eager to take advantage of the new gene therapies, both for ourselves and for our offspring, if they deliver on their promise to enhance our physical, emotional, and mental health. After all, part of the essence of being truly human is the desire to alleviate suffering and enhance human potential.

The problem is that biotechnology has a distinct beginning but no clear end. Cell by cell, tissue by tissue, organ by organ, we might willingly surrender our personhood in the marketplace. In the process, each loss will be compensated for with a perceived gain until there is little left to exchange. It is at that very point that the cost of our agreement becomes apparent. But it is also at that point that we may no longer possess the very thing we were so anxious to enrich: our humanity. In the decades to come, we humans might well barter ourselves away, one gene at a time, in exchange for some measure of temporary well-being. In the end, the personal and collective security we fought so long and hard to preserve may well be irreversibly compromised in pursuit of our own engineered perfection.

Notes

1. Robert C. Clarringer, Rolf Adolfsson, and Nenad M. Svranic, "Mapping Genes for Human Personality," *Nature Genetics,* January 1996, p. 3.
2. David Concar, "High Anxiety and Lazy Genes," *New Science,* 7 December 1996, p. 22.
3. Natalie Angier, "Parental Origin of Chromosome May Determine Social Causes, Scientists Say," *New York Times,* 12 July 1997, p. A-18.
4. Jon Beckwith, "A Historical View of Social Responsibility in Genetics," *BioScience,* May 1993, p. 330.
5. Daniel J. Kevles, *In the Name of Eugenics: Genetics and the Uses of Human Heredity* (Cambridge, Mass.: Harvard University Press, 1995), p. 269.
6. Alexander Rich and Sung Hou Kim, "The Three-Dimensional Structure of Transfer RNA," *Scientific American,* 3 January 1978, p. 52.
7. Stuart A. Newman, "Genetic Engineering as Metaphysics and Menace," *Science and Nature,* vol. 9/10, 1989, p. 118.
8. Ibid., p. 116.
9. Ibid., p. 118.
10. Tim Beardsley, "Smart Genes," *Scientific American,* August 1991, pp. 86–95.
11. Shannon Brownlee and Joanne Siberner, "The Assurances of Genes," *U.S. News & World Report,* 23 July 1990, p. 57.
12. Lisa Geller et al., "Individual, Family, and Societal Dimensions of Genetic Discrimination: A Case Study Analysis," *Science and Engineering Ethics,* vol. 2, 1996, p. 78.
13. Dorothy Nelkin and Laurence R. Tancredi, "Classify and Control: Genetic Information in the Schools," *American Journal of Law and Medicine,* vol. 17, 1991, p. 52; Irving D. Harris, *Emotional Blocks to Learning: A Study of the Reasons for Failure in School* (New York: Free Press of Glencoe, 1961), p. 36; and S. P. R. Rose, "What Should a Biochemistry of Learning and Memory Be About?," *Neuroscience,* May 1981, p. 811.
14. Nelkin and Tancredi, pp. 55–56; Gerald Coles, *The Learning Mystique: A Critical Look at "Learning Disabilities"* (New York: Pantheon Books, 1988), pp. 23–24, 43–44; and *Diagnostic and Statistical Manual of Mental Disorders,* 3rd ed. (Washington, D.C.: American Psychiatric Association, 1980). See also Joseph Biederman, Kerim Munir, and Debra Knee, "Conduct and Oppositional Disorder in Clinically Referred Children with Attention Deficit Disorders: A Controlled Family Study," *Journal of the American Academy of Child and Adolescent Psychiatry,* September 1987, p. 724; Joseph Biederman et al., "A Family Study of Patients with Attention Deficit Disorder and Normal Controls," *Journal of Psychiatric Research,* vol. 20, 1986, pp. 263–74; Gerald L. Klerman, "The Significance of the DSM III in American Psychiatry," in Andrew E. Skodol, Robert L.

Spitzer, and Janet B. W. Williams, eds., *International Perspectives on DSM III* (Washington, D.C.: American Psychiatric Press, 1983); and Lawrence M. Greenberg and William Erickson, "Pharmacotherapy of Children and Adolescents," in Cecil R. Reynolds and Terry B. Gutkin, eds., *The Handbook of School Psychology* (New York: Wiley, 1982), pp. 1023, 1025.

15. *Diagnostic and Statistical Manual of Mental Disorders,* pp. 42–43, 93–95.

16. Coles, pp. 70–90; Dorothy Nelkin and Laurence R. Tancredi, *Dangerous Diagnostics: The Social Power of Biological Information* (New York: Basic Books, 1989), pp. 125–26; and Nora D. Volkow and Laurence R. Tancredi, "Biological Correlates of Mental Activity: Studies with PET," *American Journal of Psychiatry,* April 1991, p. 439.

17. Nelson and Tancredi, *Dangerous Diagnostics,* pp. 117–21; and Greenberg and Erickson, pp. 1030–31.

18. Lee M. Silver, *Remaking Eden: Cloning and Beyond in a Brave New World* (New York: Avon Books, 1997), pp. 4–7.

19. Ibid., p. 9.

20. John H. Randall, *The Making of the Modern Mind: A Survey of the Intellectual Background of the Present Age* (Boston: Houghton Mifflin, 1940), pp. 223–24; Francis Bacon, "Novum Organum," in *The Works of Francis Bacon,* vol. 4 (London: J. Rivington and Sons, 1778), pp. 114, 246, 320, 325; idem, "The Masculine Birth of Time," in Benjamin Farrington, ed., *The Philosophy of Francis Bacon: An Essay on Its Development from 1603–1609* (Liverpool: Liverpool University Press, 1964), pp. 62, 92–93; idem, "Description of the Intellectual Globe," in *The Works of Francis Bacon,* vol. 5 (London: J. Rivington and Sons, 1778), p. 506; William Leiss, *The Domination of Nature* (Boston: Beacon Press, 1972), p. 58; and Carolyn Merchant, *The Death of Nature: Women, Ecology, and the Scientific Revolution* (San Francisco: Harper & Row, 1980), p. 172.

Form at end of book

Brain Science, Brain Fiction

When it comes to applying neuroscientific research to classroom practice, educators must look before they leap.

John T. Bruer

John T. Bruer is President of the James S. McDonnell Foundation, 1034 South Brentwood Blvd., Ste. 1850, St. Louis, MO 63117 (e-mail: bruer@jsmf.org).

During the past year, a flood of articles in popular and professional publications have discussed the implications of brain science for education and child development. Although we should consider ideas and research from other fields for our professional practice, we must assess such ideas critically. This is particularly true when we look at how a vast, complex field like brain science might improve classroom instruction.

Three big ideas from brain science figure most centrally in the education literature, and educators should know four things about these ideas to make their own critical appraisals of brain-based education. My own assessment of recent articles about brain research is that well-founded educational applications of brain science may come eventually, but right now, brain science has little to offer education practice or policy (Bruer, 1997, 1998).

Three big ideas arise from brain science: (1) Early in life, neural connections (synapses) form rapidly in the brain; (2) Critical periods occur in development; and (3) Enriched environments have a pronounced effect on brain development during the early years. Neuroscientists have known about all three big ideas for 20 to 30 years. What we need to be critical of is not the ideas themselves, but how they are interpreted for educators and parents.

Early Synapse Formation

Synapses are the connections through which nerve impulses travel from one neuron to another. Since the late 1970s, neuroscientists have known that the number of synapses per unit volume of tissue (the *synaptic density*) in the brain's outer cortical layer changes over the life span of monkeys and humans (Goldman-Rakic, Bourgeois, & Rakic, 1997; Huttenlocher & Dabholkar, 1997; Rakic, Bourgeois, & Goldman-Rakic, 1994). Not surprisingly, human newborns have lower synaptic densities than adults. However, in the months following birth, the infant brain begins to form synapses far in excess of the adult levels. In humans, by age 4, synaptic densities have peaked in all brain areas at levels 50 percent above adult levels. Throughout childhood, synaptic densities remain above adult levels. Around the age of puberty, a pruning process begins to eliminate synapses, reducing synaptic densities to adult, mature levels.

The timing of this process appears to vary among brain areas in humans. In the visual area of the human brain, synaptic densities increase rapidly starting at 2 months of age, peak at 8 to 10 months, and then decline to adult levels at around 10 years. However, in the human frontal cortex—the brain area involved in attention, short-term memory, and planning—this process begins later and lasts longer. In the frontal cortex, synaptic densities do not stabilize at mature levels until around age 16. Thus, we can think of synaptic densities changing over the first two decades of life in an inverted-U pattern: low at birth, highest in childhood, and lower in adulthood.

This much is neuroscientific fact. The question is, What does this inverted-U pattern mean for learning and education? Here, despite what educators might think, the neuroscientists know relatively little. In discussing what the changes in synaptic density mean for behavior and learning, neurocientists cite a small set of examples based on animal research and then extrapolate these findings to human infants. On the basis of observations of changes in motor, visual, and memory skills, neuroscientists agree that basic movement, vision, and memory skills first appear in their most primitive form when synaptic densities begin their rapid increase. For example, at age 8 months, when synapses begin to increase rapidly in the frontal brain areas, infants first show short-term memory skills for places and objects. Infants' performance on these tasks improves steadily over the next four months. However, performance on these memory tasks does not reach adult levels until puberty, when synaptic densities have *decreased* to adult levels.

Thing to Know No. 1: Neuroscience suggests that there is no simple, direct relationship between synaptic densities and intelligence. Increases in synaptic densities are associated with the initial emergence of skills and capacities, but these skills and capacities continue to develop after synaptic densities decrease to adult levels. Although early in infancy we might have the most synapses we will ever have, most learning occurs later, after synaptic densities *decrease* in the brain. Given the existence of the U-shaped pattern and what we observe about our own learning and intelligence over our life spans, we have no reason to believe, as we often read, that the more synapses we have, the smarter we are. Nor do existing neuroscientific studies support the idea that the more learning experiences we have during childhood, the more synapses will be "saved" from pruning and the more intelligent our children will be.

Neuroscientists know very little about how learning, particularly school learning, affects the brain at the synaptic level. We should be skeptical of any claims that suggest they do. For example, we sometimes read that complex learning situations cause increased "neural branching" that offsets neural pruning. As far as we know, such claims are based more on brain fiction than on brain science.

Critical Periods in Development

Research on critical periods has been prominent in developmental neurobiology for more than 30 years. This research has shown that if some motor, sensory, and (in humans) language skills are to develop normally, then the animal must have certain kinds of experience at specific times during its development.

The best-researched example is the existence of critical periods in the development of the visual system. Starting in the 1960s, David Hubel, Torsten Wiesel, and their colleagues showed that if during the early months of life, cats or monkeys had one eyelid surgically closed, the animal would never regain functional use of that eye when it was subsequently reopened (Hubel, Wiesel, & LeVay, 1977). They also showed that closing one eye during this time had demonstrable effects on the structure of the visual area in the animal's brain. However, the same or longer periods of complete visual deprivation in adult cats had no effect on either the animal's ability to use the eye when it was reopened or on its brain structure. Only young animals, during a critical period in their develop-

ment, were sensitive to this kind of deprivation. They also found that closing *both* eyes during the critical period had no permanent, long-term effects on the animals' vision or brain structure.

Finally, they found that in monkeys, "reverse closure" during the critical period—opening the closed eye and closing the open eye—allowed a young deprived animal to recover the use of the originally deprived eye. If the reverse suturing was done early enough in the critical period, recovery could be almost complete. These last two findings are seldom mentioned in popular and educational interpretations of critical-period research.

Over the past three decades, hundreds of neuroscientists have advanced our understanding of critical periods. We should be aware of three conclusions about critical periods that these scientists generally endorse. First, the different outcomes of closing one eye, both eyes, and reverse suturing suggest that it is *not* the amount of stimulation that matters during a critical period. If only the amount mattered, closing both eyes should have the same effect on each eye as it had when only one eye was closed. Neuroscientists believe that what matters during critical periods in the development of the visual system is the *balance* and *relative timing* of stimulation to the eyes. What does this mean? For one thing, it means that more stimulation during the critical period does not necessarily result in a better-developed visual system.

Second, neuroscientists have learned that critical periods are quite complex and that different critical periods exist for different specific functions (Daw, 1995). For example, within the visual system are different critical periods for visual acuity, binocular function, and depth perception. For humans, even in an early developing system like vision, these periods can last until early childhood. For language, the critical period for learning phonology—learning to speak without an accent—ends in early childhood, but the critical period for learning a language's grammar does not end until around age 16.

Neuroscientists now also think that for each specific function of a sensory system, like vision, there are three distinct phases within the critical period. First, there is a time of rapid change during which a function, like depth perception, quickly matures. During the second phase, sensory deprivation can result in deterioration or loss of that function. After the period of sensitivity to deprivation, there seems to be yet a third phase of the critical period. During this phase, the system retains sufficient plasticity to compensate for deprivation and regains near-normal function if appropriate sensory experience occurs.

Given these complexities, neuroscientists know that it makes little sense to speak of *a* critical period for vision or for any other sensory system, let alone of *a* critical period for brain development. Critical periods are simply windows of learning opportunity that open and then slam shut.

Finally, neuroscientists are beginning to understand why critical periods exist and why critical periods have adaptive value for an organism. They believe that as the result of evolutionary processes, highly sensitive neural systems, like vision, have come to depend on the presence of environmental stimuli to fine-tune their neural circuitry.

Relying on the environment to fine-tune the system results in neural circuits that are more sensitively tuned than they ever could be if they were hard-wired by genetic programs at birth. Relying on the presence of certain kinds of stimuli just at the right times would seem to be a highly risky developmental strategy, especially for a system like vision that is fundamental to survival. The reason it is not risky is that the kinds of stimuli needed during critical periods—patterned visual input, the ability to move and manipulate objects, noises, the presence of speech sounds—are ubiquitously and abundantly present in any normal human environment. Nature has made a bet that the stimuli will be present, but nature has placed its money on an almost sure thing. The brain expects certain kinds of stimuli to be present for normal development, and they almost always are, unless a child is abused to the point of being raised in a deprivation chamber. William Greenough and his colleagues (1992) have characterized the kind of brain modification that occurs as a result of critical periods "experience-expectant brain plasticity."

Thing to Know No. 2: If critical periods are a result of our evolutionary history and nature's bet on almost sure things occurring in a child's environment, then neuroscientific research on critical periods is likely to have little relevance to formal education. From what we know to date about critical periods, they contribute to the development of basic specieswide abilities, like vision, hearing, or language. For this reason, despite what we read, the specifics of home or preschool environments matter little, if at all, to how children's sensory and motor systems develop.

For similar reasons, critical periods say little about formal education. Formal schooling instructs children about the social and cultural particulars, not about evolution-based, specieswide skills and behaviors. Currently, we have no reason to think that there are critical periods for the acquisition of culturally and socially transmitted skills, like reading, mathematics, or music, just to name a few of the favorite examples. As far as we know, people can acquire these skills at any age; can benefit from instruction at any age; and can increase their intelligence and expertise, given the right opportunities, at any age (Greenough, 1997).

The Effects of Enriched Environments

Neuroscientists have been studying the effects of enriched environments on rats' behavior and brain development for nearly 50 years. Some of the best and most current of this work is that of Greenough and his colleagues at the University of Illinois (1992). In this research, neuroscientists study how raising rats in different environments affects their brain structure. Typically, scientists study the effects of two contrasting environments. Some rats are raised alone in small cages with only food and water available. This "isolated environment" is the typical laboratory environment for a rat.

Despite what we read, the specifics of home or preschool environments matter little, if at all, to how children's sensory and motor systems develop.

Other rats are raised in large, group cages that also contain novel objects and obstacles. Greenough calls these environments *complex,* rather than enriched. He points out that complex environments are enriched only in comparison with a rat's typical lab cage. Neuroscientists use complex environments to mimic the rats' wild or natural environment. They are not special, accelerated rodent learning environments. One should not think of them as high-quality infant care or Head Start for rats. One should think of them more as attempts to create New York City subway tunnel conditions in the laboratory.

In electron microscopic studies, Greenough and his colleagues found that young rats raised in complex environments have 25 percent more synapses per neuron in the visual areas of their brains than do rats raised in isolation. However, increases in synapses per neuron ratios do not occur to this extent in all brain areas, and some brain areas show no effects of complex rearing at all. On the basis of this research, we can see that it is definitely not the case, as we often read, that complex environments result in a 25 percent increase in brain connectivity.

More important, however, 15 years ago, Greenough and his colleagues established that the brains of *adult* rats also form new synapses in response to complex environments. Other studies in monkeys and humans have definitely established that the adult brain remains highly plastic and capable of extensive neural reorganization throughout life. The brain's ability to reorganize itself in response to new experiences is what makes it possible for us to learn throughout our lives. The ability of the mature brain to change and reorganize, a finding seldom mentioned in the education literature, is a new, exciting finding of brain science (Nelson & Bloom, 1997).

Thing to Know No. 3: Research on complex environments and related findings tells us that the brain can reorganize itself for learning throughout our lifetimes. This new insight runs counter to our current fixation on early development and critical periods. However, in thinking about how this research relates to educational practice and policy, we must be careful not to confuse *complex* with *enriched.* Neuroscientists use *complex* as a descriptive term for a laboratory simulation of a wild or natural environment. Education writers tend to use *enriched* as a value-laden term. In the popular and education literature, enriched environments tend to be culturally preferred, middle-class environments. These environments tend to include things that the writers value—Mozart, piano lessons, playing chess—and to exclude things that they scorn—video games, MTV, shooting pool. These writers tend to identify enriched environments with Cambridge, Massachusetts, and Palo Alto, California, and deprived environments with Roxbury and East Palo Alto.

As far as neuroscience goes, all these activities and environments are equally complex—and neuroscience says nothing about which are more or less enriched than others. In assessing claims about environments and the brain, we should be aware of how easy it is to slide from describing complexity to prescribing enrichment. We should be careful not to use neuroscience to provide biological pseudo-argument in favor of our culture and our political values and prejudices.

Educators should know one final thing.

Thing to Know No. 4: Research on early synapse formation, critical periods, and complex environments has a long history. Yet, we have little understanding of what this research might mean for education. Our appeals to this research are often naive and superficial. Other brain-related themes popular in the education literature—emotional intelligence, the social brain, the brain in the entire body, the intelligent immune system, down-shifting—have a much less reliable grounding in neuroscience. Educators seeking to base practice on the best science might want to assess recommendations stemming from these ideas even more carefully and critically.

References

Bruer, J. T. (1997). Education and the brain: A bridge too far. *Educational Researcher, 26*(8), 4–16.

Bruer, J. T. (1998). Let's put brain science on the back burner. *NASSP Bulletin, 82*(598), 21–28.

Daw, N. W. (1995). *Visual development.* New York: Plenum.

Goldman-Rakic, P. S., Bourgeois, J.-P., & Rakic, P. (1997). Synaptic substrate of cognitive development: Synaptogenesis in the prefrontal cortex of the nonhuman primate. In N. A. Krasnegor, G. R. Lyon, & P. S. Goldman-Rakic (Eds.). *Development of the prefrontal cortex: Evolution, neurobiology, and behavior* (pp. 27–47). Baltimore: Paul H. Brookes.

Greenough, W. T. (1997). We can't focus just on ages zero to three. *APA Monitor, 28,* 19.

Greenough, W. T., Withers, G. S., & Anderson, B. J. (1992). Experience-dependent synaptogenesis as a plausible memory mechanism. In I. Gormezano & E. A. Wasserman (Eds.). *Learning and memory: The behavioral and biological substrates* (pp. 209–299). Hillsdale, NJ: Earlbaum.

Hubel, D. H., Wiesel, T. N., & LeVay, S. (1977). Plasticity of ocular dominance columns in monkey striate cortex. *Philosophical Transactions of the Royal Society of London B, 278,* 307–409.

Huttenlocher, P. R., & Dabholkar, A. S. (1997). Regional differences in synaptogenesis in human cerebral cortex. *Journal of Comparative Neurology, 367,* 167–178.

Nelson, C. A., & Bloom, F. E. (1997). Child development and neuroscience. *Child Development, 68*(5), 970–987.

Rakic, P., Bourgeois, J.-P., & Goldman-Rakic, P. S. (1994). Synaptic development of the cerebral cortex: Implications for learning, memory, and mental illness. In J. van Pelt, M. A. Corner, H. B. M. Uylings, & F. H. Lopes da Silva (Eds.), *Progress in Brain Research* 102 (pp. 227–243). Amsterdam: Elsevier Science BV.

FRAME the DEBATE

Form at end of book

Issue 4 Summary

The three articles you have just read highlight both the hopes and the cautions associated with brain research. While brain research presents the possibility that we can be more effective in how we teach and organize schools, at the same time a number of significant risks are present. First, we risk falling into traps similar to ones into which educators have fallen in the past: by finding a new way to differentiate students (e.g., by their genes), we may find new ways to treat students differently in ways that are not supportable. That is, we risk segregating children in a manner that is discriminatory. Second, we risk running too fast and applying "findings" of brain research before they are fully understood and validated. The history of education is replete with instances in which, in their enthusiasm, educators pounced on new theories and applied them, sometimes without a full understanding of them and without proof that they were accurate.

Nature and Nurture

Questions

1. Given the evidence on each side, which appears to have the greater effect on children's development—their genetic makeup or their upbringing? Based on what you have read, what advice would you give new parents regarding the upbringing of their baby?

2. What are the primary vulnerabilities of boys? Why do boys seem more susceptible to particular types of problems?

3. How successful are schools in meeting the needs of girls? What might schools do differently to better meet girls' needs?

Introduction

The questions of *how* and *how much* "nature" and "nurture" contribute to individuals' development have vexed psychologists since the field began. Increasingly, we find evidence of nature's influence on both our physiology and our personality. In a recent book, *The Nurture Assumption: Why Children Turn Out the Way They Do,* Judith Rich Harris argues that we are primarily a product of our genes and that there is little parents and teachers can do to change our inherent characteristics. As you might imagine, many parents and teachers reacted strongly to Harris's argument and presented the counterarguments favoring "nurture." This long-standing issue is a long way from being resolved.

Equally difficult to resolve is the issue of how genes and society affect the development of males and females. Data show that boys are more aggressive: is this a case of "boys will be boys," meaning boys' genes cause them to be more aggressive, or does society encourage boys to be more aggressive? Regardless of which explanation is true, how does society react to the aggressiveness of boys? Are the greater verbal and social skills of girls due to their genes or their upbringing? Do we do girls justice in schools, or are we favoring boys and encouraging their achievement?

Do Parents Matter?

Did you think that the way parents treat their children influences how they turn out? Think again, argues a controversial new book, which contends that parents matter a whole lot less than scientists believe.

Sharon Begley

Surely there is no more cherished, yet humbling, idea than the conviction that parents hold in their hands the power to shape their child's tomorrows. And the evidence for it is as impossible to ignore as the toddler throwing a tantrum in the grocery store when Daddy refuses to buy him M&Ms: setting reasonable, but firm, limits teaches children self-control and good behavior, but being either too permissive or too dictatorial breeds little brats. Giving your little girl a big hug when she skins her knee makes her feel loved and secure, which enables her to form trusting relationships when she blooms into a young woman. Reading and talking to children fosters a love of reading: divorce puts them at risk of depression and academic failure. Physical abuse makes them aggressive, but patience and kindness, as shown by the parents who soothe their child's frustration at not being able to play a favorite piano piece rather than belittling him, leaves a child better able to handle distress both in youth and in adulthood. Right?

Wrong, wrong and wrong again, contends Judith Rich Harris. In a new book, *The Nurture Assumption: Why Children Turn Out the Way They Do; Parents Matter Less Than You Think and Peers Matter More* (462 pages. Free Press. $26), Harris is igniting a bonfire of controversy for her central claim: the belief "that what influences children's development . . . is the way their parents bring them up . . . is wrong." After parents contribute an egg or a sperm filled with DNA, she argues, virtually nothing they do or say—no kind words or hugs, slaps or tirades; neither permissiveness nor authoritarianism; neither encouragement nor scorn—makes a smidgen of difference to what kind of adult the child becomes. Nothing parents do will affect his behavior, mental health, ability to form relationships, sense of self-worth, intelligence or personality. What genes don't do, peers do.

Although Harris's book lists some 750 scientific papers, articles and books as references, maybe all she really had to do to reach this conclusion was keep good notes about the goings-on in her own suburban New Jersey colonial. Harris and her husband, Charles, had one daughter, Nomi, on New Year's Day, 1966, and adopted a second, Elaine, almost four years later. The girls grew up in the same home "filled to overflowing with books and magazines, where classical music was played, where jokes were told," recalls Harris. Both girls took ballet lessons; both learned the crawl at Mrs. Dee's Swim School. Both were read books by their parents and both delighted in birthday parties with homemade cake. Both experienced the sorrow and stress of a sick mother (Harris developed a mysterious autoimmune illness, part lupus and part systemic sclerosis, when Elaine was 6 and Nomi 10, and was often confined to bed). Yet Nomi was a well-behaved child who "didn't want to do anything *we* didn't want her to do," says Harris over iced tea in her kitchen. Elaine, adopted at 2 months, was defiant by the age of 11. She angrily announced to her parents that she didn't have to listen to them. When they grounded her once, at 15, she left for school the next morning—and didn't come back that night. Nomi was a model student; Elaine dropped out of high school.

It made Harris wonder. Why was she having about as much influence on Elaine as the fluttering wings of a butterfly do on the path of a hurricane? And it made her mad. "All of these studies that supposedly show an influence of parents on children—they don't prove what they purport to," she fumes. Having floated this idea in the scientific journal *Psychological Review* in 1995, she has now turned it into a book that is becoming the publishing phenom of the season. This week Harris is scheduled for morning television shows, radio interviews and network magazine shows. *The Free Press* has gone back for a third printing after an initial run of 15,000, and her publicists say every author's dream—Oprah—may be in her future.

This petite, gray-haired grandmother hardly seems the type to be lobbing Molotov cocktails at one of the most dearly held ideas in all of child development. Harris, 60, has no academic affiliation and no Ph.D. In 1961, she was thrown out of Harvard University's graduate department of psychology because her professors believed she showed no ability to do important original research. She got a job writing psych textbooks. Yet in August, Harris shared a $500 prize from the American Psychological Association, for the paper that best integrates disparate fields of psychology. And she has some big guns on her side. Neuroscientist Robert Sapolsky of Stanford University says her book is "based on solid science." John Bruer, president of the James S. McDonnell Foundation, which funds education programs, praises it as "a needed corrective to this belief that early experiences between the child and parents have a deterministic, lifelong effect." And linguist Steven Pinker of the Massachusetts Institute of Technology predicts that *The Nurture Assumption* "will come to be seen as a turning point in the history of psychology."

On the effect of quality time: "Parenting has been oversold. You have been led to believe that you have more of an influence on your child's personality than you really do."

So far, though, that's a minority view, and many scientists are nothing short of scathing. "I am embarrassed for psychology," says Harvard's Jerome Kagan, arguably one of the deans of child development. "She's all wrong," says psychologist Frank Farley of Temple University, president of the APA division that honored Harris. "She's taking an extreme position based on a limited set of data. Her thesis is absurd on its face, but consider what might happen if parents believe this stuff! Will it free some to mistreat their kids, since 'it doesn't matter'? Will it tell parents who are tired after a long day that they needn't bother even paying any attention to their kid since 'it doesn't matter'?" Psychologist Wendy Williams of Cornell University, who studies how environment affects IQ, argues that "there are many, many good studies that show parents can affect how children turn out in both cognitive abilities and behavior. By taking such an extreme position, Harris does a tremendous disservice."

In fact, neither scholars nor parents have always believed that parents matter. Sure, today rows upon rows of parent-advice books fill stores, parenting magazines clog newsstands, and new parents know the names Penelope Leach and T. Berry Brazelton better than they do their newborns'. But a leading tome on child development published in 1934 didn't even include a chapter on parents. It was only in the 1950s that researchers began to seek the causes of differences among children in the ways that parents raised them (time line). Now Harris is part of a growing backlash against the idea that parents can mold their child like Play-Doh.

With an impish wit and a chatty style, Harris spins a persuasive argument that the 1934 book got it right. Her starting point is behavioral genetics. This field examines how much of the differences between people reflect heredity, the genes they inherit from their parents. Over the years, researchers have concluded that variations in traits like impulsivity, aggression, thrill-seeking, neuroticism, intelligence, amiability and shyness are partly due to genes. "Partly" means anywhere from 20 to 70 percent. The other 30 to 80 percent reflects "environment." "Environment" means influences like an encounter with a bully, a best-friendship that lasts decades, an inspiring math teacher. It also includes, you'd think, how your parents reared you. But Harris argues that "environment" includes a parental contribution of precisely zero (unless you count Mom and Dad's decision about which neighborhood to live in, which we'll get to later). When she says parents don't "matter," she means they do not leave a lasting effect—into adulthood. (She accepts that how parents treat a child affects how that child behaves at home, as well as whether the grown child regards the parents with love, resentment or anger.)

On smoking: "The best predictor of whether a teenager will become a smoker is whether her friends smoke. This is a better predictor than whether her parents smoke."

To reach her parents-don't-matter conclusion, Harris first demolishes some truly lousy studies that have become part of the scientific canon. A lot of research, for instance, concludes that divorce puts kids at greater risk of academic failure and problem behavior like drug use and drinking. Other studies claim to show that parents who treat their kids with love and respect, and who get along well with others, have children who also have successful personal relationships. Yet neither sort of study "proves the power of nurture at all," Harris says emphatically. Why? They do not take into account genetics. Maybe the reason some parents are loving or competent or prone to divorce or whatever is genetic. After all, being impulsive and aggressive makes you more likely to divorce; both tendencies are partly genetic, so maybe you passed them on to your kids. Then it's their genes, and not seeing their parents' marriage fail, that explain the kids' troubles, Harris claims. And if being patient and agreeable makes you more likely to be a loving and patient parent, and if you pass that nice DNA to your kids, then again it is the genes and not the parenting that made the kids nice.

Do your own eyes tell you that being a just-right disciplinarian—not too strict, not too easy—teaches children limits and self-control? Not so fast. Harris points out that children, through their innate temperament, can elicit a particular parenting style. For example, a little hellion will likely make her parents first impatient and then angry and then resigned. It isn't parental anger and resignation that made the kid, say, a runaway and a dropout. Rather, the child's natural, genetic tendencies made her parents behave a certain way; those same tendencies made her a runaway and a dropout. Again, argues Harris, not the parents' fault. By this logic, of course, parents don't get credit, either. You think reading to your toddler made her an academic star? Uh-uh, says Harris. Maybe kids get read to more if they *like* to get read to. If so, liking books is also what makes them good in school, not listening to "Goodnight Moon."

Studies of twins seem to support Harris's demotion of parents. "[I]dentical twins reared in the same home," says Harris, ". . . are no more alike than identical twins separated in infancy and reared in different homes." Apparently, being reared by the same parents did nothing to increase twins' alikeness. Same with siblings. "[B]eing reared by the same parents [has] little or no effect on [their] adult personalities," writes Harris. "The genes they share can entirely account for any resemblances between them; there are no leftover similarities for the shared environment to explain." By "shared environment," she means things like parents' working outside the home, battling constantly, being dour or affectionate. A son might be a cold fish like Dad, or react against him and become a warm puppy. "If children can go either way, turning out like their parents or going in the opposite direction," says Harris, "then what you are saying is that parents have no predictable effects on their children. You are saying that *this* parenting style does not produce *this* trait in the adult."

What Harris offers in place of this "nurture assumption" is the idea that peer groups teach children how to behave out in the world. A second-grade girl identifies with second-grade girls and adopts the behavioral norms of that group. Kids model themselves on other kids, "taking on [the group's] attitudes, behaviors, speech, and styles of dress and adornment," Harris says. Later, a child gravitates toward the studious kids or the mischief makers or whomever. Because people try to become more similar to members of their group and more distinct from members of other groups, innate differences get magnified. The jock becomes jockier, the good student more studious. This all begins in elementary school. Harris's bottom line: "The world that children share with their peers determines the sort of people they will be when they grow up."

Is there no way parents can shape their children? Harris offers this: have enough money to live in a good neighborhood so your children associate with only the "right" peers. Dress your sons and daughters in the fashions of the moment so they are not ostracized. If their appearance is so odd that they are in danger of being shunned, spring for orthodontia. Or, Harris writes, "if you can afford it, or your health insurance will cover it, plastic surgery."

Do This! Do That! A History of Advice to Parents

Over the last century, pediatricians and scientists who study child development have kept changing the advice that they give parents about the best way to rear children. Some of the major developments:

The Early Years

Sigmund Freud concludes that early childhood shapes adult personality; the ills of adulthood are traceable to childhood. The English biologist Francis Galton uses the phrase "nature vs. nurture."

1890: The first developmental psychologists become interested in studying childhood.
1914: "Infant Care," by the U.S. Children's Bureau, urges mothers to battle infants' bad impulses. (Thumb-sucking is discouraged by "pinning sleeves" to beds.)
1925: Psychologist John Watson popularizes conditioning and "behaviorism," the idea that environment shapes children's development.
1935: Government starts welfare to ease poverty.

1940s–1950s

The baby boom begins and behaviorism dominates thinking.

1946: Dr. Spock's *The Common Sense Book of Baby and Child Care* offers alternative to behaviorism.
1952: The research of French psychologist Jean Piaget shows distinct, predictable stages in the intellectual maturation of children.

1960s–1970s

Studies show nurtured children are more likely to overcome the ills of poverty; Head Start and parent-education programs are started.

1969: English psychiatrist John Bowlby shows babies seek specific individuals for protection.

1980s–1990s

Parenting advice focuses on strengthening children's emotional development through play. New brain-imaging techniques allow scientists to see how a baby's experience influences the brain's later development.

1996: The federal welfare system is dismantled. Needy families that have children must now rely on the states.
1997: The Conference on Early Childhood Development and Learning publicizes the crucial first years of childhood.

No one denies that there is *some* truth to her argument. Even her detractors like the way she's blown the lid off dumb studies that can't tell the difference between parents' influencing their kids through genes and influencing them through actions. And they applaud her for pointing out that children of divorce are not necessarily ruined for life, notes psychologist Robert Emery of the University of Virginia. But many of the nation's leading scholars of child development accuse Harris of screwy logic, of misunderstanding behavioral genetics and of ignoring studies that do not fit her thesis. Exhibit A: the work of Harvard's Kagan. He has shown how different parenting styles can shape a timid, shy child who perceives the world as a threat. Kagan measured babies at 4 months and at school age. The fearful children whose parents (over)protected them were still timid. Those whose parents pushed them to try new things—"get into that sandbox and play with the other kids, dammit!"—lost their shyness. A genetic legacy of timidity was shaped by parental behavior, says Kagan, "and these kids became far less fearful."

On divorce: "Heredity . . . makes the children of divorce more likely to fail in their own marriages. . . . Parental divorce has no lasting effects on the way children behave when they're not at home."

"Intervention" studies—where a scientist gets a parent to act differently—also undercut Harris. "These show that if you change the behavior of the parents you change the behavior of the kids, with effects outside the home," says John Gottman of the University of Washington. Programs that teach parents how to deal with little monsters produce effects that last for years. "When parents learn how to talk to and listen to kids with the worst aggression and behavior problems, and to deal with the kids' emotions," says Gottman, "the kid becomes less impulsive, less aggressive, and does better in school." Maybe such effects aren't picked up in the studies Harris cites because such motivated—dare we say saintly?—parents are so rare. Gottman studies children at the age of 4, and then at 8. Some have parents who learned to be good "emotion coaches." They're sensitive, they validate the child's emotion ("I understand, sweetie"), they help her verbalize what she's feeling, they patiently involve her in solving the problem ("What should we do?"). Other parents didn't learn these tough skills. The 8-year-olds of emotionally adept parents can focus their attention better and relate better to other kids. "There is a very strong relationship between parenting style and the social competence of their children," says Gottman. Since the parents learned to be emotion coaches, and the kids changed over the years, the result cannot be easily dismissed as genetic (emotionally intelligent parents pass on emotional-IQ genes).

Critics also slam Harris's interpretation of twins studies. From this research she concludes that "parents do not make siblings any more alike than their genes already made them . . . [P]arenting has no influence." But some of the leaders in the field say their measurements cannot support that. "The sample sizes we use are so small that you can't detect a 10 percent or even a 20 percent effect of the family environment," says Dr. Kenneth Kendler of the Medical College of Virginia. And as Kagan points out, the vast majority of such studies rely on questionnaires to assess personality, recollections of childhood and descriptions of what goes on in the home. "Questionnaires are totally suspect," Kagan says. "The correlation between reality and what people say is just 30 or 40 percent." Such flaws could be why twins studies fail to detect an influence of parents on kids.

Finally, some researchers take issue with Harris's logic. This one is tricky, but crucial. Harris says studies of twins and siblings find no effect of "shared environment." True. But even children who grow up with the same parents do not have an identical environment. The firstborn does not have the same "environment" as her baby brother: she has younger, less experienced parents, and no midget competitors. Also, parents treat children differently, as Harris admits: she monitored Elaine's homework but not Nomi's. Children, through their innate temperament, elicit different behaviors from their parents; thus they do not share this environment called "parents." Parents, then, arguably belong in the category called "unshared environment"—which behavioral genetics suggests accounts for about half the differences among people. And besides, even what seems like an identical parenting style may be received differently by different children. One may conform, the other rebel. That does not mean that parents did not influence what their children became. It means that we are not smart enough to figure out *how* parents shape their child. Says psychologist Theodore Wachs of Purdue University, "The data do show that the same [parenting] does not have the *same* effect on kids. But that doesn't mean there is *no* effect."

In person, Harris backs off a bit from her absolutist stance. "I do think there is something to the possibility that parents determine their child's peer group, and children do learn things at home which they take to the peer group," she told *Newsweek*. She allows that children can retain many of the values and other lessons parents teach despite peer influences. "If the group doesn't care about plans for the future, then the child can retain those ideas from home," she says. "And if things like an interior life aren't discussed by peers, then that wouldn't be affected by the group either." Might different children experience the same parenting differently, and be influenced by it? Harris pauses a few seconds. "I can't eliminate that as a possibility," she says. As for her own daughter, yes, Elaine was a handful and a heartache. But she is now married, a mother and a nurse in New Jersey—and close to her parents.

On helping kids fit in: Parents "do have some control over the way their children look, and their goal should be to make them look as normal and attractive as possible, because looks do count."

If *The Nurture Assumption* acts as a corrective to the hectoring message of so many books on child rearing, then it will have served a noble function. It lands at a time when many parents are terrified that failing to lock eyes with their newborn or not playing Mozart in the nursery or—God forbid—losing it when their kid misbehaves will ruin him for life. One of Harris's "primary motivations for writing the book," she says in an e-mail, was "to lighten the burden of guilt and blame placed on the parents of 'problem' children." Her timing is perfect: millions of baby boomers, having blamed Mom and Dad for all that ails them, can now be absolved of blame for how their own children turn out. Harris is already receiving their thanks. As one mother wrote, "We parents of the difficult children need all the support and understanding we can get." Clearly, the idea that actions have consequences, that behavior matters and that there is such a thing as personal responsibility to those who trust you is fighting for its life. Near the end of *The Nurture Assumption*, Harris bemoans the "tendency to carry things to extremes, to push ideas beyond their logical limits." Everyone who cares about children can only hope that readers bring the same skepticism.

With Erika Check

Form at end of book

Boys Will Be Boys

Developmental research has been focused on girls; now it's their brothers' turn. Boys need help, too, but first they need to be understood.

Barbara Kantrowitz and Claudia Kalb

It was a classic Mars-Venus encounter. Only in this case, the woman was from Harvard and the man—well, boy—was a 4-year-old at a suburban Boston nursery school. Graduate student Judy Chu was in his classroom last fall to gather observations for her doctoral dissertation on human development. His greeting was startling: he held up his finger as if it were a gun and pretended to shoot her. "I felt bad," Chu recalls. "I felt as if he didn't like me." Months later and much more boy-savvy, Chu has a different interpretation: the gunplay wasn't hostile—it was just a way for him to say hello. "They don't mean it to have harsh consequences. It's a way for them to connect."

Researchers like Chu are discovering new meaning in lots of things boys have done for ages. In fact, they're dissecting just about every aspect of the developing male psyche and creating a hot new field of inquiry: the study of boys. They're also producing a slew of books with titles like *Real Boys: Rescuing Our Sons from the Myths of Boyhood* and *Raising Cain: Protecting the Emotional Life of Boys* that will hit the stores in the next few months.

What some researchers are finding is that boys and girls really are from two different planets. But since the two sexes have to live together here on Earth, they should be raised with special consideration for their distinct needs. Boys and girls have different "crisis points," experts say, stages in their emotional and social development where things can go very wrong. Until recently, girls got all the attention. But boys need help, too. They're much more likely than girls to have discipline problems at school and to be diagnosed with attention deficit disorder (ADD). Boys far outnumber girls in special-education classes. They're also more likely to commit violent crimes and end up in jail. Consider the headlines: Jonesboro, Ark.; Paducah, Key.; Pearl, Miss. In all these school shootings, the perpetrators were young adolescent boys.

Even normal boy behavior has come to be considered pathological in the wake of the feminist movement. An abundance of physical energy and the urge to conquer—these are normal male characteristics, and in an earlier age they were good things, even essential to survival. "If Huck Finn or Tom Sawyer were alive today," says Michael Gurian, author of *The Wonder of Boys,* "we'd say they had ADD or a conduct disorder." He says one of the new insights we're gaining about boys is a very old one: boys will be boys. "They are who they are," says Gurian, "and we need to love them for who they are. Let's not try to rewire them."

Indirectly, boys are benefiting from all the research done on girls, especially the landmark work by Harvard University's Carol Gilligan. Her 1982 book, *In a Different Voice: Psychological Theory and Women's Development,* inspired Take Our Daughters to Work Day, along with best-selling spinoffs like Mary Pipher's *Reviving Ophelia.* The traditional, unisex way of looking at child development was profoundly flawed, Gilligan says: "It was like having a one-dimensional perspective on a two-dimensional scene." At Harvard, where she chairs the gender-studies department, Gilligan is now supervising work on males, including Chu's project. Other researchers are studying mental illness and violence in boys.

While girls' horizons have been expanding, boys' have narrowed, confined to rigid ideas of acceptable male behavior no matter how hard their parents tried to avoid stereotypes. The macho ideal still rules. "We gave boys dolls and they used them as guns," says Gurian. "For 15 years, all we heard was that [gender differences] were all about socialization. Parents who raised their kids through that period said in the end, "That's not true. Boys and girls can be awfully different.' I think we're awakening to the biological realities and the sociological realities."

The Wonder (and Worry) Years

There may be no such thing as *child* development anymore. Instead, researchers are now studying each gender's development separately and discovering that boys and girls face very different sorts of challenges. Here is a rough guide to the major phases in their development.

Boys **0–3 years** At birth, boys have brains that are 5% larger than girls' (size doesn't affect intelligence) and proportionately larger bodies—disparities that increase with age.

4–6 years The start of school is a tough time as boys must curb aggressive impulses. They lag behind girls in reading skills, and hyperactivity may be a problem.

Age	1	2	3	4	5	6	7

Girls **0–3 years** Girls are born with a higher proportion of nerve cells to process information. More brain regions are involved in language production and recognition.

4–6 years Girls are well suited to school. They are calm, get along with others, pick up on social cues, and reading and writing come easily to them.

But what exactly is the essential nature of boys? Even as infants, boys and girls behave differently. A recent study at Children's Hospital in Boston found that boy babies are more emotionally expressive; girls are more reflective. (That means boy babies tend to cry when they're unhappy; girl babies suck their thumbs.) This could indicate that girls are innately more able to control their emotions. Boys have higher levels of testosterone and lower levels of the neurotransmitter serotonin, which inhibits aggression and impulsivity. That may help explain why more males than females carry through with suicide, become alcoholics and are diagnosed with ADD.

The developmental research on the impact of these physiological differences is still in the embryonic stage, but psychologists are drawing some interesting comparisons between girls and boys (chart). For girls, the first crisis point often comes in early adolescence. Until then, Gilligan and others found, girls have an enormous capacity for establishing relationships and interpreting emotions. But in their early teens, girls clamp down, squash their emotions, blunt their insight. Their self-esteem plummets. The first crisis point for boys comes much earlier, researchers now say. "There's an outbreak of symptoms at age 5, 6, 7, just like you see in girls at 11, 12, 13," says Gilligan. Problems at this age include bed-wetting and separation anxiety. "They don't have the language or experience" to articulate it fully, she says, "but the feelings are no less intense." That's why Gilligan's student Chu is studying preschoolers. For girls at this age, Chu says, hugging a parent goodbye "is almost a nonissue." But little boys, who display a great deal of tenderness, soon begin to bury it with "big boy" behavior to avoid being called sissies. "When their parents drop them off, they want to be close and want to be held, but not in front of other people," says Chu. "Even as early as 4, they're already aware of those masculine stereotypes and are negotiating their way around them."

It's a phenomenon that parents, especially mothers, know well. One morning last month, Lori Dube, a 37-year-old mother of three from Evanston, Ill., visited her oldest son, Abe, almost 5, at his nursery school, where he was having lunch with his friends. She kissed him, prompting another boy to comment scornfully: "Do you know what your mom just did? She kissed you!" Dube acknowledges, with some sadness, that she'll have to be more sensitive to Abe's new reactions to future public displays of

Some Tips for Parents

- **Common sense helps.** So does a sense of humor. Most of all, boys need to know that the two most important people in their lives, their parents, are there for them.

- **Boys need hugs, too.** Don't try to turn him into Clint Eastwood at the age of 4. You're not coddling him by showing tenderness; you're developing emotional solidarity with your son and teaching him empathy.

- **Don't sweat the gun issue.** Even if you ban all guns, chances are your son will find a way to play at fighting: fingers or carrots work equally well. There's no evidence that this kind of play will turn your boy into a killer any more than playing with trucks will make him a truckdriver.

- **It's OK to get mad.** When he's at an appropriate age, you can help him understand the difference between legitimate feelings of anger and expressing it by hitting, kicking or screaming.

- **Stay in touch.** As they get older, boys still need their parents. Look for opportunities to communicate, like picking him up at school. He'll be strapped in a seat belt, so you know he can't get away.

7–10 years While good at gross motor skills, boys trail girls in finer control. Many of the best students but also nearly all of the poorest ones are boys.

11–13 years A mixed bag. Dropout rates begin to climb, but good students start pulling ahead of girls in math skills and catching up some in verbal ones.

14–16 years Entering adolescence, boys hit another rough patch. Indulging in drugs, alcohol and aggressive behavior are common forms of rebellion.

8	9	10	11	12	13	14	15	16

7–10 years Very good years for girls. On average, they outperform boys at school, excelling in verbal skills while holding their own in math.

11–13 years The start of puberty and girls' most vulnerable time. Many experience depression; as many as 15% may try to kill themselves.

14–16 Eating disorders are a major concern. Although anorexia can manifest itself as early as 8, it typically afflicts girls starting at 11 or 12; bulimia at 15.

affection. "Even if he loves it, he's getting these messages that it's not good."

There's a struggle—a desire and need for warmth on the one hand and a pull toward independence on the other. Boys like Abe are going through what psychologists long ago declared an integral part of growing up: individualization and disconnection from parents, especially mothers. But now some researchers think that process is too abrupt. When boys repress normal feelings like love because of social pressure, says William Pollack, head of the Center for Men at Boston's McLean Hospital and author of the forthcoming *Real Boys*, "they've lost contact with the genuine nature of who they are and what they feel. Boys are in a silent crisis. The only time we notice it is when they pull the trigger."

No one is saying that acting like Rambo in nursery school leads directly to tragedies like Jonesboro. But researchers do think that boys who are forced to shut down positive emotions are left with only one socially acceptable outlet: anger. The cultural ideals boys are exposed to in movies and on TV still emphasize traditional masculine roles—warrior, rogue, adventurer—with heavy doses of violence. For every Mr. Mom, there are a dozen Terminators. "The feminist movement has done a great job of convincing people that a woman can be nurturing and a mother and a tough trial lawyer at the same time," says Dan Kindlon, an assistant professor of psychiatry at Harvard Medical School. "But we haven't done that as much with men. We're afraid that if they're too soft, that's all they can be."

And the demands placed on boys in the early years of elementary school can increase their overall stress levels. Scientists have known for years that boys and girls develop physically and intellectually at very different rates (timeline). Boys' fine motor skills—the ability to hold a pencil, for example—are usually considerably behind girls.

They often learn to read later. At the same time, they're much more active—not the best combination for academic advancement. "Boys feel like school is a game rigged against them," says Michael Thompson, coauthor with Kindlon of *Raising Cain.* "The things at which they excel—gross motor skills, visual and spatial skills, their exuberance—do not find as good a reception in school" as the things girls excel at. Boys (and girls) are also in academic programs at much younger ages than they used to be, increasing the chances that males will be forced to sit still before they are ready. The result, for many boys, is frustration, says Thompson: "By fourth grade, they're saying the teachers like girls better."

A second crisis point for boys occurs around the same time their sisters are stumbling, in early adolescence. By then, say Thompson and Kindlon, boys go one step further in their drive to be "real guys." They partake in a "culture of cruelty," enforcing male stereotypes on one another. "Anything tender, anything compassionate or too artistic is labeled gay," says Thompson. "The homophobia of boys in the 11, 12, 13 range is a stronger force than gravity."

Boys who refuse to fit the mold suffer. Glo Wellman of the California Parenting Institute in Santa Rosa has three sons, 22, 19 and 12. One of her boys, she says, is a "nontypical boy: he's very sensitive and caring and creative and artistic." Not surprisingly, he had the most difficulty growing up, she says. "We've got a long way to go to help boys . . . to have a sense that they can be anything they want to be."

In later adolescence, the once affectionate toddler has been replaced by a sulky stranger who often acts as though torture would be preferable to a brief exchange of words with Mom or Dad. Parents have to try even harder to keep in touch. Boys want and need the attention, but

Trouble Spots: Where Boys Run into Problems

Not all boys are the same, of course, but most rebel in predictable patterns and with predictable weapons: underachievement, aggression and drug and alcohol use. While taking chances is an important aspect of the growth process, it can lead to real trouble.

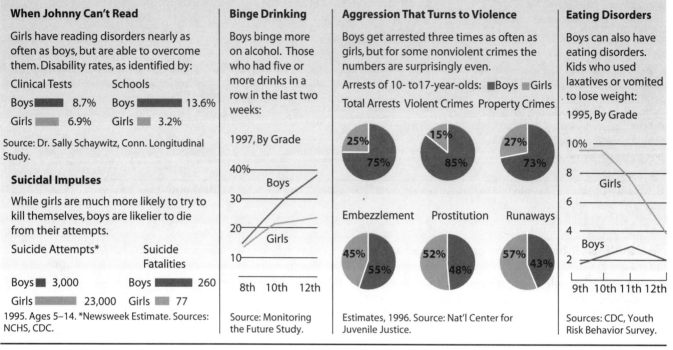

When Johnny Can't Read

Girls have reading disorders nearly as often as boys, but are able to overcome them. Disability rates, as identified by:

Clinical Tests   Schools

Boys 8.7%   Boys 13.6%

Girls 6.9%   Girls 3.2%

Source: Dr. Sally Schaywitz, Conn. Longitudinal Study.

Suicidal Impulses

While girls are much more likely to try to kill themselves, boys are likelier to die from their attempts.

Suicide Attempts*   Suicide Fatalities

Boys 3,000   Boys 260

Girls 23,000   Girls 77

1995. Ages 5–14. *Newsweek Estimate. Sources: NCHS, CDC.

Binge Drinking

Boys binge more on alcohol. Those who had five or more drinks in a row in the last two weeks:

1997, By Grade

[Graph: Boys and Girls, 8th–12th grade, from 10% to 40%]

Source: Monitoring the Future Study.

Aggression That Turns to Violence

Boys get arrested three times as often as girls, but for some nonviolent crimes the numbers are surprisingly even.

Arrests of 10- to 17-year-olds: ■ Boys ▨ Girls

Total Arrests: 25% / 75%   Violent Crimes: 15% / 85%   Property Crimes: 27% / 73%

Embezzlement: 45% / 55%   Prostitution: 52% / 48%   Runaways: 57% / 43%

Estimates, 1996. Source: Nat'l Center for Juvenile Justice.

Eating Disorders

Boys can also have eating disorders. Kids who used laxatives or vomited to lose weight:

1995, By Grade

[Graph: Girls and Boys, 9th–12th grade, from 2 to 10%]

Sources: CDC, Youth Risk Behavior Survey.

often just don't know how to ask for it. In a recent national poll, teenagers named their parents as their No. 1 heroes. Researchers say a strong parental bond is the most important protection against everything from smoking to suicide.

For *San Francisco Chronicle* columnist Adair Lara, that message sank in when she was traveling to New York a few years ago with her son, then 15. She sat next to a woman who told her that until recently she would have had to change seats because she would not have been able to bear the pain of seeing a teenage son and mother together. The woman's son was 17 when his girlfriend dumped him; he went into the garage and killed himself. "This story made me aware that with a boy especially, you have to keep talking because they don't come and talk to you," she says. Lara's son is now 17; she also has a 19-year-old daughter. "My daughter stalked me. She followed me from room to room. She was yelling, but she was in touch. Boys don't do that. They leave the room and you don't know what they're feeling." Her son is now 6 feet 3. "He's a man. There are barriers. You have to reach through that and remember to ruffle his hair."

With the high rate of divorce, many boys are growing up without any adult men in their lives at all. Don Elium, coauthor of the best-selling 1992 book *Raising a Son*, says that with troubled boys, there's often a common theme: distant, uninvolved fathers, and mothers who have taken on more responsibility to fill the gap. That was the case with Raymundo Infante Jr., a 16-year-old high-school junior, who lives with his mother, Mildred, 38, a hospital administrative assistant in Chicago, and his sister, Vanessa, 19. His parents divorced when he was a baby and he had little contact with his father until a year ago. The hurt built up—in sixth grade, Raymundo was so depressed that he told a classmate he wanted to kill himself. The classmate told the teacher, who told a counselor, and Raymundo saw a psychiatrist for a year. "I felt that I just wasn't good enough, or he just didn't want me," Raymundo says. Last year Raymundo finally confronted his dad, who works two jobs—in an office and on a construction crew—and accused him of caring more about work than about his son. Now the two spend time together on weekends and sometimes go shopping, but there is still a huge gap of lost years.

Black boys are especially vulnerable, since they are more likely than whites to grow up in homes without fathers. They're often on their own much sooner than whites. Black leaders are looking for alternatives. In Atlanta, the Rev. Tim McDonald's First Iconium Baptist Church just chartered a Boy Scout troop. "Gangs are so prevalent because guys want to belong to something," says McDonald. "We've got to give them something positive to belong to." Black educators like Chicagoan Jawanza

Kunjufu think mentoring programs will overcome the bias against academic success as "too white." Some cities are also experimenting with all-boy classrooms in predominantly black schools.

Researchers hope that in the next few years, they'll come up with strategies that will help boys the way the work of Gilligan and others helped girls. In the meantime, experts say, there are some guidelines. Parents can channel their sons' energy into constructive activities, like team sports. They should also look for "teachable moments" to encourage qualities such as empathy. When Diane Fisher, a Cincinnati-area psychologist, hears her 8- and 10-year-old boys talking about "finishing somebody," she knows she has mistakenly rented a violent videogame. She pulls the plug and tells them: "In our house, killing people is not entertainment, even if it's just pretend."

Parents can also teach by example. New Yorkers Dana and Frank Minaya say they've never disciplined their 16-year-old son Walter in anger. They insist on resolving all disputes calmly and reasonably, without yelling. If there is a problem, they call an official family meeting "and we never leave without a big hug," says Frank. Walter tries to be open with his parents. "I don't want to miss out on any advice," he says.

Most of all, wise parents of boys should go with the flow. Cindy Lang, 36, a full-time mother in Woodside, Calif., is continually amazed by the relentless energy of her sons, Roger Lloyd, 12, and Chris, 9. "You accept the fact that they're going to involve themselves in risky behavior, like skateboarding down a flight of stairs. As a girl, I certainly wasn't skateboarding down a flight of stairs." Just last week, she got a phone call from school telling her that Roger Lloyd was in the emergency room because he had fallen backward while playing basketball and school officials thought he might have a concussion. He's fine now, but she's prepared for the next emergency: "I have a cell phone so I can be on alert." Boys will be boys. And we have to let them.

With Karen Springen in Chicago, Patricia King in San Francisco, Pat Wingert in Washington, Vern E. Smith in Atlanta and Elizabeth Angell in New York.

Form at end of book

Why Smart People Believe That Schools Shortchange Girls:
What You See When You Live in a Tail

Judith Kleinfeld

Judith Kleinfeld, Ed.D., is a Professor of Psychology at the University of Alaska, Fairbanks, Alaska. Address correspondence to: Judith Kleinfeld, Director, Northern Studies Program, College of Liberal Arts, 613B Gruening Building, P.O. Box 756460, Fairbanks, Alaska 99775–6460

Abstract

Why do so many smart people believe that schools short-change girls when girls do so much better in school? Girls get better grades in every subject, go to college and graduate from college more often, and surpass boys on standardized tests of writing skills and reading comprehension. Boys do surpass girls in mathematics and science achievement and get a disproportionate number of doctorates in mathematics and the physical sciences. But more boys also end up at the bottom of the barrel, labeled impaired and assigned to special education classes. A fair judge might call the school gender wars a draw.

The reason that this charge rings true is conspicuous male success in the unrepresentative universe that the policy elite inhabits. Highly visible male success in a field comes in part from a pattern few people know about—greater male variability in many human characteristics that puts more males at the very top (but also at the very bottom) of a distribution. The schools are shortchanging students, but the shortchanged group is African-American males, not girls.

When the American Association of University Women (AAUW) launched its now famous report, *How Schools Shortchange Girls* (1992), I wondered how anyone could believe such an absurdity. Hadn't all of us spent years of our lives in schools? Didn't we all know from our own personal experience that it was the girls who usually got the higher grades, that it was the boys who got disciplined more often and more harshly, that it was the boys who

more often got held back a grade? "Having been going to school for the past billion years," as one of my own college students put it in a paper he wrote on the AAUW report, "I'm just as qualified to write about this as the University Women" (Kleinfeld, 1996:146).

I could see how people might well believe that women were shortchanged in the labor market. Women do earn less than men and hold jobs of lower prestige. Whether this pattern reflects women's personal choices or gender discrimination requires sophisticated statistical analyses to control for such influences as part-time work or work history interruptions. But wages in the labor market are like grades in school, and progress up the educational ladder is like progress up the occupational ladder. The school pattern is the opposite of the labor market pattern. Why do so many smart people seem to believe, then, that schools discriminate against girls? After all, most people don't blindly accept the "findings" of social science research, especially when these findings conflict with their personal experience. They ask themselves, "Does this research ring true?"

I got a clue to this puzzle when I had dinner with my daughter, a Yale senior, and her friends during a visit to the campus. "What are you working on now?" asked Susan, one of my daughter's roommates. "I'm reviewing the research on the issue of gender differences in school achievement, this idea that the schools shortchange girls," I told her. "You probably read in the media about the AAUW study, which argued that teachers give a lot more classroom attention to boys. That's a shocking tale! The backbone of the AAUW study was research by David and Myra Sadker who claimed to have found that boys call out answers in the classroom eight times more often than girls. The Sadkers said that the teachers paid attention to the boys when they called out but told the girls they should raise their hands when they wanted to talk.

"Now here's the disturbing part. Christina Hoff Sommers explains in *Who Stole Feminism?* that she tried to find the original research on which the Sadkers' claim was based and the research report had vanished. Can you imagine—research featured in newspapers, magazine articles, and television programs across the country? I decided to call David Sadker myself to ask for a copy of this research. I figured I shouldn't accept Christina Hoff Sommers's account without giving him a chance to respond. But he admitted he had no copy of his own research and actually referred me to his university's proposal office to search for a copy!"[1]

Susan listened politely, but her body language revealed her skepticism. She was no ideologue on gender issues, but her personal experience resonated far more with the Sadkers' claims than with Sommers's critique. Since I was reviewing the literature on gender issues, she figured she would ask me a question that troubled her. "Why do men do so much better in mathematics?" she asked me, hoping I could shed some light on what she saw with her own eyes at Yale.

My own daughter, whose political passions do not include gender issues, held the same view. "In my classes at Yale," she said, "It's the men who talk a lot. The women don't talk nearly as much, even in the small seminars." To these Yale seniors, the AAUW accusation that the schools shortchanged girls rang true. To me, a professor at the University of Alaska, a state school enrolling high school students from the middle of their high school classes, the charge seemed absurd. I had just as many, if not more, female students who excelled and dominated class discussion.

Furthermore, professors at many other colleges had noticed not male dominance but instead a troubling pattern of "male underachievement" in college that most people didn't notice or want to talk about (Kleinfeld, 1997). Eric Godfrey, a professor at Ripon College in Wisconsin, had posted this message on the Internet:

On our campus, a task force has been discussing the reason for the difference in academic performance between male and female students, which is substantially in favor of women: (1) Have you observed this phenomenon on your campus—women as a whole outperforming men as a whole? . . . One of my seniors did his research project on the subject and found that on virtually every measure of academic work women outperformed men by a statistically significant margin. (p. 4)

Of the thirty-six responses to Godfrey's posting, virtually everyone said an academic gap existed in favor of women on their campuses—the exception was a college of engineering. But the vast majority (thirty-one out of thirty-six responses) did not define this situation as a "problem." Such Internet postings are not, of course, a generalizable source of evidence, but they do suggest a possible problem which has not received serious research attention.

As I thought more about the perspective of these young women at Yale, I realized that they were living in an unrepresentative universe. These young women were living in a tail—specifically the far right hand tail of the normal curve. The male and female students at Yale were hardly representative of male and female students; they were a "select sample." But then the authors of the AAUW report themselves, researchers at the Wellesley College Center for Research on Women, inhabited another select setting, as I knew well from my own Wellesley College days. The nationally syndicated columnists who wrote about the AAUW report, the professionals and policy-makers concerned with the issue, all lived in the same unrepresentative universe.

Among such select samples, in this unrepresentative universe, males very often do better than females—far better—on intellectual tasks. The reasons are complicated, poorly understood, and rooted in part in the greater variability of males in many domains, from mental retardation and neurological disorders to mathematical precocity. That males and females can differ strongly at the tails of a distribution, even though the male and female populations actually differ very little, is well known to researchers who analyze gender differences (e.g., Eagly, 1995; Feingold, 1994). But most people interested in gender as a policy issue have not heard about the greater variability among males and how such variability, when combined with even a small difference in favor of males, has a dramatic impact on the numbers of males versus females who end up at the very top of a field.

In this article, I examine the argument that the schools shortchange girls and the reasons why so many smart people accept this charge. I first discuss the greater variability of males on many characteristics and the implications for which sex is over-represented at the top of an intellectual ranking. Second, I compare males and females on objective indicators of school success—classroom grades, rank in class, honors, getting labeled as mentally retarded or emotionally disturbed and being assigned to special education programs, and performance on standardized tests of school achievement. Third, I compare males and females on measures of academic attainment—high school drop-out rates, college entrance and graduation rates, and professional and graduate degrees. Finally, I discuss the research on teacher attention to males and females and gender differences in class participation.[2]

Gender Difference in Representative and Select Groups of Students

The study of gender differences in achievement has produced a voluminous research literature filled with contradictions and controversy. The classic study is Maccoby and Jacklin's (1974) comprehensive review of the literature, *The Psychology of Sex Differences.* Reviewing close to 1,600 studies, they found only four areas where sex differences were reasonably clear: 1) females score higher in verbal ability; 2) males score higher in spatial ability; 3) males score higher in mathematics; and 4) males are more aggressive. This classic review of the literature was based on the narrative literature reviews of the time, before the development of meta-analytic techniques, which allowed many studies in the same domain to be statistically combined in order to obtain more robust measures. Researchers examining gender differences in achievement through meta-analytic techniques generally use a statistical measure called the *standard mean difference* (D) to summarize and communicate the results.[3] The standard mean difference is a statistic which is easy to understand. Basically, D is the average difference between females and males in an area like mathematics achievement. It is calculated simply by subtracting the male mean on a test from the female mean on a test, which yields the average difference in the test scores between females and males. This difference is then divided by a measure of the variability in the test scores of females and males. Using D allows researchers to combine many different kinds of tests with many different scoring systems to come up with a strong estimate of the average difference between males and females. If females and males do not differ on the measure of intellectual performance, then D is zero. By convention: a D of .20 to .49 is considered small; a D of .50 to .79 is considered medium; and a D of .80 or higher is considered large.

After the development of meta-analytic techniques, Hyde (1981, cited in Willingham & Cole, 1997) went back and did a meta-analysis of the gender differences found in the classic Maccoby and Jacklin (1974) study. These well-established gender differences turned out to be small: verbal ability (D = .24), quantitative abilities (D = −.43); spatial abilities (D = −.49). While this interpretation has been questioned, subsequent meta-analyses of male and female differences on standardized tests have found that most are small (Willingham & Cole, 1997: 23–29).

But this is the crucial point: even *small* differences between males and females in the general population can have *important and substantial impacts* at the tails of the distribution—especially when the male population is more variable to begin with. As Willingham and Cole (1997) point out:

> Greater male variability tends to work to the advantage of males at the top of the score distribution. . . . More variable male scores exaggerate any male advantage at the top. If male scores are more variable, there is less female advantage at the top than would ordinarily result from a higher female mean. (p. 51).

Greater male variability, combined with even small differences in favor of males, results in the real-world situation that puzzles, troubles, and angers both men and women: males out-rank women at competitions at the top—SAT examinations, Graduate Record Examinations, the stars and prize-winners in a field of endeavor.

Why are males more variable than females? In part, the explanation appears to lie in biology because the greater variability among males appears even before birth. More complications of pregnancy such as toxemia or abruptio involve male fetuses (Nass, 1993). Gualtieri and Hicks (1985) point out that males are more apt to display virtually every neuro-developmental and psychiatric disorder of childhood. Proposing a "theory of selective male affliction," Geschwind and Galaburda (1985) speculate that the androgens which create the male pattern of fetal development lead to greater right-hemisphere specialization and are difficult to regulate, just as a cook can easily add too much or too little spice to a dish. The result is more variability among males at both ends of the distribution, more cases of extreme and variable patterns of intellectual ability and more cases of neurological disorders. The pattern of greater variability among males would constitute an evolutionary advantage to the human species—a source of possibly beneficial variation in the male sex where a full complement of males are not so necessary to species survival. The variability hypothesis is controversial and has been interpreted as insulting to women, consigning them to the category of the unspecialized sex, lacking in exceptional qualities (Dijkstrata, 1986, cited in Willingham & Cole, 1997).

Cultural and personality factors could also account for the greater variability among males. Males may be more apt to pursue their own interests and resist social pressures to conform. Cultural expectations for male behavior may indeed give males more permission to pursue their own interests and ambitions and to ignore what females might be more apt to consider responsibilities to other people. But these possibilities are mere speculation. We do not understand the basis for the greater male variability in intellectual domains that may be of great importance in coming to understand conspicuous male success.

Gender Differences in School Grades, Rank in Class, and Honors

If schools are shortchanging females, such discrimination should not be difficult to demonstrate. After all, virtually the entire male and female population enters school. Furthermore, schools give out grades in every subject, the currency of success in this institutional setting. Schools also compute class rank and award many honors and scholarships. We also have measures of student achievement on standardized subject area tests taken by large, national samples of students, such as the *National Assessment of Educational Progress*. We have longitudinal studies examining the performance of nationally representative samples of male and female students beyond high school, such as the *National Longitudinal Study of the High School Class of 1972*. Comparisons of performances on standardized tests in these large national samples, while not without problems, do provide an opportunity to examine the possibility that females may indeed be shortchanged because they are getting higher grades but have actually learned less in school.

From grade school through college, females receive higher grades, higher class rank, and more honors in every field except science and sports.

In the controversy about whether the schools shortchange girls, the most obvious and crucial point is passed over: females, not males, receive higher grades, hold higher class rank, and receive most academic honors and scholarships. Indeed, the problem that requires explanation is why male students do not receive their fair share of the school's rewards. The most likely explanation is that the schools "shortchange" the more active and rowdy males, who find it more difficult to conform to the school's institutional demands for quiet, orderly behavior, neat homework, and compliance with rules.

That females receive higher grades is one of the few areas of gender difference where the findings are undisputed:

Data from a wide variety of sources and educational settings show that females in all ethnic groups tend to earn higher grades in school than do males, across different ages and eras, and across different subject matter disciplines. Many researchers in past times and today consider this to be such an obvious fact that they treat it as axiomatic. (Dwyer & Johnson, 1997)

The female advantage in high school grades leads to corresponding advantages in class rank and in receipt of many high school honors and awards. A national study of the high school class of 1992, for example, found that females surpassed males in making the honor roll, being

elected to a class office, receiving an award in the field of writing or receiving another academic honor; males surpassed females in sports awards and performance at science and mathematics fairs (National Educational Longitudinal Study of 1988, Second Follow-Up, cited in Dwyer & Johnson, 1997).

In short, females surpass males in most high school competitions with the exceptions of sports, mathematics, and science. In these areas, females have made enormous progress since the women's movement. Take the most prestigious of these competitions, the Westinghouse Science Talent Search. Top finalists receive scholarships ranging from $10,000 to $40,000, and Westinghouse Science Talent Search winners are notable for later receiving the Nobel Prize. The number of female finalists increased steadily during the 1970s, 1980s, and 1990s and is now close to parity (Science Service, 1997). In 1990, 11 of the 40 finalists were female (28 percent) while in 1997, 18 of the 40 finalists were female (45 percent).

In college, the same pattern of higher female accomplishment appears. One of the most fine-grained studies, "Women at ThirtySomething: Paradoxes of Attainment," based on a large national sample of the High School Class of 1972, argues that women's "educational superiority" through high school and college compared to their "thin labor market rewards" constitutes a paradox (Adelman, 1991:v). In this national sample, women achieved higher high school grades, higher high school ranks, and higher grades in college no matter what field they studied, including mathematics and science. They also won more scholarships during the first two years after high school and earned college degrees faster.

Males more often appear at the bottom of the barrel in schools, labeled as impaired and assigned to special education classes.

Adelman presents no evidence consistent with the position that the *schools* shortchanged women. Quite the contrary, the schools rewarded women. The problem is that men and women in this large national sample chose a different curriculum in college, with women less likely to take such courses as calculus, computer science, and business, and more likely to take such courses as education, foreign languages, and the arts. Women made different choices in college. While women's choices might well be influenced by cultural expectations concerning women's roles, as well as their personal preferences, this is not a strong case for institutional discrimination on the part of schools.

The over-representation of males in special education classes and in virtually every other category of emotional, behavioral, or neurological impairment is undisputed. Even the AAUW report (1992:19) underscores this point,

"Boys outnumber girls in special education programs by startling percentages"—a phenomenon they attribute to unfair mislabeling of boys who are behavior problems in the classroom. The 1988 Elementary and Secondary School Civil Rights Survey, for example, shows that over 75 percent of the students classified as emotionally disturbed are male, and close to 75 percent of the students classified as learning disabled are male (AAUW, 1992:19).

While mislabeling rowdy boys may be part of the problem, biological variability is another part of the explanation. Research on sex differences in learning disabilities (Nass, 1993) reveals large differences in male-female ratios across many disorders:

Dyslexia 4:1

Language Disorders 3:1

Autism 4:1

Attention Deficit Disorder 3:1

Stuttering 4:1

Learning Disabilities 4:1 (p. 63)

This is the other side of the coin. Greater male variability results in more males at the bottom of the distribution, not only at the top.

On standardized tests, females surpass males at the end of high school in writing ability and certain other verbal skills; males surpass females in science and mathematics. But these average gender differences, in the general population, are small.

Standardized tests of academic achievement offer another measure of knowledge and skills. Test scores, however, have problems of their own as measures of intellectual achievement. Intense controversy surrounds the question of whether females are at a disadvantage in tests because the content of test questions is more apt to come from areas of male experience and interest or because the multiple choice format of tests gives an advantage to males, who are more apt to risk wrong answers.

In a major review of the literature, Willingham, Cole, Lewis, and Leung (1997) attempt to bring order to this complex and disputed ground as Maccoby and Jacklin (1974) did almost a quarter of a century before them. At the end of the day, a very long and tedious day, their conclusions about gender differences are remarkably similar.

Their conclusions come from a meta-analysis of the "12th-Grade Profile," a data base which includes test scores on the National Assessment of Educational Progress, High School and Beyond, the Preliminary Scholastic Aptitude Test, and other nationally representative samples of student performance at the end of high school. They examine gender differences on 74 tests grouped into 15 categories (such as Verbal—writing, Verbal—reading, Math—concepts, and Natural Science). The standard mean differences between males and females across all these tests are negligible (D = .02).

But males and females indeed differ in performance by subject area. Females surpass males in measures of writing skills (D = .57, conventionally considered a medium difference). Females also surpass males in the verbal areas of language use (D = .43) and reading comprehension (D = .20). Males, on the other hand, surpass females in mathematical concepts (D = −.11), natural science (D = −.17) and geopolitics (−.23). These differences are smaller than the female advantages in verbal areas. The area in which males surpass females by a large margin is an area not closely related to academics—mechanical/electronics (D = −.93).

Whether the female advantage in verbal skills is narrowing and even disappearing is a matter of dispute. On the major national measure, the NAEP, the female advantage in reading and writing skills appears to have remained about the same or increased in some grades (Mullis, Dossey, Foertsch, Jones, & Gentile, 1991). Some researchers argue that gender differences in verbal abilities are narrowing on the basis of other studies (e.g., Feingold, 1993; Hyde & Linn, 1988).

The female disadvantage in mathematics and science, on the other hand, does appear to be narrowing, certainly over the last three decades and possibly within the last decade in some areas (Bae & Smith, 1997; Willingham & Cole, 1997:125). As I discuss below, female high school students are showing noteworthy increases in taking advanced mathematics and science courses in high school and in taking Advanced Placement examinations in mathematics and science.

Among the talented students in a field, females surpass males in writing ability while males surpass females in mathematics, geopolitics, and science performance. At the top, gender differences are large and consequential.

In the population as a whole, gender differences, whether in writing or science, are small. But this is the crucial question: *Where is the talent? Which gender dominates the top of a field?* Among high school students in the top 10 percent of a subject area, we see an interesting picture (Willingham & Cole, 1997). In this top group, approximately 7 out of 10 of the top writers are female, and slightly over 6 out of 10 of the top students in reading are. Men dominate the top group in science by about the same margin—approximately 7 out of 10 are male. In math skills, slightly under 6 out of the 10 top scorers are males. In both history and civics, however, roughly 6 out of the 10 top scorers are also males. The top 10 percent of a high school class is not an exceptionally select group, but males are starting to pull ahead in several important areas, not only in mathematics and science.

Females now take as many high school classes in mathematics and science as do males.

The women's movement has spotlighted the issue of female success in science and mathematics. Government agencies, private foundations, and universities have supported a spate of gender equity programs, special summer and internship programs, and teacher training efforts to encourage young women in science and mathematics.[4] These efforts have born fruit. The gap between males and females in science and mathematics course-taking, for example, has essentially closed:

In the class of 1994, females were more likely than males to take algebra II in high school, and were just as likely to take calculus. With respect to science, females were just as likely as males to take biology and were more likely to take chemistry. Females have continued, however, to be less likely than males to take physics. (Bae & Smith, 1997:18)

These differences in course-taking patterns are quite small. While 22 percent of females take physics compared to 27 percent of males, 59 percent of females take chemistry courses compared to 53 percent of males (National Center for Education Statistics, 1996 and Condition of Education, 1996 cited in Sanders et al., 1997).

Males take more AP mathematics and science courses than females, but the gap is narrowing.

The number of females who enroll in Advanced Placement (AP) tests in mathematics and sciences is increasing with the result that more females are developing advanced skills. More females (52 percent) take AP examinations, and females are over-represented in tests of French, Art, Spanish, and English (Willingham et al., 1997). High school males still form the majority of AP test-takers in physics, chemistry, calculus, and Latin. But the proportion of women taking AP examinations in the natural sciences and mathematics increased from 37 percent in 1982–1983 to 43 percent in 1992–1993.

Males who take the Advanced Placement tests in mathematics and science still do better (Bae & Smith, 1997). In 1995, for example, the number of students who qualified for college credit (scores of 3 or higher) in calculus was 12 per 1,000 for males and 9 per 1,000 for females. In the sciences, the number of males qualifying for college credit was 13 per 1,000 compared to 9 per 1,000 for females. Still, as Willingham et al. (1997) emphasize, the net effect of more women taking AP tests in these areas and scoring just about the same when they do is to increase the

absolute number of talented, high achieving women in mathematics and science.

Women have become the majority of college students—especially in the African-American population—and win the majority of baccalaureate degrees.

Males and females graduate from high school in about equal numbers (National Center for Educational Statistics, 1995). Where gender issues are becoming a serious concern is in college entrance and graduation rates. Here the sex that is shortchanged is clearly males, and especially minority males from economically disadvantaged groups.

In 1995, close to 56 percent of college students were women (*Chronicle of Higher Education,* 1997). Some private liberal arts colleges, worried that even more lopsided gender ratios at their institutions would hurt recruitment, have quietly begun to institute "affirmative action" for males who apply (Gose, 1997). For minority students from economically disadvantaged groups, the gender gap in favor of females can be even more extreme. Among African-American students in 1995, for example, 62 percent were women. In obtaining college degrees, women and especially minority women continue to surpass males. In 1995, women won 55 percent of bachelor's degrees, and African-American women won 64 percent of the degrees awarded African-American students.

Women earn more master's degrees and fewer doctoral and professional degrees than men—but the gap is narrowing.

Women have made great progress in obtaining graduate degrees and professional degrees (*Chronicle of Higher Education,* 1997). In 1995, most master's degrees (55 percent) were awarded to women. Women received fewer doctoral degrees (39 percent) and fewer professional degrees (41 percent), but the gap has narrowed dramatically over the last twenty years. During the five-year period prior to 1995, for example, the proportion of women awarded doctoral degrees increased 16 percent while the proportion of women receiving professional degrees increased 7 percent. In 1995, women received 43 percent of law degrees and 39 percent of degrees in medicine. Women now receive the majority of professional degrees in veterinary medicine (65 percent) and in pharmacy (89 percent).

In short, women surpass men in college graduation rates and have made rapid progress in closing the gap in graduate and professional degrees. Men still surpass women in attaining doctoral degrees in mathematics (81 percent) and in the physical sciences (76 percent). But women have come close to parity in achieving doctorates in the life sciences (42 percent). A far greater proportion of women (20 percent) compared to college men (10 percent) sought professional degrees in such fields as law, medicine, and architecture in 1996 (Bae & Smith, 1997). Women's career aspirations have dramatically increased, but these ambitious women seek professional degrees far more than scientific careers.

The gender gap in science and mathematics has received enormous attention in the media and on the part of government agencies and foundations concerned with achieving equity. What is crucial to keep in mind is that the academic problems of minority males from economically disadvantaged groups dwarf the problems of women in science and mathematics. In 1995, for example, only 995 men in the entire country got a doctorate in mathematics compared to 271 women (*Chronicle of Higher Education*, 1997). If equity were achieved, only 724 women would be affected. In the physical sciences, 3,428 men got doctorates in 1995 compared to 1,055 women. If equity were achieved, only 2,373 women would be affected. *To close the gender gap in mathematics and physical science doctorates would affect the well-being of fewer than 3,000 women each year; to close the gender gap in college and graduate school attendance among African Americans would increase the well-being of close to 362,000 African-American men.*[5] This is the gender problem with serious social implications; yet it is all but ignored.

Gender Differences in Classroom Participation

The charge that schools are shortchanging girls is based very little on comparisons of grades or test scores, even in mathematics or science. The charge is based on the belief that females get less than their fair share of teacher attention, that they are "silenced" in the classroom. The Executive Summary to the AAUW report (1992: 2) leads with the Sadkers' research: "Girls receive significantly less attention from classroom teachers than do boys."

Three points are important to keep in mind in examining this charge. First, differences in teacher attention, even if they exist, may not matter—no study has demonstrated that teacher attention is important to academic success. Second, classroom interaction research is expensive and difficult to conduct. We have only a few local, limited studies, not large nationally representative samples as we do in the areas of grades and achievement. Third, measures of "teacher attention" or "reprimands" are highly subjective. Suppose, for example, a teacher asks a fourth-grader a question in class. In this a genuine academic question or a disguised reprimand, a way of getting an inattentive student back on task? Suppose a student answers a question and the teacher says "good." Should the teacher's response count as "praise"? For many teachers, "good" is a meaningless, automatic response.

Male and female differences in classroom participation are inconsistent, small, and variable.

The highly publicized charge that teachers, often unconsciously, discriminate against girls comes from research conducted by David and Myra Sadker (1994). One of their studies purports to find that boys called out answers eight times more than girls and that girls were reprimanded when they called out an answer. This study has mysteriously vanished as Sommers (1994) details. The second study purports to find that boys are more apt to receive praise, criticism, and remediation from the teacher (Sadker, Sadker, & Thomas, 1981). But this study, Sommers (1994) points out, did not give numbers, making it impossible to see if the attention gap was large or trivial.

The charge that boys talk more and receive more attention in class does not stand or fall with the Sadkers' research. Other studies have addressed this question. Reviewing other research on the "attention gap" in favor of males, Young (forthcoming) points out that studies of gender differences in classroom interaction yield small and inconsistent results. Studies of classroom life in elementary schools do show that "teachers give more attention to boys" but this attention "tends to be negative . . . and disciplinary" (Lindow, Marrett, & Wilkinson, 1985, cited in Young, forthcoming). Sommers (1994: 162–168) in a similar review of the literature on classroom interaction emphasizes the inconsistency of the patterns found in different studies and the difficulty of drawing conclusions about equity even when different gender patterns do occur. Whether males or females talk more in the classroom, as any teacher knows from experience, depends a great deal on the specifics of the subject, situation, and personalities in the particular class.

Law schools are the most recent front in the battle on which sex dominates the classroom. Reviewing the research and articles in the media, Young (forthcoming) concludes that this charge is probably correct: males do appear to participate more in classroom discussions in some law school classes. The aggressive, Socratic dialogue often found in law school classrooms has long been considered an excellent way to prepare future lawyers for courtroom combat. Many women preparing to become lawyers may not find the intellectual thrust and parry of Socratic questioning a congenial conversational style (Tannen, 1990; 1994). If their law school classes did not prepare them for such verbal combat in the courtroom or in negotiations, they and their clients would indeed be shortchanged.

Conclusion

I began this article with the question: Why do so many smart people believe that schools shortchange girls when girls get better grades, go to college and graduate from college more often, and score higher on standardized tests of writing skills and reading comprehension? While boys surpass girls in mathematics and science achievement, a fair judge would call it a draw. The case of male and female participation in law school classrooms is an example of why this charge rings true. Students who go to law school are a highly select group, far out in the right tail of the normal curve. The charge makes sense to them because it matches their personal experience. They do not realize that they live in an unrepresentative universe.

When we examine male and female performance in the general population, not only among select samples, we come to these conclusions.

1. On many important characteristics, males are more variable than females. When males do better than females, even if the difference is small in the population as a whole, far more males will show up in the visible category of top performers.

2. Females receive higher grades than males in virtually every school subject from grade school through college.

3. Females are far less likely than males to end up in the bottom of the academic heap, to be labeled as learning disabled, emotionally impaired, or mentally retarded and sent to special education classes.

4. On standardized tests of school achievement at the end of high school, females surpass males in writing abilities and reading comprehension while males surpass females in mathematics and science. The differences in the general population are small but the differences in groups of top performers are substantial.

5. In mathematics and science achievement, the gender gap is narrowing. Male and female high school students take about the same number and type of mathematics and science courses. The number of females taking Advanced Placement exams in mathematics and science, emerging as finalists in the Westinghouse Science Talent Search, and earning doctorates in mathematics and the natural sciences has dramatically increased.

6. A greater proportion of women compared to men enter college and earn bachelor's and master's degrees. Among African Americans and other economically disadvantaged groups, the gender gap in favor of females is large and is cause for concern.

7. While males continue to earn more doctorates in mathematics and the physical sciences than females, the numbers of females who are "shortchanged" by this inequity is small—approximately 3,000 women a year. In comparison, well over 300,000 more African-American men would have to attend college and seek advanced degrees each year to attain equity.

8. Women are aspiring to more prestigious, high-paying careers, but they choose the professions far more than positions requiring doctorates in mathematics and the physical sciences. Women have made enormous progress in attaining professional degrees, almost at parity with men in law degrees and exceeding men in veterinary degrees.

9. That boys dominate classroom discussions is the backbone of the charge that the schools shortchange girls. Studies of classroom interaction show mixed and inconsistent findings, suggesting gender patterns are quite variable and depend on the subject and situation.

The gender issue of serious proportions is the waste of talent among African-American males. This is the group that the schools are shortchanging.

Notes

1. For a more detailed description of this matter, see Kleinfeld (1996).
2. This article does not examine the issue of gender differences in self-esteem, which has become another issue in the debate on whether the schools shortchange girls, because of its tangential relationship to the central focus of this article: gender differences in academic achievement. Those concerned with the question of whether adolescent females experience a dramatic decline in self-esteem in comparison to adolescent males and the basis of this decline do not argue that the central issues concern girls' performance in school. They emphasize other issues, such as young girls' perceptions about the acceptable role of women in the adult world or girls' efforts to reach unattainable ideals of female beauty.
3. This discussion of the calculation of the standard mean difference and the statistical effects of differences in means and variability is summarized from the lucid presentation in Willingham and Cole (1997).
4. See, for example, the publications of the WEEA (Women's Educational Equity Act) Resource Center at the Education Development Center in Newton, Massachusetts, or the guide, "Gender Equity Right From the Start," a compilation of resources and instructional activities for teacher educators in mathematics, science, and technology (Sanders, Koch, & Urso, 1997).
5. Among African Americans, 917,800 females were enrolled in college, graduate, and professional programs in 1995 compared to 555,900 males (*Chronicle of Higher Education,* 1997).

References

Adelman, C. (1991). Women at thirtysomething: Paradoxes of attainment. Washington, D.C.: U.S. Department of Education, Office of Educational Improvement and Research, Office of Research.

American Association of University Women. (1992). *How schools shortchange girls: A study of major findings on girls and education.* AAUW Educational Foundation, The Wellesley College Center for Research on Women.

Bae, Y. & Smith, T. M. (1997). Women in mathematics and science. In: National Center for Educational Statistics, *The condition of education 1997,* Washington, D.C., pp. 14–21. U.S. Department of Education, Office of Research and Improvement.

Chronicle of Higher Education (1997). *Almanac Issue,* XLIV(1), August 29, 1997.

Dijkstrata, B. (1996). *Idols of perversity: Fantasies of feminine evil in fin-de-siecle culture.* New York: Oxford University Press.

Dwyer, C. A. & Johnson, L. M. (1997). Grades, accomplishments and correlates. In: W. Willingham and N. S. Cole. *Gender and fair assessment,* pp. 127–156. Mahwah, New Jersey: Lawrence Erlbaum Associates.

Eagly, A. H. (1995). The science and politics of comparing men and women. *American Psychologist 50* (3): 145–158.

Feingold, A. (1993). Cognitive gender differences: A developmental perspective. *Sex Roles 29:* 91–112.

Feingold, A. (1994). The additive effects of group differences in central tendency and variability are important in distributional comparisons between groups. *American Psychologist, 50*(1): 5–13.

Geschwind, N. & Galaburda, A. M. (1985). Cerebral lateralization: Biological mechanisms, associations and pathology. *Archives of Neurology, 42:* 428–654.

Gose, B. (1997, June 6). Liberal-Arts colleges ask: Where have the men gone? *The Chronicle of Higher Education,* A35–36.

Gualtieri, T. & Hicks, R. E. (1985). An immunoreactive theory of selective male affliction. *The Behavioral and Brain Sciences 8:* 427–441.

Hyde, J. S. (1981). How large are cognitive gender differences? A meta-analysis using w2 and d. *American Psychologist 36* (8): 892–901.

Hyde, J. S. & Linn, M. C. (1988). Gender differences in verbal ability: A meta-analysis. *Psychological Bulletin 104*(1): 53–69.

Kleinfeld, J. S. (1996). The surprising ease of changing the belief that the schools shortchange girls. In: R. J. Simon (Ed.) *From data to public policy: Affirmative action, sexual harassment, domestic violence and social welfare,* pp. 143–152. Lanham, Maryland: University Press of America.

Kleinfeld, J. (1997). None dare call it a problem: Male underachievement. *The women's Freedom Network Newsletter 4* (1): 6.

Lindow, J., Marrett, C., & Wilkinson, L. C. (1985). Overview. In: L.C. Wilkinson and C.B. Marrett (Eds.), *Gender influences in classroom interaction.* New York: Academic Press.

Maccoby, E. E. & Jacklin, C. N. (1974). *The psychology of sex differences.* Stanford, California: Stanford University.

Mullis, I. V., Dossey, J. A., Foertsch, M. A., Jones, L. R., & Gentile, C. A. (1991). *Trends in academic progress.* Washington, D.C.: U.S. Government Printing Office.

Nass, R. D. (1993). Sex differences in learning abilities and disabilities. *Annals of Dyslexia, 43:* 61–77.

National Center for Education Statistics (1995). *Dropout Rates in the United States.* U.S. Department of Education.

Sadker, M. & Sadker, D. (1994). *Failing at fairness: How America's schools cheat girls.* New York: Scribners.

Sadker, D., Sadker, M., & Thomas, D. (1981). Sex equity and special education. *The Pointer 26* (1): 33–38.

Sanders, J., Koch, J., & Urso, J. (1997). *Gender equity right from the start: Instructional activities for teacher educators in mathematics, science, and technology.* Mahwah, New Jersey: Lawrence Erlbaum Associates.

Science Service. (1997). Westinghouse Science Talent Search Science Service Database. Westinghouse Foundation.

Sommers, C. H. (1994). *Who stole feminism?* New York: Simon & Schuster.

Stumpf, H., & Stanley, J. C. (1996). Gender-related differences on the College Board's Advanced Placement and Achievement Tests, 1982–1992. *Journal of Educational Psychology 88*(2): 353–364.

Tannen, D. (1990). *You just don't understand: Women and men in conversation.* New York: Ballantine Books.

Tannen, D. (1994). *Talking from 9 to 5: How women's and men's conversational styles affect who gets heard, who gets credit, and what gets done at work.* New York: William Morrow.

Willingham, W. W., Cole, N. S. (1997). *Gender and fair assessment.* Mahwah, New Jersey: Lawrence Erlbaum Associates.

Willingham, W. W., Cole, N. S., Lewis, C., & Leung, S. W. (1997). Test performance. In: W. W. Willingham & N. S. Cole, *Gender and fair assessment,* pp. 55–126. Mahwah, New Jersey: Lawrence Erlbaum Associates.

Young, C. (Forthcoming). *Beyond the gender wars.* New York: Free Press.

Form at end of book

Issue 5 Summary

The nature-nurture question has no easy answer: clearly, both factors play a significant role in children's development. We can see that there is an interplay between them in determining how children develop. In particular, the evidence indicates that children genetically possess vulnerabilities; whether or not these vulnerabilities cause major problems in children's lives depends largely on the environment into which they are born. At present, we can do nothing to alter a child's genetic makeup. However, we have a fair amount of control over the child's environment. The responsibility of parents and educators is to ensure that the child's environment is conducive to his or her optimal development. And this responsibility needs to be recognized in the home, in the classroom, and in society in general.

Being a Child in Today's Society

Questions

1. How do the ideas of the major thinkers of education in the twentieth century—Dewey, Montessori, and Piaget—relate to the postmodern way of thinking? How do the educational programs of Bloom, Hunter, Costa, and de Bono relate to the postmodern view?

2. How do the modern and postmodern perspectives differ with regard to the universality and regularity of children's development?

3. What evidence supports the position that children are not harmed by their exposure to media such as television, the Internet, movies, and music?

Introduction

You may be surprised to learn that childhood is not a fixed phenomenon that is the same across cultures and across time. Cultures differ in their perspective on when children can work, marry, share in decision making, and be autonomous. In Western civilization, children were at various times looked on as miniature adults. In the twentieth century, Western society developed the view that children go through a universal, regular process of development. With that view came the belief that children differ significantly from adults in qualitative ways. With these understandings, society sought to make progress in better rearing and educating children.

Now we find ourselves coming into a period which some term *postmodern*. The postmodern conception of children takes a different view of development, perceiving irregularities of development as being normal and expected. The postmodern view looks more at the individuality of children, rather than at the universal patterns of their growth.

We are also at a moment when we have a new medium, the Internet, to which many children and adolescents have ready access. Like music, movies, and television before it, the Internet is seen by many as a danger to youngsters and as a source of corruption. Critics point to the dangers that the Internet poses to young people with its quick access to sites that contain graphic material of a sexual or violent nature. However, are these media to blame for the societal problems caused by children and adolescents? Further, to what extent are children and adolescents to blame for society's ills? To what extent do adults make children and adolescents scapegoats for more deeply rooted problems of society?

The Death of Child Nature:
Education in the Postmodern World

Mr. Elkind reviews the modern and postmodern conceptions of the child and the educational practices that follow from those conceptions. Becoming postmodern in education, he concludes, often means gaining a truer and deeper appreciation of the educational innovators of modernity.

David Elkind

David Elkind is a professor of child development at Tufts University, Medford, Mass.

Every child, to paraphrase Clyde Kluckhohn and Henry Murray, is like all other children, like some other children, and like no other child.[1] Children are all alike in that they are members of the same species and share the same biological and physiological characteristics, walk upright, have the potential for speech, and so on. In this species sense, we can reasonably speak of the *biological* child who is like all other children. It is also true that only subgroups of children share the same language, culture, and physical environment. When considering children who are like some other children in this cultural/environmental sense, we can speak of the *social* child. Finally, each child is different from every other in his or her unique genetic endowment and in the particular circumstances of his or her upbringing. When we speak of children in this unique, individual sense, we might speak of the *psychological* child.

Although it is unlikely that many would quarrel with this description of the three senses in which the term *child* may be used, the three are often confused, most notably in discussions of education. That is to say, individual psychological characteristics of children are often treated as biological universals. In the past, the belief in a universal psychological child (which I will simply refer to as a belief in *child nature*) had some positive consequences. It contributed, for example, to the provision of free public education. Today, however, this very same belief in a universal child nature has become a barrier to achieving an individually appropriate pedagogy for children in all their personal, ethnic, racial, and cultural diversity. In this article I attempt to substantiate this thesis.

Reprinted with permission from Phi Delta Kappan and the author.

The critique of transcendent realities and overarching generalizations is a major thrust of the movement called *post-modernism*.[2] Although different writers define this movement in different ways, there is general agreement that many of the assumptions that fueled the modern view of the world were romantic ideals that now stand in need of correction. Postmodern critiques are already common in the arts, in architecture, in science, and in industry, but they are only now beginning to be heard in the social sciences and in education.[3]

Even without invoking postmodernism, a few contemporary education reform initiatives challenge the conception of normative education tailored to the needs of a uniform child nature.[4] Likewise, a number of contemporary educational practices reflect postmodern conceptions. Nonetheless, the modern assumption of an archetypal psychological child dies hard and underlies practices that are contributing to educational dysfunction among large numbers of children. In the succeeding pages, I will try to illustrate some of the educational practices that derive from the modern conception of a common (psychological) child nature and that impede, rather than further, children's academic achievement.

In preparation for that discussion, however, let me first briefly describe the major tenets of modernism and postmodernism and show how these differing paradigmatic assumptions about the world are reflected in the modern and postmodern conceptions of the child and in some of the educational practices that flow from them. That discussion will provide the context for a critique of those contemporary educational practices that remain wedded to a modern conception of a common child nature. Such practices miseducate children in the sense that they place them at risk with no purpose.

Modernity, Child Nature, and Modern Education

Modernity was built on three unquestioned assumptions about the world. The first idea was that of *progress,* the notion that societies inevitably moved forward in a positive direction from slavery and feudalism to individual freedom and democracy. From its inception in the 16th century, experimental science was the model for the modern conception of progress, with its gradual accumulation of knowledge serving to improve the quality of life for all members of society. Later, Darwin's theory of evolution offered a scientific explanation for this progress, suggesting that societies, like species, evolve by a process of variation and natural selection, with survival of the fittest as the end result.

The notion of progress shaped the modern conception of the child and of education. Although educational philosophers differed as to whether the child's mind was a blank tablet or a full book, none doubted that education was necessary to ensure the child's steady progress toward responsible and productive adulthood. John Locke, for one, saw the child as in need of adult tutelage if he or she was to become a socially responsible and culturally literate human being.[5] In contrast, Jean-Jacques Rousseau argued that experience itself was the best teacher and that adult instruction could well be delayed until children had acquired considerable knowledge on their own.[6] Both Locke and Rousseau, however, talked about children in a universal sense and with little attention to the differential progress that might be observed thanks to dissimilarities in ability, race, ethnicity, or culture.

The notion of progress was extended to pedagogy as well as to the child. It was the rationale for the metaphor of the "ladder" of education. Knowledge, values, and skills, it was assumed, are acquired in a uniform and stepwise fashion. Subject matters were also organized according to what was regarded as a natural progression—for example, arithmetic before algebra and algebra before trigonometry. The same held true for reading, and children were taught simple folk stories and fairy tales before they were introduced to true "literature." Not surprisingly, the rate at which a child ascended this educational ladder became the only measure of individual difference. The mentally "retarded" climbed at less than the average rate, whereas the mentally "gifted" skipped steps and rose more rapidly than the norm.

A second underlying conception of modernity was that of *universality*. The emergence of science, the scientific method, and the reliance on observation and experiment was encouraged by the modern belief that nature, rather than religious or imperial authority, was the only source of knowledge and truth. Nature was assumed to operate according to universal laws that could be discovered by diligent research. The scientific belief in universal natural laws was supported by such systematic descriptions of regularities as the Newtonian laws of gravitation, the periodic table of the elements, and the Darwinian principles of evolution.

The notion of universality was also incorporated into the modern conception of the child. Educators accepted the doctrine of "formal discipline," according to which the study of Greek, Latin, and mathematics was an effective method of training *all* children to think logically and rationally. Later, with the emergence of the social sciences, universality was given a scientific imprimatur. Educational psychology, like psychology as a whole, assumed that there were universal laws of learning that held across all species and that were the same for rats as they were for children and for adults. Rat psychology led to endless controversies over such issues as the benefits of *mass* versus *distributed* learning and the extent of *transfer of training*. Using human subjects, memory was studied by means of nonsense syllables so that content would not interfere with observation of the universal memory process. Problem solving was thought to involve only trial and error or insight, inasmuch as these were the processes employed by cats and chimpanzees in their attempts to remove barriers to desired goals.

The last undergirding assumption of the modern world was that of *regularity*. Nature was lawful, and the task of science was to uncover this lawfulness. As Einstein phrased this belief, "God does not play dice with the universe." Unlawful phenomena, from this perspective, were simply phenomena that had yet to be explained or could be explained at another "level." Irregular (unlawful) phenotypes, for example, could be explained by regular (lawful) genotypes. Taking the same "levels" approach to causality, Freud argued that slips of the tongue and pen (unlawful occurrences) could be explained by deeper-level unconscious (lawful) wishes and desires.

The idea of lawfulness was also assimilated into the modern conception of a child nature. Intelligence testing demonstrated that, although children varied considerably in their intellectual abilities, these abilities were nonetheless distributed according to the normal curve of probability. They were thus lawful phenomena. Many of children's behavior disorders were also explained according to the "levels"notion of causality. Seemingly idiosyncratic learning disabilities were frequently attributed to an underlying lawfulness, namely, "minimal brain damage." Thus children's observable irregular, unpredictable surface behavior could be explained by an underlying lawful relation between the human brain and human action.

Postmodernity, the Particular Child, and Postmodern Education

Postmodernism arose as a critique of modern ideas and as an effort to correct some of the overly idealistic and romantic views of the world that they created. In this century, after two world wars, the Holocaust, the atom bomb, the degradation of the environment, and the exploitation of the earth's natural resources, it is difficult to hold to the modern conception of progress as an unbroken march toward a better world and a more humane society. Even the progress toward individual freedom and self-fulfillment that did occur was often limited to certain groups (white, Anglo-Saxon males) and did not extend to women or to minorities. To be sure, progress still happens—say, in the conquest of disease—but it is particular and domain-specific father than holding true for all of humanity.

What has come to the fore in postmodern times is the awareness of the importance of *difference.* In the modern era, difference was often seen from the standpoint of superiority. Non-Western societies, as an illustration, were regarded as inferior to Western "civilizations" because they had not progressed as far. This notion of superiority was implicit in the concept of the United States of America as a "melting pot" in which people of (inferior) cultures would be melted down and then poured into a mold from which each would be dropped out as a purified, standard American. Today, however, we recognize that people do not melt and that other cultures, ethnic groups, and races are to be appreciated and valued rather than dissolved into some common amalgam. The postmodern conception of America as a cultural, ethnic, and racial "rainbow" celebrates the valuation of difference, in contrast to the feeling of superiority inherent in the modern conceptions of social progress and of the melting pot.

Unfortunately, the idea of progress is still omnipresent in education. Nonetheless, the appreciation of difference is beginning to make some headway. The new provisions for children with disabilities and for those who come to school with English as a second language are evidence that the needs of these "different" children are at last being recognized—if not fully or properly attended to. In other domains, such as the introduction of multicultural, gender-fair, and anti-bias curricula, the acceptance of difference has met more resistance in the schools and in the local communities. But the very fact that matters of race, gender, and ethnicity are now being openly talked about reflects a new, more accepting climate for a wide range of human differences.

Just as the conception of progress was challenged by the evidence of lack of progress, the assumption of universality has also undergone revision. This is particularly true in the social sciences. When Friedrich Nietzsche, an early postmodernist, proclaimed the death of God, he was railing against metaphysics and those who exploited the belief in universal supernatural beings.[7] In a similar tone, when Michel Foucault wrote about the end of man, he was arguing against the metaphysical idea of a universal human nature and for a fuller and deeper appreciation of human individuality.[8]

And the universals of social science are proving to be less than transcendent. The "grand" social/economic theories such as those of Marx and Engels have turned out to be less than prophetic and universal. Likewise, the "grand" histories of Spengler and Toynbee now appear as flawed individual theories of history rather than as discovered universal principles of societal progression. In a similar way, the recapitulation theory—which posited that the individual in his or her development recapitulates the development of the species—can no longer be maintained. While there are still universals, particularly in the physical and biological sciences, they are much less common in the social sciences, where particularity is more likely to be the rule.

The importance of particularity, as opposed to universals, is already being recognized in education. We now appreciate that different species learn in different ways and that, even within the same species, there are differences in learning *styles.*[9] We also recognize that different subject matters require their own specific learning strategies. The idea that there are "domain-specific" modes of learning has almost completely displaced the universal ideas of "formal discipline" and of "transfer of training." When we do encounter what appear to be universals in human behavior, they are often closely linked to maturational (biological child) characteristics, such as the Piagetian stages.[10]

Finally, the modern assumption of regularity and lawfulness has been modified by the postmodern acceptance of the normality of *irregularity.* We acknowledge today that some phenomena, such as the weather, are inherently irregular. So too are phenomena such as the dispersion of cream in a coffee cup. Each time we place cream in a coffee cup, the dispersion pattern is different from what it was before. Some phenomena are, by nature, chaotic and have no underlying regularity. The *DSM IV* definition of Attention Deficit Hyperactivity Disorder (ADHD) as involving any four or five out of 18 neurological, behavioral, or attentional symptoms is a recognition that this disorder has no underlying regularity. Likewise, the implementation of multi-age grouping in some schools is tacit acceptance of the fact that development is irregular and that we need flexible classroom arrangements to deal with the "normal irregularity" of growth.

The Modern Child in the Postmodern World

Although the postmodern conception of the child as different, particular, and irregular has been assimilated into some educational conceptions and practices, the modern conception of the child as progressive, universal, and lawful remains alive and well in many others. The following are but a few examples of the persistence of modern conceptions in contemporary educational practice.

Progress

The modern belief that children should progress uniformly through the grades is causing a major problem in kindergarten and first grade. At the heart of the problem is the fact that, in the postmodern world, the majority of children (about 85%) enter school after having been enrolled in one or another early childhood program. As a consequence, schools have tightened standards and now demand that all children know their letters and numbers before being accepted into the first-grade classroom. This demand is based on the modern assumption of a common child nature such that all children of the same age will profit equally from whatever type of early childhood program they have experienced.

Yet the truth lies elsewhere. The early childhood years, roughly from age 3 to age 8, are a period of rapid intellectual growth comparable to the period of rapid physical growth of early adolescence. At such times individual differences in growth rates are most evident. With adolescents, for example, some reach their full height at 13, some at 14, some at 15, and some at 16. They may all end up being the same height, but they get there at different rates. The same is true for young children's intellectual growth. Some may attain Piaget's concrete operations at 4, some at 5, some at 6, and some at 7. They will all attain concrete operations, but at different rates—even if they have the same intellectual ability. Because these operations are a necessary prerequisite to learning numbers and letters, children of the same intellectual ability will differ widely in their ability to acquire tool skills. Moreover, different early childhood programs vary widely in the extent to which they work on tool skills.

Because of these wide individual differences in growth rate and early childhood experience, children of school age vary tremendously in their readiness for formal instruction. As a consequence, in many communities some 10% to 20% of the children are being retained or placed in transition classes, and in some school districts the numbers are as high as 50%. This is a case in which a postmodern phenomenon—large numbers of children in early childhood programs—has elicited a modern notion of a common child nature that is having dysfunctional educational outcomes for large numbers of young children.

In a similar way, because of the belief that young people progress in a uniform fashion, there is little or no accommodation of the rather abrupt changes that come about in early adolescence. The middle school concept is supposed to speak more directly to the different needs of this age group,[11] but many middle schools are such in name only. Like the junior high school, misnamed middle schools fail to incorporate the team teaching, extended class times, and integrated curricula envisioned by the inventors of the middle school. The idea that children progress in uniform fashion throughout the grades dies hard, despite abundant knowledge of the differential growth spurts that characterize early adolescence as well as early childhood.

Unfortunately, the postmodern appreciation of difference is sometimes grafted onto modern ideas of progress and, as a result, is completely undermined. A case in point is the current emphasis on "inclusion" of children with special needs in the regular classroom. This practice frequently takes away from the child the special individuality that he or she has just been given. Too often, children are included without sufficient remedial support for teachers and with too little regard to the appropriateness of inclusion of a given child in a particular classroom. Moreover, there is no accommodation to the fact that some children, such as those with spina bifida, may benefit from inclusion when they are young but not when they are teenagers. Nor is sufficient attention being paid to the number and variety of special-needs children in any given classroom. With too many special-needs children in a class, the teacher is overwhelmed and may not be able to meet the needs of other students. With too few special-needs children, the special child may stand out too much. Inclusion can be beneficial, but not for all children in all circumstances at all ages and in all ratios.

Universality

The universality component of the modern conception of the child is also difficult to dislodge. The current efforts to establish national standards presuppose that all children can attain the same standards. To be sure, those who are making up the assessment devices are making an effort to include not only quantitative tests but also qualitative measures such as portfolios, products, and performance.[12] Yet qualitative methods of assessment speak to the particularity of achievement rather than to its universality. Different children will attain and express their literacy in different ways. The real challenge of national standards, and one that has yet to be met, is how to reconcile assessments that presuppose individual differences—such as portfolios, projects, and performance—with assessments that presuppose uniformity, namely, standardized tests.

The idea of universality is also taken for granted by educational publishing, which provides standard textbooks with little acknowledgment of individual differences in learning styles, pace of learning, and so on. Publishers assume that it is the teachers' responsibility to individualize, but why should this be so? Those publishers who produce a "teacher-proof" curriculum of complete, day-to-day lesson plans and materials also presuppose a commonality or universality of learning. Yet the assumption of such universality is completely at variance with the diversity within even the most homogeneously grouped class. Educational publishers must begin to address the particularity of teachers and learners and the

Irregularity

While the new definition of ADHD and the introduction of multi-age grouping in some states and communities are bows to the presence of irregularity, the belief in an underlying regularity is tenacious. Programs such as Benjamin Bloom's mastery learning, Madeline Hunter's model of effective teaching, Arthur Costa's program for teaching critical thinking, and Edward de Bono's CoRT all assume that learning is a regular process or, at least, that its products are.[13] As Richard Gibboney documents, all these innovations have been shown to be no more successful than the programs already in place.[14] One reason is that all these initiatives are founded on modern notions of learning as universal, progressive, and lawful.

From an individual (psychological child) perspective, however, learning is always a creative activity. The learner takes something from himself or herself, something from the external world, and puts them together into a product that cannot be reduced either to the learner or to the experience. Creativity, whether in classroom learning or in the arts or in the sciences, is necessarily chaotic and irregular. The artist cannot fully explain his or her art any more than the scientist can explain his or her insights. Portfolios, projects, and performance make sense only from the perspective of learning as an individual creative process.

To be sure, there are basic skills and common knowledge that all children must acquire. Sometimes the individual must subordinate his or her individual bent to acquire basic tools of the language, concepts and mores of the culture, and so on. But this is only part of learning, not the whole process. And even such learning always has an individual coloration. Put differently, the focus on mastery, skills, and outcomes acknowledges only the accommodative side of learning and totally ignores its assimilative, creative dimension. We need to encourage and to assess both types of learning.

Although we have yet to fully appreciate the fact, the classroom is a chaotic phenomenon as well. Each time a group meets, each member of the group is in some ways different from the time the group met before. Each has had experiences that no other member of the group has encountered. In many ways, every class meeting is like every dispersion of cream in a coffee cup. This does not mean that we cannot or should not study classrooms—only that we should explore them as irregular, chaotic, and social (not as recurring physical) events. Educational research, as long as it operates according to the modern idea of regularity, will fail to capture the true dynamics of classroom interactions.

Summary and Conclusion

I have briefly reviewed here the modern and postmodern conceptions of the child and the educational practices that follow from those conceptions. The modern conception confused and merged the universal biological child with the individual psychological child. While this identification of the two different conceptions of child nature was probably necessary to the establishment of free public education, it is often a hindrance to effective contemporary educational practice. Despite a growing recognition of children as different, as particular, and as irregular, the modern conception of child nature as progressive, universal, and regular still dominates educational theory and practice. In this article, I have given only a few of the many possible examples to illustrate how modern ideas continue to undermine effective pedagogy and authentic education reform.

For purposes of space, I have limited my discussion to those aspects of education that revolve around the conception of a common child nature. Postmodern ideas, however, have implications for many other educational issues. I have already addressed the issue of school and family from this perspective,[15] but it also has implications for teacher training, curricula, school organization, and so on that cannot be dealt with here. But rethinking the conception of child nature seems a useful starting point for a broader and more wide-ranging critique of modern education.

In closing, it is important to emphasize that I am not arguing that everything postmodern is good and that everything modern is bad. There is much to be valued in modern education. Many of our foremost educational innovators were already quite postmodern. This is certainly true of John Dewey, whose project method foreshadowed the integrated curriculum.[16] It is equally true of Maria Montessori, whose recognition of young children's learning ability is now accepted in our postmodern perception of childhood competence.[17] Likewise, Jean Piaget's contention that children create their reality out of their experiences with the environment[18] is echoed in the postmodern view that all concepts are human constructions, not copies of a preexisting reality. Becoming postmodern in education, therefore, often means gaining a truer and deeper appreciation of the educational innovators of modernity.

Notes

1. Clyde Kluckhohn and Henry A. Murray, "Personality Formation: The Determinants," in idem, eds., *Personality in Nature, Society, and Culture* (New York: Knopf, 1950), pp. 35–48.

2. See, for example, Steven Connor, *Postmodern Culture* (Oxford: Basil Blackwell, 1989); and Steven Best and Douglas Kellner, *Postmodern Theory* (New York: Guilford, 1991).

3. Henry Giroux, "Postmodernism and the Discourse of Educational Criticism," *Journal of Education*, vol. 170, no. 3, 1988, pp. 6–29; and Stanley Aronowitz and Henry Giroux, *Postmodern Education* (Minneapolis: University of Minnesota Press, 1991).

4. See, for example, James Comer, "Educating Poor Minority Children," *Scientific American*, vol. 295, no. 5, 1988, pp. 42–48; and Theodore Sizer, *Horace's School: Redesigning the American High School* (Boston: Houghton Mifflin, 1992).

5. John Locke, *Some Thoughts Concerning Education*, in Charles Eliot, ed., *The Harvard Classics* (New York: Collier, 1930), pp. 9–200.

6. Jean-Jacques Rousseau, *Emile*, trans. W. Payne (New York: Appleton, 1911).

7. Friedrich Nietzsche, *Thus Spoke Zarathustra* (New York: Viking, 1966).

8. Michel Foucault, *The Order of Things* (New York: Vintage, 1973).

9. Thomas Debello, "Comparison of Eleven Major Learning Style Models: Variables, Appropriate Populations, Validity of Instrumentation, and the Research Behind Them," *Journal of Reading, Writing, and Learning Disabilities International*, vol. 6, 1990, pp. 203–22.

10. Jean Piaget, *The Psychology of Intelligence* (London: Routledge & Kegan Paul, 1950).

11. See, for example, Task Force on Education of Young Adolescents, *Turning Points: Preparing American Youth for the 21st Century* (Washington, D.C.: Carnegie Council on Adolescent Development, 1989); and Jeffrey Wiles and James Bondi, *The Essential Middle School*, 2nd ed. (New York: Macmillan, 1993).

12. Gary Sykes and Phillip Plastrick, *Standard Setting and Educational Reform* (Washington, D.C.: ERIC Clearinghouse on Teacher Education, 1993).

13. Benjamin Bloom, *Human Characteristics and School Learning* (New York: McGraw-Hill, 1976); Madeline Hunter, "Knowing, Teaching, and Supervision," in Peter L. Hosford, ed., *Using What We Know About Teaching* (Alexandria, Va.: Association for Supervision and Curriculum Development, 1984), pp. 165–76; Arthur L. Costa, *Developing Minds* (Alexandria, Va.: Association for Supervision and Curriculum Development, 1985); and Edward de Bono, *CoRT Program* (San Diego: Pergamon Press, 1988).

14. Richard A. Gibboney, *The Stone Trumpet* (Albany: State University of New York Press, 1994).

15. David Elkind, "School and Family in the Postmodern World," *Phi Delta Kappan*, September 1995, pp. 8–14.

16. John Dewey, *The Child and the Curriculum/The School and Society* (1915; reprint, Chicago: University of Chicago Press, 1956).

17. Maria Montessori, *The Absorbent Mind* (New York: Delta, 1967).

18. Jean Piaget, *Science of Education and the Psychology of the Child* (New York: Viking, 1969).

Form at end of book

Stop Blaming Kids and TV

Mike Males

Mike Males, author of The Scapegoat Generation: America's War on Adolescents (*Common Courage Press, 1996), is a social-ecology doctoral student at the University of California-Irvine.*

Children have never been very good at listening to their elders," James Baldwin wrote in *Nobody Knows My Name.* "But they have never failed to imitate them." This basic truth has all but disappeared as the public increasingly treats teenagers as a robot-like population under sway of an exploitative media. White House officials lecture film, music, Internet, fashion, and pop-culture moguls and accuse them of programming kids to smoke, drink, shoot up, have sex, and kill.

So do conservatives, led by William Bennett and Dan Quayle. Professional organizations are also into media-bashing. In its famous report on youth risks, the Carnegie Corporation devoted a full chapter to media influences.

Progressives are no exception. *Mother Jones* claims it has "proof that TV makes kids violent." And the Institute for Alternative Media emphasizes, "the average American child will witness . . . 200,000 acts of [TV] violence" by the time that child graduates from high school.

None of these varied interests note that during the eighteen years between a child's birth and graduation from high school, there will be fifteen million cases of *real* violence in American homes grave enough to require hospital emergency treatment. These assaults will cause ten million serious injuries and 40,000 deaths to children. In October 1996, the Department of Health and Human Services reported 565,000 serious injuries that abusive parents inflicted on children and youths in 1993. The number is up four-fold since 1986.

The Department of Health report disappeared from the news in one day. It elicited virtually no comment from the White House, Republicans, or law-enforcement officials. Nor from Carnegie scholars, whose 150-page study, "Great Transitions: Preparing Adolescents for a New Century," devotes two sentences to household violence. The left press took no particular interest in the story, either.

All sides seem to agree that fictional violence, sex on the screen, Joe Camel, beer-drinking frogs, or naked bodies on the Internet pose a bigger threat to children than do actual beatings, rape, or parental addictions. This, in turn, upholds the Clinton doctrine that youth behavior is the problem, and curbing young people's rights the answer.

Claims that TV causes violence bear little relation to real behavior. Japanese and European kids behold media as graphically brutal as that which appears on American screens, but seventeen-year-olds in those countries commit murder at rates lower than those of American seventy-year-olds.

Likewise, youths in different parts of the United States are exposed to the same media but display drastically different violence levels. TV violence does not account for the fact that the murder rate among black teens in Washington, D.C., is twenty-five times higher than that of white teens living a few Metro stops away. It doesn't explain why, nationally, murder doubled among nonwhite and Latino youth over the last decade, but declined among white Anglo teens. Furthermore, contrary to the TV brainwashing theory, Anglo sixteen-year-olds have lower violent-crime rates than black sixty-year-olds, Latino forty-year-olds, and Anglo thirty-year-olds. Men, women, whites, Latinos, blacks, Asians, teens, young adults, middle-agers, and senior citizens in Fresno County—California's poorest urban area—display murder and violent-crime rates double those of their counterparts in Ventura County, the state's richest.

Confounding every theory, America's biggest explosion in felony violent crime is not street crime among minorities or teens of any color, but domestic violence among aging, mostly white baby boomers. Should we arm Junior with a V-chip to protect him from Mom and Dad?

In practical terms, media-violence theories are not about kids, but about race and class: If TV accounts for any meaningful fraction of murder levels among poorer, nonwhite youth, why doesn't it have the same effect on white kids? Are minorities inherently programmable?

The newest target is Channel One, legitimately criticized by the Unplug Campaign—a watchdog sponsored by the Center for Commercial-Free Public Education—as a corporate marketing ploy packaged as educational TV. But then the Unplug Campaign gives credence to claims that "commercials control kids" by "harvesting minds," as Roy Fox of the University of Missouri says. These claims imply that teens are uniquely open to media brainwashing.

Other misleading claims come from Johns Hopkins University media analyst Mark Crispin Miller. In his critique of Channel One in the May edition of *Extra,* Miller invoked such hackneyed phrases as the "inevitable rebelliousness of adolescent boys," the "hormones raging," and the "defiant boorish behavior" of "young men." Despite the popularity of these stereotypes, there is no basis in fact for such anti-youth bias.

A 1988 study in the *Journal of Youth and Adolescence* by psychology professors Grayson Holmbeck and John Hill concluded: "Adolescents are *not* in turmoil, *not* deeply disturbed, *not* resistant to parental values, and *not* rebellious."

In the November 1992 *Journal of the American Academy of Child and Adolescent Psychiatry,* Northwestern University psychiatry professor Daniel Offer reviewed 150 studies and concluded, in his article "Debunking the Myths of Adolescence," that "the effects of pubertal hormones are neither potent nor pervasive."

If anything, Channel One and other mainstream media reinforce young people's conformity to—not defiance of—adult values. Miller's unsubstantiated claims that student consumerism, bad behaviors, and mental or biological imbalances are compelled by media ads and images could be made with equal force about the behaviors of his own age group. Binge drinking, drug abuse, and violence against children by adults over the age of thirty are rising rapidly.

The barrage of sexually seductive liquor ads, fashion images, and anti-youth rhetoric, by conventional logic, must be influencing those hormonally unstable middle-agers.

I worked for a dozen years in youth programs in Montana and California. When problems arose, they usually crossed generations. I saw violent kids with dads or uncles in jail for assault. I saw middle-schoolers molested in childhood by mom's boyfriend. I saw budding teen alcoholics hoisting forty-ounces alongside forty-year-old sots. I also saw again and again how kids start to smoke. In countless trailers and small apartments dense with blue haze, children roamed the rugs as grownups puffed. Mom and seventh-grade daughter swapped Dorals while bemoaning the evils of men. A junior-high basketball center slept outside before a big game because a dozen elders—

from her non-inhaling sixteen-year-old brother to her grandma—were all chain smokers. Two years later, she'd given up and joined the party.

As a rule, teen smoking mimicked adult smoking by gender, race, locale, era, and household. I could discern no pop-culture puppetry. My survey of 400 Los Angeles middle schoolers for a 1994 *Journal of School Health* article found children of smoking parents three times more likely to smoke by age fifteen than children of nonsmokers. Parents were the most influential but not the only adults kids emulated. Nor did youngsters copy elders slavishly. Youths often picked slightly different habits (like chewing tobacco, or their own brands).

In 1989, the Centers for Disease Control lamented, "75 percent of all teenage smokers come from homes where parents smoke." You don't hear such candor from today's put-politics-first health agencies. Centers for Disease Control tobacco chieftain Michael Eriksen informed me that his agency doesn't make an issue of parental smoking. Nor do anti-smoking groups. Asked Kathy Mulvey, research director of INFACT: "Why make enemies of fifty million adult smokers" when advertising creates the real "appeal of tobacco to youth?"

Do ads hook kids on cigarettes? Studies of the effects of the Joe Camel logo show only that a larger fraction of teen smokers than veteran adult smokers choose the Camel brand. When asked, some researchers admit they cannot demonstrate that advertising causes kids to smoke who would not otherwise. And that's the real issue. In fact, surveys found smoking declining among teens (especially the youngest) during Joe's advent from 1985 to 1990.

The University of California's Stanton Glantz, whose exposure of 10,000 tobacco documents enraged the industry, found corporate perfidy far shrewder than camels and cowboys.

"As the tobacco industry knows well," Glantz reported, "kids want to be like adults." An industry marketing document advises: "To reach young smokers, present the cigarette as one of the initiations into adult life . . . the basic symbols of growing up."

The biggest predictor of whether a teen will become a smoker, a drunk, or a druggie is whether or not the child grows up amid adult addicts. Three-fourths of murdered kids are killed by adults. Suicide and murder rates among white teenagers resemble those of white adults, and suicide and murder rates among black teens track those of black adults. And as far as teen pregnancy goes, for minor mothers, four-fifths of the fathers are adults over eighteen, and half are adults over twenty.

The inescapable conclusion is this: If you want to change juvenile behavior, change adult behavior. But instead of focusing on adults, almost everyone points a finger at kids—and at the TV culture that supposedly addicts them.

Groups like Mothers Against Drunk Driving charge, for instance, that Budweiser's frogs entice teens to drink. Yet the 1995 National Household Survey found teen alcohol use declining. "Youths aren't buying the cute and flashy beer images," an in-depth *USA Today* survey found. Most teens found the ads amusing, but they did not consume Bud as a result.

By squabbling over frogs, political interests can sidestep the impolitic tragedy that adults over the age of twenty-one cause 90 percent of America's 16,000 alcohol-related traffic deaths every year. Clinton and drug-policy chief Barry McCaffrey ignore federal reports that show a skyrocketing toll of booze and drug-related casualties among adults in their thirties and forties—the age group that is parenting most American teens. But both officials get favorable press attention by blaming alcohol ads and heroin chic for corrupting our kids.

Progressive reformers who insist kids are so malleable that beer frogs and Joe Camel and Ace Ventura push them to evil are not so different from those on the Christian right who claim that *Our Bodies, Ourselves* promotes teen sex and that the group Rage Against the Machine persuades pubescents to roll down Rodeo Drive with a shotgun.

America's increasingly marginalized young deserve better than grownup escapism. Millions of children and teenagers face real destitution, drug abuse, and violence in their homes. Yet these profound menaces continue to lurk in the background, even as the frogs, V-chips, and Mighty Morphins take center stage.

Form at end of book

Issue 6 Summary

As we come to the close of one century and the beginning of another, our views of children are changing significantly. A postmodern view of children recognizes that development is simultaneously *universal* and *individual;* it examines the *regularity* of development but does not marginalize those whose development is *irregular.* At the same time, we need to put into perspective the many serious problems that children face in our society, including poverty and violence, and be careful not to attribute society's ills to its most vulnerable members, children. We need to look closely at how society might be blaming the victim rather than looking carefully at real causes of and possible solutions to society's problems.

Multiple Intelligences

Questions

1. What are some of the applications of Gardner's theory of multiple intelligences to the classroom?

2. Why has Gardner's theory been so readily embraced by many educators?

3. What criticisms challenge Gardner's theory of multiple intelligences?

Introduction

Schools in the United States have in many ways been organized around the idea that children possess a quality called *intelligence,* a general level of mental ability. Earlier in the twentieth century, children's intelligence was measured through paper-and-pencil tests, and children were grouped in upper-level, middle-level, or lower-level classes within their grades based on their performance on these tests. Subsequently, tracking of students continued, but it was usually based on students' performance on tests of achievement rather than on tests of intelligence. Nevertheless, the idea persisted that each person possessed a quality called intelligence that could be measured.

In the 1980s, Howard Gardner presented a theory of multiple intelligences, which contends that each person has at least seven types of intelligence: linguistic, logical-mathematical, bodily-kinesthetic, visual, musical, interpersonal, and intrapersonal. His theory was quickly embraced by many educators and parents who felt that the more narrow definition of intelligence was harmful to students who excelled in other areas. Further, educators rushed to design educational applications of Gardner's theory. Critics, however, have questioned whether what Gardner describes are types of intelligence or, rather, are better considered aptitudes or abilities. By calling them "intelligences," Gardner is challenging the intelligence testing advocated by traditionalists and educators who subscribe to the idea that we are all distributed neatly along the normal curve.

How Teachers Interpret MI Theory

Teachers are planning projects, lessons, assessments, apprenticeships, and interdisciplinary curriculums around the multiple intelligences theory. Like intelligence itself, the adaptations exhibit infinite variety.

Linda Campbell

Linda Campbell is a professor in the Graduate Education Programs and Director of the Center for Community & Professional Learning at Antioch University Seattle. She is the author of the bestselling book Teaching and Learning Through Multiple Intelligences *published by Allyn & Bacon in 1996 and 1999. Her eleventh book,* Questions Answered: MI School Programs and Their Results, *1999 is published by ASCD. She may be reached at Antioch University Seattle by writing to 2326 6th Ave., Seattle, WA 98121 or by calling at 206–441–5352.*

In Eeva Reeder's math classes at Mountlake Terrace High School in Edmonds, Washington, students learn algebra kinesthetically. When studying how to graph equations, they head for the school's courtyard. There they identify X and Y coordinates in the lines of the large, square, cement blocks that form the pavement. They then plot themselves as points on the large cement axes. Reeder maintains that when her students physically pretend to be graphs, they learn more about equations in a single class session than they do in a month of textbook study.

On the Tulalip Indian reservation in Marysville, Washington, elementary school students spend their mornings rotating through learning stations. For example, to learn about photosynthesis, students might act out the process at one station, read about it at another station, and at others, sing about photosynthesis, chart its processes, discuss plant and human life cycles, and, finally, reflect on events that have transformed their lives, just as chloroplasts transform the life cycle of plants.

Meanwhile, in Pittsburgh, middle school arts teachers organize their curriculums around major student projects that emphasize both process and product. In music, creative writing, dance, and visual arts classes, students perform tasks that actual artists, musicians, and writers undertake. In a visual arts class, for example, students may work on portraiture for several weeks, learn how to work with different media, study portraits of recognized artists, and, ultimately, create, display, and reflect upon a final work, using all the principles and skills they have acquired.

Curricular Adaptations

What do these three scenarios have in common? They are all curricular interpretations of Howard Gardner's theory of multiple intelligences. As such, they share one of its central tenets: a school is responsible for helping all students discover and develop their talents or strengths. In doing this, the school not only awakens children's joy in learning but also fuels the persistence and effort necessary for mastering skills and information and for being inventive.

Since Gardner first published *Frames of Mind: The Theory of Multiple Intelligences* in 1983, educators began applying his theory in their classrooms. Just as Gardner maintains that each person has a unique cognitive profile, so too have educators shown that there is no single preferred multiple intelligences model. Individual teachers and entire schools have implemented the theory, making it the basis of their mission statements and curriculums. But they have done it in diverse, and sometimes conflicting, ways.

In the course of my university teaching, my staff development work, and my research for *Teaching and Learning Through Multiple Intelligences* (1996), I have discovered scores of approaches to multiple intelligences. Some teachers interpret the theory as an instructional process that provides numerous entry points into lesson content. Some say it suggests we need to develop each student's talents early in life. Others dedicate equal time to the arts each day. Many teachers use multiple intelligences to integrate curriculum, to organize classroom learning stations, or to teach students self-directed learning skills through project-based curriculum. Still others establish apprenticeship programs with community experts to teach students real-world skills. None of these adaptations is more correct than any other. Teachers apply the theory in the way they consider most appropriate for their students, school, and community.

Following are descriptions of five of the many multiple intelligences curricular formats currently being used: multiple intelligence-based lesson designs, interdisciplinary curriculums, student projects, assessments, and apprenticeships. All are guided in large part by students' talents, strengths, and interests.

1. Lesson Designs

Many teachers use the multiple intelligences as entry points into lesson content. As our first example showed, Reeder teaches algebra and geometry kinesthetically. Students who have trouble understanding math through paper-and-pencil exercises often grasp concepts easily when they build models or role-play math formulas.

Other teachers attempt to engage all eight intelligences in their lessons. Sharon Thetford, a multiage intermediate teacher at Tulalip Elementary School, sets up eight learning stations that her students rotate through each day. While such lesson planning is admittedly daunting at first, many teachers report that thinking in multiple modes quickly becomes second nature.

To begin lesson planning, teachers should reflect on a concept that they want to teach and identify the intelligences that seem most appropriate for communicating the content. The "instructional menus" shown on p. 95 offer some ideas for expanding pedagogical repertoires and quickly infusing variety into lessons.

Many teachers ask students to select the ways they would like to learn. Others use the menus for homework, rotating through the eight menus over eight weeks. For example, a teacher may ask students to do their homework musically for the first week. The students then share their musical reviews in class. The following week, the teacher repeats the process with a different menu. For the ninth week, the teacher may encourage students to use their favorite homework strategies. In this way, all students confront their weaknesses and engage their strengths.

Although the multiple intelligences theory provides an effective instructional framework, teachers should avoid using it as a rigid pedagogical formula. One teacher who attempted to teach all content through all eight modes each day admitted that he occasionally had to tack on activities. Even students complained that some lessons were "really stretching it." Instructional methods should be appropriate for the content.

This is not to say that a teacher should consistently avoid an intelligence because it is out of his or her comfort zone. Instead, teachers should team up with colleagues so that they can increase both their own and their students' educational options.

Teachers at Wheeler Elementary School in Louisville, Kentucky, plan and teach in teams based on their intelligence strengths. Each teacher assumes responsibility for two intelligences and contributes to his or her grade level curriculum accordingly. Students then rotate from classroom to classroom, learning from three or four teachers for each unit of study. When interviewed, students have said they appreciate the hands-on nature of their learning and each teacher's enthusiasm.

2. Interdisciplinary Curriculums

Many elementary educators have embraced multiple intelligences teaching, but high school teachers can just as easily adopt the theory. In fact, because high schools typically offer liberal arts programs, most *already* feature a comprehensive multiple intelligences curriculum. Students can quickly identify experts in specific intelligences by the subjects they teach!

Rather than totally reworking the curriculum, secondary educators need only adapt it to highlight various intelligences. For some schools this means adding a stronger arts program; for some teachers, it means adding learning stations in their classrooms or bringing in community experts in various disciplines to mentor their students.

Some secondary teachers have capitalized on their school's multiple intelligences programs by coordinating schoolwide interdisciplinary units. Although interdisciplinary instruction is popular, here is one proviso: Gardner is careful to remind educators that the core disciplines continue to offer the most sophisticated knowledge accrued over centuries. Before thinking in interdisciplinary terms, we must first possess the knowledge of the individual disciplines.

There may be as many models of multiple intelligences teaching as there are teachers!

Seattle's International Focus

An inner-city Seattle high school piloted a schoolwide multiple intelligences week on international awareness. Teachers continued to teach within their own disciplines, but all created lessons with an international focus. Literature faculty introduced short stories from the cultures of their students. Business education teachers focused on international trade issues, thereby complementing math instructors' lessons on foreign stock exchanges. Social studies teachers compared diverse forms of government and surveyed civil rights issues. Physical education teachers taught games from around the world, while health teachers conducted a unit on infectious diseases. Art and music educators engaged students in a variety of visual media and ethnomusicology. And in science classes, students studied local and global environmental issues.

The Seattle teachers became so excited over their unit plans that they invited parents to attend their classes, scheduling the classes in the late afternoon and evening for the parents' convenience. The week was a huge success: the students appreciated the cohesive curricular focus, and hundreds of parents—including immigrant parents—attended.

Montana's Use of the Arts

Montana's Framework for Aesthetic Literacy (Montana Office of Public Instruction 1994) is another approach to interdisciplinary, multiple intelligences-based curriculums. This K-12 English and language arts curriculum is taught through the visual and performing arts. Because the teachers prefer the inquiry approach over structuring curriculums thematically, they begin each unit by posing a thought-provoking, open-ended question to guide students in their studies. They might ask questions like:

What is beauty? Who determines the standards for what is beautiful?

How do we use imagination to explain our world?

How do the arts reflect their cultures?

How does balance work? Why is it important?

To seek answers, students might attend a play or a symphony, see a film, or tour a museum. They make discoveries, draw connections, construct knowledge, and seek meaning and resolution on their own.

The Montana framework suggests a three-step curricular approach. First, students are immersed in an artistic experience. Second, they study essential English and language arts concepts while also practicing diverse thinking and communication skills. Finally, they generate their own products and answers to the unit's focus question. Through this curricular sequence, students use their multiple intelligences to acquire literacy skills and to reflect on relevant and worthwhile questions.

3. Student Projects

Some educators use the theory of multiple intelligences to promote self-directed learning. They prepare students for their adult lives by teaching them how to initiate and manage complex projects. Students learn to ask researchable questions; to identify varied resources; to create realistic time lines; and to initiate, implement, and bring closure to

a learning activity. Regardless of the disciplinary focus, these projects typically draw on numerous intelligences.

Even primary-age children can learn how to execute projects. With teacher guidance, students at Project Spectrum—Howard Gardner's lab school at Harvard—study local birds and their nesting habits They design and build bird houses and then observe whether their designs successfully meet the needs of the birds or whether modifications are required.

Middle school students in the small town of Lakewood, Washington, learn biology concepts by solving a mock crime. They conduct investigations, gather and study evidence, and suggest hypotheses they must support. Once they solve the crime, they analyze the problem-solving approaches that led to the correct answer.

Some teachers encourage students to identify their own topics to pursue for classroom projects. For example, high school students in Palo Alto, California, wanted to recommend to the city how it might use a property in a redevelopment area. They did this by presenting videotape documentaries to the city council.

High school students in Ithaca, New York, became interested in cancer therapies after a classmate was diagnosed with leukemia. The students undertook research projects, interviewed medical personnel, and visited hospitals to understand the disease and identify traditional and nontraditional healing approaches.

The theory's broad view of human abilities does not dictate how and what to teach. It merely gives teachers a complex mental model from which to construct curriculum.

Projects such as these typically span two weeks to two months. Some teachers include three or more projects in a year-long curriculum, claiming that in this way, students can cover more information in greater depth than they could with conventional classroom approaches.

Project Guidelines

Because the skills of managing one's own learning must be explicitly taught, one elementary teacher (Campbell 1994) created the following project guidelines to teach his students how to conduct projects.

1. State your goal. (Example: I want to understand how optical illusions work.)

2. Put your goal into the form of a question. (Example: What are optical illusions and why do they fool our eyes?)

3. List at least three sources of information you will use. (For example, library books, eye doctors, prints of M.C. Escher's work, the art teacher.)

4. Describe the steps you will use to achieve your goal. (Find books on optical illusions and read those books, look up optical illusion in the encyclopedia, look at Escher's work.)

5. List at least five main concepts or ideas you want to research. (Example: What are optical illusions? How is the human eye tricked?)

6. List at least three methods you will use to present your project. (Example: Construct a model of how the human eye works. Hand out a sheet or optical illusions for class members to keep. Have the class try to make some.)

7. Organize the project into a time line. (Week 1: Read sources of information. Interview adults. Week 2: Look at a variety of optical illusions. Make diagram of eye.)

8. Decide how you will evaluate your project. (Examples: Practice in front of an adult and get his or her feedback. Practice in front of two friends. Fill out a self-evaluation form. Read the teacher's evaluation.)

By working through these project guidelines, students naturally engage several intelligences. In the project on optical illusions, most students used seven of the eight intelligences. Perhaps more important, by initiating and completing projects of their choice, they acquired valuable autonomous learning skills.

4. Assessments

To show what they've learned from their projects and other coursework, students should be asked to do more than fill in blanks and supply short answers to specific questions. They should demonstrate their higher-order thinking skills, generalize what they learn, provide examples, connect the content to their personal experiences, and apply their knowledge to new situations.

Multiple Intelligences Menus

Linguistic Menu

Use storytelling to explain _____

Conduct a debate on _____

Write a poem, myth, legend, short play, or news article about _____

Create a talk show radio program about _____

Conduct an interview of _____ on _____

Logical-Mathematical Menu

Translate a _____ into a mathematical formula

Design and conduct an experiment on _____

Make up syllogisms to demonstrate _____

Make up analogies to explain _____

Describe the patterns or symmetry in _____

Others of your choice _____

Bodily-Kinesthetic Menu

Create a movement or sequence of movements to explain _____

Make task or puzzle cards for _____

Build or construct a _____

Plan and attend a field trip that will _____

Bring hands-on materials to demonstrate _____

Visual Menu

Chart, map, cluster, or graph _____

Create a slide show, videotape, or photo album of _____

Create a piece of art that demonstrates _____

Invent a board or card game to demonstrate _____

Illustrate, draw, paint, sketch, or sculpt _____

Musical Menu

Give a presentation with appropriate musical accompaniment on _____

Sing a rap or song that explains _____

Indicate the rhythmical patterns in _____

Explain how the music of a song is similar to _____

Make an instrument and use it to demonstrate _____

Interpersonal Menu

Conduct a meeting to address _____

Intentionally use _____ social skills to learn about _____

Participate in a service project to _____

Teach someone about _____

Practice giving and receiving feedback on _____

Use technology to _____

Intrapersonal Menu

Describe qualities you possess that will help you successfully complete _____

Set and pursue a goal to _____

Describe one of your personal values about _____

Write a journal entry on _____

Assess your own work in _____

Naturalist Menu

Create observation notebooks of _____

Describe changes in the local or global environment _____

Care for pets, wildlife, gardens, or parks _____

Use binoculars, telescopes, microscopes, or magnifiers to _____

Draw or photograph natural objects _____

When appropriate, students may even select the way they will demonstrate what they've learned. Some teachers have used multiple intelligences menus as assessment options. The teacher specifies criteria for quality work, knowledge, and skills, but leaves students free to use flow charts, role plays, original songs, or other approaches.

Teachers at Eleanor Roosevelt Elementary School in Vancouver, Washington, have developed approaches that involve both parents and students in assessment. Students individually evaluate the skills and knowledge they have acquired and include their assessments in their portfolios. They also work in groups to assess one another's projects and evaluate their courses and teachers. Parents participate in a number of ways: by setting goals and assessing with their children, by reviewing student videotapes, by evaluating courses, and by writing informal comments during their visits to the classroom. Such diverse tools and increased participation yield more comprehensive pictures of student progress while giving students and their parents a stronger voice in schooling.

5. Apprenticeships

Gardner suggests that schools personalize their programs for students by offering them apprenticeships during the elementary and secondary school years. The apprenticeships he recommends would not track students into careers at an early age. Instead, they would contribute to a well-rounded liberal arts education and consume approximately one-third of students' schooling experience. Ideally, each student would participate in three apprenticeships: one in an art form or craft, one in an academic area, and a third in a physical discipline such as dance or sports. Students would have input into which apprenticeships they pursued.

Through such apprenticeships, students are learning something frequently lost in today's fast-paced society: that one gains mastery of a valued skill gradually, with effort and discipline over time. Once students achieve competence in the disciplines they are studying, they experiment with their own approaches and creative extensions.

Apprenticeship programs may be offered as part of the regular school curriculum or as extracurricular enrichment opportunities.

At the Key School in Indianapolis—the first multiple intelligences school in the U.S.—teachers, parents, or community members mentor students in 17 crafts or disciplines—each one called a "pod." Each student attends a pod of his or her choice four times a week to work on material related to one or more intelligences. Because each pod is open to any student in the school, children of varying ages participate in each of them.

Pod topics include architecture, cooking, and gardening, as well as themes called Sing and Song, Logowriter, Imagine Indianapolis (city planning), and Young Astronauts. In addition to the in-school experiences, a local museum offers Key students apprenticeships in ship building, journalism, animation, or weather monitoring.

The Jocko River Water Unit takes students out into their community where they learn about plant and animal life firsthand.

Programs such as this offer students powerful opportunities to work with older students or adults who have achieved competence in a discipline or craft. And when they are immersed in real-world tasks, students begin to see where their efforts may lead.

No Prescriptions

These five curricular approaches—multiple intelligence-based lesson designs, interdisciplinary curriculums, student projects, assessments, and apprenticeships—represent only a handful of adaptations of Gardner's theory of intelligence. In actuality, there may be as many models of multiple intelligences teaching as there are teachers! Educators, it appears, readily embrace the theory because it affirms what they already know and do.

Multiple intelligences does not demand an overhaul of a curriculum; it merely provides a framework for enhancing instruction and a language to describe one's efforts. Unlike most educational reforms, it is not prescriptive. Its broad view of human abilities does not dictate how and what to teach. Rather, it gives teachers a complex mental model from which to construct curriculum and improve themselves as educators.

References

Campbell, B. (1994). *The Multiple Intelligences Handbook: Lesson Plans and More.* Stanwood, Wash.: Campbell and Associates, Inc.

Campbell, L., B. Campbell, and D. Dickinson. (1996). *Teaching and Learning Through Multiple Intelligences.* Needham Heights, Mass.: Allyn and Bacon (college division of Simon and Schuster).

Gardner, H. (1983). *Frames of Mind: The Theory of Multiple Intelligences.* New York: Basic Books.

Montana Office of Public Instruction. (1994). *Framework for Aesthetic Literacy: Montana Arts and English Curriculum.* Helena, Mont.: Author.

Form at end of book

Multiple Intelligence Disorder

James Traub

James Traub is a contributing writer for The New York Times *Magazine.*

Howard Gardner first realized that he had struck a chord in the national psyche when he gave a speech to private-school administrators on his new theory of "multiple intelligences" and saw the headmasters elbowing each other to get into the hall. That was in 1983. Since that time, Gardner, a Harvard professor who still carries a book bag and wears a ski parka over his tweed jacket, has blossomed into a genuine academic superstar. He has won a MacArthur "genius" grant; his books have been translated into 20 languages; and he gives about 75 talks a year. There are now "M.I. schools" all over the country. His ideas have achieved extraordinary currency in even the most rarefied reaches of the educational world; when the directorship of one of New York's most prestigious private schools recently came open, almost every candidate for the job mentioned Gardner in his or her one-page educational-philosophy statement. In the 15 years since the publication of Gardner's *Frames of Mind,* multiple intelligences has gone from being a widely disputed theory to a rallying cry for school reformers to a cultural commonplace. And, amazingly, it has done so without ever winning over the scientific establishment.

Gardner's central claim is that what we normally think of as intelligence is merely a single aspect, or two aspects, of a much wider range of aptitudes; he has counted eight so far. Thus we have exalted the attribute measured by IQ tests—the hyperlogical style Gardner half-jokingly calls the "Alan Dershowitz" model of intelligence—and have slighted our creative and interpersonal gifts. Of course, the primary question about this theory is whether or not it's true. But an intriguing secondary question is why it's so wildly popular. "I think the whole intelligence establishment and the psychometric tradition were ready to be attacked by somebody who was credible," Gardner told me the first time I met him, in the midst of a two-day speaking tour in Chicago last December. "We know that kids who do well on tests are smart, but we also know that a lot of kids who don't do well on tests are getting it. The question is not how smart people are but in what ways people are smart." This is, of course, an immensely appealing idea. Gardner has offered an explanation for academic failure in which the problem lies in the system of measurement rather than the student or the teacher; more broadly, he has given intellectual legitimacy to critiques of the test-driven meritocracy and of the high-IQ elite it fosters. Multiple intelligence theory clearly serves many purposes. That makes it powerful, but not necessarily valid.

Psychometrics hasn't changed much since Alfred Binet devised a test at the turn of the century to predict which French children would succeed or fail in school. The instruments we now use to test a child's "intelligence quotient" measure essentially the same aptitudes that Binet did—memory, vocabulary, spatial thinking, the ability to draw analogies and solve puzzles—because these are the aptitudes historically associated with success in school and in professional life. While psychometricians disagree about the extent to which intelligence is an inherited trait rather than a result of environment and upbringing, there is broad consensus around the idea that intelligence is a single entity that can be measured with fairly great accuracy. The various mental aptitudes are understood as aspects of a single underlying trait called *g*, for "general intelligence."

Howard Gardner has approached the subject of intelligence from an entirely different angle, one that combines scientific research and speculation with personal experience. Gardner is a polymath, with a breadth of interests unusual in his field. As a boy, he was a serious pianist and a student of composition; as a young scholar at Harvard, where he has spent his entire professional life, he worked with Nelson Goodman, the philosopher of aesthetics. In one of his first books, *The Arts and Human Development,* published in 1973, Gardner noted that the developmental model created by the great Swiss psychologist Jean Piaget applied only to "those mental processes that culminate in scientific thought, an end state that can be expressed in logical terms." Gardner looked instead at the development of the cognitive processes involved in creative work. Several of his subsequent books have explored the thought processes of great artistic figures. Gardner had also begun to study brain-damaged patients at Boston's Veterans Administration Hospital. He found that many of them had suffered devastating damage to a core intellectual function that had nevertheless left other functions intact—so that some aphasics who could barely comprehend speech could nevertheless recognize a metaphor or even tell a joke. This fit with an emerging consensus in neuroscience: namely, that the brain operates in "modular" fashion, with autonomous systems devoted to different mental acts.

Gardner built on these insights in *Frames of Mind*. Rather than accepting that intelligence tests captured intelligence, he drew up a series of criteria from a wide range of disciplines and assigned the title "intelligence" to whatever mental traits satisfied them. In order to make Gardner's final cut, an aptitude had to have been isolated, or spared, in instances of brain damage; had to furnish instances of prodigies or idiots savants; had to have a unique developmental and evolutionary history; and so on. These intelligences were almost wholly independent of one another; there was no master trait—no *g*. The seven winners were "linguistic" and "logical-mathematical"—the two already recognized by psychometricians—plus "musical," "spatial," "bodily kinesthetic," "intrapersonal," and "interpersonal." Gardner has since added an eighth, the "naturalist intelligence," which is the ability to make distinctions and to form classes among objects. "Existential intelligence" has been a candidate for several years, but Gardner has not yet admitted it to the pantheon.

Gardner failed to persuade his peers. George Miller, the esteemed psychologist credited with discovering the mechanisms by which short-term memory operates, wrote in *The New York Times Book Review* that Gardner's argument boiled down to "hunch and opinion." And Gardner's subsequent work has done very little to shift the balance of opinion. A recent issue of *Psychology, Public Policy, and Law* devoted to the study of intelligence contained virtually no reference to Gardner's work. Most people who study intelligence view M.I. theory as rhetoric rather than science, and they're divided on the virtues of the rhetoric. Steven Ceci, a developmental psychologist at Cornell, praises Gardner as "a wonderful communicator" who has publicized "a much more egalitarian view of intelligence." But he points out that Gardner's approach of constructing criteria and then running candidate intelligences through them, while suggestive, provides no hard evidence—no test results, for example—that his colleagues could evaluate. Ceci adds: "The neurological data show that the brain is modular, but that does not address the issue of whether

all these things are correlated or not." Track-and-field athletes, he notes, may have special gifts in one particular event, but they will score better than the average person on every event. Psychological tests show the same kind of correlations.

Gardner describes this conventional view of intelligence as Cartesian rather than Darwinian. Cartesians, he argues, see the mind in strictly rational and ahistorical terms. "The Darwinian view," he says, "is that this is a crazy-quilt group of faculties that we have here, and they've dealt with survival over hundreds of thousands of years in very different environments. Literacy only existed twenty-five hundred years ago. What does it mean to develop a whole theory of intelligence that didn't even exist three thousand years ago? Moreover, given that we now have computers that will do our rational behavior for us, it's an open question what the intelligences are going to be that are valued fifty years from now. It might be artistic; it might be pointless kinds of things." Why should we accept a definition of intelligence that "took a certain scholastic skill—what it meant to be a good bureaucrat a hundred years ago—and make that the quintessence of intelligence"?

But that is, in a way, precisely the problem with Gardner's theory. Intelligence is not a crisp concept but a term of value—indeed, the ultimate term of value. Some in Gardner's corner, like his mentor and colleague Jerome Bruner, say they wish Gardner had employed a more neutral term like "aptitude." But if Gardner hadn't used "intelligence" he wouldn't be the colossal figure he is today. Gardner does not shy away from the "political" dimension of his argument. "My claim that there are seven or eight Xs is not a value judgment," he told me. "It's my best reading of the biological and cultural data. But my decision to call them 'intelligences' is clearly picking a fight with a group that thought it, and it alone, could decide what intelligence was."

There may well be validity to Gardner's claim that core mental aptitudes are more autonomous from one another than psychometricians like to believe. But the reason psychologists don't measure the elements of "bodily kinesthetic" intelligence isn't that they doubt the elements exist—it's that they don't think the elements matter. Some societies may be structured around musical or athletic or spiritual attainments, but ours isn't. This is where Gardner's quarrel lies. Like Robert Coles, the author of *The Moral Intelligence of Children*, and Daniel Goleman, who wrote the wildly popular *Emotional Intelligence*, Gardner believes that we have submitted too much to the tyranny of logic. What he has elaborated over the years is the most scientifically credible and deeply pondered of the various assaults on the hegemony of logic. It's an extraordinary polemic, but it's still a polemic. And so the question it leaves us with is: Are we too preoccupied with cultivating the old-fashioned intellectual gifts, or are we not preoccupied enough?

The psychometric establishment was no match for *Frames of Mind* in the court of public opinion. Gardner had offered a vision of human nature that spoke eloquently to public disillusionment with the scientific, technocratic worldview. Although Gardner had almost nothing to say about the practical applications of his theory, he had provided a paradigm that opened up new vistas for the education of children. From the outset, educators passed *Frames of Mind* around like samizdat. Tom Hoerr, the headmaster of a private school in St. Louis, told me that he bought the book soon after it was published, read it with mounting excitement, and then spent months meeting after school with his faculty to discuss it chapter by chapter. A group of teachers in Indianapolis drove 14 hours to talk with Gardner about creating a school based on his philosophy. Gardner didn't have a philosophy, and yet his reticence about the world of practice had the effect of vindicating almost any departure from the traditional curriculum or traditional pedagogy made in his name.

And so began the astonishing second life of *Frames of Mind* as a template for the transformation of the schools—a transformation much in evidence today. Open up a copy of *Education Week* and you'll see ads for conferences on the "Student at Risk" and "Restructuring Elementary Schools" and "Training for Trainers"—all with presentations on M.I. theory. One progressively minded educator recently told me, "Howard is the guru, and *Frames of Mind* is the bible." Few of the teachers and administrators I talked to were familiar with the critiques of multiple intelligence theory; what they knew was that the theory worked for them. They talked about it almost euphorically. To Dee Dickinson, an educator and consultant in Seattle, *Frames of Mind* offered a "metatheory" that tied together all the effective teaching strategies she had been promoting. "Here was a new way of looking at human capacities," she said, "and a new way of identifying people's strengths and finding effective ways of helping people use those strengths." Gardner appealed to the teachers' intuitive sense that children learn in different ways, and the teachers responded to Gardner's more explicitly political agenda of democratizing human gifts. Tom Hoerr said that what he learned from Gardner was that "working with other people, working with yourself, knowing other people, is a form of intelligence." Hoerr's own motto is: "Who you are is more important than what you know."

M.I. has now spawned a burgeoning cottage industry of consultants and manuals and videotapes. Several publishers have an entire sideline of Gardneriana, and I sent away for material from several of them. One of the items I received was *Celebrating Multiple Intelligences,* a teachers' guide written by Hoerr and his staff at the New City School, one of the most highly regarded M.I. schools. The book consists of a series of lesson plans in the various intelligences, further divided according to the students' ages. In one exercise designed to stimulate the interpersonal intelligence of students from the first through third grades, children form a circle and throw a ball of string back and forth, each time saying something complimentary about the recipient. The "learner outcome" is: "Children will focus on expressing positive comments to peers who they may or may not know well." Every exercise comes with "M.I. Extensions" designed to stimulate some other intelligence—write songs about the activity, play charades to illustrate the activity, and, above all, talk about how you felt about the activity. The sensitivity toward the variety of children's abilities is connected to a broader preoccupation with diversity. In order to "look at issues of prejudice and discrimination relating to disabilities, race, gender, and religion," the teachers devised an experiment in which "each child spent six hours a day being blindfolded, wearing ear plugs, sitting in a wheelchair, or having limited use of arms and hands." It lasted five days.

Here we come to the heart of the problem with multiple intelligences—not as theory, but as practice. M.I. theory has proved powerful not because it's true but because it chimes with the values and presuppositions of the school world and of the larger culture. When theories escape into the world, they get used in ways that their inventors could scarcely have predicted or even approved. Gardner hasn't been quite sure where his responsibility lies in such matters. He told me that he cannot be the "policeman" of the world he set into motion, though he has, increasingly, been its poster boy. Gardner has begun to speak out against some of the more extreme uses of his theory, and critics like educational historian Diane Ravitch have urged him to do more. When I showed Gardner copies of some of the exercises in *Celebrating Multiple Intelligences,* he scrutinized them carefully, frowned, and said, "The only answer I can give to this is: I would certainly not want to be in a school where a lot of time was spent doing these things."

Gardner himself is a rigorous thinker, and he now takes pains to talk about "the school virtues." He often describes himself as a "disciplinarian," by which he means that he believes in the traditional academic disciplines. The intelligences, he says, are not academic ends in themselves, but means by which legitimate academic ends may be reached. For example, if a child is not particularly strong in "logical-mathematical" intelligence, the math teacher should seek a medium in which the child feels more comfortable—language or even physical movement. In *Multiple Intelligences,* a book of practical advice published in 1993, Gardner writes, "Any concept worth teaching can be approached in at least five different ways that, roughly speaking, map onto the multiple intelligences." The model school that he sketches in the book has much in common with progressive schools generally. Students work with one another as much as with the teacher; they design and carry out long-term projects rather than completing daily assignments; they seek to master concepts rather than absorb information; they spend time in real-world environments. What's different about an M.I. school is that it observes a rigorous equality among the intelligences—no "hierarchizing" of language and logic.

Whether that's desirable or not depends in part on whether you think the schools are turning out too many Dershowitz-like whiz kids or too few. Having visited several dozen schools over the last decade or so, I would suggest the answer is clearly "too few." Maybe in Japan, or even in France, are schools producing students who are too narrow; the problem in the United States is that students are too shallow. M.I. can, in theory, be a means of teaching deeper understanding, but it's at least as likely that it will be used in the service of a specious sense of "breadth." Chester Finn, an educational reformer and former Reagan administration official, describes M.I. pedagogy as the cognitive version of the multiculturalist view that school should offer a celebration of diversity. Harold Stevenson, a psychologist at the University of Michigan, says, "What they're trying to say is, 'You may not be able to do academic things, but you move well, or you're very good at music or spatial intelligence.'" Whatever Gardner himself intends, M.I. theory legitimizes the fad for "self-esteem," the unwillingness to make even elementary distinctions of value, the excessive regard for diversity, and the decline of diligence.

Gardner and other progressive educators are surely right that traditional pedagogy, at least as it is practiced in most schools, leads to superficial understandings and the confusion of recitation with real knowledge. Good teachers challenge their students at the deepest possible level; they understand that the mastery of facts and dates is a means to an end, not an end in itself. But it's a powerful means. And it may be better for schools to err on the side of too much of it rather than too little.

There are now hundreds of schools that claim to be based in whole or in part on M.I. pedagogy. Educational journals carry glowing accounts of schools "turned around" by M.I. A researcher working for Gardner says that she finds that trivial uses of the pedagogy are giving way to more serious ones. Gardner himself guessed that, if I were to visit 50 M.I. schools, "you'd see a lot more schools that are indistinguishable from other schools than you would schools that are Mickey Mouse"—not exactly a stirring defense. Still, he said, enough schools are using his principles wisely to demonstrate the potential power of M.I.

In the middle of this past school year, I spent a day at the Key Learning Center in Indianapolis, probably the most famous of the M.I. schools. I had expected Key to be one of those schools where kids learn everything in seven or eight ways, jumping up and down in math class and singing their way through English. In fact, the math and science classes I sat in on looked perfectly familiar. Still, M.I.'s influence was as conspicuous as the drawings of the intelligences that line the entrance corridor. Every student spends as much time on music and art as English or social studies. Students are not graded. They receive, instead, "pupil progress reports" in which their academic improvement, their level of motivation, and their "performance along the developmental continuum" are measured in terms that can't be plotted on invidious bell curves.

Peter Reynolds, a bright, mop-haired seventh-grader, was assigned to serve as my "docent." Peter talked about school in a way that I couldn't have imagined doing in seventh grade. What he liked about Key, he said, was the opportunity to "interact" with people, not only other kids, but also the adults in the school. Peter explained that every year, starting in kindergarten, students are expected to devise a project and present it to teachers and peers. In first grade, he had made a study of his pet rats and talked about how they reproduced, how they used their teeth, how they responded to different stimuli. All of the presentations were videotaped, so he had an archive of his work from the age of five.

Peter happened to be presenting his project that day. He had gone to Romania with his father and a friend, and he put a crude oak-tag map up on a stand, showed photographs of the trip, and talked about the people they had met. Most of it was pitched at the level of "it was really nice" and "it was really interesting." On the other hand, I was impressed by what Gardner would have called Peter's interpersonal intelligence. He was calm and forthright, and his classmates listened respectfully and asked questions. The whole school, in fact, had a very civilized and noncompetitive atmosphere; there was none of the waving of hands and shouting "me, me, me" that I remember from junior high. Then again, what's so terrible about a little self-aggrandizing intellectual enthusiasm at age 13?

The school did have a few semi-farcical touches. There was a "flow" room designed to foster the state of unselfconscious engagement that people attain at moments of peak creativity—a practice that rested on a theory devised by Mihaly Csikszentmihalyi, a psychologist who works closely with Gardner. Kids were playing computer games, "Parcheesi," or "Guess Who?"—the kind of activities I'm happy to have my seven-year-old do at home but wouldn't expect to be part of a curriculum. But the Key school was not absurd in the way that educational traditionalists imagine. It was a serious-minded place, and the kids I met seemed enthusiastic and engaged. On the other hand, if they were engaged in deep understanding, I must have missed it. The eighth-grade "linguistics" class I sat in on read through a passage in *Life on the Mississippi* without getting within hailing distance of its meaning. The school's ambitions almost seemed to be elsewhere—in fostering a sense of personal maturity, in a genuine commitment to music, in making the children conscious of their own strengths.

What the Key school is arguably about is the fostering of a new kind of child and thus of a new kind of person—less linear and more "well-rounded," less competitive and more cooperative. This is a monumental ambition, but it's actually not far from Gardner's own vision. Something grandiose lurks beneath Gardner's modesty

and care—that's why he insisted on using that provocative word, "intelligence." Back in Chicago, I heard him tell spell-bound special-ed teachers that we are living at the edge of a paradigm shift. "This is a new definition of human beings, cognitively speaking," he said. "Socrates defined man as a rational animal; Freud defined him as an irrational animal; what M.I. theory says is that we are the animal that exhibits the eight and a half intelligences."

Form at end of book

Issue 7 Summary

Educators often look to psychology to help them find better ways to educate children and adolescents. A theory such as Howard Gardner's theory of multiple intelligences is appealing for many reasons. It suggests that children who are unsuccessful at more traditional aspects of school learning, such as verbal or mathematical thinking, may succeed in other areas, such as music or movement. If we consider musical ability and bodily-kinesthetic ability to be types of intelligence—that is, if we agree that they are human abilities that schools should develop and society should value—then Gardner's theory makes sense. Our next step is to determine ways to "intelligently" apply his theory to how we organize schools and teach.

However, many educators reject the notion that musical, bodily-kinesthetic, visual, interpersonal, and intrapersonal abilities are the major concerns of schools; they also contend that, for students to be successful adults in the workforce, they need to develop their verbal and mathematical-logical thinking. They argue that the traditional view of intelligence developed because society places greatest value on verbal and mathematical-logical thinking.

WiseGuide Wrap-Up

In Section 1, we examined many of the issues in education; in section 2, we explored issues in psychology that pertain to education. Although it is frustrating that these issues are unresolved, our struggles to understand these issues highlight an exciting aspect of educational psychology: our goal is to improve schooling and teaching, and thereby to improve students' lives. While research on the brain may not have told us very much about how to teach, in time it probably will. We continuously try to understand how parents and teachers can best promote the psychological health of children (the "nurture" part of the nature-nurture debate). We seek to determine how (or whether) the various media affect children. We look to new theories that pertain to children's learning, such as Gardner's theory of multiple intelligences, and try to find out whether they can help us reach the goal of improving children's learning and social-emotional development.

R.E.A.L. Sites

This list provides a print preview of typical **Coursewise** R.E.A.L. sites. (There are over 100 such sites at the **Courselinks**™ site.) The danger in printing URLs is that web sites can change overnight. As we went to press, these sites were functional using the URLs provided. If you come across one that isn't, please let us know via email to: webmaster@coursewise.com. Use your Passport to access the most current list of R.E.A.L. sites at the **Courselinks** site.

Site name: Brains.Org: Practical Classroom Applications for Current Brain Research

URL: http://www.brains.org/

Why is it R.E.A.L.? This site presents research in psychology and neurology that relates to education. In addition to specific topics in neuropsychology (e.g., neural pathways), the site presents information on classroom applications (e.g., classroom management).

Key topics: brain research, neuropsychology, classroom environments

Try this: Click on "Classroom Environment." How does Gene Van Tassell define taxon memory? Van Tassell concludes that students encounter many difficulties due to education's emphasis on taxon memory. Name one of these difficulties.

Site name: Initiative for Educational Equity Committee

URL: http://www.mfrl.org/compages/aauw/gequity.html

Why is it R.E.A.L.? This is a site run by the Blacksburg, Virginia, branch of the American Association of University Women. It contains links to sites in the following areas: K–12 resources, gender equity projects, science and gender equity, and gender equity education and training.

Key topics: gender equity, sex differences

Try this: Click on "Expect the Best from a Girl." According to this site, is a girl's performance in school determined by nature or nurture? Go to "Surprising But True." Do you disagree with any of the statements?

section | The Diversity of Society

3

Learning Objectives

- Comprehend the causes and effects of achievement differences among Black and White students in American schools.

- Understand the issues surrounding multiculturalism as it is applied to schooling.

- Identify the arguments for and against bilingual education.

- Analyze the positions for and against the inclusion of students with disabilities in ordinary classrooms.

WiseGuide Intro

Diversity in society is by no means new; our society and many before it have struggled with the diversity of its people. Sometimes, the struggles have concerned religion, sometimes race, sometimes nationality. Some of these struggles have been brutal. What is different about the current era? As we enter the twenty-first century, we are increasingly aware that our diversity, while the source of countless conflicts and misunderstandings, is less important than our sameness as human beings with hopes, desires, and needs. But diversity presents challenges in many parts of society, including education. In education, we seek to give students opportunities to grow, and we seek to prepare them for adulthood. But do we provide opportunities equally to all? In Reading 19, Mano Singham examines the disparity between the academic achievement of Whites and Blacks in school.

Another challenge presented by diversity is determining what is taught in schools. According to many, one function of schools is to expose young people to the culture of our society; however, given our cultural diversity, whose culture do we present? Do we present the Anglo-American culture represented by the first English settlers in the Americas and their descendants? Do we present the cultures of the countless immigrant groups who contributed to the creation of society as we know it? One of the most burning questions in education today is how to address the multicultural nature of our society. In Reading 20, Louis Denti takes a stand on the issue of multiculturalism.

A related issue is the education of students whose native language is not English. How do we educate students who do not understand the language of the majority? Different sides of this problem, which is by no means unique to American schools, are explored in Readings 21 and 22.

Finally, we examine another aspect of diversity. Human beings vary not only in race, culture, ethnicity, and language but also in their level of ability. For a very long time, those whose ability in an area differed significantly from that of the majority were labeled "disabled" and very often received education in classes and even schools apart from their peers. Recently, the inclusion movement has taken root, based on the idea that the segregation of persons with disabilities infringes on their civil rights and is not healthy for either students with disabilities or their nondisabled age-mates. In Readings 23, 24, and 25, the inclusion movement is explored from a variety of angles.

As you see, the issue of diversity is multifaceted. It is also a particularly difficult issue to address, perhaps because diversity is related to difference and we are often uncomfortable with groups who are different from ourselves. Facing diversity requires facing our fears and sometimes our own inadequacies. To face diversity successfully, in education or elsewhere in our society, we need calmness, good will, and commitment to make society better.

Culture, Ethnicity, and Language

Questions

1. Once again, you are the secretary of education. The president asks you to advise her. Specifically, she wants to know (1) the causes of the achievement gap between Black and White students, (2) the effects of the achievement gap, and (3) what can be done to close the gap.

2. What are the arguments for and against following a multicultural approach in the classroom? Why is multicultural education such a contentious issue in American education?

3. Why did bilingual education come into being? What were its goals and how effective was it in reaching its goals? Why are some trying to dismantle it now?

Introduction

Most of us have several identities. We may simultaneously be a New Yorker, an Italian American, a Catholic, a female, a White person, and a member of Generation X. Or we might simultaneously be an African American, a Hispanic, a male, a Texan, and a baby boomer. In other words, we differ from one another in many dimensions, some of which are particularly important in education—but only because we deem these dimensions to be important.

The articles you will read explore the implications of three of these dimensions—racial group, cultural group, and language group—on education. Although educators have been struggling with the impact of diversity on education for several decades, the successes have been modest and the challenges are immense. Nevertheless, the goals—high-quality education and educational opportunity for all—are worth a continued effort.

The Canary in the Mine:
The Achievement Gap between Black and White Students

The educational achievement gap is real and has serious social, economic, and political consequences, Mr. Singham points out. But the situation is by no means hopeless, if we start looking at the problem in new ways and avoid simplistic one-shot solutions.

Mano Singham

Mano Singham is associate director of the University Center for Innovations in Teaching and Education and principal researcher in the Department of Physics, Case Western Reserve University, Cleveland, Ohio.

Shaker Heights is not your typical community. It is a small inner-ring bedroom suburb of Cleveland, covering an area of about five square miles and having a population of 30,000. It is a carefully planned city with tree-lined streets winding past well-maintained homes and manicured lawns, lakes, parks, and red-brick schools nestled in campus-like grounds. The city is about one-third African American and two-thirds white, with a sprinkling of other minorities. Although income levels in the city range from the poor (about 10% below the poverty level) to millionaires, the image of Shaker Heights is that of a primarily middle- and upper-middle-class community (median family income of $66,000) that is home to many of the academics, professionals, and corporate executives of all ethnic groups who work in the Cleveland area. It is also a highly educated community, with more than 60% of all residents over the age of 25 holding at least a bachelor's degree—a figure *three times* the national average.

Shaker Heights prides itself on the excellence of its school system, taxing itself voluntarily with one of the highest rates in the state of Ohio in order to maintain the wide range of academic and extracurricular programs that provide the students who take advantage of them with an education that would be the envy of any child in the nation. Hence the city tends to attract as residents relatively well-off people who seek both an integrated community and a high-quality education for their children. Every year, the school district sends off about 85% of its graduating seniors to four-year colleges, many of them prestigious, and boasts a remarkably high number of the National Merit Scholarship semifinalists, way out of proportion to the small size of its student enrollment (about 5,500).

But all is not well, and the problem is immediately apparent when you walk into classrooms. Although the school population has equal numbers of black students and white ones, in the highest-achievement tracks (the Advanced Placement sections) you find only a handful of blacks (about 10%), while the lowest-achievement tracks (called "general education") are populated almost exclusively by blacks (about 95%). When educational statistics are disaggregated by ethnicity, it is found that black Shaker Heights students on average do better than black students elsewhere, just as white Shaker Heights students do better than their counterparts in other school systems. The real puzzle has been why, although both communities have equal access to all the school district's educational opportunities, the academic performance of black Shaker Heights students lags significantly behind that of their white peers. For example, the average black SAT score in 1996 was 956 (compared to a national black average of 856), while the average for white students was 1198 (compared to a national white average of 1049).

This ethnic educational achievement gap is hardly news. It is a well-studied and well-established fact that, using almost any measure (the famous 15-point average I.Q. gap between blacks and whites sensationalized by *The Bell Curve*, SAT scores, college and high school grade-point averages, graduation and dropout rates), black students nationwide do not perform as well as whites.[1] While the phenomenon itself is indisputable, there is no clear consensus on the causes, and favored explanations seem to depend on where one stands on the ideological spectrum.

The so-called liberal interpretation is that this gap is the result of economic disparities between the two ethnic communities that can be traced back to the legacy of slavery and other forms of oppression that blacks have suffered. Support for this view (which I will call the socioeconomic model) comes from the fact that educational achievement correlates more strongly (although not perfectly) with economic status than with any other single variable. Proponents of this model argue that, since the black community lags badly behind the white in both income and wealth, the educational disparities are *caused* by the socioeconomic disparities. Once economic disparities disappear, proponents of this model say, educational (and other social) disparities will vanish along with them.

Those at the so-called conservative end of the ideological spectrum are not convinced that economic factors are the primary cause of black educational underachievement. As evidence, they point to the fact that other minority groups such as Asians, some of whom are economically worse off than blacks, excel in school. They believe that, while the legacy of slavery and segregation was indeed harsh, the civil rights legislation of the Fifties and Sixties has removed all legal roadblocks to black advancement and we have now achieved a color-blind society. This view leads them to conclude that various social pathologies within the black community (lumped under the euphemism "black culture") must be at fault. They point to unstable families; poor parenting skills; lack of drive and ambition; negative peer pressure and poor choice of role models; high levels of teenage pregnancies, drugs, and crime; and lack of parental involvement in their children's education as the causes of a lack of interest in education among black students.

Favored explanations for the achievement gap seem to depend on where one stands on the ideological spectrum.

Believers in this type of explanation (which I will call the sociopathological model) tend to lecture black communities constantly about the need for a wholesale spiritual awakening to traditional virtues and the work ethic. While they appreciate the hardships that blacks suffered in the past, their solution is to say, in effect, "Get over it. The real victims and perpetrators of that unjust system are dead. Stop looking to the past and claiming to be a victim. Pull yourself up by your bootstraps, and take advantage of what is now equally available to everyone." This group concedes that, while racial prejudice still exists, it is essentially a *personal* matter that should be dealt with on a personal level.

A third view (which I will call the genetic model) is best represented by Charles Murray and Richard Herrnstein, authors of *The Bell Curve,* who, after making the appropriate regretful noises to indicate their lack of racial prejudice, essentially conclude that the educational disparity is a fact of nature, the result of long-term evolutionary selection that has resulted in blacks' simply not having the genetic smarts to compete equally with whites. Instead of engaging in well-meaning, heroic, but ulti-

mately futile efforts to solve an inherently insoluble problem, the authors argue, the best thing to do would be to accept this situation and then determine how to minimize its adverse social consequences.

The good news is that there is little evidence for the belief that black students are somehow genetically inferior to whites and that this constitutes an insurmountable barrier to their ever achieving academic equality.[2] The further good news is that there are some very promising studies that indicate that the achievement gap in education can he narrowed dramatically and even eliminated. The bad news is that it is not going to be easy to achieve this goal. The problem needs to be addressed on many fronts—educationally, socially, and psychologically—and there is no single "magic bullet" that is going to take care of it.

The first thing to note is that there is one odd feature that characterizes the discussion of any social problem that is analyzed on the basis of how different ethnic groups compare. Statistics for whites are usually taken as a measure of the "natural" state of society, and black statistics are used as a measure of the problem. If the problem is viewed in this way, then the solution lies in getting black people to "act white," i.e., to adopt the values, behavior, attitudes, and mannerisms of white people, so that blacks will perform as well as whites. Much of the preaching of virtues to the black community about their social pathology (the sociopathological model) seems to have this belief as a basis.

There are many problems with this approach. One is that black people are not as impressed with the virtues of whites as whites are and see no need to emulate them. Given the behavior of whites during the time of slavery, to ask blacks to regard whites as role models for virtuousness seems presumptuous, to put it mildly. James Baldwin captured this difference in perception when he said in *The Fire Next Time,* "White Americans find it as difficult as white people elsewhere do to divest themselves of the notion that they are in possession of some intrinsic value that black people need or want. . . . [T]here is certainly little enough in the white man's public or private life that one should desire to imitate."[3]

It would also be presumptuous to assume that rejecting the white behavior model is an act designed merely to give perverse satisfaction to blacks, even though it might hurt their chances of economic and educational success in life. Researcher Signithia Fordham, in her studies of black high school students in Washington, D.C., found that there was a marked difference in attitudes toward academic and career success between the generation of blacks that came of age during the civil rights struggle and their children.[4]

For black parents, the success of any one black person in any new field was perceived also as a vicarious victory for the whole black community because that individual was opening doors that had hitherto been closed to blacks. Other blacks could then emulate the example of the pioneer and follow in his or her footsteps. Thus eventually the community as a whole could pull itself out of the miserable conditions that were the legacy of slavery. So the black community rejoiced when Thurgood Marshall became a Supreme Court justice, when Ralph Bunche became an undersecretary-general of the United Nations and a winner of the Nobel Prize, when Arthur Ashe became Wimbledon and U.S. Open tennis champion, and when others became lawyers, doctors, nurses, college professors, and other kinds of professionals and administrators. It seemed to be only a matter of time before all members of the black community would obtain their share of the American dream that had long been denied them.

There was a price that was paid by these trailblazers, though. They recognized that all eyes were on them to see if they would measure up. Ever mindful of their responsibility not to jeopardize the chances of those who were to come after them, these black pioneers had to prove themselves "worthy" in white eyes, and this was done by "acting white" (at least in their work environment), by adopting the values and behavior of the white-dominated establishment they were trying to penetrate. In his autobiography, Malcolm X speaks sardonically of what he calls these "firsts," black people who were hailed as the first to occupy any position that had previously been denied to blacks. He said that very often it was these people, even more than whites, who would vociferously condemn other blacks like himself who did not buy into the notion of having to act white in order to advance themselves and their community. But by and large, such "white" behavior was tolerated and excused by blacks as a temporary strategy for the long-term benefit of their community.

But Fordham found that young black people now, following Malcolm X's lead, see things quite differently. What they have observed is that the success of the pioneers did not breed widespread success. A few more blacks made it into the professions but nowhere near the numbers necessary to lift up the whole community. Fordham reports that young black people see the strategy of using individual success to lead to community success as a fatally flawed one. They have replaced it with a largely unarticulated but nevertheless powerfully cohesive strategy that is based on the premise that the only way that the black community as a whole will advance is if all its members stick together and advance together. This way they can keep their ethnic identity intact (i.e., not have to "act white"). Hence the attempt by any individual black to achieve academic success is seen as a betrayal because it would involve eventually conforming to the norms of white behavior and attitudes.

This view causes immense problems for those black students who have higher academic aspirations. Many are torn between wanting to achieve academic success because of their parents' expectations and sacrifices on their behalf and the natural desire to stay in step with their peers and retain important adolescent friendships. Many of them adopt a middle road, keeping their grades just high enough to avoid trouble at home and preserve good relations with their teachers but no more. Fordham calls their strategy "racelessness"—behaving in what they see as a race-neutral manner so as not to draw attention to themselves. They also tend to study alone and in secret so that they cannot be accused of breaking ranks with their peers. This pattern of isolated study leads to disastrous consequences when these same students confront the more challenging college environment.

By itself, Fordham's explanation of why black students underperform may not be sufficiently compelling. But Claude Steele of Stanford University (along with Joshua Aronson) has done research that indicates that other complementary factors contribute to poor academic performance by blacks.[5] Steele's research on college students at Stanford and the University of Michigan indicates that when students are placed in a situation in which a poor performance on a standardized test would support a stereotype of inferior abilities because of the student's ethnicity or gender, then the student's performance suffers when compared with those who do not labor under this preconception. For example, when black students and white ones were given tests that they were told measured their academic abilities, black students did worse than whites. But when a control group of black students and white ones were given the same test but were told that the test did not have any such significance but was merely a laboratory tool, the difference in performance disappeared. He calls this phenomenon "stereotype threat."

What is interesting about Steele's research results is that they do not apply only to black/white comparisons. The same phenomenon occurred with men and women. The women's performance deteriorated when they were told that the standardized mathematics test they were taking had shown gender differences, whereas the male/female difference disappeared in the control group when the women were told that the identical test had not shown any gender differences. The white men, who were outperforming black and women students, were themselves not immune to the stereotype threat. When they were told that the same tests were being used to compare their abilities with Asians, their performance deteriorated.

Another interesting fact that Steele uncovered is that the "threat" of stereotyping that depresses performance does not have to be very obvious. Just being required to check off their gender or ethnicity on the answer sheet was sufficient to trigger the weaker performance by the students. Steele concludes that the fear that a poor performance on a test will confirm a stereotype in the mind of an examiner imposes an anxiety on the test-taker that is difficult to overcome. Given the widespread suspicion that blacks cannot cut it in the academic world or that women are not good in math, both these groups enter any test-taking situation with a disadvantage compared with those who do not have this fear. Steele suggests that it is this fear that causes these groups to disinvest in education, to assert that it is not important and that they are not going to expend any effort on mastering it. That way, a poor performance is only a measure of the individual's lack of interest in the subject and is not a sign of his or her inability to master it.

Anthropologist John Ogbu's and other researchers' studies of the effects of minority/dominant relationships on academic performance are more complex.[6] They looked at studies of the performance of different ethnic minority groups in the same society (such as African Americans, Hispanics, Asians, and Native Americans in the U.S.) and of the same ethnic minority groups in different societies (such as Koreans in Japan and the U.S.). Their results indicate that the performance of any given minority depends on a complex interplay of factors, such as whether the minority is a voluntary one (such as Asians now and earlier generations of Jews, Irish, and Germans) or an involuntary one (such as blacks due to enslavement, Native Americans due to conquest, and Hispanics due to colonization), and the perceptions of the dominant community toward the minority. For example, Koreans and the Buraku (a tribe in Japan that is ethnically identical with other Japanese) do poorly in Japanese schools, where both groups are considered to be academically inferior. But members of the same groups excel when they come to the U.S., which tends to view any Koreans or Japanese (being Asian) as academic high fliers.

Ogbu points out the importance to academic performance of the perception of the relationship between effort and reward. People are more likely to work harder if they can see a benefit in return and have a realistic expectation of receiving that benefit. In the case of education, this link lies in the belief that educational effort leads to academic credentials, which in turn lead to gainful employment.

This effort/reward scenario lies at the basis of the white work ethic and forms an important component of the lectures delivered to blacks by those who adhere to the sociopathological view of underachievement. Ogbu points out that the effort/reward relationship is not at all obvious to blacks. For years blacks were denied employment and education commensurate with their efforts. It did not

matter how much they valued education or strove to master it; higher levels of education and employment were routinely denied them purely on the basis of their ethnicity. Hence it is unreasonable to expect them to see the work/credential/employment linkage as applying to them, as most whites do.

But it could be argued that this difference in perception is something that will disappear with time (or, as some might contend, should have disappeared by now if not for blacks' clinging to their "victim" status.) But Ogbu points out that there is a more pernicious effect still at work. He finds that the value of the "reward" lies very much in the eye of the beholder, because this perception is strongly affected by the group with which one compares oneself. Ogbu argues that members of voluntary minorities (i.e., the immigrant groups against whom blacks are routinely and adversely compared) judge their status and rewards against those of their peers *whom they left behind in their native country*. So even if they are working in lower-status jobs in the U.S. than those they left behind to come here, they tend to be earning more than their peers who stayed at home, and they also feel that their children (for whom they made the sacrifice to come to the U.S.) will have greater educational opportunities and chances for advancement than the children of their peers back home. Hence they have a strong sense of achievement that makes them strive even harder and instill these values in their children.

But blacks (an involuntary minority) have a different group as a basis for comparison. They have no reference points to groups outside the U.S. They compare their achievement with that of white people (usually suburban, middle-class whites), and they invariably suffer in the comparison. Ogbu says that in his interviews with "successful" blacks (however one measures that), it does not take long for the sentiment to be expressed that, of course, if they had been white, they would be even more successful, would have advanced more in their careers, or would have made more money. So for blacks, the perceived link between effort and reward is far weaker than it is for whites and voluntary minorities, and we should not be too surprised if the weakness of this link manifests itself in a lower commitment to academic effort.

The causes of black underachievement identified by Fordham, Steele, and Ogbu cannot simply be swept away by legislative or administrative action, by exhortations, or by identifying people with racial prejudice and weeding them out of public life. They lie in factors that are rooted deeply in history and that will not go away by themselves and may even worsen if not addressed. The good news is that there are specific *educational* strategies that provide hope for change.

One study originated around 1974 at the University of California, Berkeley, and was the result of an observation by a mathematics instructor named Uri Treisman.[7] He noticed (as had countless other college instructors) that black and Hispanic students were failing in the introductory mathematics course in far greater numbers than were members of any other ethnic group and were thus more likely to drop out of college. This occurred despite remedial courses, interventions, and other efforts aimed directly at this at-risk group. Treisman inquired among his colleagues as to the possible reasons for this phenomenon and was given the usual list of suspect causes: black students tended to come from homes characterized by more poverty, less stability, and a lack of emphasis on education; they went to poorer high schools and were thus not as well prepared; they lacked motivation; and so forth. Rather than accept this boilerplate diagnosis, Treisman actually investigated to see if it was true. He found that the black students at Berkeley came from families that placed an intense emphasis on education. Their parents took great pride in and were highly supportive of their going to college. Many of these black students had gone to excellent high schools and were as well prepared as any other group. There was also a wide diversity among them—some came from integrated middle-class suburban neighborhoods; others, from inner-city segregated ones. Clearly the conventional wisdom did not hold, and the cause of their poor achievement lay elsewhere.

What Treisman then did was to narrow his investigation to just two groups—blacks and the high-achieving ethnic Chinese minority. He studied all aspects of the two groups' lives to see what factors might be contributing to their hugely different performances, and what he found was interesting. He discovered that, while both blacks and Chinese socialized with other students in their group, the Chinese also *studied* together, routinely analyzing lectures and instructors, sharing tips and explanations and strategies for success. They had an enormously efficient information network for sharing what worked and what didn't. If someone made a mistake, others quickly learned of it and did not repeat it. In contrast, the black students partied together, just like the Chinese, but then went their separate ways for studying, perhaps as a result of the high school experience Fordham describes. This tendency resulted in a much slower pace of learning, as well as the suffering that comes with having to learn from mistakes. Black students typically had no idea where they stood with respect to the rest of the class, and they were usually surprised by the fact that they received poor grades despite doing exactly what they thought was expected of them, such as going to class, handing in all their assignments on time, and studying for as many hours as other students.

Treisman addressed this problem by creating a workshop for his mathematics students. In these workshops, students were formed into groups and worked on mathematics problems together. Discussion and sharing of information were actively encouraged and rewarded. By this means, Treisman sought to introduce to *all* his students (not just those who happened to chance upon this effective strategy) the value of group academic effort and sharing as methods of achieving academic success. One notable feature of this experiment was that the working groups were mixed ethnically and in terms of prior achievement. The second noteworthy feature was that the students were given *very challenging* problems to work on, much harder than the ones that they would normally have encountered in the regular courses.

The Chinese students, unlike the blacks, studied together, routinely analyzing lectures and sharing tips and strategies.

It is interesting that both these features, although they preceded Claude Steele's research, avoided triggering the stereotype threat identified by him. The ethnically mixed nature of the groups avoided the perception that this was a remedial program aimed at blacks, while the explicitly challenging nature of the problems posed to the students meant that there was no stigma attached to failing to solve them. Failure was simply due to the difficulty of the problems, not to membership in an ethnic group that was assumed to be incapable of achieving academic success. In addition, when students did succeed in solving a problem, they experienced a sense of exhilaration and power at having achieved mastery of something difficult, which, as anyone who has experienced it will testify, is the only real and lasting incentive to high achievement. What Treisman found was that, as a result of his workshops, black students' performance improved by as much as one letter grade.

Much research supports the effectiveness of Treisman's strategy. Traditional "remedial" courses designed for underachieving students are largely based on the assumption that poor performance is due to lack of adequate preparation: that weaker students are handicapped by a lack of so-called basic skills. Hence these courses tend to have a strong emphasis on drilling students on the basics. But what such courses ignore is that students fall behind academically for a variety of reasons, not the least of which is that they have not mastered the higher-level reasoning and problem-solving skills that are the prerequisites for success in real life. So even if you drill students in the basics so that they reach the same hypothetical starting line as others, they start falling behind again as soon as they encounter new material because they do not know how to process the new information efficiently. Even worse, the drilling methods often used in remedial courses bore the students (turning them off to education even more) and tend to reinforce the low-level thinking skills that caused them to fall behind in the first place at the expense of the higher-level ones, thus compounding the problem instead of solving it. On the other hand, if students are given interesting and challenging problems to work on, things that pique their interest and are relevant to their lives, they are more likely to acquire the so-called basic skills as a means to solving the problems of interest.

In his book *Color-Blind* Ellis Cose describes another success story of black education, this time at Xavier University, a historically black college in New Orleans.[8] This university took to heart the message of psychometrician Arthur Whimbey, who argued in *Intelligence Can Be Taught* that students can be taught to perform better academically by a suitably planned program that stresses the importance of higher-level thinking skills.[9] When the school adopted a Whimbey-inspired curriculum, incoming freshmen so improved their academic performance that Xavier is now the single biggest supplier of black graduates to medical schools, despite its relatively small enrollment. Once again it must be emphasized that what was stressed in this program was the challenging nature of the academic program, the drive for *excellence* as opposed to remediation.

I have argued here that perceiving the academic performance of white students as the norm and that of blacks as a measure of the problem naturally leads to the proposing of solutions that have as their basis the attempt to persuade blacks to "act white" or at least to adopt white values. But the implicit notion that black behavior and values are somehow inferior to whites' makes these solutions offensive and unacceptable to many blacks.

There is an even more serious objection to this strategy of trying to get everyone to adopt the "white ethic" as a means of reducing the educational achievement gap. It is that it might be masking the true nature of the problem by assuming that there is no real problem in the educational delivery system as such but only in the way that it is received by different groups: that is, black students don't respond to education in the proper manner.

An alternative explanation is that the primary problem lies not in the way black children view education but in the way we teach *all* children, black, white, or other. The traditional model of education is one that largely requires children to work alone or to listen to an instructor. It is a passive model, based on the assumption that extrinsic rewards (such as credentials and jobs) are sufficient motivators for students to go to school and learn. Education is regarded as medicine; it is good for you but not necessarily

pleasurable or worth doing for its own sake. Much emphasis is placed on teaching students "facts" that are unrelated to their interests or immediate experience but that they are told will be useful to them in the future. There is very little emphasis on exploiting the intrinsic curiosity that children have about the world around them or on using this as a springboard for challenging, self-motivated, and self-directed investigative studies.

Alternative, "active learning" methods of education (which have variants that come under the labels of "inquiry" or "discovery" learning) have as their primary motivator *intrinsic* rewards, the satisfaction that students experience when they, by their own efforts, solve some complex and challenging problem. Anyone who has struggled to understand a complex issue he or she cared deeply about and has succeeded knows the feeling of exhilaration and confidence in one's abilities that ensues. It is truly a high. Unfortunately, this happens far too rarely in education. Instead, most students (irrespective of gender or ethnicity) see the classroom as a place where they are made to learn material and jump through assessment hoops that have no meaning for them, with the carrot being rewarding employment far into the future.

Research indicates that active learning methods produce significant academic gains for students, with more on-task behavior in class. These methods also reduce the achievement gap—but not, as it might be feared, by "dumbing down" the curriculum or depressing the performance of traditional high achievers. These students gain too, but the most dramatic gains tend to be for those who are not well served by the traditional passive model (i.e., involuntary minorities and women). This is because these students are the ones who lagged behind more in the traditional classroom and thus have more room to improve their performance.[10]

Such a deep-rooted criticism of the current education system is hard for many people to accept, especially those who are already highly credentialed academically. After all, they reasonably point out, the system worked for me, and I became a success. In addition, the U.S. has become an economic, scientific, and technological superpower. So how could its education system be so bad?

The issue is not whether any given education system is good or bad, and framing the question in this way is to go down a blind alley. The issue is what fraction of the student population you want to achieve excellence. The fact is that there never was a majority of students "just like us." What is true is that there has always been a relatively small fraction of students (possibly as high as 25%) from families that expect them to pursue a college education. For this fraction, the links between effort, credentials, and rewards are sufficiently realistic and compelling to act as an extrinsic motivator for academic effort. But even in these families, many students sense that school is not a very interesting or challenging place, and they simply go through the motions, hoping to escape with just enough success to avoid parental censure before they enter the real world and do something meaningful with their lives. Once they do get into real jobs and are confronted with challenging problems, some of them soon develop the higher-level thinking skills required for success.

But in those communities and families in which the perception of the link between effort and reward is weaker (as is the case with low-income families of all ethnicities and with involuntary minorities), these extrinsic rewards become even less compelling as motivators for academic effort and excellence, and the students' performance suffers. In fact, the effort/reward link may actually work *against* education since life on the streets may seem to provide a more realistic expectation of material reward. As long as society requires only a small fraction of educated people and does not care about gender or ethnic or socioeconomic equity issues, then the present system of education is quite adequate. What the academic achievement gap may really be telling us is that, while the symptoms of the education system's ills are more clearly visible in the black community than in the white, there are fundamental problems with the way education is delivered to *all* students.

The academic achievement gap may really be telling us that there are fundamental problems with the way education is delivered to *all* students.

It used to be that coal miners took canaries into the mines as detectors of noxious gases. If the canary died, then the miners realized that they were in a region of danger and took the necessary precautions. The educational performance of the black community is like the canary, and the coal mine is the education system. The warning signals are apparent. But treating the problem by trying to make blacks "like whites" would be like replacing the canary in the coal mine with a bird that is more resistant to poisonous gases. It simply ignores the real problem.

While we cannot chance history, we should not try to dismiss it as irrelevant either. We must come to terms with its very real and serious consequences for our lives *now* if we are to go beyond shallow analyses of important problems such as the achievement gap in education. Such shallow analyses, in the long run, do more harm than good because they force even well-meaning people to choose between two unsavory options: either to adopt a race-neutral socioeconomic explanation that clashes with everyday experience (and is hence secretly rejected though lip service is paid to it) or to look for pathologies in the character or culture of the involuntary minority communities. Neither option reflects the reality.

The educational achievement gap is not an artifact. It is real and has serious social, economic, and political consequences. Its roots lie in complex and historically rooted ethnic relationships and characteristics. But the situation is by no means hopeless. We can be encouraged by very promising experiments that have narrowed this gap. But we have to start looking at the problem in new and deep ways, and we must avoid the temptation to seek simplistic one-shot solutions if we are going to make any real headway.

Notes

1. Richard J. Herrnstein and Charles Murray, *The Bell Curve* (New York: Free Press, 1994).
2. Mano Singham, "Race and Intelligence: What Are the Issues?," *Phi Delta Kappan,* December 1995, pp. 271–78; Stephen Jay Gould, *The Mismeasure of Man* (New York: Norton, 1981); and R. C. Lewonton, Steven Rose, and Leon J. Kamin, *Not in Our Genes* (New York: Pantheon, 1984).
3. James Baldwin, *The Fire Next Time* (New York: Dial Press, 1963), p. 108.
4. Signithia Fordham, "Racelessness as a Factor in Black Students' School Success," *Harvard Educational Review,* February 1988, pp. 54–84.
5. Claude M. Steele. "Race and the Schooling of Black Americans," *Atlantic,* April 1992, pp. 68–78; Claude M. Steele and Joshua Aronson, "Stereotype Threat and the Intellectual Test Performance of African Americans," *Journal of Personality and Social Psychology,* vol. 69, 1995, pp. 797–811; and David J. Lewin, "Subtle Clues Elicit Stereotypes' Impact on Black Students," *Journal of NIH Research,* November 1995, pp. 24–26.
6. See, for example, John Ogbu, "Immigrant and Involuntary Minorities in Comparative Perspective"; Yongsook Lee, "Koreans in Japan and the United States"; and Nobuo K. Shimahara, "Social Mobility and Education: Burakumin in Japan," in John Ogbu and Margaret Gibson, eds., *Minority Status and Schooling* (New York: Garland, 1991).
7. P. Uri Treisman, "Studying Students Studying Calculus," *College Mathematics Journal,* vol. 23, 1992, pp. 362–72.
8. Ellis Cose, *Color-Blind: Seeing Beyond Race in a Race-Obsessed World* (New York: HarperCollins, 1997).
9. Arthur Whimbey with Linda Shaw Whimbey, *Intelligence Can Be Taught* (New York: Dutton, 1975).
10. David W. Johnson, Roger T. Johnson, and Karl A. Smith, *Active Learning: Cooperation in the College Classroom* (Edina, Minn.: Interaction Book Co., 1991); Mark Keegan, "Psychological and Physiological Mechanisms by Which Discovery and Didactic Methods Work." *School Science and Mathematics,* vol. 95, 1995, pp. 3–10; Chet Meyers and Thomas B. Jones, *Promoting Active Learning* (San Francisco: Jossey-Bass, 1993); Jane Butler Kahle, "Systemic Reform: Challenges and Changes," *Science Educator,* Spring 1997, pp. 1–5; and Jane Butler Kahle and Arta Damnjanovic, "The Effect of Inquiry Activities on Elementary Students' Enjoyment, Ease, and Confidence in Doing Science: An Analysis by Sex and Race." *Journal of Women and Minorities in Science and Engineering,* vol. 1, 1994, pp. 17–28.

Form at end of book

Multiculturalism and Schools:
The Struggle toward Open-Mindedness

Is "educating for diversity" worthwhile? Or is it just more smoke and mirrors?

Louis Denti

Louis Denti, Ph.D., is a professor in the Division of Special Education and Rehabilitative Services, San José State University, California. He directs the Alternative Education Program and co-directs the Center on Applied Ethics in Education.

Recently, a close friend of mine made an off-the-cuff remark engendering a sharp, somewhat caustic reply from me. He said, "Differences will always be viewed as negative in public schools. Those educators who don't realize this basic truth are naive and deluded by the fantasy of multiculturalism."

I furrowed my brow and attacked. "Do you mean race, gender, nationality, sexual orientation, disability, dressing styles, personal appearance, or the way people act? Do schools inadvertently or consciously support this negative point of view?"

He backed away and then replied sarcastically, "The norms of the system dictate that a narrow band of students will always be at the top of the class and all other students will be measured against them. Those well-defined norms will shut out most of the lower-ability students. Sorry, but appreciation for cultural and ethnic differences will never be fully realized. Just look around. . . . Do you really see that much change or just 'do-gooder' lip-service?"

I immediately launched into a diatribe about new dynamic instructional models that support and encourage teaching from a multicultural perspective, teacher education programs that emphasize cross-language acquisition, and school-to-work programs that guarantee low-income minority students jobs upon completing high school. "All these changes and many more," I pleaded vociferously, "embrace cultural diversity." I was desperate in my need to maintain a degree of optimism and not succumb to his *fait accompli*.

He laughed, shrugged, and arrogantly pronounced, "Someday you will understand that multiculturalism, though interesting, is but a passing fancy in American education. We must be realists and quit trying to solve all the world's problems. Some kids will never fit in, just as some kids will always fail. It will never change." Just as the conversation began to intensify, he indicated he had to leave for an appointment.

After my friend departed, I felt angry and disheartened because I was not able to articulate my concerns in an intelligible way. I realized that we were both white males and our ideologies about cultural differences were rooted, in not only our upbringing, but our experiences and interactions with persons from different ethnic, linguistic, and cultural backgrounds. I was trying to grapple with the complexity of multiculturalism and its importance in shaping our future educational landscape. My friend, on the other hand, was not allowing for what he perceived to be another politically correct fad. He was opposed—his position was fixed.

Reckoning with the Phenomenon of Multiculturalism

Shelby Steele likens multiculturalism to a social policy of compensatory deference. Basically, people of color are shown deference to compensate for their sufferings—a maneuver, according to Steele, that makes deference synonymous with social virtue. As Steele states, "Social reform becomes a series of expedient devices—group preferences, quotas, set-asides, redistricting, race and gender norming."[1]

One readily conjures up an archetypal image of sin and salvation, wherein liberals atone for victimizing the poor by compassionate excrescence. Steele levels a blow against what he terms the "vernacular of social virtue—diversity, multiculturalism, pluralism, role models, self-esteem and the endless stream of euphemisms associated with political correctness. . . . It is a deferential language that enables us to signal our social virtue through talk alone. Compensatory deference is what defines political correctness, just as its absence defines incorrectness," states Steele.[2]

Steele reminds us to define our terms. Rhetoric, political posturing, newspeak, and reciting *mea culpas* in a confessional will not right the wrongs so evident in our society toward persons who are different because of race, class, ethnicity, or disability. Adopting an ultraconservative agenda may offset liberal excesses, but it also increases tension between the races, producing more intolerance. Laws such as California's Proposition 187, which denies illegal immigrants educational opportunities and social services, and Proposition 209, which bans racial and gender preferences in public education, hiring, and contracting, are harsh reminders of the high price persons who are different by virtue of their race or ethnicity pay in American society.

Adopting an ultraconservative agenda may offset liberal excesses, but it also increases tension between the races, producing more intolerance.

A backlash to liberalism, evident in California, will be the mainstay on the political front for several years. However, button-down tactics without a vision can be disempowering, vindictive, and out of step with the times. As the acclaimed author and historian Carlos Cortes states, "Currently ninety-seven out of every one hundred births [worldwide] are either Asian, African, or Latino."[3] One would be hard-pressed to ignore the changing landscape of worldwide population trends and the resulting effect on interaction patterns between minority and majority groups. As a matter of fact, majority and minority status becomes a moot issue when one considers the changing demographics in America. Jesus Garcia and Sharon Pugh and Robert Lichter indicate that by the year 2000 whites will constitute only 55.9 percent of the U.S. population, down from 75.5 percent in 1980.[4] This is consistent with international trends that indicate that by the turn of the century 5 billion of the 6 billion people on earth will be nonwhite.

In *Culture of Complaint: A Passionate Look into the Ailing Heart of America*, Robert Hughes points out, "Any effort to discover the historical realities of the West, historians now acknowledge, must begin with multiculturalism—that is, above all, by recognizing that the West was not a terra nullius into which the whites marched; that it was a highly charged arena in which various cultures, the invading Anglo-American and the already resident Indian and Spanish, impacted on one another, never with simple results."[5] The same highly charged arena is as evident today as was true in centuries past. Only nowadays, a thin veneer of pseudo-acceptance covers the fear and anxiety caused by the mere mention of the politically charged term multiculturalism. Sanding that veneer with a barbed tongue and carelessly coating the historical landscape with separatism, racism, and "what-about-me-isms" (Hughes's term) seemingly has become "patriotically correct." However as Hughes points out, "Cultural separatism within this republic is more a fad than a serious proposal; it is not likely to hold, but if it did, it would be an educational disaster for those it claims to help, the young, the poor and the black. It would be a gesture not of 'empowerment' but of 'emasculation.' "[6]

We can try to legislate it away, but eventually we as a nation will have to deal with it. We will have to come to terms with our disparate perceptions, beliefs, and attitudes.

Cortes indicates that America cannot run from a multicultural world, though we have tried by fleeing to suburbia and building walled cities and communities. We must learn to make the best of it, which will require a renewed interest in the democratic ideals of egalitarianism—*e pluribus unum*.[7] My friend shudders at the thought of such high-minded ideals.

Multiculturalism is not a patina phenomenon, a gloss on the political landscape. It envelops us and maps our consciousness. We can try to legislate it away, but eventually we as a nation will have to deal with it. We will have to come to terms with our disparate perceptions, beliefs, and attitudes.

Fundamentalism versus Multiculturalism

One usually equates fundamentalism with a conservative religious agenda. However, Webster defines it as a movement or point of view characterized by rigid adherence to fundamental or basic principles. In his book *Care of the Soul*, Thomas Moore defines fundamentalism as a defense against the overtones of life, the richness and polytheism of imagination.[8] My friend's views on culture and ethnicity fit this definition rather nicely. He winnows out elements of despair and hopelessness, casting out my naiveté on his sea of doubt. His axiomatic formulations—difference is seen as negative, norms of the system never change, idealists are throwbacks to another time—challenge my penchant for community building as well as my belief that harmonious interactions with persons from diverse backgrounds are possible in public schools and the broader community.

One must attest that poetic images of living in harmony are definitely tainted by the stark realities painted by John Ogbu and Maria Matute-Bianchi, wherein they describe this country's present social approach to several immigrant and minority populations as "caste-like." They claim that certain populations are perceived by the majority as forming a layer of U.S. society that is not expected to excel academically or economically.[9] Accordingly, academic underachievement and social withdrawal, when viewed as inevitable, fuel a more fundamentalist and separatist position of "us" and "them." Statements such as the following abound: "We give 'em all these benefits, and look at the way they live." "I have friends who are (fill in the ethnic blank), who have made something of themselves." "I don't think we should give them a free ride to college." "Half the time they throw away their school lunches while their moms and dads drive around in big cars."

These caustic and prejudicial statements offer simplistic answers for what many perceive as disturbing trends emanating from cultural diversity. In some ways they place things in boxes and categories of right and wrong so the issues are more or less black and white. "Someday you will understand that multiculturalism is yet another passing fancy," is my friend's cutting reminder. A reminder that tears at the richness of experience and expression gained from difference; the richness gained from seeing beyond the outward manifestations of color, race, ethnicity, class, gender, sexual orientation, disability, and peering into the soul of the person, the community—into the soul of hope.

By disrupting various assumptions about culture, race, class, and ethnicity through knowledge, experience, and dialogue, the "soul of hope" begins to emerge, promoting an enhanced understanding of these delicate, threatening, and complex issues. Challenging a person's perspectives about race, ethnicity, and culture with questions such as "How did you come to know that to be true?" "Do you have some experience with what you just described?" and "Where did you learn the ideas you just shared?" can help ferret out the difference between what a person knows to be real and what a person says is real. I wish I had been prepared with those very questions in my brief discourse with my friend. Perhaps the interaction would have taken a different course. I do know that as a result of the interaction I have been rethinking how schools address the demands of an ever-changing ethnic and cultural mix in schools.

Culture and Voice in Schools

Within schools there has been a narrow fascination with persons from different cultures. The American archetype—white, middle class child from an urban or suburban city—still permeates the educational psyche. Though all demographic projections indicate that poor, urban, and racial minority students will increasingly dominate public schools in the next decade and well into the

21st century, the nostalgic belief that an ideal student exists creates a false sense of security and reality for educators. Of course the construction of that image helps to maintain a degree of sanity for educators—for any deviance from the institutional order appears as a departure from reality. When we talk about persons from different races, ethnic backgrounds, or disability groups in schools, the conversation usually revolves around where to place or how to deal with these individuals, versus honoring their contributions and involvement within the fabric of the institution. One needs only to observe myriad classes for limited English, bilingual, special needs, at-risk, and Chapter 1 students, along with the fragmented services offered these individuals, to gain a quick understanding of what second-class citizenry looks like in schools. Finding a place for treatment becomes more important than creating a service-delivery model that incorporates difference as a normative vision of the school.[10]

As Gay states, "Many educators mistakenly continue to equate the inclusion of diversity in school programs with lowering standards of performance and to equate student learning differences with academic deficiencies or cultural inferiorities. They, therefore, either insist upon all students having identical learning experiences to avoid charges of discrimination, or designing a variety of special purpose programs to serve the diverse needs of learners in isolation from the instructional mainstream."[11] Friere, in his book *Pedagogy of the Oppressed,* indicates that language and culture constitute the curriculum. To include language and culture as a "gift" denies one voice and a stake in the process of shaping one's educational path. Therefore, not including multiculturalism as a salient aspect of any instructional endeavor in public schools robs children of the gift of hearing each other's language and attending to their voices.[12] As Nadine Ruiz points out, to think that voice and language are one and the same is a delusion. The richness of one's language is strengthened by the power of one's voice. That voice, which derives from the family and community, must be allowed a forum in our public schools."[13]

Curriculum and Instruction Based on Multiculturalism

It goes without saying that teachers create the social environment for learning for children in school classrooms. The way one teaches determines whether students will access the curriculum and profit from instruction. If materials and methods are ethnically and culturally insensitive or inappropriate, students find it difficult to identify with their backgrounds and share experiences about their lives. According to Gay, "The instructional demand should be consistent with such principles of learning as continuity, similarity, interest, motivation, and individualization. The curriculum design message of these principles is that students are more likely to learn and retain better what they learn when their school experiences resemble and build upon their out-of-school experiences."[14]

The way one teaches determines whether students will access the curriculum and profit from instruction.

Moreover, understanding how to develop appropriate curriculum to maximize and honor diversity requires a basic grasp of American education, multicultural education, and curriculum development. Gay explains that American education is skills specific and based on instrumental value. For instance, history is taught to further understand the past and forecast the future. The intent of multicultural education, on the other hand, is to "improve the academic success of a broader spectrum of students, to develop knowledge and appreciation of cultural pluralism, and to better equalize social, economic, and political opportunities among ethnic and cultural groups."[15] Hooks elaborates further,

Multiculturalism compels educators to recognize the narrow boundaries that have shaped the way knowledge is shared in the classroom. It forces us all to recognize our complicity in accepting and perpetuating biases of any kind. Students are eager to break through barriers to knowing. They are willing to surrender to the wonder of relearning and learning ways of knowing that go against the grain. When we, as educators, allow our pedagogy to be radically changed by our recognition of a multicultural world, we can give students the education they desire and deserve.[16]

Learning and instruction do not have to be compromised for students who are poor or of a different race.[17] Nothing better exemplifies this than the movie *Stand and Deliver*. The love of learning for the teacher, Jaime Escalante, along with his high expectations, challenges his Latino students to rise above their destiny as second-class citizens and take their rightful place alongside their ancestors—the great Mayan mathematicians. Escalante's relentless pressure and encouragement to ensure student success reinforces the notion that strength of conviction and intention by a teacher can overcome many institutional and societal odds. He exemplifies what might be possible in schools and communities that value and honor diversity. He challenges ad hominem assumptions about intelligence, ability, and determination in a group of students who had been "written off" by his high school faculty and administration.

Unfortunately, Escalante constantly had to prove to a reticent faculty that his methods of teaching would empower his students to compete in the broader society. Like Escalante, when teachers attempt to change instructional

arrangements to accommodate diversity in their classrooms, other teachers question the viability and rationale of departing from the traditional curriculum. The innovators are judged to be shortchanging the average or high-achieving student. As a result, they feel abandoned by other teachers and leaders and traditional sources of support. Moreover, state and district standards do not allow for an issues-oriented curriculum that facilitates the teaching of critical-thinking skills through ethnicity, gender, and social class perspectives. When teachers are required to teach to irrelevant standards, instead of involving students in a meaning-centered curriculum, instruction suffers from "pedagogical emaciation." Students, in essence, are starved for instruction that is relevant. Ask any high school student, "What did you learn in school today, yesterday, or last week?" and you are lucky to get a shrug or a grunt.

The innovators are judged to be shortchanging the average or high-achieving student. As a result, they feel abandoned by other teachers and leaders and traditional sources of support.

Would it not be wonderful to ask the same question and hear a high school sophomore launch into a passionate discussion about the pros and cons of democracy as it relates to immigration laws? Imagine this sophomore writing letters to legislators; interviewing students from different ethnic backgrounds that may be affected by immigration laws; talking to parents about how immigration has shaped their family destiny; role-playing conservative and liberal talk-show hosts; writing a major group research paper on the topic; or taking a trip to the mayor's office to discuss the way the city deals with immigration. The teacher in this scenario would provide direct instruction on the topic as needed to ensure that students comprehend the basic issues. Using primary source materials, the teacher could enliven the discussion even further. This teacher could act as a co-investigator trying to learn as much as possible with the students. Student excitement would thus be directly related to the teacher's excitement, and the learning so contagious that a high school student might even initiate a conversation with his or her parent about the class (radical thought).

For as Banks indicates: "When content is organized around key interdisciplinary concepts such as culture, communication, and values, the teacher can structure lessons and units that facilitate the inclusion of content from diverse cultures as well as content that will help students to develop the knowledge, values, commitments, and skills needed to participate in effective personal, economic, and civic action."[18] Similarly, Mark Lacelle-Peterson and Charlene Rivera offer a few suggestions regarding access for all diverse learners. Referring to English language learners (ELLs) and educational equity, they state, "Meaningful participation in learning, implies both full participation in well-taught, challenging classes that aim to meet the same educational goals set for all students. The goals for students and the criteria by which their success in meeting those goals will be measured must be made explicit."[19] They also recognize that "like monolingual English-speaking students, ELLs need both access to higher level courses and the guidance and encouragement to take them."[20] However, as Linda Darling-Hammond cautions, "Unless educational assessment and teaching truly re-forms around equity and access to educational opportunity, testing will limit students' life choices and their avenues for demonstrating competence."[21]

Societal roadblocks are constantly being erected to minimize the value of schooling and undermine the credibility of the teacher.

Of course it would be shortsighted to think that pedagogy per se could overcome the obstacles confronting today's educators regarding quality curriculum and instruction. Societal roadblocks are constantly being erected to minimize the value of schooling and undermine the credibility of the teacher. However, if the teacher has high, yet realistic, expectations for all students, and is willing to create a learning environment extolling the virtues of multiculturalism, then students will, at the very least, feel as if they have a voice in their own learning. At best, they will sharpen their critical-thinking skills, develop an enhanced social perspective, learn about and experience social justice, and actively create a world they want to live and participate in. Real education for real students. . . . Not education divorced from the intricacies of living, nor biased in favor of a single point of view. I can see my friend smirking at the foregoing line. Ah! disdain for idealism. You never know, he may be right given the persistence of discrimination in schools today.

Conclusion

In many ways multicultural education, paradoxically, seeks to unify as well as allow for diversity. This paradox requires an ebb and flow of discourse in order to find a common ground of expression and action. Multicultural education, like liberatory education, calls for active participation, whether that be in overcoming oppression through literacy programs like Paulo Friere's phonics and written composition approaches for peasants in Brazil, or rewriting American history to reflect differing racial, ethnic, and cultural contributions. Shelley F. Fishkin says, "We

must not allow ourselves to be drawn into outmoded debates. The old battle lines are irrelevant. 'Traditional' American culture has always been multicultural. Our teaching must take into account our increasingly complex understanding of what our common culture is and how it evolved. Doing so will force us to examine how an unequal distribution not of talent but of power permitted a blatantly false monocultural myth to mask and distort the multicultural reality."[22]

Mihaly Csikszentmihalyi, in his insightful book *The Evolving Self,* echoes a similar value when he states, "If there are to be a thousand years longer in which we will evolve, however, it will be necessary to find better ways to build selves. . . . And despite greater individuality, it will be a self identified with the greatest good—not only with kin and country, but with humanity as a whole, and beyond humanity, with the principle of life itself, with the process of evolution. It is difficult to see at this point how humanity can survive otherwise."[23] Some eighty years ago, the philosopher Henri Bergson believed this evolution would be spontaneous, contrary to a designed evolutionary process. He coined the term *élan vital* to express "a prolific unity, of an infinite richness, superior to any that the intellect could dream of."[24] It is in that *élan vital* and process of evolution that the spirit of multiculturalism finds its way, and will continue to do so, even when the forces of monoculturalism try to wall it out literally and then figuratively.

Education for diversity encompasses virtues such as respect for persons, civility, integrity, and care. It is these virtues that give us a sense of unity as citizens. Teaching about tolerance for difference is not enough. We must embrace the virtues of respect and care for others and include these teachings in our institutions and homes in order to make us stronger as a community, nation, and global village.

As for my friend and me: we will continue to struggle toward openmindedness, railing and bristling against one another's perceptions on multiculturalism and schools. Who knows, we might agree to disagree—or even compromise!

Notes

1. Shelby Steele, "How Liberals Lost Their Virtue over Race," *Newsweek,* January 1995, 41.
2. Ibid.
3. Carlos Cortes, "Keynote Address on Multiculturalism," (San Jose State University College of Education Dean's Retreat, Asilomar, Calif., 1994).
4. Jesus Garcia and Sharon Pugh, "Multicultural Education in Teacher Preparation Programs," *Phi Delta Kappan* (November 1992): 214–219, and Robert L. Lichter, "The Role of the Faculty in Meeting the National Need for African-American, American Indian, and Latin Scholars," in *Introduction to the Stony Brook Conference Proceedings,* ed. M. Adams and E. Wadsworth (Stony Brook, N.Y.: State University of New York, 1988).

5. Robert Hughes, *Culture of Complaint: A Passionate Look into the Ailing Heart of America* (New York: Time Warner Co., 1994), 127–128.

6. Ibid., 153.

7. Cortes, "Keynote Address."

8. Thomas Moore, *Care of the Soul* (New York: Harper Perennial, 1992).

9. John U. Ogbu and Maria E. Matute-Bianchi, "Understanding Sociocultural Factors: Knowledge, Identity and School Adjustment," in *Beyond Language: Social and Cultural Factors in Schooling Language Minority Students* (Los Angeles: Office of Bilingual Education, California State Department of Education, Evaluation, Dissemination, and Assessment Center, California State University, 1986).

10. Louis Denti and Michael S. Katz, "Escaping the Cave to Dream New Dreams, A Normative Vision for the Field of Learning Disabilities," *Journal of Learning Disabilities* 28, no. 7 (1995): 415–424.

11. Geneva Gay, "Designing Relevant Curricula for Diverse Learners," *Education and Urban Society* 20, no. 4 (1988): 327–340.

12. Paulo Friere, *Pedagogy of the Oppressed,* trans. M. Bergman-Ramos, (New York: Herder & Herder, 1970).

13. Nadine T. Ruiz, personal communication, 20 September 1997.

14. Gay, "Designing Relevant Curricula," 331.

15. Ibid., 332.

16. bell hooks, *Teaching to Transgress* (New York: Routledge, 1994), 44.

17. Flora I. Ortiz, Hispanic-American Children's Experiences in Classrooms: A Comparison between Hispanic and Non-Hispanic Children," in *Class, Race and Gender in American Education,* ed. L. Weiss (Albany, N.Y: State University of New York Press, 1988).

18. James A. Banks, "A Curriculum for Empowerment, Action, and Change," in *Empowerment through Multicultural Education,* ed. C. Sleeter (Albany, N.Y.: State University of New York Press, 1991), 133.

19. Mark W. Lacelle-Peterson, and Charlene Rivera, "Is It Real for All Kids? A Framework for Equitable Assessment Policies for English Language Learners," *Harvard Educational Review* 64, no. 1 (1994): 55–75.

20. Ibid.

21. Linda Darling-Hammond, "Performance-based Assessment and Educational Equity," *Harvard Educational Review* 64, no. 1 (1994): 5–30.

22. Shelley F. Fishken, "The Multiculturalism of 'Traditional Culture,'" *The Chronicle of Higher of Education,* vol. XLI, no. 26 (1995): 48.

23. Mihaly Csikszentmihalyi, *The Evolving Self* (New York: Harper Perennial, 1994), 82.

24. Rupert A. Sheldrake, *The Presence of the Past: Morphic Resonance and the Habits of Nature* (New York, Times Books, 1988), 311–312.

Form at end of book

Language Wars:
Spanish Speakers Fight to Overturn Bilingual Education

Andrew Phillips

In California

With a touch of defiance and no shortage of pride, Alice Callaghan calls herself a "flaming street activist." She has been arrested a dozen times or so (she's lost count) protesting the Vietnam War, standing up for illegal immigrants, and defending the rights of homeless people in Los Angeles's vast skid row. She is, in short, no one to mess with, something she is proving again with her latest cause: dismantling a controversial educational program that she says keeps poor Spanish-speaking kids trapped in poverty. From a storefront community centre in the heart of the city's garment district, Callaghan has spurred a movement to do away with California's system of bilingual education. It is the latest hot-button issue to confront the voters of the state that so often sets political trends for the rest of the United States. And if the polls are right, they will follow her lead in a ballot next week—and support a measure to eliminate a system once seen as a fundamental right of California's fast-growing Latino population.

Callaghan is originally from Calgary but has been in Los Angeles for 40 years—much of it as an Episcopal priest working with Spanish-speaking immigrants. At the centre she runs, called Las Familias del Pueblo, dozens of squealing children tear around as they wait for their parents to finish work in the sweatshops nearby. Almost no one speaks English. Callaghan acknowledges that ending bilingual education—which in California means teaching primarily in Spanish—is an unusual cause for her. It allies her with conservatives who are uncomfortable with the rising influence of Spanish-speakers, and pits her against Latino activists who see eliminating bilingual programs as yet another right-wing attack on their community. But for Callaghan, the issue is clear: the parents who come to Las Familias know that in America, English is the language of success. "They don't want their kids selling tamales or cleaning offices," she says. "They want something better for them." It was, in fact, Mexican immigrants themselves who began the current drive against bilingual education.

The debate could have turned ugly. California's recent history has been scarred by bitter controversies over such issues as eliminating social benefits for illegal immigrants (passed in 1994) and doing away with affirmative action for minorities (adopted in 1996). Now, emotions on both sides are rising as Californians prepare to vote on June 2 on a raft of measures—including Proposition 227, the initiative to end most bilingual education. But the surprise is that the debate has been relatively civil. And for some analysts, an important part of the reason is that California's Latinos are acting less and less like a minority under siege. In some areas—including Los Angeles—they are nearly the majority, and surveys show that most will support Proposition 227. "We were a beleaguered minority," says Gregory Rodriguez, a researcher at the Pepperdine Institute for Public Policy in Malibu. "Today, we're a potential majority, and we're starting to feel our power."

In fact, after decades of staying on the margins of American political and economic life, the 30 million Americans of Hispanic background are influential and fashionable as never before. Census projections show that they will surpass blacks as the biggest American minority group by 2005, and will form fully one-fifth of the U.S. population by 2035. Marketers have discovered their $500-billion purchasing power—up 67 per cent since 1990. Major corporations are pouring money into advertising campaigns aimed at Latinos, fuelling a growth in Hispanic advertising agencies (there are now 160, up from half a dozen in 1980). New magazines are popping up—such as *People en Español and Latina,* a glossy quarterly aimed at young Hispanic women. All across Los Angeles, billboards proclaim that the city's No. 1 TV station for news is Spanish-language KMEX—flagship of the national Univision network. Business is so good that Univision's share price more than doubled in the past year.

Politicians, too, have woken to the importance of the Latino vote. The four leading candidates for governor of

By Andrew Phillips, *Maclean's,* June 1, 1998.

California last week staged the first-ever statewide debate on Spanish-language TV (they debated in English and were simultaneously translated into Spanish). Republicans, especially, are worried that their past support for measures widely seen as anti-Hispanic under Gov. Pete Wilson may doom them among the fastest-growing sector of the electorate. "The trend is obvious and the political danger is real," California Republican strategist Stuart Spencer wrote in a memo to party leaders. The party's response: it named a 27-year-old Latino, Mike Madrid, as its statewide political director.

Hispanic power is evident in many key states where national elections are decided—New York, Texas, Florida, Illinois and New Jersey. But nowhere is it more obvious that in California, whose fight over bilingual education is being watched carefully by politicians and educators nationwide. If Proposition 227 passes, they say, it could provoke similar measures in other parts of the United States. Like many such issues, it is about much more than education—ethnicity, class, culture, and how best to integrate the second-biggest wave of immigration this century into the American mainstream. And it reflects a seismic shift in the ethnic makeup of California.

Statewide, Latinos make up nearly 30 per cent of the population, with blacks at 7 per cent and Asians at 9.1 per cent. But the Latino community is growing faster than the others, fuelled by immigration and a high birthrate. Los Angeles County, 80-per-cent white as recently as the late 1960s, now has no ethnic majority. Hispanics have long spilled out of traditional barrios like East Los Angeles, where English signs are almost as rare as in east-end Montreal and billboards for Maxwell House coffee read, "*Bueno hasta la última gota*" (Good to the last drop). But, just as important, U.S.-born Latinos are moving quickly into the middle class and fleeing the city for the suburbs. A 1996 study by Rodriguez of the Pepperdine Institute showed that half own their own homes and have family incomes over $50,000. Overall, Latino incomes are still only two-thirds those of whites and just behind those of blacks. But the averages are pulled down by mixing in new immigrants with those born in the United States. "We've been led to believe what screwups we are," says Rodriguez, "but when you take out the immigrant generation, Latinos are moving up like other groups."

It is not the newly comfortable Latinos, however, who most concern Alice Callaghan. For all the economic gains U.S.-born Hispanics are enjoying, the new immigrants from Mexico and Central America who pour into Southern California still face little but poverty. The men and women who send their children to Las Familias typically take home only about $200 for a week's worth of sewing clothes in the surrounding factories. Almost all are in the United States illegally, but it was they who sparked

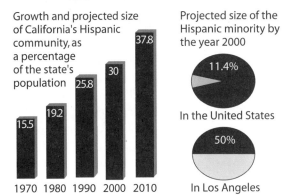

A NEW POWER IN NUMBERS

Growth and projected size of California's Hispanic community, as a percentage of the state's population

1970: 15.5
1980: 19.2
1990: 25.8
2000: 30
2010: 37.8

Projected size of the Hispanic minority by the year 2000

11.4%
In the United States

50%
In Los Angeles

Source: U.S. Department of Commerce, Bureau of the Census.

the fight against bilingual education. In 1996, about 90 of them pulled their children out of the nearby Ninth Street Elementary School because the bilingual program they were in was failing to teach them English. Like most of the 410,000 pupils in California's so-called bilingual classes, they were being taught almost entirely in their native language—in this case, Spanish.

The school refused to switch them into English classes, so the parents staged a two-week boycott with Callaghan's help. It drew statewide headlines and forced the school to change. One of the parents, 33-year-old Fredesvinda Angel, who came to Los Angeles from Mexico 10 years ago, explained through an interpreter that her daughter, Jessica, was losing the little English she had picked up the longer she stayed in school. "She learns Spanish at home," said Angel. "The important thing is that she has to learn English at school, so she can go on and get a good job."

Their boycott drew the attention of a Silicon Valley entrepreneur named Ron Unz, a onetime Republican candidate for governor. He contacted Callaghan, and used his own money (about $1 million so far) to start a campaign to do away with bilingual education, which he has called "completely illogical, if not loony." His campaign, dubbed "English for the children," gathered almost half a million signatures to put Proposition 227 on next week's ballot. It would abolish bilingual education, and instead put students with limited English into one year of English immersion before moving them into regular classes.

The irony is that bilingual education was launched in the late 1960s in California as a way of easing children with little or no English into the state's school system. And since 80 per cent of them were Spanish-speaking, it became inextricably entwined with a drive by Latino nationalists to boost their language and culture. Today, about 1.4 million students in California's schools, a quarter of the total, speak only limited English—more than any other state. The theory was that they would spend a short time being taught in their native tongue before being moved into the English system.

But as the years dragged by, many children ended up in bilingual programs for most of their school careers—often spending almost all day in Spanish. And many English-speaking students were directed into bilingual classes simply because they had Spanish names. Evidence mounted that even many Latino children born and raised in the United States were graduating unable to compete in English. "Kids are coming out with diplomas that mean nothing," says Henry Gradillas, a former principal of a tough high school in East Los Angeles who is campaigning for Proposition 227. "They're born here and they end up competing for the lousiest jobs with new immigrants straight from Mexico."

On the other side, most Latino organizations and teachers' unions say abolishing bilingual classes will have disastrous results—forcing Spanish-speaking children into an all-English environment before they are ready. Bilingual education, they say, is being scapegoated for the failures of California's much-criticized public school system. And Unz's Proposition 227 is a blunt instrument: it will force all school boards to adopt the same solution instead of tailoring programs to local conditions. "It's throwing the baby out with the bathwater," says Antonio Villaraigosa, the 45-year-old Speaker of the California legislature and the state's highest-ranking Hispanic official. "It's another wedge issue that divides and polarizes people."

Villaraigosa himself is a prime example of how California's Latinos are leveraging their newfound influence. Until recently, their increasing numbers were not reflected at the polls. Many Hispanic immigrants did not become U.S. citizens, but the emotional campaigns to deny benefits to illegal immigrants and end affirmative action galvanized them. They felt under attack, and defended themselves by taking out citizenship and registering to vote. More Hispanics were elected to office, and the most successful ones, such as Villaraigosa, are reaching beyond ethnic politics. He started out as a poor kid in East L.A., with an abusive father who left the family when Antonio was 5; at 15 he had "Born to raise hell" tattooed on his right arm, and at 20 he was acquitted on an assault charge. Now, the tattoo is long gone. "My son started to notice it, so I had it removed. And yes, it was painful," Villaraigosa said in an interview. He calls himself "a politician who happens to be Latino, not a Latino politician. You can't be ethnic-based any more. In the California of the future there will be no majority. You have to be a coalition-builder."

Others who have made the difficult journey out of the barrio without the help of bilingual education are passionately opposed to abolishing it. "Ultimately, the children will be harmed," says Antonia Hernandez, a lawyer and president of the Mexican American Legal Defense and Educational Fund. Hernandez, who grew up speaking Spanish at home, today serves on a host of distinguished boards of directors and is among the new Latino professional class that is helping to reshape California. She does not want today's kids to go back to the hardship she experienced, growing up in East Los Angeles as the daughter of working-class Mexican immigrants. She met her first Hispanic teacher in Grade 6. "I made it in spite of the [English-only] system. I didn't really learn to think in English until law school. Before then I used to translate everything into Spanish and back into English," she recalls. "Count all the kids that didn't make it. Don't count me."

These days, though, her views are increasingly under attack—even among Hispanics. Edward Zapanta lives only six kilometres from his boyhood home in East Los Angeles, but it might as well be another country. Now a neurosurgeon in an upper-middle-class neighborhood of Pasadena, just north of Los Angeles, he sits on the boards of two major corporations, the Times Mirror Co. and Southern California Edison, and is a trustee of the University of Southern California.

Unlike many Latinos today, Zapanta grew up speaking English at home. He learned Spanish later, to understand his many Spanish-speaking patients, and confesses to speaking it poorly. His wife, Norene Murray, is an Anglo, and none of his four children speaks Spanish. Zapanta takes pride in the success of Hispanics, but has little time for nationalist arguments. He supports doing away with ethnic preferences in universities and does not support bilingual education. Latino children, Zapanta argues, "are living here. They will have to compete in English. Spanish should be kept alive at home." That kind of unsentimental thinking may not please Hispanic leaders more concerned with culture than economics. But these days, it's the majority view among Latinos determined to seize control of their future.

With Anne Gregor in Los Angeles.

Form at end of book

Bilingual Education:
The Controversy

Our commonly held notion of how earlier generations of immigrants were educated—often used as the chief argument in support of English immersion—is a myth, Mr. Rothstein reveals.

Richard Rothstein

Richard Rothstein is a research associate of the Economic Policy Institute, Washington, D.C. This article is adapted from a chapter in his book, The Way We Were? *(Century Foundation Press, 1998), and is reprinted with permission from the Twentieth Century Fund/Century Foundation, New York, N.Y. The book is available from the Brookings Institution, 1775 Massachusetts Ave. N.W., Washington, D.C. 20036; ph. 800/275-1447. ©1998, Twentieth Century Fund/Century Foundation.*

Bilingual education, a preferred strategy for the last 20 years, aims to teach academic subjects to immigrant children in their native languages (most often Spanish), while slowly and simultaneously adding English instruction.[1] In theory, the children don't fall behind in other subjects while they are learning English. When they are fluent in English, they can then "transition" to English instruction in academic subjects at the grade level of their peers. Further, the theory goes, teaching immigrants in their native language values their family and community culture and reinforces their sense of self-worth, thus making their academic success more likely.

In contrast, bilingual education's critics tell the following, quite different, story. In the early 20th century, public schools assimilated immigrants to American culture and imparted workplace skills essential for upward mobility. Children were immersed in English instruction and, when forced to "sink or swim," they swam. Today, however, separatist (usually Hispanic) community leaders and their liberal supporters, opposed to assimilation, want Spanish instruction to preserve native culture and traditions. This is especially dangerous because the proximity of Mexico and the possibility of returning home give today's immigrants the option of "keeping a foot in both camps"—an option not available to previous immigrants who were forced to assimilate. Today's attempts to pre-serve immigrants' native languages and cultures will not only balkanize the American melting pot but hurt the children upon whom bilingual education is imposed because their failure to learn English well will leave them unprepared for the workplace. Bilingual education supporters may claim that it aims to teach English, but high dropout rates for immigrant children and low rates of transition to full English instruction prove that, even if educators' intentions are genuine, the program is a failure.

The English First Foundation, a lobbying group bent on abolishing bilingual education, states that most Americans "have ancestors who learned English the same way: in classrooms where English was the only language used for all learning activities."[2] According to 1996 Republican Presidential nominee Bob Dole, the teaching of English to immigrants is what "we have done . . . since our founding to speed the melting of our melting pot. . . . We must stop the practice of multilingual education as a means of instilling ethnic pride, or as a therapy for low self-esteem, or out of elitist guilt over a culture built on the traditions of the West."[3]

Speaker of the House Newt Gingrich chimed in as well:

If people had wanted to remain immersed in their old culture, they could have done so without coming to America. . . . Bilingualism keeps people actively tied to their old language and habits and maximizes the cost of the transition to becoming American. . . . The only viable alternative for the American underclass is American civilization. Without English as a common language, there is no such civilization.[4]

This viewpoint has commonsense appeal, but it has little foundation in reality.

Bilingual Education: The History

Despite proximity to their homeland, Mexican Americans are no more likely to reverse migrate than were Europeans in the early 20th century. One-third of the immigrants who came here between 1908 and 1924 eventually abandoned America and returned home.[5]

What's more, the immigrants who remained did not succeed in school by learning English. During the last great wave of immigration, from 1880 to 1915, very few Americans succeeded in school, immigrants least of all. By 1930, it was still the case that half of all American 14- to 17-year-olds either didn't make it to high school or dropped out before graduating. The median number of school years completed was 10.

Far from succeeding by immersing themselves in English, immigrant groups did much worse than the native-born, and some immigrant groups did much worse than others. The poorest performers were Italians. According to a 1911 federal immigration commission report, in Boston, Chicago, and New York 80% of native white children in the seventh grade stayed in school another year, but only 58% of Southern Italian children, 62% of Polish children, and 74% of Russian Jewish children did so. Of those who made it to eighth grade, 58% of the native whites went on to high school, but only 23% of the Southern Italians did so. In New York, 54% of native-born eighth-graders made it to ninth grade, but only 34% of foreign-born eighth-graders did so.[6]

A later study showed that the lack of success of immigrants relative to the native-born continued into high school. In 1931, only 11% of the Italian students who entered high school graduated (compared to an estimated graduation rate of over 40% for all students). This was a much bigger native/immigrant gap than we have today.

While we have no achievement tests from that earlier period by which to evaluate relative student performance, I.Q. tests were administered frequently. Test after test in the 1920s found that Italian immigrant students had an average I.Q. of about 85, compared to an average for native-born students of about 102. The poor academic achievement of these Italian Americans led to high rates of "retardation"—that is, being held back and not promoted (this was the origin of the pejorative use of the term "retarded").

A survey of New York City's retarded students (liberally defined so that a child had to be 9 years old to be considered retarded in the first grade, 10 years old in the second grade, and so on), found that 19% of native-born students were retarded in 1908, compared to 36% of Italian students. The federal immigration commission found that the retardation rate of children of non-English-speaking immigrants was about 60% higher than that of children of immigrants from English-speaking countries.[7] The challenge of educating Italian immigrant children was so severe that New York established its first special education classes to confront it. A 1921 survey disclosed that half of all (what we now call) "learning disabled" special education children in New York schools had Italian-born fathers.[8]

As these data show—and as is the case today—some groups did better than others, both for cultural reasons and because of the influence of other socioeconomic factors on student achievement. If Italian children did worse, Eastern European Jewish children did better. This is not surprising in light of what we now know about the powerful influence of background characteristics on academic success. In 1910, 32% of Southern Italian adult males in American cities were unskilled manual laborers, but only one-half of 1% of Russian Jewish males were unskilled. Thirty-four percent of the Jews were merchants, while only 13% of the Italians were. In New York City, the average annual income of a Russian Jewish head-of-household in 1910 was $813; a Southern Italian head-of-household averaged $688.[9]

But even with these relative economic advantages, the notion that Jewish immigrant children assimilated through sink-or-swim English-only education is a nostalgic and dangerous myth. In 1910, there were 191,000 Jewish children in the New York City schools; only 6,000 were in high school, and the overwhelming majority of these students dropped out before graduating. As the Jewish writer Irving Howe put it, after reviewing New York school documents describing the difficulties of "Americanizing" immigrant children from 1910 to 1914, "To read the reports of the school superintendents is to grow impatient with later sentimentalists who would have us suppose that all or most Jewish children burned with zeal for the life of the mind."[10] There may have been relatively more such students among the Jewish immigrants than in other immigrant communities, Howe noted, but they were still a minority.

Immersing immigrants in an English-language school program has been effective—usually by the third generation. On the whole, immigrant children spoke their native language; members of the second generation (immigrants' native-born children) were bilingual, but not sufficiently fluent in English to excel in school; members of the third generation were fluent in English and began to acquire college educations. For some groups (e.g., Greek Americans), the pattern more often took four generations; for others (e.g., Eastern European Jews), many in the second generation may have entered college.

This history is not a mere curiosity, because those who advocate against bilingual education today often claim that we know how to educate immigrant children because we've done it before. However, if we've never successfully educated the first or even second generation of children from peasant or unskilled immigrant families, we are dealing with an unprecedented task, and history can't guide us.

To understand the uniqueness of our current challenge, compare the enormous—by contemporary standards—dropout rate of New York City Jewish students in 1910 with that of Mexican students in the Los Angeles school district today. Like New York in 1910, Los Angeles now is burdened with a rising tide of immigrants. In 1996, there were 103,000 Hispanic students in grades 9–12 in Los Angeles (out of the city's total K–12 Hispanic population of 390,000). Hispanic high school students were about 26% of the total Hispanic student population in Los Angeles in 1996,[11] compared to 3% for Jews in New York in 1910 (only 6,000 high school students out of 191,000 total Jewish enrollment). In Los Angeles today, 74% of Mexican-born youths between the ages of 15 and 17 are still in high school; 88% of Hispanic youths from other countries are still in attendance.[12] More than 70% of Hispanic immigrants who came to the United States prior to their sophomore year actually complete high school (compared to a 94% high school completion rate for whites and a 92% rate for blacks).[13] English immersion programs for Jews early in this century (and certainly similar programs for Italians) cannot teach us anything that would help improve on today's immigrant achievement or school completion, much of which may be attributable to bilingual education programs, even if imperfectly administered.

If the notion is misleading that English immersion led previous generations of immigrants to academic success, so too is the claim that bilingual education repudiates the assimilationist approach of previous immigrants. In reality, today's Hispanics are not the first to seek bicultural assimilation. Some 19th- and early 20th-century European immigrants also fought for and won the right to bilingual education in the public schools.[14] Native-language instruction was absent from 1920 until the mid-1960s only because a fierce anti-German (and then anti-immigrant) reaction after World War I succeeded in banishing it from American classrooms. Even foreign-language instruction for native-born students was banned in most places. If Chicago's Bismarck Hotel found it necessary to rename itself the "Mark Twain," it should not be surprising that bilingual education programs were also abolished.

Today's Hispanics are not the first to seek bicultural assimilation.

Before World War I, immigrant groups often pressed public schools to teach children in their native language. The success of these groups depended more on whether adult immigrant activists had political power than on a pedagogical consensus. The immigrants' objective, as it is today, was to preserve a fragment of ethnic identity in children for whom the pull of American culture seemed dangerously irresistible. In this, they were supported by many influential educators. William Harris, the school su-

perintendent in St. Louis and later U.S. commissioner of education, argued for bilingual education in the 1870s, stating that "national memories and aspirations, family traditions, customs and habits, moral and religious observances cannot be suddenly removed or changed without disastrously weakening the personality." Harris established the first "kindergarten" in America, taught solely in German, to give immigrant students a head start in the St. Louis schools.[15]

Nineteenth-century immigrant parents were often split over the desirability of bilingual education, as immigrant parents are split today. Many recognized that children were more likely to succeed if schools' use of the native language validated the culture of the home. But others felt that their children's education would be furthered if they learned in English only.

The first bilingual public school in New York City was established in 1837 to prepare German-speaking children for eventual participation in regular English schools. The initial rule was that children could remain in German-language instruction only for 12 months, after which they would transfer to a regular school. But the German teacher resisted this rule, believing that, before transferring, the children needed more than the limited English fluency they had acquired after a year of German instruction. The record is unclear about how often the rule was stretched.

Many immigrant children, not just Germans, did not attend school at all if they could not have classes in their native language. In his 1840 address to the New York legislature, Gov. William Seward (later Lincoln's secretary of state) explained that the importance of attracting immigrants to school—and of keeping them there—motivated his advocacy of expanded native-language instruction: "I do not hesitate to recommend the establishment of schools in which [immigrant children] may be instructed by teachers speaking the same language with themselves." Only by so doing, Gov. Seward insisted, could we "qualify . . . [them] for the high responsibilities of citizenship."

Buoyed by Seward's endorsement, Italian parents in New York City demanded a native-language school as well, and in 1843 the Public School Society established a committee to determine whether one should be established. The committee recommended against an Italian-language school, claiming the Italian community was itself divided. "Information has been obtained," the committee stated, "that the more intelligent class of Italians do not desire such a school, and that, like most [but not, apparently, all] of the better class of Germans, they would prefer that those of their countrymen who come here with good intentions should be Americanized as speedily as possible."[16]

Bilingual education, though sometimes controversial, was found nationwide. In Pennsylvania, German

Lutheran churches established parochial schools when public schools would not teach in German; in 1838, Pennsylvania law converted these German schools to public schools. Then, in 1852, a state public school regulation specified that "if any considerable number of Germans desire to have their children instructed in their own language, their wishes should be gratified."[17]

In 1866, succumbing to pressure from politically powerful German immigrants, the Chicago Board of Education decided to establish a German-language school in each area of the city where 150 parents asked for it. By 1892 the board had hired 242 German-language teachers to teach 35,000 German-speaking children, one-fourth of Chicago's total public school enrollment. In 1870, a public school established in Denver, Colorado, was taught entirely in German. An 1872 Oregon law permitted German-language public schools to be established in Portland whenever 100 voters petitioned for such a school. Maryland, Iowa, Indiana, Kentucky, Ohio, and Minnesota also had bilingual education laws, either statewide or applying only to cities with large immigrant populations. In Nebraska, enabling legislation for bilingual education was enacted for the benefit of German immigrant children as late as 1913.[18]

There was considerable variation in how these programs arranged what we now call the "transition" to English. In St. Louis, Harris' system introduced English gradually, beginning in the first grade. The 1888 report of the Missouri supervisor of public instruction stated that "in some districts the schools are taught in German for a certain number of months and then in English, while in others German is used part of the day and English the rest. Some of the teachers are barely able to speak the English language." Ohio's 1870 rules provided that the lower grades in German-language public schools should be bilingual (half the instructional time in grades 1 through 4 could be in German), but in grades 5 through 8 native-language instruction had to be reduced to one hour a day. Baltimore permitted public schools in the upper grades to teach art and music in German only, but geography, history, and science had to be taught in both English and German. In some Midwestern communities, there was resistance to any English instruction: an 1846 Wisconsin law insisted that public schools in Milwaukee must at least teach English (as a foreign language) as one academic subject.[19]

While Germans were most effective in demanding public support for native-language instruction, others were also successful. In Texas in the late 19th century, there were seven Czech-language schools supported by the state school fund. In California, a desire by the majority to segregate Chinese children seemed to play more of a role than demands by the Chinese community for separate educa-tion. San Francisco established a Chinese-language school in 1885; the city later established segregated Indian, Mongolian, and Japanese schools.[20]

San Francisco's German, Italian, and French immigrants, on the other hand, were taught in their native languages in regular public schools. Here, bilingual education was a strategy designed to lure immigrant children into public schools from parochial schools where they learned no English at all. According to San Francisco's school superintendent in 1871, only if offered native-language instruction could immigrant children be brought into public schools, where, "under the care of American teachers," they could be "molded in the true form of American citizenship."[21]

Support for bilingual education was rarely unanimous or consistent. In San Francisco, the election of an "anti-immigrant" Republican school board majority in 1873 led to the abolition of schools in which French and German had been the primary languages of instruction and to the firing of all French- and German-speaking teachers. After protests by the immigrant community, bilingual schools were reestablished in 1874. In 1877, the California legislature enacted a prohibition of bilingual education, but the governor declined to sign it. William Harris' bilingual system in St. Louis was dismantled in 1888, after redistricting split the German vote and the Irish won a school board majority.[22]

Support for bilingual education was rarely unanimous or consistent.

In 1889, Republican Gov. William Hoard of Wisconsin sponsored legislation to ban primary-language instruction in public and private schools, claiming the support of German immigrant parents. The *Milwaukee Sentinel* published a front-page story about "a German in Sheboygan County . . . who sent his children away to school in order that they might learn English." The father, reported the *Sentinel,* complained that "in the public schools of the town, German teachers, who . . . did not know English . . . had been employed . . . , [and] he felt it essential to the welfare of his children, who expected to remain citizens of this country, to know English."[23]

But both the newspaper and Wisconsin's Republican politicians had misjudged the immigrants' sentiments. In response to the anti-bilingual law, enraged German Americans (who had previously supported Republican candidates) mobilized to turn the statehouse over to Democrats and to convert the state's 7-to-2 Republican majority in Congress to a Democratic majority of 8-to-1. The Democrats promptly repealed the anti-bilingual education law.

An almost identical series of events took place in Illinois, where formerly Republican German American voters mobilized in both East St. Louis and Chicago to elect a liberal Democrat, Peter Altgeld, governor in 1890, largely because of his bilingual school language policy. These upheavals in two previously safe Republican states played an important role in the election of Democrat Grover Cleveland as President in 1892. Nonetheless, the controversy continued, and in 1893 the *Chicago Tribune* began a new campaign against German-language instruction. In a compromise later that year, German instruction was abolished in the primary grades but retained in the upper grades, while Chicago's mayor promised German Americans a veto over future school board appointments to ensure that erosion of primary-language instruction would not continue.[24]

But these controversies ended with World War I. Six months after the armistice, the Ohio legislature, spurred by Gov. James Cox, who was to be the Democratic Presidential candidate in 1920, banned all German from the state's elementary schools. The language posed "a distinct menace to Americanism," Cox insisted. The *New York Times* editorialized in 1919 that, although some parents "want German to be taught [because it] pleases their pride . . . , it does not do their children any good." Within the following year, 15 states in which native-language instruction had flourished adopted laws requiring that all teaching be in English. By 1923, 35 states had done so.[25] Only when Nebraska went so far as to ban native-language instruction in parochial as well as public schools did the Supreme Court, in 1923, strike down an English-only law.[26]

During the next 30 years, bilingual instruction had its ups and downs, even where English was not the native language. In 1950, Louisiana first required English, not French, to be the language of public school instruction. In the Southwest, where teaching in Spanish had long been common, the practice continued in some places and was abolished in others. Tucson established a bilingual teaching program in 1923, and Burbank established one in 1931. New Mexico operated bilingual schools throughout most of the 20th century, up until the 1950s. The state even required the teaching of Spanish to English-speaking children in elementary school. But in 1918, Texas made teaching in Spanish a crime, and, while the law was not consistently enforced (especially along the Mexican border), as recently as 1973 a Texas teacher was indicted for not teaching history in English.[27] In the same year, Texas reversed itself and adopted bilingual education as its strategy.

When bilingual education began to re-emerge in the 1970s—spurred by a Supreme Court finding that schools without special provisions for educating language-minority children were not providing equal education—the nation's memory of these precedents had been erased. Today many Americans blithely repeat the myth that, until the recent emergence of separatist minority activists and their liberal supporters, the nation had always immersed its immigrant children in nothing but English and this method had proved its effectiveness.

Bilingual Education: Mixed Evidence

This mixed history, however, does not prove that bilingual education is effective, any more so than English immersion or intense English-language instruction. To an unbiased layperson, the arguments of both advocates and opponents of bilingual education seem to make sense. On the one hand, it's reasonable to insist that children who don't speak English continue their education in a language they understand in history, literature, math, and science, while they learn English. It's also reasonable to expect, however, that this might make it too tempting to defer English-language instruction. Moreover, the best way to do something difficult—e.g., making the transition to English—is simply to do it without delay. It makes sense to acknowledge that children may adapt better to school if the school's culture is not in conflict with that of the home. But some immigrant parents may be more intent on preserving native culture for their children than are the children themselves.

Modern research findings on bilingual education are mixed. As with all educational research, it is so difficult to control for complex background factors that affect academic outcomes that no single study is ultimately satisfying. Bilingual education advocates point to case studies of primary-language programs in Calexico, California; Rock Point, Arizona; Santa Fe, New Mexico; New Haven, Connecticut; and elsewhere that show that children advance further in both English and other academic subjects when native-language instruction is used and the transition to English is very gradual. Opponents point to case studies in Redwood City and Berkeley, California: in Fairfax, Virginia; and elsewhere that prove that immersion in English or rapid and intensive English instruction is most effective.[28] Overall, the conflicting evidence from these case studies does not suggest that abolition of bilingual education or even the substitution of parental choice for pedagogical expertise in determining whether bilingual approaches should be used would improve things much.

The problem is especially complex because not only economic factors but also generational variation apparently affects the achievement of immigrant youths. In

1936, the principal of a high school in New York City that enrolled large numbers of Italian immigrants wrote:

The problem of juvenile delinquency . . . baffles all the forces of organized society. . . . The highest rate of delinquency is characteristic of immigrant communities. . . . The delinquent is usually the American-born child of foreign-born parents, not the immigrant himself. Delinquency, then, is fundamentally a second-generation problem. This intensifies the responsibility of the school.[29]

The same is true today. The challenge now facing immigrant educators is that academic achievement for second-generation Hispanic and Asian children is often below that of children who arrive in the U.S. as immigrants themselves.[30] Many of these children of the second generation seem to speak English, but they are fully fluent in neither English nor their home language. Many of their parents, frustrated that their own ambition has not been transmitted to their children, may become convinced that only English immersion will set their children straight, while others seek bilingual solutions to prevent the corruption of American culture from dampening their children's ambition.

In the absence of persuasive evidence, the issue has become politicized. In a country as large as ours, with as varied experience, there is virtually no limit to the anecdotes and symbols that can be invoked as substitutes for evidence.

Opponents of bilingual education promote Hispanic parents to the media when they claim they want their children to learn English without bilingual support; the clear implication is that only liberal ideologues and separatists support native-language instruction. These claims, like those circulated by the *Milwaukee Sentinel* a century ago, may not reflect the feelings of most parents. And the technology of teaching a new language to immigrant children is complex; both bilingual education advocates and opponents claim their goal is full English literacy as rapidly as possible. But there's no reason to expect that politicized parent groups are the best judges of language acquisition research.

There are also successful adult immigrants who brag of their English fluency, acquired either with or without bilingual education. As always, such anecdotal evidence should be treated with caution. Richard Rodriguez' autobiography, *Hunger of Memory,* describes his successful education in an English-only environment. But Rodriguez, unlike most immigrants, was raised in a predominantly English-speaking neighborhood and was the only Spanish speaker in his class.[31] His experience may be relevant for some immigrants, but not relevant for many others.

Whichever method is, in fact, more effective for most immigrant children, there will be many for whom

the other method worked well. It may be the case that immigrant children's social and economic background characteristics should affect the pedagogy chosen. Even if some Russian Jewish immigrants did not require bilingual education to graduate from high school, perhaps Italians would have progressed more rapidly if they'd had access to bilingual instruction. Today, the fact that some (though not all) Asian immigrants seem to progress rapidly in school without native-language support provides no relevant evidence about whether this model can work well for Mexican or Caribbean children, especially those low on the ladder of socioeconomic status and those whose parents have little education. Nor does it tell us much about what the best pedagogy would be for Asians who generally do less well in school, such as Hmong, Laotian, and Cambodian children.[32]

It is certain, however, that the American "melting pot" has never been endangered by pluralist efforts to preserve native languages and cultures. Bilingual instruction has *never* interfered with the powerful assimilationist influences that overwhelm all children whose parents migrate here. And this is equally true of Spanish-speaking children today.

After the last 20 years of bilingual education throughout America, Spanish-speaking children continue to assimilate. From 1972 to 1995, despite rapidly accelerating immigration (more Hispanic youths are first-generation immigrants today than 20 years ago), the Hispanic high school completion rate has crept upward (from 66% to 70%). Hispanic high school graduates who enroll in college jumped from 45% to 54% (for non-Hispanic whites, it's now 64%). And the number of Hispanic high school graduates who subsequently complete four years of college jumped from 11% to 16% (for non-Hispanic whites, it's now 34%).[33] A study of the five-county area surrounding Los Angeles, the most immigrant-affected community in the nation, found that from 1980 to 1990, the share of U.S.-born Hispanics in professional occupations grew from 7% to 9%, the share in executive positions grew from 7% to 10%, and the share in other administrative and technical jobs grew from 24% to 26%.[34] Overall, 55% of U.S.-born Hispanics are in occupations for which a good education is a necessity, in an area where bilingual education has been practiced for the last generation.

Perhaps we can do better. Perhaps we would do better with less bilingual education. But perhaps not. All we can say for sure is that the data reveal no apparent crisis, and the system for immigrant education with which we've been muddling through, with all its problems, does not seem to be in a state of collapse.

The best thing that could happen to the bilingual education debate would be to remove it from the political realm. Soundbite pedagogy is no cure for the complex interaction of social, economic, and instructional factors that determine the outcome of contemporary American schools.

Notes

1. Technically, "bilingual education" refers to all programs designed to give any support to non-English-speaking children, including programs whose main focus is immersion in English-speaking classrooms. In public debate, however, the term generally refers to only one such program, "transitional bilingual education (TBE)," in which native-language instruction in academic subjects is given to non-English speakers. In this article, I use the term in its nontechnical sense to refer only to "TBE" programs.
2. Web site, English First Foundation: http://englishfirst.org.
3. Mark Pitsch. "Dole Takes Aim at 'Elitist' History Standards," *Education Week,* 13 September 1995, p. 18.
4. Newt Gingrich, *To Renew America* (New York: HarperCollins, 1995), pp. 161–62.
5. Irving Howe, *World of Our Fathers* (New York: Simon and Schuster, 1983), p. 58.
6. Michael R. Olneck and Marvin Lazerson, "The School Achievement of Immigrant Children: 1900–1930," *History of Education Quarterly,* Winter 1974, pp. 453–82, Tables 3, 5, 6.
7. David K. Cohen, "Immigrants and the Schools," *Review of Educational Research,* vol. 40, 1970, pp. 13–27.
8. Seymour B. Sarason and John Doris, *Educational Handicap, Public Policy, and Social History* (New York: Free Press, 1979), pp. 155–56, 340–51.
9. Olneck and Lazerson, Tables 11 and 12.
10. Howe. pp. 277–78.
11. *Fall 1995 Preliminary Ethnic Survey* (Los Angeles: Information Technology Division, Los Angeles Unified School District, Publication No. 124, 1996).
12. Georges Vernez and Allan Abrahamse, *How Immigrants Fare in U.S. Education* (Santa Monica, Calif.: RAND Corporation, 1996), Table 3.2.
13. These figures are not strictly comparable; estimates are based on data in Vernez and Abrahamse, Table 4.2, and in National Center for Education Statistics, *Dropout Rates in the United States: 1995* (Washington, D.C.: Office of Educational Research and Improvement, U.S. Department of Education, NCES 97-473, 1997), Table 9.
14. Native-language instruction in public schools was also common in the Southwest, particularly in Texas, New Mexico, and Arizona, which were formerly part of Mexico and whose native populations, not their immigrants, were originally Spanish-speaking Mexicans. It was also common in Louisiana, where French-language public schools were established well after the Louisiana Purchase to preserve native French culture.
15. Diego Castellanos, *The Best of Two Worlds: Bilingual-Bicultural Education in the United States* (Trenton: New Jersey State Department of Education, CN 500, 1983), pp. 23–25.
16. Sarason and Doris, pp. 180–81, 194.
17. Heinz Kloss, *The American Bilingual Tradition* (Rowley, Mass.: Newbury House, 1977), pp, 149–50.
18. Ibid., pp. 61, 86, 180; Castellanos, p. 19; and Mary J. Herrick, *The Chicago Schools: A Social and Political History* (Beverly Hills, Calif.: Sage, 1971), p. 61.
19. Kloss, pp. 69, 86, 158–59, 190; and Castellanos, pp. 24–25,
20. Kloss, pp. 177–78, 184.
21. Castellanos, p. 23; and Paul E. Peterson, *The Politics of School Reform, 1870–1940* (Chicago: University of Chicago Press, 1985), p. 55.
22. Peterson, pp. 55–56; Castellanos, p. 25; and James Crawford, *Bilingual Education: History, Politics, Theory, and Practice* (Trenton, N.J.: Crane Publishing Company, 1989), p. 22.
23. "The School Question," *Milwaukee Sentinel,* 27 November 1889.
24. Herrick, p. 61; Kloss, p. 89; Peterson, pp. 10, 58; William F. Whyte, "The Bennett Law Campaign in Wisconsin," *Wisconsin Magazine of History,* vol. 10, 1927, pp. 363–90; and Bernard Mehl, "Educational Criticism: Past and Present," *Progressive Education,* March 1953, p. 154.
25. Crawford, pp. 23–24; and David Tyack, "Constructing Difference: Historical Reflections on Schooling and Social Diversity," *Teachers College Record,* Fall 1993, p. 15.
26. *Meyer v. Nebraska,* 262 US 390 (1923).
27. Castellanos, pp. 43, 49; Crawford, p. 26; and idem, *Hold Your Tongue* (Reading, Mass.: Addison-Wesley, 1992), p. 72.
28. See, for example, Rudolph Troike, "Research Evidence for the Effectiveness of Bilingual Education," *NABE Journal,* vol. 3, 1978, pp. 13–24; *The Bilingual Education Handbook: Designing Instruction for LEP Students* (Sacramento: California Department of Education, 1990), p. 13; Iris Rotberg, "Some Legal and Research Considerations in Establishing Federal Bilingual Policy in Bilingual Education," *Harvard Educational Review,* May 1982, pp. 158–59; and Rosalie Pedalino Porter, *Forked Tongue: The Politics of Bilingual Education* (New York: Basic Books, 1990) p. 141.
29. Leonard Covello, "A High School and Its Immigrant Community—A Challenge and an Opportunity," *Journal of Educational Sociology,* February 1936, p. 334.
30. Ruben G. Rumbaut, "The New Californians: Research Findings on the Educational Progress of Immigrant Children," in idem and Wayne Cornelius, eds., *California's Immigrant Children: Theory, Research, and Implications for Educational Policy* (San Diego: Center for U.S.-Mexican Studies, University of California, 1995).
31. For a discussion of Rodriguez as prototype, see Stephen D. Krashen, *Under Attack: The Case Against Bilingual Education* (Culver City, Calif: Language Education Associates, 1996), p. 19.
32. Rumbaut, Table 2.6.
33. *Dropout Rates in the United States: 1995,* Table A-37; and National Center for Education Statistics, *The Condition of Education 1997* (Washington, D.C.: U.S. Department of Education, NCES 97-388, 1997), Indicators 8, 22.
34. Gregory Rodriguez, *The Emerging Latino Middle Class* (Malibu, Calif.: Pepperdine University Institute for Public Policy, 1996), Figure 22.

Form at end of book

Issue 8 Summary

In the Issue 8 Introduction, a person was described as a New Yorker, an Italian American, a Catholic, a female, a White person, and a member of Generation X, and another person was described as an African American, a Hispanic, a male, a Texan, and a baby boomer. Despite the many differences between these two people, the minute they both arrive in China, they are both simply *Americans.* Their many differing qualities are irrelevant. Someday, the differences among students may be irrelevant when they arrive in the classroom. At the same time, however, we seek to respect and celebrate our differences. The goal is to create classrooms that respect diversity but do not discriminate based on diversity. So far, that goal has been elusive. As we enter the twenty-first century, we struggle to understand how we can make access to learning equal to all; we struggle to determine how to address in classrooms our cultural diversity and yet maintain a coherent curriculum; and we struggle to discern how best to teach the increasingly large numbers of children who enter our school systems without speaking English. These issues, with their political overtones and emotional overlays, will bedevil us for many years to come.

Inclusion of Students with Disabilities

Questions

1. In what ways is the inclusive education movement similar to previous civil rights movements? How is it different?

2. In your capacity as secretary of education, you are asked by the president to make a recommendation regarding whether the federal government should advocate inclusive education. The president asks you to state your position and present supporting arguments. What is your response?

3. Underlying the inclusion debate is a set of different assumptions made by both camps. What are the assumptions, or the beliefs about education, made by the pro-inclusionists? What assumptions underlie the arguments of the anti-inclusionists?

Introduction

The education of students with disabilities has had a tortuous path. Several decades ago, many students with disabilities simply had no access to public education; if they received any education, it was at their parents' expense. In the 1970s, a landmark federal law guaranteed children a free and appropriate education regardless of their disability. Suddenly, school systems had to accommodate all children, whether they had visual impairments, hearing impairments, mental retardation, autism, or physical disabilities. The next question was *where* would such children be placed? Initially, children with disabilities were placed in special schools or sometimes in special classes in ordinary schools. But parents exerted pressure on school districts to integrate their children into ordinary classes. By the 1990s, the movement for *inclusive education* had become very strong. Increasingly, school districts were being pressured by parent groups to educate their children in neighborhood schools in the same classes as their nondisabled peers.

Inclusion has been the subject of enormous debate, both inside schools and outside of them. The articles you will read present differing views on whether or not inclusion is good policy and *why*. As you read them, think of yourself in different roles: as a child with a disability, as the parent of a child with a disability, as a nondisabled child, as the parent of a nondisabled child, as a classroom teacher, and as a taxpayer. You may find that the different roles give you very different views on whether or not education should be fully inclusive.

Inclusive Education:
A Modern-Day Civil-Rights Struggle

John A. Kovach and Don E. Gordon

John A. Kovach is Assistant Professor of Sociology at Pennsylvania State University, Delaware County Campus. He has served as an Associate Director at the National Center for Education in the Inner Cities and has researched and written on poverty and education, Native American adult education, and urban education policy issues.
Don E. Gordon is a research assistant at the Temple University Center for Research in Human Development and Education.

Because public schools reflect the society at large, issues of integration, inclusion, and educational equity often kindle our national debates. Education occupies a unique, often contradictory position in our society, frequently serving as a scaffolding that helps ensure the continuation of the status quo but always holding the potential to be a force for dramatic change. For this reason, when civil-rights struggles ascend to the level of legislation, they often hinge on the issue of equal schooling. As with society at large, schoolwide interventions that seek to alleviate inequity often end up strengthening the existing order. Pull-out special education programs, for example, were developed to help students with a variety of special needs get "up to speed" before returning to the regular classroom. A number of studies have shown that students placed in these programs actually receive inferior instruction and fall further behind students in regular classrooms (Reynolds 1994; Reynolds and Zetlin 1993).

Some critics have argued that this situation of unequal schooling outcomes occurs because true change actually requires a complete revamping of the social structure—in this case, the organization of schools along with change in community institutional structures—rather than a slight modification of the existing system (Apple 1996). This debate is particularly pertinent to the issue of special education, simply because students that are classified for these programs are disproportionately from poor and minority backgrounds (Raison, Hanson, Hall, and Reynolds 1995). Ironically, then, programs that were established to help students with special needs have frequently ended up consigning them to "separate and unequal" status, often in the same school buildings as their more fortunate peers. This issue of *educational* segregation is doubly relevant because the enactment of the Education for All Handicapped Children Act in 1975 represented the culmination of a long civil-rights struggle to provide not only for handicapped children but for all children with special needs. This act (PL 94-142) established that even students who are most difficult to teach—whether due to innate cognitive, social, or emotional reasons—are entitled to the best education possible.

The issue of inclusive education, which is so central to the reform agenda of the 1990s, is best seen as an issue of civil rights. If it can be demonstrated that the best education available is in the regular classroom, and that inclusive classrooms prove beneficial for regular and special-needs students alike, then implementing such classrooms is the fairest and most effective strategy for ensuring that the rights of all students to an equal education are met.

By considering what can be done to reduce educational segregation and the inequities that accompany it while focusing attention on larger social structural factors that create the context for success or failure, we may increase the life chances of all children and youth. We must also emphasize contemporary urban realities and reforms that can impact achievement and life chances of inner-city youth, because minority and poor populations disproportionately dominate the urban terrain in the United States. So how do we reduce educational segregation to achieve equity in an era of urban decline and decay? Even as schools have had some success at integration that transcends neighborhood boundaries, educational segregation remains a barrier to educational equity as we approach the next millennium.

Segregated Schools

Within the educational community there has long been a recognition of the problems created by segregation. Coleman (1966) found that a decade after the *Brown v. the*

Board of Education decision U.S. schools were still largely segregated; 80 percent of European-American students attended public schools that were 90–100 percent European-American, and 65 percent of African-American children attended schools that were more than 90 percent African-American. In addition, almost all students in the South and Midwest were in schools that were 100 percent segregated.

These basic findings about school segregation have not changed much over the past 30 years. In 1968, 76 percent of African-American students and 55 percent of Hispanic students attended predominately minority schools. In 1991, 66 percent of all African-Americans and 74.3 percent of Hispanics were still in segregated schools. In states such as Illinois, Michigan, New York, and New Jersey, more than 50 percent of the schools are 90–100 percent minority. Additionally, African-Americans and other minorities tend to find themselves in schools where overall achievement is low.

In *Pennsylvania Human Relations Commission v. School District of Philadelphia* (1995), Commonwealth Court Judge Doris Smith declared that, despite 25 years of court-ordered desegregation, the School District of Philadelphia remained a segregated system. As a result, she ordered officials to implement new strategies to achieve equity in educational achievement and life chances for all students. But efforts to achieve integration and educational equity, as measured by achievement and outcomes, have not specifically addressed the widespread problem of within-school segregation that accompanies categorical placements. Even within relatively high-achieving schools, minority students tend to be placed disproportionately in pull-out programs characterized by low expectations and an increased risk of educational failure (Kantor and Brenzel 1993; Oakes 1992). In fact, African-American children are three times as likely as European-Americans to be labeled as retarded or behaviorally disturbed (Heller, Holtzman, and Messick 1982). The creation of a second system for special-needs students, albeit well-intentioned, has a negative effect on academic performance as well as social adjustment. Wells and Serna (1996) have shown that educational segregation leads to increased racial and socioeconomic segregation within schools, with low-income African-American and Hispanic students most frequently placed in the lowest-level classes even when they have equal or higher test scores or grades. Similarly, Oakes and Welner (1995) and Oakes (1985) showed how tracking in schools functions to reproduce inequities. Tracking and pull-out programs have long-lasting effects as these students fall steadily further behind their peers and become increasingly bored in school. These effects are worse for minority children who may already carry feelings of self-doubt or academic inadequacy with them to school. In the end, educational segregation in the form of tracking or pull-out special education programs reinforces interpersonal conflicts and self doubts in minority children due to relationships between race, socioeconomic status, and academic track (Kovach 1995; Byrne 1988; Espinosa 1986; Matute-Bianch 1986; Ogbu 1979). The effects of this educational segregation are, no doubt, long lasting due to their psychological as well as educational significance.

Provision of quality education is now the central civil-rights issue facing the United States today.

To alleviate educational segregation, we must shift away from special programs within schools toward more powerful instruction capable of leading to educational success for *all* children and youth. The broader issue of racial segregation should remain on the agenda, but we must progress to a new chapter in educational policy. Within the context of economic decline, especially in our nation's inner cities, and increased diversity of special-needs students living in these areas, provision of quality education is now the central civil-rights issue facing the United States today. To address this problem effectively, however, we must understand the current economic and political realities that create the conditions for both success and failure of inclusion initiatives that impact educational segregation.

The Inner City in Decline

The United States leads the industrialized world in the number of children living in poverty (Johnson, Miranda, Sherman, and Weill 1991). As a result of the decline of the manufacturing base of the U.S. economy and the economic restructuring of the past decade, the number of children and families living at risk in inner cities has increased (Kirst and Kelly 1995). The quality of life available to these children and families is threatened by poverty, lack of employment opportunities, disorderly and stressful environments, poor health care, children born by children, and highly fragmented patterns of service. With one in three African-Americans living in poverty—as compared to one in ten European-Americans—and given the disproportionate numbers of minority families trapped in the inner city, economic decline is highly relevant to any initiatives designed to impact educational equity and increased life chances for minority youth.

Urban schools, while reeling from the effects of economic structural changes that have reshaped the inner-city landscape, are particularly challenged in attempting to serve an increasingly diverse, academically at-risk student population (Garcia 1995). These children from poor, inner-city neighborhoods are more likely to contract measles, tuberculosis, lead poisoning, and many other diseases and conditions (Yancey and Saporito 1994). As poverty rises in urban neighborhoods, both children and young adults are more likely to witness a homicide, know someone with syphilis, be subject to high levels of crime, receive inadequate health care, and suffer from a variety of physical, psychological, and social problems. Thus, we see a marked achievement gap between urban schools and national norms. Indeed, we can predict the mean reading score of a school by the aggregated rates of childhood poverty and the various epidemiological problems that are also correlated with the racial composition of a school. The more a school draws from poor or minority neighborhoods riddled with social problems, the worse its students perform academically (Yancey and Saporito 1994). Many of these children from families who reside in the inner city suffer from severe problems related to inadequate learning and low self-esteem. These social and economic realities, combined with educational inequities stemming from educational segregation, effectively doom most minority and poor children in our inner cities to a second-class citizenship status. Any paradigm for change must acknowledge the need for insights and expertise drawn from many disciplines and professions, collaboration among family, school, and community, and recognition that schools do not operate in a social or institutional vacuum.

Catalysts and Caveats for Change

Much of what transpires in the realm of education policy is shaped by current economic realities that make it more difficult for the state to provide increased revenues for education or social and public services. In the inner cities especially, the shrinking tax-revenue base of the state, economic restructuring, loss of a manufacturing base that formerly provided many jobs for the urban working class, and increased pace of technological change has contributed to the rapid obsolescence of manufacturing plants and capital equipment in the country as a whole, leaving in its wake poverty, unemployment, economic stagnation, and urban decay. Along with these changes, we have seen a concomitant rise in the number of children and families living in poverty, especially in the inner cities (Kirst and Kelly 1995). Faced with expenditures that are outpacing revenues, states have reduced support for adequate health care, environmental protections, and the network of social services that function as a lifeline for the growing number of poor persons throughout the United States. Furthermore, poor, minority, urban residents, on the whole, do not represent a significant constituency to national or state-level politicians, seldom impacting leaders beyond local mayors and representatives. The battle for state revenues takes place within a political arena in which increasingly conservative, affluent upper-middle-class and economically threatened middle-class suburban citizens are in a coalition pitted against the urban poor in a battle for dwindling state revenues and resources.

Urban schools are also challenged to serve an increasingly diverse student population that is academically at risk (Garcia 1995). For this reason, many urban school districts have been motivated to place increasing numbers of children in special-education classes as a way of maintaining current budget levels (Reynolds 1994). These programs contribute to a sense of disjointedness in schools (Wang, Reynolds, and Walberg 1994/1995). Programs are offered in eight or nine varieties, with greatly disproportionate numbers of minority children labeled for special places and so-called disabilities. States further concretize this structure within schools through special-education subsidies of about $20 billion per year. Some inner-city school districts allot a quarter of the budget to special education. Ultimately, we must somehow address the larger social and economic contexts undergirding such changes in schools in creating policy initiatives for reducing educational segregation and increase equity of outcomes and the life chances of all children and youth.

These forces of change in economic, residential, and fiscal conditions create a set of constraints directly affecting the operation of schools—especially urban schools serving disproportionate numbers of minority students (Bartelt 1995). Thus, differential outcomes result, in part, from the decreased access to cultural and educational resources for poor minority students as disproportionate numbers of them are labeled as "learning disabled" or "at risk." In the end, these students are inadequately prepared to take on productive roles in an increasingly credential-conscious and highly competitive workplace. We must consider this macroecology of social relationships as they relate to educational institutions, especially urban schools, if we want to effect long-term, significant change relative to educational inequities suffered by minority students.

Although most educational professionals may be aware of the importance of macroecological factors as they impinge on day-to-day practice, they deal with these factors as if they were unalterable. To move successfully toward educational equity will require an approach that simultaneously focuses on the problem of educational segregation and provides a strategy for long-term structural change.

Reducing Educational Segregation

Inclusive education and initiatives focusing on serving students at the margins of schools are two important mechanisms for intervention that can lead to learning success for all students and a reduction in inequities caused by educational segregation. While a fairly substantial body of literature now shows the effectiveness of inclusive education (Lombardi 1995; Hardie 1993; Friend and Cook 1993), there seems to be less of an understanding concerning the importance and potential benefits of focusing on marginal students.

Inclusion, or integration of children with disabilities into regular classrooms, positively affects both student learning and social relations with classmates (Lombardi 1995). This approach reduces risk factors that most often affect minority and urban school students and, therefore, can be important for reducing educational segregation and the achievement gap between minority and nonminority students. Thus, Goals 2000 and the Improving America's Schools Act of 1993 both call for an inclusive approach to achieving higher educational outcomes for all students, including those with special needs. Although the creation of a separate system for special-needs students was well intentioned, the system has not resulted in improved learning for such students. Segregation of special students in separate classrooms is actually deleterious to their academic performance and social adjustment; special students generally perform better on average in regular classrooms (Lombardi 1995; Baker, Wang, and Walberg 1994/1995; Hardie 1993).

New political pressures are forcing schools to reexamine noninclusive programs and practices. Parents and legal experts are increasingly demanding that schools scientifically and legally justify the use of noninclusive practices. As schools are challenged to serve an increasingly diverse student population effectively, the concern is not *whether* to provide inclusive education, but how to *implement* inclusive education in ways that are both feasible and effective in ensuring schooling success for all children, especially those with special needs (Reynolds 1994).

Serving Students at the Margins

Serving students at the margins of achievement levels is an approach that connects attention, resources, and services with students who may be at risk, learning disabled, low achieving, or gifted and talented. By dispensing with labels and other traditional approaches, all students can get attention and be helped (Wang, Reynolds, and Walberg 1993). Marginal students at both ends of the achievement continuum often have unusual needs and can challenge teachers to the limits of their commitments, insights, and skills. At the lower achievement margins of schools, one finds alienation, segregation, rejection, and many highly reluctant learners. Many of these students are struggling in their academic programs or in their social behavior; they are often at risk in their private lives and live in disordered communities (Harrison 1995). At the higher end of the achievement continuum, students may be inadequately served due to the inequitable distribution of resources or may suffer from the inattention of school personnel who assume that, because these students are achieving, they have fewer special needs requiring intervention (Wang et al. 1993).

A focus on marginal students can be a useful and efficient strategy for confronting and reducing risk factors of educational segregation and differential outcomes for minority students in both suburban and urban schools. This strategy is also helpful for successful implementation of educational initiatives that are designed to include students with special needs in regular education classes. A focus on serving children at the margins in schools is important for bridging the minority achievement gap because, in urban schools, a disproportionate number of these students at both ends of the achievement continuum are members of racial and ethnic minorities (Wang et al. 1993). In addition, focusing on children at the margins—instead of a programmatic focus relying heavily on labeling children and assigning them to special programs—can be important for local school empowerment. In general, special education programs increase the levels of state control and involvement in local schools due to the additional funding that schools receive from the state for the operation of these special programs.

A problem with this state and federal involvement in special education programs is that the nature of rules and regulations excludes local control and reinforces an attitude of distrust of local educators. Federal programs are problematic in that they mainly tend to be framed in narrow categorical types, organized around factors thought to predispose students to poor learning ability. Most operate and are funded on the basis of input variables, with little attention paid to outcomes, Students qualify for assistance based on certain defined characteristics; as they enter the programs, their school districts immediately qualify for special subsidies. Whether the programs do these children any good does not seem to matter in the way that the reward system is structured. With the current focus on outcomes-based initiatives that is found in most school districts, pressures will surely mount to change what has become the standard operating procedure for special education programs. In Philadelphia, for example, the recently installed school superintendent raised concern among teachers when he suggested that their new contract, which is currently under negotiation, should include outcomes-based pay raises and incentives (Mezzacappa 1996).

Inclusion initiatives are certainly important, but simply because they have been demonstrated to be successful on a small pilot basis does not mean that they will enjoy the same success when brought to scale in large urban school districts across the country. In fact, when large districts have attempted to implement district-wide

> **Without a self-conscious link to a larger social vision for change, inclusion initiatives will have limited long-term impact on children's lives.**

inclusion initiatives results have been mixed because inclusion approaches focus only on factors related to curriculum and instruction; the paradigm does not account for contemporary economic and political realities that impact the life chances of urban children and youth. Without a self-conscious link to a larger social vision for change and an accompanying connection to coalitional groups and organizations involved in a larger social movement, inclusion initiatives will have limited long-term impact on children's lives.

Long-Term Structural Change

If any within-school approaches to educational equity are truly to have any impact, such reforms must simultaneously be directed toward change at the macroecological or structural level. The critical question here becomes one of determining who the major actors will be in a movement for structural change that considers the social impact and human factors related to economic change and restructuring. Whether in cities, suburbs, or rural areas, the impetus for such change must ultimately come from a coalitional group of teachers, parents, school administrators, community agencies, and civil-rights activists who work together, through progressive organizations, to provide coordinated social services and transform schools from a disconnected nonsystem into an institution that is joined with the community and larger society as an active agent of social change (Schorr and Schorr 1988). This is not to say in some grandiose and obvious way that we must all work together for educational equity. Instead, we believe that the political climate is perhaps right, and we must rely on historically proven strategies to achieve such change.

The Clamor for Change

The growth in categorical programs occurred rapidly in a period of relatively high economic growth during the 1950s through 1970s. A declining total school-age population made it relatively easy for schools to accommodate new and expensive programs in the 1980s (Wang and Reynolds 1994). Some of the surplus regular-classroom teachers who would otherwise have been laid off were able to move to special education assignments. Beginning in the early 1980s, the general school-aged population started to increase, while real family income began to decline. Consequently, public deficits began to grow at alarming rates while popular resistance to increases in public expenditures mounted. This shift created a relatively new and

vigorous competition for funds between two quite different systems of education, along with resistance to new taxes. This resistance, of course, could serve as a new, positive force for change if community members and conservative politicians were to question the benefits of narrowly framed programs in schools. The general public seems to be asking why so many students are set aside in categorical programs, while conservative politicians are motivated by attempts to trim expenditures that may be of questionable value from state and federal budgets. These new pressures to examine categorical programs have resulted in a cascade of reform initiatives. Already there is a strong movement to abandon the categorical approach for mildly disabled children. For example, a recent report by the RAND Corporation made a strong case for attending to the unique needs of non-English and limited-English-speaking students within the regular educational framework (McDonnell and Hill 1993). New Jersey is currently supporting inclusion in an effort to educate children with disabilities in regular education settings. Accompanying this change, New Jersey has set arbitrary funding limits for special education services (O'Neill 1996). All of these current developments represent a window of opportunity for change toward increasing educational equity if the dismantling of programmatic segregation is pursued as a civil-rights issue and strategies for change extend beyond the walls of the school into the local community and beyond.

Recommendations for Reform

If reform is truly to impact educational segregation while, at the same time, affecting educational equity, a two-pronged approach is essential. There must be an emphasis on removing categorical programs that are at the heart of continuing within-school segregation. Furthermore, if reform initiatives are to increase life chances for all children and youth, especially in inner cities, there must be some long-range agenda and strategy for changing the larger social context within which schools must operate. The first requisite of this approach for change involves categorical programs that exacerbate problems related to educational segregation of minority students. Suggestions for dealing directly with this problem and other long-neglected concerns of minority children include (Kovach 1991; Quality Education for Minorities Project 1989):

- make public schools inclusive and integrated;
- eliminate tracking at all educational levels;
- increase the number of minority teachers;
- eliminate the practice of ability and age grouping in elementary grades;

- provide a preparatory year ("grade 13") for minority students entering college;

- provide quality out-of-school educational experiences for poor and minority students; and

- abolish remedial and pull-out classes in favor of keeping students of mixed abilities together in the classroom.

Of course, all of these recommendations must take place within the context of increased public dialogue if they are to serve intended target groups and make an impact. A coordinated initiative employing these suggestions would surely help to break some of the stereotypes that have rationalized segregation within the schools.

To impact educational equity issues effectively, especially in the inner city, there must also be an approach designed to affect structural change. Educational equity initiatives that are not connected to change in larger structural factors are doomed to failure simply because it is highly unlikely that any semblance of equity can be achieved within the present social context of growing inequality in U.S. society. Although change on this social structural level appears much more difficult to achieve, suggestions derived from historically proven strategies for change could be applied in the present context. For example, when considering the popular struggles of the past 30 years—e.g., the movements for civil rights, African-American liberation, welfare rights, women's rights, and the student movement of the 1960s—it becomes apparent that all of these movements had their own rules, logic, and direction that flowed from historically specific circumstances. These contemporary struggles are both a reflection of an institutionally determined logic and a challenge to that logic. Furthermore, all of these movements were successful to the extent that their initial organizing and actions were outside of established institutional channels for change.

Massive socioeconomic changes of the past decade have reshaped the workplace and along with it families, communities, the structure and functioning of urban neighborhoods, and public schools in those communities. These changes have made an independent struggle for change not only possible but imperative. We see a reflection of this response with the increased militancy of coalitions of activists from the schools, community, and social-service organizations and agencies that are collaborating in organizing grass-roots actions outside of established channels for change in the inner city that seek improved social and economic circumstances and life chances for those in forgotten urban neighborhoods. For significant change to occur, these coalitional groups must root their efforts in goals that are structured by what is possible given the social, political, and economic conditions of the 1990s. Viewed in this context, the prospects and opportunities for change during the remainder of this decade are very positive.

The problem of segregation within schools is nuanced and very complex. For educational professionals and reformers, this moment in history represents an opportunity for significant reforms that advance civil rights and increase educational equity and life chances for all children and youth. What we have suggested here is not necessarily the need for more programs to address differential outcomes that emanate from educational segregation, but rather the need for an integrated approach to the equitable allocation of our educational resources. In addition, there must be significant attention directed toward change in the social context that exists beyond the walls of the school. What is needed is a call for better and more rational delivery of services, not more of the same. Concomitantly, if we are to improve the life chances of minority students and distribute educational resources more equitably, there must be a larger organizing nucleus for affecting social and economic change in the inner city and expanding the opportunity structure within the community.

The public wants to see us produce results if they are going to spend more on schooling. Such pressure can be a positive force for those of us involved in education reform, because it will compel us to focus on translating what we know into policy and practice. We will therefore develop and support mechanisms facilitating the application of multidisciplinary knowledge in a coordinated and connected way to address the pressing civil-rights issue of unequal education. In the end, such a coordinated approach, coupled with the actions of community groups who have united with progressive organizations on a national level, has the potential to link education with the broader community in a way that will build on positive attributes, effect progressive change, and increase life chances for all children and youth.

References

Apple, M. W. 1996. *Cultural politics and education.* New York: Teachers College Press.

Baker, E. T., M. C. Wang, and H. J. Walberg. 1994/1995. The effects of inclusion on learning. *Educational Leadership* 52(4): 33–35.

Bartelt, D. 1995. The macroecology of educational outcomes. In *School-community connections: Exploring issues for research and practice,* ed. L. C Rigsby, M. C. Reynolds, and M. C. Wang, 159–91. San Francisco: Jossey-Bass.

Byrne, B. M. 1988. Adolescent self-concept, ability grouping, and social comparisons: Reexamining academic track differences in high school. *Youth and Society* 20(1): 46–67.

Coleman, J. S. 1966. *Equality of educational opportunity.* Washington, D.C.: U.S. Government Printing Office.

Espinosa, R. 1986. Concentration of California students with low achievement: A research note. *American Journal of Education* 95(1): 77–95.

Friend, M., and L. Cook. 1993. Inclusion. *Instructor* 103(4): 52–56.

Garcia, E. 1995. The impact of linguistic and cultural diversity on America's schools: A need for new policy. In *Making a difference for students at risk: Trends and alternatives,* ed. M. C. Wang and M. C. Reynolds, 156–80. Thousand Oaks, Calif.: Corwin Press.

Hardie, A. 1993. Inclusion: Accepting children with disabilities. *Texas Child Care* 17(2): 2–8.

Harrison, E. C. 1995. Curbing violence: A challenge for the nation's schools. In *Dealing with youth violence: What schools and communities need to know,* ed. R. M. Duhon-Sells, 16–23. Bloomington, Ind.: National Educational Service.

Heller, K. A., W. H. Holtzman, and S. Messick. 1982. *Placing children in special education: A strategy for equity.* Washington, D.C.: National Academy Press.

Johnson, C., L. Miranda, A. Sherman, and J. Weill. 1991. *Child poverty in America.* Washington, D.C.: Children's Defense Fund.

Kantor, H., and B. Brenzel. 1995. Urban education and the truly disadvantaged: The historical roots of the contemporary crisis, 1945–1990. In *The "underclass" debate: Views from history,* ed. M. B. Katz, 366–402. Princeton, N.J.: Princeton University Press.

Kirst, M., and C. Kelly. 1993. Collaboration to improve education and children's services. In *School community connections: Exploring issues for research and practice,* ed. L. C. Rigsby, M. C. Reynolds, and M. C. Wang, 21–45. San Francisco: Jossey-Bass.

Kovach, J. A. 1991. Risks associated with poverty: An analysis of problems and reform needs of urban schools. In *Handbook of special education: Research and practice,* Vol. 4, ed. M. C. Wang, M. C. Reynolds, and H. J. Walberg, 199–215. New York: Pergamon Press.

Kovach, J. A. 1995. Decreasing educational segregation in urban schools: The role of inclusive education and the need for structural change. *Applied Behavioral Science Review* 3(2): 165–75.

Lombardi, T. 1995. Research base on the effects of inclusion. *LINK* 14(1): 15–22.

Matute-Bianch, M. 1986. Ethnic identities and patterns of school success and failure among Mexican-descent and Japanese-American students in a California high school: An ethnographic analysis. *American Journal of Education* 95(1): 233–55.

McDonnell, L. M., and P. T. Hill. 1993. Newcomers in American schools: Meeting the educational needs of immigrant youth. Santa Monica, Calif.: RAND Corporation. ERIC ED 362 589.

Mezzacappa, D. 1996. City schools to alter way special education is funded. *The Philadelphia Inquirer,* 10 April.

Oakes, J. 1985. *Keeping track: How schools structure inequality.* New Haven, Conn.: Yale University Press.

Oakes, J. 1992. Can tracking research inform practice? Technical, normative, and political considerations. *Educational Researcher* 21(4): 12–21.

Oakes, J., and K. Welner. 1995. Liability grouping: The new susceptibility of school tracking systems to legal challenges. Paper presented at the annual meeting of the American Educational Research Association, San Francisco, April.

Ogbu, J. 1979. Minority education and caste: The American system in cross-cultural perspective. *Crisis* 86(1): 17–21.

O'Neill, J. 1996. N.J. schools to be held to new standard. *The Philadelphia Inquirer,* 2 May.

Quality Education for Minorities Project. 1989. *Education that works: An action plan for the education of minorities.* Cambridge, Mass.: Action Council on Minority Education.

Raison, J., L. Hanson, C. Hall, and M. C. Reynolds. 1995. Another school's reality. *Phi Delta Kappan* 76(6): 480–82.

Reynolds, M. C. 1994. A brief history of categorical school programs, 1945–1993. In *Rethinking policy for at-risk students,* ed. K. K. Wong and M. C. Wang, 3–24. Berkeley: McCutchan.

Reynolds, M. C., and A. G. Zetlin. 1993. A manual for 20/20 analysis: A tool for instructional planning. Philadelphia: Center for Research in Human Development and Education. ERIC ED 358 183.

Schorr, L. B., and D. Schorr. 1988. *Within our reach: Breaking the cycle of disadvantage.* New York: Anchor Press.

Wang, M. C., and M. C. Reynolds. 1994. Special education: Accelerated reforms. Research report to the Office of Educational Research and Improvement, National Center on Education in the Inner Cities, Temple University Center for Research in Human Development and Education.

Wang, M. C., M. C. Reynolds, and H. J. Walberg. 1993. Reform all categorical programs. *Education Week* 12(26): 64.

Wang, M. C., M. C. Reynolds, and H. J. Walberg. 1994/1995. Serving students at the margins. *Educational Leadership* 52(4):12–17.

Wells, A. S., and I. Serna. 1996. The politics of culture: Understanding local political resistance to detracking in racially mixed schools. *Harvard Educational Review* 66(1): 93–118.

Yancey, W. L., and S. J. Saporito. 1994. Urban schools and neighborhoods: A handbook for building an ecological database. Research report to the Office of Educational Research and Improvement, National Center on Education in the Inner Cities, Temple University Center for Research in Human Development and Education.

FRAME the DEBATE

Form at end of book

Inclusion:
Time to Rethink

David S. Martin

David S. Martin is Professor of Education at Gallaudet University in Washington, D.C. His research interests include the teaching of higher-level thinking strategies, teacher education programs, equity in testing for deaf professionals, curriculum development, and social-studies education. Dr. Martin is counselor of the Pi Rho Chapter of Kappa Delta Pi and Chair of the Society's Publications Committee.

The study of special education as a sub-field reveals a rather short history in comparison with the history of the entire educational enterprise. For a long period in U.S. history, and in the history of many other countries, the concept of educating learners with significant disabilities did not even exist. Sadly, in some countries, even today this concept is unthinkable. In the United States, rather early in the 19th century, special separate programs and institutions were organized for learners with serious disabilities. This change brought such learners out of hiding from homes into situations in which they were grouped together and educated separately, sometimes in residential facilities and sometimes in separate day classrooms. The identification of more moderate learning disabilities, of course, did not occur until much later, and thus these children were not separately identified and were taught together with other children, often without great success. Against this historical background we face the continuous question of what placement is most appropriate for the needs of special learners.

Abuses in Separate Programs

What were the negative practices of separate placements for special-needs learners that led to a call for reform in the latter 20th century? A rapid review of literature as well as interviews and anecdotal records indicates several categories. First, as is well known, was the abuse of low expectation; with rare exceptions, special-needs learners in separate settings were not provided with high expectations in regard to behavior or academic achievement by their teachers, parents, or administrators. A separate body of re-

search and education has supported the self-fulfilling nature of low expectations in many educational settings. Thus, special-needs learners in separate settings in the past often did not achieve highly for at least partly this reason.

Second, educators desiring to have classrooms with few if any exceptionalities saw separate settings as convenient places to "remove" a problem. In more crass language, they frequently viewed separate classes or schools as useful "dumping grounds."

Third, it is a short logical step to predict that teachers themselves would regard such settings to be less than desirable places of employment, with the result that many teachers avoided work with exceptional children. It is testimony to the wonderful dedication of some special educators of the 19th and early 20th centuries that they worked so diligently out of a sense of mission with exceptional children in such institutions and programs; however, these dedicated teachers found little true recognition or reward in those roles.

Finally, although this list could be lengthened easily, the placement of exceptional learners in such environments only perpetuated the stereotyping of these learners —e.g., a majority of deaf children placed in residential schools were expected to enter vocations such as printing because of the attitude that "the deaf are good at that because they don't need to have much interaction with other people and they are not distracted by a lot of noise on the job." Stereotyping, then, closed the circle back to the original point of low expectations, and the result was continuously self-reinforcing thinking within the society. In the meantime, more moderate disabilities such as learning disabilities were not even identified clearly until the latter part of the 20th century, and children with such disabilities were usually classified as simply less able or, often, in far more pejorative terms such as "slow."

The Advent of Change

Against this backdrop of history in special education, the calls for reform grew more and more strident through the years following World War II. Several different pieces of important legislation and litigation relate to this topic. Legislation may be divided into two broad categories: civil-rights legislation and special education legislation. Philosophically, civil-rights legislation—e.g., *Brown v. the Board of Education* in 1954—relates as much to special-needs learners as does specifically educational legislation. The right to equal treatment under the law, which may at times mean spending more than equal resources, is part of the core behind careful thinking about placement of special-needs learners. The Civil Rights Act of 1964, though not directly related to disabilities, is also relevant. More directly pertinent are P.L. 102-166: the Civil Rights Act of 1991 and P.L. 101-335: Americans with Disabilities Act of 1990. Finally, P.L. 101-336: Handicapped Children's Protection Act of 1986 is in a sense also a civil-rights piece of legislation.

In the arena of special education legislation, P.L. 94-142: Education of All Handicapped Act of 1975 is rightly considered a landmark. Subsequently, that law was reauthorized as P.L. 101-476: Individuals with Disabilities Education Act of 1990 (IDEA), and is under reauthorization debate as of early 1997, having been postponed from its scheduled reauthorization of 1995. Prior to the enactment of P.L. 94-142, approximately 1,000,000 children with disabilities had been totally excluded from the public school system, and perhaps another 4,000,000 were not receiving appropriate educational preparation. It is instructive to review a key segment of P.L. 94-142 in regard to the placement question. In everyday references, that law was and still is often referred to as the "mainstreaming" law; however, the term "mainstreaming" does not even occur in the act. The critical concept in the law in regard to placement, on the other hand, was that of "least restrictive environment" (LRE). The concept was carefully developed to indicate that on an *individual* basis each special-needs child was to be assessed and placed in the educational environment that was the least restrictive for him or her. But just what did "least restrictive" mean? The term was intended as a relative, *not* absolute, concept. Thus, the LRE as intended was to identify the particular educational setting that would be the most facilitative of that child's development. A child with one particular type and level of disability in the original law would benefit from a different kind of setting than another child with a different type or level of disability; there was to be no single LRE for all children with special needs.

A great many cases have reached our nation's courtrooms on issues of inclusion. Among the most important have been *Pennsylvania Association of Retarded Citizens v. Commonwealth of Pennsylvania* (1971) and *Mills v. Board of Education of the District of Columbia* (1972), both of which successfully addressed exclusion of "handicapped" students from appropriate educational programming.

In fact, for a number of children with disabilities who had been educated in separate classes or even schools, LRE *did* mean placement within a regular public school setting with nondisabled children, generally with some type of support. However, for others, the LRE would be one in which separate education in some form would be the most facilitative.

Confusing LRE with Mainstreaming

For a variety of reasons during the 1980s, LRE became synonymous for many educators and laypersons with the term *mainstreaming*, which, of course, referred to the education of a special-needs learner with nondisabled learners in the same regular classroom on a regular basis. Certainly one reason for this confusion was the negative image that some people, including some parents, still had about certain of the ills that had been connected with some—but by no means all—special programs or schools. In fact, many had not recognized that important positive benefits had accrued to children in some special settings by teachers who in the latter part of the 20th century were now prepared very specifically for work with children having particular disabilities. The expertise of these specially prepared teachers would then be diluted or even lost to many special-needs children in a mainstreamed environment. However, in the minds of a number of parents, a mainstreamed education equaled a higher quality education.

A second reason for the confusion of LRE with mainstreaming was fiscal. In many school districts and states, the continued placement of special-needs learners in separate settings, particularly residential, would mean that the school district would be responsible for the additional funds required for such placement, appearing on the surface to be far more "expensive" than mainstreaming that same learner.

A third reason was governmental and political. The change in the relationship between general and special education is, of course, the underlying theme of the entire inclusion issue. Under the Reagan Administration, then Assistant Secretary of Education Madeleine Will in 1986 introduced the Regular Education Initiative (REI), which called for general education personnel to become more responsible for the education of students who have special needs. This movement, which can be considered the beginning of inclusionism, argued that the pull-out system placed a stigma on the special-needs learner and did not serve his or her individual needs. Proponents of REI cited fragmentation in the delivery of special education programs, noting also that there was little cooperation between regular and special educators.

The Concept of Inclusion

During the 1990s, the term "inclusion" has entered the language of special education as the latest policy interpretation of LRE, particularly under the implementation of IDEA. "Full inclusionists"—whether educators, policy makers, or parents—have defined inclusion in such a way that separate programs and classes would be virtually abolished, incorporating *all* special-needs learners into classes with nondisabled learners. Some writers in education, including many who have forgotten or never knew the original intention of LRE, even *equate* LRE now with inclusion. In this way, we have to a great extent lost the original intention of LRE as it was expressed in the original legislation.

"Full inclusionists" have defined inclusion in such a way that separate programs and classes would be virtually abolished.

If certain ills existed with separate education, what ills have occurred with this application of inclusion to *all* students with special needs? This question is best answered by reference to what had been originally conceived as the conditions under which "mainstreaming" could succeed.

For students with mild and moderate disabilities, the most appropriate circumstances for inclusion would include:

- a regular-classroom teacher who has had some preparation in the disability areas of all disabled children in his or her classroom;

- regular support services for the teacher and the learner;

- the provision of appropriate special materials for the learner;

- parents who are supportive of the placement; and

- learners—particularly older children who have the privilege of attending placement meetings—who themselves are also in favor of that placement.

We could develop additional conditions for success, but these would be ideal. Clearly, if these conditions did not apply, or if the type and level of disability of the learner were severe to the extent that these conditions could not possibly apply even with training or funding, then such "inclusion" placement is *not* appropriate for that student.

Because the full provision of the conditions for success mentioned above are not inexpensive, it is easy to understand that many inclusion placements have had less than full funding. It is then easy to understand why teacher unions have taken positions of at least caution and often outright opposition to inclusion. It is also easy to understand that inclusion can be, if properly done, even *more* expensive than placement in separate situations with properly trained teachers and appropriate materials and support.

Current literature supports an increasing caution about full inclusion. For example, Kauffman and Hallahan (1995) warned against embracing the "illusory rhetoric" of full inclusion and maintained that the inclusion movement offers only the illusion of support for all students. In the specific area of deaf education, Liu (1995) indicated that deaf children are frequently not able to meet their educational, cultural, or social needs in inclusion settings; he stated that those advocating full inclusion have mistakenly pursued equal treatment instead of equal opportunity and asked that the problem be approached instead from a cultural-pluralism perspective rather than from a disabilities perspective. Cohen (1995) noted that, instead of safeguarding the rights of disabled children, inclusion may deny children the right to attend school in alternative settings. If it is true that some aspects of separate placements in the past were less than appropriate in certain cases, but it is also true that the proper implementation of inclusion is not only expensive and inappropriate for some learners, then what alternatives exist?

Recent publications provide further directions for research and policy development. Salisbury, Evans, and Palombaro (1997) have addressed the collaborative problem-solving behavior that promotes the inclusion of young children in primary grades. Turnbull and Ruef (1997) discussed the role of family perspectives on inclusive lifestyle issues. Tomlinson, Callahan, Tomchin, Eiss, Imbeau, and Landrum (1997) wrote about ways to help teachers to address academic diversity in the classroom which builds on the concept that prior research shows that many veteran teachers are either unwilling or unable to differentiate instruction for diverse learners. Culross (1997) addressed issues of inclusion in gifted and talented education. Taylor, Richards, Goldstein, and Schilit (1997) discussed ways to teach social strategies for special children in regard to cooperative interaction with others in inclusive settings. Finally, Heumann and Hehir (1996), Stussman (1996), Knoblauch (1996), and the American Federation of Teachers (1996) joined to address inclusion in an issue of the *ERIC Review*. I encourage readers to consult these provocative and up-to-date resources.

Viable Alternatives

The question, then, revolves around how educators may guarantee individualized and specialized education for special-needs learners while at the same time giving them access to learning that has high standards and prepares them for social and occupational interaction with the mainstream of society. To that end, several alternatives that combine both foci do exist.

I am currently working in the field of deaf education, which is particularly impacted by inappropriate application of inclusion policies. Although deaf education is in many ways unique within this field of special education, we may borrow from it a number of concepts that may well apply to the field of special education at large as potentially useful and workable alternatives to a dichotomy between full inclusion and complete separation. However, for certain deaf children, a clearly identified and well-programmed separate education in either day classes or residential programs is *highly* appropriate *and* least restrictive. Therefore, let us look at some alternatives and their potential application to special education at large.

1. Certainly one alternative is the full, appropriate application of the conditions for successful inclusion, as listed earlier. This alternative, however, rests on the assumption that the placement—even with this level of support and preparation—is deemed appropriate for the specific cultural, linguistic, social, emotional, and academic needs of the individual child.

2. A second alternative is one that is being implemented with gradually increasing frequency and is sometimes known as "reverse mainstreaming." This concept involves a separate placement for the special-needs learner, but with regular daily or weekly interaction with nondisabled learners for certain activities at the site where the special-needs learners are being educated. Both disabled and nondisabled learners benefit from interaction in social and academic arenas. Such arrangements are particularly viable in schools in which a special class is located among many, other "regular" classrooms.

3. A third model, which is a variation of the second, is exemplified by an Immersion/Inclusion Program, such as the one currently being used at the Willie Ross School for the Deaf in Longmeadow, Massachusetts. This program involves a "two-way street" in which, on a daily basis, some deaf students are transported to a nearby public school for instruction in certain subjects for which they are ready, while at the same time regular public school nondisabled students and some "inclusion" deaf students come to the School for the Deaf for specialized experiences that they cannot get at their regular school site. The interaction, therefore, is enhanced by this bidirectional integration.

4. Still another model, also a variation of the second alternative, may be found in the TRIPOD Program located in southern California, again for deaf students. In this program, similar to that at Willie Ross, deaf and hard-of-hearing students have their "home base" in a separate placement, but other activities apply as well. Approximately one-third of the students are deaf and the other two-thirds are hearing; interaction uses sign language for everyone. In addition, for those deaf students who may benefit from some auditory instruction, training is offered. Teachers who are responsible for working most closely with deaf and hard-of-hearing students are specifically prepared and certified in deaf education, but all students have the "regular" curriculum as their expectations for academic achievement. In addition, the program runs centers in other schools, and pairs of teachers—one deaf and one hearing—are responsible for teaching these integrated classes of deaf and hearing children.

5. A final alternative relates to curriculum expectations. Since the inception of the new special education laws, important and positive changes have developed in programs in a number of cases, particularly in deaf education. For example, several residential schools have officially adopted the "regular education" curriculum of their respective states—e.g., the Maryland School for the Deaf. Additionally, five of the major professional organizations related to deaf education in 1996 officially adopted a resolution that teachers being prepared to work with deaf and hard-of-hearing children would have the same subject-matter preparation as teachers of nondisabled children, with the implication that the curriculum for those children would have the same targets for academic work as for other learners.

Thus, old stereotypes of the negative aspects of separate education in most cases no longer apply. Nonetheless, pressure is building—particularly from within the organized teacher ranks—for alternatives to full inclusion, which many feel is no longer appropriate for a general policy for all special-needs learners. There are undoubtedly other examples and models that could be cited as viable alternatives, and I invite interaction and exchange of information about such alternatives, through perhaps a network or at the very least through letters to the editor of this journal.

An ideal of equality lies at the philosophical heart of much special education legislation in this country since World War II. Ironically, if we carry out inclusion without providing appropriate accessibility, then the entire act of inclusion is rendered meaningless. In this context, "accessibility" refers to sufficient accommodations by nondisabled persons and in facilities that afford disabled learners an equal-access footing with others. For physically disabled learners, access refers to, for example, ramps for wheelchairs; on the other hand, for deaf learners, access refers to the provision of sign-language interpreters so that visual language is available at all times.

Critical Next Steps

A number of policy and procedural actions are essential at this time.

1. Educators and parents alike must demand that the concept of a continuum of placement options be preserved for all students with identified disabilities. This policy demand must be made not only at the federal regulatory level, but also at state and school-district levels.

2. Conventional teacher-preparation programs require one course in the introduction to special education, because many states require only that for certification or licensure of regular-education teachers. However, that one course is not sufficient to prepare most "regular" teachers for working with a learner who has a diagnosed disability. Instead, components of *additional* teacher-education courses should incorporate materials and methods for working with special-needs learners. In addition, practicum placements for future teachers must include experiences with "included" children and methods for implementing their individualized education plans. Future teachers must also be prepared to know when and how to seek the help of other professionals in regard to the needs of disabled learners.

3. State and local funding bases of special education must be changed through legislation so that there is no longer a fiscal advantage for administrators of special education in public school districts to place special-needs learners in regular classrooms as opposed to a separate placement that might at first appear to cost the school district additional funds. The initiative for this legislation can partly rest on a careful analysis of the *true* cost of appropriate inclusion, which may include special assistance, additional training and materials, and support services. A study of these costs will make the point quite clear to legislators that separate programs for some disabled students make both educational and

physical sense. Of course, it is *cheaper* to do a poor job of inclusion than to pay fully for an appropriate separate placement; that comparison is unfair and inappropriate.

4. Once such funding formulae are in place, a parallel activity should be the reorientation of administrators and decision makers in the area of special education. They must be truly familiar with both the alternatives and the consequences for the actual needs of disabled learners for every placement. Organizations like the American Association of School Administrators, the National Elementary School Principal Association, and the National Secondary School Principal Association must take the leadership in such an educational process by working with universities to improve preservice administrator-preparation and professional-development programs. The Council for Exceptional Children should also play a cooperative role in this preparation and the professional development of special-education administrators.

5. Educators must broaden the understanding of the general public of what placement options mean and the appropriateness of inclusion for some students and not for others. A most important aspect of this public-information effort will, of course, be with parents. Special-education administrators and school programs in general can play a vital role in providing parents such information about the meaning of alternative placement the moment the needs of a special child are known.

6. Educators and policy makers must disseminate information to the media about successful alternatives to full inclusion, both programmatically and individually. A carefully chosen case study of a special-needs child can have impact far beyond a mountain of legislative discussion or justification of regulations.

7. We must form partnerships between special education leaders and teachers, administrators, and regular education teachers for collaboration on alternatives and cooperation within the school to make these alternatives become realities. This cooperative effort will prevent the general public from viewing the opposition of teacher unions to inclusion as nothing more than self-protection or not wanting additional responsibilities. Yet teachers definitely want to do what is best for children, and their expressed concerns grow from the realization that at this time they are not able and not prepared to provide what special children need in some inclusion situations.

8. Finally, researchers in university and school settings must play a role in collecting and analyzing data on successful alternatives and reasons for them. By doing so, a body of literature may now grow to broaden the concept of placement.

The essence of appropriate actions in this arena is to make the concept of placement "inclusive" and to move away from "inclusion" as the only alternative. Let us begin our efforts on all of these fronts.

References

American Federation of Teachers. 1996. Excerpts from policies and position statements on inclusive schools, *ERIC Review,* 4(3): 30–31.

Cohen, O. P. 1995. Full inclusion and deaf education: Redefining equality. *Journal of Law and Education* 24(2): 241–66.

Culross, R. R. 1997. Concepts of inclusion: Did you know? *Teaching Exceptional Children* 29(3): 24–25.

Heumann, J. E., and T. Hehir. 1996. Inclusion and the Individuals with Disabilities Education Act. *ERIC Review* 4(3): 12–13.

Kauffman, J. M., and D. P. Hallahan, eds. 1995. *The illusion of full inclusion: A comprehensive critique of a current special education bandwagon.* ERIC ED 376 639.

Knoblauch, B. 1996. Selected inclusion resource organizations. *ERIC Review* 4(3): 20–23.

Liu, A. 1995. Full inclusion and deaf education: Redefining equality. *Journal of Law and Education* 24(2): 241–66.

Salisbury, C. L., I. M. Evans, and M. M. Palombaro. 1997. Collaborative problem-solving to promote the inclusion of young children with significant disabilities in primary grades. *Exceptional Children* 63(2): 195–209.

Stussman, B. 1996. Inclusion: It's not all academic. *ERIC Review* 4(3): 15–17.

Taylor, R. L., S. B. Richards, P. A. Goldstein, and J. Schilit. 1997. Teacher perceptions of inclusive settings. *Teaching Exceptional Children* 29(3): 50–53.

Tomlinson, C. A., C. M. Callahan, E. M. Tomchin, N. Eiss, M. Imbeau, and M. Landrum. 1997. Becoming architects of communities of learning: Addressing academic diversity in contemporary classrooms. *Exceptional Children* 63(2): 269–82.

Turnbull, A. P., and M. Ruef. 1997. Family perspectives on inclusive lifestyle issues for people with problem behavior. *Exceptional Children* 63(2): 211–27.

Form at end of book

The Dismantling of the Great American Public School

Follies of inclusion are examined in terms of the potential costs to gifted classmates.

Karen Agne

Karen Agne, Ph.D., is an assistant professor of education in the Center for Educational Studies and Services at State University of New York, Plattsburgh. She is a twenty-year veteran of the Illinois Public Schools, where she served as a gifted instructional specialist for ten years.

Everybody's talking about it. Public education, rarely a topic of discussion unless teachers are on strike or tax referendums proposed, is now under review everywhere people gather. The same concerns are being voiced in the checkout line, the dentist's office, the shopping mall. So prevalent is this topic that it's not necessary to take a formal survey to get the data. Just listen and take notes.

"We took our kids out of public school and put them in Catholic school, and we're not even Catholic. The teacher was taking half the morning to get around to the 'regular' kids."

"I'm staying home now to teach my kids. They weren't learning anything at school. We have a Home-Schooling Mothers group. Do you want to join?"

"We had to move because that school had no program for our child; he's accelerated."

"I'm not a teacher, but I'm home schooling. I got tired of hearing my child cry and complain every day about going to school. She was bored silly."

"I don't want to be teaching. It's hard work and I'm afraid I might not be doing it right, but at least he gets individual attention now."

"Public schools are just for kids with problems."

What happened? How did it all slip away while we weren't looking? "How could this be happening in this country?" parents want to know. In a word, inclusion happened. What does inclusion mean? Take a look:

A kindergarten teacher attempts to explain directions to the tiny charges seated on the rug before her. But a child with Down syndrome, focused on her own agenda, remains the center of attention as she crawls about pinching the bottoms of each child she reaches.

Ear-piercing screams come from a third-grade classroom where a behaviorally disabled child is expressing her displeasure at not being first to observe the science artifact being passed amongst her classmates. Her exhausted teacher says, "Oh, this happens every day. I have to call for help to watch my class while I take her out." The eight-year-old child refuses to walk and continues her high-pitched screams, punching and kicking at her teacher, as she is carried bodily down the hall. Returning, the teacher offers, "They'll just bring her right back in here and we'll go through this again. This year I just pray to get through each day."

Several children talk or play together in one corner while classmates read or write. "What are they doing?" I ask. "Oh, they don't understand what we're working on," replies the teacher. "I'm told they're supposed to be here. I've tried, but I don't know what to do with them. An aide comes in for half an hour." This scene is repeated throughout the various classrooms of schools in several counties I've observed.

In some elementary schools teachers team up to get through the day. A disruptive, emotionally disturbed child is sent to sit in the other classroom to "calm down," after which time he may return to his assigned classroom. "This helps give the other children a little break from him," the teachers explain.

A special education teacher shares that she is paid to "teach" one student all year. At eleven years of age, this brain-damaged child is confined to a wheelchair. He cannot speak, he must be fed and diapered, and he "has never, in the three years that I've worked with him, ever demonstrated evidence of understanding anything," she explains. But this child is mandated by law to receive regular classroom time. This means that he is wheeled into a classroom each day. Every twenty minutes he begins gasping and must be suctioned to prevent choking. His specially trained teacher says, "I hate having to take him in there. Where's the benefit? He understands nothing. The other kids are frightened by his constant choking, and they can't just ignore the suctioning procedure. I worry about how much of their learning is lost. I worry that he's being used. But if anyone protests, the parents just holler 'Hearing! Hearing!' So there's nothing anyone can do." This single child is granted more than $140,000 per year to meet his special needs.

What I have related here is but a sampling of many such scenarios I have witnessed. How prevalent must this tendency be throughout the country? No one will speak of it, to avoid reproach as cruel, inhuman, or uncaring. The approach described here can hardly be considered advantageous to either the special needs students or their classmates, let alone their teachers. As a result, concerned parents around the country are quietly taking their "unchallenged" children out of our public schools.

While disquieted parents express their disappointment regarding the state of the public school, few ever utter a word suggesting that children with special needs be sent elsewhere, to other rooms or buildings. They lament only that the present approach, with everyone in the same group for academic activities, isn't working for all students; that, indeed, the majority of schoolchildren is falling behind.

Liberty and justice for all, in today's schools, has come to mean that everyone of the same age shall be lumped together in the same classroom, with the same teacher, regardless of a multitude of mental, emotional, and physical needs and requirements.

Liberty and justice for all in today's schools has come to mean that everyone of the same age shall be lumped together in the same classroom . . .

By analogy, if a horticulturist were to provide the same amount and type of food, water, soil, and light to every one of the hundreds of plants in her care, easily half would not survive. Moreover, it would surely require many years for the same professional to acquire enough varied knowledge and skill to ensure that each plant will survive, much less thrive.

Now, if every ten months each gardener's stock was replaced with a collection of completely new and different plants, only then would his task begin to compare even slightly with that of today's professional teacher. And the hopeful survivor in her care is of significantly deeper complexity; whose survival, yea, whose desired advancement, is of monumental importance in comparison.

Yet regular in-service teachers, already overtaxed and underpaid, are expected to take on even more responsibility and to educate themselves for the expertise necessary to care for these new special needs. Although special educa-

tion teachers receive years of training and experience designed to prepare them for working with children of diverse learning needs, most regular classroom teachers receive none. Some new in-service recruits may have taken a three-hour course, suggested or required in their preparation. But, as many colleges of education adjust requirements to include a course in special education—a Band-Aid approach to the problem—countless teachers express resentment.

"If I had wanted to teach special education I would have trained for it. I'm not cut out for that. It take a certain type of person. This isn't fair to me or to the special students assigned to my classroom."

But, wait a minute—if teachers and parents are so opposed to what's happening in public schools, who's responsible for these changes? How did this happen? Who or what, is to blame? And why is nothing being done about it?

How about P.L. 94-142, or IDEA, the well-known mainstreaming law? Heralded by social scientists and inclusion advocates as an educational equalizer, this "one size fits all approach"[1] is anything but equal. It has systematically removed the individual attention required by the most needy few, while simultaneously denying it to the mainstream majority of students. So, why has this faulty approach remained on the education scene? Because it's cheap! Politicians love it. Supporting this movement makes them appear benevolent but allows them to move funding, for which education is in dire need, to more popular, vote-procuring issues. No need to hire the quantity of specialists required to maintain settings in which student-teacher ratios used to be no more than eight to one. No press to provide accelerated programs for gifted students, for we're pretending that all students are gifted these days. No, these requisites no longer mesh with the "one size fits all" plan.

In spite of studies reported by the U.S. Department of Education showing that students with disabilities included in the regular classroom fail more often than do those taught in special settings,[2] proponents continue to press for inclusion. They urge modifying teaching methods and beliefs in ways designed to camouflage the problems and shoehorn all students into one "equal" mold. Some of these changes include the following:

- Knowledge of facts is not important.

- Students needn't know correct grammar, spelling, or punctuation to graduate.

- Memorization, multiple-choice exams, rewards, and competition are all old-fashioned.

- Ability grouping (except for athletics) must be eliminated.

- Honor rolls, advanced or honor classes, valedictorian, and salutatorian recognition must be eliminated.

- Assign group rather than individual grades.

- Use portfolios for "authentic" assessment.

- Raise standards, but don't use tests to detect mastery.

- Cooperative learning should be practiced 80 percent of the time in the classroom.

- Peer tutoring should be encouraged.

- Disruption in classrooms reflects teacher failure.

- Acceleration robs students of "normal" socialization.

- All students are gifted.[3]

A majority of these ideas are being parroted by educationists, 17 percent of whom have never been a classroom teacher and 51 percent of whom have not been a K–12 teacher in more than sixteen years.[4]

A look at our present school system reflects an anti-intellectual society, forged by a misguided, synthetic egalitarianism. The most able students in our society are being taught to devalue their abilities and also themselves. In many cases they are taught little else in today's schools.

Bumper stickers read, "My athlete can beat up your honor student!" Able students purposely underachieve in order to avoid labels like "geek," "nerd," and "dweeb." It's great to be a superior athlete but not even okay to be a superior scholar in an institution established to disseminate learning. Something is wrong with this picture.

A capable student finally drops out of public school, finding no peers, no appropriate programs, and no superintendent who will permit grade acceleration. Cause for great concern? Yes, but when this student can then proceed to pass college entrance exams and be accepted into several college programs without a high school degree, something is definitely amiss in our formula for assessment and decision-making. Clearly, this is not equal educational opportunity, for there is nothing so unequal as equal educational treatment of students with diverse abilities.

When we permit a few educationists to promote the overuse of certain methods as "best for all students"—when in fact these methods (cooperative learning, peer tutoring) obviously exploit the ablest students and systematically prevent their progress—we establish serious consequences in our schools.

But when the Office of Gifted and Talented is eliminated; only two cents of every dollar for K–12 education is allotted to serve our most promising students; honors classes are dismantled; and a state rules that only disabled students may receive funding for special education; our public school system, yea, our society is dangerously compromised.

Until we come to realize that education can never be equal unless each student is allowed and enabled to progress at his own highest rate, our efforts to reform our public school system will continue to fail. In our urgency to reform we seem to have fallen into a common trap produced by myopic vision. We can see only one way—either-or. This eliminates the possibility of a flexible middle, a healthy balance that permits commitment to all needs, however diverse.

For instance, regarding the inclusionists' list, much benefit may be afforded memorization capabilities. The fact that all children cannot commit certain information to memory, however, should not dictate eliminating that challenge for others. Many professions depend on rote memorization capability. Indeed, daily life may be enhanced by one's memorized information, selected thoughts, and ideas. There is a special feeling of security that comes with "owning" information. Students love participation in theatrical production, a wonderful way to practice memorization. The activity of brain calisthenics can be fun and rewarding.

Portfolios are not even a good, let alone "best," form of assessment, as Vermont discovered. Several years after the state adopted portfolio assessment, its schools were able to manage only 33 percent reliability.[6] That's because portfolios by nature are purely subjective, making them seriously unreliable for overall assessment purposes. Additionally, they are extremely time-consuming for students and teachers alike, while requiring enormous storage space, a luxury lacking in most schools.

"Authentic assessment," like "inclusion," sounds nice and appears more benevolent, but its purpose is to resolve one of the major problems of inclusion. Many included students cannot pass basic skills tests. But performance-based assessment methods are impractical for large-scale assessment and are not supported by many educational evaluation experts. Major concerns include the neglected issues of reliability and validity, the lack of consensus of how this form of assessment should be used, its ineffectiveness in complex subject areas, and the fear that reliance on such an approach reduces motivation for capable students. A common conclusion of educational psychometricians is that "authentic assessment is a fad that will be of only historical interest" in years to come.[7]

Multiple choice and standardized exams, on the other hand, although highly reliable and useful for determining mastery of basic skills, are certainly inadequate for measuring all human capabilities, especially those deemed most important, such as creativity and high-level problem solving. Shouldn't these factors serve to inform us that both methods are necessary for the most efficient and effective evaluation?

Cooperative learning, which may promote motivation for some students, enhanced socialization, and just plain fun in the classroom, is essential for many learning projects and endeavors. Although currently touted as some great panacea, it's hardly new. Effective teachers have always relied on student grouping, teams, squads, and the like for selected classroom purposes. Too much reliance on group learning, "discovery" methods, and peer teaching, however, can become counterproductive. Misinformation and unnecessary remediation may rob precious learning time. Teachers need to direct as well as facilitate. Students need individual study and on-task time. Each student must also be encouraged to seek her own directions, interests, and challenge levels.

Clearly, none of the various notions, methods, and ideas on the foregoing list of "inclusion-ordered" approaches is, by itself, effective. Each must be varied with the "old-fashioned" methods to ensure "best for all" learning. There must be a balance to serve students of all types and abilities equally.

Students must have some experience with others of like ability. Identical age grouping assumes that all students of the same age can learn together adequately. Yet one common definition of a gifted student is a comprehension level two chronological years beyond his same-age peers. When a child reads at three, circling alphabet letters in kindergarten is clearly not a challenge. When she relishes multiplication computer games at home, we must be prepared to ask more of her than to count to ten. We dare not pretend that there is no such thing as a gifted student or that all children are gifted.

When a child reads at three, circling alphabet letters in kindergarten is clearly not a challenge.

Learners must also have time for individual study. Assigned seats placed in rows may well signal emphasis on control rather than learning, but occasionally this arrangement is perfect for the discerning teacher's purpose. Successful education for all requires appropriate individual challenge and remediation, as well as caring interaction and socialization among students. Most important of all is the teacher/student relationship, which is diminished when teachers must devote excessive time to many children with multiple needs. With distance-learning access on the rise, the opportunity for one-to-one interaction between each learner and her teacher becomes all the more crucial. A healthy mentoring relationship between the teacher and the student has always been and remains a pivotal factor for education excellence.

Successful schools must be prepared to offer all these approaches in order to serve all learners equally. It is not about either-or. People are not designed for either-or treatment. Incredibly, miraculously varied in their needs and capabilities, they also require an education with techniques and methods that can fulfill these unparalleled individual distinctions.

Successful schools must be prepared to offer all these approaches in order to serve all learners equally. It is not about either-or.

Such an education requires much support, much expertise, varied and multiple personnel needs, and therefore, enormous monetary backing. How much are our children worth? How much is our future worth? How can a nation that currently enjoys such increased prosperity afford not to invest in its children? There can be no either-or. All children must be served.

It is possible to build a great public school system, great because it offers everything needed for all its students; those who learn less easily, those who excel, and all those in between. But we can never achieve this ideal state until fanatical inclusionists and overzealous egalitarians allow a complete portrayal of our students, including encouraging and enabling the very highest capabilities among us.

In a poignant article, the father of a physically handicapped child afflicted with the rare Cornelia de Lange syndrome pleaded,

The advocates of full inclusion speak glibly of giving teachers training necessary to cope with the immense variety of challenges which handicapped children bring to the classroom. No amount of training could prepare a regular teacher for Mark. The requisite expertise and commitment are found only among teachers who have chosen to specialize in the handicapped. Special education is by no means the unmitigated disaster its critics charge. The drive to ditch this flawed program in favor of a radical alternative will almost certainly result in just such a disaster. One can only hope that we will not repeat the pattern of sabotaging our genuine achievements in the pursuit of worthy-sounding but deeply wrongheaded ideas.[8]

Notes

1. Albert Shanker, "Full Inclusion Is Neither Free Nor Appropriate," *Educational Leadership* (December/January 1995).
2. Lynn Schnaiberg, "E.D. Report Documents 'Full Inclusion' Trend," *Education Week,* 19 October 1994, 17, 19.
3. Robert Slavin, "Cooperative Learning and the Cooperative School," *Educational Leadership* 45, no. 3 (1987): 7–13; Ellen D. Fiedler, Richard E. Lange, and Susan Winebrenner, *Roeper*

Review, 16 (1993): 4–7; and John Goodlad and Thomas Lovitt, *Integrating General and Special Education* (New York: Merrill, 1993), 171–201.

4. Koretz et al., *RAND Corporation* (1992) studied the Vermont statewide assessment program. Average reliability coefficients ranged from .33 to .43. If the reliability of test scores is under .50, there is no differentiation in the performance of an individual student from the overall average performance of students. See also James Popham, *Classroom Assessment: What Teachers Need to Know* (Boston: Allyn and Bacon, 1995), 171–173 and Blaine Worthen, Walter Borg, and Karl White, *Measurement and Evaluation in the Schools* (New York: Longman, 1993), 441–442.

5. Public Agenda, a nonpartisan, nonprofit organization, *Different Drummers: How Teachers of Teachers View Public Education,* an opinion poll comparing ideas of the general public, in-service teachers, and teacher educators, (New York: October 1997).

6. Ellen Winner, *Gifted Children: Myths and Realities* (New York: Basic Books, 1996) and Karen Diegmueller, "Gifted Programs Not a Right, Connecticut Court Rules," *Education Week,* 30 March 1994, 8.

7. Thomas Brooks and Sandra Pakes, "Policy, National Testing, and the Psychological Corporation," *Measurement and Evaluation in Counseling and Development* 26 (1993): 54–58; James S. Terwilliger, "Semantics, Psychometrics, and Assessment Reform: A Close Look at "Authentic" Tests, ERIC Document Reproduction Service #ED397123, 1996; and Louis Janda, *Psychological Testing: Theory and Applications* (Boston: Allyn and Bacon, 1998), 375.

8. Arch Puddington, "Life with Mark," *American Educator* (1996): 36–41.

Form at end of book

Issue 9 Summary

Inclusive education—the idea that, regardless of disability, all children should be educated together in the same class in their local school—is one of the most hotly debated issues in American education. Pro-inclusionists note that students with disabilities are discriminated against when they are segregated in separate classes or schools; they argue that students with and without disabilities benefit when they are educated together. Anti-inclusionists contend that equal access to education does not necessarily mean the same education for all; they note that teachers in ordinary classes are not prepared to teach students with disabilities and that the rights of the nondisabled students are abridged when a child with special needs is in their class.

Inclusion has become one of the most divisive issues in American education today. People are either staunchly pro-inclusion or anti-inclusion. Even many who are ardent advocates for the rights of people with disabilities contend that, in the end, inclusion cannot succeed, because there are simply too many obstacles (e.g., classes are too large to accommodate students with special needs; parents of nondisabled students are strongly against it; teachers are ill-prepared to accommodate students with disabilities). However, if that argument had been accepted in the 1950s and 1960s, no attempts to integrate Whites and Blacks would have been attempted.

If you were to live on Mars and everybody on Mars were red, what would you never know about yourself? You would probably never know that you were red. It is through our diversity, through the contrasts that we face, that we understand ourselves better. However, for various reasons, we have difficulty facing diversity, and too often diversity becomes a source of conflict rather than an opportunity for learning. Where better than school should we explore our diversity for the sake of greater understanding and growth? Whether you are for or against multicultural education, bilingual education, or inclusive education, your future professional life as a teacher will be replete with opportunities to promote your students' growth by the exploration of the diversity among us.

R.E.A.L. Sites

This list provides a print preview of typical **Coursewise** R.E.A.L. sites. (There are over 100 such sites at the **Courselinks**™ site.) The danger in printing URLs is that web sites can change overnight. As we went to press, these sites were functional using the URLs provided. If you come across one that isn't, please let us know via email to: webmaster@coursewise. com. Use your Passport to access the most current list of R.E.A.L. sites at the **Courselinks** site.

Site name: HORIZONS Newsletter
URL: http://horizons.educ.ksu.edu/
Why is it R.E.A.L.? This site is published about five times a year by the Midwest Desegregation Assistance Center. It presents national and regional information about education and equity. Select one of the recent issues of HORIZONS and explore the articles pertaining to integration of children.

Key topics: desegregation, integration, ethnicity, multicultural education
Try this: Select one of the recent issues of HORIZONS and explore the articles pertaining to integration of children.

Site name: Yahoo! Bilingual Education
URL: http://dir.yahoo.com/Education/Bilingual/
Why is it R.E.A.L.? This site gives a variety of Internet links pertaining to bilingual education, including journal articles, professional organizations, government agencies responsible for bilingual education, research centers, and advocacy groups.

Key topics: bilingual education, research, government, Internet links
Try this: Click on "National Association for Bilingual Education," then go to "About NABE." Why does this organization believe that "bilingual/multicultural education is imperative if U.S. children are to succeed in the 21st Century"?

Site name: Inclusive Education
URL: http://www.uni.edu/coe/inclusion/index.html
Why is it R.E.A.L.? This site, presented by the Renaissance Group, presents the "whats" and "how to's" of inclusive education. Specific topics include teaching strategies, legal requirements, the philosophy of inclusive education, and Internet links.

Key topics: inclusive education, Internet links, resources, law
Try this: Describe this site's recommendations for inclusive education teaching strategies.

section 4 | Testing, Grouping, and Teaching

Learning Objectives

- Understand the benefits and drawbacks of both standardized testing and performance-based assessment.

- Articulate the issues underlying homogenous grouping of students.

- Comprehend the arguments for and against the phonics and whole language approaches to teaching reading and identify how the two methods can be combined.

- Know the problems associated with the category "learning disabilities."

WiseGuide Intro

In the previous three sections, we examined issues in society and in the fields of education and psychology. This section, however, focuses on the practical realities of schooling: how do we assess students' knowledge, how do we group students, and how do we teach them? While these issues may seem simple, they are, in fact, rather complex, and educators continue to struggle with them.

First, we examine the question of how to test children. As a student, you have probably been tested dozens of times. In some cases, you were probably tested using standardized, multiple-choice tests. Were these tests valid? Did they have a reasonable purpose? A newer approach to assessment is performance-based testing. This approach, which requires students to carry out the actual tasks they have been taught, has been welcomed by many educators. One of the primary advantages of performance-based assessment, according to its advocates, is its direct bearing on teaching. Two readings on assessment are presented in this section. In Reading 26, Thomas Haladyna, Nancy Haas, and Jeanette Allison review the history of standardized testing, examine the valid and invalid uses of test scores, and explore the effect of testing on both students and teachers. Jay McTighe, in Reading 27, explores the uses of performance-based tests and discusses the implications of performance-based tests for teaching.

Next, we explore the issue of ability grouping, or tracking. For decades, American educators have been debating the merits of grouping students by ability. Advocates of tracking argue that it is a more efficient way to deliver instruction because the students in the class are alike. Opponents of tracking argue that it creates self-fulfilling prophecies and leads to a social ordering of children. The argument put forth by Jeannie Oakes and Amy Stuart Wells in Reading 28 is that detracking of students (placing them in mixed ability classes), combined with high academic standards, will cause all students to achieve more academically. Sally M. Reis and her co-authors in Reading 29 are concerned that mixing students of different ability levels places students in a "one-size-fits-all" environment, where their specific needs will go unattended. They advocate a differentiated approach to instruction, in which teachers vary their teaching to meet students' individual needs.

One of the most hotly debated issues in education is the teaching of reading. The phonics approach, in which students are taught to associate letters and letter combinations with specific sounds, was popular for many years. It was succeeded by a whole language approach to teaching reading that emphasized the use of context and prediction in understanding printed words. As with the nature-nurture argument, both sides of the phonics–whole language debate concede the validity of the other method: the remaining debate concerns *how much* of each approach is appropriate in teaching reading. In Reading 30, Patrick

Groff argues for placing greater emphasis on a phonics approach, while in Reading 31 Bill Honig argues for a more blended approach. Finally, in Reading 32, Dorothy Strickland presents a model called *whole-part-whole,* which seeks not only to balance the two approaches but also to merge them intelligently in a way that will improve students' reading skills.

In the last portion of this section, we examine the difficult issue of learning disabilities. Since this category of disability gained general acceptance in the 1970s, the number of students considered to have learning disabilities has grown tremendously, yet the category remains ambiguous; few educators would agree on a precise definition of it. Many disagree on the cause or causes of learning disabilities and disagree further on appropriate interventions. Probably the learning disability that has received the most attention is *dyslexia,* which affects the ability to read. In Reading 33, Robert Sheppard describes how dyslexia affects the lives of students in Canada and examines the impact of reducing special education services. In Reading 34, Louise Spear-Swerling and Robert J. Sternberg critique the learning disabilities category, looking specifically at its definition and the criteria used to diagnose learning disabilities in students.

How We Test Children

Questions

1. Why has standardized testing been so popular in the United States? What needs does standardized testing appear to meet?

2. What are the effects of standardized testing on students and their teachers?

3. What are the basic purposes of performance-based assessment? What assumptions underlie a performance-based approach to assessment?

Introduction

Testing students has been such a prominent part of education in the United States that many educators and parents cannot imagine schooling without testing. The purposes of testing, according to some, are to determine how to group students, to determine whether students are eligible for more advanced programs, to determine whether students need remedial or other special help, and to determine whether students are ready to move on to the next grade. Testing is also used to hold schools and teachers accountable for teaching and to hold students accountable for learning. But traditional testing has been criticized. Some have questioned the validity of the tests. Do they measure what we seek to measure? Are the test questions related to the curriculum of the classroom? In addition, some believe that test scores are misused by those who do not fully understand them, leading to poor decision making. Is it fair or helpful to compare students continually with a hypothetical norm rather than to look at their academic progress? Despite the continued criticism of standardized testing, it continues to thrive and may even be growing.

Many educators have sought to develop alternatives to standardized testing. One alternative approach is performance-based assessment. This approach is based on the idea that assessment should be intrinsically linked with teaching; in performance-based assessment, the assessment of a student is linked directly to the task he or she has learned. This approach solves some of the problems associated with standardized testing, but it introduces some new problems. If we do not compare students with other students, how do we determine whether a student's achievement is appropriate for his or her grade? How do we determine eligibility for special programs? How do we hold schools, teachers, and students accountable?

Continuing Tensions in Standardized Testing

Every spring, anxiety increases in American classrooms as teachers and students get ready for the "test."

Thomas Haladyna, Nancy Haas and Jeanette Allison

Thomas Haladyna is Professor, Educational Psychology, Nancy Haas is Associate Professor, Instructional Design, and Jeanette Allison is Assistant Professor, Early Childhood Education, Arizona State University West, Phoenix.

Those test scores usually appear on the first page of the newspaper, building a sense of their importance. Students talk about taking the test. Legislators talk about the test scores. School board members either break out the champagne to celebrate high scores or blame the superintendent, who in turn blames the teachers, for low scores. Poor scores prompt editorial writers to lament the sorry state of schools, often criticizing the quality of teaching, as if nothing else contributed. Teachers question the usefulness of the test scores. What are the conditions behind these tests that summon such varied responses?

In this article, the authors examine the tensions resulting from the use of these test scores. Three interwoven themes provide a background for these tensions. The first theme is that mass education was a great social experiment, first tried in the United States in the mid 1800s. The nation sought not only to provide education opportunities to all of its citizens, but also to maintain efficiency in doing so. The second theme is that achievement tests always have been used by the public to evaluate educational progress. Policymakers, including state and national legislators and school boards, make policy decisions and allocate resources based on test scores. It stands to reason that large-scale standardized testing at the national, state and school district levels is likely to continue. The third theme is that U.S. schools have used tests to weed out students and eliminate them from further education opportunities, rather than using tests to identify problems in learning that need intervention. Amid this tension, many students are not being well served—in particular, those who live in

poverty and/or lack the language skills necessary to succeed in school and in society. This article examines the roles that educators might play in the future of standardized testing.

A standardized achievement test is designed to provide norm-referenced interpretations of student achievement in specific content areas at certain points in their education careers. Norm-referenced interpretations are relative, showing how students compare with others in the nation.

Part One: A Brief History of Standardized Testing in the U.S.

The impetus for standardized tests emerged in the 1800s and has continued. Problems with standardized testing today are really not very different from old ones.

The Inception of Standardized Testing

The first documented achievement tests were administered in the period 1840 to 1875, when American educators changed their focus from educating the elite to educating the masses. Cremin (1964) pointed out that the earliest tests were intended for individual evaluation, but test results were inappropriately used to compare schools and children without regard for non-school influences. As millions of immigrants came to the United States in the 19th century, the standardized test became a way to ensure that all children were receiving the same standard of education. In fact, however, test results were often used to emphasize the need for school reform (Office of Technology Assessment, 1992).

Ability (Intelligence) Testing

At the turn of the century, the focus shifted from achievement testing to ability testing for the purpose of sorting and classifying students. Schools wanted to identify and weed out students who were not going to succeed academically. Consequently, many ethnic groups new to the

United States faced discrimination on the basis of new "intelligence" tests, such as the Binet Intelligence Scale.

In 1922, Walter Lippmann wrote a series of articles in the *New Republic* protesting the misuse of standardized ability tests, which echo the protests of current critics. Lippmann characterized intelligence tests as

[ ] gross perversion by muddleheaded and prejudiced men. Intelligence is not an abstraction like length and weight; it is an exceedingly complicated notion which nobody has yet succeeded in defining. If the impression takes root that these tests really measure intelligence, that they contribute a sort of last judgment on the child's capacity, that they reveal "scientifically" his predetermined ability, then it would be a thousand times better if all the intelligence testers and their questionnaires were sunk without warning in the Sargasso Sea. (cited in Perrone, 1976, pp. 14–15)

Despite criticism, standardized ability testing quickly took hold in the United States. According to Deffenbaugh (1925), both ability and achievement tests were being used to sort and classify students, reflecting education's lingering elitism, as well as educators' failure to address the problems of low achievers.

The Beginning of Multiple-Choice, Standardized Achievement Tests

As noted earlier, two prevailing goals in American education have been 1) providing equal access to public education and 2) efficient delivery. The drive for greater efficiency turned American schools away from essay tests and toward multiple-choice tests. Critics and test specialists argued vehemently about the strengths and weaknesses of the two types of tests (e.g., O'Dell, 1928), an argument that continues today (Haladyna, 1994; Shepard, 1994).

Technological advances meant that multiple-choice tests could offer test data about many students at a very small cost. This method facilitated comparisons among teachers, schools, school districts and even states. The Stanford Achievement Test is recognized as the first of the large-scale publishers' tests (Haladyna, in press). First published in 1923, it continues to be an acknowledged leader in its field. Other popular standardized tests that can trace their origins to that era include the Iowa Test of Basic Skills (ITBS), the American College Testing Program, Scholastic Aptitude Test, the California Achievement Test and the Metropolitan Achievement Test. The ACT Assessment and the Scholastic Aptitude Test (SAT) became the nation's leading college admissions tests.

Haertel and Calfee (1983) stated that these tests at first only vaguely and generally reflected school learning, without any mention of a curriculum or instructional objectives. Prescriptive and didactic textbooks, however,

began to have an influence on the tests. Diagnosis and prescription became central themes in standardized testing. Critics noticed that these tests measured concrete, lower-level school outcomes very well, but neglected more complex types of learning. By the 1950s, the Bloom taxonomy (Bloom, Engelhart, Furst, Hill, & Krathwohl, 1956) emerged, which justified teaching by objectives and raising the quality of testing to measuring more than simple memory-type learning. The biggest disappointment with the standardized achievement test was its remote connection to classroom teaching and the school district curriculum. This mismatch led to a different approach to testing.

Criterion-Referenced Testing

Originating from Ralph Tyler's work in the 1930s, teaching and testing by instructional objectives came into vogue in the 1970s. The criterion-referenced test was supposed to be linked to objectives or learning domains that were easily tested. This kind of testing fostered systematic instruction. Proponents of criterion-referenced testing, such as James Popham (1995), called for tests that inform teachers about their successes and failures. Publishers' standardized achievement tests, however, are non-specific and unfocused with respect to the variety of objectives that teachers address in their classrooms. Interest in the criterion-referenced test has waned, because many of its outcomes seemed easy to teach and easy to test. Furthermore, the criterion-referenced test lacked the normative data that nationally normed standardized achievement tests could provide.

Testing in the Latter Part of the 20th Century

Three factors affected standardized testing in the latter part of the 20th century: 1) changing demographics caused by immigration, 2) technological challenges introduced during the Cold War and exacerbated by the computer age and 3) racial inequality. Arthur Jensen (1980) wrote essays and published studies that fueled concern over intelligence and racial differences. Studies show that low degrees of scholastic aptitude (i.e., intelligence) predict low levels of education, and that for most people low levels of education lead to unproductive lives (Herrnstein & Murray, 1994). Reversing this trend, while difficult, continues to be a goal in American education. The question remains: Can we educate all students enough so they can function in society in more positive ways?

Problems We Face Today

How do we measure achievement of today's students? For what purposes should standardized achievement tests be used? Do standardized achievement tests adequately measure school achievement, or are performance tests and portfolios more appropriate? Tensions continue to mount as both educators and non-educators seek answers to these questions.

Year after year, polls show that the public wants the information from publishers' standardized achievement tests; 68 percent of respondents to a USA/Gallup poll favor President Clinton's national testing program, and other polls continue to show support for standardized testing (Rose, Elam & Gallup, 1997). Parents are increasingly willing to pay for independent evaluations of their children's achievement in basic skills, as evidenced by the rise of private testing and tutoring centers.

Until a time when they are specifically designed to reflect curriculum and instruction, publishers' standardized achievement tests do not seem to be appropriate measures of instruction or curriculum. They do not reflect how instruction has affected learning and how demographics produces differences in performance. When the achievement tests are given, however, newspapers clamor to publish the scores, and then try to interpret what they mean. Reporters seem to have an innate need to line up the scores from top to bottom and then attempt to make judgments related to the effectiveness of schools. Even college admissions tests are used in this invalid way. The ACT and SAT were never intended to evaluate states or school districts, and the sampling of students is never adequate for this purpose. Nonetheless, members of the press continue to chant the mantra about how schools and, specifically, teachers are failing.

The Message from Testing's History

Four major conclusions emerge from our history of standardized testing:

- Testing has been and will always remain a basis for knowing about how schools affect students, despite the potential for misinterpretation and misuse of test scores

- Two governing principles continue to influence school testing: 1) all students must be given equal opportunities regarding their education and 2) schooling must be offered in an efficient manner

- The increase in the amount of testing, as well as the misuse of test scores, increases tensions in education, to the detriment of children and teachers

- Schooling plays an important role in each citizen's life; those with more education lead more productive lives, and the "quality" of that education is unfairly driven by test scores. (Office of Technology Assessment, 1992)

Standardized testing is entrenched in American education. The public continues to support testing because it perceives that test scores are valid indicators of children's learning. While it seems unlikely that educators will be able to change the public's taste for large-scale standardized tests, it is possible to ensure that the test results are responsibly interpreted and used.

Part Two: The Role of Professional Organizations

Many national and international organizations have issued position papers or statements on standardized testing, including the: Association for Childhood Education International (1991), Association for Supervision and Curriculum Development (1987), Council for Exceptional Children (1993), National Association for the Education of Young Children (1988), National Association of Early Childhood Teacher Educators (1989), National Association of Elementary School Principals (1989), National Association of State Boards of Education (1988), National Council of Teachers of English (1989), National Council of Teachers of Mathematics (1989), National Commission on Testing and Public Policy (1990), American Psychological Association [APA], National Council on Measurement in Testing, and American Educational Research Association (1985), and the National Education Association (1972). These organizations recognize the mounting evidence that standardized testing often has detrimental and counterproductive effects on children and teachers.

Kamii (1990) summarized the growing concerns of professional organizations, teachers and parents about standardized testing: "[We] are not against accountability. We are all for it. Our reasons for opposing the use of achievement tests are that they are not valid measures of accountability and that they are producing classroom practices harmful to young children's development" (p. ix). Below is the gist of what organizations conclude about standardized testing:

- Testing increases pressure and stress on children, which sets them up for failure, lowered self-esteem and potential health risks

- Testing compels teachers to spend valuable time preparing children to take tests and teaching to the test, undermining what otherwise could be sound, responsive teaching and learning

- Testing limits children's education possibilities, which results in a mediocre curriculum and learning

- Testing discourages social and intellectual development, such as cooperation, creativity and problem-solving skills, as time is spent instead on learning exactly what appears on the test

- Testing leads to harmful tracking and labeling of children, especially those of minority and low socioeconomic backgrounds.

The professional organizations have stated, in no uncertain terms, that testing does not provide useful information about individual children; yet, test scores often become the basis for making decisions about retention, promotion, kindergarten entrance, ability grouping and special education placements (Council for Exceptional Children, 1993; National Association for the Education of Young Children/Council for Exceptional Children, 1996).

Professional organizations have redoubled their efforts to protect children and teachers. They propose the cessation of all standardized testing below the 4th grade. Realizing, however, that schools are under public pressure to test children, they have made detailed recommendations about testing practices. For instance, the National Association for the Education of Young Children (NAEYC, 1988) issued strong recommendations about the selection, administration, interpretation and use of tests and scores, charging that:

The most important consideration in evaluating and using standardized tests is the utility criterion: The purposes of testing must be to improve services for children and ensure that children benefit from their educational experiences. The ritual use even of "good tests" (those judged to be valid and reliable measures) is to be discouraged without documented research showing that children benefit from their use. (p. 53)

The above excerpt alludes to something very ironic about testing practices: There is no evidence that supports its pervasive use. What are its direct benefits to children? What great advantage does testing provide teachers?

Professional advocate organizations agree that testing needs to be more humane, meaningful and varied (see, especially, Association for Childhood Education International/Perrone, 1991; Bredekamp & Copple, 1997; Council for Exceptional Children, 1993; National Association for the Education of Young Children, 1988; National Association for the Education of Young Children/Council for Exceptional Children, 1996; Perrone, 1976, 1977, 1981, 1991).

Many educators agree that continuing standardized testing is basically irresponsible (e.g., Meisels, 1987; Shepard & Smith, 1986; Weber, 1977).

- All standardized testing of children—preschool through later elementary—should cease or at least be severely reduced

- Teachers and parents should oppose all standardized testing, especially group-administered tests

- If tests are given, teachers and parents should oppose using test results alone to make any important judgments about a child

- Testing must recognize and be sensitive to individual diversity (age, ability, gender, culture, language and race)

- Tests should be used solely for their intended purpose

- Administrators and teachers must critically evaluate and select tests for validity

- Administrators and policymakers have the responsibility to ensure that schooling is both psychologically and morally prudent for children

- Administrators and teachers must be knowledgeable about interpreting test results, and cautious and conservative when sharing test results publicly.

Increasingly, professional organizations argue that standardized testing is an extremely high-stakes practice in which children's worth is "measured" by a score that is not likely to be validly interpreted. Furthermore, teachers' effectiveness is often unfairly judged on the basis of a classroom average. Annual, standardized tests make no allowance for the fact that students' development and cognitive abilities in the early years are uneven. While children's developmental growth is not uniform, standardized test norms are based on average growth without regard to unique developmental patterns. Individual character is lost and children who do not fare favorably on standardized tests (i.e., those with special needs and language barriers) remain "guilty until proven innocent" (Bredekamp & Copple, 1997; Meisels, 1987, 1993; Shepard, 1994; Smith, 1991).

Despite strong support, no convincing evidence exists that standardized testing is beneficial. It can, however, increase chaos and reduce teachers' sense of efficacy (Hartman, 1991; Rosenholtz, 1989). The scope of the curriculum is also reduced. As a result, teachers spend precious time focusing on the mechanics of test-taking, and on narrow test content (Haladyna, Nolen & Haas, 1991; Nolen, Haladyna & Haas, 1992).

In fact, Perrone (1991) stated that many school districts do not use any standardized testing programs, and they can produce alternative "evidence" of students' productivity and teachers' effectiveness (see also Bredekamp & Copple, 1997; Bredekamp & Rosegrant, 1992, 1995; Meisels, 1993). The use of student portfolios, for example, is gaining many supporters, including parents. The portfolio appears to directly reflect what students are learning in ways that standardized tests never can. One advantage of the portfolio over any test is the perspective of time. A good portfolio shows a student's growth in some important ability, such as writing, over the entire school year. This growth can be assessed by lay persons and parents, without the need for technical data.

Another advantage of the portfolio is that the students' personal written reflections it contains also show how motivation and attitude can affect students' growth. Thus, the portfolio yields a much richer assessment, especially when its contents are directed from a school district curriculum.

Professional organizations need to promote such alternative assessments. More important, organizations must be more active in assessment design, thereby providing school districts and instructional programs with valid and more humane methods to assess students.

Part Three: Valid and Invalid Interpretations and Uses of Test Results

The misinterpretation and blatant misuse of test scores is pervasive. Some questions to consider are:

What time span does a test score represent? Test scores can reflect the sum of a child's learning over several years. Most policymakers, however, as well as the lay public, want to know how much learning occurred in a particular school year. A standardized test given once a year is not a good measure of this kind of learning. These standardized tests are not precise enough, nor is instruction geared to reflect exactly what the test measures. At best, we get a rough year-to-year measure of student learning that does not accurately measure the sum of school learning because the school curriculum is seldom specifically correlated to what the test measures. If the curriculum and instruction *did* match the test, we would have another kind of problem, "teaching to the test," which will be discussed in another section.

The causes of a test score or set of scores are complex and difficult to assess. There are, in fact, many causes, some of which reside in school and some of which originate in the home or community. It would be incorrect to attribute test results solely to the teacher's expertise. So many other factors affect test results. In Arizona, for example, 28 percent of the students live in poverty. It is no stretch of the imagination to reason that these students lack the same opportunities the other 72 percent enjoys.

Standardized tests' very name conveys to laypersons a precision that no publisher would support. Each test is a *sample* of a large body of knowledge that teachers often feel compelled to teach. When teachers decide to "teach to the test," a practice that most of them deplore, the interpretation of the test score is corrupted. The standardized test score

should never be a precise measure of student learning; it was meant to be merely a general survey instrument.

It has been widely reported that the pressure for unfair accountability causes a number of teachers to tamper with their teaching methods in order to get high scores (Haladyna et al., 1991; Mehrens & Kaminski, 1989; Weber, 1977). While no one is proud of these practices, they are extensive and can be traced to the reductionist thinking that a test score precisely measures a teacher's or school's merit. The invalid interpretation of test scores, coupled with constant public scrutiny and the need for higher performance from chronically low-scoring students, drives some teachers into this unethical trap.

Valid Uses of Test Scores

National rank. One of the major selling points for any standardized survey achievement test is that it can rank students through percentiles. In a competitive world, such information helps shape expectations. We cannot overlook such national ranking, since test scores drive decisions about college admission. Yet, it would be unwise to create false expectations from test performance using national rank, unless mitigating circumstances could explain why certain students scored higher or lower than expected.

Future achievement. The best predictors of future test scores are past test scores. The best predictors of student grades are prior grades. These simple truisms show that a constancy in standardized test scores exists that teaching cannot influence. If these tests truly sample general achievement, then one test score can generally predict future test scores and, thus, future achievement. Intervention or changes may affect future achievement, but test scores are fairly dependable predictors of future test performance.

Curriculum evaluation. At the individual level, a set of test scores is hardly dependable enough to provide good information, but at a school or school district level subscores provide enough information, such as mathematics computation and mathematics problem solving, to furnish central administration and teachers with ideas about student performance relevant to curricula. If the scores for mathematics problem solving are low compared with other areas, the curriculum could be revised, which will, in turn, ultimately change instruction and future test results. This is a positive use of standardized test information. The negative side of this evaluation issue, and a common problem, is that if your curriculum is focused on content and processes that are not well represented on the publishers' tests, then test results can be very misleading about your instructional program's effectiveness.

Policy decisions. The primary education policymakers are school boards and federal and state legislators. They need information to make policies and allocate resources. Standardized test scores provide information that can be useful, but also misleading. A key requirement for making interpretations about the adequacy of student learning and program effectiveness is the linkage of any standardized test to the current curriculum.

In an experiment tried in a small Western school district, the first author met with members of a school district who were trying to justify their programs to an increasingly critical public. An examination of standardized achievement test results showed the district to be slightly above average, reflecting the community's social class and economic wealth. Teachers were asked to examine each test item. The test items were divided into two parts: instructionally relevant and instructionally irrelevant. On relevant items, the district's performance was well above the national average. On irrelevant items, its average was slightly below the national average. The lesson to be learned: if we test what we teach, we are more likely to get positive results than if we test what we do not teach.

Grouping students for instruction. In the early years of the 20th century, schools customarily used test scores to group students for instruction. Students who needed more time and patience were grouped for remedial instruction, while advanced students were permitted to work ahead. Multiage grouping strategies seem to have many positive benefits, according to Ong, Allison and Haladyna (submitted for publication). Since tests scores have good predictive value regarding performance and future performance, it is desirable to have good test information when determining groupings for instruction.

Diagnosis of weak areas in the curriculum. Traditional, standardized test scores provide convincing breakdowns of student performance by specific topics. These breakdowns can help school districts and schools plan for shifts in instructional emphasis to shore up lagging performance in critical areas. If a school's mathematics computation scores are low, a re-emphasis in all the grades might result in a more positive result the following year.

Invalid Uses of Test Scores

Invalid uses of test scores contribute mightily to the increasing tensions associated with standardized testing.

Cash for high test scores. Currently, Arizona is considering legislation that will reward teachers if their students' test scores are high. They would receive a $1,200 bonus in pay. Connecting pay bonuses to students' test performance has a great many flaws, not the least of which is that some

teachers and school leaders will do almost anything, even cheat, to achieve a high score (Mehrens & Kaminski, 1989; Nolen, Haladyna, & Haas, 1992). Some educators might then produce fraudulent results by dismissing students who are likely to score low, reading the answers to students, or simply correcting students' answer sheets after the test. Such practices have been well documented, when teachers and other educators feel no recourse other than to tamper with the testing process.

Graduation or certification testing. Many states are experimenting with graduation or certification testing. Oregon, for example, has developed the Certificate of Initial Mastery, which requires additional qualifications to receive a high school diploma. Graduation or certification testing is certainly legitimate, because it reflects the public's current interest in having high standards in public schools. It remains to be proven, however, that making pass/fail decisions on the basis of test scores is always valid. The City of Chicago, for example, recently failed 8th-grade students on the basis of test scores from the Iowa Test of Basic Skills.

The schools' failure to provide students opportunities to learn the Iowa Test material, however, may provide a legal basis for striking down such action. How the passing score is set represents another important issue. Downing and Haladyna (1996) identified the types of validity evidence needed in such high-stakes testing and the legal implications of such testing. While states like Oregon go about high school certification using validity evidence as a guidance tool, do all sponsors of such tests stick to the *Standards for Educational and Psychological Testing* (APA et al., 1985)?

Evaluating teaching. Many researchers and experts in teacher evaluation strongly reject the idea of using test scores to evaluate teaching (Berk, 1988; Haertel, 1986). The most common argument against this practice is that students' learning capabilities can be affected by many powerful factors outside of school. Some of these factors are mental ability and social capital (Coleman, 1987), a broad, encompassing concept that includes family and home factors as well as neighborhood factors. Coleman argued that in the most extreme circumstances, no amount of teaching will overcome profoundly low social capital. Teachers from low-income areas already know this. Any progress they make with these vulnerable children will never earn them plaudits as teachers, despite the fact that they heroically work under adverse conditions.

Evaluating schools and school districts. This practice hardly seems defensible, because factors well beyond the teacher's control influence student learning. How, then, can school districts and schools be held accountable for test scores, particularly when the standardized achievement does not sample the domain of instruction found at the school? A good case in point arises in Arizona, where every elementary and secondary school student took a version of the Iowa test. A study by Noggle (1987) showed only a 26 percent correlation between an Iowa test and the state's content standards.

Curriculum alignment. Some schools ask teachers to abandon the regular curriculum in order to prepare students for the standardized achievement test; in other schools, the curriculum is aligned directly with the test (Nolen et al., 1992). Abandoning the curriculum seems to disrupt students and disturb the learning process. Curriculum continuity and coherence are critical in the formative years, especially as children learn how to read and write. Allowing the test to dictate the curriculum results in a watered down curriculum.

Teaching to the test. Nolen et al. (1992) showed that some schools abandon part of the academic year in favor of test preparation, and develop instructional packets to coach students for the test. Suspending normal instruction clearly has a negative effect on student development.

Part Four: Effects on Students and Teachers

The effects of testing on students and teachers have been studied by Smith (1991), Paris, Lawton, Turner and Roth (1991), and the authors of this article (Haas, Haladyna & Nolen, 1990; Hartman, 1991; Nolen et al., 1992).

Student Effects

Students are adversely affected by standardized tests in three ways: 1) it heightens student anxiety about the testing experience, 2) it decreases student motivation and learning and 3) students, by the time they are in high school, do not believe the tests hold much value (Paris et al., 1991).

Test anxiety. Test anxiety is a chronic problem for as many as 25 percent of all students (Haladyna et al., 1991). Pressure to perform well on tests may exacerbate students' natural anxiety, or create other, related problems. Hartman (1991) and Haas et al. (1990) collected many anecdotal comments from teachers who described their students' test anxiety. The tests left many of the students feeling angry, frustrated, tired and upset. One teacher complained:

The CAT [California Achievement Test] is a nightmare of testing these children. And I mean a nightmare: Kids crying and throwing up, breaking their pencils, going to the bathroom,

saying "I don't want to come to school" after going 15 minutes of a two-week ordeal. (Hartman, 1991, p. 53)

Another teacher said:

The children are tense. They don't eat or sleep well the night before the test. Many parents put tremendous pressure on the children to score high. (Haas et al., 1990, p. 50)

Nolen et al. (1992) reported a variety of student problems, including truancy, upset stomach, irritability, crying, wetting or soiling, excessive bathroom breaks, concern over the time limit, "freezing" up on timed parts of the test, headaches, hiding, refusing to take the test, and increased aggression. The prevalence of these incidents, as reported by teachers, ranged from 6.7 percent for wetting and soiling to 44 percent for excessive concern over time limits. The extensiveness of this anxiety is considerable, and would seem to correlate with damage to students' self-concept, and their attitudes toward school and the subject matter.

Loss of valuable learning time. Another dimension of this problem is that the students spend an enormous amount of time studying for, and taking, this test. Nolen et al. (1992) reported that only 12.5 percent of the teachers surveyed at the elementary level spent no time preparing for the test, while others reported spending up to two months in preparation. While this time may be viewed as learning time, students are robbed of time to spend on curriculum-appropriate learning. A junior high school teacher summarized this problem in the following way:

Because of the standardized test, I have found that my creativity and flexibility as a teacher have been greatly reduced. I spend a great deal of time zeroing in on skills that I know are on the test. This leaves only a bare minimum of opportunity to explore writing and enrichment reading. In reviewing the test I find that what I am going over is the same thing that the teachers in one grade lower and one grade higher are covering as well. This makes for a very redundant curriculum. Also, the skills we emphasize before the tests do not help them to perform better on a day-to-day basis. (Haas et al., 1990, p. 63)

The cognitive losses brought on by excessive over-studying of test-specific material may be difficult to assess. The point is, spending class time learning test-specific material detracts from learning other material that needs to be covered.

Inadequate effort or inattention to perform. A number of reports focus on student motivation to perform. A 7th-grade teacher reported:

This testing is unacceptable. In my homeroom this year out of 28 students, 19 showed up for part of the testing. Many of those students "bubbled" randomly. The situation exists in many classrooms in this district. The students are highly transient and from poor homes. They expect to do poorly and don't try. (Haas et al., 1990, p. 62)

Another teacher said:

Any little thing could distract them. So it might be a pencil that dropped. It might be something, say we're sitting here and there's a bird out there on the wire and they might look over and see that bird. For ten questions they're looking at the blue jay on the wire and mark anything! . . . Here [the administration] has a test score that they are using to evaluate me on the entire school year and it's all based on the blue jay that was sitting on the rail out there! (Hartman, 1991, p. 66)

Paris et al. (1991) reported lack of student effort to be a problem that increases with age. Students in the early grades think that the test is relevant to measuring what they have learned, but by high school most students know that the test does not reflect their intelligence or learning and has no bearing on their future. They believe tests that really count toward their future are the college admissions tests—the ACT or SAT. Reports indicate that students pay less attention to the test because they are unmotivated or find the tasks too hard.

Effects on Teachers

This section addresses problems that afflict teachers under the conditions introduced by testing. Mary Lee Smith (1991) put it succinctly:

To understand the perceived effects of external testing on teachers, one needs only to ask. Their statements on questionnaires, in interviews, and during conversations in meetings and lounges reveal the anxiety, shame, loss of esteem, and alienation they experience from publication and use of test scores. (p. 8)

Teachers suffer when standardized tests are used as the sole indicator of student learning. Haas et al. (1990) interviewed nearly 400 teachers, whose comments echoed much of those from Smith's (1991) observations.

Invalidity of test interpretation and use. As stated earlier, test results often are interpreted and used in an invalid manner. If a school's scores are lower than what parents expect, the teachers may be shamed into thinking that they have not done a good enough job. Even teachers who are lucky enough to teach in affluent areas, where test scores are generally very high, may realize they had very little to do with that achievement. Using test scores without a context brings shame and embarrassment to many teachers. They know that it is invalid to use these test scores to hold teachers accountable, but they are powerless in the face of the media commentary and political attacks.

Another factor contributing to the invalidity problem is the presence of children from different cultures who may have English language deficiencies that inhibit learning and affect the measurement of their learning. A 2nd-grade teacher put it this way:

My students are mostly Native American and Hispanic [of] low SES [socioeconomic status], and as a result are exposed to many hardships. It hardly seems fair to compare their scores to students of the same age who have grown up with a well developed foundation in the English language. I think a national standardized norm-referenced test is a good idea for some things but the results should be taken into consideration with cultural and SES factors. (Haas et al., 1990, p. 102)

A 6th-grade teacher said: "How can the test be appropriate for my Navajo and Hispanic students when the only time they speak English is when they are in school?" (Haas et al., 1991, p. 36).

Teachers seem to be divided roughly into two camps. Both camps admit that the tests reflect poorly on what they teach and how well they teach. Unfortunately, the first camp may resort to some type of strategy to improve student performance on invalid tests, even to the point of cheating. Members of the second camp merely ignore the test and teach according to their beliefs. The second group, while having to endure criticism for low test scores, may still be more satisfied.

Curriculum mismatch. Most teachers recognize that mandated publishers' tests do not match well with state-dictated standards, district curriculum, textbook series or what they themselves deem to be appropriate content. One 1st-grade teacher said:

I feel that by mandating the standardized test in the primary grades, we are allowing test makers to design curriculum, at least in my district. A much better measure of what children are learning is through the district's curriculum referenced tests. Much valuable time is being lost to test preparation. (Haas et al., 1990, p. 37)

Because the state mandates a test that does not match what teachers are expected to teach, they have to either ignore the state's test and do what they think is professionally and responsibly correct, or cave in and teach to the test. This sets up teachers' sense of apathy that Smith (1991) summarizes as, "Why should we worry about these scores when we all know they are worthless?" (p. 9).

Teacher distress. As reported in the previous section, students suffer from the testing experience. Teachers see first-hand the effects of testing on students, especially young students. These teachers also see the effects of testing on themselves, their colleagues and even the administrators. In the words of a 6th-grade teacher:

The test adds stress to everyone. In this district administrators are made to think that the test reflects on how well they do their job, which makes them more concerned for themselves than for the children. The children in this school are scared to death because they have been warned by their parents to do well and make them proud. The parents take the results of the test personally, as if they were being evaluated. (Haas et al., 1990, p. 49)

This feeling of remorse about what is happening to students and colleagues seems to gnaw at these teachers. A feeling of hopelessness seems to pervade this atmosphere. It is hard for teachers to be satisfied with their chosen profession when the consequences of published tests can be used against them in so many ways.

Part Five: Where Do We Go from Here?

As we have learned, publishers' standardized achievement tests are not going away. In fact, standardized testing is gaining in popularity, despite its obvious harmful effects. Educators must continue to inform the public about these tests' negative effects, without compromising their integrity or commitment to sound curriculum, good instruction and appropriate assessment. Audiences for this message include: 1) state legislators and school board members, 2) the media, 3) parents, 4) the general public and 5) the few fellow educators who do not understand this message. It is important that educators be united about standardized testing.

What Message Do We Send to These Audiences?

To reiterate, accountability is a good idea. It is important to know where each student stands relative to standards, and to know what to do to help them improve. Simplistic uses of test scores that are only remotely connected to classroom teaching will not achieve this accountability. Test scores alone are not the complete picture, because they ignore environmental factors. What the authors advocate is a broad assessment that includes worthwhile outcomes of student learning, as well as information about factors that exist within and outside of school that affect learning. Additionally, test batteries should be aligned with the curriculum of the school district and instruction.

To advance this continuous dialogue with the public regarding students' education, we support four propositions that guide us toward responsible standardized testing:

Test score interpretations must be valid. Learning is a lifetime endeavor. These standardized survey tests only *sample* the large domain of knowledge. When we see scores, we need to ask what the test measures and what factors probably contribute to this level of performance. In other words, a test score represents only one level of learning out of a very large domain. We must squarely face the

fact that these tests are not adequate reflections of a school district curriculum or instructional emphasis at the classroom level. As a measure of lifelong learning, we might want to speculate about which factors contributed to high or low performances. Some of these factors are: the quality and quantity of instruction, motivation, cognitive ability, amount and quality of family support, attitude, adequacy of instructional materials, and quality of educational leadership, both within the school and at the district level. Do not make judgments simply from a test score. Be careful about assigning a single cause to test scores, such as the teacher being solely responsible for the student outcomes. Such irresponsible interpretation unfairly judges teachers and children.

Test score uses must be valid. Insist that test scores be used only for valid purposes. Ask for evidence about the validity of any test use. Evaluating teachers on the basis of test scores is invalid, because no evidence can show that the test is well-matched to instruction; nor can it be shown whether other, non-school factors were taken into account. Test scores are simply inadequate to the task of evaluating teaching and teachers. Tests that are supposed to keep students accountable for their education are defensible if students are given adequate preparation for the test, as well as remedial instruction, when necessary.

Keep standardized tests standardized. Once the standardized test is accurately interpreted and used fairly and defensibly, the administration of the test ought to be standardized, as well. Too many reports from all parts of the United States concern educators who capitulated to the pressures of being accountable by doing something unethical. To reiterate:

- Do not teach to the test. Do not alter the curriculum to conform to the test's content.

- Do not change the test administration times or conditions.

- Determining who should be tested should be spelled out as part of policy. Excluding certain students from testing is one way to inflate test scores, which may lead to invalid interpretations.

- Excluding students from testing is sometimes appropriate, however, as when the test result does not validly reflect students' knowledge. Language barriers, emotional difficulties, health and illness factors, and physical and mental handicaps are prominent factors that may hinder students' ability to perform well. The exclusion should be standardized from class to class, school to school, and district to district.

Examine and evaluate the consequences of standardized testing. Students should not take tests unless the interpretations and uses of test results are fair and useful. If it is shown that the consequences of testing have harmful effects on students, then such testing cannot be justified. As pointed out in Part Three, many educators have argued that standardized testing below grade 3 seldom provides true measures of student ability or development.

In addition, the reporting of test scores by racial or ethnic categories seldom serves useful purposes. These reports often perpetuate negative stereotypes of minority groups, masking relevant factors, such as poverty, that may account for a poor performance. If test interpretation and use lead to unequal treatment of students instead of providing equal opportunities, then we must take steps to resolve the problem. More and more states, for example, are adopting stiff high school graduation requirements. If students are not instructed adequately, then large numbers of students will not complete high school. Test scores already tell us that the most likely group of students destined to fail these graduation tests will be those living in poverty and those with the added task of trying to learn to read, write, speak and understand English. As we examine and evaluate the consequences of standardized testing, we will probably continue to offer the public what they demand, but we should insist that the testing is done in a manner that does not harm those whom the tests are intended to serve.

References

American Psychological Association, American Educational Research Association, National Council on Measurement in Education. (1985). *Standards for educational and psychological testing*. Washington, DC: American Psychological Association.

Association for Children Education International/Perrone, V. (1991). On standardized testing. A position paper. *Childhood Education, 67,* 131–142.

Association for Supervision and Curriculum Development. (1987). Testing concerns. In *Forty years of leadership: A synthesis of ASCD resolutions through 1987* (pp. 17–19). Alexandria, VA: Author.

Berk, R. A. (1988). Fifty reasons why student achievement gain does not mean teacher effectiveness. *Journal of Personnel Evaluation in Education, 1*(4), 345–364.

Bloom, B. S., Engelhart, M. D., Furst, E. J., Hill, W. H., & Krathwohl, D. R. (1956). *Taxonomy of educational objectives.* New York: D. McKay.

Bredekamp, S., & Copple, C. (Eds.). (1997). *Developmentally appropriate practice in early childhood programs* (Rev. ed.). Washington, DC: National Association for the Education of Young Children.

Bredekamp, S., & Rosegrant, T. (Eds.). (1992). *Reaching potentials: Appropriate curriculum and assessment for young children: Volume 1.* Washington, DC: National Association for the Education of Young Children.

Bredekamp, S., & Rosegrant, T. (Eds.). (1995). *Reaching potentials: Transforming early childhood curriculum and assessment: Volume 2.* Washington, DC: National Association for the Education of Young Children.

Coleman, J. S. (1987). Families and schools. *Educational Researcher, 16,* 32–38.

Council for Exceptional Children. (1993). *Division for Early Childhood recommended practices: Indicators of quality in programs for infants and young children with special needs and their families.* Washington, DC: Author.

Cremin, J. (1964). *The transformations of the school: Progressivism in American education, 1876–1957.* New York: Vintage Books.

Deffenbaugh, W. S. (1925). *Uses of intelligence tests in 215 cities. City School Leaflet No. 20.* Washington, DC: Bureau of Education, U.S. Department of the Interior.

Downing, S. M., & Haladyna, T. M. (1996). Model for evaluating high-stakes testing programs: Why the fox should not guard the chicken coop. *Educational Measurement: Issues and Practice, 15,* 5–12.

Haas, N. S., Haladyna, T. M., & Nolen, S. B. (1990, April). *War stories from the trenches: What teachers and administrators say about the test.* Paper presented at a symposium at the annual meeting of the National Council on Measurement in Education, Boston.

Haertel, E. (1986). The valid use of student performance measures for teacher evaluation. *Educational Evaluation and Policy Analysis, 8,* 45–60.

Haertel, E., & Calfee, R. (1983). School achievement: Thinking about what to test. *Journal of Educational Measurement, 20,* 119–130.

Haladyna, T. M. (1994). *Developing and validating multiple-choice test items.* Hillsdale, NJ: Lawrence Erlbaum Associates.

Haladyna, T. M. (in press). *Review of the Stanford Achievement Test* (8th ed.). Mental Measurement Yearbook.

Haladyna, T. M., Nolen, S. B., & Haas, N. S. (1991). Raising standardized achievement test scores and the origins of test score pollution. *Educational Researcher, 20*(5), 2–7.

Hartman, J. A. (1991). *How mandated student assessment programs affect kindergarten teachers: Two steps forward, three steps backward.* Unpublished doctoral dissertation. Urbana, IL: The University of Illinois.

Herrnstein, J., & Murray, C. (1994). *The bell curve: Intelligence and class structure in American life.* New York: Free Press.

Jensen, A. R. (1980). *Bias in mental testing.* New York: The Free Press.

Kamii, C. (Ed.). (1990). *Achievement testing in the early grades: The games grown-ups play.* Washington, DC: National Association for the Education of Young Children.

Mehrens, W. A., & Kaminski, J. (1989). Methods for improving standardized test scores: Fruitful, fruitless, or fraudulent? *Educational Measurement: Issues and Practices, 8,* 14–22.

Meisels, S. J. (1987). Uses and abuses of developmental screening and school readiness testing. *Young Children, 42,* 4–6, 68–73.

Meisels, S. J. (1993). Remaking classroom assessment with The Work Sampling System. *Young Children, 48*(5), 34–40.

National Association for the Education of Young Children. (1988). Position statement on standardized testing of young children 3 through 8 years of age. *Young Children, 43*(3), 42–47.

National Association for the Education of Young Children/Council for Exceptional Children. (1996). *Guidelines for preparation for early childhood professionals.* Washington, DC: Authors.

National Association of Early Childhood Teacher Educators. (1989). Resolution: Testing in the early years. *The Journal of Early Childhood Teacher Education, 10*(1), 16–17.

National Association of Elementary School Principals. (1989). Standardized tests. In *Platform 1988–1989* (p. 7). Alexandria, VA: Author.

National Association of State Boards of Education. (1988). *Right from the start.* Alexandria, VA: Author.

National Commission on Testing and Public Policy. (1990). *From gatekeepers to gateways: Transforming testing in America.* Chestnut Hill, MA: Boston College.

National Council of Teachers of English. (1989). Testing and evaluation. In *NCTE forum: Position statements on issues in* education from the National Council of Teachers of English (pp. VI:1–VI:4). Urbana, IL: Author.

National Council of Teachers of Mathematics. (1989). *Curriculum and evaluation standards for school mathematics.* Reston, VA: Author.

National Education Association. (1972). Moratorium on standardized testing. *Today's Education, 61,* 41.

Noggle, N. L. (October 1987). *Report on the match of the standardized tests to the Arizona Essential Skills.* Tempe, AZ: College of Education.

Nolen, S. B., Haladyna, T. M., & Haas, N. S. (1992). Uses and abuses of achievement test scores. *Educational Measurement: Issues and Practices, 11,* 9–15.

O'Dell, C. W. (1928). *Traditional examinations and new type tests.* New York: Century.

Office of Office of Educational Research and Improvement. (1996). *Youth indicators 1996.* Washington, DC: U.S. Department of Education.

Office of Technology Assessment. (1992). *Testing in American schools: Asking the right questions.* Washington, DC: Author.

Ong, W. S., Allison, J. M., Haladyna, T. M. (submitted for publication). *A comparison of reading, writing and mathematics achievement in comparable single-age and multi-age classrooms.*

Paris, S., Lawton, T. A., Turner, J. C., & Roth, J. L. (1991). A developmental perspective on standardized achievement testing. *Educational Researcher, 20,* 12–20, 40.

Perrone, V. (1976). *On standardized testing and evaluation.* Olney, MD: Association for Childhood Education International.

Perrone, V. (1977). *The abuses of standardized testing* (Fastback 92). Bloomington, IN: Phi Delta Kappa Educational Foundation.

Perrone, V. (1981). Testing, testing, and more testing. *Childhood Education, 58,* 76–80.

Perrone, V. (1991). *Standardized testing. ERIC Digest.* Urbana, IL: ERIC Clearinghouse on Elementary and Early Childhood Education.

Popham, W. J. (1995). *Classroom assessment: What teachers need to know.* Boston: Allyn & Bacon.

Rose, L. C., Elam, S. M., & Gallup, A. C. (1997). The 29th annual Phi Delta Kappa/Gallup poll of the public's attitudes toward the public schools. *Phi Delta Kappan, 79(1),* 41–58.

Rosenholtz, S. J. (1989). *Teachers' workplace: The social organization of schooling.* New York: Longman.

Shepard, L. A. (1994). The challenges of assessing young children appropriately. *Phi Delta Kappan, 76(3),* 206–212.

Shepard, L. A., & Smith, M. L. (1986). Synthesis of research on school readiness and kindergarten retention. *Educational Leadership, 44,* 78–86.

Smith, M. L. (1991). Put to the test: The effects of external testing on teachers. *Educational Researcher, 20,* 8–11.

Weber, G. (1977). *Uses and abuses of standardized testing in the schools.* Washington, DC: Council for Basic Education.

Form at end of book

What Happens between Assessments?

Not only assessment needs to change. Curriculums and instructional strategies, too, must reflect a *performance* orientation. Here are seven principles for performance-based instruction.

Jay McTighe

Jay McTighe is Director of the Maryland Assessment Consortium, c/o Urbana High School, 3471 Campus Dr., Ijarnsville, MD 21754 (e-mail: jmctighe@aol.com).

Growing concern over the inadequacy of conventional tests has spurred interest in performance assessments, such as performance tasks, projects, and exhibitions. To many supporters, these performance assessments are better suited than traditional tests to measure what really counts: whether students can apply their knowledge, skills, and understanding in important, real-world contexts. More teachers are using performance assessments in their classrooms, and such assessments are beginning to influence district- and state-level testing programs as well.

Increasing the use of performance assessments—in and of itself—will not significantly improve student performance, however. To borrow the old farm adage: "You don't fatten the cattle by weighing them." If we expect students to improve their performance on these new, more authentic measures, we need to engage in "performance-based instruction" on a regular basis.

But what does it really mean to teach for performance? Working the past six years with hundreds of teachers using performance assessments, I have seen how the development of assessment tasks and evaluative criteria can influence instruction. Based on this experience, I offer seven principles of performance-based instruction, illustrated by vignettes from classrooms in which these principles are being applied.

Establish Clear Performance Targets

As part of a unit on nutrition, a middle school health teacher presents her students with the following performance task.

You are having six of your friends over for your birthday party. You are preparing the food for the party, but your mother has just read a book on nutrition and tells you that you can't serve anything containing artificial sweeteners or lots of salt, sugar, or saturated fats. Plan a menu that will make your friends happy and still meet your mother's expectations. Explain why your menu is both tasty and healthy. Use the USDA Food Pyramid guidelines and the Nutrition Facts on food labels to support your menu selection.[1]

To teach effectively, we need to be clear about what we expect students to know, understand, and be able to do as a result of our instruction. But performance-based instruction calls for more. We also need to determine *how* students will demonstrate the intended knowledge, understanding, and proficiency. When establishing performance targets, consider Gardner's (1991) contention that developing students' *understanding* is a primary goal of teaching. He defines understanding as the ability to apply facts, concepts, and skills appropriately in new situations.

When students have opportunities to examine their work in light of known criteria and performance standards, they begin to shift their orientation from "What did I get?" to "Now I know what I need to do to improve."

The principle of *establishing clear performance targets* and the goal of *teaching for understanding* fit together as a powerful means of linking curriculum, instruction, and assessment. A performance-based orientation requires that we think about curriculum not simply as content to be covered but in terms of desired *performance of understanding.* Thus, performance-oriented teachers consider assessment up front by conceptualizing their learning goals and objectives as performance applications calling for students to demonstrate their understanding. Performance assessments, then, become targets for teaching and learning, as well as serving as a source of evidence that students understand, and are able to apply, what we have taught.

Establishing clear performance targets is important for several reasons. Teachers who establish and communicate clear performance targets to their students reflect what we know about effective teaching, which supports the importance of instructional clarity. These teachers also recognize that students' attitudes and perceptions toward learning are influenced by the degree to which they understand what is expected of them and what the rationale is for various instructional activities. Finally, the process of establishing performance targets helps identify curriculum priorities, enabling us to focus on the essential and enduring knowledge in a crowded field.

Strive for Authenticity in Products and Performances

Fifth graders conduct a survey to gather data about community attitudes toward a proposal that public school students wear uniforms. The students organize the data and then choose an appropriate graphic display for communicating their findings. Finally, students write letters to the editor of the local paper to present their data and their personal views on the proposal. A direct link to the larger world is established when two student letters are published in the newspaper.

Leading reformers recommend that schools involve their students in authentic work. Performance tasks should call upon students to demonstrate their knowledge and skills in a manner that reflects the world outside the classroom. Although diagramming sentences may help students understand sentence structures and parts of speech, this is not really an authentic activity, because few people outside of school diagram sentences. When students engage in purposeful writing (for example, to persuade an identified audience), however, they are using their knowledge and skills in ways much more congruent with the demands of real life.

As in the larger world, authentic work in schools calls for students to apply their knowledge and skills, with the result typically being a tangible product (written, visual, or three-dimensional) or a performance. These products and performances have an explicit *purpose* (for example, to explain, to entertain, or to solve a problem) and are directed toward an identified *audience*. Because real-world issues and problems are rarely limited to a single content area, authentic work often provides opportunities for making interdisciplinary connections.

Emphasizing authentic work does not lessen the importance of helping students develop basic skills. On the contrary, basic knowledge and skills provide an essential foundation for meaningful application. The "basics" are not ends in themselves, however; they serve a larger goal:

to enable students to thoughtfully apply knowledge and skills within a meaningful, authentic context.

Research and experience confirm that when learners perceive classroom activities as meaningful and relevant, they are more likely to have a positive attitude toward them (McCombs 1984, Schunk 1990). In addition, many teachers have observed that when given the opportunity to produce a tangible product or demonstrate something to a real audience (for example, peers, parents, younger or older students, community members), students often seem more willing to put forth the effort required to do quality work.

Remember that what we assess sends a strong signal to students about what is important for them to learn. When authentic performance tasks play a key role in teaching and assessing, students will know that we expect them to apply knowledge in ways valued in the world beyond the classroom.

Publicize Criteria and Performance Standards

Before beginning a laboratory experiment, a high school science teacher reviews the Science Department's performance list for a lab report with her students. The list, containing the criteria for a thorough report, clearly conveys the teacher's expectations while serving as a guide to the students as they prepare their reports. Before she collects the reports, the teacher allows students to exchange papers with their lab partners, give feedback to one another based on the performance list criteria, and make needed revisions.

Like the problems and issues we confront in the real world, authentic classroom performance tasks rarely have a single, correct answer. Therefore, our evaluation of student products and performances must be based upon judgment and guided by criteria. The criteria are typically incorporated into one of several types of scoring tools: a rubric, a rating scale, or a performance list.[2] With all of these tools, the criteria help to spell out the qualities that we consider to be most significant or important in student work.

Teachers at elementary schools in Anne Arundel County, Maryland, use a "Writing to Persuade" rubric to help students learn the qualities of effective persuasive writing. A large poster of the rubric, containing the criteria in the form of questions, is prominently displayed in the front of the classroom to provide a reference for teachers and students. For example: "Did I clearly identify my position?" " Did I fully support my position with facts or personal experiences?" "Did I effectively use persuasive language to convince my audience?"

Evaluative criteria clearly are essential for summative evaluations, but teachers also are recognizing their role in *improving* performance. By sharing the criteria with students, we begin to remove the mystery of how work will be evaluated, while highlighting the elements of quality and standards of performance toward which students should strive. Teachers also can help students internalize these elements of quality by having them use scoring tools themselves to evaluate their own work or that of their peers. When students have opportunities to examine their work in light of known criteria and performance standards, they begin to shift their orientation from "What did I get?" to "Now I know what I need to do to improve."

Provide Models of Excellence

A middle school art teacher displays five examples of well-constructed papier-mâché sculptures of "figures in action." The examples illustrate the criteria by which the sculptures will be evaluated: composition (figure showing action), strength and stability of armature (underlying structure), surface construction (application of papier-mâché), finishing techniques (texture, color, details), and overall effect. The teacher notes that the quality of her students' sculptures has markedly improved since she began sharing and discussing actual models of excellence.

Providing students with lists of criteria or scoring rubrics is a necessary piece of performance-based instruction—but it isn't always sufficient. Not every student will immediately understand the criteria or how to apply them to their own work ("What do you mean by well organized?"). Wiggins (1993) suggests that if we expect students to do excellent work, they need to know what excellent work looks like. Following his idea, performance-based instruction calls for providing students with models and demonstrations that illustrate excellence in products or performances.

This approach, of course, is not unknown in schools. Effective coaches and sponsors of extracurricular activities often involve their club or team members in analyzing award-winning school newspapers or yearbooks, or reviewing videotapes of excellent athletic or dramatic performances. But providing models of quality work is also an essential piece of performance-based instruction in classrooms.

Teachers can use examples of excellent work during instruction to help students understand the desired elements of quality. Some teachers also present students with examples of mediocre and excellent work, asking them to analyze the differences and identify the characteristics that distinguish the excellent examples from the rest. In this way, students learn the criteria of quality through tangible

models and concrete examples. In some classrooms, students actually help to construct the scoring tools (rubric, rating scale, or performance list), based on their growing knowledge of the topic and the criteria they have identified in the examples. (The potential benefits of providing students with tangible examples underscore the value of saving examples of student work from performance tasks for use as models in future years!)

Some teachers are wary of providing models of quality, fearing that students may simply copy or imitate the examples. This is a real danger with activities for which there is a single correct answer (or one "best" way of accomplishing the task). With more open-ended performance tasks and projects, however, we can minimize this problem by presenting students with multiple models. In this way, students are shown several different ways to satisfy the desired criteria, thus discouraging a cookie-cutter approach.

By providing students with criteria *and* models of excellence, teachers are often rewarded with higher quality products and performances. In addition, they are helping students become more self-directed; students able to distinguish between poor- and high-quality performance are more likely to be able to evaluate and improve their own work, guided by a clear conception of excellence.

Teach Strategies Explicitly

An elementary teacher introduces his students to two strategies—summarizing and predicting—to enhance their comprehension of text materials. He describes each strategy and models its use by thinking aloud while applying it to a challenging text. During the lesson, the teacher refers to large posters spelling out a written procedure and visual symbol for each strategy. Following the lesson, he distributes bookmark versions of the posters. Over the next two weeks, each student works with a reading buddy to practice using the strategies with both fiction and nonfiction texts while the teacher monitors their progress and provides guidance.

In every field of endeavor, effective performers use specific techniques and strategies to boost their performance. Olympic athletes visualize flawless performances, writers seek feedback from "critical friends," law students form study groups, coaches share tips at coaching clinics, busy executives practice time management techniques.

Students also benefit from specific strategies that can improve their performance on academic tasks. For example, webbing and mapping techniques help students see connections, cognitive reading strategies boost comprehension (Palinscar and Brown 1984; Haller, Child, and Walberg 1988), brainstorming techniques enhance idea generation, and mnemonics assists retention and recall.

Few students spontaneously generate and use strategies on their own, however, so we need to explicitly teach these thinking and learning strategies. One straightforward approach is to use the direct instruction model, in which teachers

1. introduce and explain the purpose of the strategy;

2. demonstrate and model its use;

3. provide guided practice for students to apply the strategy with feedback;

4. allow students to apply the strategy independently and in teams; and

5. regularly reflect on the appropriate uses of the strategy and its effectiveness.

In addition to direct instruction, many teachers find it helpful to incorporate thinking and learning strategies into tangible products, such as posters, bookmarks. visual symbols, or cue cards (McTighe and Lyman 1988). For example, students in a middle school mathematics class I am familiar with have constructed desktop spinners depicting six problem-solving strategies they have been taught. When working on open-ended problems, the students use the spinners to indicate the strategy they are using. Their teacher circulates around the room, asking students to think aloud by explaining their reasoning and problem-solving strategies. Later. she leads a class discussion of solutions and the effectiveness of the strategies used. The spinners provide students with a tangible reminder of the value of using strategies during problem solving. These and other cognitive tools offer students practical and concrete support as they acquire and internalize performance-enhancing strategies.

Use Ongoing Assessments for Feedback and Adjustment

A middle school social studies teacher notes that the quality of her students' research reports has markedly improved since he began using the writing process approach of brainstorming, drafting, reviewing feedback, and revising. Through the use of teacher and peer reviews of draft reports, students are given specific feedback on strengths, as well as on aspects of their reports that may be unclear, inaccurate, or incomplete. They appreciate the opportunity to make necessary revisions before turning in their final copy.

The Japanese concept of *Kaizen* suggests that quality is achieved through constant, incremental improvement. According to J. Edwards Deming, guru of the Total Quality Management movement, quality in manufacturing is not achieved through end-of-line inspections; by then, it is too late. Rather, quality is the result of regular inspections (assessments) *along the way,* followed by needed adjustments based on the information gleaned from the inspections.

Performance-based instruction underscores the importance of using assessments to guide improvement throughout the learning process, instead of waiting to give feedback at the end of instruction.

How do these ideas apply in an academic setting? We know that students will rarely perform at high levels on challenging learning tasks on the first attempt. Deep understanding or high levels of proficiency are achieved only as a result of trial, practice, adjustments based on feedback, and more practice. Performance-based instruction underscores the importance of using assessments to provide information to guide improvement throughout the learning process, instead of waiting to give feedback at the end of instruction.

Once again, effective coaches and sponsors of clubs often use this principle as they involve their students in scrimmages, dress rehearsals, and reviews of bluelines. Such activities serve to identify problems and weaknesses, followed by more coaching and opportunities to practice or revise.

The ongoing interplay between assessment and instruction so common in the arts and athletics is also evident in classrooms using practices such as nongraded quizzes and practice tests, the writing process, formative performance tasks, review of drafts, and peer response groups. The teachers in such classrooms recognize that ongoing assessments provide the feedback that enhances their instruction and guides student revision. *Kaizen,* in the context of schools, means ensuring that assessment enhances performance, not simply measures it.

Document and Celebrate Progress

Early in the school year, a middle school physical education teacher has her students analyze their current fitness levels based on a series of measures of strength, endurance, and flexibility. The initial results are charted and used to establish personal fitness goals. The teacher then guides students in preparing individualized fitness plans to achieve their goals. Subsequent fitness tests at the middle and end of the year enable the teacher and her students to document their progress and, if necessary, establish new goals. The teacher believes that the focus on improvement based on a personal benchmark allows every student to achieve a measure of success while cultivating the habits necessary for lifelong fitness.

Perhaps one of the greatest challenges in this current era of school reform is the gap between our goal of higher standards of performance for all and the realization that some students are functioning well below these lofty standards. Many educators struggle daily with this tension: How do we preserve students' self-esteem without lowering our standards? How do we encourage their efforts without conveying a false sense of accomplishment? Perceptive teachers also recognize that students' own beliefs about their ability to be successful in new learning situations are a critical variable. Confronted with rigorous performance standards, some students may well believe that the target is beyond their grasp and may not, as a result, put forth needed effort.

There are no easy solutions to this dilemma. But reflect for a moment on the natural inclination displayed by parents and grandparents of toddlers and preschoolers. They regularly support new performance by encouraging small steps ("C'mon, you can do it!"), celebrating incremental achievements ("Listen, everyone! She said, 'dada'!"), and documenting growth (witness the refrigerator displays ranging from scribbles of color to identifiable pictures). These celebrations encourage children to keep trying and to strive for greater competence. They focus on what youngsters *can do* and how they have *improved* as a means of spurring continued growth.

Performance-based instruction demands a similar tack. Acknowledging the limitations of one-shot assessments, such as tests and quizzes, as the primary measures of important learning goals, some educators are moving toward creating collections of student work over time. One manifestation of this is the growing interest in and use of portfolios. Consider an analogy with photography. If a test or quiz represents a snapshot (a picture of learning at a specific moment) then a portfolio is more like a photo album—a collection of pictures showing growth and change over time.

Performance tasks should call upon students to demonstrate their knowledge and skills in a manner that reflects the world outside the classroom.

Just as portfolios can be extremely useful as a means of documenting student progress, they also provide a tangible way to display and celebrate student work. Grade-level teams at North Frederick Elementary School in Frederick, Maryland, for example, sponsor a "portfolio party" each fall and spring. Parents, grandparents, school board members, central office staff, business partners, and others are invited to review student work collected in portfolios. Before the party, teachers guide students in selecting examples from their portfolios that illustrate progress in key learning areas. During the party, students present their portfolios to the guests, describe their work during the year, highlight the progress they have made, and identify related goals for future improvement.

Principal Carolyn Strum says the school's portfolio program has had at least four benefits: (1) the systematic collection of student work throughout the year helps document student progress and achievement; (2) student work serves as a lens through which the faculty can reflect on their successes and adjust their instructional strategies; (3) school-to-home communication is enhanced as students present and explain their work to their parents and other adults; and (4) students assume greater ownership of their learning and display obvious pride when involved in selecting and showing off their accomplishments and growth.

Developing content standards, creating more authentic performance assessments, and establishing rigorous student performance standards will not—in and of themselves—substantially boost student achievement. But the seven principles above reflect promising ways that teachers and schools are beginning to rethink their curriculum and instructional strategies to ensure that *performance* is more than something measured at the end of a unit.

Notes

1. This performance task was developed in 1994 by R. Marzano and D. Pickering, Mid-Continent Regional Educational Laboratory Institute, Aurora, Colorado.
2. For a detailed discussion and examples of classroom performance lists, see M. Hibbard and colleagues, (1996), *Performance-Based Learning and Assessment*, (Alexandria, Va.: Association for Supervision and Curriculum Development).

References

Haller, E., D. Child and H. Walberg. (1988). "Can Comprehension Be Taught: A Qualitative Synthesis." *Educational Researcher* 17, 9: 5–8.

Gardner, H. (1991). *The Unschooled Mind.* New York: Basic Books.

McCombs, B. (1984). "Processes and Skills Underlying Intrinsic Motivation to Learn: Toward a Definition of Motivational Skills Training Intervention." *Educational Psychologist* 19: 197–218.

McTighe, J., and F. Lyman. (1988). "Cueing Thinking in the Classroom: The Promise of Theory-Embedded Tools." *Educational Leadership* 45, 7: 18–24.

Palinscar, A., and A. Brown. (1984). "Reciprocal Teaching of Comprehension Fostering and Comprehension Monitoring Activities." *Cognition and Instruction* 1: 117–176.

Schunk, D. (1990). "Goal Setting and Self-Efficacy During Self-Regulated Learning." *Educational Psychologist* 25, 1: 71–86.

Wiggins, G. (1993). *Assessing Student Performance: Exploring the Limits and Purposes of Testing.* San Francisco, Calif.: Jossey-Bass.

FRAME
the
DEBATE

Form at end of book

Issue 10 Summary

Two very different approaches to assessment are presented in these readings. Standardized testing compares the performance of one student with the performance of many; performance-based assessment examines a student's performance relative to the specific tasks taught to the student. Standardized testing uses tasks that are derived from the knowledge taught; performance-based assessment requires students to demonstrate use of the knowledge. Standardized testing is usually based on tests developed nationally; performance-based tests are drawn directly from the classroom curriculum. Standardized tests have usually been rigorously studied and validated; performance-based assessment is typically created by teachers themselves and is usually unresearched.

Neither approach to testing successfully meets all the needs educators have regarding student assessment. The two approaches described in these articles in many ways complement one another; educators might consider how they can intelligently use both approaches to assessment to ensure that students receive the best possible education.

Questions

1. Congratulations! Because of your winning responses to prior questions, you have kept your job as secretary of education. Once again, the president calls on you to make a recommendation about the stand she should take on ability grouping in American schools. Identify whether you support homogeneous or heterogeneous grouping, and make a case for your position.

2. What is the relationship between tracking and differentiated instruction, as described by Sally M. Reis and her co-authors? To what extent is differentiated instruction practical in a large classroom?

Introduction

How to group students within a grade has been a problem in education for decades. When a school has enough students in a single grade to create more than one classroom, school personnel must determine the basis by which they assign students to classroom 1 versus classroom 2. For many years, students have been grouped homogeneously on ability or academic achievement. That is, students who score higher on ability tests (usually, group intelligence tests) or, later, achievement tests are placed in the "upper" class, and the remaining students are placed in the "lower" class. Larger schools might have three, four, or more classes per grade, differentiated by student performance. This practice, known as tracking, is commonplace in American schools. Advocates of tracking argue that this approach allows instruction to occur more efficiently because teachers can better meet students' needs if their students do not fall along such a broad range.

Some schools in the United States (and many schools elsewhere) do not track students in the early grades. Rather, students are mixed heterogeneously. Thus, any given class includes students of varying ability levels or achievement levels, presenting teachers with a difficult task. However, advocates of heterogeneous grouping argue that the social benefits of heterogeneous grouping outweigh the drawbacks. They contend that ability grouping damages the self-esteem of students in the lower classes and prevents students from learning mutual respect; consequently, they recommend that schools detrack and mix students of varying abilities and achievements in the same classes.

Detracking for High Student Achievement

Bucking the politics of exclusivity and privilege, ten schools attempt to provide access to high standards for all students. A research team documents successes and challenges.

Jeannie Oakes and Amy Stuart Wells

Jeannie Oakes is Professor and Amy Stuart Wells is Associate Professor at the Graduate School of Education and Information Studies, UCLA, Los Angeles, CA 90095 (e-mail: oakes@ucla.edu and aswells@ucla.edu).

Standards reform in the United States aims at providing all children with a more challenging curriculum and holding schools accountable for their achievement. High academic standards, proponents argue, will alleviate inequalities in curriculum, instruction, and expectations for students. Purportedly, standards will also bring excellence by requiring all students to demonstrate higher levels of achievement and by providing all students with equal educational opportunities while preparing a more informed citizenry and a better trained work force.

But what about the firmly entrenched system of tracking that exposes students to dramatically different and unequal levels of curriculum? Consider the daily experiences of many lower-track students—particularly low-income students of color—whose classrooms offer fewer resources, low-level curriculum, and less powerful learning environments. How can these students reach higher standards?

The Reform Possibilities

For three years, we have followed the progress of 10 U.S. secondary schools where administrators and teachers have worked to restructure their schools in ways that could bring all students to high academic standards.[1] The schools, which vary in size from 500 to 3,000 students, have racially and socioeconomically mixed student populations. They are widely dispersed across the country, with one in the Northeast, three in the Midwest, one in the South, two in the Northwest, and three in various regions of California.

Faculties at these schools became disenchanted with their tracking systems, which had created academic, racial,

and socioeconomic divisions among students. White and middle-class students were overrepresented in honors and advanced classes, while lower-income African American and Latino students were disproportionately represented in general and remedial classes. These educators saw detracking as a way to pursue both excellence and equity. In addition to reducing or eliminating tracks, the schools created new schedules, reorganized teachers into teams, provided all students access to honors programs, instituted integrated curriculums, and created opportunities for students to get extra academic support—all in an effort to make standards-based education possible.

Toward Detracked Courses

For most schools, the first step was to do away with low-level classes. Union High School (all school names are pseudonyms) eliminated remedial tracks, leaving only one regular and one advanced track. Grant High School's English department eliminated its low-level 12th grade electives; all current electives are of equal rigor and offer an honors option.

When students develop insight into their own ways of knowing and learning, they become highly motivated students in the broader sense of the word, thirsty for a greater understanding of the world around them.

Other schools required students to take a core of heterogeneous courses. Two middle schools, King and Explorer, developed a common curriculum for all students. Some of the high schools required all students to pass benchmark classes—English I at Green Valley, biology at Grant, and algebra at Union. At Central High, all students begin 9th grade on a college-prep trajectory in English, science, and math.

Many schools simultaneously opened the top levels by allowing almost everyone access to honors programs. Others provided honors activities within heterogeneous classes. Teams at Explorer Middle School offer either multilevel activities or pullout challenge classes, available to all

---

students, several times a week. Traditionally low-achieving students and mainstreamed special education students frequently participate.

Green Valley also offers challenge projects within heterogeneous English classes. Students must complete at least one challenge class per quarter to receive an *A* in the class. Grant High's honors-option language arts classes allow any student who completes the work to receive an honors designation on his or her transcript. Plainview started a "Jaime Escalante" campaign that encourages minority students to enroll in advanced placement classes.

Double Doses of Curriculum

Many schools created opportunities for students to get extra help to master more challenging curriculum. Central High's faculty designed a customized calendar to provide a "double dose" of instruction for students having difficulty.[2] The intercessions allow low-achieving students a chance to repeat classes they had previously failed, without affecting their course load during the normal sessions. Several schools offer resource classes for low-achieving students; students enroll in these classes in place of an elective. Union High encourages capable students to double up in math courses and offers a support class, Transitions to College Math, for students who need a review of algebra concepts while enrolled in Algebra II or geometry. Bearfield Middle's math teachers offer tutoring sessions before or after school.

Grant High operates a math homework center one day a week in which teachers, community volunteers, and upper-level students tutor students who need help. In addition, two math teachers offer a summer challenge program in which minority students can complete a year's worth of math in an eight-week course. Students who complete the summer challenge may then skip to a higher-level math class in the fall. The class has already produced increased enrollments in calculus among formerly underrepresented minority groups.

Accommodating Diversity

Many teachers adopted classroom strategies that allow students to demonstrate their ability in previously unrecognized ways. Teachers at Explorer Middle School use Socratic Seminars, where students discuss open-ended questions in a format described by one teacher as "analogous to a conversation around the dinner table. . . . It allows those kids who don't feel comfortable in other settings a chance to speak their minds . . . because they know they can't be wrong."

Grant High School developed a Marine Science curriculum that relies very little on textbooks; instead, students take frequent field trips and complete small-group projects. Students might make anatomical models of fish out of play dough, or collect and identify various forms of ocean plant and animal life. All Marine Science students are required to design and teach a week of science classes at a local elementary school and guide a group of children on a beach walk.

Several high schools adopted programs that provide low-achieving students access to a broad span of math concepts. Interactive Math at Central and Liberty and Integrated Math at Grant interweave concepts from algebra, statistics, geometry, probability, and logic, with the conceptual demands increasing each year. Bob Jackson, math chair at Grant, credited the Integrated Math program for enabling a diverse group of students to learn math well:

They're the kind of kids who probably would have been doomed to spending two years in arithmetic and not doing anything substantive. And with the new mathematics, I can't believe the type of things and level they've achieved right now.

The math chair at Central High, Faith Jacobs, told us that you can't detrack in a traditional curriculum. Her colleague Christie Jeffries summed up their new curriculum: "We teach problem solving, writing, and communicating your mathematical thoughts." She also emphasized problem finding as an important dimension of mathematics: "They have to figure out what problems to do before they can even do the problems."

A Green Valley team of teachers piloting an integrated math and engineering program were excited about the content of combined mathematics and vocational studies. Math teacher Gloria Pedroza said,

It is really good math. It isn't watered down, and it is very much applied. You won't ever get this question from a kid: "When will I ever use this?"

Many schools developed multicultural curriculums, such as Grant's required 9th grade World Cultures course and Liberty's Ethnic Studies class, which engage students who show little interest in traditional curriculum and allow low-achieving minority students to display their culturally specific knowledge. Many schools offer African American or Mexican American History, African American or Latin American Literature, Ethnic Literature, and Women's Literature. As an English teacher at Green Valley stated, "We have got to find ways for all kids to find entry and go as far as they can."

King Middle School's Project Equal incorporates multicultural literature into the curriculum and the library. Last year, several 8th grade teachers attended a course on how to teach a unit on the Holocaust. Teachers at other schools studied culturally related learning styles.

We also found teachers who based their curriculum and pedagogy on theories of the multidimensional nature of intelligence and giftedness. Plainview English teacher Olivia Jeffers developed an interdisciplinary, individualized course that a multiracial group of both high- and low-track students take to help satisfy college-entrance English requirements. Students choose much of their own reading and work on research projects at their own pace. Jeffers does not feel that she is holding the high-achieving students back by having them in the same room with low-achieving students. In fact, she sees it as quite the opposite. She described the benefit of the detracked classroom for a high-achieving white student from a wealthy suburban family:

In class discussions, this girl not only contributes her ideas, but she also gets insight from somebody else who hasn't had her experience, or doesn't own a horse, or a place out in the country—a kid who gets on the bus every day and lives in two rooms. She listens to kids who've had to struggle just to survive.

Jeffers says she has constructed a learning environment for students where she can find "the genius within them." She finds that when students develop insight into their own ways of knowing and learning, they become highly motivated *students* in the broader sense of the word, thirsty for a greater understanding of the world around them.

Like Jeffers, other teachers changed their conceptions of ability after creating environments in which all students could be smart. One teacher told us, "Heterogeneous grouping has made teachers think differently about all kids; they see more potential."

Another teacher stated, "The program has done amazing things for standard-track kids. All of sudden, somebody says, You can do this!'"

A Cautionary Note

Most of the educators we studied changed their practices in the belief that colleagues, families, and students would happily support reform that enhanced the achievement of students previously in the low track, without harming—and perhaps even enriching—the experiences of students who would otherwise be in high tracks. Yet they quickly learned that their challenges were compounded by formidable cultural and political obstacles. They ran headlong into deeply held beliefs and ideologies about intelligence, racial differences, social stratification, and privilege. Conventional conceptions of intelligence, ability, and giftedness combined with the local community culture and politics around race social class to fuel enormous resistance.

In the end, none of the schools achieved the extent of detracking and curriculum reform hoped for. Their promising efforts toward high standards for all students were cut short by fears that the advantages of high-achieving students would be compromised.

One school started a "Jaime Escalante campaign" in which minority students are encouraged to enroll in advanced placement classes.

The experience of the gifted education specialist at Explorer Middle School, which offered challenge courses to *all* students, captures the essence of the battles. Parents of identified gifted students severely criticized her for not offering their children separate enrichment classes. What upset the parents most was not the quality of the curriculum. It was that their children were no longer being singled out and treated differently:

They didn't ask, "Well, what are our kids learning in your classes?" I found that really dismaying, because I was prepared to tell them what we do in class. I had course outlines. I send objectives, goals, and work requirements home with every class, and nobody asked me anything about that. . . . I'm dealing with their egos, more than what their kids really need educationally.

This political battle was ostensibly fought over which kids—gifted or not gifted, and according to which definition—would have access to which curriculum and which teacher. The cultural underpinnings of such battles, however, are far more profound. At risk for the families of high-track students is the entire system of meritocracy on which they base their privileged positions in society. As this system begins to crack, these parents often employ tactics that make reform politically impossible. Given that detracking is basic to standards-based reform, policymakers and educators stand forewarned.

Notes

1. Funded in part by the Lilly Endowment, the study used qualitative methods to examine changes in school organization, grouping practices, and classroom pedagogy. Our research associates were Robert Cooper, Amanda Datnow, Diane Hirshberg, Martin Lipton, Karen Ray, Irene Serna, Estella Williams, and Susie Yonezawa. For a detailed report, see *Beyond the Technicalities of School Reform: Policy Lessons from Detracking Schools,* by Jeannie Oakes and Amy Stuart Wells (Los Angeles: UCLA Graduate School of Education and Information Studies 1996).
2. MacIver uses the term *double dose* to describe strategies that provide low-achieving students with extra time and instruction on the regular curriculum, rather than a separate remedial curriculum. See *Helping Students Who Fall Behind,* by Douglas MacIver (Baltimore: Center for Research on Students Placed at Risk, Johns Hopkins University 1991).

Form at end of book

A Response:
Equal Does Not Mean Identical

Detracking alone is not the best means to raise student achievement. Students with different abilities, interests, and levels of motivation should be offered differentiated instruction that meets their individual needs.

Sally M. Reis, Sandra N. Kaplan, Carol A. Tomlinson, Karen L. Westberg, Carolyn M. Callahan, and Carolyn R. Cooper

Sally M. Reis is Professor of Educational Psychology at the University of Connecticut, School of Education, Department of Educational Psychology, 249 Glenbrook Rd., University-64, Storrs, CT 06269-2064. Sandra N. Kaplan is Professor of Education at the University of Southern California. Carol A. Tomlinson is Associate Professor of Education at the University of Virginia. Karen L. Westberg is Associate Professor of Education at the University of Connecticut. Carolyn M. Callahan is Professor of Education at the University of Virginia. Carolyn R. Cooper is a consultant in the field of gifted and talented education. The authors are members of the Executive Committee of the National Association of Gifted Children.

Latoya was already an advanced reader when she entered 1st grade in a large, urban school district. Her teacher noticed the challenging chapter books Latoya brought to school and read with little effort. After administering a reading assessment, the school's reading consultant confirmed that Latoya was reading at the 5th grade level. Latoya's parents reported with pride that she had started to read independently when she was 3 years old and "had read every book she could get her hands on."

Teachers who offer differentiated curriculum and instruction view students as individuals with their own skills, interests, styles, and talents.

In the March 1998 issue of *Educational Leadership*, Jeannie Oakes and Amy Stuart Wells argue in their article "Detracking for High Student Achievement" that high academic standards "will also bring excellence by requiring all students to demonstrate higher levels of achievement and by providing all students with *equal* [emphasis added] educational opportunities while preparing a more informed

citizenry and a better trained work force" (p. 38). But what about Latoya? If, as it sounds, *equal* means *identical,* will equal educational opportunities sufficiently challenge Latoya in reading?

Equal and Identical Are Not the Same

Providing identical educational opportunities for all students will not enable Latoya to increase her reading level, nor will they help her attain more advanced and more sophisticated levels of accomplishments in reading. Rather, if appropriate curriculum and instruction are not supplied, she will systematically be held back and will stagnate in a system that offers identical opportunities for all students. What she needs is different content, resources, and support! It is clear that in Latoya's class *all children should not be reading at the 1st grade level just because they are 1st graders.* If Latoya has not made any further progress in reading by the end of the school year, she will have wasted valuable opportunities. To achieve at increasingly higher levels in reading and to continue to develop her talents, she will require different, not equal, resources, teaching strategies, and content. How can equal curriculum, instruction, and expectations address the diverse learning needs in Latoya's classroom?

Why Is Differentiation Difficult?

Latoya is now a 5th grader. When Latoya was in 1st grade, her teacher had to simultaneously meet Latoya's educational needs and address the needs of her classmates, many of whom neither recognized initial consonant sounds nor had begun to read. Four years later, Latoya's 5th grade teacher, looking for information in Latoya's permanent file, noticed the reading assessment completed in 1st grade and read with amazement about her early, advanced reading. As a 5th grader, Latoya is still reading only slightly above the 5th grade level. Her teacher could find no evidence that any curricular or instructional adjustments had been made in previous years to meet Latoya's learning needs. Discouraged about what she perceived as the school system's inability to develop Latoya's talents in reading, the 5th grade teacher contacted the special education coordinator and asked about provisions to challenge advanced students in reading. The special education coordinator responded with amazement. "We don't need any services for gifted students. We expect high levels of achievement from all students. And anyway, we don't have any gifted kids in this school." The classroom teacher was left wondering what she could do to motivate Latoya, who still seems to have a talent in reading but is achieving only slightly above grade level. Latoya's story is true.

The needs of students like Latoya are often unmet in their classrooms. All children need to learn and to increase their current levels of achievement, yet whole-group, single-size-fits-all instruction rarely offers the kinds of adaptation required to meet the needs of a diverse group of learners. Differentiation is defined in various ways, but it is usually regarded as accommodating learning differences in children by identifying students' strengths and using appropriate strategies to address a variety of abilities, preferences, and styles. Then, whole groups, small groups, and individual students can equally engage in a variety of curriculum enrichment and acceleration experiences.

How can equal curriculum, instruction, and expectations address the diverse learning needs in a classroom?

Teachers who offer differentiated curriculum and instruction view students as individuals with their own skills, interests, styles, and talents. They tailor their curriculum and instruction to meet the needs of advanced learners by using such strategies as curriculum compacting. This technique eliminates or streamlines content that students already know and replaces it with more challenging material, often based on students' interests (Reis & Renzulli, 1992; Renzulli, 1978). Other strategies include tiered instruction and assignments, which provide different learning opportunities for students at different achievement levels. Independent study and opportunities for individually prescribed levels of content and instruction are also important differentiation strategies (Renzulli, 1977; Tomlinson, 1996, 1997).

Unfortunately, recent research indicates that only a small number of teachers offer differentiation in their classrooms (Archambault et al., 1993; Tomlinson et al., 1995). Similar research about high-achieving learners in heterogeneous classrooms indicates that many children are unchallenged and are not given appropriate levels of curriculum and instruction (Cohen, 1997). In one study, observers in 46 classrooms found that high-achieving students were asked to do exactly what students who achieved at average levels were doing in 84 percent of the activities. Very little differentiation of content or instruction was provided (Westberg, Archambault, Dobyns, & Salvin, 1993).

Whole-group, single-size-fits-all instruction rarely offers the kinds of adaptation required to meet the needs of a diverse group of learners.

We have also investigated why many teachers do not offer differentiation. In a survey of randomly selected 3rd and 4th grade teachers in public schools, 61 percent indicated that they had no training in meeting the needs of high-achieving students in heterogeneous classrooms. Fifty-four percent of the responding teachers in private or independent schools indicated that they had no background or training in meeting the needs of such students (Archambault et al., 1993). We also know that preservice and novice teachers understand, but do not have the background and skills to assess or address, the diversity in levels of achievement and aptitude for learning in the classroom (Tomlinson et al., 1995). The good news is that when trained in differentiation, 90 percent of classroom teachers were able to compact curriculum for students who had already mastered the content (Reis et al., 1993). In the same study, we also learned that more training time and differing types of professional development experiences, such as peer coaching, resulted in higher levels of success in implementing curriculum compacting. In another study, we found that when training and support are provided, many classroom teachers can and do furnish differentiation to above-average and advanced students in both heterogeneous and homogeneous groups (Westberg & Archambault, 1995).

It's Not the Grouping That Matters, It's What Happens in the Group

Does providing differentiated curriculum and instruction mean that we create inequalities, even if it occurs within various grouping options? If one reads the article "Detracking for High Student Achievement" by Oakes and Wells (1998), it would certainly appear so. "But what about the firmly entrenched system of tracking that exposes students to dramatically different and unequal levels of curriculum?" they ask (p. 38). What does tracking have to do with Latoya? The issue is *not* grouping or tracking, which we regard as two quite different concepts. Tracking is the general, and usually permanent, assignment of students to classes that are taught at a certain level and with whole-group instruction. Grouping is a more flexible, less permanent arrangement of students that takes into account factors in addition to ability, such as motivation, interests, instructional levels, and student effort (Renzulli &

Reis, 1991). What is important, in our belief, is what happens within the different types of grouping arrangements used in schools—age groups, instructional groups, or interest groups. We believe that assigning children to predetermined tracks on the basis of ability or achievement is wrong, but so is whole-class instruction with no instructional modification that systematically holds back children like Latoya. All learners in our schools, including those who are advanced, should be challenged academically. The context in which that learning takes place is negotiable, but whether it takes place is not negotiable.

All Parents Want Their Children Challenged

To argue that parents of high-achieving or gifted students want to create or continue a system of "meritocracy on which they base their privileged positions in society" (Oakes & Wells, 1998, p. 41) seems to perpetuate a false belief that pits parents of high-achieving students against all others, a condition simply not backed up either by data presented in the article or by our experiences. Some parents of students identified as gifted may have separate classes as their goal, but in our collective years of experience working with these parents, they have not been the majority.

The thousands of parents with whom we speak each year are more interested in finding the best possible education for their children. In a small manufacturing city in Connecticut, a city where over 55 percent of the population is Hispanic, parents of high-achieving Hispanic students argued for a return to some form of grouping for their children. Their middle school had eliminated all forms of grouping in all classes. With no appropriate differentiation in the classroom, parents saw that their children were not being academically challenged. Many teachers told the parents that they simply could not meet the needs of students representing a seven- or eight-year range of achievement in some of their classes. The teachers themselves asked for help in flexibly grouping students into clusters within specified classes so that they could better address students' differing instructional needs.

In a magnet school for high-achieving Hispanic students in Los Angeles, talented students are flexibly grouped for instruction in all content areas. Providing for the academic readiness of learners happens in all sorts of forms in all sorts of schools where educators strive for the maximum development of student potential.

All parents want their children to achieve at high levels and to learn at an appropriate pace, depth, and level of complexity. To blame parents for wanting challenge for their children or to accuse them of creating a meritocracy ignores the very real evidence that some students are not being challenged in school. Instead of attacking the parents of these students, we invite them to participate in the dialogue on school improvement by encouraging open discussion about how schools can address the needs of all children and, indeed, how parents can be active partners in achieving this goal.

References

Archambault, F. X., Jr., Westberg, K. L., Brown, S., Hallmark, B. W., Zhang, W., & Emmons, C. (1993). Classroom practices used with gifted third and fourth grade students. *Journal for the Education of the Gifted, 16*(2), 103–119.

Cohen, C. S. (1997). *The effectiveness of peer-coaching on classroom teachers' use of differentiation for gifted middle school students.* Unpublished doctoral dissertation, University of Connecticut.

Oakes, J., & Wells, A. S. (1998). Detracking for high student achievement. *Educational Leadership, 55*(6), 38–41.

Reis, S. M., & Renzulli, J. S. (1992). Using curriculum compacting to challenge the above-average. *Educational Leadership. 50*(2), 51–57.

Reis, S. M., Westberg, K. L., Kulikowich, J., Caillard, F., Herbert, T., Plucker, J., Purcell, J. H., Rogers, J. B., & Smist, J. M. (1993). *Why not let high ability students start school in January? The curriculum compacting study.* (Research Monograph 93106). Storrs, CT: University of Connecticut. The National Research Center on the Gifted and Talented.

Renzulli, J. S. (1977). *The enrichment triad model.* Mansfield Center, CT: Creative Learning Press.

Renzulli, J. S. (1978). What makes giftedness? Re-examining a definition. *Phi Delta Kappan, 60,* 180–184, 261.

Renzulli, J. S., & Reis, S. M. (1991). The reform movement and the quiet crisis in gifted education. *Gifted Child Quarterly. 35*(1), 26–35.

Tomlinson, C. A. (Developer). (1996). Differentiating instruction for mixed-ability classrooms. [Professional Inquiry Kit]. (Available from ASCD)

Tomlinson, C. A. (Developer). (1997). Differentiating instruction. [Facilitator's Guide and Videos]. (Available from ASCD)

Tomlinson, C. A., Callahan, C. M., Moon, T. R., Tomchin, E. M., Landrum, M., Imbeau, M., Hunsaker, S. L., & Eiss, N. (1995). *Preservice teacher preparation in meeting the needs of gifted and other academically diverse students,* (Research Monograph 95134). Charlottesville, VA: University of Virginia, The National Research Center on the Gifted and Talented.

Westberg, K. L., & Archambault, F. X., Jr. (Eds .) (1995). *Profiles of successful practices for high ability students in elementary classrooms.* (Research Monograph 95122). Storrs, CT: University of Connecticut. The National Research Center on the Gifted and Talented.

Westberg, K. L., Archambault, F. X., Dobyns, S. M., & Salvin, T. J. (1993). The classroom practices observation study. *Journal for the Education of the Gifted. 16*(2), 120–146.

Form at end of book

Issue 11 Summary

Educators have struggled for many decades with the issue of equality. When we seek equality for all students, does that mean that we treat all students equally by providing them with the same type of instruction? Or does it mean that we treat them equally by providing them with instruction that meets their individual needs? Can we afford to organize schools such that we meet students' individual needs?

Very commonly, teachers teach "to the middle"—that is, to the average level in their class. Students above that level may be bored; those below that level may be lost. This pattern is true whether classes are grouped homogeneously or heterogeneously, the only difference being that, in a homogeneously grouped classroom, the range of student levels is more narrow. The concept of differentiated teaching is intriguing because, in theory, this method means that no students will be bored or lost. However, the reality may be very different from the theory. To implement differentiated instruction, teachers will have to think about their lessons and organize their classrooms differently. Further, they may need to obtain support in the form of smaller classes or teachers' aides. Is society willing to spend more on education to pay for smaller classes or more teachers' aides? Is society truly committed to the idea that all students with appropriate education can succeed?

The Reading Controversy

ISSUE 12

Questions

1. What are the benefits of a phonics approach? What are its limitations?

2. What are some ways that the whole language approach and the phonics approach can be combined to promote the learning of reading?

3. Why do you think the field of education has tended to embrace the "extremes" of the phonics approach and the whole language approach? Why has it been difficult to persuade educators to use both methods?

Introduction

Learning how to read is one of the most fundamental tasks of the elementary school years, but *how* to teach reading is a much-debated issue. Two schools of thought have dominated the debate. Advocates of the phonics approach believe that students need to learn the associations between symbols and sounds in order to decode printed words. Whole language advocates believe that students need to learn about the context of writing and to use prediction to help them make sense of what they read.

As you might imagine, phonics advocates criticize the whole language approach because they believe that students learning through a whole language-based curriculum will lack the basic word attack skills to decipher words. Whole language advocates criticize the phonics approach as focusing on words out of context *(bat . . . cat. . . . sat)* or requiring the reading of banal sentences ("The fat cat sat on the mat") and thereby dampening students' intrinsic motivation to read.

Which method works best? The state of California, which some years ago embraced the whole language approach, has now had an about-face and rejects whole language entirely, blaming it for the increase in reading problems. Lurching from one approach to another is probably not advisable: recent critiques of reading research have indicated that students, in fact, need both approaches at different times in the process of learning to read.

Where's the Phonics?
Making a Case for Its Direct and Systematic Instruction

Patrick Groff

Groff was a professor of education at San Diego State University. He may be contacted at 5152 College Gardens Court, San Diego, CA 92115, USA.

In their article in the May 1997 issue of *The Reading Teacher,* Diane Lapp and James Flood accurately frame the current dispute among reading instruction specialists as to how phonics information is learned best by beginning readers. Since 1973, one side of this controversy has contended that beginning readers' acquisition of phonics knowledge is *not* an indispensable part of their written word recognition development. According to Frank Smith (1973) teaching children to master phonics information, and apply it when reading, is one of the 12 easy ways to make learning to read difficult. Kenneth Goodman (1973) concurs with this assessment.

The other side of this controversy (Chall, 1983; Share & Stanovich, 1995) points to relevant experimental research findings that suggest phonics knowledge is a prerequisite to novice readers' accurate identification of written words. Arguments to the contrary are held by these advocates to be "outdated and not congruent with the latest [empirical] research evidence" (Share & Stanovich, 1995, p. 36).

As Lapp and Flood rightly observe, most teachers today agree that children's acquisition of phonics skills is an essential part of their reading development. Teachers, by and large, also concur that "children who start slowly in acquiring decoding skills rarely become strong readers" (p. 698). There appears to be widespread assent among teachers that "early acquisition of decoding skills leads to wider reading [by children] in and out of school" (p. 698).

Nonetheless, it also is true, as Lapp and Flood point out, that "ideas about how and when to teach phonics are recurring points of contention" among teachers and teacher educators" (p. 696). These issues indeed remain "controversial" among reading education professionals.

The Integrated-Balanced Approach

Lapp and Flood offer to resolve this dispute over how phonics should be taught to children by proposing an "integrated-balanced" approach to its instruction. In the example of a reading lesson that they describe, the large majority of available teaching time is given to the development of children's listening comprehension. The teacher reads a given story aloud to children three times. In preparation for the first of these read-alouds, students speculate about the meanings of pictures in the story and make predictions as to what will happen. After this initial read-aloud, children share their thoughts about the story's content and decide if their predictions were correct or not.

As the teacher reads the story a second time, pupils listen for "color words," words that help the reader "see" the story's content. Following this, the teacher writes a list of these words, which the children copy. Then, pupils again discuss the story, particularly the author's use of color words.

After a final read-aloud, the children copy a list of words from the story that contain a prominent spelling pattern such as *at*.

At last, students read the story independently. Following this self-sustained reading, they create artwork and participate in roleplaying activities related to the story. When possible, during this time the teacher works with groups of children and individuals who are not progressing satisfactorily in attaining phonics skills.

Lapp and Flood contend that the attention given to word recognition in this lesson is a satisfactory version of "explicit" phonics teaching. In my opinion, it clearly is not.

Questions about the Exemplar Lesson

Lapp and Flood are convinced they have described the approach to phonics instruction that will best serve beginning readers' written word recognition needs, "create

Groff, Patrick. (1998, October). Where's the Phonics? Making a Case for Its Direct and Systematic Instruction. *The Reading Teacher,* 52(2), 138–141.

harmony in the learner's mind," and "make them lifelong independent readers" (p. 699). However, their beliefs in this respect give rise to a number of troublesome uncertainties.

Lapp and Flood, for example, claim that "there is no strong research base to support this practice" of "teach[ing] phonics systematically and explicitly, separate from rather than as an integrated segment of text" (p. 696). They contradict themselves elsewhere, however, when they assert that "a trend in the data favors explicit phonics [instruction] because it provides children with close approximations between letters and sounds" (p. 699).

In fact, an increasing preponderance of experimental evidence supports the teaching of isolated letter-speech sound correspondences (phonics). A new mandate for explicit phonics instruction in public schools in California entitled *Teaching Reading* (California State Board of Education, 1996), for example, is based on a *Collection of Articles on Beginning Reading Instruction* (California State Board of Education, 1997) that confirms the validity of explicit reading instruction. A highly impressive article in this collection is the report of a synthesis of 30 years of experimental research on reading conducted by the National Institute of Child Health and Human Development (Grossen, 1997). The report concludes that several empirical studies find that a "mixture of decoding and comprehension instruction in the same instructional activity is clearly less effective" (p. 14) than separation of the two activities as done in explicit phonics instruction.

Hysteria or Rational Deduction?

Lapp and Flood charge that "educators today are being pressured by hysteria from the media, parents, and legislatures to teach phonics systematically and explicitly" (that is, not in the manner that they recommend). It is not hysteria, however, but rather findings of highly respected experimental research that create the present opposition to an integrated-balanced phonics program that Lapp and Flood advocate. This empirical evidence consistently indicates that explicit phonics teaching is superior.

Much experimental evidence indicates that considerable time should be devoted in reading lessons to explicit and comprehensive development of beginning readers' phonics skills (see for example, Beck & Juel, 1995; Grossen, 1997; Grossen & Carnine, 1990; Hirsch, 1996; Liberman & Liberman, 1990; Pressley & Rankin, 1994; Share & Stanovich, 1995; Williams, 1991). The consensus of pertinent empirical investigations is that the more phonics information that children acquire, and learn to apply to decode written words, the better. There is not sufficient time available in beginning reading instruction periods to conduct the many integrated-balanced activities that Lapp and Flood propose and at the same time teach phonics information satisfactorily.

As detailed by Lapp and Flood, the integrated-balanced approach to phonics teaching presumes that unless most of the time available for beginning reading lessons is given over to elaborate and time-consuming discussions by beginning readers of simplistic, easily comprehended stories read aloud to them, these children will be unable to learn phonics information satisfactorily. It appears that Lapp and Flood greatly underestimate the extent to which typical beginning readers understand that print carries messages. Almost all children at school-entry age realize that unsophisticated, uncomplicated stories read aloud to them portray a cast of recognizable characters, who behave in predictable ways or carry out understandable actions to some reasonable end.

The most effective beginning reading programs also put the least possible demands on pupils' reading comprehension by making sure that stories children read independently contain very few words that are outside their speaking/listening vocabularies (Grossen, 1997). So, after a child decodes a familiar word when reading, through the application of phonics information, he or she experiences no confusion about word meaning. By minimizing the task of comprehension of word meanings, children can devote most of their mental energy to developing accurate and rapid (automatic) word recognition skills. Almost nothing relates more closely to reading comprehension of neophyte readers than does this automatic word recognition (Samuels, 1994).

Integrated-Balanced Phonics Goes Wrong

Lapp and Flood's integrated-balanced phonics instruction plan clearly does not place the highest possible priority on teaching beginning readers the alphabetic code (i.e., how letters represent speech sounds and how these sounds then can be blended together to produce recognizable spoken words). Instead, it emphasizes development of children's oral language competencies.

Lapp and Flood's belief that 5- to 7-year-old readers "are unable to learn [phonics information] through analytic abstract or auditory experiences" is refuted by the bulk of relevant empirical evidence (Grossen, 1997; Liberman & Liberman, 1990). Moreover, Lapp and Flood's reference to the controversial views of Carbo (1987) as proof of their view on phonics teaching compromises its credibility.

Unfortunately, Lapp and Flood also demand that phonics instruction serve a function for which it was never designed. They state "systematic, decontextualized phonics" teaching "may at best produce better reading comprehension scores . . . only through Grade 3" (p. 696). Only rarely have reading educators argued, however, that phonics knowledge plays a dominant role in upper-grade children's reading comprehension. Other factors, such as the large number of unfamiliar topics and word meanings in upper-grade textbooks, have a greater influence on students' reading comprehension in these grades than do phonics skills (Chall, Jacobs, & Baldwin, 1990). All teachers should be aware, nonetheless, that explicit phonics instruction prepares primary-grade children to automatically recognize the words that are part of their oral vocabulary.

Conclusions

Too many questions can be raised about validity of the Lapp-Flood integrated-balanced phonics instruction approach to accept the claim that it will produce "lifelong independent learners who are able and excited readers," and who have access to "the wonderful world of books" (p. 699). No one knows, of course, which kind of phonics instruction develops "lifelong" results. Such research has never been conducted. Access to books depends most heavily on the size of a school's library budget.

It is well established, on the other hand, that the great majority of experimental findings on reading development make clear that explicit, direct, systematic, intensive, comprehensive, and early teaching of phonics information is the most productive way to develop children's automatic word recognition skills. Independent repeated readings of a story by pupils also assist greatly to that end. However, the phonics instruction scheme that Lapp and Flood recommend does not include or emphasize either of these practices.

The Lapp-Flood approach does not prepare children to read stories independently in the most effective way possible. That is, the indirect, implicit, and nonintensive mode of phonics instruction that it incorporates has not been found experimentally to be superior to explicit phonics teaching.

The Lapp-Flood approach takes up too much of children's time by having them listen repeatedly to stories,

rather than adequately preparing them to read independently. As Liberman (1989) convincingly explains, pupils' listening ability and the successful recognition of written words are two fundamentally different processes. The former develops naturally without any conscious effort on the child's part. In learning to read, the child does not enjoy any such biological advantage. Instead, pupils are faced with the task of paying close attention to arbitrarily shaped optical forms and must learn to associate these letters with an equally prescriptive set of speech sounds. The fact that illiterate children have no conscious awareness of the speech sounds that make up their oral language greatly compounds the problem they face in learning to read.

Despite these facts, the integrated-balanced instruction that Lapp and Flood advocate for helping children acquire letter-speech sound associations tips the scale emphatically in favor of implicit, contextualized learning of phonics skills. They make this appear to be a reasonable, moderate, and harmonious way to direct students' learning. However, when examined through the magnifying lens of experimental evidence, Lapp and Flood's approach proves to be inferior to explicit phonics instruction.

References

Beck, L. L., & Juel, C. (1995). The role of decoding in learning to read. *American Educator, 19,* 8, 21–25, 39–42.

California State Board of Education. (1996). *Teaching reading.* Sacramento, CA: California Department of Education.

California State Board of Education. (1997). *Collection of articles on beginning reading instruction.* Sacramento, CA: California Department of Education.

Carbo, M. (1987). Reading style research: "What works" isn't always phonics. *Phi Delta Kappan, 68,* 431–435.

Chall, J. S. (1983). *Learning to read: The great debate.* New York: McGraw-Hill.

Chall, J. S., Jacobs, V. A., & Baldwin, L. E. (1990). *The reading crisis: Why poor children fall behind.* Cambridge, MA: Harvard University Press.

Goodman, K. S. (1973). The 13th easy way to make learning to read difficult. *Reading Research Quarterly, 8,* 484–493.

Grossen, B. (1997). *30 years of research: What we know about how children learn to read.* Santa Cruz, CA: Center for the Future of Teaching and Learning.

Grossen, B., & Carnine, D. (1990). Translating research on initial reading instruction into classroom practice. *Interchange, 21,* 15–23.

Hirsch, E. D. (1996). Reality's revenge: Research and ideology. *American Educator, 20,* 4–6, 31–46.

Lapp, D., & Flood, J. (1997). Where's the phonics? Making a case (again) for integrated code instruction. *The Reading Teacher, 50,* 696–700.

Liberman, A. M. (1989). Reading is hard just because listening is easy. In C. von Euler, I. Lundberg, & G. Lennerstrand (Eds.), *Brain and reading* (pp. 197–205). London: Macmillan.

Liberman, I. Y., & Liberman, A. M. (1990). Whole language vs. code emphasis: Underlying assumptions and their implications for reading instruction. *Annals of Dyslexia, 40,* 51–76.

Pressley, M., & Rankin, J. (1994). More about whole language methods of reading instruction for students at risk for early reading failure. *Learning Disabilities Research & Practice, 9,* 157–168.

Samuels, S. J. (1994). Word recognition. In R. B. Ruddell, M. R. Ruddell, & H. Singer (Eds.), *Theoretical models and processes in reading* (4th ed., pp. 359–380). Newark, DE: International Reading Association.

Share, D. L., & Stanovich, K. E. (1995). Cognitive processes in early reading development: Accommodating individual differences into a mode of acquisition. *Issues in Education, 1,* 1–57.

Smith, F. (1973). *Psycholinguistics and reading.* New York: Holt, Rinehart & Winston.

Williams, J. P. (1991). The meaning of a phonics base for reading instruction. In W. Ellis (Ed.), *All language and the creation of literacy* (pp. 9–19). Baltimore: Orton Dyslexia Society.

Form at end of book

Reading the Right Way

What research and best practices say about eliminating failure among beginning readers.

Bill Honig

Bill Honig is author of Teaching Our Children to Read: The Role of Skills in a Comprehensive Reading Program, *published by Corwin Press. He is visiting distinguished professor of education at San Francisco State University and president of the Consortium of Reading Excellence, 5500 Shellmound St., Suite 140, Emeryville, Calif. 94608. E-mail: Honig@sirius.com*

Teaching children to read is the key to subsequent educational success and should be the most important priority of elementary school.

Yet in many inner-city, suburban and rural schools, large and growing numbers of children are reaching upper elementary levels unable to read and understand grade-appropriate material—as many as 70 to 80 percent in some inner-city schools and 30 percent in some suburban schools. The magnitude of this problem causes not only innumerable personal tragedies but also significantly drives instruction down and jeopardizes the future of our public schools.

What is most frustrating is that much of this reading failure could be prevented if schools just applied what is known about beginning reading instruction. While the field of reading seems mired in contentious debate—principally pitting phonics against whole language as the best instructional approach—a powerful and persuasive consensus has developed among educational, cognitive and medical researchers, as well as our best teachers, about the causes and cures of reading failure.

Ripe for Improvement

These ideas have been successfully implemented in thousands of classrooms in diverse settings with spectacular results. They draw from the whole language movement but also include organized skill development components such as phonemic awareness, phonics and decoding. As such, effective reading programs use elements from both traditions that have proven successful while discarding those that have proven ineffective.

Although this comprehensive approach is not driving reading instruction in most classrooms, teachers are hungry for information about specifics and willing to apply them in their classrooms and schools. Reading instruction is ripe for improvement because teachers daily face children who are not learning to read, and they realize a gap in instruction exists. In such situations, administrative leadership is crucial.

Before change can occur, administrators need a detailed knowledge of the reading process so they don't get taken in by specious advice.

Although for most children the reading battle is lost in kindergarten and 1st grade, the best place to begin the search for remedies is to observe students who have difficulty reading in upper grades. In the course of working with school districts nationwide to improve reading performance, I have asked more than 10,000 teachers to describe such students. They uniformly state (consistent with the research) that reading-deficient children in the upper primary grades exhibit:

- poor decoding skills (students struggle with too many individual words and don't know how to effectively tackle a new word);

- weak vocabulary;

- the inability to read strategically and actively;

- poor spelling;

- too few reading opportunities outside of school; and

- poor motivation, lack of confidence or avoidance behavior, all stemming from experiencing too much reading failure.

Rule of Thumb

Recent research has developed a powerful explanatory theory of why poor readers exhibit these behaviors. The theory is based on the two ways that proficient readers gain meaning from text: (1) from the *word*—the vocabulary concept underlying an individual word and (2) from the *passage*—from stringing those words together and thinking about their meaning.

This research shows that in proficient reading, word recognition is primarily an automatic, unconscious and rapid process. Conversely, passage understanding is primarily an active, engaged, thinking process of weaving individual words into a meaningful whole, thinking about what the author is saying and connecting it to other ideas.

If readers take too much time and mental effort decoding individual words, they can't attend to passage meaning. The rule of thumb is this: A student should recognize 18 or 19 out of 20 words automatically or reading comprehension suffers, a construct referred to as automaticity. Additionally, by sixth grade if students are reading below 100 to 120 words a minute, they probably cannot attend to meaning properly. The 1992 National Assessment of Educational Progress showed that more than 40 percent of American 4th-graders read too slowly to understand what they were reading.

A balanced reading program should include strategies to develop both automatic word recognition *and* passage comprehension. Many reading programs used in schools fall short of this balanced approach. They de-emphasize the word side and the tools by which students become automatic with a growing number of words and over-rely on the passage side. These inadequate programs are based on the theory that the arduous instructional task of developing word recognition skills for many children can be avoided or minimized because the passage can supply word meaning. Vast amounts of research and experience now dispute this view.

One strand of studies, focusing on computer eye research, has disposed of the claims that proficient readers skip a large number of words. Actually, studies suggest, they read virtually every word and see all the letters in each word. (Try skipping a *not* in expository text.)

Other studies show that using context can help decode words only about 10 to 25 percent of the time and this rate is too slow for fluency. It is the poorer readers who rely on context-based decoding strategies. Finally, studies have demonstrated that using indirect methods first (such as context) and waiting to directly instruct those who fail to intuit the alphabetic system significantly decreases the odds that those struggling students will learn to read properly.

In 1st grade, recognizing individual words contributes about 80 percent of meaning. (The words and concepts of the story are simple and if the words are recognized the meaning of the story is apparent.) In later grades, other factors increase in importance such as strategic reading ability or the ability to discuss what has been read, but recognizing individual words still remains crucial to reading for understanding.

Decoding Skills

Becoming automatic with a growing number of words depends on knowing how to use the alphabetic system to decode words. (Decoding is the ability to read through a word from left to right, generate the sounds that are connected to all the letters or letter patterns in that word and manipulate those sounds until they connect to a word in the student's speaking vocabulary). This finding is one of the most validated in reading research and equipping each child with the ability to decode simple words should be a major goal of kindergarten and early 1st-grade reading instruction.

First-grade decoding ability predicts 80 to 90 percent of reading comprehension in 2nd and 3rd grade and still accounts for nearly 40 percent of reading comprehension by 9th grade!

Why should the ability to sound out a pseudo-word like *mot* in mid-1st grade and *lote* or *blar* by late 1st be so predictive of later reading ability? (A pseudo-word assures that the child has not seen and memorized the word and so is a true test of decoding ability.) The reason has to do with storing words efficiently in memory for subsequent rapid retrieval.

Thoroughly decoding a word the first few times it is read forces a reader to connect information about the unique pattern of each of the letter/sound combinations to the meaning of the word. When a word is read, the letters of the word are stored in one part of the brain, the sounds in another and the meaning of the word in another so it is necessary to establish neural connections among these parts. Subsequent successful readings strengthen these mental connections and quicken the retrieval process until it occurs automatically. Additionally, early readers who want to read for meaning independently need a strategy for figuring out words that they have not yet seen in print.

Theories that questioned the importance of alphabetic decoding of individual words have not withstood scientific and empirical scrutiny. Furthermore, the children's inability to figure out the sounds of printed words is implicated in most cases of reading deficiency. Compared to full alphabetic screening of a word, no other method produces fast enough retrieval for the huge numbers of words in English—there are too many words to memorize without using the generative nature of the alphabetic system. Contextual cues are essential for increasing vocabulary, resolving ambiguity in decoded words or confirming a decoded word ("Does it make sense or does it sound right?"). But context-driven decoding even aided

10 Components for a Comprehensive Reading Strategy

A strong consensus has developed on the program components necessary to reduce reading failure and improve reading performance among students.

No single program will suffice, but literature on the best practices in reading instruction points to 10 major interventions, all of which must be effectively organized and integrated in an elementary reading program if that school is to reach the standard that 85 to 90 percent of students can read grade-appropriate material from the end of 1st grade on.

The absence or ineffectiveness of any one of these components will lower the number of students who can handle grade-appropriate materials. Thus it is the cumulative effect of these elements that produces high literacy rates in a school. Some of these strands are ongoing; some are appropriate for a particular time.

No. 1: A pre-K to 5th grade (or ending elementary grade level) oral language program in which children are read to a little above their reading level and ideas are discussed.

No. 2: A kindergarten to 5th grade writing program stressing both narrative and expository writing, which uses accepted rubrics (telling a story, organizing a report, arguing a point, etc.) and writing as a means of discussing important ideas.

Decoding Tools

No. 3: Teaching each child to phonologically decode. Equipping each student with this tool (preferably by mid-1st grade) requires:

- A kindergarten skills development program of basic phonemic awareness (hearing and manipulating sounds in spoken words), upper- and lower-case letter recognition and concepts in print, especially recognizing a word in print. A supplemental phonemic awareness program is needed for those children not making progress by mid-kindergarten.

- A late-kindergarten/1st-grade strand of organized and systematic phonics to teach students how the alphabetic system works. This strand should include enough of the letter/sound correspondence system to allow students to become automatic with a sufficient number of words. This phonics strand should also allow students to develop some proficiency in word attack skills (sounding out, seeing common letter patterns, seeing parts of words and generating and selecting from legitimate alternative pronunciations) to start to read beginning materials independently in which only about one in 20 words needs to be figured out. It also should use decodable text to practice and perfect the recognition of words based on the patterns being taught and the use of spelling and word-building activities.

Most children should be able to read and understand non-predictable beginning materials by mid-1st grade—some will require more time, others will have mastered these skills to be reading (not pretend reading) by late kindergarten. Continued support of enhancing these skills during late 1st and 2nd grade also should be provided.

No. 4: An ongoing diagnostic assessment and intervention component to know which children are progressing and which need more intensive instruction. (Students who have learned to decode will get 18, 19 or 20 words right on a mid-1st grade standard decoding test of simple pseudo-words, while students who don't understand the alphabetic system will get none, one or two right.) A tutoring or intervention program can assist students in kindergarten, 1st and later grades who, after intensified assistance by the teacher, still are not making proper progress.

No. 5: An independent reading program that gets students to read simple trade books in 1st grade and approximately 25 to 35 narrative and informational books a year beginning in 2nd grade. Fifth grade elementary students need to read over a million words of text outside school assignments (approximately 20 minutes a night four nights a week) to learn enough vocabulary words to stay grade-appropriate readers.

Discussion Opportunities

No. 6: An advanced skill development support in syllabication, word roots, fluency, more complex letter sound correspondences and mechanics from 2nd grade on.

No. 7: A comprehension development program that includes (1) teaching strategic reading, especially for expository text (emphasized in 3rd through 5th) and (2) discussion or book club groups.

No. 8: Vocabulary instruction in word webs, word choice and word histories.

No. 9: A developmental (linguistically based) spelling program starting in late 1st or early 2nd grade.

No. 10: Parent and community involvement that encourages reading to children, having children read to them and turning off the TV for a nightly reading period.

Diagnostics Too

This comprehensive, strategic approach has several implications.

In early primary grades it is important that enough time for both skill and language-rich activities be allocated (at least two to three hours a day, including reading in the subject matter areas in early primary). Schools must purchase a mix of good literature (both narrative and informational text), predictable text and decodable text and ensure that the support programs, such as Chapter 1 and tutoring, are integrated into teaching reading right from the start.

This strategy also requires a diagnostic approach. Programs should allow for some skill grouping because such groups are essential for diagnostic teaching and children learn at different rates.

You need to know which children are making satisfactory progress and which are not and do something to correct the deficiencies quickly.

—Bill Honig

Dealing with Non-English-Speaking Learners

Some educators question whether young students who are learning to speak in English also can be taught to read in English and can profit by phonemic awareness, phonics and decoding instruction in kindergarten and 1st grade.

The pedagogical argument against skills instruction is that these children are so overwhelmed by learning English that teaching them phonics will be confusing and interfere with their oral language learning. Consequently, many school programs for second-language learners are strong on oral language development but weak on reading skills.

A large body of evidence now refutes this hypothesis. The research shows that kindergarten and 1st-grade children benefit tremendously by skills instruction. By neglecting these skills, many will not learn to read well and will be deprived of the very tool (fluent reading) that will enable them to build their English vocabulary.

Development Classes

In English language development classes or sheltered English classes, students can learn to decode in about the same time as English-speaking children (perhaps lagging a month or two) because even limited oral vocabularies are enough to teach the alphabetic principle.

As such, they are much like children who come from extremely low socio-economic conditions. Both groups have limited English oral vocabularies but are taught to read in 1st grade by teachers using the best practices described here.

One added component is necessary for these children: Teachers must ascertain if the child knows the meaning of the word being decoded since decoding and becoming automatic with that word requires connecting letters, sounds and the meaning of the word.

A recent series of studies (which can be obtained from Dale Willows, School of Education, Ontario Institute of Studies in Education, 252 Bloor Street West, Toronto, Ontario, Canada M5S 1V6) have shown that contrary to the prevailing dogma, second-language students who receive decoding early do just as well as English speakers who receive the same training in learning to read in English, and they significantly outperform English speakers who do not receive such instruction. Second-language learners who do not receive skill instruction lag way behind the other three groups—another example of the harm that neglect or indirection does for our most vulnerable children.

Bilingual Programs

In Latin America, Spain and the most effective bilingual programs in the United States, beginning reading is now incorporating specific instruction in phonemic awareness, phonics and decoding since Spanish also is an alphabetic system. Spanish traditionally has been taught using syllables—*ma, me, mi, mo, mu; ba, be, bi,* etc. Since Spanish has only a limited number of syllables and they are short and regular, many students can learn to read by memorizing the syllables, reading and intuiting the alphabetic system.

However, even in Spanish many children are hampered by low levels of phonemic awareness and an incomplete understanding of how sound maps to print. They, too, will be helped by decoding instruction. A good bilingual program using these techniques should have almost all children actually reading simple materials and cracking the code by late kindergarten.

Many new bilingual materials contain these decoding strategies, while others have not budged from relying solely on the more traditional syllable-driven instructional strategy.

One weak part of bilingual programs is the absence of a transition strategy. Many programs move students into 3rd and 4th grade just when English materials begin to contain large numbers of new words not in the student's speaking vocabulary and more complex linguistic patterns. Many English-speaking students who have not reached basic fluency by the end of 3rd grade go into a 4th-grade slump because they flounder with too many basic words.

Similarly, many bilingual students who have not had a strong English-as-a-second-language component starting in the early grades and have not become automatic in print with a core group of English words have an extremely difficult year when they transition. These students are forced to do double duty by simultaneously trying to learn to read basic words while struggling with the huge number of new words appearing in text that are not in their speaking vocabulary. Reading scores of many students who read well in Spanish plummet during their transition years because of the lack of proper preparation to read in English.

—Bill Honig

---

by partial alphabetic clues is too slow and unreliable to serve as a fluent decoding tool.

For example, a recent large-scale study in New Zealand found that 1st-graders who use sounding-out strategies for new words as opposed to context-based strategies (skipping the word, reading to the end of the sentence etc.) read significantly better in 2nd and 3rd grades than do poorer and second-language learners. These more vulnerable children tended to use the less-effective context-based method.

" . . . in proficient reading, word recognition is primarily an automatic, unconscious and rapid process."

Extensive research and practical experience has demonstrated that learning to read does not come as naturally to most children as learning to speak does. It needs to be taught. As many as 50 percent of children will intuit the alphabetic system from the instructional strategies now in vogue—exposure to print and print activities and mini-lessons in the context of reading a story. However, many students need an organized program that teaches phonemic awareness, letter sound correspondences and decoding skills to learn to read. This need is especially true of the dyslexic, low socioeconomic and second-language children who fail under our present emphasis on indirect strategies.

Moreover, many 1st-grade students may seem to be progressing because they are memorizing words. Yet many remain unable to decode words and will subsequently suffer reading problems. Thus, every student needs to be evaluated to determine if he or she understands and can use the alphabetic system. Finally, almost all students' learning will be accelerated or consolidated by helping them understand the alphabetic system.

Decoding ability, vocabulary level and spelling are extremely highly correlated with reading comprehension. Pedagogically, they are connected. The best method for building vocabulary is to read extensively, and children cannot read extensively, especially when text becomes conceptually and structurally more difficult in 3rd and 4th grade, unless they have become automatic with a large number of words and proficient at decoding and learning new words. Similarly, learning spelling patterns helps accelerate decoding and developing automaticity with written words.

A vast amount of research also has shown that learning decoding and independent reading of simple nonpredictive text in 1st grade is developmentally appropriate. (Approximately 95 percent of children are mature enough to learn basic phonemic awareness and letter recognition in kindergarten and phonics and decoding in 1st grade.) These studies also found that if students are not taught these skills early, most will never recover. Only one out of eight children reading below grade level by the end of 1st grade will ever read grade-appropriate materials, though expensive and well-designed intervention can beat these odds.

Decoding gives students a sense of success, confidence and independence in figuring out and remembering a new word. This independence leads to real, not pretend, reading: Students know they can look at a previously unread simple text and read it. Non-decoders seldom experience this success and continually experience frustration in attempting to read.

Researchers estimate that nearly half of special education students would not need that expensive program if they were taught initially to read properly. Unfortunately, few schools make the ability to decode a primary objective in 1st grade, check to see which children can do it and then help the ones who can't.

Instructional Implications

To acquire the ability to decode a simple word by mid-1st grade, students must have reached basic levels of phonemic awareness (the ability to hear and manipulate the sounds in spoken words), recognize letters and have acquired basic concepts in print, preferably by the end of kindergarten. Then, by mid-1st grade, they learn about half of the basic letter/sound correspondences (at least the consonants and short vowels and a smattering of blends, long vowels and more complex vowels) and the patterns of words using these sounds. They also master a core of high-frequency words and phonograms, how to map sounds to letter/letter patterns in sequence in written words (blending or sounding out) and how to apply this knowledge in figuring out a word that has not been read before but is in the student's speaking vocabulary.

Many students figure out how to sound out or blend after a few attempts; many others find this skill difficult and need several months to master this skill. In late 1st and 2nd grades, students need to extend their letter-sound knowledge to the more complex patterns and learn to use larger orthographic patterns when they sound out a word.

Four major deficiencies in reading instruction prevent students from learning how to decode:

- Nearly 20 percent of our students do not develop threshold levels of phonemic awareness in kindergarten. (This means they can not distinguish the discrete sounds in words and manipulate and sequence them, which is necessary to connect sounds and letters in words.) And, these children were not diagnosed and given assistance.

- Students were not taught enough about the main letter/sound correspondences and thus did not learn the alphabetic system.

- About a third of our students have difficulty in learning how to read through a word or how to sound it out and have not been taught how to do it.

- Students have not had the opportunity to practice reading a large number of words based on the beginning letter/sound patterns in text. As a result, they have not become automatic at recognizing those words.

Phonemic Awareness

One critical breakthrough in the reading field in the past decades is how important being able to hear and manipulate the discrete sound parts of words—phonemic awareness—is to learning to read. Most phonemic awareness is learned in the process of learning how print maps to sound in phonics instruction. However, threshold levels are necessary to learn phonics. If a child cannot tell what the last sound in *cat* is, that child is going to find it impossible to connect that sound with the written symbol *t* or to read through a word while keeping the letters and sounds in proper sequence.

Most children acquire basic phonemic awareness in kindergarten by such activities as rhyming and sound-word games. Unfortunately, about a sixth of our children have phonological wiring problems. Without assistance of about 12-14 hours (about 20 minutes a day) during the latter third of the kindergarten year, they will not acquire basic phonemic awareness. Many of these children end up in special education or Title I programs because they never were taught properly at the outset, and many others flounder with their reading problems remaining undetected. The implications are obvious—kindergarten programs must identify and assist those children who, without intervention, will have an extremely difficult time learning to read.

One reason for the growth of the whole language movement was the reality that many children never seemed able to learn phonics and decoding. Educators naturally were inclined to find other ways for them to learn to read. As mentioned earlier, these other ways (predictions using context and first-letter cues) are too slow and inaccurate to replace phonological decoding, and teaching children to rely on them produced large numbers of poor readers. Now we know that one key reason why many of these students didn't learn to decode was that they could not hear and abstract the sounds. The obvious solution is to ensure that children are properly prepared to learn phonics and decoding.

Phonics Instruction

Most children need an organized program that directly teaches the basic consonant/vowel combinations and that follows principles of linguistic sequencing. Such a program introduces words based on short vowel patterns and simple consonants in early 1st grade and then follows with the more complicated vowel marker patterns (*e* controlled, *r* controlled and vowel combinations and consonant blends and digraphs, such as *ch*). Those basic high-frequency words that cannot be sounded out also need to be taught in some sequence.

The sound/symbol correspondences (and high-frequency words) must be practiced and reinforced extensively in connected or decodable text. These materials contain good stories but are designed to contain large numbers of words easy enough for children to read

because they represent the patterns previously taught. For example, changing the gingerbread man with its difficult "g" sound to the pancake man, which reinforces short and long "a" sounds. The problem is this: Many materials in use for teaching reading in 1st grade are highly predictable in their vocabulary with too few decodable words. Thus, the materials are not effective for developing independent decoding skills. The opposite problem is no better; literature books that contain too many difficult words are too hard for many children beginning to read.

Finally, activities that allow students to spell and manipulate words by sorting, and changing them (change *sit* to *set* to *sat*) are an essential part of the curriculum for beginning readers. Just allowing students to play with the structure of words will help many students to understand the alphabetic principle.

Studies have shown that programs incorporating these elements (as well as reading to children, discussions and language-rich activities) are about twice as effective as the more indirect or unfocused methods now in wide use.

Massive Retraining

The other major reasons for the growth of whole language approaches that deemphasized decoding were the sterile, unproductive nature of much phonics instruction (worksheets and paucity of connected text), and the lack of motivational and authentic reading experiences accompanying skills instruction. The decoding instruction being advocated today is much more akin to a thinking phonics program that strives for understanding of the alphabetic principle and uses engaging activities to help students learn it.

Secondly, in the latest synthesis, decoding instruction is only part of a broader language arts curriculum that does stress reading to children, writing, shared reading activities and discussion of literature.

None of these ideas will be simple to implement. They call for the use of the right materials, restructuring of schools around these ideas and massive retraining of teachers. (A high percentage of those who have graduated from university teacher training programs in the past 10 years have minimal understanding of linguistics, spelling and teaching the alphabetic code.) Without aware and dedicated leadership, this problem will not be corrected.

Form at end of book

What's Basic in Beginning Reading?
Finding Common Ground

As the debate continues between phonics and holistic approaches to reading instruction, a method called *whole-part-whole* strikes a welcome balance.

Dorothy S. Strickland

Dorothy S. Strickland is the State of New Jersey Professor of Reading at Rutgers University Graduate School of Education, 10 Seminary Place, New Brunswick, NJ 08901-1183.

"These storybooks are very nice, but don't you think they need the skills first?" "When I was in school every child could read. Back in those days, teachers stressed the basics." "Why don't they teach phonics anymore?"

As a frequent speaker before school boards, parent groups, and educators, I have learned that certain questions and comments are inevitable. Most often they are raised by a parent whose child is having difficulty with reading. Sometimes they come from school board members troubled by media reports of low test scores. Occasionally they are even asked by an educator, who admits to a degree of uneasiness about difficult and challenging changes in instructional practice. Many questions focus on beginning reading. Most often, that means phonics.

Teachers began to realize that skills are worthless as isolated knowledge but powerful as strategies used purposefully and masterfully.

The queries are right on target in recognizing that reading instruction has changed. Ironically, however, many of the changes we see today were also prompted by concern about low achievement. Educators sought instructional alternatives to the kind of teaching that encouraged the accumulation of isolated skills and left many children devoid of long-term competence and with little ability to apply those skills during actual reading and writing. Faced with large numbers of such children, teachers began to realize that skills are worthless as isolated knowledge but powerful as strategies used purposefully and masterfully. Thus, rather than abandon skills instruction, many teachers made a conscious effort to approach skills differently—as strategies taught within the context of learning to read and write.

The model known as *whole-part-whole* instruction provides a balanced conceptual framework for thinking about and planning skills instruction. It addresses the need for teaching that (1) is grounded in fundamental understandings about whole texts such as stories, informational books, and poems; (2) allows for in-depth focus on specific skills; and (3) includes planned practice within the context of meaningful reading and writing.

The Whole-Part-Whole Framework

The debates about beginning reading reveal that the conceptual framework guiding a teacher's decision making is a powerful instructional force. Teachers who use what is termed a *bottom-up* approach tend to focus on isolated skills, such as letter names and specific sound-letter relationships. They believe that once these are in place, meaning will follow. Those who favor a *top-down* conceptual framework concentrate on lots of reading aloud and response to literature, with a more incidental approach to teaching letters and sounds. They tend to focus on skills as students reveal needs.

Whole-part-whole instruction provides the balance between these two approaches. For example, if the target strategy is the use of a particular sound-letter relationship of the letter *s*, the teacher may begin by sharing an enlarged text that features words with the letter or letters being taught; or the teacher may use a chart to write text generated by the students. In either case, the initial response is for the purpose of developing comprehension and interpretation. This may involve group discussion, drawing or writing activities, and shared rereading with the teacher. After the children are familiar with the text, the teacher guides them to look at specific features of certain words and to note how the words look and sound. In this case, the letter *s* would be featured and children would be guided to note how words starting with the letter *s* look and sound at the beginning. This would lead to a variety of activities focusing on the letter *s*. Finally, the students return to reading and writing with whole text to apply what they have learned.

These lessons are meant to go well beyond the teaching and learning of a single sound-letter correspondence. The teacher is also striving to help the children understand the alphabetic principle and its application to reading and writing. The approach also emphasizes helping children become independent, self-improving learners. Dorothy Fowler's article "Balanced Reading Instruction in Practice" describes in greater detail instructional activities that a 1st grade teacher uses with her students in a typical language arts block of time, and Figure 1 shows the process.

- *Start with whole text.* Grounding instruction in whole texts provides the basis for meaningful literacy activities. Examples include the shared reading of poems or stories using big books or charts. An active demonstration of the teacher's own composing and spelling processes is extremely powerful, as he or she models at the chalkboard, thinking aloud about what word will come next or how a word is spelled.

- *Focus on knowledge about the parts of language that may be useful for reading and writing.* Responding to all texts only at the holistic level is not enough. Instruction should include a planned, systematic effort to highlight specific textual features and literary devices as a variety of materials are read, written, and discussed over time. Highlighting specific textual features helps children form generalizations about language that they can apply to their own independent efforts to read and write.

- *Return to whole texts for application and practice.* Planned opportunities to apply what has been learned about the parts of language allow students to move from simply knowing about a generalization to using that knowledge in a purposeful way. This also acknowledges the fact that isolated language elements behave differently depending on context. For example, the letter *s* behaves differently when paired with *t* as opposed to *b*. Words such as *lead* or *wind* not only mean different things in different contexts, they may be pronounced differently. Effective beginning readers use word meaning and sentence structure, along with sound-letter relationships, to approach unknown words.

Moving from whole to part and back to whole again thus provides a framework for planning that addresses skills in a manner that is meaningful, strategic, and more characteristic of the way proficient readers ac-

tually use skills when they read and write. Although the focus here is on beginning reading, the whole-part-whole framework can be used to teach any skill.

Speaking of Phonics and Phonemic Awareness . . .

Until recently, no aspect of reading instruction was more discussed, more hotly debated, and less understood than phonics and its role in learning to read. For better or worse, the topic of phonemic awareness is currently running a close second. While phonics refers to instruction in the sound-letter relationships used in reading and writing, phonemic awareness refers to a child's understanding that speech itself is composed of a series of individual sounds.

Children who are phonologically aware can discriminate between and manipulate sounds in words and syllables in speech. They know when words rhyme or do not rhyme. They can indicate when a series of words begin or end with the same sound, and they can break down or blend a series of sounds such as /k/-/a/-/t/ in *cat*. Most important, these children can shift their attention away from the content of speech to focus on the form of speech before they return to its meaning.

Although the role of phonemic awareness in children's literacy development is still not completely clear, most researchers agree that "training in phonological awareness is both possible and advantageous for children" (Ayres 1993, p. 153). Questions remain, however, about how much phonemic awareness is a necessary prerequisite to developing ability in decoding and how much is acquired in a reciprocal, mutually supportive relationship with learning to read (Perfetti et al. 1987, Weaver 1998).

The debates about phonics and phonemic awareness have less to do with their value than with the amount and type of instruction they require. The controversy generally pits systematic, intensive instruction against holistically oriented approaches. Briefly stated, those promoting systematic, intensive phonics advocate an emphasis on phonics that is highly sequenced, skills- or code-driven, and initiated early in the child's schooling. Children begin by learning about the parts of words and build toward whole words. The approach stresses correct identification and automaticity of response. Much of the research cited to support this view comes from experimental studies where children's demonstration of performance is based on the results of standardized tests (Chall 1983, Adams 1990).

Holistically oriented approaches include philosophies and practices frequently associated with terms such as *whole language, integrated language arts,* and *literature-based curriculum.* In operation, these terms share certain characteristics; however, they are not synonymous.

Although virtually all holistically oriented teaching includes to some extent such elements as greater emphasis on writing and its relationship to reading, greater use of trade books, increased attention to the integration of the language arts, and greater reliance on informal classroom assessment, teachers vary in their implementation of and adherence to various philosophies. Those who emphasize meaning are likely to cite basic research on how children learn to read and write, as well as classroom-based studies on long-term effects (Krashen 1993, Weaver 1994).

My experience suggests that these differences are much less apparent in the classroom than they are in the debate. In practice, teachers who advocate holistic approaches are apt to include strong word-recognition programs with phonics as a key tool for word recognition; and teachers who support intensive, systematic phonics often read aloud to children and encourage invented spelling. Although the matter of emphasis is important, it is unlikely that you will find classrooms that reflect polar ends of an instructional continuum. A conceptual framework such as the whole-part-whole model allows for flexibility based on student needs.

Finding Common Ground

Most controversies have points of agreement. Educators on both sides of the phonics debate agree that, ultimately, reading and writing for meaning is paramount. Both sides are keenly aware of the importance of good literature in the lives of children and the need for responsive adults who support children's natural inclinations toward making sense with print. Needless to say, both sides recognize the importance of the alphabetic code in learning to read and write.

Responding to all texts only at the holistic level is not enough. Instruction should include a planned, systematic effort to highlight specific textual features and literary devices.

Today's educators are seeking to provide a comprehensive and balanced instructional program that is engaging and rich with meaning, yet grounded in curricular expectations that are visible to teachers, parents, and students. To plan such a program, they would do well to consider points of agreement, along with the following instructional guidelines (Strickland 1998):

1. Skills and meaning should never be separated. Instructional techniques that help children understand and use the alphabetic code should be applied hand in hand with those that guide students in reading comprehension and thoughtful response to literature and the effective use of the writing process.

2. Instruction is systematic when it is planned, deliberate in application, and proceeds in an orderly manner. This does not mean a rigid progression of one-size-fits-all teaching. Rather, it means a thoughtfully planned program that accounts for learner variability. Encouraging invented spelling works side by side with instructing students in word recognition skills, including phonics. Each informs the other.

3. Intensive instruction on any particular skill or strategy should be based on need. Thus, intensity will vary both with individuals and groups. Children who are fluently reading words that contain specific phonics elements should not have to endure intensive phonics instruction in those elements. The best tests of a phonics element are the ability to read words containing that element within connected text and the successful use of that element in invented spellings.

4. There is no substitute for ongoing documentation and monitoring of learning to determine the order in which skills should be addressed and the level of intensity required to help a child or group of children succeed in a particular area. The use of running records and analyses of invented spelling serve this purpose well.

5. To track specific goals and objectives within an integrated language-arts framework, teachers must know the instructional objectives their district requires at the grade level they teach. They also should be extremely familiar with the objectives at the grade levels above and below theirs. Alignment of curricular goals with instructional standards and assessment helps give everyone involved (teachers, administrators, and parents) a clear sense of direction.

Educators on both sides of the phonics debate agree that, ultimately, reading and writing for meaning is paramount.

The phonics debates have been with us for a long time, evoking contrasting points of view. Many educators are feeling increasingly uncomfortable with the growing polarization and politicization of issues. Most classroom teachers find themselves in a different arena from that of the staunch advocates on either side of the issues. Too often these opponents have become entrenched in their positions, having based their reputation on being right. Meanwhile, classroom teachers watch with growing impatience as the debates escalate, with little light shed on the topic for their benefit and that of the children they teach.

Effective teachers recognize phonics and phonemic awareness as useful tools for successful reading and writing. But they also are aware of the dangers of overreliance

Figure 1 — A Whole-to-Part-to-Whole Conceptual Framework Blending Skills with Meaning

Whole	to	Part	to	Whole
Learning with, through, and about whole written texts*		Learning about how the parts (textual features) of language function in written texts		Learning to apply what was learned with, through, and about written texts

*Whole texts include predictable stories, dictated stories, content area materials, letters, charts containing songs, rhymes, messages, and lists.

Source: Strickland, D.S. (1989). "Teaching Skills in a Literature-Based Curriculum." Handout presented at the annual conference of the International Reading Association, New Orleans.

References

Adams, M. (1990). *Beginning to Read: Thinking and Learning About Text.* Cambridge, Mass.: Harvard University Press.

Ayers, L.R. (1993). "The Efficacy of Three Training Conditions on Phonological Awareness of Kindergarten Children and the Longitudinal Effect of Each on Later Reading Acquisition." Unpublished doctoral diss., Oakland University, Rochester, Mich.

Chall, J. (1983). *Learning to Read: The Great Debate.* New York: McGraw-Hill.

Krashen, S. D. (1993). *The Power of Reading: Insights from the Research.* Englewood, Colo.: Libraries Unlimited.

Perfetti, C., I. Beck, L. Bell, and C. Hughes. (1987). "Phonemic Knowledge and Learning to Read Are Reciprocal: A Longitudinal Study of First Grade Children." *Merrill-Palmer Quarterly 33,* 283–319.

Strickland D. (1998). *Teaching Phonics Today: A Primer for Educators.* Newark, Del.: International Reading Association.

Weaver, C. (1994). *Reading Process and Practice.* Portsmouth, N.H.: Heinemann.

Weaver, C. (1998). "Experimental Research: On Phonemic Awareness and on Whole Language." In *Reconsidering a Balanced Approach to Reading,* edited by C. Weaver, Urbana, Ill.: National Council of Teachers of English.

Form at end of book

on one method of word recognition and the potential deterrent to successful reading. If the debate is to serve any productive purpose, it must be used as the basis for constructive dialogues and collaborative efforts to examine and take advantage of the best research and practice available. This must be done in a way that makes sense and is most effective for students, teachers, and parents.

Issue 12 Summary

Some children arrive at elementary school already knowing how to read. Some leave elementary school unable to read. Then there are the large numbers of children who learn how to read during elementary school. Somehow, educators must meet the needs of all three groups.

Teaching children how to read, in many cases, is not easy. We are asking students to make sense of a complex array of symbols that (1) are associated with different sounds at different times, (2) have so many irregularities that the rules sometimes seem worthless, and (3) yield different word meanings in different contexts. It is not surprising that no single method of teaching reading is going to work for all children at all times. Consequently, it behooves us as educators to know a variety of methods and to know the specific instances when they are likely (or unlikely) to be effective. Children differ in how they learn to read, and their needs are different at different points in the learning process. Elementary teachers are responsible for knowing the various approaches, knowing when to apply them, and maintaining their flexibility. When their teaching method is not working with a student, it is not time to hammer away at the same method or to blame the student; rather, it is time to exercise flexibility and try a different approach.

ISSUE 13

Learning Disabilities

Questions

1. What new understandings have emerged to explain dyslexia? What are the specific difficulties encountered by individuals with dyslexia?

2. What is the relationship of learning disabilities and intelligence? What are the implications of this relationship for teaching?

Introduction

Learning disabilities come in many forms. This category is highly heterogeneous; it encompasses a wide variety of students with a wide variety of problems. A student might have difficulty reading, writing, or doing mathematics; may possess a short attention span; may have difficulty organizing things; or may have some motor difficulties. The most common type of learning disability is reading disability, or *dyslexia*. In recent years, some progress has been made in understanding this learning disability, at least in some cases.

However, learning disabilities are still complex phenomena. A generation ago, "learning disabilities" was a little used, poorly understood term. Now it is a widely used, poorly understood term. Educators have not been able to establish a definition of "learning disabilities" or to determine their causes and the best educational practices to address such disabilities in children.

The articles you will read concern two aspects of learning disabilities: the increasing understanding of dyslexia and the difficulty in defining and diagnosing learning disabilities.

Why Kids Can't Read

As science cracks the code, parents fight for their children's right to specialized education

Robert Sheppard

They are imps, all of them—and they know it. The mere hint of a visitor in their class has them all primed to perform. "Listening position," orders teacher Bernadette (Learn with Bern) Siracky, and most of them hop to: backs straight, hands where they can be seen. The test words are rolled out with the crack of a drill sergeant. "What are your lips doing?" asks Siracky. "What is your tongue doing? What are your teeth doing?" Words are physical commodities here at Calgary's Foothills Academy, a unique private school for the so-called learning disabled. Words are rolled about in the mouth like hard candy. Their rhythms are thumped against the side of the desk. Siracky uses anything to inject them into the brains of otherwise healthy, intelligent children who have been told they cannot read, they cannot learn.

"You know, Miss Siracky all of us here have been on TV at least twice, or had our pictures in the newspaper," says Sean with all the world-weariness of a 10-year-old. Sean knows that he is in a special school, subsidized largely by private benefactors, with a waiting list of 1,000 for the 35 spots that open each year. What Sean probably does not realize is that his presence at Foothills Academy is an indictment of a public system that is floundering—almost indecently in some cases—in its attempts to deal with its weakest learners, with those who cannot make sense of words.

Ten years ago, universities were churning out special-education teachers and school boards were racing to develop individualized communications programs and separate facilities for students needing extra help. But more recently, cash-strapped boards have retrenched, leaving parents of children with learning disabilities, attention deficit or emotional problems no alternative but to resort to the squeaky-wheel approach—or scramble for the growing number of private alternatives. In Calgary, the number of specialized classrooms for the learning disabled plummeted from 148 in 1994 to one in 1997, although there are plans to reinstate a few this fall. In wealthy Mississauga, Ont., where the Peel District School Board was a mecca for special needs families, the number of communications programs for learning disabled kids has been reduced from 90 to 50 since 1993.

It is a pattern repeated across the country. Last month, in Prince Albert, Sask., a justice from the Court of Queen's Bench decided it was time for the courts to decide whether the learning disabled were getting the education they deserved. In a rare lawsuit, parents who had been supplementing a modest version of the Foothills Academy program in their local public school, won the right to challenge the province and their boards in court over their refusal to sustain and expand the program.

The Prince Albert case portends a far-reaching change for the education of those with learning disabilities—genetic, lifelong afflictions that may affect as many as 4.5 million Canadians, 730,000 of them school age. Dyslexia, the most common form of learning disorder, is often not discovered until age 9 or 10, when children can no longer struggle through on memorization. For some, a reading disability is merely a frustration for an otherwise rational mind to get around. For many, it is the barrier preventing even the most elemental connection of one bit of knowledge to another. Several studies have suggested that those with learning problems are over-represented in jails, reform schools and the ranks of the working poor. A study by a New York City clinician in the mid-1980s found that almost 50 per cent of adolescents who committed suicide had been previously diagnosed with learning disabilities. As Halifax psychologist Wayne MacDonald says: "You can pay me now, or pay me later. In the long run, society is paying the price for these wasted lives."

While schools are scaling back on specialized programs, researchers and innovative private academies are discovering new techniques to reach the weakest learners, and science is zeroing in on the hard-wired limits of the brain—indeed, on the very roots of reading. In a break-

By Robert Sheppard, *Maclean's*, Sept. 7, 1998.

through last March, Sally Shaywitz, a senior scientist in the department of pediatrics at Yale University in New Haven, Conn., published actual photographs of the reading brain using sophisticated magnetic resonance imaging. Her research proves that there is a neurological basis for reading disorders: the reading path in the dyslexic brain is dramatically different than that of a normal reader's. Scientists are excited at the possibility of providing a pictorial benchmark of the reading brain to explore whether early intervention programs might actually rewire the neural network. Geneticists now believe that the neurological base for dyslexia may be hereditary, and that it is linked to the same chromosome that contributes to such relatively commonplace maladies as hay fever, migraine headaches, asthma, thyroid disease and allergies.

Dyslexia, the most common of the learning disorders, often goes undetected until age 9 or 10.

In her airy office at Toronto's Hospital for Sick Children, festooned with Ikea boxes full of research results and a wide assortment of children's dolls, psychologist Maureen Lovett says the notion of dyslexia—"word blindness"—has been well documented for more than 100 years. But it is only relatively recently that researchers have recalled it is not the eye but the ear—the way words sound in the brain—that is at the base of reading and writing disorders. And it is only in the past three or four years that her researchers, working in seven experimental public school classrooms in Toronto and Mississauga, made the breakthrough they were hoping for.

In intensive daily sessions, Lovett's team found they could teach the 44 component sounds of the English language and improve their students' reading skills within just a few months. "But there was this amazing failure to transfer what they learned," says Lovett. "They could read 'pine,' but they could not read 'wine' or 'sign.' " Then her team added on what Lovett calls strategy-based or "talking-to-yourself" learning: rhyming patterns used to coax the sounds of similar words through reluctant brains. The results were more lasting.

That kind of double-pronged technique is exactly what Foothills Academy in Calgary has been practicing for most of its 18 years. The cost of the program, per student, is $14,500 annually—although most are highly subsidized. New arrivals, all of whom read at half their normal grade level, are bombarded with 70 hours of phonemic awareness to teach the sounds of language and the way they are formed by the tongue and larynx. Then comes a myriad of coping strategies—everything from desk thumping to looking in mirrors to see the way the mouth forms sounds. Students are taught how to order words, and their lives as well. In fact, the biggest part of the program is

teaching specific organizational techniques: from words to sentences to thought structures and homework responsibilities. "Kids come here, they can't read a damn thing," says Gordon Bullivant, Foothills' loquacious, chain-smoking executive director. "We mother-hen them for three years. Then they are out, back to the real world." Only one pupil has returned after three years; 86 per cent of Foothills' former students have gone on to some form of post-secondary education.

In Charlottetown, Kay MacPhee is finding similar success with the use of nonsense words to teach the sounds of reading. As principal of the Prince Edward Island School for the Hearing Impaired, MacPhee had great success teaching deaf children to read "through the tiny speck of hearing they had." When a doctor friend asked her to try her luck with the learning disabled, she rose to the challenge. Says the retired principal: "It took longer with the learning disabled because you had to bypass the strategies they were already using—mostly memory and that will only take you so far."

Four years ago, MacPhee formed her own tutorial company, Spell Read Canada. Her partner is Kay Reeves, a woman who came to her in 1992 at the age of 44, wanting to learn how to read. Now, mostly through word of mouth, they have 24 students from as far away as Washington and Texas spending the summer in their Charlottetown classrooms. Among their pupils is a 38-year-old Nova Scotia businessman, putting his company on hold for a month so he can learn to read.

So why are the public schools not knocking on their doors? MacPhee—and Lovett in Toronto—are almost apologetic. Give the public system time, they say, there is some resistance to be knocked down. Bullivant, who also happens to be the current president of the Learning Disabilities Association of Canada, is more blunt: "It is all a question of dollars. You can teach children to read—but you have to spend the time and the money."

Learning disabilities can challenge families to their core. Take Charlie's story. By all accounts, Charlie R. was a likable boy from small-town Saskatchewan who did his chores, kept a bee farm and helped handicapped kids with their swimming lessons. From the beginning, Charlie's teachers recognized that he had a reading problem. He could not pronounce many words properly. Even when he seemed to learn to read some words, he would be totally flustered by those same words on a new page. Charlie was held back a grade in order to "catch up" with other children. A couple of times a week he and a small group of children with similar problems were given special reading lessons. Art, music and gym were eliminated from his schedule so he could concentrate on the tougher subjects. His mother was told to take privileges away so he would be forced to do his assignments. Nothing worked. The other kids ridiculed him. Charlie hid his homework in the hedge, or brought it to school scrunched into a ball so he would not have to turn it in.

Just before he left school for good, a 15-year-old enmeshed in drugs and alcohol—"the only things that made me feel good," he told his family—Charlie was diagnosed as being seriously dyslexic. He read and wrote at a Grade 3 level with 20-per-cent comprehension. It was a staggering realization that had been hidden from his family, friends and teachers. Looking back, Charlie's mother says: "The knowledge of what a learning disability really is and how it encompasses one's whole life had been missed. Can you imagine Charlie living all those years, trying his best to fit in? That would be like going to work every day and being asked to do a job that you could not do. And tomorrow you have to get up and go to work again to try to bluff your way through it one more day."

Charlie's is an extreme case, but in many ways not atypical. Parents have sold property or given up lucrative jobs and relocated in efforts to help their learning disabled offspring. Like Charlie's family, many parents have found it too painful to tell their stories without maintaining anonymity. In an effort to crack the problem with research funding, the National Institute for Health in Bethesda, Md., declared the 1990s the decade for the learning disabled. Some of that funding has made its way to Canada: Lovett's group at the Hospital for Sick Children is participating in a three-city study—Toronto, Atlanta and Boston—to determine, she says, "what works best for what kind of child."

In the United States, almost five per cent of school-age children are classified as learning disabled and are therefore eligible for extra funding. In Canada, classification standards vary by province, but typically between three and four per cent of the student population is diagnosed as learning disabled. Manitoba and Alberta are currently conducting high-level reviews of their special education programs. This fall, Alberta has promised to add 590 new full-time intern teachers to provide literacy assessment and assistance in kindergarten plus Grades 1 and 2. In populous Ontario, the government has maintained its special education budget at $1.2 billion, the lion's share of which goes to programs for the learning disabled at the rate of $1,200 and $2,700 per student, depending on age and category. Large, sophisticated boards such as Mississauga's Peel District School Board have schools dedicated to those with severe learning problems, as well as discreet classrooms and review committees to go over assessments and individualized programs. And many school boards in the Maritimes and Ontario have adopted the New Zealand-created Reading Recovery program, an intensive word awareness strategy designed for Grade 1.

Worthy as these efforts may be, they must be viewed against a backdrop of stop-and-go funding and a pro-

longed retrenchment. Judy Tilston, the elected chair of the Calgary Board of Education, is also the mother of a learning disabled youngster who is about to enter high school this month. The prospect, she says, "scares me spitless. There is not a lot of extra support out there. He will be going to a high school with one learning strategist on staff—a good one I am told—and 2,200 kids." When it comes to the learning disabled, Tilston says, "There is no question that this board has really strong feelings that the public system is not meeting these needs appropriately. But the reality is we don't have the money. We don't even come close." In most provinces, public schools get a little extra for learning disabled students. "But we are already taking a ton of money out of the general instruction grant to help our special needs population," says Tilston. "It is just not enough."

In Peel, the public board has cut back on specialized programs, but increased the number of teachers with a specialty in learning disabilities for its general classrooms, notes John Amon, former director of the board's special education program. "We made a shift to reduce costs at the expense of a service-delivery system," he explains, referring to the cutbacks in the segregated programs and facilities, "not, I like to think, at the expense of learning disabled students."

For many special needs advocates, that is a debatable point. At the school board level, the biggest fights have been over what is commonly called mainstreaming, or what some refer to as "the myth of inclusion." Should students with serious reading or attention problems be taught in a mainstream class with some extra help, or in a segregated environment? "Generally speaking, parents of physically or mentally disabled kids want inclusion in mainstream classrooms," says Anne Price, executive director of the Calgary Learning Centre, a non-profit agency that coordinates educational research and testing. "Parents of learning disabled kids want segregated classrooms because they know their kids do not perform well in larger groups."

School board administrators argue that the shift to mainstream instruction is not being driven by cost-cutting alone. They focus on issues of self-esteem and fairness to other slow learners, including those with English as a second language. Many Ontario school boards will not test ESL students for learning disabilities until they have been in the system for at least two years, setting up an intolerable wait in some situations. Edward Blackstock chief psychologist for the Peel District School Board, is unequivocal in his preference: "We on the front lines believe more strongly in specialized classes than the research shows."

Cutbacks have led to fierce fights around the special education watering hole. Yude Henteleff, a prominent Winnipeg lawyer who has been a tireless advocate on behalf of the learning disabled for nearly 30 years, says he has been increasingly called upon to mediate disputes between parents of special needs children and parents of extremely bright or "gifted" children—all fighting over limited funds. An unforgiving critic of the special education system, not just in Manitoba but in many other parts of the country, Henteleff cites certain school districts that will not offer special help to a poor learner unless that child falls two years behind; others will cut extra tutorials or special classes once a student starts to show some progress—a catch 22, many parents feel.

Not all cases of learning disabilities lead to failure. Twenty-year-old Krista Ferguson has just completed her first year in a teacher's program at Lakehead University in Thunder Bay, Ont. Bright, vivacious and outgoing, she says many of her friends do not know that she mixes up letters and numbers, has great difficulty spelling simple words such as "which," multi" and "unite" and, "Oh yeah, I can't tell time." She says she can read certain types of clocks, but has trouble remembering whether "quarter to" is 15 minutes before the hour or after.

Ferguson, who grew up in a bedroom community north of Toronto, was identified at an early age as having a learning disability. But hiving her off into a segregated classroom with kids with behavioral problems, attention deficit disorder and different degrees of learning disorders just made her withdraw. "I would just try to fade into the background," says Ferguson, "and hope my teachers would ignore me."

Having her daughter formally identified as learning disabled was an enormous dilemma, says Karen Ferguson. "You don't want to label your children because it will stigmatize them. But they don't have any self-esteem anyway because they know they are not accomplishing what they want." Once she was labelled, there was a new frustration, says her mother: "Her marks were reflecting something that wasn't happening. You got the feeling they were giving the child an A so the parents wouldn't complain."

Krista Ferguson struggled for years, but succeeded because of a supportive family, extra tutoring and what she calls her coping mechanisms. She sounds out words differently in her head to help with the spelling, and she tries to avoid certain situations. "I'll probably be the only primary schoolteacher who will have to use a calculator to add one plus one," says Ferguson, half in jest. "But at least I will have a better understanding of what it is like for a student to have an invisible disability."

Making the transition to the workplace is something Morrey Siegel can address. Thirty-two and frighteningly articulate, he is one of the early pioneers of the learning disabled movement, having been diagnosed 25 years ago with dyslexia and severe hyperactivity—what is now called attention deficit disorder—before there were programs in place to deal with these problems. Siegel's parents had him assessed at Toronto's Clarke Institute of Psychiatry and paid for extra tutors at school. Learning was a struggle, and still is. "This is a lifelong disability," says Siegel. "You don't educate your way out of it." It was only after he finished school—and earned two diplomas in business and property assessment at Seneca College—that he felt the doors closing. He wanted to be a civil servant. Both the Ontario and federal governments had employment equity programs, but he did not fit the criteria. "They call this the invisible disability," says Siegel. "I did not fit their stereotype of a disabled person. The system says, 'We've got these programs for you. We want you.' But they are not there."

Today, students are being taught self-advocacy tips and have the benefit of modern technology. Computers can spell-check homework, or scan documents and sound them back to poor readers. In Alberta, learning disabled students as young as 8 are being allowed extra time on provincewide tests. But with such advances come questions of fairness. In the United States, where students with learning disabilities have statutory rights and are federally funded, there has been a vocal backlash against those who are perceived to be taking advantage of the system. In that country, nearly 4.5 per cent of its grade school population is in publicly funded learning disabilities programs at a cost of nearly $9 billion a year—roughly four times the cost of its Head Start program for poor kids.

In the United States, learning disabilities are defined simply as an unexplained difference between a student's potential and actual performance. As a result, middle-class students with high IQs and average achievement are receiving special tutoring, computer equipment and extra time on university entrance exams for scarce places. Mark Kelman, a Stanford University law professor and co-author of a new book called *Jumping the Queue: An Inquiry into the Legal Treatment of Students with Learning Disabilities,* argues that the disability movement has been overtaken by middle-class parents worried that their kids are not getting ahead. But psychologist Marc Wilchesky, co-ordinator of the learning disability program at Toronto's York University, believes that only a small minority of students are trading on the label for some advantage. "This is a very motivated hard-working group," says Wilchesky. "Ninety per cent of these students stay on to complete their degrees, which is a much higher retention rate than the regular student population."

To date, Canadians have not been so litigious as their neighbors south of the border—but that may be changing. In June, the Canadian Human Rights Commission ruled in favor of a federal civil servant in Etobicoke, Ont., who had been denied a promotion nine years ago because she had auditory dyslexia and could not learn French. The commission awarded Nancy Green more than $70,000 for lost wages and $5,000 for hurt feelings. It also ordered the federal government to develop a program to recognize and accommodate people with learning disabilities in the federal civil service.

Then there is the precedent being set in Prince Albert. For five years, a group of families in the Saskatchewan farm community ran charities and late-night bingos to supplement a scaled-down version of the Foothills Academy program in their local public school. Last year, when they ran out of steam and the four school boards involved refused to expand the program to more grades, six families and the support group calling itself the Concerned Parents for Children with Learning Disabilities took the unusual step of asking the courts to declare that their children were not being taught in a way they can learn. Last month, Justice Gene Anne Smith of the Saskatchewan Court of Queen's Bench rejected the province's and the school boards' attempts to dismiss the matter out of hand, saying there are fundamental rights at stake—the rights of children who cannot learn easily or in a traditional manner. The case will now go to full trial, probably in the fall. The school boards have argued that such a legal exercise can only be an "inconclusive seminar on special education." But for those families battling the system, what lies in the balance is nothing less than the gift of reading.

Form at end of book

Curing Our "Epidemic" of Learning Disabilities

If educators wish to help children who are low achievers, they must discard the concept of learning disabilities entirely, in favor of a new way of thinking about children's learning problems, Ms. Spear-Swerling and Mr. Sternberg maintain.

Louise Spear-Swerling and Robert J. Sternberg

Louise Spear-Swerling is a professor in the Department of Special Education, Southern Connecticut State University, New Haven. Robert J. Sternberg is IBM Professor of Psychology and Education at Yale University, New Haven.

At a recent party, where most of those present were the parents of school-age children, one of us overheard the following exchange. One parent, discussing her daughter's difficulties in learning to read, mentioned to another parent that the child was suspected by school personnel of having learning disabilities. "My son's teacher thinks that he has learning disabilities, too," confided the second parent. "Both of my children have already been diagnosed as learning-disabled," interjected a third parent, who was nearby.

It seems that a veritable plague of learning disabilities has descended on some of our schools. In the past 20 years or so, the number of children diagnosed as learning disabled has steadily increased, and children with learning disabilities (LDs) now form the single largest category of students receiving special education services.[1] Is there really an epidemic of learning disabilities, perhaps caused by some hidden toxin in our air, food, or water? Or instead is it that—as more than one parent has suggested to us—the concept of learning disabilities merely serves to excuse the failure of schools and teachers to do an adequate job of teaching all children?

In our opinion, neither scenario is accurate. True, some children have actual disabilities in learning, and some teachers do a poor job of teaching. However, the fundamental problem is the concept of learning disabilities itself, and the way it has distorted our view of chil-

dren's difficulties in learning. Furthermore, the flaws in the learning-disabilities concept cannot be repaired through minor tinkering. If educators wish to help children who are low achievers, they must discard the concept of learning disabilities entirely, in favor of a new way of thinking about children's learning problems.

What exactly is the concept of learning disabilities? The centerpiece of educational definitions of learning disabilities and the characteristic that is usually emphasized in school identification of children with LDs is an ability/achievement discrepancy—typically operationalized as an I.Q./achievement discrepancy.[2] Children with learning disabilities are seen as having low achievement relative to the achievement that would be expected based on their I.Q. scores. In addition, learning disabilities are assumed to be the result of a disorder intrinsic to the child, such as a central nervous system dysfunction.[3] Children whose learning difficulties are caused primarily by environmental disadvantage or by poor teaching—as well as by other so-called exclusionary conditions such as sensory impairment or emotional disturbance—are not supposed to be identified as having learning disabilities. Finally, learning disabilities are thought to involve a unique or distinctive syndrome, one qualitatively different from other kinds of learning problems. For example, learning disabilities involving reading, the kind most often identified,[4] are assumed to involve a distinctive syndrome of poor reading that is different from "ordinary" poor reading.

However, it turns out that all these aspects of the learning-disabilities concept are problematic—none more so than the notion of an I.Q./achievement discrepancy. Both educationally and psychologically, the discrepancy construct fails to work.

Educationally, one might reasonably assume that the separate classification and treatment of children under the learning-disabilities umbrella is based on these children's need for a distinctive kind of educational program. Yet there is little evidence to support this assumption. For example, children with learning disabilities in reading unquestionably need instructional help—but they do not appear to need a qualitatively different kind of remedial program than do other poor readers, such as those without I.Q./achievement discrepancies.[5] Moreover, the discrepancy construct and the concept of learning disabilities in general provide little insight into the best way to teach children with learning difficulties. Indeed, some evidence suggests that, by lowering expectations for children who have been labeled as having LDs and by limiting these children's experience with certain kinds of academic tasks, the concept of learning disabilities may, in some instances, worsen rather than improve children's educational prospects.[6]

Psychologically, the discrepancy construct is inherently problematic for many reasons. As operationalized in most schools, I.Q./achievement discrepancy criteria rest on the assumption that I.Q. is a perfect predictor of achievement. However, although I.Q. is generally a good predictor of school achievement, it is certainly not a perfect predictor. In fact, sometimes I.Q. is a downright mediocre predictor of achievement. In the beginning elementary grades, for instance, I.Q. typically accounts for only 10% to 25% of the variance in reading achievement.[7]

These inaccuracies in prediction become particularly problematic at the extremes of I.Q. because of a statistical phenomenon known as regression to the mean. Regression effects were first studied by Sir Francis Galton in the 19th century.[8] Galton tried to predict certain behavioral and biological variables from other variables. For instance, he found that, although the sons of very short fathers tended to be shorter than average height, they usually were not as short as their fathers. Similarly, although the sons of very tall fathers tended to be taller than average, they usually were not quite as tall as their fathers, In sum, Galton found that in predicting one variable from another, extreme scores on one variable (e.g., father's height) tended to predict less extreme scores on the other variable (e.g., son's height).

Like the rest of us, children with LDs are influenced by their biology.

Because of regression, those with higher-than-average I.Q. scores—for example, 120—can be expected to score somewhat lower in achievement, or somewhat closer to the mean. On the other hand, those with I.Q.s lower than average—let's say, 80—can actually be expected to have achievement somewhat higher than 80—again, closer to the mean. Thus, without correction for regression, some high-I.Q. children will be thought to have discrepancies when they actually do not, and some low I.Q. children will be thought to lack discrepancies when they actually have them. In other words, the discrepancy construct

tends to over-identify as learning disabled high-I.Q. children and to under-identify low-I.Q. children. To make a bad situation worse, many of the tests used in the LD field have inadequate reliabilities,[9] and, with tests of low reliability, regression effects become even more problematic.

Of course, regression effects work both ways. That is, if one were attempting to use reading achievement to predict I.Q., then individuals with high scores in reading would, because of regression, tend to have I.Q. scores that were somewhat lower than their reading scores; individuals with low scores in reading would tend to have I.Q. scores that were somewhat higher than their reading scores. However, in school identification of learning disabilities, I.Q. is generally used to predict reading achievement, rather than the other way around.

In calculating discrepancies, it is possible to correct for regression through a method known as regression analysis.[10] However, this method requires, among other things, that all the correlations between the specific I.Q. test used, on the one hand, and the specific achievement tests used, on the other, be known. Because these different correlations are usually not known in educational practice and because the fact that regression is an issue at all is sometimes unrecognized, most schools do not use regression analysis.[11]

However, from a psychological standpoint, perhaps the most dubious thing of all about the discrepancy construct involves the issue of I.Q. Many contemporary researchers share a broad, multidimensional view of intelligence.[12] I.Q. tests do tap a *subset* of important cognitive abilities, but the idea that overall intellectual potential can be captured in a single number such as an I.Q. score is one with which many contemporary investigators would strongly disagree. Of course, the discrepancy construct assumes that I.Q. measures exactly the latter kind of broad "potential" for learning.

Because of the myriad problems with the discrepancy construct, a number of researchers have suggested that minor learning disabilities —and specifically those involving reading, the most widely researched area of learning disabilities—should no longer be defined with reference to an I.Q./achievement discrepancy.[13] Unfortunately, however, for those who are committed to the traditional concept of learning disabilities, the fatal flaws in the concept are not restricted to the discrepancy criterion.

Another serious flaw in the concept involves long-held assumptions about the causation of learning disabilities, specifically, that learning disabilities are caused by a biological abnormality, such as by a central nervous system defect or dysfunction. Research on the role of biology in learning disabilities, and specifically in reading disability, has been reviewed extensively by Gerald Coles and by ourselves, among others.[14] This research does not support the assumption that learning disabilities are caused by a biological abnormality, at least not for most school-identified children with LDs.

However, we are not claiming that biological influences and predispositions are irrelevant to the problems of children with LDs. For instance, compelling evidence exists for strong genetic influences on temperament, personality, and abilities.[15] Like the rest of us, children with learning disabilities are influenced by their biology. The point is that, in most cases of school-identified learning disabilities, there is little evidence that these biological influences constitute actual abnormalities or defects; rather, they probably fall along a continuum with the biological influences experienced by everyone. Furthermore, biological influences such as genetic factors do not act alone to determine cognitive or academic skills but assert themselves only in a complex interaction with the environment.

Finally, there is little evidence that children categorized as having LDs suffer from a unique or distinctive syndrome of poor learning. For instance, the popular view that reading disability is characterized by frequent reversal errors or transpositions of letters and therefore involves a "special" kind of poor reading is not correct.[16] Most children with reading disability appear to have a core of linguistic, and specifically phonological, deficits. These kinds of deficits also characterize poor readers who lack I.Q./achievement discrepancies and who would not be classified as having learning disabilities.[17]

Let us consider a real-life example of the glaring inadequacies that pervade the concept of learning disabilities, as operationalized by I.Q./achievement discrepancy criteria. Richard and Alex are two third-grade boys from a suburban school district in Connecticut who are near the bottom of their respective classes in reading. On an individually administered standardized reading test, they both achieved standard scores of 76. Because this test has a mean score of 100 and a standard deviation of 15, both boys were functioning more than $1^1/_2$ standard deviations below the mean in reading. In addition, neither boy had experienced obvious environmental disadvantage or had another handicapping condition that would account for his poor reading. In other words, both boys met exclusionary criteria for learning-disabilities services.

Only Alex, however, actually qualified for these services. Alex's full-scale I.Q. score was 99. This score, compared to Alex's reading score, yielded an I.Q./achievement discrepancy of 23 points, which qualified him for learning-disabilities services according to Connecticut guidelines on learning disabilities. In contrast, Richard's full-scale I.Q. score was 91, which did not yield a large enough discrepancy to classify him as having LDs. Note that both boys had I.Q. scores within the average range and that, when test error of measurement is taken into ac-

count, their true scores might even have been equal. Furthermore, I.Q. tests provide little information about important cognitive abilities, such as creativity, or about other characteristics that are important in achievement, such as motivation. Do we really want to say that Alex's overall intellectual ability is greater than Richard's or that Alex has more potential in reading than Richard does?

Of course, one might argue that Connecticut guidelines simply use an overly stringent discrepancy criterion. Indeed, there are some states with less stringent discrepancy criteria in which Richard would also qualify for LD services—as well as some states with *more* stringent criteria, in which even Alex would not qualify. Unlike most other handicapping conditions, one can make a "learning disability" vanish or reappear just by relocating to another state![18]

We would like to see LD specialists become, simply, learning specialists.

Most important, this kind of argument sidesteps the real problem, which is that the discrepancy criterion involves an arbitrary, artificial construct that provides little insight into children's learning difficulties. Modifying the discrepancy construct by setting a more or less stringent cutoff for educational services or by using alternative measures of potential such as listening comprehension does not address the more fundamental problems with the construct or with the concept of learning disabilities as a whole.

However, there is knowledge that can provide educators with useful insight into children's learning difficulties—but this knowledge has nothing to do with I.Q. or with I.Q./achievement discrepancies. First, because the problems of children who are experiencing difficulties in learning can be interpreted only with reference to development in normally achieving children, it is essential to know about the course of typical development in the domain in question. In the case of Richard and Alex, of course, this domain is reading. For example, readers who achieve normally at the first-grade level frequently confuse letters such as *b* and *d*. Richard and Alex are functioning at a first-grade level in reading, so the fact that both boys are still making these kinds of reversal errors is neither particularly surprising nor indicative of a pathological brain dysfunction.

Knowledge about typical development also provides clear implications for instruction. For example, phonological abilities such as phonological awareness and word decoding are central to acquiring reading skills in the early elementary grades.[19] Phonological abilities are certainly not the only abilities that are involved in acquiring a high level of reading skill, but for *beginning* readers much hinges on being able to figure out how the alphabet works. It turns out that, although Richard and Alex are weak in virtually all areas of reading, their phonological awareness and decoding skills are especially weak. These weaknesses do not bode well for the future and must be addressed instructionally if either Richard or Alex is to progress in reading.[20]

This last example leads us to a second type of knowledge that provides insight into learning difficulties—a child's profile of cognitive skills in a particular domain. For instance, suppose that Richard's (but not Alex's) reading difficulties were associated primarily with weaknesses in overall language comprehension and reading comprehension and that his decoding skills were adequate for his age. Obviously, Richard's instructional program would now need to differ from Alex's in some substantial ways. What is informative, however, is not the presence or absence of an I.Q./achievement discrepancy, but rather the specific profile of cognitive abilities that are important in a given domain.

Finally, we must emphasize that when we use terms such as "profile of cognitive abilities," we are talking about abilities that are shaped by experience and instruction as well as by inborn capacities. Unlike some critics of the learning-disabilities field, we do not think that children's learning problems are largely the fault of teachers, the education system, or society in general. Rather, we believe that children come to school with individual differences in specific cognitive abilities that render some children more susceptible than others to school failure. Nevertheless, whether or not children actually fail may depend a great deal on their experiences in school. With the right kinds of educational experiences, a given child's vulnerability to school failure might never be realized, or at least might be greatly ameliorated.

In previous works, we have described a way of conceptualizing children's difficulties in reading that embodies the ideas that we have just discussed.[21] These ideas—that problems in learning to read need to be viewed in relation to typical reading acquisition, that these problems can be understood by examining their cognitive underpinnings, and that children's intrinsic characteristics interact with environmental factors and with experience to produce a particular outcome—certainly did not originate with us. Indeed, they are well-represented in scientific thinking about reading disability.[22] Unfortunately, however, these ideas do not exemplify typical thinking about reading disability or about other learning disabilities in educational circles or in the popular press.

Although we have focused on the domain of reading, the basic ideas that we have mentioned can be applied to any of the domains under the learning-disabilities umbrella. For instance, the discrepancy construct is no more valid or enlightening for children who have "math disability" or "writing disability" than for those with "reading disability." Instead, educators who wish to help children with difficulties in a particular domain need to know about the course of typical development in that domain, about the specific cognitive abilities that are crucial at various points in development, about the cognitive abilities in which a particular child is weak, and about how best to develop these abilities.

Clearly, *both* Richard and Alex need help in reading. Viewing Alex as having a mysterious reading disorder—or viewing Richard as a "dumb" poor reader—is neither accurate nor helpful. However, although neither boy is likely to be helped by the concept of learning disabilities, is also obvious that neither will be helped by instruction that ignores his cognitive weaknesses. Instead, each boy needs to have his cognitive weaknesses addressed—as well as his strengths exploited—in an effective, individually tailored instructional program. This kind of program certainly might be developed and implemented by the boys' third-grade teacher. However, because the range of individual differences in children's cognitive skills is quite large, even at the beginning of kindergarten,[23] we think that some children will always benefit from the help of specialists such as reading consultants, special education teachers, and so on.

Thus we would like to see professionals in the field of learning disabilities change their ideas and their approaches rather than change careers. The necessary changes would not be minor. Among other things, they would involve dramatic alterations in procedures for identifying children for educational services, in funding practices, and in the roles of learning-disabilities specialists.

For example, current educational guidelines for identifying children with LDs, with an ability/achievement discrepancy at their core, not only lack scientific validity but also are poor education policy. All low achievers, not just those who meet some arbitrary and illogical discrepancy cutoff, need educational help. The precise nature of this help may certainly need to differ depending on the individual child, but the essential point for policy makers is that there is no scientific basis for singling out only one group of low achievers for educational services. Thus we would like to see low achievers identified for educational services based on low achievement rather than on an ability/achievement discrepancy.

Changes in school identification procedures will depend on concomitant changes in funding practices; as long as state and federal funds are tied to the current system of LD identification, educators will find it difficult or impossible to adopt a different system. Changes in identification procedures would also alter the roles of learning-disabilities specialists, who would no longer need to devote themselves to documenting I.Q./achievement discrepancies or to distinguishing the "real" cases of learning disabilities from other instances of low achievement. Instead, learning-disabilities specialists could focus their time and energies on instruction, on consultation and collaboration with other practitioners, and on educationally relevant forms of assessment.

We are not suggesting that learning-disabilities specialists assume a purely pragmatic stance that ignores cognitive processes. Rather, we would like to see learning-disabilities specialists become, simply, learning specialists. Learning specialists could specialize in knowledge about the cognitive processes involved in typical acquisition of academic skills, in knowledge about the ways in which children might go awry in acquiring important cognitive and academic skills, and in adapting instruction for children with a variety of cognitive and academic difficulties. Without some truly sweeping changes, the entire field of learning disabilities will continue to rest on a crumbling conceptual foundation. On the other hand, with the right kinds of changes, those in the learning-disabilities field have the capacity to make a real difference in the lives of low achievers.

That many children experience school failure is beyond dispute. However, the solutions to any problem may stand or fall on how we frame that problem. The concept of learning disabilities has not and will not provide a solution to the problem of school failure. To cure our "epidemic" of learning disabilities, we need to begin by dispensing with the concept of learning disabilities itself.

Notes

1. Janet W. Lerner, *Learning Disabilities: Theories, Diagnosis, and Teaching Strategies* (Boston: Houghton Mifflin, 1993); and *To Assure the Free, Appropriate Education of All Handicapped Children (1978–1990): 13th Annual Report to Congress on the Individuals with Disabilities Education Act* (Washington, D.C.: U.S. Department of Education, 1991).

2. W. Frankenberger and J. Harper, "States' Criteria and Procedures for Identifying Learning Disabled Children: A Comparison of 1981/82 and 1985/86 Guidelines." *Journal of Learning Disabilities,* vol. 20, 1987, pp. 118–21; and Keith E. Stanovich, "Discrepancy Definitions of Reading Disability: Has Intelligence Led Us Astray?," *Reading Research Quarterly,* vol. 26, 1991, pp. 7–29.

3. National Joint Committee on Learning Disabilities, letter to member organizations, 1988.

4. Louisa C. Moats and G. Reid Lyon, "Learning Disabilities in the United States: Advocacy, Science, and the Future of the Field." *Journal of Learning Disabilities,* vol. 26, 1993, pp. 282–94; and Corinne R. Smith, *Learning Disabilities: The Interaction of Learner, Task, and Setting* (Needham Heights, Mass.: Allyn and Bacon, 1991).

5. Linda S. Siegel, "I.Q. Is Irrelevant to the Definition of Learning Disabilities," *Journal of Learning Disabilities,* vol. 22, 1989, pp. 469–78.

6. Richard I. Allington and Anne McGill-Franzen, "School Response to Reading Failure. Instruction for Chapter 1 and Special Education Students in Grades Two, Four, and Eight." *Elementary School Journal,* vol. 89, 1989, pp. 529–42: and Anne McGill-Franzen, "Compensatory and Special Education: Is There Accountability for Learning and Belief in Children's Potential?" in Ellreda H. Hiebert and Barbara M. Taylor, eds. *Getting Reading Right from the Start: Effective Early Literacy Interventions* (Boston: Allyn and Bacon, 1994), pp. 13–35.

7. Keith E. Stanovich, Anne Cunningham, and Dorothy Feeman, "Intelligence, Cognitive Skills, and Early Reading Progress," *Reading Research Quarterly,* vol. 19, 1984, pp. 278–303.

8. Robert B. McCall, *Fundamental Statistics for Psychology* (New York: Harcourt Brace Jovanovich, 1980).

9. Moats and Lyon, op. cit.

10. Linda J. Hargrove and James A. Poteet, *Assessment in Special Education* (Englewood Cliffs, N.J.: Prentice-Hall, 1984); and Lerner, op. cit.

11. Frankenberger and Harper, op. cit.

12. See, for example, Stephen J. Ceci, *On Intelligence—More or Less: A Biological Treatise on Intellectual Development* (Englewood Cliffs, N.J.: Prentice-Hall, 1990); Howard Gardner, *Frames of Mind: The Theory of Multiple Intelligences* (New York: Basic Books, 1983); Robert J. Sternberg, *Beyond I.Q.: A Triarchic Theory of Human Intelligence* (New York: Cambridge University Press, 1985); and idem, *The Triarchic Mind: A New Theory of Human Intelligence* (New York: Viking, 1988).

13. Jack M. Fletcher et al., "Cognitive Profiles of Reading Disability: Comparisons of Discrepancy and Low Achievement Definitions," *Journal of Educational Psychology,* vol. 86, 1994, pp. 6–23; Richard K. Olson et al., "Genetic Etiology of Individual Differences in Reading Disability," in L. V. Feagans, E. J. Short, and L. J. Meltzer, eds., *Subtypes of Learning Disabilities: Theoretical Perspectives and Research* (Hillsdale, N.J.: Erlbaum, 1991), pp. 113–35; and Linda S. Siegel, "Evidence That I.Q. Scores Are Irrelevant to the Definition and Analysis of Reading Disability," *Canadian Journal of Psychology,* vol. 42, 1988, pp. 201–15.

14. Gerald S. Coles, *The Learning Mystique: A Critical Look at "Learning Disabilities"* (New York: Pantheon, 1987); and Louise Spear-Swerling and Robert J. Sternberg, *Roads to Reading Disability: When Poor Readers Become "Learning Disabled"* (Boulder, Colo.: Westview Press, 1996).

15. Thomas J. Bouchard, "Genes, Environment, and Personality," *Science,* vol. 264, 1994, pp. 1700–1701; and Robert Plomin, "The Nature and Nurture of Cognitive Abilities," in Robert J. Sternberg, ed., *Advances in the Psychology of Human Intelligence,* vol. 4 (Hillsdale, N.J.: Erlbaum, 1988), pp. 1–33.

16. Donald Shankweiler et al., "Identifying the Causes of Reading Disability," in Philip B. Gough, Linnea C. Ehri, and Rebecca Treiman, eds., *Reading Acquisition* (Hillsdale, N.J.: Erlbaum, 1992), pp. 275–305.

17. Fletcher et al., op. cit.; and Keith E. Stanovich and Linda S. Siegel, "Phenotypic Performance Profile of Children with Reading Disabilities: A Regression-Based Test of the Phonological-Core Variable-Difference Model," *Journal of Educational Psychology,* vol. 86, 1994, pp. 24–53.

18. Moats and Lyon, op. cit.

19. Marilyn Jaeger Adams, *Beginning to Read: Thinking and Learning About Print* (Cambridge, Mass.: MIT Press, 1990); Jeanne Chall, *Stages of Reading Development* (New York: McGraw-Hill, 1983); and Louise Spear-Swerling and Robert J. Sternberg, "The Road Not Taken: An Integrative Theoretical Model of Reading Disability." *Journal of Learning Disabilities,* vol. 27, 1994, pp. 91–103, 122.

20. B. Byrne, P. Freebody, and A. Gates, "Longitudinal Data on the Relations of Word-Reading Strategies to Comprehension," *Reading Research Quarterly,* vol. 27, 1992, pp. 140–51.

21. Spear-Swerling and Sternberg, "The Road Not Taken"; and idem, *Roads to Reading Disability.*

22. See, for example, Fletcher et al., op. cit.: Isabelle Y. Liberman and Alvin M. Liberman, "Whole Language Versus Code Emphasis: Underlying Assumptions and Their Implications for Reading Instruction," *Annals of Dyslexia,* vol. 40, 1990, pp. 51–76; Shankweiler et al., op. cit.: Keith E. Stanovich, "Matthew Effect in Reading: Some Consequences of Individual Differences in the Acquisition of Literacy," *Reading Research Quarterly,* vol. 21, 1986, pp. 360–406; idem, "Discrepancy Definitions of Reading Disability"; Stanovich and Siegel, op. cit.; and Frank R. Vellutino and Donna M. Scanlon, "The Effects of Instructional Bias on Word Identification," in

Laurence Rieben and Charles A. Perfetti, eds., *Learning to Read: Basic Research and Its Implications* (Hillsdale, N.J.: Erlbaum, 1991), pp. 189–203.

23. Lois G. Dreyer, "The Development of Phonologic and Orthographic Knowledge in Kindergarten Children: Relationship to Emerging Word Reading Ability," paper presented at the annual meeting of the American Educational Research Association, New Orleans, April 1994.

Form at end of book

Issue 13 Summary

Unlike mental retardation, hearing impairment, visual impairment, or physical disability, "learning disabilities" is a vague concept. Some would argue that the term "learning disabilities" is useless because it categorizes under one "umbrella" several disorders that have only one thing in common: they interfere with children's academic performance. Trying to understand learning disabilities and trying to find the best practice to educate children with learning disabilities are very difficult when the category describes many disorders. Therefore, efforts have been made to isolate specific learning disabilities, such as dyslexia, and to tease out the relationship of learning disabilities to general mental ability (or intelligence), in the hopes of developing a better understanding of this phenomenon. Gradually, our understanding has grown and, we hope, in the century to come, we will become more successful in developing strategies to help students with learning disabilities experience academic success.

WiseGuide Wrap-Up

This section focused on a set of issues pertaining to how we organize schools—namely, how we test children, how we group children, how we teach children, and how we categorize children who differ from the norm. In each case, the articles presented were selected to highlight the difficult decisions faced by educators who are struggling with these issues.

Every college student who is preparing to be a teacher has had the experience of having been a student. On the one hand, this gives the future teacher some insight regarding the experience of a student trying to learn. On the other hand, this tends to cause new teachers to recreate in their own classrooms the ways in which they themselves were taught, repeating many of the same mistakes. It is very difficult to break into the cycle of new teachers using the methods they experienced when they were students. However, we are constantly learning about better ways to test, group, and teach students; in order to implement these new ways, new teachers have to be prepared to let go of the methods with which they are familiar. To do this, new teachers need to struggle with these questions (how to test, how to group, how to teach), and they need to have the courage to give up the familiar and to experiment with the unknown.

R.E.A.L. Sites

This list provides a print preview of typical **Coursewise** R.E.A.L. sites. (There are over 100 such sites at the **Courselinks**™ site.) The danger in printing URLs is that web sites can change overnight. As we went to press, these sites were functional using the URLs provided. If you come across one that isn't, please let us know via email to: webmaster@coursewise. com. Use your Passport to access the most current list of R.E.A.L. sites at the **Courselinks** site.

Site name: Guidelines for the Development and Management of Performance Assessments

URL: http://www.campus.cua.edu/www/eric_ae/digests/tm9604.htm

Why is it R.E.A.L.? This site, written by Edward D. Roeber of the Council of Chief State School Officers, gives useful information on the planning, implementation, and interpretation of performance-based assessments. The site is part of the ERIC Clearinghouse on Assessment and Evaluation. It includes specific suggestions and a bibliography.

Key topics: assessment, performance-based assessment, research

Try this: According to Edward D. Roeber, what is a major key to the success of an entire performance assessment project?

Site name: How to Work Effectively with a Heterogeneous Classroom

URL: http://www.maec.org/hetclass.html

Why is it R.E.A.L.? This site was created by the Mid-Atlantic Equity Consortium. It highlights specific methods that promote learning in the heterogeneously mixed classroom. The content of the site is adapted from the book *How to Differentiate Instruction in Mixed-Ability Classrooms,* published by the Association for Supervision and Curriculum Development.

Key topics: heterogeneous grouping, ability grouping, effective teaching

Try this: Name some ways that the "flow of instruction in a differentiated classroom" could be improved.

section 5 | The Impact of Technology

Learning Objectives

- Articulate the reasons for the growing interest in media literacy.

- Understand the value and methods of promoting teleliteracy in students.

- Identify ways teachers can use television to encourage their students to think critically.

 **WiseGuide Intro**

One of the most powerful influences on children and adolescents is what is shown on television—both the programs *and* the advertisements. Children and adolescents (as well as adults) spend countless hours in front of the television set. Some educators celebrate the influence of television, arguing that it exposes us at lightning speed to information from around the globe, it provides our diverse nation with a common experience, and it keeps us company when we are lonely. Others decry the influence of television, arguing that it is aimed at the lowest common denominator, it does nothing to challenge the mind, and it fosters passivity. Critics contend that television has made us so passive that we stop thinking critically and mindlessly accept what we are told by news anchors, salespeople, and Hollywood stars.

Two of the weightiest criticisms of television is that it involves a purely visual mode and that it causes children to read less. Interestingly, television had an opposite effect on me. As a teenager, I saw a dramatization on television of the novel *Old Goriot* by nineteenth-century French novelist Honoré de Balzac; it inspired me to read Balzac's novels, and I developed a passion for them that I still have not quenched. Other television viewers no doubt have been stimulated by programs on painting, dance, music, the sciences, travel, and history.

Thus, we find in television a medium that has enormous potential to promote an interest in subjects, but television's potential has probably not been realized. A difficult task for teachers is to find a way to make television worthwhile for students; if deployed wisely by teachers, television can motivate students and promote their learning of a variety of subjects. But how do we marshal this medium for our own purposes? In Reading 35, Marnie W. Curry-Tash argues that teachers should promote media literacy, the ability to access and evaluate communications—more specifically, teleliteracy. She contends that, by analyzing the purpose and strategies of television commercials, students can become more critical thinkers. David B. Owen, Charles L. P. Silet, and Sarah E. Brown, in Reading 36, propose that not only advertisements but also television programs themselves can be the basis for student learning. Specifically, they argue that students can learn to analyze the content of television programs, attending to such factors as gender roles, the portrayal of ethnic diversity, and the presentation of sex and violence. They argue that students can be taught to engage in "critical viewing" by becoming more reflective and evaluative, skills they may be able to generalize to other activities.

Television
and Other Media

Questions

1. What arguments are presented by the authors to establish the possible negative effects of television?

2. How, according to the authors, can a teacher promote higher-level thinking in students using television viewing?

3. Curry-Tash describes the role of television in creating a "democratic, global village." What do you think is the relationship between television and the concepts of "democracy" and a "global village"?

Introduction

Few would argue that television entertains us, informs us, keeps us from boredom, distracts us from our troubles, and makes us feel connected, but does television *educate* us? The authors of the articles in this section show various ways that teachers can use television to promote learning and critical thinking by students. The authors are not encouraging students to watch educational television; rather, they contend that, by watching advertisements, dramas, and comedies with a critical eye, students can develop a form of literacy—teleliteracy. The same critical thinking skills that students bring to watching television can also be brought to other sources of information, including books, magazines, and even teachers' lessons.

The Politics of Teleliteracy and Adbusting in the Classroom

Marnie W. Curry-Tash

Marnie W. Curry-Tash teaches in an interdisciplinary freshman program at Concord High School, California. Her e-mail address is ttmct@lanminds.com.

Last year, I watched the Super Bowl via satellite on a TV powered by an electric generator in remote northern Uganda, where I was stationed working with Sudanese refugees. As advertisements featuring opulent, ultra-developed images of the United States flickered across the screen, I noted with uneasiness not only the dramatic discrepancy in lifestyles between Uganda and the U.S. (this is not to deny the widening gap between rich and poor in our own country), but also the far-reaching impact of American media. At $1 million for a thirty-second spot, I realized that the cost of just one minute of a commercial break would vastly exceed the United Nation's yearly budget to provide relief and developmental assistance to the 100,000 refugees who suffered in my backyard (based on the 1996 budget total of $1,305,347 [UNHCR, Programme Briefing Note, Sub-office Adjumani/Pakelle, April 1996]). Perched between two worlds, I struggled to reconcile my place between the two. My internal wrestlings reminded me of my California classroom where just a year before my sophomores, the Monday after the Super Bowl, spontaneously recreated the Budweiser frog commercial with a robust, choral croaking of the syllables, "Bud-Weis-Er." Here too, was evidence of the beguiling seductiveness of American mass media and of advertising in particular.

Supplement these anecdotes with the knowledge that the advertising industry expends $130 billion a year and that their images appear on 162 million TV sets glowing in living rooms across the U.S. an estimated seven hours a day. Consider also the 260,000 billboards and 23,076 newspapers and magazines clamoring for our attention. And finally, think about the fact that upon graduation, our students will have seen between 350,000 and 640,000 TV commercials! Added together, these statistics testify to the urgent need for language arts teachers to take seriously the recent addition of media literacy to the *Standards for the English Language Arts* (1996, Urbana, IL: NCTE/IRA) and perhaps more importantly, to devote at least a portion of our attention to the commercial interests undergirding the media industry.

By the time they graduate, our students will have viewed almost half a million TV commercials. How can we bring this expertise into the classroom?

I suspect that some of us might grimace at the prospect of yet another demand placed on our curriculum and wonder how we will squeeze in yet another topic. But because curriculum does not exist in a vacuum and because I believe that we as reflective practitioners must articulate why we teach what we teach, I frame my proposal within a theoretical framework which speaks to the significance of such studies in terms of cultural imperialism, democracy, popular culture, and multiculturalism. My argument starts with a macro or global analysis of TV and then leads into an examination of how media (TV and commercials in particular) functions at a micro or personal level. Finally, I propose how these issues can be transformed into challenging and meaningful curriculum.

Please note that *adbusting* as an expression originates from the title of The Media Foundation's quarterly magazine entitled *Adbusters*. I am indebted to this organization for its savvy word spins and ideas about how to interrupt the power of commercials in my classroom. In this article, to "adbust" means to engage in critical evaluations of the content and broader implications of commercial advertisements.

What Is Media Literacy?

Any discussion of media literacy must offer a definition and place it in a historical context. The internationally accepted definition of media literacy is "the ability to access, analyze, evaluate and produce communication in a variety of forms" (Leveranz: and Tyner 1993, 21). Currently media education is experiencing a renaissance of sorts after a fallow period in the 1980s. During the 1970s though, media literacy gained popular currency after the 1972 Surgeon General warned TV viewers of the connection between TV violence and anti-social behavior. This advisory spurred an explosion of curricula and educational media, which was generously funded by the U.S. Department of Education, the National Endowment for the Arts, and the Rockefeller Foundation (Leveranz and Tyner, 22). The resulting abundance of curricula on "visual literacy" saturated schools so much that media education lost its attractiveness and became another passing educational fad. Many of my colleagues, recalling their 1970s classrooms, have told me with a wistful smile, "Oh yeah, I used to teach a unit on advertising analysis."

So how is the current reinvigorated media literacy movement different from two decades ago? I think the key difference lies in the reorientation of media education away from a transmission model, whereby a passive viewer receives information and is instantly influenced by the content therein. Instead, many media educators today believe that, just as media constructs a version of world and self, viewers actively "read" and construct a "television text" in a way that can be oppositional or subversive (Apple 1993, 102). Drawing on critical pedagogy, which demands an understanding of the economic, social, political, historic, and cultural forces shaping media, this conception of audience recognizes the liberatory potential in communication which engages viewers as active agents with voices and alternate visions of reality. Ultimately, advocates of media literacy hope to foster in students "the kind of critical autonomy it takes to be informed citizens in a democratic society" (Leveranz and Tyner, 22). In this vision, students move beyond being consumers of information and become critics and producers of knowledge.

Media literacy today also benefits from the growing attention given to the raging debate over the value of popular culture. While some defenders of classic Western traditions contend that "the expanding sphere of popular culture . . . [is] a tasteless and dangerous threat to notions of civility and order" (Giroux 1989, 237), proponents of popular culture like David Bianculli, TV critic for the New York *Daily News,* attack those who thumb their noses at TV as intellectual elites. Rather than viewing popular culture as a vulgar phenomenon of common people, Bianculli believes that TV should be regarded as an art, deserving of appreciation and serious scholarship (Bianculli 1992, 25, 142).

As a reformed anti-TV snob, I now agree with him that a blanket rejection and condemnation of TV divorces us from what is happening in the world (or at least one important version of what is happening in the world). Without TV, I would never have witnessed the collapse of the Berlin Wall, the release of Nelson Mandela from prison, the Rodney King beating, the Challenger explosion, the Clarence Thomas confirmation hearings, Ken Burns' documentary on the Civil War, or the funeral of Princess Diana. Likewise, without some exposure to "Beverly Hills 90210," "Melrose Place," and Bart Simpson, I would have no concept of the issues and influences affecting my students. Nonetheless, I must also acknowledge that what Bianculli views as "art" is a production created by a media industry enmeshed in certain political and economic systems. Thus, one must always ask whose vision of reality is served through the media (Apple, 96). For similar reasons, we must avoid the temptation to dismiss media as trivial knowledge since it holds enormous political significance.

A Democratic, Global Village?

In 1962 Marshall McLuhan coined the term the electronic "global village" to describe the exploding power, proliferation, and interdependence of electronic media. His notion of a "village," which conveyed a sense of global interconnectedness and even intimacy, has been eclipsed, in my opinion, by the emergence of corporate conglomerates which now dominate and control the TV networks. Neil Postman alludes to this phenomenon when he observes that TV network news is a "mix and match," "homogenized" affair which essentially delivers the same content (Postman and Powers 1992, 54–5). My viewing of NBC's live telecast of the Super Bowl in Uganda is another manifestation of this shift. While no one can deny that TV coverage of certain events like the Civil Rights protests, the Kent State shootings, the attempted ouster of Soviet President Gorbachev, and the Valdez oil spill provoked international attention and added momentum to popular movements, we must not overlook the hegemonic impact of America's increasingly dominant, commercial-driven popular culture on the rest of the world.

Any attempt at teleliteracy in the classroom, then, needs to recognize that the "whole point of television in America is to get you to watch so that programmers, performers, and others can rake in the money" (Postman and Powers, 3). One example of how these commercial interests pervade our TV viewing is reported by John Simpson (1995):

Advertisers are not good people for news organizations to rely on: during the Gulf War NBC lost $25 million in revenue because companies which had bought space in the news bulletins canceled their advertisements—they were afraid their products would appear alongside reports of American casualties . . . Most of the companies which advertise on television want them [the audience] to feel good so, therefore, do the people in charge of providing the news. The freest society in the world has achieved the kind of news blackout which totalitarian regimes can only dream about. (92)

This account illustrates how the interlocking interests of business, advertising, and media inevitably determine what vision of the world and of reality will be constructed for us on our TV sets.

Yet another disturbing dimension of this scenario is the visual effect of a news story on a devastating mud slide in South America being juxtaposed to a commercial for Colgate, Scope, or Polident which features smiling white teeth. As Postman points out, the "natural" disaster becomes a surreal and trivial distant event whose impact is washed away by a commercial break that runs longer than the actual news report on the tragedy (Postman, 126). This example becomes even more problematic when one deconstructs the content of the news report and learns how "land-ownership patterns" in South America force poor families to live on dangerous hillsides where not only can they barely cultivate enough food for survival, but they are vulnerable to destructive mud slides (Apple 1993, 104). Michael Apple demonstrates how TV coverage casting the landslide as a "natural" disaster reinforces certain economic structures and in doing so exemplifies the potent ability of the media to shape our understanding of the world. This illustration demonstrates how TV news (and popular culture in general) is a site of struggle and resistance wherein some people benefit/profit and some people get represented, while others do not.

Teleliteracy on the Micro and Personal Level

Media also shapes our identity as a nation and as individuals. One example of this surfaces in Bianculli's *Teleliteracy: Taking Television Seriously* (1992) when, making a comparison between elitist attacks on TV and Plato's denunciation on the popular poetry and drama of his time, Bianculli writes, "I found a pattern that went through the ages with revealing, and depressing, regularity. While the common people—the consumers—generally were eager to entertain and be entertained by new art forms, the ruling and intellectual elite responded with stubborn conservatism" (Bianculli, 24). What concerns me about this description is how he uncritically conceives the common people, not as citizens, but as consumers. If we are to really take TV seriously, we need to recognize how the commercial-driven media seeks to define and position its mass audience as consumers.

One extreme example of this trend is Chris Whittle's brainchild, Channel One. Offering up daily two-minute doses of school-sanctioned and mandated advertising, Channel One has transformed some 12,000 schools across the country (approximately 40% of secondary schools) into commercial zones serving corporate greed (KIII 1994, 1). Horace Mann's democratic ideal of public education, where the emphasis rested on cultivating the common good and on preparing students for meaningful citizenship, seems lost behind the guise of free technology and world "news." In fact, Whittle's public relation materials to prospective advertisers pitch Channel One as "more than television; [rather, it is] a direct pipeline" to teens, promising an *entrée* into "the American consumer market" sure to help "establish brand loyalties and perceptions that will last a life time" (Molnar 1996, 66). I wonder, are we training our students to "world class standards" in order for them to become consumers in the twenty- first century?

The advertising industry expends $130 billion a year.

Ronald Collins and Michael Jacobson (1992) eloquently articulate this concern by reminding us:

There is a long standing American ideal of simple honest living, of moderation in the marketplace. Frugality used to be a key word in America's civic vocabulary. Yet ever since World War II we have allowed business people to exalt one value— consumption—to the near exclusion of all others. This treads on our moral and civic tradition like a bulldozer in a flower garden. In this one-value universe, the ideal of consumption obliterates other important social and environmental values. (56)

When elementary students spend $15 billion a year, and influence their parents to spend an additional $160 billion per year, we can begin to understand the high stakes beneath seemingly innocuous Saturday morning cartoon toy promotions and fast food commercials. Teens, not surprisingly, spend even more of their own money— an estimated $57 billion, while still influencing family expenditures to the tune of $36 billion (Molnar, 21). Obviously, we need to educate students to rethink their consumption and grapple with the reality that North Americans, who represent only 5% of the world's population consume one third of the earth's resources and produce almost half of the non-organic waste (Adbusters 1994, 7).

Media literacy offers opportunities for us to connect with our students' lived culture.

The influence of media and TV on national and personal identities also surfaces in the portrayal (or lack thereof) of certain segments of the population (e.g., women, "minorities," gays, etc.). The recurrent images of women viewed as sex objects and of African American boys (and men) depicted as gangster criminals reinforce inaccurate, denigrating stereotypes. Similarly, the absence of certain populations also relegates already marginalized people into invisible spaces, which ultimately promulgates a distorted vision of nation and self within the mass audience.

Adbusting in the Classroom

Incorporating media literacy into our classrooms does not have to subvert the standard curriculum. There are many meaningful opportunities and techniques by which we can integrate media literacy in our conventional teaching programs. Teachers can utilize media as a bridge from students' lives into more traditional elements of the curriculum. Just as one teacher used her African American students' familiarity with rap music to launch into a more academic exploration of poetic devices like literal and figurative meaning, as well as rhyme scheme, alliteration, and onomatopoeia (Ladson-Billings 1995, 161), TV commercials can be integrated into a unit on persuasion and fused with either George Orwell's *Animal Farm* (1946) or Frederik Pohl's *The Space Merchants* (1952) since both novels satirically portray societies where persuasion, either in the form of propaganda or advertising, alters and corrupts the fabric of daily existence.

Media as an instructional tool places a premium on the lived, cultural knowledge of students and offers teachers a means of honoring students, while still pushing them towards academic success. (What's more, ubiquitous VCR technology allows us to tape commercials at low cost, so this methodology is fairly accessible.) My approach to media literacy, which I think could be easily applied to other forms of media besides commercials, is comprised of three steps, detailed below.

Marking the Invisible Visible

When students ask during a discussion of *Animal Farm*, "Why are the animals so stupid? Can't they *see* that Squealer's duping them?," I shift them towards reckoning with how they too have unknowingly been manipulated by advertisements. In playful confrontation, I'll ask a female student, "Why are you wearing make-up?" Or I'll ask a basketball player, "Why are you wearing Air Jordans?" From there, we take the plunge and begin to unravel the complex issues and interests at work behind commercials.

Initially my students refuse to believe that advertisers manipulate them into spending money on certain products (after all, they consider the animals stupid for falling prey to Squealer's PR and want to distinguish themselves as being much too sophisticated to be likewise duped). They dismiss the effect of commercials and tell me I'm ridiculous when I inquire why commercials (which make up 19 minutes of every prime time hour) aren't listed in their *TV Guide*. Students are also skeptical about my claim that everything in a commercial is intentional and that advertisers hire psychologists to assist them in engineering a media experience that fosters need and desire within the target audience.

In order to crack open their resistance, I've used a variety of successful activities over the years, including:

- Viewing *Deadly Deception: General Electric, Nuclear Weapons & Our Environment* (1991), a 29-minute video produced by INFACT, a grassroots consumer action group which conducted a successful boycott against General Electric in the late 1980s. This Academy Award winning video offers an interesting perspective in that: 1) it is itself a piece of propaganda, and 2) it weaves excerpts from the "We bring good things to life" commercial campaign with vivid imagery suggesting there is another side to this slogan.

- Viewing *Still Killing Us Softly* (1987), a 30-minute video examining the cumulative, unconscious effect on women, men, and children of how women are portrayed in ads.

- Listening and analyzing the lyrics of Tracy Chapman's "Material World" or Madonna's "Material Girl."

- Conducting a Jingle Jam, where cooperative groups of students compete to brainstorm as many commercial jingles as they can recall. Usually, this reveals just how thoroughly we absorb these catchy, persistent tunes.

Making Personal Connections

Once students begin to seriously question the content of advertisements, as well as the motives of advertisers, I assign a media journal where students not only keep track of how many hours a day they spend engaged with mass media, but where they also critically reflect on the issues discussed in class. Sample prompts include:

- Think back to your first day of being ultraconscious about your media intake. How did this feel? What did you notice about the ease or difficulty of logging your media hours?

- Over the course of your life so far, what has TV meant to you? What moments from it stick with you as memorable? Why? And with what effect?

- Imagine that yesterday you were cut off from all media . . . you had absolutely no exposure to magazines, radio, TV, newspapers, movies, or music.

What would this day be like for you? How would it differ from what really happened for you yesterday? Consider what role mass media plays in your life.

- Parents often express concern about their children's exposure to media. What do you think a parent's responsibility is when it comes to the following issues: violence on TV, sexually explicit advertisements or music, quantity of TV viewing time?

- Having spent time this week in class analyzing commercials (and I hope paying extra attention to them outside of the classroom), reflect on the relationship of ads to society—do they mirror what's going on in society? Or, do they shape what happens in society? What is the overall impact of ads on our lives?

- Calculate the percentage of waking time you've spent on mass media this week. How do you feel about this figure? How has your understanding of mass media changed over the course of this week? Do you think mass media has a positive or negative impact on America? Why?

In addition to this personal reflection, students learn to recognize various advertising claims (Jeffrey Shrank's 1975 book is helpful) and to understand how these strategies relate to Abraham H. Maslow's hierarchy of needs (Maslow 1970, 97–104).

Becoming Knowledge Producers

Then, depending on the time available, my class completes one or two of the following cooperative group projects:

- Close analysis of a TV commercial (captured on video) and then presented in a class oral presentation.

- The creation of a collage poster of print ads wherein each group examines an assigned topic like: gender, alcohol, tobacco, race, disabilities/handicaps, youth/elderly, socio-economic status, and materialism. The final product must include written analysis which incorporates relevant statistical information. (For example, the number of deaths from tobacco-related diseases, or in the case of race, students take a page-by-page tally of several different magazines to determine the total number of ads featuring people and the percentage of those which depict people of color.)

- Production of a counterad or countermercial spoofing an existing campaign. Some examples include: for Marlboro, "Come to where the cancer is"; for Slim-So-Fast, "Fat-So-Fast is yours with the help of this yo-yo dieting aid"; or for Obsession perfume, "Be obsessed by Calvin Swine." The Media Foundation of Vancouver offers excellent sample parodies of video and print ads (contact them at 1-800-663-1243).

In each project, I challenge students to employ the creative and manipulative genius of professional advertisers. I want them to: polish their presentations, carefully craft their words, agonize about how to organize text and visual images, and above all, persuade their audience. Underlying this expectation is my desire to equip students with the skills necessary to become active agents who question rampant consumerism as a social ideal and who recognize how the media attempts to manipulate its target audience.

Culminating writing activities have varied over the years, but have explored questions such as:

- Are we consumers or citizens?

- How does the scarcity of minorities in advertisements affect people of color, caucasians, and our society?

- How are women/men portrayed in advertisements and what's the effect?

- What is the connection between our investigation of advertising and the novel we read? What is the significance of that connection?

- Is materialism wrecking America and/or the planet?

At this point in the unit, I am primarily interested in having students process and crystallize their personal beliefs regarding the problematic issues bound up in the advertising industry's mission.

Conclusion

The new *Standards for the English Language Arts* (1996) challenges us to expand the scope of our conception of literacy. The addition of media literacy offers opportunities for us to: connect with our students' lived culture; extend the significance and relevance of a classic text like *Animal Farm,* and perhaps most importantly, problematize media's commercial interests which have troubling implications for our society and our future. The implicit politics of this latter task may cause some teachers to feel uncomfortable, but I contend that to omit this element from our investigations of media is itself a political act. Integrating the techniques of Adbusting into our curricula will equip our students with the critical awareness needed to be civic-minded community members, thoughtful citizens, and discriminating consumers. Otherwise, who benefits?

Works Cited

Adbusters. 1994. *Spoof Ad Calendar 1994.* Vancouver, Canada: The Media Foundation.

Apple, Michael. 1996. *Cultural Politics and Education.* New York: Teachers College Press.

———. 1993. *Official Knowledge: Democratic Education in a Conservative Age.* New York: Routledge.

Bianculli, David. 1992. *Teleliteracy: Taking Television Seriously.* New York: Simon & Schuster.

Chasnoff, Debra, prod./dir. 1991. *Deadly Deception: General Electric, Nuclear Weapons, & Our Environment.* Boston: INFACT.

Collins, Ronald K. L. and Michael F. Jacobson. 1992. "Are We Consumers or Citizens?" *Utne Reader* 49 (Jan./Feb.): 56–57.

Giroux, Henry A. 1989. *Cultural Pedagogy, the State and Cultural Struggle.* Albany, NY: SUNY Press.

KIII Press Release. 1994. www.k3.com/news/94.10.02.html

Ladson-Billings, Gloria. 1995. "But That's Just Good Teaching! The Case for Culturally Relevant Pedagogy." *Theory into Practice 34.3* (Summer): 159–165.

Lazarus, Margaret, prod./dir. 1987. *Still Killing Us Softly.* Cambridge, MA: Cambridge Documentary Film.

Leveranz, Deborah and Kathleen Tyner. 1993. "Inquiring Minds Want to Know: What Is Media Literacy?" *The Independent* (Aug./Sept.): 21–25.

Maslow, Abraham H. 1970. *Motivation and Personality.* New York: Harper & Row.

McLuhan, Marshall. 1962. *The Gutenburg Galaxy: The Making of Typographic Man.* Toronto: University of Toronto Press.

Molnar, Alex. 1996. *Giving Kids the Bu$iness.* Boulder, CO: Westview Press.

Orwell, George. 1946. *Animal Farm.* New York: Harcourt, Brace and Co.

Pohl, Frederik and C. M. Kornbluth. 1952. *The Space Merchants.* New York: St. Martin's Press.

Postman, Neil and Steve Powers. 1992. *How to Watch TV News.* New York: Penguin.

Simpson. John. 1995. Quoted in *Life History and Narrative.* J. Amos Hatch and Richard Wisniewski, eds. London: Falmer Press.

Shrank, Jeffrey. 1975. *Deception Detection: An Educator's Guide to the Art of Insight.* Boston: Beacon.

Standards for the English Language Arts. 1996. Urbana, IL: NCTE/IRA.

Form at end of book

Teaching Television to Empower Students

Our students are experienced consumers of television. How can we harness their expertise?

David B. Owen, Charles L. P. Silet, and Sarah E. Brown

David P. Owen, Charles L. P. Silet, and Sarah E. Brown teach at Iowa State University in Ames, Iowa.

One of the most effective ways to cultivate cooperative learning is to teach television. When you teach television, you can transform the dynamics of the traditional classroom where the teacher knows the subject, the students do not, and motivation is always an issue. Effective teachers have always been able to create a motivating connection between their subject matter and the students' world. With television, however that connection is already present, and the teacher's role is to use and shape an existing interest, not create it in the first place.

As we all know, students enter the classroom with thousands of hours of viewing experience, the raw data of television, and teachers come with knowledge of the analytic and critical skills that can transform students' preconceived attitudes toward television into real understanding of the medium.

What Do Students Know?

We find that the best way to begin media analysis is to have our students complete an inventory of their viewing and reading habits. In the first class meeting we pass out a two-page questionnaire in which we ask them to provide us information about what they read and view aside from school assignments. The purpose of this is both for us to learn which media sources our students consume and, equally important, for our students to become aware of how they gain access to information and entertainment.

For instance, we ask about the books, newspapers, and magazines they read. We are interested in both the frequency (often, occasionally, rarely, never) as well as the specific titles. We also ask them about movies (in theaters and on videos), concerts (popular and classical), theater, CDs purchased and listened to, radio, any source from which they derive information or entertainment. Finally, we ask them about their television-viewing habits: what shows they watch, how often, and who their favorite television personalities are. We even inquire whether they take the trouble to record shows they cannot see when broadcast, such as soap operas.

This gives us a reasonably detailed knowledge of our students' media exposure, which provides us with a context within which to communicate with our students about the media world they inhabit.

Periodically we ask the students to participate in more directed television viewing. We ask them to keep a video log for a week in which they not only list the shows they watch but also comment on the characters and themes and on their reactions to them. While the media surveys listed above are general in nature, these logs are much more formally directed and detailed and can be used for class discussion and reflection.

Finally, we conduct another kind of survey when we are through teaching television and ask our students some evaluative questions concerning how their viewing habits have changed. For instance, we ask them, "When you watch television now, how is the experience different than before?" We also ask students if they notice a difference in their television viewing habits: do they watch different shows, are there shows they no longer watch, do they watch more or less television now, and so on. In general, this last survey allows us to judge how successful our teaching has been and also indicates to the students how their critical viewing skills have empowered them.

Three Principles

We have discovered that teaching television is a circular process which revolves around three principles. First, most students have preconceived viewing habits which lead them to believe that television is essentially "just entertainment." Second, students must change their initial viewing habits in order to become critical viewers. And third, if students develop active, critical viewing habits, they will come of their own accord to begin to understand the breadth and sutlety of television's power and the serious personal and cultural consequences it has for all of us.

Television As Entertainment

Most students come to school having watched an extraordinary amount and variety of television. They have a stupefying amount of what we call "telinfo" (television information). For instance, they bring the ability to sing or whistle theme songs from shows like "Friends" or "The Simpsons" or "The Brady Bunch" as well as advertising jingles like "You deserve a break today" (McDonalds). They can instantly recognize products' slogans ("Just do it!" [Coke] "Pizza! Pizza!" [Little Caesar's Pizza]), logos (the Swoosh [Nike], color associations ("If it's yellow, it's Cheerios!" "If it's orange, it's Wheaties!"). They know in extraordinary detail the history of their favorite television characters and their relations with other characters (what they wear, what they eat, who their friends are and have been, what they do, favorite expressions). Because students know so much detail, they think they already understand television.

Change of Viewing Habits

Our first task, consequently, is to jolt our students out of their customary viewing habits and help them develop a reflective attitude. We do that by starting quite simply. We begin teaching television by having the students analyze color magazine advertisements, for instance, ones for Stetson perfume, a Mont Blanc fountain pen, and a Dodge automobile. We project a color image of the ad and ask the students to do two things. First, we have them describe without any analysis, commentary, or evaluation what they *see* and write those things down individually. Then, in a class discussion, we ask them to use their lists to say what they see and write their observations on the board. We keep asking them, whatever they respond, "What else?," until they have fairly exhausted describing the ad. As we have already said, at this stage we do not allow students to use any evaluative language in their descriptions.

The next step, after establishing this exhaustive description, is to have students begin to analyze and evaluate what they see. Once again we have them make a list, this time of what the various details *mean* to the viewer, and then share their insights in a class discussion. For example, in the fountain pen ad, where in their first list they would mention merely that the decoration on the pen was of a gold color, in the second list they might comment that the gold suggests something about wealth, status, power, and

so on. In addition, they might observe that the gold color also appears elsewhere in the ad, as on the pen's tip and the reflection along the barrel, which thereby not only shapes the ad's meaning but also its composition as a whole. We tend to spend 30 to 45 minutes on this single exercise.

When we are through, students often comment that they had no idea one could look at a single picture meaningfully in such detail and depth. This simple ad exercise, then, provides a paradigm for how to look at all visual images, including television. It also exemplifies the three guidelines which we have formulated from our experience and which help us shape our pedagogy:

1. start with the students' own experience and perceptions;

2. move from the simple to the complex;

3. shift the students' viewing from passive to active.

This initial exercise begins the process of transforming viewing habits from a casual, uncritical acceptance of visual material to a more attentive, analytical questioning of what is being presented to them. This is essential for creating visual literacy.

Recognition of Television's Power

For our students to reach the point where they can recognize television's sophisticated messages, they must become active, critical, reflective viewers. The catch phrase we use to describe our two-step learning process is, "What do you see, and what does it mean?"

The second step is to develop habits of critical viewing. Once students are seeing more detail, then we repeatedly encourage them to interpret what this detail means. For example, again in the same activity, the insights growing out of cooperative interaction reveal a much greater complexity of meaning than what they as individuals had first noted. As students become better observers and learn to analyze what they have observed, they will spontaneously come to recognize that television is a powerful cultural force. Once sensitized to viewing critically, they are never again able, as they frequently tell us, "to watch television in the same way." When we start hearing students volunteer this observation, we know that by working together we have all succeeded.

A Sample Unit

After having surveyed our students' viewing experience and having completed the exercise on viewing print advertisements, students are ready to move on to use the same process but apply it now to advertisements that appear on television, advertisements which incorporate all of the visual materials from the print medium but add to them the qualities of movement and sound. Since ads "tell a story," we begin focusing on questions of narrative that the visual produces, and the examination of narrative becomes one of the foundations of our approach to television. As the students soon learn, this is a vastly more complicated visual experience to understand.

From the ads we move on to an examination of news broadcasts—local, national, PBS, CNN, "60 Minutes," "Nightline," "20/20," etc. From there we turn to dramas. We begin with soap operas because their deliberate narrative and visual pacing makes them the most accessible drama to analyze. Next we examine the increasingly complex world of drama from shows like "Dr. Quinn, Medicine Woman" to the more visually and thematically sophisticated shows like "ER," "NYPD Blue," "Homicide," or "The X-Files." We complete the unit by looking at situation comedies, which,we have found to be the most difficult for our students to take seriously enough to analyze. We examine sitcoms all the way from the animated "Simpsons," with their cartoon characters, through "Seinfeld" and "Friends" to the much more complex and socially critical comedies like the recently concluded "Roseanne."

We have discovered that this progression of genres from ads to news to dramas to sitcoms is important in developing our students' willingness to take television seriously enough to give it the critical attention it deserves. Students *know* ads are manipulating them, but they discover right at the beginning how much more extensively and subtly they are doing so than they first suspected. News programs, from the students' perspective, are by definition serious television since they give us the "facts" about our world. Here, again, their analysis reveals to them how complex the relation is between the viewer and what is on the screen, how the "facts" of the news program are shaped by the ways in which they are selected and presented.

Students are now ready to deal with the even more complex and problematic programming of "fictional" television. Because dramas obviously take on serious issues such as crime, poverty, sexuality, family relationships, and other social issues, students are open to the idea that these programs have meaning beyond their entertainment value.

Finally, we save comedy for last because students have the most difficulty in seeing the social content and "seriousness" there. Our experience is that by following this sequence, students are ready on their own initiative at the end to watch comedy shows more closely, think about what they see, and recognize that they are more than just a way to pass time. Past episodes of "Roseanne," for instance, are not only funny but also are richly nuanced presentations of genuine problems that the students are actually encountering in their everyday worlds.

Student Activities

Students actively engage in selecting and evaluating television examples. We as teachers may choose the genres to be studied and the general approach, but students select specific shows to work with within those broad categories. Students seem much more motivated when they can pick shows they feel they know something about and then, by analyzing them in detail, learn that the shows are much more complex than they had originally believed. We also have students work in groups both when analyzing and when presenting their findings. Our experience has been that this active approach is essential for students to develop true media literacy.

Student Contracts

Each student submits a contract which indicates his/her commitment to the unit based on one of the following conditions:

1. I will choose four shows which all appear in the same time slot but on different channels, e.g., Thursday at 7:00 p.m. on ABC, CBS, NBC, FOX, or PBS.

2. I will choose four shows which all fall under the same category. At least two will appear at different time slots. I will choose one of the following categories: news, drama (crime shows, medical shows, lawyer shows), soap opera (daytime), melodrama (evening), science fiction, situation comedy, sports, MTV, talk show, or verisimilitude (tabloid journalism).

3. I will choose four different shows which all appear during a specific block of time, say, two hours (for example, weekdays from 7:00–9:00 a.m. or 3:00–5:00 p.m.), and I will make inferences about what characterizes this time frame.

4. Whichever choice I make, I will prepare a written report which summarizes my understanding of the shows, their relationships, and the consequences for television viewers.

Analysis of Show

Following the submission of this commitment, students prepare to bring to each cooperative learning/discussion group meeting an analysis of one of their shows which is based on questions such as these:

1. What is the plot of the show? Write a concise plot summary.

2. What is the audience focus of this show? Age? Sex? Education? Economic status? Primary interests? Occupation? Size of audience? Social group?

3. Is this the appropriate viewing audience? Why or why not? What is the appropriate viewing audience?

4. What emotional appeals do the producers of the show use to get its viewers "hooked," e.g., power, family life, humor, drama, vicarious living, emotions?

5. How is violence portrayed in this show? Is it appropriate? Is it realistic?

6. How is sex portrayed in this show? Is it appropriate? Is it realistic?

7. How does the show address issues of diversity, racism, and sexism?

8. Are these accurate depictions of society and real life?

9. How can you tell the difference between fantasy and fiction in this show?

10. What have you learned by analyzing this show? Write a brief summary, including what surprised you, what angered you, and whether your opinion of this show has changed. Use specific evidence to support your answers.

There appears to be a direct, inverse relation between the decline in professional attention to television and its ascent in cultural influence.

In addition to such higher-order thinking, students use specific techniques first practiced in class such as these: taking notes on scratch paper while watching; viewing the show more than once; paying close attention to commercials for audience focus; rewinding and replaying specific areas of the show; keeping tallies of violent acts, sexually explicit content, or inaccurate depiction of diversity issues regarding gender, race, and class; and asking someone else's opinion, such as talking about findings with others or watching the show with a friend or family member.

Discussion Topics

Given this individual preparation, the learning/discussion groups meet four times. Each meeting serves as a cooperative effort to answer questions pertaining to a different focus topic for that meeting. This is important so that students are continually building upon their knowledge and covering in depth these four "core" areas. The four topics follow.

Meeting One: Advertising. How did advertising affect your viewing? Who was the target audience? How did it fit into the program that you were watching? Was it effective? Was it misleading? Come to a group consensus about the role of advertising in television based on each individual's work and the group's discussion. Use specific examples from both to support answers.

Meeting Two: Diversity. How were the issues of diversity handled in the shows watched? What kind of ethnic groups were represented? Were they treated fairly? Were their roles realistic? Was one particular race or ethnic group always playing the same role? How does that make you feel? What does this say about our society? Come to a group consensus about the way the television industry treats different races and ethnic groups based on each individual's work and the group's discussion. Use specific examples from both to support answers.

Meeting Three: Gender Roles. How were the issues of gender roles handled in the shows watched? What roles did men play? Women? Are they realistic? Are they fair? Do they accurately reflect society? Does the portrayal of gender roles on television influence the way people perceive roles in real life? Come to a group consensus about the way television treats the sexes based on each individual's work and the group's discussion. Use specific examples from both to support answers.

Meeting Four: Violence and Sex. How are violence and sex portrayed in the shows watched? Were they portrayed together? What do we learn about sex and violence from the television? How are we supposed to know what is real and what is not real? What is acceptable and what is not acceptable? Does television accurately reflect society's view of violence and sex? Come to a group consensus about the way violence and sex are portrayed on television based on each individual's work and the group's discussion. Use specific examples from both to support answers.

When the groups meet, each member of the group has a specific job. A *recorder* is responsible for filling out the group's answers on the worksheet to be turned in. An *instigator* is responsible for keeping the discussion moving along and monitoring the time. A *questioner* is the "devil's advocate" in the discussion, questioning and probing those who are talking. Finally, a *reporter* is responsible for sharing with the class as a whole some of the most interesting things the group discussed. In addition, each group is to prepare a written report of its findings on each of the topics.

Student Projects

In addition to the genre and topical activities listed above, innumerable other kinds of projects are possible.

Epitaphs: Students construct two epitaphs, putting to rest a television show they have analyzed. The epitaphs are to contain style techniques from a poet they had recently studied. Of the two epitaph creations, one is to be transformed into a symbolic and representative gravestone.

Pilot show based on short-story techniques: Students create a pilot for a sitcom or drama using aspects of short story construction such as plot, character, setting, fantasy and escape, and imagination. After writing their pilot, they find actors, produce and edit it. They must take into consideration all aspects of the television process: advertising, camera angles, lighting, sound, and so on.

Transcript exercise: In order to help make students aware of the powerful images they see on television, students transcribe a talk show or sitcom. Have students first read portions of the transcript, then watch the actual footage. Compare and contrast the differences between the written text and the text as performed.

Role-play and conflict management: Take a scene from a sitcom or drama. Set it up in class and have students role-play a realistic outcome. Other student "observers" pay close attention to how the conflict is resolved and whether it is resolved realistically. Then watch the clip from the actual television show. Does the role-play mirror the way the situation was resolved on television? Is either realistic? Does television even influence how students solve problems in their real lives?

Plan a day's programming: Students must plan one entire programming day for a television station. It should be programmed in terms of an "ideal" broadcast day. They must take into consideration FCC regulations of quality children's programming and what kind of advertising they will allow and when. They may want to cancel shows they feel are harmful to children or change time slots of adult programming to later hours. Finally they may create their own plot lines for shows which they feel need a voice on their station.

Getting Started to Teach Television

We make three suggestions.

First, you have to know what is on television. Even if you do not watch much television, the vast majority of your students do. So, you must have some general notion of what shows are on, when they appear, who is in them, and what they are about. You need to have some familiarity with sitcoms, evening dramas, soap operas, talk shows, game shows, sports, news, advertising, the lot. This way you can demonstrate your knowledge of your subject in class and be able to respond intelligently to students' ob-

servations about the shows they watch. You should not feel compelled to know *more* than your students do about various shows because, quite frankly, you probably will not be able to do so. Nevertheless, you need to demonstrate a "good faith" effort to understand the media world that they live in.

Second, you need to read about television. This you can do on three levels. On the easiest level, read the articles on television that appear in the daily newspaper. Some of them will simply be celebrity profiles, others might describe a new show, while still others might provide items of information, such as discussions of violence on television or the new ratings system. On a more sophisticated level you can also find in the popular press extended critiques and analyses of individual shows, of series, of trends, of the industry as a whole, and so on. Lastly, a body of criticism published in professional journals examines television from a variety of intellectual disciplines: aesthetics, psychology, cultural studies, sociology, etc. These journal articles can provide background and a diversity of approaches that will help you develop your own critical viewing skills.

Third, you need to be sensitive that critically examining television may involve controversy. Prepare yourself, your administrators, and the parents of your students for whatever examination of television you intend to pursue. Discuss with the appropriate administrators what you plan to do so that both you and they can be aware of potential problems. It is important to realize that some parents greatly restrict the television their children watch, censor it, or even forbid watching it. These restrictions can arise for religious, moral, or practical reasons; and, of course, they need to be addressed. In your planning, you may need to provide alternative activities at various points to accommodate any students who might, for whatever reason, have restrictions on viewing. As always in the public schools, teachers walk a very fine line between challenging students and alienating their parents. You need to remember that television is a "hot-button" topic.

Conclusion

Almost every large-scale analysis of education from the 1960s on to the current administration's Department of Education report, *Strong Families, Strong Schools: Building Community Partnerships for Learning* (1994, Washington, DC: U.S. Department of Education), mentions the central importance of children's television viewing as one of the most powerful—possibly *the* most powerful—factors in developing their definitions of self and connection with the world. If television is largely responsible for forming the students who populate our nation's classrooms, should not we, as educators, be training ourselves and our students to understand and cope with the power of the medium?

Since its beginnings after World War II, television has attracted the attention of educators, social critics, and the public. In the 1970s, however, the number of critical commentaries began to decline, and with the widespread use of the personal computer in the 1980s, focus has largely shifted away from television's cultural role. Yet, there appears to be a direct, inverse relation between the decline in professional attention to television and its ascent in cultural influence. We all are convinced that television today is the most powerful educator in America.

Therefore, we think it needs to be viewed with the greatest attention and concern, and to develop such reflective viewing we need to make television studies a routine, perhaps central, part of public education. Either we empower ourselves and our students by understanding television or television will retain its power over us.

Form at end of book

Issue 14 Summary

One often hears that television and other media have enormous power in influencing our lives. If this is true, it is surprising how little attention we have paid to harnessing the power of television and other media to promote learning in our children and adolescents. We complain about television and decry its negative effects, but, most important, we keep watching. And so do our children and teenagers; until we closely examine how to use television to achieve our goals as teachers, we will be letting this enormously powerful medium go to waste.

WiseGuide Wrap-Up

Most Americans use television to get their morning news, their evening news, and their evening's entertainment. Many use television to enjoy spectator sports. With the advent of cable and satellite dishes, many can now get scores of channels, yet, despite the ready access to television programs, television has very little to do with classroom learning. How is television used in or by schools? Typically, teachers show educational programs (not everyone's favorite type of television program) or entertainment programs on rainy days, when students cannot go into the schoolyard during recess. The authors of the two articles in this section contend that television can be used educationally in another way: to direct students to think evaluatively and analytically about the programs and commercials they see.

There is another way in which television educates us. Programs that are entertaining can also educate; let's call this "back door" educational television. Historical drama can teach students, perhaps unconsciously, about the way of life of a particular period. Dramas that take place in other cultures can almost subliminally inform viewers about life in cultures other than their own. Well-written dramas can provoke thinking about moral dilemmas or help viewers consider the implications of the decisions they make in their lives. Well-written comedies can use humor to highlight aspects of the human condition with which they can identify.

The responsibility for making television programs educational as well as entertaining falls not only in the hands of the television writers and producers but also in the hands of parents, teachers, and viewers, who make choices about what children watch and how they make sense of what they watch.

R.E.A.L. Sites

This list provides a print preview of typical **Coursewise** R.E.A.L. sites. (There are over 100 such sites at the **Courselinks**™ site.) The danger in printing URLs is that web sites can change overnight. As we went to press, these sites were functional using the URLs provided. If you come across one that isn't, please let us know via email to: webmaster@coursewise. com. Use your Passport to access the most current list of R.E.A.L. sites at the **Courselinks** site.

Site name: Center for Educational Priorities

URL: http://www.cep.org/

Why is it R.E.A.L.? This site is a clearinghouse for information on education as it relates to American popular culture. In particular, the center examines the impact of television and other media on children and their learning.

Key topics: culture, education, television, media

Try this: Visit the "Study Guide to Kids' TV," then click on "Kids' TV Problems." According to Harper's, what has happened to the written vocabulary of the average 6- to 14-year-old American child in less than fifty years? Summarize Leon Botstein's views on the ultimate effect television has on education. Do you agree or disagree with his notions regarding language?

Site name: Media Literacy Education Bibliography

URL: http://www.indianapolis.in.us/maci/mlbib.html

Why is it R.E.A.L.? This site provides an annotated bibliography on media literacy. Most of the books reviewed here are intended to help parents and educators understand how television has an impact on their children's lives and to understand how to make children more critical consumers of television.

Key topics: bibliographies, media literacy, television

Try this: What does this site report about brain research on children who grow up in a media-saturated world? How can teachers incorporate these findings in their teaching methods?

section 6 | Growing Up Safe

Learning Objectives

- Know the causes of violence in childhood and its effects.

- Identify methods for helping children express their anger in a healthy manner.

- Understand multiple approaches to promoting character education and moral development in children.

- Articulate the issues in the debate about character education, indicating the differing philosophies and assumptions underlying the various positions.

WiseGuide Intro

One of the saddest realities of life is that children sometimes cause great tragedy. In very recent times, we have seen horrible scenes of children killing other children, as well as adults. Fortunately, these instances of murder by children are rare, but they do occur, and lesser forms of violence are far more common. Where does violence in children come from?

Educators and psychologists agree that violence, like other human behavior, comes from a combination of biological makeup and how we are brought up. Thus, some children may demonstrate violent behavior because of mental illness that has an underlying physical cause. Others may be violent because they have learned that violent behavior is an effective means to an end; in addition, they may have never learned a moral code, a set of beliefs about what is right and what is wrong.

Regardless of the underlying causes, society and, in particular, educators must deal with the harsh realities of violence in childhood. In this section, we grapple with this issue from a variety of perspectives. In Reading 37, Jonah Blank profiles a student who killed three classmates and wounded five others in order, he said, to get attention from his peers. Dale Ann D. Roper, in Reading 38, analyzes the anger that underlies childhood violence. She differentiates healthy and unhealthy expressions of anger and provides teachers with strategies for dealing with anger and creating a healthy classroom environment. Timothy C. Brennan, Jr., in Reading 39, tells the story of how his school became the center of media attention when a thirteen-year-old boy attended school with a "hit list" of his enemies. He concludes that children learn from everything they see; for children, he contends, we are all teachers.

How do we intervene positively in the development of children and, in particular, in the development of their character? Many educators and psychologists have struggled over the question of how we influence children's moral and social growth. Alfie Kohn, in Reading 40, argues that true moral growth in children comes from neither teaching moral behavior (a behaviorist idea) nor allowing children to discover their own internal morality (a romantic notion). Rather, Kohn contends, we must use constructivist principles of teaching to help students develop their own understanding of moral issues. To do this, we need to organize schools differently, such that students have opportunities to make decisions and examine moral issues. Perry L. Glanzer, in Reading 41, disagrees with Kohn, arguing that schools should teach commonly accepted moral principles, albeit with a sensitivity to the moral codes of the families that the school serves. In Reading 42, Jacques S. Benninga and Edward A. Wynne disagree with Kohn for different reasons than does Glanzer. They contend that Kohn's approach treats children like miniature adults and confers too much freedom on them. They believe that children should feel a sense of belonging to and responsibility for others, and that this will instill moral behavior in our children. Finally, in Reading 43, Sanford N. McDonnell, former chairman of the McDonnell-Douglas Corporation, expresses the belief that schools need to promote "core" American values or universal values common to most religions. His approach to character education is eclectic and includes cooperative learning, students' active participation in rule making, student responsibility, literature used to provoke discussion of moral dilemmas, and sports used to promote the understanding of fairness and of right and wrong.

In a multicultural society and in a society where church and state are separate, it is difficult for schools to embrace a single approach to teaching character education or moral development. However, because of the violence we witness in our schools and neighborhoods and because of our goal to help children become healthy, happy members of society, we cannot neglect the social, moral, and ethical part of children's development.

Violence in Childhood

Questions

1. Brainstorm explanations for the increase in violence by children. Which of the explanations that you have generated seem to be most valid?

2. If society were truly committed to reducing violence by children, what might we do? What specific changes could we make to address this problem?

3. Parents often look to schools to solve students' behavioral problems. Schools often look to parents to do so. How could parents and schools work together to solve the problem? Try to be as specific as possible.

Introduction

As horrible as instances of adult violence are, instances of violence by children are particularly disturbing. When we read about children gunning down their peers in a high school library or see a television news story about two children in a British shopping mall kidnapping and killing a younger child, it gives most of us a certain chill. It goes against the expectation (reasonable or not) that children are innocent and basically good. While violence by adolescents is not new, statistics show increasing levels of violence by children. What is happening in our society that is causing this terrible development? What needs of our children are not being met such that they experience this degree of anger? How can we better meet our children's needs at school and at home to ensure that their emotional development is healthy?

The Kid No One Noticed

Guns, he concluded, would get his classmates' attention.

Jonah Blank

Paducah, KY.—When Michael Carneal warned friends last Thanksgiving to stay away from their high school lobby, it was not, he now says, because he knew that a tragedy would occur there once the long weekend came to an end. "Just about every day I told people that something was going to happen on Monday." He had developed a habit of making frequent but empty threats, he says, after logging onto a Web site called "101 Ways to Annoy People."

This week, Michael Carneal pleads guilty but mentally ill to three counts of murder and five of attempted murder—the result of a threat that proved anything but empty. When he gunned down eight classmates at a prayer circle in the lobby of Heath High School last December 1, he was a frail 14-year-old, a little over 5 feet tall and weighing 110 pounds. Now, at 15, he is a few inches taller and 20 pounds heavier. He has spent the past 10 months in juvenile detention, which he prefers to high school. He likes the food, sleeps well, and, he says, "people respect me now."

Of all the school shootings that made headlines in America over the past year, the Paducah killings may be the most baffling. Nearly every theory trotted out at the time of the tragedy now seems hollow: the obsession of a gun nut or the revenge of a bully's victim, atheistic nihilism or the influence of violent movies, the traumas of a dysfunctional childhood or the ravages of criminal insanity—all important social problems but, in this case, each a dead end. What's striking about Michael Carneal is how ordinary he is. But he had an extraordinary craving for "respect."

"This is the only adventure I've ever had."

U.S. News has obtained a copy of the psychiatric report prepared as evidence for his trial—an evaluation by doctors who spent several days interviewing him, his family, and five of his friends. "Michael Carneal was not mentally ill nor mentally retarded at the time of the shootings," the doctors found. His lawyers agree that he was not legally insane at the time but say he is mentally ill and needs treatment. The Carneal quotes in this article come from the psychiatric report.

In school shootings from Mississippi to Arkansas to Oregon, an inner darkness seems to have preceded the mayhem: membership in a satanic cult, a history of torturing animals, or a fanatical fascination with firearms and explosives. But whatever demons may have lurked in Michael's heart remain well hidden. Examine the psychiatric reports and the police records, talk to anyone in Paducah who is still willing to talk, and a picture gradually comes into focus: Michael Carneal is, and was, insecure, self-centered, and hungry for attention, a boy wrestling with the frustrations of puberty and desiring the approval of his peers—hardly different from millions of kids across America. In some ways, though, he seemed younger than most teenagers. While his contemporaries were listening to gangsta rap, Michael still liked Smurfs. On Heath High's social ladder, he was barely clinging to the lower rungs.

Heroes

A few Friday nights ago, while Michael read a Stephen King book in his cell, his ex-schoolmates donned camouflage fatigues. The Heath Pirates were playing a football archival, the Ballard Bombers, and the kids were decked out in military garb to show their school spirit. Even after a 35–0 defeat, Heath High's heroes were clearly the boys in football gear. They were the ones who would be talked about until the next Friday, the ones for whom the cheerleaders cheered, for whom the band played. Until the shooting, Michael was a band member, a skinny freshman with a baritone horn.

Once he wrote a secret story, a tale in which a shy kid named Michael was picked on by "preps"—the popular kids—but was saved by a brother with a gun. "Michael" gave the corpses of the slain preps to his mother as a gift. The story might have set off alarms, but it remained hidden until after the shootings.

The actual Michael Carneal had no heroic brother, no fictional alter ego to save him from a threat that seemed quite real. He felt alienated, pushed around, picked on. "I didn't like to go to school," he said. "I didn't feel as if anyone really liked me." But he cited little evidence of bullying. Once in middle school, someone pulled his pants down; friends say such things were happening to kids all the time. In his own view, however, he was a castaway, at the mercy of cruel Pirates.

He was never very close to his father, a lawyer. His older sister, Kelly, got much of the family's attention. A popular girl, she became the school valedictorian half a year after the shootings. "He tries to be as good as me," she told psychiatrists, "and he can never size up." Michael compensated by becoming a class clown, what one friend called an "energetic prankster who would get attention any way he could." Michael later told doctors he stole CDs, sold parsley to a classmate as marijuana, and downloaded Internet pornography, which he passed around the school.

He was not a gun enthusiast; he may have handled firearms only a few times in his life. His friends noticed no pronounced interest in violent movies, music, TV, or video games. He dismissed the media-spread notion that his rampage was inspired by a scene in the movie *The Basketball Diaries,* which he described as boring. "I don't know why it happened, but I know it wasn't a movie."

One possible element was hardly mentioned at the time: unrequited love, or unrequited lust. Gwen Hadley, mother of one of the victims, confirms to *U.S. News* what many students had suspected: "Michael was in love with my daughter Nicole, and Nicole had no interest in him." Michael told his doctors he liked Nicole but said they never dated. Gwen Hadley says he had phoned Nicole almost nightly in the weeks before the shootings, ostensibly to discuss chemistry.

Their photos tell the whole story: Nicole was tall, pretty, and, in a school where many a girl seems to be a bottle blond, she had enough self-assurance to remain a defiant brunette. But Michael, with his thick glasses, had the owlish aspect of a pubescent Steve Forbes. Nicole played in the band with Michael and did not treat him with disdain. On a few occasions, they did homework together in his home.

Michael told psychiatrists he had begun to date but had never so much as kissed a girl. He was upset when students called him a "faggot," and he almost cried when a school gossip sheet labeled him gay. Classmates now say kids toss such taunts around freely, but, for Michael, the barbs stung. Alone in his room, with his Internet porn for company, the lack of a girlfriend was a source of physical frustration and social embarrassment. When he fired into the prayer circle, his first bullet struck Nicole Hadley.

The why may never be fully explained, but the what of those final days is now tragically clear. On Thanksgiving, Michael stole two shotguns, two semiauto-

matic rifles, a pistol, and 700 rounds of ammunition from a neighbor's garage. He hauled the cache home on his bike and sneaked it through a bedroom window. "I was feeling proud, strong, good, and more respected," he would tell the psychiatrists. "I had accomplished something. I'm not the kind of kid who accomplishes anything. This is the only adventure I've ever had."

The next day, he stole two more shotguns, these from his parents' bedroom. A day later, on Saturday, he took "the best" guns to a friend's house; the boys admired the long arms and shot targets with a pistol. On Sunday, after church and homework, he wrapped his arsenal in a blanket. He did not plan to shoot anyone, he said, but just wanted to show the guns off. "Everyone would be calling me and they would come over to my house or I would go to their house. I would be popular. I didn't think I would get into trouble."

On Monday, he put the bundle into the trunk of his sister's Mazda. In his backpack was a Ruger .22 pistol. He rode with Kelly to school and found his friends, as usual, hanging out in the front lobby. A few feet away, the morning prayer circle was ending. His moment had arrived: He announced what was in the blanket and waited for the adulation he was certain would follow.

The boys talked about the guns for a minute or two but were not especially impressed. In western Kentucky, firearms are a part of everyday life. As the discussion turned to new CDs, Michael reached into his backpack. He put plugs in his ears and rammed the ammo clip into his Ruger. "I pulled it out," he recalled, "and nobody noticed." Witnesses thought they were merely watching the class clown. Three shots killed three girls who had played beside Michael in the band: Nicole Hadley, Kayce Steger, and Jessica James. The remaining five shots wounded five other students.

"I Had Guns"

When he opened fire, Michael said, he was trying to get people to notice him: "I don't know why I wasn't bluffing this time. I guess it was because they ignored me. I had guns, I brought them to school, I showed them to them, and they were still ignoring me." He didn't think the light-calibered Ruger could kill, he said, nor did he aim at anyone in particular. But after another student—a football player—talked him into dropping the gun, the meaning of his actions sank in. "I said, 'Kill me, please. Please kill me.' I wanted to die. I knew what I had done."

Now, the families of his victims are searching for a sliver of meaning. At a two-day quilting bee, where they stitched together panels of sympathy sent from as far away as France and Japan, mothers and fathers grasped at the hope of preventing the next schoolyard shooting.

"We've got to teach parents to love and respect their kids," said Jessica James's father, Joe, who took up quilting especially for the occasion. "We don't have homes any more," added his wife, Judy. "We only have places where kids come to sleep." Yet the Carneal family, by all external appearances and in the judgment of several psychiatrists, was in no way dysfunctional.

"I just wanted the guys to think I was cool."

The families see Michael as a cold, deliberate killer and believe the sure threat of harsh punishment might have prevented the tragedy. But Michael, who faces a life sentence with no chance of parole for 25 years, seems not to have pondered the consequences of his actions. His best explanation for pulling the trigger is pathetically childish: "I just wanted the guys to think I was cool."

Gwen Hadley, for all her efforts at positive renewal, knows that her daughter won't be the last schoolgirl cut down for no reason. "It's going to happen again," she said. "This can happen anywhere, at any time." Then she put another stitch in the quilt of hope.

Form at end of book

Facing Anger in Our Schools

Dale Ann D. Roper

Dale Ann D. Roper is Coordinator of Adult Religious Education at St. Clare of Assisi Catholic Church in Houston. She plans programs, recruits and trains volunteers, facilitates group discussions, and makes presentations on positive discipline, substance abuse counseling, and religious education.

On 24 March 1998, two boys, ages 11 and 13, shot 16 people at an Arkansas school, killing 5. On 21 May, an Oregon student opened fire in a school cafeteria, killing two classmates. Fatal incidents at schools in Kentucky, Mississippi, Alaska, Pennsylvania, and Tennessee have added to the academic year's death toll (Poland 1998).

People have blamed the media, society, poor family values, and schools. Whatever the catalyst, educators have long sought ways to improve safety and security as the level of violence increased in public schools; indeed, these precautions may have helped curb the increase in the incidence of violence. Still, the intensity of attacks is rising. Have poorly developed stress and anger-coping skills led to more recent incidents of violence?

Looking at Violence

Violence affects everyone in a society, not just teachers, administrators, parents, and students. The Children's Defense Fund (1997) reported juvenile gun violence was increasing at an alarming rate. In 1982, 390 teenagers, ages 13 to 15, were arrested for murder; a decade later, the total was 740 (Gest, Witkin, Hetter, and Wright 1994).

Such statistics may focus attention solely on efforts for protection against violence and on demands for harsher punishment of the perpetrators. Punishment may demonstrate short-term power and control over a misbehaving angry child, but the long-term result may be increased resentment, with tendencies toward revenge or retreat (Nelsen 1987). Angry behaviors escalate later. We *feel* anger; it exists for a reason and deserves respect and attention (Lerner 1985).

Educators can help develop that respect and create a greater awareness for the need to change unhealthy behavioral reactions to stress and anger. They can teach skills that move people from reactionary violent behavior to healthy behavior choices.

Looking at Anger

Anger can be a natural and healthy response to trauma. It can motivate people to find solutions to problems they might otherwise ignore. Unhealthy use of anger may result in win-lose situations with one person demonstrating power over another. Creating win-win situations lets everyone experience power (Nelsen, Lott, and Glenn 1993). Covey (1994) presented a three-step win-win process: (1) think win-win; (2) seek first to understand, then be understood; (3) synergize based on principles of valuing the difference and searching for third alternatives. In other words, by working together and learning from one another, we create win-win results. Unfortunately, many individuals have a hard time handling anger in healthy ways.

Juvenile anger and violence in schools are symptoms of growing national problems affecting students and, ultimately, leading to teacher ineffectiveness and alienation. One way to combat this social malady is to teach children healthy responses to anger and techniques for win-win solutions to problems. It is not easy to change habitual expressions of anger (Ginott 1971). New knowledge comes hard. Therefore, administrators, teachers, parents, and students must develop a clearer understanding of anger.

Physiological Effects of Anger

When we become angry, our bodies respond by preparing to flee the situation or fight for protection. The "fight or flight" reaction produces immediate changes in the body: increased heart rate, muscular tension, general metabolic rate, blood pressure, and rate of breathing (Ornish 1984). These natural responses are similar for both genders in all cultures (Barrington 1992/93). Anger increases hormonal changes at an incredible rate. The adrenal glands produce a rush of hormones, elevating heart rate and increasing strength. The rush can be so great that one may not be aware of his or her own strength and could unintentionally hurt someone. The body also becomes increasingly sensitive to touch. The slightest touch from another person may feel threatening, excessive, and intrusive, eliciting overreactive anger. The face becomes flushed, the mouth becomes dry, and the sense of smell is greatly increased. The vision of an angry person may become intensely focused on its source.

Observers experience the same adrenaline rush as those involved in an angry exchange. Indeed, observers of violence may play an important role in escalating mass violence (Baron 1977). Picture a high school cafeteria fight between two students angry with each other. Students across the cafeteria may stand on or leap over tables to get a better view. If one excited student, while rushing to see the fight, interferes with another student, a new fight may break out and an angry free-for-all or riot may occur. Moving out of tunnel vision and becoming aware of the peripheral excitement is crucial for teachers responsible for controlling the situation (Barrington 1992/93).

Similarities between Excitement and Anger

Physiological responses to excitement are the same as the physiological responses to anger (Barrington 1992/93). They may feel the same to the individual experiencing them, and the resulting behaviors may look the same to the observer. Anger and excitement can be easily confused, and both can result in aggressive, socially unacceptable behaviors.

Children extremely excited after winning a ball game or completing a complex task will experience the same adrenaline rush as when they are angry. If they have never learned to distinguish the adrenaline rush of excitement from that of anger, they could be easily provoked into confrontation. On the football field, players slap and hit one another after a great play, often wrestling to the ground in celebration. If someone from the opposite team happens to touch them, it can trigger fights between opposing players. Though often accepted on the sports field, these behaviors are perceived as violence elsewhere and can result in arrests or injuries. People acting out explosive, culturally influenced anger or feelings of excitement make it difficult for observers to determine which emotion is being expressed.

Effects of Unhealthy Anger on Society

Teachers sometimes complain that both boys and girls act as though they are unable to control behavior when excited or angry. Students say they want to change but insist they cannot. This excuse becomes, for some students, a license for undisciplined excitement or angry, hostile behavior.

Parents traditionally have regarded some aggression in boys as desirable and natural (Sears, Maccoly, and Levin 1957). In the United States, boys have learned to be more openly aggressive or forceful. Football players might be encouraged to play hard and look mean. The goal is not to anger the players but to excite them to play aggressively enough to intimidate the other team and hopefully win the game. The greater the excitement, the easier it is to move into habitual angry behaviors without realizing what is happening. Indeed, competition is more likely to enhance aggressive inclinations than decrease them (Berkwitz 1962). Such aggression, however, leads to problems in the classroom.

Women have traditionally been discouraged from recognizing or displaying aggressive behavior in direct ways (Lerner 1985). They were more likely to attack others verbally or covertly. Yet women subjected to strong annoyances tend to become aggressive to others, too (Baron 1977). The passive-aggressive behaviors of women seem to be changing. Today's teachers find more girls acting openly aggressive.

Anger has been equated historically with "bad" events or actions. In the Old Testament, anger was associated with floods, famines, plagues, and punishment for bad behavior. When children display anger, adults may call them "bad." Unable to distinguish feelings from actions, these children can grow up feeling frightened and threatened by their own anger and that of others. When they display normal angry or excited behaviors at home, they risk being abused physically, emotionally, or verbally. If not taught differently, these children are likely to feel threatened by anger as adults and may react in the same unhealthy ways. The cycle continues from one generation to the next.

Students who act inappropriately demonstrate just one symptom of an angry society. Chemical abuse and media tolerance for uncontrolled violence add to teachers' problems. The more violence observed, the more acceptable it becomes. Children exposed to violent anger in their homes and the media have a wide range of techniques with which to harm others (Baron 1977).

When anger and abuse become routine, it begins to feel normal. Living without anger and abuse may feel painfully wrong. Some people learn to hold angry feelings inside and even deny their anger, because it is too difficult to face. Unable to express anger at home for fear of abuse, children often develop habits of venting their unacknowledged anger at unsuspecting victims or at themselves. Indeed, the abused are likely to become abusers or victims of others' abuse (Black 1990).

Effects of Unhealthy Anger in Schools

School may seem the safest place to express anger, because students know the system and feel confident they will not be physically abused there. Students sometimes create hostile situations in school so they can vent built-up aggressive feelings. They may use aggression to control or manipulate (Berkwitz 1962).

Students intimidate with looks, actions, verbal threats, and open defiance. Abused at home, they become the abusers at school. They move back into the role of victim, feeling abused when there are consequences to pay for poor behavior. Teachers must understand that there are intrinsic rewards received in both roles. The abuser may experience temporary power and control, while the abused may later receive attention or gifts. Such students are at-risk for dropping out of school, running away from home, getting in legal trouble, burdening society, and committing suicide.

Relating Unhealthy Anger to Teacher Burnout

A hidden cost of this situation is the number of teachers who face burnout. Such impaired motivation to work has become common in today's complex world (Potter 1987). It begins with small warning signals: feelings of frustration, emotional outbursts, withdrawal, health problems, alienation, substandard performance, and increased drug and alcohol use. If the symptoms are ignored, a person might eventually dread going to work and lack energy and enthusiasm at home. Along with continually addressing students' unhealthy, angry behavior, teachers must manage their own anger.

Healthy expression of anger is possible when clear personal and professional boundaries exist. Expressing anger is crucial to feelings of well-being (Black 1990). Poorly defined or inconsistently maintained boundaries may cause teachers to swing between conforming to the demands of others and rigidly enforcing rules to meet personal needs for control. Some students, perceiving the confusion, use the opportunity to manipulate the situation with inappropriate behaviors. If allowed to continue, everyone in the class is affected. It becomes increasingly hard to focus on tasks. Serious roadblocks to learning are likely to result. Yet teachers can use new strategies to help

discouraged, misbehaving students learn better, handle anger, and feel wanted.

Strategies to Handle Anger

The following strategies, based on Barrington (1992/93) and personal experience with stress management, can help teachers expand their ability to handle anger, alleviate physiological responses to stress and anger, and improve the learning environment.

1. When angry in class, try taking a self-imposed time-out. Do some deep breathing and hand-muscle exercises. Try some heel/knee lifts at your desk. These exercises increase large-muscle activity and decrease the flow of adrenaline in your body, helping you feel calmer.

2. When a student is angry with you, avoid eye contact. It can fuel an escalating power struggle. Instead, look over the student's right shoulder or ear as you talk. If the student is unable to gain composure with you, allow someone else to use nonviolent intervention to calm the student.

3. When you witness an angry confrontation, identify for yourself whether you feel angry or excited. Use physical activities to relieve physiological effects. Be prepared to follow school policies and nonviolent intervention techniques. Do not underestimate the effects on you and your students of observing anger between others.

4. If you believe the whole class has been affected, stop the lesson and have the class do simple exercises. Give everyone a chance to work off the extra adrenaline rush that comes with anger and excitement. By breaking the pattern of behavior interfering with the learning process, you will create a more cooperative learning environment.

5. When angry outside of class, take a brisk walk. Do some deep-breathing exercises. Listen to soft music or guided imagery tapes to reduce your heart rate and blood pressure.

6. Avoid competitive games, which can escalate angry behavior. Also avoid aerobics and weight lifting; the adrenaline surge from anger may result in overexertion and personal injury.

A Short-Term Solution for the Unruly Class

If a class is having trouble handling anger, take time to teach about it. Few students have had training on anger.

They must learn to view anger as a natural response to a threatening situation. They can recognize the feeling and learn how to control their behavior. An overwhelmed teacher no longer in control should consider the following emergency plan, developed from Barrington (1992/93), Dinkmeyer, McKay, and Dinkmeyer (1980), Glenn (1989), Nelsen, Lott, and Glenn (1993), and Prothrow-Stith (1987).

1. Develop a clear understanding of the situation, and identify student behaviors that trigger emotional reactions in you and others. Consider your thoughts and feelings. What is behind the anger? Is there a basic need for respect or a fear of rejection? Is safety for self or others the issue, or is it fear of a lack of administrative and parental support?

2. Identify your classroom responsibilities and expectations. Be certain they are realistic, then detach with care. Detaching means you no longer feel responsible for or guilty about others' inappropriate choices (Beattie 1987). You do not stop caring, but you acknowledge students are accountable for their choices. Clarify your needs and goals, then determine the personal and professional boundaries you must set with the class. Identify rules necessary to maintain these boundaries. Choose a few positive incentives that will help motivate student cooperation.

3. Include students in your overall behavior plan. Begin by explaining your perspective. Review what has been happening and your expectations. Then identify the problem as you see it. Invite students to identify their responsibilities, needs, and goals in writing. Involve them in setting rules, then make a decision and explain to the class the new rules, including consequences and incentives. The most important factor is mutual respect.

4. Respect students' right to choose personal behaviors. Help them to understand and respect your responsibility to follow through with the incentives and consequences they helped establish. Student participation, clarity, and consistency should be the plan's focus.

Creating Cooperative Classes

If educators want classes without inappropriate, angry behavior, the best time to win student cooperation is during the first weeks of a new school year. Discussions on anger, cooperation, and the purpose for learning the subject matter ensure that the class establishes acceptable goals. Students need opportunities to express themselves in pos-

itive ways at the beginning of the school year. They must discover the classes' relevance to their lives, develop skills for cooperative learning and dealing with anger, and establish mutual respect. One way to ensure the development of cooperation is through cooperative play activities. Rohnke (1984) promoted cooperative play to bring people together in an atmosphere of trust, break down artificial barriers, and increase participants' sense of personal confidence.

Creating a positive learning atmosphere in the first few weeks of school will set the tone for the rest of the year. Teachers who help students understand and control anger while demonstrating the relevance of lessons are more likely to win cooperation. Frequent review of goals, rules, incentives, consequences, and relevance to learning helps reduce the display of angry behaviors in the classroom.

Neither society nor students will change overnight. For many students, school may be the only place they will have the chance to learn how to handle anger in an appropriate way. If we as teachers refuse to offer this training, then we are enabling inappropriate behavior to perpetuate itself.

Teachers must keep parents and administrators informed of concerns and plans to address issues of anger in the classroom. Their help and support is vital. Neighborhood churches and synagogues may also offer parenting courses.

In moments of discouragement, teachers must acknowledge their feelings. By joining other creative teachers, we can begin to work on the anger at the core of the violence problem. Fight-or-flight reactions, strong controls, and tight security are not the only choices to handle violence in our schools. We can address our own anger and help students understand and handle theirs in healthy ways. Together, we can promote positive change in a violent society.

References

Baron, R. A. 1977. *Human aggression.* New York: Plenum Press.

Barrington, K. 1992/93. Teaming teachers for success. Teacher-training program. Deer Park, Tex.: Deer Park Independent School District.

Beattie, M. 1987. *Codependent.* Center City, Minn.: Hazelden.

Berkwitz, L. 1962. *Aggression: A social psychological analysis.* New York: McGraw-Hill.

Black, C. 1990. *Double duty.* New York: Ballantine Books.

Children's Defense Fund. 1997. In America . . . : Facts on youth, violence, and crime. Washington, D.C.: CDF.

Covey, S. 1994. *First things first.* New York: Simon & Schuster.

Dinkmeyer, D., G. D. McKay, and D. Dinkmeyer Jr. 1980. *For effective teaching.* Circle Pines, Minn.: American Guidance Service.

Gest, T., G. Witkin, K. Hetter, and A. Wright. 1994. Violence in America. *U.S. News & World Report* 5(17 January):22–26.

Ginott, H. 1971. *Between parent and teenager.* New York: Avon Books.

Glenn, H. S. 1989. *Developing capable people.* Video. Orem, Utah: Sunrise Productions.

Lerner, H. G. 1985. *The dance of anger.* New York: Harper and Row.

Nelsen, J. 1987. *Positive discipline.* New York: Ballantine Books.

Nelsen, J., L. Lott, and S. H. Glenn. 1993. *Positive discipline in the classroom.* Rocklin, Calif.: Prima Publishing.

Ornish, D. 1984. *Stress, diet & your heart.* New York: Signet.

Poland, S. 1998. Making crisis planning a top priority: What happened in Jonesboro could happen in your schools. *School Board News* 18(9): 2,4.

Potter, B. A. 1987. *Preventing job burnout.* Menlo Park, Calif.: Crisp Pub.

Prothrow-Stith, D. 1987. *Violence prevention: Curriculum for adolescents.* Newton, Mass.: Education Development Center.

Rohnke, K. 1984. *Silver bullets: A guide to initiative problems, adventure games, and trust activities.* Dubuque, Iowa: Kendall-Hunt.

Sears, R. R., E. Maccoly, and H. Levin. 1957. *Patterns of child rearing.* Evanston, Ill.: Row, Peterson.

Form at end of book

Uneasy Days for Schools

Behavior is learned by children during every waking moment, not just in the classroom.

Timothy C. Brennan Jr.

Brennan is superintendent of Parsippany-Troy Hills Public Schools in New Jersey.

On a Friday afternoon in late May, a 13-year-old boy in one of my district's middle schools produced a list of people he wanted "to be gone or die." Several hours later, I stood in the principal's office, holding the list in my hand and looking hard at the youngster's uneasy smile in a photo from the school files. He was too timid, I speculated, to threaten his antagonists with a punch in the nose. Or perhaps not verbal enough to ward them off with a well-chosen quip. He had decided instead to compose a list of students and teachers who had given him problems. The names of his 20 "enemies" were accompanied by an illustration and several pages of how-to text that was at once childish and troubling.

Two parents had called the school earlier in the day, alarmed by remarks the boy had made to their daughters about a "hit list." When confronted, the youngster had readily produced it, scribbled on the front of a manila folder containing his plans. He assured the principal that he would never hurt anyone except in self-defense. Ten years ago this might have meant a trip to the guidance counselor and a heart-to-heart with Mom and Dad. Not now. That luxury had been washed away by TV images from Oregon and Arkansas of bloodied kids with tears running down their chubby cheeks and yellow crime-scene tape tied to monkey bars.

"The crisis-management procedure is underway," said my no-nonsense principal, a gentle man whose idea of handling problems is to place all cards on the table and take forthright action. "He's been seen by the psychologist." The boy's father had come to pick him up. He was told by the principal that the boy could not return to school until he had been examined by a psychiatrist and

that his son must remain at home until the school received the doctor's results. Dad was concerned and cooperative. The boy lived with his father and grandfather. There was no mention of his mother.

After we alerted the police, the principal and I were joined by a youth-services detective. "The data needs to be evaluated before we make it public," said the principal. He agreed to send a letter to parents on Monday. "But if my child's name were on that list I'd want to know now—today," I said. In Oregon a few weeks earlier, turning a child over to his parents had proved tragically ineffective, so we decided to have police coverage at the school. The detective left with phone numbers to call all the people on the list.

I briefed members of the Board of Education about the incident. One of them called me Sunday night as I was returning from a family party. "The newspaper's got the story," she said. "Some people are keeping their kids home from school tomorrow." I called the reporter, then rang the police. By 3:45 Monday morning, the principal and I were discussing how parents might be concerned about similarities between our case and recent incidents around the country.

Monday's headline ran across the entire front page of the local paper and referred to a "Hit List." About 30 parents, many of whom had left their kids at home, met with the principal while I conferred with our crisis team. An image of American childhood in the late 20th century came to mind. Like cakes that should be allowed to bake slowly in a warm oven, our children too often get the heat turned up and the time cut back. On the outside they look finished, perhaps even crusty. But inside, they have not had time to coalesce. Under stress they are likely to collapse.

By midmorning the first TV crew arrived at the school. For the next 24 hours, six stations and one network shot footage and sent live feeds to their local newscasts. This was a media circus, but the reporters were no clowns. Even though the kids waved and virtually poured themselves out of school-bus windows trying to get on TV, most reporters took pains to make sure they weren't identifiable on camera. Late Tuesday afternoon, a court order put the boy under "house arrest." His grandfather voluntarily turned over two weapons which had been kept at the house. "Here's the fodder for tomorrows news programs," I thought, driving home, listening to a talk-show host playing segments of someone else's interview with me.

The next morning's news carried the story that Monica Lewinsky had switched attorneys. There was that same picture of her in the beret, being hugged by the president as he moved through the crowd. I thought about sending her a thank-you note. The media spotlight turned off our little school even more quickly than it had turned onto it. A sense of relative quiet returned. Parents were still calling: one to thank us for keeping the children safe, another to wonder out loud whether a child's rights had been forgotten, a third volunteering to organize a fundraiser to buy metal detectors.

For all the attention, something obvious and important had been missed. Childhood in America used to have a tripart support system: home, church and school. When I was a kid, my friends and I believed that God was watching us. Few young people now believe in an attentive God. My mother worked at my dad's paint store from about the time that I was 10, yet until we were well into high school, my sister and I decided on what we would do after school

on the basis of what "Mommy said." The voices of parents still matter, but now they compete with relentless electronic images of effortless pleasure and colorful violence.

Through our school's few days of fear and notoriety, we heard: "The school should . . . We need to start teaching these kids earlier that . . . The teachers have to let these kids know . . ." Many of the suggestions were good, but we must expand the concept of "teacher" and school." Behavior is learned by children during every waking moment. To the extent that we are observed in action by children, we are all teachers. We become their models and what they watch forms the memories from which their actions are drawn.

Role modeling is the most powerful form of teaching, even as it was when Aristotle crystallized the idea for his students in ancient Greece: "The soul never thinks without a picture."

Form at end of book

Issue 15 Summary

We live in a society that tolerates a fair amount of violence, in part because we do not want to live under a repressive government and we want to protect certain freedoms. We also hold beliefs about how reasonable people should behave. For many, acts of violence are puzzling contradictions to our expectations, yet violence is a part of our lives.

Violence in schools is not uncommon. It most often takes the form of children bullying others; many turn a blind eye to it, believing that that is simply how children behave. But, in doing so, we send a message to children that violent behavior is tolerable. When adults behave violently in front of children, they send an even worse message: that violent behavior is an acceptable way to reach your goals. As a society, we have to take responsibility for the message that we send children about violence, a message sent in our music, our television programs, our movies, and our own behavior.

Character Education

Questions

1. How do the arguments of Perry L. Glanzer and Alfie Kohn relate to the differences between the behavioral and constructivist approaches to psychology and education?

2. A parent approaches you and says, "My family has a different religion, a different ethnic background, and a different set of values than most of the families in this neighborhood. I don't think you should be teaching values in the schools because the beliefs of my culture may not be represented." What is your response? Does character education have a place in our schools?

3. Congratulations! The president has accepted your resignation as secretary of education. She asks you, as a last act, to make a set of five recommendations regarding how schools can improve students' character education. What are your five recommendations?

Introduction

Is it in the domain of schools to develop children's character or morality? Some would answer no, identifying character development as the responsibility of a child's family or church. Many would say yes, claiming that schools should promote moral development as well as cognitive development. They further contend that it is impossible to spend six hours a day with children without confronting a wide variety of moral issues. If one accepts character education as a responsibility of schools, the next question is *how* to promote the development of children's characters. What methods should be used, and what theories underlie these methods? Further, how do we know which moral beliefs we want to inculcate in children?

Educators have long struggled with these questions. They are all the more difficult in a multicultural society such as ours. In a monocultural society, there is usually wide agreement about the values that schools should teach. In a multicultural society, where cultures' values are likely to differ, determining the values to be taught is problematic. The difficulty is made more complex by the fact that teachers are often not from the same cultural background as that of their students.

The articles that you will read present different perspectives on the issue of character education. Before you read them, ask yourself the questions posed in the first paragraph. After you have read the articles, ask yourself the questions again and see if your answers have changed.

How Not to Teach Values:
A Critical Look at Character Education

What goes by the name of character education
nowadays is, for the most part, a collection of
exhortations and extrinsic inducements designed to
make children work harder and do what they're told,
Mr. Kohn maintains. He subjects this approach to
careful scrutiny, arguing that there are better ways to
promote social and moral development.

Alfie Kohn

*Alfie Kohn writes and lectures widely on education and human
behavior. His five books include* Punished by Rewards *(Houghton
Mifflin, 1993) and, most recently,* Beyond Discipline: From
Compliance to Community *(Association for Supervision and
Curriculum Development, 1996). He lives in Belmont, Mass. © 1997,
Alfie Kohn.*

Teachers and schools tend to mistake good behavior for good
character. What they prize is docility, suggestibility; the child
who will do what he is told; or even better, the child who will do
what is wanted without even having to be told. They value most
in children what children least value in themselves. Small
wonder that their effort to build character is such a failure; they
don't know it when they see it.

—John Holt
How Children Fail

Were you to stand somewhere in the continental United
States and announce, "I'm going to Hawaii," it would be
understood that you were heading for those islands in the
Pacific that collectively constitute the 50th state. Were you
to stand in Honolulu and make the same statement, however, you would probably be talking about one specific island in the chain—namely. the big one to your southeast.
The word *Hawaii* would seem to have two meanings, a
broad one and a narrow one; we depend on context to tell
them apart.

The phrase *character education* also has two meanings. In the broad sense, it refers to almost anything that
schools might try to provide outside of academics, especially when the purpose is to help children grow into good
people. In the narrow sense, it denotes a particular style of
moral training, one that reflects particular values as well as
particular assumptions about the nature of children and
how they learn.

Unfortunately, the two meanings of the term have
become blurred, with the narrow version of character education dominating the field to the point that it is frequently mistaken for the broader concept. Thus educators
who are keen to support children's social and moral development may turn, by default, to a program with a certain
set of methods and a specific agenda that, on reflection,
they might very well find objectionable.

My purpose in this article is to subject these programs to careful scrutiny and, in so doing, to highlight the
possibility that there are other ways to achieve our broader
objectives. I address myself not so much to those readers
who are avid proponents of character education (in the
narrow sense) but to those who simply want to help children become decent human beings and may not have
thought carefully about what they are being offered.

Let me get straight to the point. What goes by the
name of character education nowadays is, for the most
part, a collection of exhortations and extrinsic inducements designed to make children work harder and do what
they're told. Even when other values are also promoted—
caring or fairness, say—the preferred method of instruction is tantamount to indoctrination. The point is to drill
students in specific behaviors rather than to engage them
in deep, critical reflection about certain ways of being. This
is the impression one gets from reading articles and books
by contemporary proponents of character education as
well as the curriculum materials sold by the leading national programs. The impression is only strengthened by
visiting schools that have been singled out for their commitment to character education. To wit:

A huge, multiethnic elementary school in Southern California
uses a framework created by the Jefferson Center for Character
Education. Classes that the principal declares "well behaved" are
awarded Bonus Bucks, which can eventually be redeemed for an
ice cream party. Or an enormous wall near the cafeteria,
professionally painted Peanuts characters instruct children:
"Never talk in line." A visitor is led to a fifth-grade classroom to
observe an exemplary lesson on the current character education

topic. The teacher is telling students to write down the name of the person they regard as the "toughest worker" in school. The teacher then asked them. "How many of you are going to be tough workers?" (Hands go up.) "Can you be a tough worker at home, too?" (Yes.)

A small, almost entirely African American school in Chicago uses a framework created by the Character Education Institute. Periodic motivational assemblies are used to "give children a good pep talk," as the principal puts it, and to reinforce the values that determine who will be picked as Student of the Month. Rule number one posted on the wall of a kindergarten room is "We will obey the teachers." Today, students in this class are listening to the story of "Lazy Lion," who orders each of the other animals to build him a house, only to find each effort unacceptable. At the end, the teacher drives home the lesson: "Did you ever hear Lion say thank you? " (No.) "Did you ever hear Lion say please? " (No.) "It's good to always say . . . what? " (Please.) The reason for using these words, she points out, is that by doing so we are more likely to get what we want.

A charter school near Boston has been established specifically to offer an intensive, homegrown character education curriculum to its overwhelmingly white, middle-class student body. At weekly public ceremonies, certain children receive a leaf that will then be hung in the Forest of Virtue. The virtues themselves are "not open to debate," the headmaster insists, since moral precepts in his view enjoy the same status as mathematical truths. In a first-grade classroom, a teacher is observing that "it's very hard to be obedient when you want something. I want you to ask yourself 'Can I have it—and why not?' " She proceeds to ask the students, "What kinds of things show obedience?" and, after collecting a few suggestions, announces that she's "not going to call on anyone else now. We could go on forever, but we have to have a moment of silence and then a spelling test."

Some of the most popular school-wide strategies for improving students' character seem dubious on their face. When President Clinton mentioned the importance of character education in his 1996 State of the Union address, the only specific practice he recommended was requiring students to wear uniforms. The premises here are first, that children's character can be improved by forcing them to dress alike, and second, that if adults object to students' clothing, the best solution is not to invite them to reflect together about how this problem might be solved, but instead to compel them all to wear the same thing.

A second strategy, also consistent with the dominant philosophy of character education, is an exercise that might be called "If It's Tuesday, This Must Be Honesty." Here, one value after another is targeted, with each assigned its own day, week, or month. This seriatim approach is unlikely to result in a lasting commitment to any of these values, much less a feeling for how they may be related. Nevertheless, such programs are taken very seriously by some of the same people who are quick to dismiss other educational programs, such as those intended to promote self-esteem, as silly and ineffective.

Then there is the strategy of offering students rewards when they are "caught" being good, an approach favored by right-wing religious groups[1] and orthodox behaviorists but also by leaders of—and curriculum suppliers for—the character education movement.[2] Because of its popularity and because a sizable body of psychological evidence germane to the topic is available, it is worth lingering on this particular practice for a moment.

In general terms, what the evidence suggests is this: the more we reward people for doing something, the more likely they are to lose interest in whatever they had to do to get the reward. Extrinsic motivation, in other words, is not only quite different from intrinsic motivation but actually tends to erode it.[3] This effect has been demonstrated under many different circumstances and with respect to many different attitudes and behaviors. Most relevant to character education is a series of studies showing that individuals who have been rewarded for doing something nice become less likely to think of themselves as caring or helpful people and more likely to attribute their behavior to the reward.

"Extrinsic incentives can, by undermining self-perceived truism, decrease intrinsic motivation to help others," one group of researchers concluded on the basis of several studies. "A person's kindness, it seems, cannot be bought."[4] The same applies to a person's sense of responsibility, fairness, perseverance, and so on. The lesson a child learns from Skinnerian tactics is that the point of being good is to get rewards. No wonder researchers have found that children who are frequently rewarded—or in another study, children who receive positive reinforcement for caring, sharing, and helping—are less likely than other children to keep doing those things.[5]

In short, it makes no sense to dangle goodies in front of children for being virtuous. But even worse than rewards are *awards*—certificates, plaques, trophies, and other tokens of recognition whose numbers have been artificially limited so only a few can get them. When some children are singled out as "winners, " the central message that every child learns is this: "Other people are potential obstacles to my success."[6] Thus the likely result of making students beat out their peers for the distinction of being the most virtuous is not only less intrinsic commitment to virtue but also a disruption of relationships and, ironically, of the experience of community that is so vital to the development of children's character.

Unhappily, the problems with character education (in the narrow sense, which is how I'll be using the term unless otherwise indicated) are not restricted to such strategies as enforcing sartorial uniformity, scheduling a value of the week, or offering students a "doggie biscuit" for being good. More deeply troubling are the fundamental assumptions, both explicit and implicit, that inform character education programs. Let us consider five basic questions that might be asked of any such program: At what level are problems addressed? What is the underlying theory of human nature? What is the ultimate goal? Which values are promoted? And finally, How is learning thought to take place?

1. At What Level Are Problems Addressed?

One of the major purveyors of materials in this field, the Jefferson Center for Character Education in Pasadena, California, has produced a video that begins with some arresting images—quite literally. Young people are shown being led away in handcuffs, the point being that crime can be explained on the basis of an "erosion of American core values," as the narrator intones ominously. The idea that social problems can be explained by the fact that traditional virtues are no longer taken seriously is offered by many proponents of character education as though it were just plain common sense.

But if people steal or rape or kill solely because they possess bad values—that is, because of their personal characteristics—the implication is that political and economic realities are irrelevant and need not be addressed. Never mind staggering levels of unemployment in the inner cities or a system in which more and more of the nation's wealth is concentrated in fewer and fewer hands; just place the blame on individuals whose characters are deficient. A key tenet of the "Character Counts!" Coalition, which bills itself as a nonpartisan umbrella group devoid of any political agenda, is the highly debatable proposition that "negative social influences can [be] and usually are overcome by the exercise of free will and character."[7] What is presented as common sense is, in fact, conservative ideology.

The character education movement seems to be driven by a stunningly dark view of children—and of people in general.

Let's put politics aside, though. If a program proceeds by trying to "fix the kids"—as do almost all brands of character education—it ignores the accumulated evidence from the field of social psychology demonstrating that much of how we act and who we are reflects the situations in which we find ourselves. Virtually all the landmark studies in this discipline have been variations on this theme. Set up children in an extended team competition at summer camp and you will elicit unprecedented levels of aggression. Assign adults to the roles of prisoners or guards in a mock jail, and they will start to become their roles. Move people to a small town, and they will be more

likely to rescue a stranger in need. In fact, so common is the tendency to attribute to an individual's personality or character what is actually a function of the social environment that social psychologists have dubbed this the "fundamental attribution error."

A similar lesson comes to us from the movement concerned with Total Quality Management associated with the ideas of the late W. Edwards Deming. At the heart of Deming's teaching is the notion that the "system" of an organization largely determines the results. The problems experienced in a corporation, therefore, are almost always due to systemic flaws rather than to a lack of effort or ability on the part of individuals in that organization. Thus, if we are troubled by the way students are acting, Deming, along with most social psychologists, would presumably have us transform the structure of the classroom rather than try to remake the students themselves—precisely the opposite of the character education approach.

2. What Is the View of Human Nature?

Character education's "fix-the-kids" orientation follows logically from the belief that kids need fixing. Indeed, the movement seems to be driven by a stunningly dark view of children—and, for that matter, of people in general. A "comprehensive approach [to character education] is based on a somewhat dim view of human nature," acknowledges William Kilpatrick, whose book *Why Johnny Can't Tell Right from Wrong* contains such assertions as: "Most behavior problems are the result of sheer 'willfulness' on the part of children."[8]

Despite—or more likely because of—statements like that, Kilpatrick has frequently been invited to speak at character education conferences.[9] But that shouldn't be surprising in light of how many prominent proponents of character education share his views. Edward Wynne says his own work is grounded in a tradition of thought that takes a "somewhat pessimistic view of human nature."[10] The idea of character development "sees children as self-centered," in the opinion of Kevin Ryan, who directs the Center for the Advancement of Ethics and Character at Boston University as well as heading up the character education network of the Association for Supervision and Curriculum Development.[11] Yet another writer approvingly traces the whole field back to the bleak world view of Thomas Hobbes: it is "an obvious assumption of character education," writes Louis Goldman, that people lack the instinct to work together. Without laws to compel us to get along, "our natural egoism would lead us into 'a condition of warre one against another.' "[12] This sentiment is echoed by F. Washington Jarvis, headmaster of the Roxbury Latin School in Boston, one of Ryan's favorite examples of what character education should look like in practice. Jarvis sees human nature as "mean, nasty, brutish, selfish, and capable of great cruelty and meanness. We have to hold a mirror up to the students and say, 'This is who you are. Stop it.' "[13]

Even when proponents of character education don't express such sentiments explicitly, they give themselves away by framing their mission as a campaign for self-control. Amitai Etzioni, for example, does not merely include this attribute on a list of good character traits; he *defines* character principally in terms of the capacity "to control impulses and defer gratification."[14] This is noteworthy because the virtue of self-restraint—or at least the decision to give special emphasis to it—has historically been preached by those, from St. Augustine to the present, who see people as basically sinful.

In fact, at least three assumptions seem to be at work when the need for self-control is stressed: first, that we are all at war not only with others but with ourselves, torn between our desires and our reason (or social norms); second, that these desires are fundamentally selfish, aggressive, or otherwise unpleasant; and third, that these desires are very strong, constantly threatening to overpower us if we don't rein them in. Collectively, these statements describe religious dogma, not scientific fact. Indeed, the evidence from several disciplines converges to cast doubt on this sour view of human beings and, instead, supports the idea that it is as "natural" for children to help as to hurt. I will not rehearse that evidence here, partly because I have done so elsewhere at some length.[15] Suffice it to say that even the most hard-headed empiricist might well conclude that the promotion of prosocial values consists to some extent of supporting (rather than restraining or controlling) many facets of the self. Any educator who adopts this more balanced position might think twice before joining an educational movement that is finally inseparable from the doctrine of original sin.

3. What Is the Ultimate Goal?

It may seem odd even to inquire about someone's reasons for trying to improve children's character. But it is worth mentioning that the whole enterprise—not merely the particular values that are favored—is often animated by a profoundly conservative, if not reactionary, agenda. Character education based on "acculturating students to conventional norms of 'good' behavior . . . resonates with neoconservative concerns for social stability," observed David Purpel.[16] The movement has been described by another critic as a "yearning for some halcyon days of moral niceties and social tranquillity."[17] But it is not merely a *social* order that some are anxious to preserve (or recover): character education is vital, according to one vocal proponent, because "the development of character is the backbone of the economic system" now in place."[18]

The character education programs—and theorists who promote them—seem to regard teaching as a matter of telling and compelling.

Character education, or any kind of education, would look very different if we began with other objectives—if, for example, we were principally concerned with helping children become active participants in a democratic society (or agents for transforming a society *into* one that is authentically democratic). It would look different if our top priority were to help students develop into principled and caring members of a community or advocates for social justice. To be sure, these objectives are not inconsistent with the desire to preserve certain traditions, but the point would then be to help children decide which traditions are worth preserving and why, based on these other considerations. That is not at all the same as endorsing anything that is traditional or making the preservation of tradition our primary concern. In short, we want to ask character education proponents what goals they emphasize—and ponder whether their broad vision is compatible with our own.

---

4. Which Values?

Should we allow values to be taught in school? The question is about as sensible as asking whether our bodies should be allowed to contain bacteria. Just as humans are teeming with microorganisms, so schools are teeming with values. We can't see the former because they're too small; we don't notice the latter because they're too similar to the values of the culture at large. Whether or not we deliberately adopt a character or moral education program, we are always teaching values. Even people who insist that they are opposed to values in school usually mean that they are opposed to values other than their own.[19]

And that raises the inevitable question: Which values, or whose, should we teach? It has already become a cliché to reply that this question should not trouble us because, while there may be disagreement on certain issues, such as abortion, all of us can agree on a list of basic values that children ought to have. Therefore, schools can vigorously and unapologetically set about teaching all of those values.

But not so fast. Look at the way character education programs have been designed and you will discover, alongside such unobjectionable items as "fairness" or "honesty," an emphasis on values that are, again, distinctly conservative—and, to that extent, potentially controversial. To begin with, the famous Protestant work ethic is prominent: children should learn to "work hard and complete their tasks well and promptly, even when they do not want to," says Ryan.[20] Here the Latin question *Cui bono?* comes to mind. Who benefits when people are trained not to question the value of what they have been told to do but simply to toil away at it—and to regard this as virtuous?[21] Similarly, when Wynne defines the moral individual as someone who is not only honest but also "diligent, obedient and patriotic,"[22] readers may find themselves wondering whether these traits really qualify as *moral*—as well as reflecting of the virtues that are missing from this list.

Character education curricula also stress the importance of things like "respect," "responsibility," and "citizenship." But these are slippery terms, frequently used as euphemisms for uncritical deference to authority. Under the headline "The Return of the 'Fourth R' "—referring to "respect, responsibility, or rules"—a news magazine recently described the growing popularity of such practices as requiring uniforms, paddling disobedient students, rewarding those who are compliant, and "throwing disruptive kids out of the classroom."[23] Indeed, William Glasser observed some time ago that many educators "teach thoughtless conformity to school rules and call the conforming child 'responsible.' "[24] I once taught at a high school where the principal frequently exhorted students to "take responsibility." By this he meant specifically that they should turn in their friends who used drugs.

Exhorting students to be "respectful" or rewarding them if they are caught being "good" may likewise mean nothing more than getting them to do whatever the adults demand. Following a lengthy article about character education in the *New York Times Magazine,* a reader mused, "Do you suppose that if Germany had had character education at the time, it would have encouraged children to fight Nazism or to support it?"[25] The more time I spend in schools that are enthusiastically implementing character education programs, the more I am haunted by that question.

In place of the traditional attributes associated with character education, Deborah Meier and Paul Schwarz of the Central Park East Secondary School in New York nominated two core values that a school might try to promote: "empathy and skepticism: the ability to see a situation from the eyes of another and the tendency to wonder about the validity of what we encountered."[26] Anyone who brushes away the question "Which values should be taught?" might speculate on the concrete differences between a school dedicated to turning out students who are empathic and skeptical and a school dedicated to turning out students who are loyal, patriotic, obedient, and so on.

Meanwhile, in place of such personal qualities as punctuality or perseverance, we might emphasize the cultivation of autonomy so that children come to experience themselves as "origins" rather than "pawns," as one researcher put it.[27] We might, in other words, stress self-determination at least as much as self-control. With such an agenda, it would be crucial to give students the chance to participate in making decisions about their learning and about how they want their classroom to be.[28] This stands in sharp contrast to a philosophy of character education like Wynne's, which decrees that "it is specious to talk about student choices" and offers students no real power except for when we give "some students authority over other students (for example, hall guard, class monitor)."[29]

Even with values that are widely shared, a superficial consensus may dissolve when we take a closer look. Educators across the spectrum are concerned about excessive attention to self-interest and are committed to helping students transcend a preoccupation with their own needs. But how does this concern play out in practice? For some of us, it takes the form of an emphasis on *compassion;* for the dominant character education approach, the alternative value to be stressed is *loyalty,* which is, of course, altogether different.[30] Moreover, as John Dewey remarked at the turn of the century, anyone seriously troubled about rampant individualism among children would promptly target for extinction the "drill-and-skill" approach to instruction: "The mere absorbing of facts and truths is so exclusively individual an affair that it tends very naturally to pass into selfishness."[31] Yet conservative champions of character education are often among the most outspoken supporters of a model of teaching that emphasizes rote memorization and the sequential acquisition of decontextualized skills.

Or take another example: all of us may say we endorse the idea of "cooperation," but what do we make of the practice of setting groups against one another in a quest for triumph, such that cooperation becomes the means and victory is the end? On the one hand, we might find this even more objectionable than individual competition. (Indeed, we might regard a "We're Number One!" ethic as a reason for schools to undertake something like character education in the first place.) On the other hand, "school-to-school, class-to-class, or row-to-row academic competitions" actually have been endorsed as part of a character education program,[32] along with contests that lead to awards for things like good citizenship.

The point, once again, is that it is entirely appropriate to ask which values a character education program is attempting to foster, notwithstanding the ostensible lack of controversy about a list of core values. It is equally appropriate to put such a discussion in context—specifically, in the context of which values are *currently* promoted in schools. The fact is that schools are already powerful socializers of traditional values—although, as noted above, we may fail to appreciate the extent to which this is true because we have come to take these values for granted. In most schools, for example, students are taught—indeed, compelled—to follow the rules regardless of whether the rules are reasonable and to respect authority regardless of whether that respect has been earned. (This process isn't always successful, of course, but that is a different matter.) Students are led to accept competition as natural and desirable, and to see themselves more as discrete individuals than as members of a community. Children in American schools are even expected to begin each day by reciting a loyalty oath to the Fatherland, although we call it by a different name. In short, the question is not whether to adopt the conservative values offered by most character education programs, but whether we want to consolidate the conservative values that are already in place.

5. What Is the Theory of Learning?

We come now to what may be the most significant, and yet the least remarked on, feature of character education: the way values are taught and the way learning is thought to take place.

The character education coordinator for the small Chicago elementary school also teaches second grade. In her classroom, where one boy has been forced to sit by himself for the last two weeks ("He's kind of pesty"), she is asking the children to define tolerance. When the teacher gets the specific answers she is fishing for, she exclaims, "Say that again," and writes down only those responses. Later comes the moral: "If somebody doesn't think the way you think, should you turn them off?" (No.)

Down the hall, the first-grade teacher is fishing for answers on a different subject. "When we play games, we try to understand the—what?" (Rules.) A moment later, the children scramble to get into place so she will pick them to tell a visitor their carefully rehearsed stories about conflict resolution. Almost every child's account, narrated with considerable prompting by the teacher, concerns name-calling or some other unpleasant incident that was "correctly" resolved by finding an adult. The teacher never asks the children how they felt about what happened or invites them to reflect on what else might have been done. She wraps up the activity by telling the children, "What we need to do all the time is clarify—make it clear—to the adult what you did."

The schools with character education programs that I have visited are engaged largely in exhortation and directed recitation. At first one might assume this is due to poor implementation of the programs on the part of individual educators. But the programs themselves—and the theorists who promote them—really do seem to regard teaching as a matter of telling and compelling. For example, the broad-based "Character Counts!" Coalition offers a framework of six core character traits and then asserts

that "young people should be specifically and repeatedly told what is expected of them." The leading providers of curriculum materials walk teachers through highly structured lessons in which character-related concepts are described and then students are drilled until they can produce the right answers.

Teachers are encouraged to praise children who respond correctly, and some programs actually include multiple-choice tests to ensure that students have learned their values. For example, here are two sample test questions prepared for teachers by the Character Education Institute, based in San Antonio, Texas: "Having to obey rules and regulations (a) gives everyone the same right to be an individual, (b) forces everyone to do the same thing at all times, (c) prevents persons from expressing their individually [sic]"; and "One reason why parents might not allow their children freedom of choice is (a) children are always happier when they are told what to do and when to do it, (b) parents aren't given a freedom of choice; therefore, children should not be given a choice either, (c) children do not always demonstrate that they are responsible enough to be given a choice." The correct answers, according to the answer key, are (a) and (c) respectively.

The Character Education Institute recommends "engaging the students in discussions," but only discussions of a particular sort: "Since the lessons have been designed to logically guide the students to the right answers, the teacher should allow the students to draw their own conclusions. However, if the students draw the wrong conclusion, the teacher is instructed to tell them why their conclusion is *wrong*."[33]

When education is construed as the process of inculcating *habits,* then it scarcely deserves to be called education at all.

Students are told what to think and do, not only by their teachers but by highly didactic stories, such as those in the Character Education Institute's "Happy Life" series, which end with characters saying things like "I am glad that I did not cheat," or "Next time I will be helpful," or "I will never be selfish again." Most character education programs also deliver homilies by way of posters and banners and murals displayed throughout the school. Children who do as they are told are presented with all manner of rewards, typically in front of their peers.

Does all of this amount to indoctrination? Absolutely, says Wynne, who declares that "school is and should and must be inherently indoctrinative."[34] Even when character education proponents tiptoe around that word, their model of instruction is clear: good character and values are *instilled in* or *transmitted to* students. We are "planting the ideas of virtue, of good traits in the young," says William Bennett.[35] The virtues or values in question are fully formed, and, in the minds of many character education proponents, divinely ordained. The children are—pick your favorite metaphor—so many passive receptacles to be filled, lumps of clay to be molded, pets to be trained, or computers to be programmed.

Thus, when we see Citizen-of-the-Month certificates and "Be a good sport!" posters, when we find teachers assigning preachy stories and principals telling students what to wear, it is important that we understand what is going on. These techniques may appear merely innocuous or gimmicky; they may strike us as evidence of a scattershot, let's-try-anything approach. But the truth is that these are elements of a systematic pedagogical philosophy. They are manifestations of a model that sees children as objects to be manipulated rather than as learners to be engaged.

Ironically, some people who accept character education without a second thought are quite articulate about the bankruptcy of this model when it comes to teaching academic subjects. Plenty of teachers have abandoned the use of worksheets, textbooks, and lectures that fill children full of disconnected facts and skills. Plenty of administrators are working to create schools where students can actively construct meaning around scientific and historical and literary concepts. Plenty of educators, in short, realize that memorizing right answers and algorithms doesn't help anyone to arrive at a deep understanding of ideas.

And so we are left scratching our heads. Why would all these people, who know that the "transmission" model fails to facilitate intellectual development, uncritically accept the very same model to promote ethical development? How could they understand that mathematical truths cannot be shoved down students' throats but then participate in a program that essentially tries to shove moral truths down the same throats? In the case of individual educators, the simple answer may be that they missed the connection. Perhaps they just failed to recognize that "a classroom cannot foster the development of autonomy in the intellectual realm while suppressing it in the social and moral realms," as Constance Kamii and her colleagues put it not long ago.[36]

In the case of the proponents of character education, I believe the answer to this riddle is quite different. The reason they are promoting techniques that seem strikingly ineffective at fostering autonomy of ethical development is that, as a rule, they are not *trying* to foster autonomy or ethical development. The goal is not to support or facilitate children's social and moral growth, but simply to "demand good behavior from students," in Ryan's words.[37] The idea is to get compliance, to *make* children act the way we want them to.

Indeed, if these are the goals, then the methods make perfect sense—the lectures and pseudo-discussions, the slogans and the stories that conk students on the head with their morals. David Brooks, who heads the Jefferson Center for Character Education, frankly states, "We're in the advertising business." The way you get people to do something, whether it's buying Rice Krispies or becoming trustworthy, is to "encourage conformity through repeated messages."[38] The idea of selling virtues like cereal nearly reaches the point of self-parody in the Jefferson Center's curriculum, which includes the following activity: "There's a new product on the market! It's Considerate Cereal. Eating it can make a person more considerate. Design a label for the box. Tell why someone should buy and eat this cereal. Then list the ingredients."[39]

If "repeated messages" don't work, then you simply force students to conform: "Sometimes compulsion is what is needed to get a habit started," says William Kilpatrick.[40] We may recoil from the word "compulsion," but it is the premise of that sentence that really ought to give us pause. When education is construed as the process of inculcating *habits*—which is to say, unreflective actions—then it scarcely deserves to be called education at all. It is really, as Alan Lockwood saw, an attempt to get "mindless conformity to externally imposed standards of conduct."[41]

Notice how naturally this goal follows from a dark view of human nature. If you begin with the premise that "good conduct is not our natural first choice," then the best you can hope for is "the development of good habits"[42]—that is, a system that gets people to act unthinkingly in the manner that someone else has deemed appropriate. This connection recently became clear to Ann Medlock, whose Giraffe Project was designed to evoke "students' own courage and compassion" in thinking about altruism, but which, in some schools, was being turned into a traditional, authoritarian program in which students were simply told how to act and what to believe. Medlock recalls suddenly realizing what was going on with these educators: "Oh, *I* see where you're coming from. You believe kids are no damn good!"[43]

The character education movement's emphasis on habit, then, is consistent with its view of children. Likewise, its process matches its product. The transmission model, along with the use of rewards and punishments to secure compliance, seems entirely appropriate if the values you are trying to transmit are things like obedience and loyalty and respect for authority. But this approach overlooks an important distinction between product and process. When we argue about which traits to emphasize—compassion or loyalty, cooperation or competition, skepticism or obedience—we are trafficking in value judgments. When we talk about how best to teach these things, however, we are being descriptive rather than just prescriptive. Even if you like the sort of virtues that appear in character education programs, and even if you regard the need to implement those virtues as urgent, the attempt to transmit or instill them dooms the project because that is just not consistent with the best theory and research on how people learn. (Of course, if you have reservations about many of the values that the character educators wish to instill, you may be *relieved* that their favored method is unlikely to be successful.)

I don't wish to be misunderstood. The techniques of character education may succeed in temporarily buying a particular behavior. But they are unlikely to leave children with a *commitment* to that behavior, a reason to continue acting that way in the future. You can turn out automatons who utter the desired words or maybe even "emit" (to use the curious verb favored by behaviorists) the desired actions. But the words and actions are unlikely to continue—much less transfer to new situations—because the child has not been invited to integrate them into his or her value structure. As Dewey observed, "The required beliefs cannot be hammered in; the needed attitudes cannot be plastered on."[44] Yet watch a character education lesson in any part of the country and you will almost surely be observing a strenuous exercise in hammering and plastering.

For traditional moralists, the constructivist approach is a waste of time. If values and traditions and the stories that embody them already exist, then surely "we don't have to reinvent the wheel," remarks Bennett.[45] Likewise an exasperated Wynne: "Must each generation try to completely reinvent society?"[46] The answer is no—and yes. It is not as though everything that now exists must be discarded and entirely new values fashioned from scratch. But the process of learning does indeed require that meaning, ethical or otherwise, be actively invented and reinvented, from the inside out. It requires that children be given the opportunity to make sense of such concepts as fairness or courage, regardless of how long the concepts themselves have been around. Children must be invited to reflect on complex issues, to recast them in light of their own experiences and questions, to figure out for themselves—and with one another—what kind of person one ought to be, which traditions are worth keeping, and how to proceed when two basic values seem to be in conflict.[47]

In this sense, reinvention is necessary if we want to help children become moral people, as opposed to people who merely do what they are told—or reflexively rebel against what they are told. In fact, as Rheta DeVries and Betty Zan add (in a recent book that offers a useful antidote to traditional character education), "If we want children to resist [peer pressure] and not be victims of others' ideas, we have to educate children to think for themselves about all ideas, including those of adults."[48]

Traditionalists are even more likely to offer another objection to the constructivist approach, one that boils down to a single epithet: *relativism!* If we do anything other than insert moral absolutes in students, if we let them construct their own meanings, then we are saying that anything goes, that morality collapses into personal preferences. Without character education, our schools will just offer programs such as Values Clarification, in which adults are allegedly prohibited from taking a stand.

In response, I would offer several observations. First, the Values Clarification model of moral education, popular in some circles a generation ago, survives today mostly in the polemics of conservatives anxious to justify an indoctrinative approach. Naturally, no statistics are ever cited as to the number of school districts still telling students that any value is as good as any other—assuming the program actually said that in the first place.[49] Second, conservative critics tendentiously try to connect constructivism to relativism, lumping together the work of the late Lawrence Kohlberg with programs like Values Clarification."[50] The truth is that Kohlberg, while opposed to what he called the "bag of virtues" approach to moral education, was not much enamored of Values Clarification either, and he spent a fair amount of time arguing against relativism in general.[51]

If Kohlberg can fairly be criticized, it is for emphasizing moral reasoning, a cognitive process, to the extent that he may have slighted the affective components of morality, such as caring. But the traditionalists are not much for the latter either: caring is seen as an easy or soft virtue (Ryan) that isn't sufficiently "binding or absolute" (Kilpatrick). The objection to constructivism is not that empathy is eclipsed by justice, but that children—or even adults—should not have an active role to play in making decisions and reflecting on how to live. They should be led instead to an uncritical acceptance of ready-made truths. The character educator's job, remember, is to elicit the right answer from students and tell those who see things differently "why their conclusion is *wrong*." Any deviation from this approach is regarded as indistinguishable from full-blown relativism; we must "plant" traditional values in each child or else morality is nothing more than a matter of individual taste. Such either/or thinking, long since discarded by serious moral philosophers,[52] continues to fuel character education and to perpetuate the confusion of education with indoctrination.

To say that students must construct meaning around moral concepts is not to deny that adults have a crucial role to play. The romantic view that children can basically educate themselves so long as grown-ups don't interfere is not taken seriously by any constructivists I know of—certainly not by Dewey, Piaget, Kohlberg, or their followers. Rather, like Values Clarification, this view seems to exist principally as a straw man in the arguments of conservatives. Let there be no question, then: educators, parents, and other adults are desperately needed to offer guidance, to act as models (we hope), to pose challenges that promote moral growth, and to help children understand the effects of their actions on other people, thereby tapping and nurturing a concern for others that is present in children from a very young age.[53]

Character education rests on three ideological legs: behaviorism, conservatism, and religion. The third raises the most delicate issues.

Character education rests on three ideological legs: behaviorism, conservatism, and religion. Of these, the third raises the most delicate issues for a critic; it is here that the charge of *ad hominem* argument is most likely to be raised. So let us be clear: it is of no relevance that almost all of the leading proponents of character education are devout Catholics. But it is entirely relevant that, in the shadows of their writings, there lurks the assumption that only religion can serve as the foundation for good character. (William Bennett, for example, has flatly asserted that the difference between right and wrong cannot be taught "without reference to religion."[54]) It is appropriate to consider the personal beliefs of these individuals if those beliefs are ensconced in the movement they have defined and directed. What they do on Sundays is their own business, but if they are trying to turn our public schools into Sunday schools, that becomes everybody's business.

Even putting aside the theological underpinnings of the character education movement, the five questions presented in this article can help us describe the natural constituency of that movement. Logically, its supporters should be those who firmly believe that we should focus our efforts on repairing the characters of children rather than on transforming the environments in which they learn, those who assume the worst about human nature, those who are more committed to preserving than to changing our society, those who favor such values as obedience to authority, and those who define learning as the process of swallowing whole a set of preexisting truths. It stands to reason that readers who recognize themselves in this description would enthusiastically endorse character education in its present form.

The rest of us have a decision to make. Either we define our efforts to promote children's social and moral development as an *alternative* to "character education," thereby ceding that label to the people who have already appropriated it, or we try to *reclaim* the wider meaning of the term by billing what we are doing as a different kind of character education.

The first choice—opting out—seems logical: it strains the language to use a single phrase to describe practices as different as engaging students in reflecting about fairness, on the one hand, and making students dress alike, on the other. It seems foolish to pretend that these are just different versions of the same thing, and thus it may be unreasonable to expect someone with a constructivist or progressive vision to endorse what is now called character education. The problem with abandoning this label, however, is that it holds considerable appeal for politicians and members of the public at large. It will be challenging to explain that "character education" is not synonymous with helping children to grow into good people and, indeed, that the movement associated with the term is a good deal more controversial than it first appears.

The second choice, meanwhile, presents its own set of practical difficulties. Given that the individuals and organizations mentioned in this article have succeeded in putting their own stamp on character education, it will not be easy to redefine the phrase so that it can also signify a very different approach. It will not be easy, that is, to organize conferences, publish books and articles, and develop curricular materials that rescue the broad meaning of "character education."

Whether we relinquish or retain the nomenclature, though, it is vital that we work to decouple most of what takes place under the banner of "character education" from the enterprise of helping students become ethically sophisticated decision makers and caring human beings. Wanting young people to turn out that way doesn't require us to adopt traditional character education programs any more than wanting them to be physically fit requires us to turn schools into Marine boot camps.

What does the alternative look like? Return once more to those five questions: in each case, an answer different from that given by traditional character education will help us to sketch the broad contours of a divergent approach. More specifically, we should probably target certain practices for elimination, add some new ones, and reconfigure still others that already exist. I have already offered a catalogue of examples of what to eliminate, from Skinnerian reinforcers to lesson plans that resemble sermons. As examples of what to add, we might suggest holding regular class meetings in which students can share, plan, decide, and reflect together.[55] We might also provide children with explicit opportunities to practice "perspective taking"—that is, imagining how the world looks from someone else's point of view. Activities that promote an understanding of how others think and feel, that support the impulse to imaginatively reach beyond the self, can provide the same benefits realized by holding democratic class meetings—namely, helping students become more ethical and compassionate while simultaneously fostering intellectual growth.[56]

A good example of an existing practice that might be reconfigured is the use of literature to teach values. In principle, the idea is splendid: it makes perfect sense to select stories that not only help students develop reading skills (and an appreciation for good writing) but also raise moral issues. The trouble is that many programs use simplistic little morality tales in place of rich, complex literature. Naturally, the texts should be developmentally appropriate, but some character educators fail to give children credit for being able to grapple with ambiguity. (Imagine the sort of stories likely to be assigned by someone who maintains that "it is ridiculous to believe children are capable of objectively assessing most of the beliefs and values they must absorb to be effective adults."[57])

Perhaps the concern is not that students will be unable to make sense of challenging literature, but that they will not derive the "correct" moral. This would account for the fact that even when character education curricula include impressive pieces of writing, the works tend to be used for the purpose of drumming in simple lessons. As Kilpatrick sees it, a story "points to these [characters] and says in effect, 'Act like this; don't act like that.' "[58] This kind of lesson often takes the form of hero worship, with larger-than-life characters—or real historical figures presented with their foibles airbrushed away—held up to students to encourage imitation of their actions.

Rather than employ literature to indoctrinate or induce mere conformity, we can use it to spur reflection. Whether the students are 6-year-olds or 16-year-olds, the discussion of stories should be open-ended rather than relentlessly didactic. Teachers who refrain from tightly controlling such conversations are impressed again and again by the levels of meaning students prove capable of exploring and the moral growth they exhibit in such an environment. Instead of announcing, "This man is a hero; do what he did," such teachers may involve the students in *deciding* who (if anyone) is heroic in a given story—or in contemporary culture[59]—and why. They may even invite students to reflect on the larger issue of whether it is desirable to have heroes. (Consider the quality of discussion that might be generated by asking older students to respond to the declaration of playwright Bertolt Brecht: "Unhappy is the land that needs a hero.")

More than specific practices that might be added, subtracted, or changed, a program to help children grow into good people begins with a commitment to change the way classrooms and schools are structured—and this brings us back to the idea of transcending a fix-the-kid approach. Consider the format of classroom discussions. A proponent of character education, invoking such traditional virtues as patience or self-control, might remind students that they must wait to be recognized by the teacher. But what if we invited students to think about the best way to conduct a discussion? Must we raise our hands? Is there another way to avoid having everyone talk at once? How can we be fair to those who aren't as assertive or as fast on their feet? Should the power to decide who can speak always rest with the teacher? Perhaps the problem is not with students who need to be more self-disciplined, but with the whole instructional design that has students waiting to be recognized to answer someone else's questions. And perhaps the real learning comes only when students have the chance to grapple with such issues.

One more example. A proponent of character education says we must make students understand that it is wrong to lie; we need to teach them about the importance of being honest. But why do people lie? Usually because they don't feel safe enough to tell the truth. The real challenge for us as educators is to examine that precept in terms of what is going on in our classrooms, to ask how we and the students together can make sure that even unpleasant truths can be told and heard. Does pursuing this line of inquiry mean that it's acceptable to fib? No. It means the problem has to be dissected and solved from the inside out. It means behaviors occur in a context that teachers have helped to establish, therefore, teachers have to examine (and consider modifying) that context even at the risk of some discomfort to themselves. In short, if we want to help children grow into compassionate and responsible people, we have to change the way the classroom works and feels, not just the way each separate member of that class acts. Our emphasis should not be on forming individual characters so much as on transforming educational structures.

Happily, programs do exist whose promotion of children's social and moral development is grounded in a commitment to change the culture of schools. The best example of which I am aware is the Child Development Project, an elementary school program designed, implemented, and researched by the Developmental Studies Center in Oakland, California. The CDP's premise is that, by meeting children's needs, we increase the likelihood that they will care about others. Meeting their needs entails, among other things, turning schools into caring communities. The CDP offers the additional advantages of a constructivist vision of learning, a positive view of human nature, a balance of cognitive and affective concerns, and a program that is integrated into all aspects of school life (including the curriculum).[60]

Is the CDP an example of what character education ought to be—or of what out to replace character education? The answer to that question will depend on tactical, and even semantic, considerations. Far more compelling is the need to reevaluate the practices and premises of contemporary character education. To realize a humane and progressive vision for children's development, we may need to look elsewhere.

Notes

1. See, for example, Linda Page, "A Conservative Christian View on Values," *School Administrator.* September 1995, p. 22.
2. See, for example, Kevin Ryan, "The Ten Commandments of Character Education," *School Administrator,* September 1995, p. 19; and program materials from the Character Education Institute and the Jefferson Center for Character Education.
3. See Alfie Kohn, *Punished by Rewards: The Trouble with Gold Stars, Inventive Plans, A's, Praise, and Other Bribes* (Boston: Houghton Mifflin, 1993); and Edward L. Deci and Richard M. Ryan, *Intrinsic Motivation and Self-Determination in Human Behavior* (New York: Plenum, 1985).
4. See C. Daniel Batson et al., "Buying Kindness: Effect of an Extrinsic Incentive for Helping on Perceived Altruism," *Personality and Social Psychology Bulletin,* vol. 4, 1978. p. 90; Cathleen L. Smith et al., "Children's Causal Attributions Regarding Help Giving," *Child Development,* vol. 50, 1979, pp. 203–10; and William Edward Upton III, "Altruism, Attribution, and Intrinsic Motivation in the Recruitment of Blood Donors," *Dissertation Abstracts International* 34B, vol. 12, 1974, p. 6260.
5. Richard A. Fabes et al., "Effects of Rewards on Children's Prosocial Motivation: A Socialization Study," *Developmental Psychology,* vol, 25. 1989, pp. 509–15; and Joan Grusec, "Socializing Concern for Others in the Home," *Developmental Psychology,* vol. 27, 1991, pp. 338–42.
6. See Alfie Kohn, *No Contest: The Case Against Competition,* rev. ed. (Boston: Houghton Mifflin, 1992).
7. This statement is taken from an eight-page brochure produced by the "Character Counts!" Coalition, a project of the Josephson Institute of Ethics. Members of the coalition include the American Federation of Teachers, the National Association of Secondary School Principals, the American Red Cross, the YMCA, and many other organizations.
8. William Kilpatrick, *Why Johnny Can't Tell Right from Wrong* (New York: Simon & Schuster, 1992), pp. 96, 249.
9. For example, Kilpatrick was selected in 1995 to keynote the first in a series of summer institutes on character education sponsored by Thomas Lickona.
10. Edward Wynne, "Transmitting Traditional Values in Contemporary Schools," in Larry P. Nucci. ed., *Moral Development and Character Education: A Dialogue* (Berkeley. Calif.: McCutchan, 1989), p. 25.
11. Kevin Ryan, "In Defense of Character Education," in Nucci, p. 16.
12. Louis Goldman, "Mind, Character, and the Deferral of Gratification." *Educational Forum,* vol. 60, 1996, p. 136. As part of "educational reconstruction," he goes on to say, we must "connect the lower social classes to the middle classes who may provide role models for self-discipline" (p. 139).
13. Jarvis is quoted in Wray Herbert, "The Moral Child," U.S. *News & World Report,* 3 June 1996, p. 58.
14. Amitai Etzioni, *The Spirit of Community: The Reinvention of American Society* (New York: Simon & Schuster, 1993), p. 91.
15. See Alfie Kohn, *The Brighter Side of Human Nature: Altruism and Empathy in Everyday Life* (New York: Basic Books, 1990): and "Caring Kids: The Role of the Schools," *Phi Delta Kappan,* March 1991, pp. 496–506.
16. David E. Purpel. "Moral Education: An Idea Whose Time Has Gone," *The Clearing House,* vol. 64, 1991, p. 311.
17. This description of the character education movement is offered by Alan L. Lockwood in "Character Education: The Ten Percent Solution," *Social Education,* April/May 1991, p. 246. It is a particularly apt characterization of a book like *Why Johnny Can't Tell Right from Wrong,* which invokes an age of "chivalry" and sexual abstinence, a time when moral truths were uncomplicated and unchallenged. The author's tone, however, is not so much wistful about the past as angry about the present: he denounces everything from rock music (which occupies an entire chapter in a book about morality) and feminism to the "multiculturalists" who dare to remove "homosexuality from the universe of moral judgment" (p. 126).
18. Kevin Walsh of the University of Alabama is quoted in Eric N. Berg, "Argument Grows That Teaching of Values Should Rank with Lessons," *New York Times,* 1 January 1992, p. 32.
19. I am reminded of a woman in a Houston audience who heatedly informed me that she doesn't send her child to school "to learn to be nice." That, she declared, would be "social engineering." But a moment later this woman added that her child ought to be "taught to respect authority." Since this would seem to be at least as apposite an example of social engineering, one is led to conclude that the woman's real objection was to the teaching of *particular* topics or values.
20. Kevin Ryan, "Mining the Values in the Curriculum." *Educational Leadership,* November 1993, p. 16.
21. Telling students to "try hard" and "do their best" begs the important questions. *How,* exactly, do they do their best? Surely it is not just a matter of blind effort. And *why* should they do so, particularly if the task is not engaging or meaningful to them, or if it has simply been imposed on them? Research has found that the attitudes students take toward learning are heavily influenced by whether they have been led to attribute their success (or failure) to innate ability, to effort, or to other factors—and that traditional classroom practices such as grading and competition lead them to explain the results in terms of ability (or its absence) and to minimize effort whenever possible. What looks like "laziness" or insufficient perseverance, in other words, often turns out to be a rational decision to avoid challenge: it is rational because this route proves most expedient for performing well or maintaining an image of oneself as smart. These systemic factors. of course, are complex and often threatening for educators to address: it is much easier just to impress on children the importance of doing their best and then blame them for lacking perseverance if they seem not to do so.
22. Edward A. Wynne, "The Great Tradition in Education: Transmitting Moral Values," *Educational Leadership,* December 1985/January 1986, p. 6.
23. Mary Lord, "The Return of the 'Fourth R,' " U.S. *News & World Report,* 11 September 1995, p. 58.
24. William Glasser, *Schools Without Failure* (New York: Harper & Row, 1969), p. 22.
25. Marc Desmond's letter appeared in the *New York Times Magazine,* 21 May 1995, p. 14. The same point was made by Robert Primack, "No Substitute for Critical Thinking: A Response to Wynne," *Educational Leadership,* December 1985/January 1986, p. 12.
26. Deborah Meier and Paul Schwarz, "Central Park East Secondary School," in Michael W. Apple and James A. Beane, eds., *Democratic Schools* (Alexandria, Va.: Association for Supervision and Curriculum Development, 1995), pp. 29–30.
27. See Richard de Charms, *Personal Causation: The Internal Affective Determinants of Behavior* (Hillsdale. N.J.: Erlbaum, 1983). See also the many publications of Edward Deci and Richard Ryan.

28. See, for example, Alfie Kohn, "Choices for Children: Why and How to Let Students Decide," *Phi Delta Kappan,* September 1993, pp. 8–20; and Child Development Project, *Ways We Want Our Class to Be: Class Meetings That Build Commitment to Kindness and Learning* (Oakland. Calif.: Developmental Studies Center, 1996).

29. The quotations are from Wynne, "The Great Tradition," p. 9; and Edward A. Wynne and Herbert J. Walberg, "The Complementary Goals of Character Development and Academic Excellence," *Educational Leadership,* December 1985/January 1986, p. 17. William Kilpatrick is equally averse to including students in decision making; he speaks longingly of the days when "schools were unapologetically authoritarian," declaring that "schools can learn a lot from the Army," which is a "hierarchial [sic], authoritarian, and undemocratic institution" (see *Why Johnny Can't,* p. 228).

30. The sort of compassion I have in mind is akin to what the psychologist Ervin Staub described as a "prosocial orientation" (see his *Positive Social Behavior and Morality,* vols. 1 and 2 [New York: Academic Press, 1978 and 1979])—a generalized inclination to care, share, and help across different situations and with different people, including those we don't know, don't like, and don't look like. Loyally lending a hand to a close friend is one thing; going out of one's way for a stranger is something else.

31. John Dewey, *The School and Society* (Chicago: University of Chicago Press, 1900; reprint, 1990), p. 15.

32. Wynne and Walberg, p. 17. For another endorsement of competition among students, see Kevin Ryan, "In Defense," p. 15.

33. This passage is taken from page 21 of an undated 28-page "Character Education Curriculum" produced by the Character Education Institute. Emphasis in original.

34. Wynne, "Great Tradition," p. 9. Wynne and other figures in the character education movement acknowledge their debt to the French social scientist Emile Durkheim, who believed that "all education is a continuous effort to impose on the child ways of seeing, feeling, and acting which he could not have arrived at spontaneously. . . . We exert pressure upon him in order that he may learn proper consideration for others, respect for customs and conventions, the need for work, etc." (See Durkheim, *The Rules of Sociological Method* (New York: Free Press, 1938], p. 6.)

35. This is from Bennett's introduction to *The Book of Virtues* (New York: Simon & Schuster, 1993), pp. 12–13.

36. Constance Kamii, Faye B. Clark, and Ann Dominick, "The Six National Goals: A Road to Disappointment," *Phi Delta Kappan,* May 1994, p. 677.

37. Kevin Ryan, "Character and Coffee Mugs," *Education Week,* 17 May 1995, p. 48.

38. The second quotation is a reporter's paraphrase of Brooks. Both it and the direct quotation preceding it appear in Philip Cohen, "The Content of Their Character: Educators Find New Ways to Tackle Values and Morality," *ASCD Curriculum Update,* Spring 1995, p. 4.

39. See B. David Brooks, *Young People's Lessons in Character: Student Activity Workbook* (San Diego: Young People's Press, 1996), p. 12.

40. Kilpatrick, p. 231.

41. To advocate this sort of enterprise, he adds, is to "caricature the moral life." See Alan L. Lockwood, "Keeping Them in the Courtyard: A Response to Wynne," *Educational Leadership,* December 1985/January 1986, p. 10.

42. Kilpatrick, p. 97.

43. Personal communication with Ann Medlock, May 1996.

44. John Dewey, *Democracy and Education* (New York: Free Press, 1916; reprint, 1966), p. 11.

45. Bennett, p. 11.

46. Wynne, "Character and Academics," p. 142.

47. For a discussion of how traditional character education fails to offer guidance when values come into conflict, see Lockwood, "Character Education."

48. Rheta DeVries and Betty Zan, *Moral Classrooms, Moral Children: Creating a Constructivist Atmosphere in Early Education* (New York: Teachers College Press, 1994), p. 253.

49. For an argument that critics tend to misrepresent what Values Clarification was about, see James A. Beane, *Affect in the Curriculum* (New York: Teachers College Press, 1990), pp. 104–6.

50. Wynne, for example, refers to the developers of Values Clarification as "popularizers" of Kohlberg's research (see "Character and Academics," p. 141), while Amitai Etzioni, in the course of criticizing Piaget's and Kohlberg's work, asserts that "a typical course on moral reasoning starts with something called 'values clarification'" (see *The Spirit of Community,* p. 98).

51. Kohlberg's model, which holds that people across cultures progress predictably through six stages of successively more sophisticated styles of moral reasoning, is based on the decidedly nonrelativistic premise that the last stages are superior to the first ones. See his *Essays on Moral Development, Vol. 1: The Philosophy of Moral Development* (San Francisco: Harper & Row, 1981), especially the essays titled "Indoctrination Versus Relativity in Value Education" and "From *Is* to *Ought.*"

52. See, for example, James S. Fishkin, *Beyond Subjective Morality* (New Haven, Conn.: Yale University Press, 1984): and David B. Wong, *Moral Relativity* (Berkeley: University of California Press, 1984).

53. Researchers at the National Institute of Mental Health have summarized the available research as follows: "Even children as young as 2 years old have (a) the cognitive capacity to interpret the physical and psychological states of others, (b) the emotional capacity to effectively experience the other's state, and (c) the behavioral repertoire that permits the possibility of trying to alleviate discomfort in others. These are the capabilities that, we believe, underlie children's caring behavior in the presence of another person's distress. . . . Young children seem to show patterns of moral internalization that are not simply fear based or solely responsive to parental commands. Rather, there are signs that children feel responsible for (as well as connected to and dependent on) others at a very young age." (See Carolyn Zahn-Waxler et al., "Development of Concern for Others," *Developmental Psychology,* vol. 28, 1992. pp. 127, 135. For more on the adult's role in light of these facts, see Kohn, *The Brighter Side.*)

54. "Education Secretary Backs Teaching of Religious Values," *New York Times,* 12 November 1985, p. B–4.

55. For more on class meetings, see Glasser, chaps. 10–12: Thomas Gordon, *T.E.T: Teacher Effectiveness Training* (New York: David McKay Co., 1974), chaps. 8–9: Jane Nelsen, Lynn Lott, and H. Stephen Glenn, *Positive Discipline in the Classroom* (Rocklin, Calif.: Prima, 1993); and Child Development Project, op. cit.

56. For more on the theory and research of perspective taking, see Kohn, *The Brighter Side*, chaps. 4–5: for practical classroom activities for promoting perspective-taking skills, see Norma Deitch Feshbach et al., *Learning to Care: Classroom Activities for Social and Affective Development* (Glenview, Ill.: Scott, Foresman, 1983). While specialists in the field distinguish between perspective taking (imagining what others see, think, or feel) and empathy (*feeling* what others feel), most educators who talk about the importance of helping children become empathic really seem to be talking about perspective taking.

57. Wynne, "Great Tradition." p. 9.
58. Kilpatrick, p. 141.
59. It is informative to discover whom the proponents of a hero-based approach to character education themselves regard as heroic. For example, William Bennett's nominee for "possibly our greatest living American" is Rush Limbaugh. (See Terry Eastland, "Rush Limbaugh: Talking Back," *American Spectator,* September 1992, p. 23.)
60. See Victor Battistich et al., "The Child Development Project: A Comprehensive Program for the Development of Prosocial Character," in William M. Kurtines and Jacob L. Gewirtz. eds., *Moral Behavior and Development: Advances in Theory, Research, and Applications* (Hillsdale, N. J.: Erlbaum, 1989): and Daniel Solomon et al., "Creating a Caring Community: Educational Practices That Promote Children's Prosocial Development," in Fritz K. Oser, Andreas Dick, and Jean-Luc Patry, eds., *Effective and Responsible Teaching* (San Francisco: Jossey-Bass, 1992). For more information about the CDP program or about the research substantiating its effects, write the Developmental Studies Center at 2000 Embarcadero, Suite 305, Oakland, CA 94606.

FRAME the DEBATE

Form at end of book

The Character to Seek Justice:
Showing Fairness to Diverse Visions of Character Education

Overall, Alfie Kohn [in Reading 40] fails to address the deeper issues that influence our understanding of morality, Mr. Glanzer maintains.

Perry L. Glanzer

Perry L. Glanzer is an education policy analyst with Focus on the Family, Colorado Springs, Colo.

Dennis Prager, a Jewish author and talk show host in Los Angeles, tells of having asked U.S. high school seniors what they would do if their dog and a stranger were both drowning. In the 15 years that he has been asking the question, two-thirds of the seniors have said they would *not* save the stranger first. He gets different answers at religious schools. Secular students say that they love their dogs but don't even know the stranger. "They have been raised on love as their only value," says Prager. "We religious [people] . . . believe that humans are created in God's image and dogs are not. Therefore, even though I do love my dogs more than strangers—I admit that—I would save a stranger before either of my dogs. That is how I would behave because I have a value system."[1]

Prager tells this story to illustrate the importance of world views when discussing moral questions. His simple tale reveals that students' beliefs about humanity and the world around them will deeply influence how they understand and apply virtues such as love. While educators may believe it is a fairly straightforward task to teach a list of virtues, in fact, it is not. As Warren Nord, a philosopher from the University of North Carolina, points out, character education is influenced by a whole host of other beliefs connected to our world view:

Morality is very much bound up with our identities, with our place in a community or tradition, with our understanding of nature and human nature, with our convictions about the afterlife, with our hopes and our fears, our feelings of guilt, our experiences of the sacred, our assumptions about what the mind can know, and our understanding of what makes life meaningful. We make sense of what we ought to do, of what kind of a person we should be, in light of all of these aspects of life—at least if we are at all reflective.[2]

Character—like music, athletics, crafts, or any other human endeavor—requires rigorous training.

Nord's list includes a number of highly controversial and contentious issues. Sadly, most packaged curricula that I have read and most character education conferences that I have attended avoid such topics, although they are directly connected to character education.

Alfie Kohn's article in the February 1997 *Kappan* brought a refreshing change to the discussion by raising five questions about the world views behind the character education movement.[3] The questions touched upon the level, goals, choices, assumptions about human nature, and theory of learning that influence certain types of character education.

Yet Kohn's analysis disappointed me for a variety of reasons. Some of his criticisms, especially of habit formation, were misdirected or demonstrated some faulty assumptions. Most problematic of all, Kohn merely offered to place another controversial world view behind his own brand of character education program instead of offering a proposal for how justice can be done to the variety of world views that parents and children hold. In what follows, I will outline my disagreements with Kohn's overview of these five basic questions. In addition, I want to suggest some important steps that could be taken by character educators that would help them do justice to the diversity of families in our public schools.

1. At What Level Are Problems Addressed?

According to Kohn, people who think immoral behavior is primarily dependent on "bad values" must also believe "that political and economic realities are irrelevant and need not be addressed."[4] I know of few proponents of character education (in Kohn's narrow sense) who would draw such a sharp distinction. I would actually agree that structural injustices, as well as the character of the people within those structures, should be considered when pursuing moral development. Yet Kohn makes the stronger case that attempts to "fix the kids" (which Kohn equates with teaching children virtuous habits) ignore the evidence from social psychology demonstrating a prior need to fix the kid's environment. Kohn's underemphasis on the child's personal character development is problematic for a couple of reasons.

First, attempts at systemic change will fail if the individuals within the system lack the character to bring about those changes. Kohn suggests that people often lie because they don't feel safe enough to tell the truth. Thus, he concludes, "The real challenge for us as educators is to examine that precept in terms of what is going on in our classrooms, to ask how we and the students together can make sure that even unpleasant truths can be told and heard. . . . Our emphasis should not be on forming individual characters so much as on transforming educational structures."[5] But how do children learn to tell the truth in situations that are not safe? In the adult world, telling the truth to one's boss, principal, or spouse can be downright scary. Children need to develop the moral courage to voice truths or perform other moral behaviors in unsafe environments, especially if they are to participate in the promotion of social justice.

For example, when meaningful changes were being made in the early 1960s to correct racial injustice in the public schools, Robert Coles, a Harvard psychologist, became fascinated by the moral heroism of the children initiating school desegregation efforts. In particular, Ruby Bridges, a 6-year-old African American girl from New Orleans, caught his attention. During the months she walked to school through heckling mobs who spat at her and called her names, Ruby smiled at her antagonists, expressed forgiveness for them, and even prayed for them.[6] I believe that character educators also want children to show the kind of moral heroism that Ruby did—the kind that fosters social change. Children and adults with strong moral character are the ones who will transform unjust systems.

The second problem is that Kohn fails to realize how his world view as a social scientist results in downplaying the importance of a child's exercise of will. In other words, social psychologists often experience their own "fundamental attribution error" because the scientific world view has difficulty attributing anything to the will of an individual. As psychiatrist Jeffrey Satinover has noted:

From a scientific perspective there is never any room whatever for freely acting agents. At best, a given analysis only leaves us with remaining areas for which we have not (yet) discovered, or are (as yet) incapable of discovering, the true, prior causes. It is in the very nature of science and the scientific method that it cannot at all address or understand free agency.[7]

Thus social scientists such as Kohn will rarely attribute a child's moral behavior to the child's will, because they can always find environmental factors to explain it. For this reason, educators should be wary of the deterministic tendencies of social science that can lead to an inadequate view of human nature.

2. What Is the View of Human Nature?

Ironically, Kohn actually argues that it is the character education movement that "seems to be driven by a stunningly dark view of children . . . and of people in general."[8] In contrast, I find most of the character education movement to be fairly optimistic, albeit in the wrong ways. Throughout history, many religious (e.g., Jewish, Christian) and philosophical (e.g., Platonist, Aristotelian) traditions have understood that the development of character requires the rigorous training of the whole being in the same way as athletic or musical development requires extensive training. The power to make good choices and develop good character is aided by this training.

Conversely, one receives the impression from some character education programs and curricula that children need merely to be taught some virtues, exposed to a few posters and pep rallies, and maybe taught to exercise a little discipline to instill particular virtues. This seems like a very optimistic view of human nature. I find little awareness that character—like music, athletics, crafts, or any other human endeavor—requires rigorous training. The optimism of the character education movement is also demonstrated by the fact that one finds little mention in the curricula of evil or vice. While Kohn quotes such writers as William Kilpatrick, Edward Wynne, and Kevin Ryan to prove that the doctrine of original sin lurks behind many character education programs, I cannot seem to find it in most curricula.

Yet Kohn claims that character education proponents, such as Amitai Etzioni and others, share three assumptions that show a dangerous resemblance to the doctrine of original sin: "first, that we are all at war not only with others but with ourselves, torn between our desires and our reason (or social norms); second, that these desires are fundamentally selfish, aggressive, or otherwise unpleasant; and third, that these desires are very strong, constantly threatening to overpower us if we don't rein them in. Collectively, these statements describe religious dogma, not scientific fact."[9]

But Kohn here reveals his own set of three faulty assumptions. First, he assumes that one can make a clear distinction between religious dogma and scientific fact when it comes to views about human nature. In reality, there are a variety of ideological camps within the whole field of psychology, and their understandings of human nature contain a mixture of theory and fact.

Second, Kohn makes some faulty generalizations about religion or at least a faulty assumption about Christian beliefs. The religious beliefs that Kohn describes are closer to Buddhist doctrine than to historical Christian teaching, such as that of St. Augustine. While Buddhism claims that suffering comes from desire and that desires should be eliminated, Christian theologians who wrote about original sin, such as Augustine, claimed that one's reason and will should direct one's desires to the right end. Desires such as love are good, but to direct one's love toward the wrong being or object is not a virtue, but a vice.[10] In Augustine's view, the love of money is greed, all-consuming romantic love is lust, and the inordinate love of a sports team or of one's career would be idolatry.

Third, Kohn seems to assume that one can equate "the bleak world view of Thomas Hobbes" with a Judeo-Christian view of human nature. But for Jews and Christians, children are made in the image of God, and in truth, it would be natural (i.e., the way humans were created) for children's desires to be rightly ordered and directed. Thus a Christian theologian such as St. Augustine would agree with Kohn that children's naturally good desires should be unleashed—in the right direction. Hopefully, Kohn also believes that good desires for things such as sex should be channeled in morally appropriate ways. The belief that humans are "fallen" does not discount children's potential to direct their desires in the right direction, but it acknowledges the gap that they and we as adults experience between what we want to be and what we do. Kohn may find his perspective has more in common with a Judeo-Christian world view, rightly understood, than he realizes. What would help Kohn—and students—is an accurate understanding of the various world views that underlie the psychological, philosophical, and theological views of human nature.

3 and 4. What Is the Ultimate Goal? Which Values?

Kohn argues that proponents of character education have a "profoundly conservative, if not reactionary, agenda" that has the ultimate goal of ensuring social stability or social order.[11] He doubts that this agenda would cohere with other objectives such as helping students become advocates for social justice. At this point, I find Kohn's point re-

markably refreshing, albeit for different reasons. In his book *After Virtue*, philosopher Alasdair MacIntyre argues that the virtues a community prizes and teaches are related to what that community believes is the human "telos" or end.[12] This connection between the goal of character educators and the virtues they want to instill is striking. Educators and most character education programs serve a political vision, either liberal or conservative, that is justified by appealing to the preservation of democracy. To achieve this end, conservatives, as Kohn notes, want schools to promote such virtues as patriotism, hard work, and citizenship. In contrast, liberals, such as Kohn, desire educators to teach skepticism and tolerance. Yet the important point is that all these virtues serve an end, a moral vision of what is good for the American community. In studying character education in the former Soviet Union, I have found that Soviet educators in a similar manner taught children to love the motherland, to be patriotic, and to work hard, for the obvious reason that these virtues would help build communism.[13]

Religious parents are understandably suspicious of systems of morality that are justified on such pragmatic grounds and that reflect political visions. For instance, Christian parents do not want their children to learn virtue merely to help democracy keep idling along (although it is a beneficial side effect). They pray for them to imitate Christ in the same way that Ruby Bridges did. Of course, Christians should not expect public schools to inculcate *uniquely* Christian virtues. Thus they should not find it surprising that few character education programs teach such virtues as forgiveness, faith, or love for one's enemies.

However, Christian parents—all parents, for that matter—have the right to expect character education programs to do justice to their particular world view. Kohn is right; virtues serve certain ends. Yet the answer is not to promote Kohn's ends or Kohn's list of virtues. Instead, the various ends and virtues should be openly discussed and agreed upon by the families in the community. Furthermore, ways should be sought to do justice to these various world views.

5. What Is the Theory of Learning?

According to Kohn, the character educators he describes see children as "so many passive receptacles to be filled, lumps of clay to be molded, pets to be trained, or computers to be programmed." As a result, their methods of learning treat children as "objects to be manipulated rather than as learners to be engaged." Actually, I share much of Kohn's concern about the methods as he characterizes them. Educators' methods of character education should leave children "with a *commitment* to that behavior, a reason to continue acting that way in the future."[14] That being said, I still am troubled by parts of Kohn's argument. Kohn not only criticizes the methods used in character education, but also the very importance of developing habits of character. He writes:

When education is construed as the process of inculcating *habits*—which is to say, unreflection actions—then it scarcely deserves to be called education at all. It is really . . . an attempt to get "mindless conformity to externally imposed standards of conduct."[15]

Apparently, Kohn believes that the development of moral habits is only important for those with an overly pessimistic view of human nature. Yet one does not have to be a cynic about human nature to acknowledge that children must learn good habits. Kohn fails to differentiate between human capacity and development. While most humans are born with the natural capacity to compete in a sport, play an instrument, or perform surgery, they still must develop these capacities (hitting a curve ball, finding certain chords, or accurately cutting human tissue) in order to become skilled in these practices. In the same way, moral growth still requires that children acquire certain habits of behavior.

Moreover, it is difficult for athletes, musicians, or surgeons to come through under pressure without this extensive training of their whole being. Similarly, in our moral lives we cannot think long and critically about every action. Most of our behavior stems from habit. It is those habits of behavior that we need to develop if we are to sustain our moral lives in the flurry of life.[16]

Of course, unlike the development of specific skills for certain vocations, society should expect and encourage all children to develop good moral habits. Yet this does not mean that habit formation encouraged by character educators must necessarily become "mindless conformity to externally imposed standards of conduct." Educators can still encourage children to develop an internal commitment to developing habits of character, just as the majority of athletes and musicians choose to subject themselves to grueling training to develop certain habits. Yes, children should be taught to think critically about their habits and to develop an internal commitment to good ones, but that does not lessen their need to form virtuous habits.

Overall, Alfie Kohn fails to address the deeper issues that influence our understanding of morality. To help children become the critical thinkers that Kohn wants, these issues must be addressed. Instead, he appears satisfied to substitute an approach to character education that rests on social psychology, liberalism, and naturalistic philosophy (of the pragmatic variety) for one that he claims rests upon "behaviorism, conservatism, and religion (i.e., of the conservative Catholic variety]." Yet par-

ents and children, whom the education system should serve above all, are likely to have world views that combine aspects of these views and many others. How can public schools do justice to the variety of world views their students represent? Kohn never addresses this absolutely essential moral question—the one that should be asked from the very beginning.

In closing, I would like to offer a couple of suggestions for creating a just approach to character education. First, the diversity of families within a school district must be considered. Any approach to character education must do justice to the variety of world views represented. Public schools are designed to serve a diverse range of families, and character education should be no exception. Second, character education programs, especially at the elementary level, should attempt to instill commonly agreed upon virtues or habits of behavior. Children need them, and cross-cultural and psychological studies have affirmed that agreement on these matters does exist.[17]

Third, in developing character education programs and curricula, especially at the secondary level, writers or educators should give serious consideration to how students will discuss important underlying questions. Why should we develop virtue? In what ways should these virtues be shown? How will character education address the reality of moral failure? What will motivate or empower us to attain these virtues? Furthermore, educators must allow children to *discuss* and *explore* the variety of answers that are offered, even if they are *religious* answers. Charles Haynes, a leading authority on religion and the public schools, comments on the significance of this issue:

Character education can be hollow and misleading when taught within a curriculum that is silent about religion. When religion is largely ignored, students get the false and dangerous message that religious ideas and practices are insignificant for human experience.[18]

Teachers could aid this process by creating a community of inquiry that allows deeper philosophical and religious issues to be discussed.

Sadly, I have seen few character education programs that actually address the issue of world views.[19] Yet I believe that greater dialogue with philosophical and theological traditions of ethical thought could inform such perspectives as Kohn's, those of many other educators, and those of students themselves. In this way, they would be forced to wrestle with the deeper questions that relate to differing world views. All in all, this approach strikes a balance between two enduring tensions facing character education. Communities must inculcate virtuous habits in their young, yet they must also be open to having their visions of virtue critiqued and examined. When children—or even psychologists—are allowed to explore various perspectives, sometimes the truth of their discoveries can pierce through their own world view. Interestingly, Robert Coles, a refreshingly honest psychologist, traced the moral heroism of Ruby Bridges and others like her not to some psychological theory, but to the religious beliefs and behavior of their parents. He wrote:

I have tried to comprehend [the moral courage of children such as Ruby]—with little luck, as far as psychiatric characterization goes. If I had to offer an explanation, though, I think it would start with the religious tradition of black people. . . . In home after home I have seen Christ's teachings, Christ's life, connected to the lives of black children by their parents.[20]

Could we learn something from these parents' lives and world views about how to teach our children values?

Notes

1. Dennis Prager and Jonathan Glover, "Can We Be Good Without God? A Debate Between Dennis Prager and Jonathan Glover at Oxford University." *Ultimate Issues,* vol. 9, 1993, p. 13.

2. Warren A. Nord, *Religion and American Education: Rethinking a National Dilemma* (Chapel Hill: University of North Carolina Press, 1995), p. 341.

3. Alfie Kohn, "How Not to Teach Values: A Critical Look at Character Education," *Phi Delta Kappan,* February 1997, pp. 428–439.

4. Ibid., p. 430.

5. Ibid, p. 437.

6. Robert Coles, *The Moral Life of Children* (Boston: Houghton Mifflin, 1986), pp. 22–23.

7. Jeffrey Burkes Satinover, "Psychology and the Abolition of Meaning," *First Things,* February 1994, p. 15.

8. Kohn, p. 431.

9. Ibid.

10. Augustine, "On the Morals of the Catholic Church," in Waldo Beach and H. R. Niebuhr, eds., *Christian Ethics: Sources of the Living Tradition* (New York: Ronald Press Company, 1955), pp. 110–18.

11. Kohn, pp. 431–32.

12. Alasdair MacIntrye, *After Virtue,* rev. ed. (Notre Dame, Ind.: University of Notre Dame Press, 1984).

13. See George Avis, ed., *The Making of the Soviet Citizen: Character Formation and Civic Training in Soviet Education* (London: Croom Helm, 1987); and Abraham Kreusler, *Contemporary Education and Moral Upbringing in the Soviet Union* (Ann Arbor, Mich.: University Microfilms International, 1976).

14. Kohn, p. 435.

15. Ibid., p. 434.

16. For a discussion of this subject, see Dallas Willard, *The Spirit of the Disciplines* (San Francisco: Harper San Francisco, 1988).

17. See C. S. Lewis, *The Abolition of Man: How Education Develops Man's Sense of Morality* (New York: MacMillan, 1947): and Larry Nucci, "Children's Conceptions of Morality, Societal Convention, and Religious Prescription," in Carol Harding, ed., *Moral Dilemmas: Philosophical and Psychological Issues in the Development of Moral Reasoning* (Chicago: Precedent Press, 1985).

18. Charles Haynes, "Character Education in the Public Schools," in idem and Oliver Thomas, eds., *Finding Common Ground* (Nashville: Freedom Forum First Amendment Center, 1994), chap. 14, p. 2.

19. One teacher-training program that seriously considers the issue of world views is offered by Children of the World, 910 Calle Neocio, Suite 300, San Clemente, CA 92673.

20. Coles, p. 34.

Form at end of book

Keeping in Character:
A Time-Tested Solution

The positive outcomes of for-character education, the authors contend, counter such misleading pictures as the one sketched by Alfie Kohn in his February *Kappan* article [Reading 40].

Jacques S. Benninga and Edward A. Wynne

Jacques S. Benninga is a professor of education and director of the Bonner Center for Character Education and Citizenship at California State University, Fresno. Edward A. Wynne is a professor of education at the University of Illinois, Chicago, and editor of the For-Character Education Web Page (www.uic.edu/~edaw/main.html).

In the February 1997 *Kappan*, Alfie Kohn attacked modern character education for a myriad of alleged deficiencies. This essay constitutes our response to his criticisms. The basic structure of true "for-character" education relies on an approach that

- is relevant for students of all ages;

- has been time-tested and refined over 2,500 years;

- is as responsive to today's children as it was to yesterday's;

- has broad support among American citizens, including teachers and students; and

- has a research base to justify its continuation.

Increasing Disorder

Before we turn to particulars, it is important for readers to understand exactly why we and so many other American adults are worried about the character of the nation's youth. It is not, as Kohn implies, because we dislike young people. Instead it is because we love them and want them to stop killing and abusing themselves and one another at record rates.

Statistics document the record-breaking rates of distress afflicting young Americans and form an essential backdrop for any discussion of for-character practices. The annual rates of death of young (15- to 19-year-old) white males by homicide and suicide are at their highest points since national record-keeping began in 1914.[1] The rates of out-of-wedlock births to young (15- to 19-year-old) white females are also at or near their highest points since national record-keeping began in 1936. What's more, these high rates have occurred during an era of generally more accessible contraception, abortion, and sex education. All these indicators focus on whites—members of our most advantaged group. This suggests that the "causes" for the bulk of the disorder only incidentally involve poverty and race.

Any for-character school or classroom will include a number of for-character activities.

As if we needed any more bad news, the Centers for Disease Control released an important report in February 1997. That report found that "nearly three-quarters of all the murders of children in the industrialized world occur in the United States" and that the U.S. has the "highest rates of childhood homicide, suicide, and firearms-related deaths of any of the world's 26 richest nations."[2]

All these relatively precise measures of disorder indirectly measure many other uncountable forms of profound despair, injury, and wrong-doing that affect the young.

- Most murders of young persons are committed by young murderers.

- Every identified young death by homicide undoubtedly subsumes many other less violent crimes, such as battery, woundings, and beatings.

- Out-of-wedlock births are also indices of victimization of vulnerable females by males or of risky acts of promiscuity.

- The suicides are also indicators of previously attempted suicides and other symptoms of deep depression.

High school students themselves are very well situated to see what is happening among their peers. They clearly recognize that many deeply flawed contemporary education policies have enmeshed our young in a disorderly, low-demand world—a world in which too many adults confuse being caring with being permissive. Recent evidence from a national sample of high school students shows that 50% of the respondents said that "schools fail to challenge pupils to do their best," 71% said that there were "too many disruptive students," 79% said that learning would improve if "schools ensured students got their work done on time and completed their assignments," 86% said that schools should teach students the value of "hard work," 71% would require after-school classes for students who get D's and F's in major subjects, 73% said requiring exit tests before graduation would cause students to learn more, and 50% said that "too many students get away with being late to class or not doing their work."[3] As we will show, these student opinions are quite congruent with the for-character approach.

Some Qualifications

We have both done considerable research and writing on issues involving student character. For instance, each of us, acting separately and with the help of local educators, has organized school recognition programs, one in the Chicago area and the other in the Fresno area. These programs identify elementary and secondary schools that maintain exemplary character formation policies and curricula. Over 13 yearly cycles, approximately 400 elementary, middle, and secondary schools have participated in these programs. Thus we have examined a variety of good, bad, and indifferent for-character activities. From that base, after some important background information, we will assess Kohn's key contentions.

One other qualification should be expressed. Many of Kohn's criticisms are essentially aimed at the ambitious claims made for packaged character education curricula. We and many leading figures in the character education movement are not sanguine about expecting notable results from any such quick-fix approach.[4] However, well-conceived packages may be useful if they are part of a holistic school- or classroom-wide for-character approach. Indeed, it is to express our distance from quick-fix activities that we use the phrase "for-character education" rather than the more common "character education." Such use stresses the need to integrate for-character elements into many typical school activities. Thus there can be for-character policies, for-character cocurricular activities, and even for-character lunchroom policies. To further stress the issue of systematically planning for-character activities, one of the authors even published a list of 100 for-character activities that can be used in and around schools.[5] Though 100 is not a sacred number, the point is that any for-character school or classroom will include a number of for-character activities, most of which will be integrated into its day-to-day operations.

Character and For-Character Education

The word *character* derives from the Greek word "to mark" or "to engrave" and is associated with the writings of philosophers such as Plato and Aristotle. People with good character habitually display good behavior, and these people are known by their behavior. Thus a generous person may be seen giving notable gifts, or a brave person may perform heroic acts. A courteous person behaves properly and with civility toward others.

There may be no specific consensus on a list of desirable character traits or habits. But considerable agreement exists on the desirable virtues—moral qualities regarded as good or meritorious—that underlie these traits. Throughout history thoughtful philosophers and educators have been concerned about the cultivation of such virtues as honesty, kindness, courage, perseverance, and loyalty and about the cultivation of their concomitant traits. The renewed interest in such virtues is evident in the huge success of *The Book of Virtues,* by William Bennett. The book is a collection of inspiring classic literature for children and adults. It addresses 10 particular virtues. In recent years, we have also witnessed the publication of a spate of nonsectarian character-oriented books by psychologists, educators, and distinguished scholars.[6]

The consensus is that traits—and, to some degree, virtues—are not innate. They must be acquired through learning and practice in homes, schools, neighborhoods, churches, and other agencies. They must be transmitted to be internalized. However, a child's state of mind *is* relevant to this process. That is, for-character educators do not advocate having children behave solely according to a set of principles or rules without understanding them. Rather, for-character educators agree with William Frankena, who proposed that "we regard the morality of principles and the morality of traits of character, or being and doing, not as rival kinds of morality between which we must choose, but as two complimentary aspects of the same morality."[7]

The character tradition stresses the importance of whole environments operating systematically to foster good character formation. But environments mean not only the physical elements surrounding students, but also the people surrounding them, the good or bad examples they provide, and the expectations they establish. Profound character education involves managing classrooms or whole schools so that they will advance student character.

Here is where Alfie Kohn missed the mark. His criticisms extend far beyond the defects of relying solely on packages. He takes offense because for-character educators have developed a perspective, a "particular style of moral training." And it is true that there are good and bad ways to teach character. Kohn then proposes his alternative to character education. Let us, in his words, get straight to the educational point. His alternative is a set of various approaches that we have met before, collected under the umbrella of developmental education. The umbrella currently includes such panaceas as the whole-language approach, constructivism, and, most recently, democratic education. These approaches have already been tried in our own era, without generating either "good people" or notable academic learning.[8]

True, the policies have attractive labels. But such labels are deceptive. Who, for example, could be against democratic education? Yet such ambitious labels are riddled with inconsistencies that foreclose careful analysis. For example, many educators now favor emotive terminology, such as "educating for democracy," without being able to define or evaluate the policies advocated to advance such ends. Various notions, such as self-esteem education and inclusion, are now contained in the "democratic education" package. Few of these programs have undergone rigorous evaluation to determine their effects, and, when they have been evaluated, the results often fail to support their ambitious claims.

But that doesn't seem to matter to some. In the words of educational theorist Amy Guttman, democratic education "commits us to accepting nondiscriminatory and nonrepressive policies as legitimate even when they are wrong."[9] Even when such practices lead to lower academic achievement, she states, they are necessary to advance the "virtues of citizenship," and even when student participation threatens to produce disorder within schools, it may be defended on "democratic grounds."[10]

These conceptions of democracy are probably not what America's founders had in mind two centuries ago, but they seem to be exactly what Alfie Kohn believes. That is, he wants us to engage elementary school children in "deep, critical reflection about certain ways of being"; to teach reflection over diligence, respect, patriotism, and responsibility; to teach self-determination and skepticism over self-control and obedience. He does not suggest where skepticism should begin or end. Still, he is at least skeptical about patriotism: he compares the Pledge of Allegiance to the Flag to a form of "loyalty oath to the Fatherland" (with its obvious Nazi overtones). It would seem consistent with such cynicism to approve as well of 10-year-olds' skepticism toward their parents, although wiser students may choose to reserve their skepticism for persons who recommend such questionable doctrines.

The Five Questions

Kohn poses five basic questions that might be asked of character education programs. In answer to the first question— "At what level are problems addressed?"—

Kohn reiterates the liberal argument that crime and urban decay are political outcomes of unemployment and the consolidation of great wealth in the hands of the few. These "bad things" are the cause of any character problems our young people might have. In other words, "It's all someone else's fault!" Our reply is brief, since we are neither criminologists nor economists—but neither, we believe, is Kohn.

- The data we have already cited on steadily rising youth disorder dealt just with whites. Presumably, such a group, even though afflicted with disorder, is not composed of poor inner-city residents.

- The long-term economic trends affecting most young white Americans involve economic improvements over their parents. Our college students, when we ask them for a show of hands on such matters, usually agree that they will be better off than their parents regarding such things as length of education, quality of housing, length of life span, and quality of health. It appears that the long-term increase in disorder is not caused by the spread of grinding poverty.

- The causal connection, if any, between crime and personal income is actually hotly debated. As James Wilson and Richard Hermstein have emphasized, the overall statistical relationship between crime and the unemployment rate is not very strong.[11] Though many criminals may be poorly educated and are often unemployed, the factors underlying the development of the criminal personality are more complicated.

View of Human Nature

Next, Kohn addresses for-character's view of human nature. And surprise, the for-character educators do not see everything as sweetness and roses. "Fix-the-kids," say prominent for-character educators, who take a "dim view of human nature" (William Kilpatrick), who hold a "pessimistic view of human nature" (Edward Wynne), who say that "children are self-centered" (Kevin Ryan), and who seek to "control [children's] impulses and defer [their] gratification" (Amitai Etzioni).

Kohn is absolutely right! We are horrified and distressed at the harm so many young people are doing to themselves and to one another. We also desperately want to change the destructive conduct of many young people—to protect them and their possible victims. As for being anti-youth, our opinions and prescriptions are generally similar to those approved by young people themselves, as reported in the national high school student poll quoted near the beginning of this article. Are the students also anti-youth?

If modern for-character educators are not utopian in their attitudes toward children, they certainly are not alone. In a recent national survey of American adults, 72% of the respondents said there was an excess of "drugs and violence in their local schools." When the responses were broken down by race, the comparable figures were 58% (whites) and 80% (blacks).[12] Are the blacks who think there's too much violence in their children's schools also anti-youth?

There are important historic precedents for our current concerns. Many of history's best minds have realized that most children and adults don't naturally set about "doing good for intrinsic reasons," as Kohn would suggest. A revealing dialogue from Plato's *Republic* (Book II) is instructive. Glaucon, a character in *The Republic,* maintains in a discussion with Socrates that it is natural for people to pursue their own interests despite the needs of others or the need for an orderly society. As evidence, Glaucon tells the story of Gyges, an otherwise rather decent shepherd. Gyges found a magic ring that enabled him to become invisible. The result? Gyges "seduced the queen and with her help attacked and murdered the king and seized the throne."[13] Of course, the tale of Gyges is a story—all made up. However, does anyone doubt the psychological truth of the ring story? When people receive uncontrolled power, there is a real possibility that they will abuse it. Or, as James Madison put it, "If men were angels, no government would be necessary."

Similarly, Horace Mann, the founder of public education in the U.S., believed that "moral education is a primal necessity of social existence. The unrestrained passions of men are not only homicidal, but suicidal."[14] But contrary to what Kohn would surmise, Mann hoped to form a literate, diligent, productive, and responsible citizenry committed to the conception that the best society was one in which people governed themselves through elected officials and representative institutions. Both Aristotle and Plato advocated a curriculum of music, literature, mathematics, and gymnastics that would result in a "well-balanced and harmonious character."

It would certainly be wrong to characterize these men or the contemporary for-character educators mentioned by Kohn as promoting a totalitarian educational agenda based on their conceptions of an unschooled human nature. To the contrary, it seems more reasonable to conclude that the current for-character perspective represents the collective and rather consistent perspective of the best minds of the past 2,500 years. Such a conclusion seems more promising than the utopian, New Age perspective proposed by Kohn.

Furthermore, the Founders of our nation, from their extensive reading of history, concluded that the greatest threat to democracy was the danger of tyranny that might evolve from the failure of powerful men to meet their civic responsibilities. To prevent such destructive patterns, citizens had to possess such virtues as self-discipline, responsibility, and prudence. Lacking such virtuous citizens, any democracy would gradually decay into a morass of selfishness and jealousy.

John Adams and his wife Abigail exemplified this "republican virtue" in their role as parents. Adams, absent for long periods from his family, wrote to his wife, "Train [our children] to virtue. Habituate them to industry, activity, and spirit."[15] Similarly, George Washington compiled and learned early a set of 110 "Rules of Civility and Decent Behavior in Company and Conversation," which thereafter governed his private behavior and tempered his impulsiveness.[16] The models left us by these men are still worth emulating.

Rather than holding a dark, bleak vision of human nature, these leaders had purpose and courage in the face of danger and suffering. They were indifferent to material circumstances and believed that their legacies would consist of the good and virtuous lives they lived. It is understandable that some citizens in our hedonistic and pedestrian era (What is the going price for a night in Lincoln's bed?) have trouble interpreting their heroic stoicism. Still, we owe it to our young people to try and hold high models up before them. Kohn has missed the point here.

The Ultimate Goal

Kohn next attacks for-character educators for their "profoundly conservative, if not reactionary, agenda." Rather than teach the virtuous life, he wants educators to train children as "advocates for social justice." Rather than set standards for behavior, he wants educators to promote skepticism in children. Rather than, as Aristotle suggested, "learning that there are things which one is expected to do even when all concerned are aware that one does not feel like doing them . . . [and] that there are things worth doing and aiming for which are not immediately pleasant,"[17] Kohn wants us to emphasize "the cultivation of autonomy so that children come to experience themselves as 'origins' rather, than 'pawns.' " Thus children should be allowed to participate "in making decisions about their learning and about how they want their classroom to be." We should, Kohn states, stress compassion over loyalty, cooperation over competition. autonomy over punctuality, self-determination over self-control. In truth, those of us concerned with the formation of character engage in no such dichotomous thinking. We want to develop all the virtues.

But children cannot be treated like miniature adults. Nowhere is this issue better exemplified than in recent public service television spots for the United Negro College Fund. In these brief ads, small children are pictured piloting advanced aircraft, sitting behind corporate desks, and teaching, in a university classroom, while the announcer suggests: "A mind is a terrible thing to waste." The point behind these gripping presentations is clear: children are only *potentially* capable of doing the jobs suggested by the images. They are certainly not ready in the early stages of life for the responsibilities that are inherent in adult positions. They need encouragement and training to realize their potential. Their minds are not those of adults. As both Piaget and Kohlberg have shown us, they are not miniature versions of what they will become. Rather, they are, as we now know, thinkers of a qualitatively different kind from the thinkers we hope they will become. This point seems to have been overlooked by Kohn, who seems to believe that by defining the best outcomes for adults we can infer direct implications for classrooms of children. This is just not so.

Allowing students too much freedom to "cultivate autonomy" and too much freedom to "make decisions about their learning" can be detrimental. Three quick examples may suffice to make this obvious point.

- A *New York Times* article (independently verified by one of the authors) told of one "democracy first" public high school in which a discussion took place among the students and teachers—the whole school community—about whether the students should be allowed to bring knives and to have sex on a school picnic. (They eventually voted the proposal down.)[18]

- Robert Howard described an elementary school classroom in which the students, with their classroom teacher's approval, decided that a student who was guilty of spitting on a classmate was to be punished by standing in the middle of his classmates who would each, in turn, spit on the offender. (A more experienced teacher intervened and stopped the punishment.)[19]

- Timothy Lensmire invited the students in his third-grade writing project to insert the names of fellow pupils in the stories they composed. He wrote a book on the project and its outcomes. The young authors discovered that using the names of classmates gave them the power to embarrass and shame their peers. Some students so named became very upset. Eventually, Lensmire was distressed about the pain and selfishness his innovation was generating, but—like Hamlet—he could not decide what to do. Fortunately, the principal stepped in and ended the project. Lensmire's book was sympathetically reviewed in an academic journal.[20] The reviewer disapproved of the principal's intrusion,

calling it "institutionalized violence," and commented that, if the project had continued, Lensmire could have transformed his classroom into a court and could have had his writers and injured students hold an in-class lawsuit over the conflict—that is, if someone did not beat up someone else first.

These activities bear some vague, though distorted and uninformed, resemblance to our republican form of government. We say "distorted" because they involve so little accountability for the misuse of student power. Nothing happens to authors who recklessly hurt other students' feelings. As for the picnic, if the "no knives and no sex" resolution had failed, would the students have been collectively liable for any harmful—or deadly—results? These are just the sort of in-school activities that cultivate poor character in students. Though we feel such activities are comparatively rare in our schools, we believe many readers will be able to identify less dramatic examples of similar tendencies.

What For-Character Educators Want

So what do for-character educators want? What is our ultimate goal? Simply stated, we want children and adolescents to learn to feel a sense of belonging to and responsibility for others. This goal and its rationale come from the work of Emile Durkheim almost 100 years ago. In Durkheim's view, morality and religion, the *collective conscience* as he called them, are the cohesive bonds that hold the social order together. A breakdown of these values, he believed, would lead to social instability and individual feelings of anxiety and dissatisfaction, sometimes resulting in depression, suicide, and other forms of disorder.

Durkheim exhaustively studied the topic of suicide.[21] He concluded that it—and by extension other types of youth disorder—was largely caused by the affliction of not being immediately needed. Suicide was not particularly related to poverty or to evident social injustice. Instead, people with simple, proximate obligations to others (e.g., mothers, manual laborers, teachers) tended to choose to live through the inevitable "slings and arrows of outrageous fortune." They rejected suicide because it was a betrayal of those immediate obligations. (Who will feed the chickens? Who will change the baby's diapers?) These notions are certainly generalizable. Conversely, people with abstract and unclear obligations to others are much more prone to suicide. Young people, especially in our country and in our era, are one class with very remote and vague obligations to others.

Recent sociological studies have reached conclusions generally congruent with Durkheim's broad propositions.[22] One of the authors once examined records of adolescents who had committed suicide. One pitiful file told of a boy whose last act before committing suicide was to kill his beloved dog. Once the ties of responsibility were destroyed, the boy no longer had any obligation to endure the typical buffets of life. In effect, we are often saved by our obligations to others.

Durkheim's theory implies that the young are ignored, unwanted, and lacking in serious responsibilities. The solution involves creating more structured and intense responsibilities. Thus he implies that being extremely permissive toward the young makes things worse. When people are really important to us, we surround their conduct with many forms of constraint and their misconduct with notable and fast consequences. We demand that the surgeon who will cut us open first wash his or her hands. When we go to an expensive restaurant for a fine meal, we want the waiter to display a little style. When we're playing a sport to win, we want our teammates to go all out. We put people who are really important to us under pressure, and so they feel important.

But too many of today's young people are rarely expected to help support their families, nor are they called on to carry out demanding household chores. Instead, their most typical characteristic is that they are often not very much needed by anyone else. They are ignored. Their roles are largely ornamental. If many of them died, the day-to-day work of the world would continue for the immediate future. People given such freedom can find themselves bored and tempted toward irresponsible and dangerous behavior. The traditional character prescription still applies: "For Satan finds some mischief still for idle hands to do."

We believe that children need age-appropriate but significant responsibilities, in order to feel socially integrated and respected. Adults with authority (i.e., parents, teachers, coaches) should feel comfortable disciplining youngsters who fail to carry out those significant duties. It is, furthermore, the responsibility of adults to critically examine children's and adolescents' social environments and to design and manage them so those environments help our young people grow into mature and moral adults.

These intuitions, based on our collective research, are corroborated by findings about what works with regard to for-character education. Activities in which students assume responsibility (including the acceptance of authority and consequences) for their own learning and behavior and the learning and behavior of others "will result in positive changes in selected prosocial character traits." Moreover, "classroom and school climates that embody such factors as clear standards, mutual respect between students and teachers, and shared governance have been found to be associated with some limited, but nonetheless important, positive changes in student character."[23]

Which Values?

In his fourth question, Kohn wonders, "Which values" should we teach? We agree with him that "whether or not we deliberately adopt a character or moral education program, we are always teaching values." We would say, more precisely, we are always teaching virtues. But which virtues? Though Kohn agrees with the teaching of non-controversial virtues, such as fairness or honesty, he objects to such "conservative" and "potentially controversial" guidelines as "work hard and complete your tasks." Here again, Kohn rebukes for-character educators for sneaking in their propagandistic biases—e.g., the Protestant work ethic or obedience. He would prefer that we teach empathy and skepticism.

The for-character tradition recognizes that no single virtue should always dominate, although the virtues are systematically related to form a unity of perspective. Virtuous people we know or read about and admire—e.g., George Washington, Martin Luther King, Mother Teresa—all possessed a measure of the Socratic virtues: wisdom, temperance, justice, and courage. A certain well-roundedness is desirable, and an excess in any one virtue can lead to imbalances. For example, the fictional Hamlet was reflective and loyal, but indecisive. Richard Nixon was diligent and far-sighted, but also vindictive.

A certain well-roundedness is desirable, and an excess in any one virtue can lead to imbalances.

We do not feel qualified to strongly recommend any particular mix of values to educators or parents. We are far more concerned with the openness of the decision-making process, realizing that conflicts do occur over moral priorities. Since their inception American public schools have successfully and regularly resolved conflicts over what should be taught. Such disputes are the day-to-day routines of our democratic processes. Differences are scrutinized, pros and cons are subjected to public debate, compromises are negotiated, and votes are cast.

There are, of course, many sources that offer specific answers to the question of which virtues we should teach. One such set is embodied in the principles laid out in the U.S. Constitution, the Bill of Rights, and other founding documents (e.g., justice, the rights and responsibilities of citizenship, freedom of the press, freedom of religion, and so on). Another set of answers is the common core of virtues alluded to throughout this article: honesty, love, compassion, duty, respect, responsibility, diligence, and so on. A third set of answers can be found in the growing number of communities that have adopted common core virtues for their own children. Yet another set of answers can be found in the six pillars growing out of the Aspen Declaration of 1992: caring, civic virtue and citizenship, justice and fairness, respect, responsibility, and trustworthiness. Since America is the world's most religious industrialized country, it would be incongruous if some of that tradition did not influence the setting of priorities with regard to virtue. This might touch on such matters as chastity, the sanctity of marriage, honoring one's parents or others in authority, or displaying charity. The list goes on.

What Is Our Theory of Learning?

The pedagogical principles we advocate are simple and direct.

- Identify and list the virtues and relevant behavior traits one hopes children will learn. (There are a variety of virtues to choose from and a variety of sources for those virtues.)

- Establish those identified virtues or traits as goals for students and the faculty.

- Provide occasions for students, either individually or as part of well-designed groups, to practice the behaviors associated with such traits or virtues.

- Praise students, either individually or as a group—publicly or privately—when desirable behavior, consistent with expectations, is displayed.

- Identify undesirable traits and prohibit them. Publicize and justify such prohibitions, and establish and enforce clear, unpleasant, and appropriate consequences for such misbehavior by individuals or groups.

- Use the school's formal curriculum and ceremonies to support such activities.

- Hire, train, and retain staff members who actively support such policies.[24]

Kohn characterizes this approach as nothing more than "exhortation and directed recitation . . . teaching as a matter of telling and compelling." Teachers in for-character classrooms, he states, are encouraged to engage in a variety of measures to get students to conform: praising children who respond correctly, prohibiting wrongdoing, and inculcating habits such as perseverance, delay of gratification, and self-control. He's correct. But this approach is far more than simplistic "exhortation." We believe that straightforward tactics will improve academic and for-character learning and help save students' lives.

As to for-character vocabulary, we intend such words as *instill in, transmit to,* and *habit formation* to describe the process of character development and mature moral deci-

sion making. These are, however, not our words. They are the words of Plato and Aristotle, of Kant and Piaget. They are the collective knowledge of our best minds over time.

So how do schools best help shape the character of the young? Our answer is clear. Effective schools share the same systemic characteristics researchers have observed in highly effective parents.[25] Similarly, less-effective schools share characteristics of less-effective, laissez-faire parents. That is, well-grounded teachers and schools set high expectations and nourish children's earned sense of competence and self-reliance. They rely on extrinsic control, clarity, consistency, nurture and honesty of communication to shape their students' character. They are primarily concerned for the well-being of the children. We believe that schools with these characteristics are more likely to graduate students who are accomplished academically and who demonstrate the habits and character traits that lead to productive citizenship. We believe that this is what good schools have always been about.

The Bog of Intrinsic Motivation

Kohn strongly opposes all measures that involve incentives, since they rely on external motivation. His position is, in effect, that, as long as such constraints are applied, students will not be free. That is, they will not practice learning for intrinsic reasons. The matter can be put in a more critical way: Kohn is less interested in stimulating students toward excellence in academics or character formation than many other educators. His case requires him to find strong evidence that recognition, praise, and other earned rewards do not habituate people to be kind, honest, or diligent. In other words, well-deserved praise does not encourage people to make a habit of their praised conduct. This is a rather fantastic position, countered by recent research and everyday experience.[26]

Allow us to provide just one instance of such everyday experience of the deep power of extrinsic motivation over learning. As part of a study of a typical suburban high school, one of the authors identified various systems to motivate learning that were used in that school. Each system was accompanied by its own unique intrinsic and extrinsic rewards. The most powerful and effective learning systems were associated with interscholastic competitive team athletics.

This "discovery" simply represents the researcher's having stumbled into a widely recognized pattern. In many schools, a great deal of attention is given to athletics. Much of this attention consists of public praise, publicity, and other forms of conspicuous display. The point so often forgotten, though, is that such extrinsic motivation systems work very well! Student athletes work long and hard to learn how to improve their skills, and often they succeed. The members of the swimming team, for example, practiced arduously for four hours a day over the 20-day Christmas vacation. And when the members of the girls' varsity volleyball team returned to school in the fall, their coach publicly tested each player to see if she had managed to improve her jumping and speed since their last practices. All the other school teams applied equivalent begin-the-season tests. It was understood by the athletes that training started well before each season began. Obviously, extrinsic motivation to learn has not turned off student athletes; it has just made them work harder at learning their skills.

Finally, Kohn offers his example of a good school program that promotes children's moral and social development. He presents the Child Development Project (CDP), whose premise is that, "by meeting children's needs, we increase the likelihood that they will care about others." However, one of the authors helped conduct a four-year direct comparison of students in CDP schools with students attending a public school with a strong for-character program.

In contrast to the CDP schools, the for-character school established specific, measurable goals, standards, and performance indicators; conducted frequent, systematic assessments of performance; measured and rated school performance relative to the goals and published the results; publicly recognized schools, classes, and individuals for achieving goals; and supported school personnel in their efforts to achieve school goals. In other words, it was not the type of school in which Kohn would enroll his children.

Although there were major differences between the CDP program and the for-character program, both seem to have had positive effects on students, and, of the hundreds of variables studied, there were numerous areas in which neither program was significantly or consistently differentiated from the other.[27] But the teachers in the for-character school, as opposed to teachers in the CDP schools, rated their school as more businesslike, creative, and innovative, with more involved and supportive parents, a more supportive and accessible principal, a more traditional academic focus, a pleasanter atmosphere, and better relations between teachers and students. And students in the for-character school scored higher on measures of self-esteem in the third and fourth grades than did students in the CDP schools. These positive results in a school with clear for-character policies should not extinguish other experiments designed to improve student character. However, the results do counter such misleading pictures as the one sketched by Alfie Kohn.

Notes

1. The U.S. Department of Health and Human Services, Public Health Service, Bureau of Vital Statistics, and predecessor agencies have compiled annual vital statistics reports on specific topics for appropriate years (homicide and suicide, 1914–94; out-of-wedlock births, 1940–93).
2. Judith Haveman, "A Nation of Violent Children: A New Survey Finds the Epidemic Is Confined Almost Exclusively to the U.S.," *Washington Post National Weekly Edition,* 17 February 1997, p. 34.
3. Jean Johnson and Steve Farkas, *Getting By: What American Teenagers Really Think About Their Schools* (New York: Public Agenda, 1997).
4. Over the past few years many books have documented exemplary programs in character education. None of these school programs relied primarily on packaged character education programs, though some did use them. See Jacques S. Benninga, ed., *Moral, Character, and Civic Education in the Elementary School* (New York: Teachers College Press, 1991); Philip F. Vincent, *Promising Practices in Character Education: Nine Success Stories from Around the Country* (Chapel Hill, N.C.: Character Development Group, 1996); and Edward A. Wynne. *A Year in the Life of an Excellent Elementary School* (Lancaster, Pa.: Technomics, 1993).
5. "List of 100 For-Character Activities and Policies," in Edward A. Wynne and Kevin Ryan, *Reclaiming Our Schools: A Handbook on Teaching Character, Academics, and Discipline* (New York: Merrill, 1997), pp. 197–202.
6. See, for example, Stephen L. Carter. *Integrity* (New York: HarperCollins, 1996): William Damon, *Greater Expectations: Overcoming the Culture of Indulgence in America's Homes and Schools* (New York: Free Press, 1996); Jack Frymier et al., *Values on Which We Agree* (Bloomington, Ind.: Phi Delta Kappa Educational Foundation, 1995); Gertrude Himmelfarb, *The Demoralization of Society: From Victorian Virtues to Modern Values* (New York: Alfred A. Knopf., 1995); William Kilpatrick, Gregory Wolfe, and Suzanne M. Wolfe, *Books That Build Character: A Guide to Teaching Your Child Moral Values Through Stories* (New York: Simon & Schuster, 1994); Alex Molnar, ed., *The Construction of Children's Character: 96th NSSE Yearbook: Part II* (Chicago: National Society for the Study of Education, University of Chicago Press, 1997); and Wynne and Ryan, op. cit.
7. William K. Frankena, *Ethics* (Englewood Cliffs. N.J.: Prentice-Hall, 1963), p. 53.
8. See, for example, Robert E. Slavin, "Reforming State and Federal Policies to Support Adoption of Proven Practices." *Educational Researcher,* December 1996, p. 4, in which Slavin comments that "year after year, the achievement of American children remains unchanged. . . . Yet, in what other area of American life would we be satisfied to say that things have simply become no worse over the past quarter century?" Slavin was writing about the academic achievement of youths; we have shown that the moral indicators have declined over this same time period.
9. Amy Gutmann, *Democratic Education* (Princeton, NJ: Princeton University Press, 1987), p. 288.
10. Ibid.
11. James Q. Wilson and Richard J. Herrnstein, *Crime and Human Nature* (New York: Simon & Schuster, 1985).

12. Jean Johnson and John Immerwahr. *First Things First: What Americans Expect from the Public Schools* (New York: Public Agenda, 1994).

13. Plato, *The Republic,* trans. H.D.P. Lee (Baltimore: Penguin Books, 1955), pp. 90–91.

14. Horace Mann, as quoted in Lori Sandford Wiley, *Comprehensive Character-Building Classroom* (Manchester, N.H.: Character Development Foundation, 1997), p. 28.

15. Lawrence Cremin, *American Education: The Colonial Years* (New York: Harper Torchbook, 1970), p. 479.

16. Richard Brookhiser, "A Man on Horseback," *Atlantic,* January 1996, p. 61.

17. Sarah Broadie, *Ethics with Aristotle* (New York: Oxford University Press, 1991), p. 109.

18. Edward A. Wynne, "Character and Academics in the Elementary School," in Benninga, ed., p. 142.

19. Robert W. Howard, "Lawrence Kohlberg's Influence on Moral Education in Elementary Schools," in Benninga, ed., pp. 61–62.

20. John Willinsky, "The Underside of Empowerment," *Educational Researcher,* March 1995, pp. 31–32.

21. Emile Durkheim, *Suicide: A Study in Sociology,* trans. John A. Spaulding and George Simpson (Glencoe, Ill.: Free Press, 1951).

22. R. W. Marris, "Sociology of Suicide," in Seymour Perlin, ed., *A Handbook for the Study of Suicide* (New York: Oxford University Press, 1975), pp. 93–112.

23. James S. Leming, *Character Education: Lessons from the Past, Models for the Future* (Camden, Me.: Institute for Global Ethics, 1993), p. 16.

24. Edward A. Wynne, "Transmitting Character in Schools—Some Common Questions and Answers," *The Clearing House,* January/February 1995, pp. 151–53.

25. See Eleanor Maccoby, *Social Development: Psychological Growth and the Parent/Child Relationship* (New York: Harcourt Brace Jovanovich, 1980), pp. 382–83; and Diane Baumrind, "The Development of Instrumental Competence Through Socialization," in Anne D. Pick, ed., *Minnesota Symposium on Child Psychology,* vol. 7 (Minneapolis: University of Minnesota Press, 1973).

26. Judy Cameron and W. David Pierce, "The Debate About Rewards and Intrinsic Motivation: Protests and Accusations Do Not Alter the Results." *Review of Educational Research,* vol. 66, 1996, pp. 39–51.

27. Jacques S. Benninga et al., "Effects of Two Contrasting School Task and Incentive Structures on Children's Social Development," *Elementary School Journal,* vol. 92, 1991, pp. 149–67.

Form at end of book

Ethics and Freedom

A corporate executive applies the Boy Scout Law to the workplace and the schoolhouse.

Sanford N. McDonnell

Sanford McDonnell is chairman emeritus of McDonnell Douglas, c/o The Boeing Co., Building 100 Dock, McDonnell Boulevard and Airport Road, St. Louis, Mo. 63134.

In 1983, after years of telling young boys to practice the values of the Scout Oath and Scout Law—to be trustworthy, loyal, helpful, friendly, courteous, kind, obedient, cheerful, thrifty, brave, clean and reverent—I asked myself how well was I doing against that code of ethics, and I realized I had a lot of room for improvement.

Then, as chairman of McDonnell Douglas, I began thinking about our employees. Surely they knew we wanted them to behave ethically. But by what values?

You see, McDonnell Douglas had a code of conduct, as most organizations do. Ours was a "thou shalt not" set of rules, but we didn't have a positive "thou shalt" code of ethics. So I gave a small task force of people who reported directly to me the Scout Law and asked them to draft a company code that covered its 12 points.

After numerous iterations, we came up with a code of ethics that covered all the points except "A scout is reverent." As a Christian, I wanted to think all of our employees believed in God, but I agreed with the task force that we should not use our executive position in the corporation to pressure our employees to be reverent.

When we adopted that code of ethics at our April 1983 board of directors meeting, we didn't just hang it on the wall. We set up an eight-hour training program to teach us all, beginning with me and my direct reports, how to apply the code in our daily business lives.

By the time I retired in 1988 we had trained well over 50,000 employees. This training program was part of the corporation's comprehensive, proactive ethics program. It grew more and more effective each year and is stronger than ever today.

Roots of Character

After starting this program, I felt the need to check into the character of the young people coming out of the schools into the community and into McDonnell Douglas and other companies. In the process of that investigation I went back into history and found out the following about character education.

In 1748, Baron Charles de Montesquieu published his magnum opus, "The Spirit of Laws," which had a profound effect upon our founding fathers. In it, Montesquieu developed the concept of the separation of powers, which formed the basis of our Constitution more than 200 years ago.

Montesquieu also explored the relationship that must exist between a people and different forms of governments for the government to survive. For example, a dictatorship depends upon fear. When fear disappears the dictatorship is overthrown. A monarchy depends upon the loyalty of the people.

The most desirable form of government is a free republic, but it is also the most fragile because it depends upon a virtuous people. What did Montesquieu mean by a "virtuous" people?

Well, virtuous means living by high ethical values. And one of the best definitions of ethics was given by Dr. Albert Schweitzer, who said, "In a general sense, ethics is the name that we give to our concern for good behavior. We feel an obligation to consider not only our own personal well-being but also that of others and of human society as a whole."

"Character without knowledge is weak and feeble, but knowledge without character is dangerous and a potential menace to society."

Montesquieu meant, therefore, that in a free republic the leaders and a majority of the people must be committed to doing what's best for the nation as a whole. When that commitment breaks, people can no longer be depended upon to behave in the best interests of their nation. The result is laws, regulations, red tape and controls—things designed to force people to be trustworthy. These are instruments of bondage, not freedom.

Vital School Role

Throughout most of our history, certain basic, ethical values were considered fundamental to the character and people of this nation. These values were passed on from generation to generation in the home, the school and the religious institution—each one undergirding and reinforcing the others. We had a consensus not only on values but on the importance of those values, and from that consensus, we knew who we were as a people and where we were going as a nation.

Today in America we have far too many 12-year-olds pushing drugs, 14-year-olds having babies, 16-year-olds killing each other and young people of all ages admitting at epidemic levels to lying, cheating and stealing. We have crime and violence everywhere and unethical behavior in business, the professions and government. In other words, a crisis of character all across America is threatening to destroy the goodness which, as Alexis de Tocqueville put it, is the very foundation of our greatness and ability to remain free.

That is the bad news. The good news is that we know what to do about it. We know that we must get back to the core values of our American heritage in our homes, our schools, our businesses, our government and, indeed, in each of our daily lives. And we know that the schools have the greatest potential for helping us do so.

When our country was founded, Harvard, Yale and Princeton were already in existence as theological seminaries whose whole thrust was teaching the values of our Judeo-Christian faith. And from kindergarten through the university level, character education was considered just as important as intellectual knowledge.

A Win-Win Approach

Ten years ago when I retired as chairman and CEO of McDonnell Douglas, I formed a business-education-community partnership in St. Louis that led to the creation of character education program called PREP (Personal Responsibility Education Process). PREP, a K–12 program, is now in its 10th year and operates in 34 public school districts representing 426 individual schools with almost 250,000 students throughout the metropolitan area and two outlying counties. To my knowledge, PREP is the country's largest public school experiment in character education.

PREP is still in a development mode in many of the districts, but where implemented properly, it has produced very encouraging and sometimes dramatic results. Behavior problems have decreased as academic performance has improved. The teachers are happier, the students are happier, the parents are happier and the community is happier. It is a win-win program that exemplifies why character education should be an integral part of the formal education system from kindergarten through graduate school.

It is obvious that without order in classrooms, teachers are not able to teach. What is not always so obvious but is equally true is that by creating a moral and caring community environment in the schools by teaching kids, for example, to really care about others, students feel better about themselves and work harder. PREP has proven this time and time again.

PREP does not represent a single program. We have a large data bank of programs that are being used in St. Louis or elsewhere from which a school district can pick the approach that it believes best fits its school environment. In fact, each school within a district selects its preferred program.

To make an effective choice, each school or district is encouraged to use "Eleven Principles of Effective Character Education," a document published by the Character Education Partnership, a national organization based in Washington, D.C. (see page 263). Each district must reach a consensus on what values it wants its students to learn. Some can only agree on eight values while others find a consensus around as many as 30 values. But every district, independent of one another, has selected honesty, responsibility and respect.

Once a month, representatives from each of the 34 participating school districts attend a PREP Development Team meeting to exchange information about their respective programs.

A Working Partnership

The Character Education Partnership, which I also chair, defines character, good character, as "understanding, caring about and acting on core ethical values such as honesty, responsibility, respect, kindness and caring for others." Kevin Ryan, a Boston University professor and a member of the board of directors of CEP, has a simpler definition of character: "knowing the good, loving the good and doing the good."

In other words, building good character must involve the cognitive, the emotional and the dynamic: the head, the heart and the hand.

For many reasons, formal character education now has been largely removed from the public schools. But while we can't teach religion in the public schools any-more, we can teach the universal values common to all the great religions. Developing character in this compre-hensive sense requires a comprehensive educational approach—one that uses all aspects of schooling (acade-mic subject matter, the instructional process and the man-agement of the school environment) as opportunities to develop character.

The following are examples of activities that can be used to develop character:

- Classical literature is full of moral dilemmas. The teacher involves the students in classroom discussion by asking such questions as "What is the moral of this story?" "What was the right thing to do and why?" and "What would you have done?"

- At the beginning of the school year, the teacher asks the students to decide on the classroom rules and how those rules should be enforced to make the classroom a good place in which to learn. When the process is followed, a moral, civil, caring community is created by the students. It also helps the teacher maintain classroom order and provides rules to follow when inevitable violations occur.

- Cooperative learning, where students are paired to work on projects and homework, teaches children teamwork, respect for others and caring.

- Service projects inside and outside school teach students to care about others.

- Organized team sports provide coaches with a chance to undergird and reinforce the school's chosen values.

Restoring Goodness

Above all, CEP believes the school itself must embody character. It must be a moral community that helps stu-dents form caring attachments to adults and to each other. These relationships nurture both the desire to be a good person and the desire to learn.

Character without knowledge is weak and feeble, but knowledge without character is dangerous and a potential menace to society. America can't regain the goodness de Tocqueville wrote about by graduating young people from our schools who are brilliant but dishonest, who have great intellectual knowledge but don't really care about others or who are great thinkers but are irresponsible.

America can restore goodness by teaching our young to do what is right, to tell the truth, to serve others, to work hard and to learn as much as they can. We must en-courage them when hardship comes to have courage, to try again when they fail and to never give up. That is char-

acter education. It is one of the most important, if not the most important, answers to our national crisis of charac-ter and should be part of all efforts to reform education.

We know how to provide character education and we are doing it in many parts of the nation. Our goal, however, must be to provide character education as soon as possible in every school in America. For, as Martin Luther King Jr. stated: "Intelligence plus character—that is the goal of true education.

Eleven Principles of Effective Character Education

While no single script exists for what constitutes effective character education in schools, educational leaders can be guided by some important basic principles.

The following 11 statements, drawn up and published by the Character Education Partnership, serve as criteria that schools can use to plan a character education program or evaluate an existing one.

An expanded, four-page version of these principles is available by calling the Character Education Partnership at 800-988-8081 or 202-296-7443.

No. 1: Character eduction promotes core ethical values as the basis of good character.

No. 2: Character must be comprehensively defined to include thinking, feeling and behavior.

No. 3: Effective character education requires an intentional, proactive and comprehensive approach that promotes the core values in all phases of school life.

No. 4: The school must be a caring community.

No. 5: To develop character, students need opportunities for moral action.

No. 6: Effective character education includes a meaningful and challenging academic curriculum that respects all learners and helps them succeed.

No. 7: Character education should strive to develop students' intrinsic motivation.

No. 8: The school staff must become a learning and moral community in which all share responsibility for character education and attempt to adhere to the same core values that guide the education of students.

No. 9: Character education requires moral leadership from both staff and students.

No. 10: The school must recruit parents and community members as full partners in the character-building effort.

No. 11: Evaluation of character education should assess the character of the school, the school staff's functioning as character educators and the extent to which students manifest good character.

Form at end of book

Issue 16 Summary

The character education issue is layered with dilemmas. Is character education the responsibility of schools? If so, how do we influence children's characters? Finally, what values do we seek to teach in character education? The many schools of thought regarding how we teach reading, mathematics, science, and social studies suggest different approaches to character education. A behaviorist would teach specific values, while a constructivist would create situations that provoke students to examine their own values. Just as there are some who argue that there is a *canon* of literature and history that all students in the United States should know, so are there those who argue that the values taught in character education are the traditional values of American society. And, just as there are some who argue that the multicultural nature of our society should be reflected in the literature and history that we teach, so are there those who argue that the values that we teach should reflect the various cultures that constitute our society.

These debates are happening right now. You will often seen news articles about debates and even political battles about curriculum in local boards of education or in state education agencies. And these are among the most important debates occurring in our schools. Don't stand by—as a citizen and a future teacher, weigh in with your opinion.

The problem of violence in our schools and the issue of character education highlight the fact that schools do not exist in a bubble. They exist in a society, and they contribute to the shaping of that society. What we do in schools—what we teach, how we teach, how we group children, how we treat children— matters enormously. When you become a teacher, you are taking on a huge responsibility—namely, to do your absolute best to ensure that your students leave your classroom better off than when they entered it. They may be better informed, more self-assured, happier, or more socially comfortable. Have you heard the expression "First, do no harm"? It pertains to teachers just as much as it pertains to doctors. First, do no harm, but then do something to make a difference in your students' lives. When that happens, you will know that you made the right choice entering the teaching profession.

R.E.A.L. Sites

This list provides a print preview of typical **Coursewise** R.E.A.L. sites. (There are over 100 such sites at the **Courselinks**™ site.) The danger in printing URLs is that web sites can change overnight. As we went to press, these sites were functional using the URLs provided. If you come across one that isn't, please let us know via email to: webmaster@coursewise. com. Use your Passport to access the most current list of R.E.A.L. sites at the **Courselinks** site.

Site name: Children, Media and Violence
URL: http://interact.uoregon.edu/MediaLit/FA/MLmediaviolence.html
Why is it R.E.A.L.? This site links readers to a wide variety of information pertaining to how the media affect children's behavior. The topics include the effects of television, rock music and videos, censorship, and parental responsibility.
Key topics: children, television, violence, research
Try this: Click on "Children's Understanding of What Is Real on Television — A Review of Literature." What problems are encountered when investigating children's understanding of television?

Site name: Children and TV Violence
URL: http://www.cmhc.com/factsfam/violence.htm
Why is it R.E.A.L.? This site is sponsored by the Mental Health Net to help parents understand the effects of television on their children.
Key topics: children, television, violence
Try this: According to this site, what are some effects of television violence on children and teenagers?

Site name: For-Character Education
URL: http://www.uic.edu/~edaw/main.html
Why is it R.E.A.L.? This site, prepared by Professor Edward A. Wynne of the University of Illinois at Chicago, presents information for educators on character education. The site is designed to help educators learn how to promote character education by presenting readings, readers' views, and links to related web sites.
Key topics: character education, moral development, Internet links
Try this: Read "Twenty Ways Educators Can Help Students Acquire Good Character." Choose five of these suggestions and provide criticism from an opposing view.

Index

Note: Names and page numbers in **bold** type indicate authors and their articles.

Ability grouping, and gifted students, 146
Achievement
    African Americans, 105–111
    and socioeconomic status, 105–106
Adams, John, 255
Adams, M., 189
Adolescents, male, 69–70
Adrenaline, and anger/excitement, 227
Advertising
    and alcohol use, 90
    and cigarette smoking, 89
    teaching abuses of, 210
African American achievement gap, 105–111
    effort/reward relationship, 108
    and ethnic identity issues, 107
    psychological factors, 107–108
    versus successful blacks, 107
    successful educational strategies for,
        109–111
    theories of, 105–106
African Americans
    and male development, 70
    and tracking, 105
After Virtue (MacIntyre), 249
Agne, Karen, 143
Airasian, Peter W., 33
Alcohol use, advertising influence issue, 90
Allison, Jeanette, 152
American College Testing Program, 153
Americans with Disabilities Act of 1990, 138
America Reads Challenge, 21
Anger, 226–228
    effects in schools, 228
    effects on society, 227–228
    compared to excitement, 227
    management strategies, 228
    physiological effects of, 226–227
    and teacher burnout, 228
    teacher emergency response to, 229
Apple, Michael, 133, 208, 209
Apprenticeships, and MI theory, 96
Aptitude tests, and MI theory, 4
Archambault, F.X., Jr., 174
Aronson, Joshua, 107
Ashe, Arthur, 107
Assessment of students
    and MI theory, 95–96
    ongoing, value of, 166
    portfolio assessment, 145, 155–156, 167
    See also Standardized tests
Attention deficit disorder, 51, 84
    and boys, 67–68
Authentic assessment, 145

Authentic work, 164
Awards
    gender differences, 75
    negative aspects of, 235
Ayers, L.R., 189

Bae, Y., 76, 77
Baker, E.T., 133
Baldwin, James, 88, 106
Baron, R.A., 227
Barrington, K., 227
Bartelt, D., 132
Beattie, M., 227, 228, 229
Beck, L.L., 179
Beckwith, Jonathan, 50
Begley, Sharon, **62**
Bell Curve, The (Murray and Herrnstein), 106
Bennett, William, 7, 240, 241, 253
Benninga, Jacques S., 252
Bergson, Henri, 116
Berk, R.A., 161
Berkwitz, L., 228
Berliner, David C., 4, 15
Bianculli, David, 208, 209
Biddle, Bruce J., 4, 15
Bilingual education, 118–127
    California, 118–120
    effectiveness of, 125–126
    Hispanic American view of, 118, 119, 120
    historical view, 121–125
    opponents of, 118, 119, 121, 126
    reading instruction, 185
Binet, Alfred, 97
Binge drinking, gender differences, 70
Black, C., 228
Blank, Jonah, 223
Bloom, B.S., 153
Book of Virtues, The (Bennett), 253
Bottom-up approach, reading instruction, 188
Bowlby, John, 64
Brain
    and critical periods, 57–58
    enriched environments, effects of, 58
    measures of brain activity, 51–52
    modular operation of, 98
    physical aspects and intelligence, 56–57
    physical development, 56–57
Brain activity electrical mapping (BEAM), 51
Brain research, and education, 45–47
Brazelton, T. Berry, 63
Bredekamp, S., 155
Brennan, Timothy C., Jr., 231
Bridges, Ruby, 248, 251

Brooks, David, 240
Brown, A., 167
Brown, Sarah E., 213
Brown v. the Board of Education, 130–131, 138
Bruer, John T., 56, 63
Bullivant, Gordon, 194
Bunche, Ralph, 107
Byrne, B., 131

California, bilingual education, 118–120
California Achievement Test, 153
Callaghan, Alice, 118, 119
Callahan, Carolyn M., 173
Campbell, Linda, 92, 96
Carbo, M., 180
Care of the Soul (Moore), 113
Carneal, Michael, 223–225
Cartesian view, of intelligence, 98
Ceci, Steven, 98
Center for Commercial-Free Public
    Education, 89
Certification testing, 157
Chall, J.S., 178, 180, 189
Channel One, 89, 209
Character education, 234–259
    Character Education Partnership
        guidelines, 263
    for-character education, 253–254
    goal of, 237, 249, 255–256
    ideological basis of, 242
    learning theory applied to, 239–242,
        249–251, 258
    literature, use of, 243
    lying, teaching about, 243
    meanings of, 234
    morality and worldview, 247
    and motivation, 235, 258–259
    necessity for, 252–253
    PREP (Personal Responsibility Education
        Process), 262
    Scout Oath, 261
    Values Clarification program, 241
    values taught, 237–239, 257–258
    view of human nature in, 236–237,
        248–242, 254, 255
Character Education Institute, 239
Character Education Partnership, 262–263
Child, D., 167
Child Development Project, 243, 259
Child nature
    meaning of, 82
    modern child, 84–86
    and modern education, 82–83
    and postmodern education, 83–84

Child–rearing
    history of practices, 64
    and male development, 68, 70–71
    parents versus genetics influences, 62–66
Chu, Judy, 67
Cigarette smoking
    and advertising, 89
    predictors of, 89
Cities, poverty and urban schools, 131–132
Civil Rights Act of 1964, 138
Civil Rights Act of 1991, 138
Classroom participation, gender differences, 78
Clinton, Bill, 16, 22, 234
Cognitive development, constructivist view, 30
Cohen, C.S., 174
Cohen, O.P., 139
Coleman, J.S., 130, 157
Coles, Robert, 98, 248
Collins, Ronald, 209
Color-Blind (Cose), 110
Comprehensive Test of Basic Skills (CTBS),
    increase in scores, 4
Concerned Parents for Children with Learning
    Disabilities, 197
Constructivist teaching, 28–31
    appeal of method, 35–36
    basic principles of, 33–34
    forms of, 34
    goals of, 28
    instructional limitations of, 36–37
    issues/concerns related to, 31
    opposition to, 34–38
    proponents of, 30–31
    teacher's role, 28–30
    theoretical basis of, 30, 34
    time factors in, 37–38
Contracts, teleliteracy instruction, 215
Convergent thinking, negative aspects of, 24
Cooperative learning
    anger management, 229
    character development, 263
    pros/cons of, 146
Cooper, Carolyn R., 173
Cortes, Carlos, 113
Cose, Ellis, 110
Covey, S., 228
Creativity, Gardner's study, 98
Cremin, J., 152
Criterion-referenced tests, 153
Critical periods, and brain, 57–58
Csikszentmihalyi, Mihaly, 100, 116
Culross, R.R., 139
Culture of Complaint: A Passionate Look into
    the Ailing Heart of America (Hughes), 113
Curriculim development, and MI theory,
    93–94
Curry-Tash, Marnie W., 207

Dalton Plan, 44
Darling-Hammond, Linda, 116
Darwin, Charles, 45
Darwinian view, of intelligence, 98
Dawkins, Richard, 50
Daw, N.W., 57
Decoding
    benefits to learner, 186
    meaning of, 183

Decoding instruction, 183, 185–186
    tools for, 184
Deffenbaugh, W.S., 153
Deming, J. Edwards, 166
Democracy, and education, 44, 45
Denti, Louis, 112
Detracking, 170–172
    detracked courses, approach to, 170–171
    versus differentiation, 173–175
    diversity accommodation, 171–172
Developmental stages, male versus female,
    68–69
DeVries, Rheta, 241
Dewey, John, 25, 44, 241
Dickinson, Dee, 99
Dijkstrata, B., 74
Dinkmeyer, D, 229
Discussion time
    reading instruction, 184
    teleliteracy topics, 216
Divorce, and male development, 70
Dole, Bob, 121
Downing, S.M., 157
Drug therapy, for behavior disorders, 52
Durkheim, Emile, 256–257
Dwyer, C.A., 75

Eagly, A.H., 73
Eating disorders, gender differences, 70
Ebstein, Richard, 48
Education
    and child nature, 82–86
    and cognitive theory, 45
    and democracy, 44
    inequality and women, 72–73
    myths related to, 4–6
Education for All Handicapped Children
    Act, 130
Educational reform
    change strategies, 10
    needs for future, 10–12, 16–18
    principles of, 10
Elkind, David, 82
Emery, Robert, 65
Emotional intelligence, 31
Emotional Intelligence (Goldman), 98
Employment, preparing students for, 6, 8, 16
Employment screening, and genetic
    discrimination, 51
English First Foundation, 121
Enriched environment, effects on
    brain/learning, 58
Environmental factors, genes versus parental
    influence issue, 62–66
Escalante, Jaime, 115
Espinosa, R., 131
Ethics, definition of, 261
Etzioni, Amitai, 248, 254
Evolving Self, The (Csikszentmihalyi), 116
Excitement, compared to anger, 227

Facilitative role, of teacher, 30
Farley, Frank, 63
Feingold, A., 73, 76
Finn, Chester, 100
Fishkin, Shelley F., 116
Flood, James, 178

Flow, theory of, 100
Fordham, Signithia, 106
Foucault, Michel, 84
Fowler, Dorothy, 189
Frames of Mind: The Theory of Multiple
    Intelligences (Gardner), 92, 98
Framework for Aesthetic Literacy Instruction,
    and MI theory, 94
Freud, Sigmund, 64, 83
Friend, M., 133
Fundamentalism
    definitions of, 113
    versus multicultural education, 113–114
Future Shock (Toffler), 24

Galton, Francis, 64
Garcia, E., 131, 132
Garcia, Jesus, 113
Gardner, Howard, 92, 94, 96, 97–101, 167
    biographical information, 97–98
Gardner, John, 9
Gary Plan, 44
Gender differences
    awards and honors, 75
    binge drinking, 70
    classroom participation, 78
    eating disorders, 70
    grades, 75
    graduate level study, 77–78
    infants, 68
    learning problems, 76
    Maccoby/Jacklin conclusions, 74
    male versus female development, 67–71
    mathematics and science, 76–77
    motor skills, 69
    reading problems, 70
    subject area performance, 76
    suicidal feelings, 70
    variability among males, 74
    violence, 70, 227
Genetic discrimination
    and education, 51–52
    and employment screening, 51
    IQ and African Americans, 106
Genetic influence
    genes versus parental influence issue, 62–66
    learning disabilities, 194
Genetic studies
    future view, 52–53
    political/social implications, 49–50
    recent developments, 48–49
Gen Rich concept, 52
Gerstner, Louis V., Jr., 15
Geschwind, N., 74
Gest, T., 226
Gilbert, Walter, 49
Gilligan, Carol, 67, 68
Gingrich, Newt, 121
Ginott, H, 226
Giraffe Project, 240
Giroux, Henry A., 208
Glanzer, Perry L., 247
Global village concept, and mass media,
    208–209
Godfrey, Eric, 73
Goldman, Daniel, 98
Goldman-Rakic, P.S., 56

Goodling, Bill, 22
Goodman, K.S., 178
Gordon, Don E., 130
Gose, B., 77
Gottman, John, 65
Grades, gender differences, 75
Gradillas, Henry, 120
Graduate level study, gender differences, 77–78
Graduation testing, 157
Greenough, W.T., 58
Groff, Patrick, 178
Gronlund, Norman E., 24
Grossen, B., 179
Gualtieri, T., 74
Gurian, Michael, 67

Haas, Nancy, 152, 158, 159
Haertel, E., 153, 157
Haladyna, Thomas, 152, 153, 155, 156, 158
Haller, E., 167
Hardie, A., 133
Harris, Judith Rich, 62–66
Harrison, E.C., 133
Harrnstein, J., 153
Hartman, J.A., 158
Haynes, Charles, 250
Heller, K.A., 131
Hernandez, Antonia, 120
Higher-order thinking skills, importance of, 25
Hirsch, E.D., 179
Hispanic Americans, rise in political power, 118–119
Hobbes, Thomas, 236, 249
Hoerr, Tom, 99
Holmbeck, Grayson, 89
Honig, Bill, 182
Howard, Robert, 256
How Schools Shortchange Girls, 72
Hubel, D.H., 57
Hughes, Robert, 113
Human Genome Project, 49
Humanities, study of, 17
Huttenlocher, P.R., 56

Immigrants
    bilingual education, history of, 123–125
    educational failure of, 122–123
    language immersion programs, 122, 123
    See also Bilingual education
Improving America's Schools Act, 133
Inclusive education, 130–146
    legislation related to, 138
    and marginal students, 133
    negative aspects of, 142–145
    policy/procedure actions for, 141
    positive effects of, 133
    publications related to, 139
    and structural level changes, 134
    variations of, 140
    within-school guidelines, 134, 139
INFACT, 89, 210
Infants, gender differences, 68
Intelligence
    Cartesian view, 98
    Darwinian view, 98
    multiple intelligences (MI) theory, 97–101

Intelligence Can Be Taught (Whimbey), 110
Intelligence tests, opposition to, 152–153
International studies, and MI theory, 93–94
Intervention studies, nature/nurture issue, 65
Iowa Test of Basic Skills, 153
    increase in scores, 4
IQ/achievement discrepancy, learning disabled, 198, 199–200
Irregularity, and modern world, 86

Jacklin, C.N., 74, 76
Jarvis, F. Washington, 236–237
Jefferson Center for Character Education, 240
Jensen, A.R., 153
Jensen, Arthur, 49
Johnson, C., 131

Kagan, Jerome, 63, 65
Kalb, Claudia, 67
Kamii, C., 154
Kant, Immanuel, 10
Kantrowitz, Barbara, 67
Kaplan, Sandra N., 173
Katzen, quality concept, 166
Kaufhold, Jack, 24
Kaufman, J. M., 139
Kelman, Mark, 196
Kendler, Kenneth, 65
Key Learning Center, MI-oriented school, 96, 100
Kilpatrick, William, 236, 240, 254
Kim, Sung Hou, 50
Kindlon, Dan, 69
Kirst, M., 131, 132
Kleinfeld, Judith, 72, 73
Knoblauch, B., 139
Knowledge, constructivist view, 29, 33
Kohlberg, Lawrence, 241, 256
Kohn, Alfie, 234, 247–259
Koshland, Daniel, 49
Kovach, John A., 130, 131, 134
Krashen, D.D., 190

Lacelle-Peterson, Mark, 116
Ladsonƒ Billings, G., 210
Lapp, Diane, 178, 179
Las Familias del Pueblo, 118
Leach, Penelope, 63
Learning disabilities
    educational definition of, 198
    effects on family, 195
    epidemic issue, 198
    genetic analysis for, 51–52
    genetic factors, 194
    IQ/achievement discrepancy, 198, 199–200
    prevalence of, 195
    reading instruction approaches, 194–195
    and reading problems, 193–197, 200–201
    signs of, 197
    technological aids for, 196
    and workplace, 196
Learning problems, gender differences, 76
Learning theory, and character education, 239–242, 249–251, 258
Least restrictive environment (LRE), compared to mainstreaming, 138

Lensmire, Timothy, 256
Lerner, H.G., 226, 227, 229
Lessons, design and MI theory, 93
Leveranz, D., 208
Liberman, A.M., 179, 180
Li, Christine P., 19
Lichter, Robert, 113
Lindow, J., 78
Linn, Robert L., 24
Lippman, Walter, 153
Literature, in character education, 243
Liu, A., 139
Locke, John, 83
Lombardi, T., 133
Lovett, Maureen, 194, 195
Lying, in character education, 243
Lyman, F., 167

Maccoby, E.E., 74, 76
McCombs, B., 167
McDonnell, L.M., 134
McDonnell, Sanford N., 261
MacIntyre, Alasdair, 249
McKinsey Global Institute, 6
McLuhan, Marshall, 208
MacPhee, Kay, 194
McTighe, Jay, 163, 167
Mainstreaming, compared to least restrictive environment (LRE), 138
Malcolm X, 107
Male development, 67–71
    and African Americans, 70
    and child-rearing, 68, 70–71
    crisis phases, 69
    and divorce, 70
    phases of development, 68–69
Males, Mike, 88
Managerial role, of teacher, 29–30
Mann, Horace, 8, 255
Marginal students, inclusion for, 133–134
Marshall, Ray, 16
Marshall, Thurgood, 107
Martin, David S., 137
Maslow, Abraham, 25
Mass media
    advertising abuses, teaching of, 210
    global village concept, 208–209
    influence on personal/identity level, 209–210
    media literacy, 207–208
    teleliteracy instruction, 208–217
Mathematics instruction, 19
Mathematics performance, gender differences, 76–77
Matute-Bianchi, Maria, 114, 131
Media literacy
    current movement, 208
    definition of, 207–208
    teleliteracy instruction, 208–217
Medlock, Ann, 240
Mehrens, W.A., 156, 157
Meier, Deborah, 238
Meisels, S.J., 155
Metropolitan Achievement Test, 153
    increase in scores, 4
Mezzacappa, D., 133

Miller, Mark Crispin, 89
Minorities
    in special education programs, 132
    and tracking, 131
    in urban schools, 132
Modern world
    modern child, 84–86
    postmodernism, 83–84
    principles related to progress, 83
Molnar, A., 209
Montesquieu, Charles de, 261
Moore, Thomas, 113
Moral Intelligence of Children, The (Coles), 98
Morality
    moral heroism, example of, 248
    and worldview, 247
    See also Character education
Mothers Against Drunk Driving, 90
Motivation
    and African American achievement
        gap, 108
    and character education, 235, 258–259
    and learning, 110
    and rewards/awards, 235
Motor skills, gender differences, 69
Mullis, I.V., 76
Multicultural education, 112–116
    versus fundamentalism, 113–114
    learning and instruction, 114–116
    necessity of, 113, 114
Multiple-choice tests, standardized tests, 153
Multiple intelligences (MI) theory
    development of theory, 97–98
    opposition to, 98–99
    types of intelligences, 98
Multiple intelligences (MI) theory and
        teaching, 92–96, 100–101
    apprenticeships, 96
    assessment of students, 95–96
    classroom atmosphere, 100–101
    curriculum development, 93–94
    lesson design, 93
    MI menus, 95
    projects, 94–95
    teachers' guide for, 99
Mulvey, Kate, 89
Musick, M.D., 21

Nass, R.D., 74
National Assessment of Educational Progress
        (NAEP), 19, 22
    increase in scores, 4
National Assessment Governing Board
        (NAGB), voluntary national test
        development, 19–20
National tests
    guidelines for use, 20–21
    opposition to, 22–23
Nation at Risk, current position on, 7–13
Nature/nurture, parental influences issue,
        62–66
Neill, Monty, 22
Nelkin, Dorothy, 51
Nelson, C.A., 57
Neural efficiency analyzer, 51–52
Neurons, synapse formation, 56–57

New City School, MI-oriented school, 99
Newman, Stuart, 50
Nietzsche, Friedrich, 84
Noggle, N.L., 158
Nolen, S.B., 157, 158
Nord, Warren, 247
*Nurture Assumption: Why Children Turn Out
        the Way They Do; Parents Matter Less Than
        You Think and Peers Matter More* (Harris),
        62–66

Oakes, Jeannie, 131, **170**, 173, 174, 175
O'Dell, C.W., 153
Offer, Daniel, 89
Ogbu, John, 108, 114, 131
O'Neill, J., 134
Ormrod, Jeanne, 25
Ornish, D., 226
Owen, David B., 213

Palinscar, A., 167
Parents
    lack of influence issue, 62–66
    and teen behavior, 89–90
Paris, S., 158, 159
Pedagogy of the Oppressed (Friere), 114
*Pennsylvania Human Relations Commission
        v. School District of Philadelphia*, 131
Performance-based instruction
    authentic assessment, 145
    authentic work, emphasis on, 164
    documentation of progress, 166–167
    models of excellence as examples, 165
    ongoing assessment in, 166
    performance standards, exposure of
        students to, 164–165
    performance targets, 163–164
    specific teaching strategies, 165–166
Perrone, V., 155
Phillips, Andrew, 118
Phonemic awareness, 186–187
    instructional approach, 187
    meaning of, 186–187, 189
    pros/cons of, 189
Phonics instruction
    integrated-balanced instructional
        approach, 178
    materials for, 187
Piaget, Jean, 25, 30, 34, 64, 97, 256
Pinker, Steven, 63
Pohl, F., 208, 209
Pollack, William, 69
Popham, W.J., 153
Portfolio assessment, 145, 155–156
    benefits of, 167
Position emission tomography (PET), 51–52
Poverty, decline of urban schools, 131–132
Prager, Dennis, 247
PREP (Personal Responsibility Education
        Process), 262
Private schools, 5
Progress, and modern world, 85
Progressive Education Movement, 44
Projects
    and MI theory, 94–95
    on teleliteracy, 211, 217

Project Spectrum, 94
Proposition 227, 118
Prothrow-Stith, D., 229
Pugh, Sharon, 113
Purpel, David, 237

Quie, Albert, 9

Raison, J., 130
Rakic, P., 56
Ravitch, Diane, 99
Reading comprehension, reading skills related
        to, 186
Reading instruction, 19
    balanced program, elements of, 183
    bilingual education, 185
    bottom-up approach, 188
    components of, 184
    decoding, 183, 185–186
    decoding versus whole language approach,
        187, 190
    discussion time, 184
    exposures necessary for, 186
    instructional guidelines, 190
    non-English-speaking learners, 185
    phonemic awareness, 186–187, 189
    phonics, 178
    phonics instruction, 187
    time factors, 184
    whole-language approach, 189–190
    whole-part-whole approach, 188–189
Reading problems
    areas of deficiency, 182, 186
    gender differences, 70
    and learning disabilities, 193–197, 200–201
    and poverty, 132
Reading Recovery program, 195
R.E.A.L. sites
    Brains.Org: Practical Classroom
        Applications of Current Brain
        Research, 102
    Center for Educational Priorities, 219
    Children, Media and Violence: Media
        Literacy Online Project, 265
    Children and TV Violence, 265
    Empower America: Empowering Our
        Schools, 40
    For-Character Education Web Page, 265
    Guidelines for the Development and
        Management of Performance
        Assessments, 204
    Home School Legal Defense Association
        Home Page, 40
    HORIZONS Newsletter, 148
    How to Work Effectively with a
        Heterogeneous Classroom, 204
    Hurry Up! It's Time to Go, 102
    Inclusive Education Web Site, 148
    Initiative for Educational Equity
        Committee, 102
    Media Literacy Education Bibliography,
        219
    Multicultural Education, 148
    Phonics and Whole Language
        Research, 204
    Postman Links, 219

Separation of Church and State
    HomePage, 40
    Studies in Moral Development, 265
    Yahoo Bilingual Education, 148
Regular Education Initiative (REI), 138
Regularity, and modern world, 83
Reich, Robert, 16
Reis, Sally M., 173, 174
Remediation, double dose instruction, 171
Renzulli, J.S., 174
Republic (Plato), 255
Rewards, negative aspects of, 235
Reynolds, M.C., 130, 132, 133
Rich, Alexander, 50
Rifkin, Jeremy, 48
Rivera, Charlene, 116
Rohnke, K., 229
Roper, Dale Ann D., 226
Rose, L.C., 154
Rothstein, Richard, 16, **121**
Rousseau, Jean-Jacques, 83
Ruiz, Nadine, 114
Ryan, Kevin, 236, 238, 254

Sadker, David, 72, 73, 78
Sadker, Myra, 72, 78
St. Augustine, 249
Salidbury, C.L., 139
Samuels, S.J., 179
Sanders, J., 77
Sapolsky, Robert, 63
Satinover, Jeffrey, 248
Schemata, 29
Scheurman, Geoffrey, 28
Scholastic Aptitude Test (SAT), 153
    decline of scores, 4
School segregation
    effects of, 131, 137
    versus inclusion, 132–133
    legislation related to, 131, 138
School violence
    and anger, 226–228
    crisis management, example of, 231–232
    Paducah school shooting, 223–225
Schorr, L.B., 134
Schunk, D., 167
Schwarz, Paul, 238
Schweitzer, Albert, 261
Sears, R.R., 227
Share, D.L., 178, 179
Shepard, L.A., 153, 155
Sheppard, Robert, 193
Silet, Charles L.P., 213
Simpson, J., 208
Singham, Mano, **105**
Smith, M.L., 155, 158, 159
Smith, F., 178
Smith, Marshall S., 19
Socioeconomic status, and achievement,
    105–106
Sommers, Christina Hoff, 73, 78
Spear-Swerling, Louise, 198

Special education
    least restrictive environment (LRE), 138
    legislation related to, 138
    mainstreaming, 138
    and minority students, 132
Spock, Benjamin, 64
Standardized tests
    alternatives to, 155–156
    criterion-referenced tests, 153
    decline in scores myth, 4–5
    effects on students, 158–159
    effects on teachers, 159–160
    historical view, 152–154
    intelligence test, 152–153
    multiple-choice tests, 153
    negative use of scores, 157–158
    parental support of, 154
    positive use of scores, 156–157
    professional organizations' view of,
        154–155
    responsible testing guidelines, 160
    teaching for the test, 24–25, 158, 160
Stand and Deliver, 115
Stanford Achievement Test, 153
Steele, Claude, 107
Steele, Shelby, 112
Stereotyping, and African American
    achievement gap, 107–108
Sternberg, Robert J., 198
Stevenson, David L., 19
Strickland, Dorothy S., 188, 190
Suicidal feelings
    Durkheim on, 256–257
    gender differences, 70
Sylwester, Robert, 44

Tancredi, Laurence, 51
Teachers
    behavioral view of, 28–30
    burnout, 228
    constructivist role of, 28–30
*Teaching and Learning Through Multiple
    Intelligences* (Campbell), 92
Technical skills, and education, 5
Teleliteracy, 208–217
    adbusting instruction, 210
    and change of viewing habits, 214
    critical viewing as goal, 214
    discussion topics, 216
    examination of specific shows, 215
    on personal level, 209–211
    preparation for teaching, 217
    projects, 211, 217
    show analysis, 215–216
    student contracts, 215
    student knowledge of, 213–214
Television viewing
    benefits of, 208–209
    teleliteracy instruction, 208–217
    and violence, 88–89
Test anxiety, and standardized tests, 158

Third International Mathematics and Science
    Study (TIMSS), 20
Thompson, Michael, 69
Toffler, Alvin, 24
Tomlinson, Carol A., 139, **173, 174**
Tracking
    and African Americans, 105
    detracking, 170–172
    negative effects of, 131
    positive use of, 173–175
Traub, James, 97
Treisman, Uri, 109
Tucker, Marc, 16
Turnbull, A.P., 139
Turner's syndrome, 48
Twin studies, nature/nurture issue, 65

Uniforms for students, 235
Universality, and modern world, 83, 85–86
Unplug Campaign, 89
Unz, Ron, 119

Values Clarification program, 241
Villaraigosa, Antonio, 120
Violence
    gender differences, 70, 227
    and television viewing, 88–89
    See also School violence
Violent crime, and boys, 67, 70
Vygotsky, Lev, 30

Walberg, H., 167
Walsh, Mary E., 33
Wang, M.C., 133, 134
Watson, John, 64
Weaver, C., 189, 190
Weber, G., 155, 156, 159
Wellman, Glo, 69
Wells, Amy Stuart, 170, 173
Westberg, Karen L., 173, 174
Whimbey, Arthur, 110
Whole-language reading approach, 189–190
    versus decoding, 187, 190
Whole-part-whole approach, reading
    instruction, 188–189
Who Stole Feminism? (Sommers), 73
Why Johnny Can't Tell Right from Wrong
    (Kilpatrick), 236
Wiggins, G., 167
Williams, J.P., 179
Williams, Wendy, 63
Willingham, W.W., 74, 76, 77
Wilson, Woodrow, 31
Winnetka Plan, 44
Wolpe, Howard, 5
World Wide Web sites. *See* R.E.A.L. sites
Wynne, Edward A., 236, 239, 241, **252,** 254

Yancey, W.L., 131, 132
Young, C., 78

Zan, Betty, 241
Zapanta, Edward, 120

Frame the Debate
Review Form

Name _____ Date _____

Issue _____

1. Prior to reading about and discussing this issue, my personal beliefs were:

_____

_____

_____

_____

2. Describe the credentials and/or credibility of experts cited in each of the readings for this issue.

_____

_____

_____

_____

3. Summarize the main idea presented in each of the readings for this issue.

_____

_____

_____

_____

4. Summarize the facts that support each main idea.

_____

_____

_____

_____

5. Identify any opinions expressed.

_____

_____

_____

_____

_____

6. List any examples of bias or faulty reasoning.

_____

_____

_____

_____

_____

7. How does this issue correlate with material presented in class and/or in your textbook?

_____

_____

_____

_____

_____

8. Based on further consideration of this issue, my personal beliefs are now/still:

_____

_____

_____

_____

_____